AN UNDISCIPLINED ECONOMIST

CARLETON LIBRARY SERIES

The Carleton Library Series publishes books about Canadian economics, geography, history, politics, public policy, society and culture, and related topics, in the form of leading new scholarship and reprints of classics in these fields. The series is funded by Carleton University, published by McGill-Queen's University Press, and is under the guidance of the Carleton Library Series Editorial Board, which consists of faculty members of Carleton University. Suggestions and proposals for manuscripts and new editions of classic works are welcome and may be directed to the Carleton Library Series Editorial Board c/o the Library, Carleton University, Ottawa K1S 5B6, at cls@carleton.ca, or on the web at www.carleton.ca/cls.

221 *Surveyors of Empire*
Samuel Holland, J.F.W. Des Barres, and the Making of The Atlantic Neptune
Stephen J. Hornsby

222 *Peopling the North American City*
Montreal, 1840–1900
Sherry Olson and Patricia Thornton

223 *Interregional Migration and Public Policy in Canada*
An Empirical Study
Kathleen M. Day and Stanley L. Winer

224 *How Schools Worked*
Public Education in English Canada, 1900–1940
R.D. Gidney and W.P.J. Millar

225 *A Two-Edged Sword*
The Navy as an Instrument of Canadian Foreign Policy
Nicholas Tracy

226 *The Illustrated History of Canada*
25th Anniversary Edition
Edited by Craig Brown

227 *In Duty Bound*
Men, Women, and the State in Upper Canada, 1783–1841
J.K. Johnson

228 *Asleep at the Switch*
The Political Economy of Federal Research and Development Policy since 1960
Bruce Smardon

229 *And We Go On*
Will R. Bird
Introduction and Afterword by David Williams

230 *The Great War as I Saw It*
Frederick George Scott
Introduction by Mark G. McGowan

231 *The Canadian Oral History Reader*
Edited by Kristina R. Llewellyn, Alexander Freund, and Nolan Reilly

232 *Lives in Transition*
Longitudinal Analysis from Historical Sources
Edited by Peter Baskerville and Kris Inwood

233 *W.A. Mackintosh*
The Life of a Canadian Economist
Hugh Grant

234 *Green-lite*
Complexity in Fifty Years of Canadian Environmental Policy, Governance, and Democracy
G. Bruce Doern, Graeme Auld, and Christopher Stoney

235 *Canadian Expeditionary Force, 1914–1919*
Official History of the Canadian Army in the First World War
G.W.L. Nicholson
Introduction by Mark Osborne Humphries

236 *Trade, Industrial Policy, and International Competition, Second Edition*
Richard G. Harris
Introduction by David A. Wolfe

237 *An Undisciplined Economist*
Robert G. Evans on Health Economics, Health Care Policy, and Population Health
Edited by Morris L. Barer, Greg L. Stoddart, Kimberlyn M. McGrail, and Chris B. McLeod

An Undisciplined Economist

Robert G. Evans on Health Economics, Health Care Policy, and Population Health

Edited by
MORRIS L. BARER,
GREG L. STODDART,
KIMBERLYN M. MCGRAIL,
AND CHRIS B. MCLEOD

Carleton Library Series 237

McGill-Queen's University Press
Montreal & Kingston • London • Chicago

ISBN 978-0-7735-4715-5 (cloth)
ISBN 978-0-7735-4716-2 (paper)
ISBN 978-0-7735-9946-8 (ePDF)
ISBN 978-0-7735-9947-5 (ePUB)

Legal deposit third quarter 2016
Bibliothèque nationale du Québec

Printed in Canada on acid-free paper that is 100% ancient forest free (100% post-consumer recycled), processed chlorine free

This book has been published with the help of funding received from CIFAR (Canadian Institute for Advanced Research).

Publication of this book has been supported through grants received from the Institute of Health Services and Policy Research, and the Institute of Population and Public Health, Canadian Institutes of Health Research.

Publication of this book has also been supported by the Centre for Health Services and Policy Research, in the School of Population and Public Health at the University of British Columbia.

McGill-Queen's University Press acknowledges the support of the Canada Council for the Arts for our publishing program. We also acknowledge the financial support of the Government of Canada through the Canada Book Fund for our publishing activities.

Library and Archives Canada Cataloguing in Publication

Evans, Robert G., 1942–, author, honouree
An undisciplined economist: Robert G. Evans on health economics, health care policy, and population health/edited by Morris L Barer, Greg L. Stoddart, Kimberlyn M. McGrail, and Chris B. McLeod.

(Carleton Library Series; 237)
Includes bibliographical references and index.
Issued in print and electronic formats.
ISBN 978-0-7735-4715-5 (cloth). – ISBN 978-0-7735-4716-2 (paper). – ISBN 978-0-7735-9946-8 (PDF). – ISBN 978-0-7735-9947-5 (ePUB)

1. Medical economics – Canada. 2. Medical policy – Canada. 3. Public health – Canada. I. Barer, Morris Lionel, 1951–, editor II. Stoddart, Gregory Lloyd, 1948–, editor III. McGrail, Kimberlyn, 1966–, editor IV. McLeod, Christopher B., editor V. Title.

RA410.55.C35E968 2016 338.4'336210971 C2016-901412-6
C2016-901413-4

This book was typeset by Interscript in 10.5/13 Sabon.

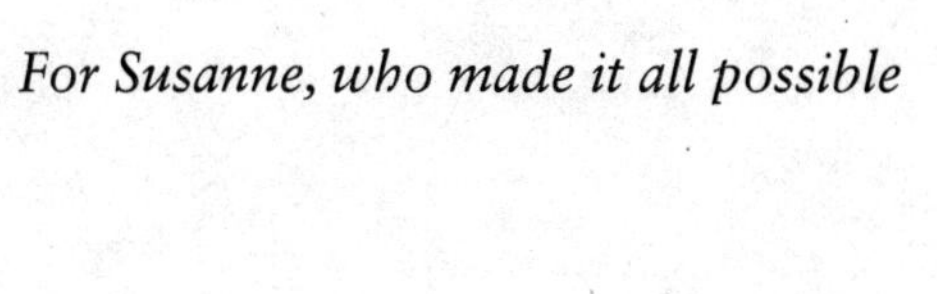

For Susanne, who made it all possible

Contents

Editors' Foreword

In 1969 the University of British Columbia (UBC) had the wisdom and good fortune of asking Robert Evans to join its Department of Economics. That same year he published his first paper on health care. Over the subsequent four decades (and now well into a fifth), Evans became one of the fathers of health economics as a subdiscipline, and Canada's best-known and most influential health care policy analyst and commentator. Along the way, he was also instrumental in the evolution of the field of Population Health, through his leadership of the program of the same name sponsored by the Canadian Institute for Advanced Research. This book is the tale of the intellectual journey of discovery of a quintessential public servant.

THE BOOK

Over the course of his storied career, Bob has authored, co-authored, and edited or co-edited well over 300 books, monographs, journal articles, reports, and other commentaries. What the reader will find in the short collection offered here represents the culmination of an exceedingly challenging editorial task – reducing the full list to a number manageable within a single book, while at the same time ensuring that the included selections achieve key objectives. We had three. The first was to assemble some of the pieces of work that have had the most enduring influence on how others have come to think about particular topics, or on a discipline or field of inquiry. The second objective was to bring together in one easy-to-access location, for new students to the fields that Bob so influenced, the ideas that every student of health care policy or health economics or population health, wherever trained, should have grasped firmly by the time of graduation. Those of us who had the privilege of going through our own training at a time when Bob's work was current and easily accessible tend to forget that, unbelievable though it may seem, new students may never have heard of the man. Perhaps this volume will go some small way to correcting that. The third and final objective was to create a collection that combined seminal and timeless works with some of Bob's lesser-known, but often equally compelling, writings. These may never have been formally published, or have ended up being released in forms not easily accessible. We hope that by including a few less-known selections we will pique the reader's curiosity and thirst for more. To that end, we also provide (at the end of each section, and in the editors' postscript) information on where to find other works by Robert Evans.

THE AUTHOR

Given its limited capacity, this book cannot convey the full reach and influence of the author. One can gain a sense of the intellect, the breadth, the remarkable capacity to synthesize across seemingly unrelated realms, but his contributions were not limited to the written word. We do our best here to compensate. It is no overstatement for us to claim, with conviction, that Bob has had a profound influence on a wide community that extends well beyond other (national and international) researchers. His ideas, his turns of phrase, his practical yet insightful approaches to analyzing vexing public policy issues, have had significant influence on many publics, on the media, on the evolution of health care systems, on health policy-makers, and on politicians. His contributions are truly worthy of emulation by all those interested in health research and in the positive impact that a public-spirited health researcher can have on the quality of life of the citizens of a country.

For more than four decades, Bob has had a profound influence on health care policy in Canada and internationally, as well as on the disciplines of economics, health economics, and the social sciences more generally. Since the late 1980s, he has also played a leadership role in the evolution and advancement of the public and policy discourse around the key influences on the health of populations. He has, we would argue, had more impact and influence in the translation of health policy research for the benefit of users of that information than any other single researcher in Canada over this period.

Canadians tend to take for granted a health care system that (despite its problems) survives in the form we find it today in significant part because of the tireless efforts of this man. He has campaigned relentlessly against the propagation of simple-minded and seemingly sensible ideas about health care that are not, in fact, consistent with research-based evidence. Under the "Evans lens," claims about user charges and private insurance as means of health care financing and cost control, about the "unsustainability" of publicly funded health care systems, about the implications of an aging population for health care costs, and about the costs, pricing, and therapeutic effects of many prescription pharmaceuticals, have been repeatedly exposed as self-interested, often pernicious, promotion. If embraced, many of the ideas behind these claims would have resulted in a health care system in Canada both more expensive and less effective than the one Canadians have available to them today.

On the academic front, Bob has been among a small handful of distinguished international health economists (another of whom, Anthony Culyer, has penned one of the section forewords for us) whose work has shaped the field. He was the first to develop the theory of, and provide empirical support for, the fundamentally important phenomenon of "supplier-induced demand" in the "market" for physician services. The notion that physicians have, and exercise, considerable latitude over which patients to see, how often, and what services to provide to them, may seem trivial now, but was a point of vigorous debate, particularly among economists, as recently as two decades ago. These ideas continue to have far-reaching implications in health policy, affecting everything from contemporary fee negotiations to discussions about primary care reform.

In the early 1980s, Bob wrote and published a book on health economics, *Strained Mercy*, which was much more than a textbook (though it has certainly been heavily used for that purpose and, remarkably, continues to be used 30 years later). It offered insights into the special relationships between, and the incentives governing, the decisions of patients, health care professionals, and policy-makers, not to be found in other books of the genre. It influenced, and continues to influence, many other writers and commentators on economics, health economics, and health care systems, even today.

In the late 1990s, Bob pioneered an accounting approach to analyzing models of, and approaches to, health care financing that added remarkable clarity to many of the recurring debates on health care reform. He pointed out what now seems obvious – that increasing costs to the system automatically increase by an equal amount incomes drawn from the system, and require an equal increase in the revenues generated to support the system – but was at the time viewed as a revelation (enlightening for some, an "inconvenient truth" for many others). From this simple proposition can be elaborated a framework that has been used widely to expose the rationales behind, and implications of, a broad and ingenious variety of financing and organizational reforms proposed by those on all sides of the political and interest spectrum.

But Bob was (and is) much more than an economist, or a health economist. While many distinguished scholars have gained international reputations based on their stellar work in one field, Evans has distinguished himself internationally in two. He has been extremely influential in shaping the field of Population Health, which is now relatively commonplace, but a quarter of a century ago was a field of inquiry that did not exist. He was the inaugural head of the groundbreaking Population Health Program of the Canadian Institute for Advanced Research (CIAR, now CIFAR). It is not an overstatement to suggest that, in the absence of the amazing intellectual reach and leadership provided by Bob and his close colleague Clyde Hertzman, the work of that CIAR program would not have gained international recognition as a key building block for the birth of the field. He served as lead editor, and contributing author, on the program's influential first book, *Why Are Some People Healthy and Others Not?*, published in the mid-1990s but still viewed widely as the original blueprint for many of the Population Health developments since. The contributions here were profound – they have influenced patterns of public investment in health-improving initiatives, and even the organization of public services, in Canada and in other OECD countries. He was subsequently involved in co-editing a second book based on the work of that same program – *Healthier Societies: From Analysis to Action* – published in 2006.

One of the things that has set Bob apart from others working the same terrain (or even working different terrains) is his breathtaking ability to move comfortably beyond his first discipline, not only to be able to make intellectual contributions to and within other areas of inquiry, but to bridge and synthesize research evidence drawn from multiple disciplines. This ability is dramatically showcased in the first book noted above (from which we have included a chapter in Section D), but is nowhere more evident than in his 1996 paper, "Health, Hierarchy, and Hominids" (also in Section D), and in his highly acclaimed 2002 monograph for the UK Office of Health Economics, *Interpreting and Addressing Inequalities in Health: From Black to Acheson to Blair to ... ?* (not included in this collection because of its length). His disciplinary travels have taken him from economics, to health economics (he served as the first president of the Canadian Health Economics Research Association in the early 1980s, and on the executive board of the International Health Economics Association), health services research, political science, psychoneuroimmunology, genetics, the study of non-human primate social behaviour, and early childhood development. In recognition of this work he was in 2002 appointed as one of the CIAR's first two Institute Fellows (the other being the internationally renowned cosmologist Werner Israel).

Along the way, Bob was (arguably) the first health economist to move the subdiscipline of health economics from a focus on health *care* to a broader focus on health. His role in the evolution of the field of population health is the most obvious, but not the only, example of this. His constant reminders (to anyone who would listen) that economic evaluations, or examinations of productivity in the health care sector, for example, must focus on the appropriate metrics of success or impact (improved health, not simply more health care), have not always had the influence that they deserve, to the detriment of much of the work in those sub-fields.

In his role as expert to and for the public, Bob has been, for most of the last four decades, the "go-to person" in Canada when the media, commissions of inquiry, ministries of health, or federal or provincial politicians wanted advice on matters related to health care reform or health care "crises," of which there is a seemingly endless supply. He has been exceedingly generous with his time whenever the media have come calling, being featured regularly on radio and television, and a frequent contributor to "op-eds" for local and national newspapers. He is renowned for being able to convey complex ideas to any audience with a sense of humour and clarity rarely found in academic scholars. He has a remarkable capacity to make others stop and think, because he so convincingly dismantles widely held beliefs. And he believes strongly in the importance of making the time to be publicly accessible to communicate the results of his work to audiences likely to be affected by it. More than one observer has remarked that he is a national treasure.

Bob's capacity for translating research evidence in the health policy field into concrete and applied recommendations has been recognized through his appointment to a BC royal commission in the early 1990s, and to the prime minister's National Forum on Health later that decade. He also made important, but less publicly visible, contributions to the report of the Commission on the Future of Health Care in Canada (Romanow Commission, 2002). And he has willingly shared his knowledge and expertise internationally, through conference presentations too numerous to count, but also through consultations for countries as disparate as China, Egypt, Greece, and Sweden.

In late 2005, *Healthcare Policy* began to be published by Longwoods Publishing. Not only was Bob asked to serve as the chair of a distinguished international editorial advisory board, but he was also invited by the publisher and editor-in-chief to make a standing contribution to each issue, as the self-described "Undisciplined Economist." The publisher has remarked on a number of occasions that the Evans column is the most frequently read piece in each and every issue of the journal.

Bob was appointed as an Officer of the Order of Canada in 2004, but this is only the most notable of an array of evidence of the esteem and respect with which this man is regarded, both within, but also well beyond, his research communities. In November 1998, he became the inaugural recipient of the British Columbia Health Association Legacy Award for contributions to health policy in BC. The following year he received a UBC Killam Senior Research Prize. He was elected as a Fellow of the Royal Society of Canada in 2000, and the same year was honoured with the Distinguished Academic Career Achievement Award from the Confederation of University Faculty Associations of British Columbia. The following year brought three additional significant distinctions: he was the first Canadian (and second-ever non-American) to receive the Baxter International Foundation Prize for Health Services Research; he was the recipient of the Edward K. Barsky Award from Physicians' Forum in the US, "for his leadership in promoting economic justice in health care delivery around the world"; and he was successful in competing for one of the early, and rare, Senior Investigator Awards from the Canadian Institutes of Health Research (CIHR). In 2002 he received two additional prestigious awards – the Health Services Research Advancement Award from the Canadian Health Services Research Foundation and UBC's highest honour for its faculty, the Jacob Biely Faculty Research Prize. In July 2004 he was named a Distinguished University Scholar at UBC, and in January 2005 was named a UBC University Killam Professor. In April of that year he was elected a fellow of the newly formed Canadian Academy of Health Sciences. Also in 2005, Evans was one of two finalists for CIHR's Michael Smith Prize in Health Research. In 2014 he received an honorary doctorate from the Université de Montréal.

What is most notable about this collection of honours over the past two decades is that they have come from a diverse set of organizations in Canada and abroad, representing the public, health care institutions, health care professional organizations, health services research (and research funding) organizations, a private foundation, a broadly based health research organization, and his academic colleagues. He is, for example, an honorary life member not only of the Canadian Association for Health Services and Policy Research, but also of the Canadian College of Health Leaders. Finally, we would be remiss if we did not note that Bob is a remarkably warm, generous, and unpretentious human being. We all consider ourselves fortunate to have had the opportunity to learn from him, to work with him, and to have him as a colleague.

THE CONTENT

In the beginning it seemed like such a wonderful, and simple, idea – pull together Bob's best works, wrap them between book covers, and distribute widely. Alas, we were overwhelmed with an embarrassment of riches and a herculean task of selection and organization. The objectives and the selection criteria (described above) seemed sensible and practical, until they ran hard up against the reality of this author's body of work. It was not as if the best and most important pieces came with flashing lights or signs that said "Pick me," and there was no "right" way to organize whatever gems we chose. We went through a number of organizing frameworks before settling on the four-section structure that the reader will find here. That structure is a direct reflection of the most common foci or themes within Bob's collected works. The first section contains a number of his most withering attacks on the assumptions, values, and favourite techniques that plague the discipline of economics and the subdiscipline of health economics. These criticisms are more than simply disputes about abstract notions. The choices that the researcher makes affect his or her results and the implications that follow (or, more succinctly, "garbage in, garbage out"); when those results are taken seriously by individuals with policy responsibilities, the implications can be far-reaching, and harmful.

Much of Bob's work has focused, in one form or another, on the key policy challenges facing health care systems in all developed economies. While his "playground" was often Canada, significant chunks of his best work emerged out of international comparisons (largely Canada-US).

Within the broad "health care policy" rubric, however, was a large cluster of papers that focused more specifically on the question of how health care should be financed, and the implications of different financing decisions. There were enough key contributions in this area that we devoted a separate section, Section B, to those papers. Other papers touching on a wider variety of health care policy topics populate Section C.

The final section of this collection, Section D, contains a selection of works drawn from Bob's work in the Population Health field. The astute reader will note that these cover a more narrow chronological range, reflecting the fact that this work did not begin to draw his intellectual curiosity until the Population Health Program was created by CIAR in the late 1980s. The section, and the book, closes with a revised, and previously unpublished, version of a presentation from 2013. It focuses largely on the determinants of health in populations, but also brings the reader full circle back to the vexing problems that populate Section A.

The papers for each section were chosen using a semi-structured process whereby the four editors, a few friends (including two of those who wrote section forewords, Theodore Marmor and Anthony Culyer), and the author himself independently rated each of Bob's works as Category I (must be included), Category II (would be good to include), or Category III (not essential). Including any paper that was rated as Category I or II by any of the seven members of the selection committee would have left us with a volume containing over 60 papers. Through several iterations, involving many hours of rereading papers and many more hours of group discussion, we managed to reduce 60+ to about 30. We thought we were done, but alas, our publisher informed us that this would fill two volumes. Needless to say, the cutting room floor was littered with gems. As compensation, we provide a number of suggestions for further reading at the end of each section.

The papers included in this volume have been taken from a wide range of locations. Most were originally published in leading, peer-reviewed, health care policy or health services research journals. A few first appeared as chapters in other collections. Three are rather different, in some important ways. First, readers may note that Chapter 3 has a different style than most of the other chapters. This is the only one of the papers penned by Bob for his "Undisciplined Economist" column that is included. These columns were all of an "editorial/commentary" style, shorter and more direct than a traditional academic paper, and intended for a somewhat different audience. Other papers from that column appear in the Further Readings list for Section D, and of course the rest (all well worth reading) can be found in back issues of *Healthcare Policy*. Second, Chapter 8 is one of two previously unpublished pieces, a result not of poor quality (indeed, it is the editors' view that this is the best extant treatment of the topic, by anyone) but of unfinished business. It was originally intended as a chapter in an updated version of Bob's seminal textbook, *Strained Mercy*, which, for a variety of reasons, was never completed. Finally, Chapter 16 is an edited transcript of a recent public lecture.

We realized, when we were done, that this process was much like the process of picking a men's Canadian Olympic hockey team – we could have chosen two or three different, non-overlapping, sets of 20 papers, and each of them would have been a compelling collection of insights and timeless contributions well worth the read. Alas, once again, our publisher would not have been amused. At the end of the day, we are comfortable that we have included here an interesting and important mix of the best-known, the best, some terrific but more obscure, and some previously unpublished.

IN CLOSING

One of us (Greg Stoddart) has referred to Bob as "the Wayne Gretzky of health economics," not only because he performs his craft at a higher level than anyone else, but also because he elevates the game of all those around him. We consider ourselves extremely fortunate to have been among those who have had our games elevated. We hope you enjoy the read as much as we have enjoyed the process of creating this timeless legacy to a great mind and a wonderful colleague and friend.

Morris Barer, University of British Columbia
Greg Stoddart, McMaster University (Emeritus)
Kim McGrail, University of British Columbia
Chris McLeod, University of British Columbia

April 2015

Acknowledgments

This project would not have been completed without contributions from a number of key individuals, each of whom did some of the heavy lifting at critical junctures. We are deeply indebted to five key members of the team – Karen Cardiff, Megan Engelhardt, Judy Hamel, Kyla Madden, and Dawn Mooney. There were permissions to reprint to secure from original sources (Karen, Megan) and from co-authors (Megan); there was the huge and thankless task of converting all of the papers from the original (largely pdf) format to a common format usable by the publisher (Judy, Megan, Karen); there was the challenge of recreating all of the tables and figures (Dawn); and then there was the careful assembly of the entire book (Megan). Kyla was our key contact at McGill-Queen's University Press (MQUP), and has been a source of immense patience, encouragement, and support throughout the life of the project. Her first, and perhaps most important, contribution was deciding that this project was of interest to MQUP. The fact that she saw this as worth pursuing served as fuel when we needed it most. She also provided timely advice on structure, content, organization, more mundane matters, such as reference formats and indexing, publication options, review options, approaches to promotion, and on and on. Many other members of the MQUP team, including Ryan Van Huijstee, Patricia Kennedy, Jennifer Roberts, and Jack Hannan, helped during the later stages of book editing, production, and promotion.

We owe a particular debt of gratitude to the five individuals – Tony Culyer, Jerry Hurley, Ted Marmor, John Frank, and Alan Bernstein – who signed on (with enthusiasm) for the job of writing forewords for each of the book's sections. These are each fitting in their own way, reflective of the relationships each had (and has) with Bob, and wonderful in their stylistic variety. The final product was also improved as a result of us attending to the thoughtful suggestions provided by two external reviewers.

We are grateful for the financial support for this project provided by UBC's Centre for Health Services and Policy Research, the Institutes of Health Services and Policy Research, and Population and Public Health (Canadian Institutes of Health Research), and the Canadian Institute for Advanced Research (CIFAR). Without that support, this project would not have seen the light of day.

The debt to the last of these (CIFAR) extends well beyond their financial support for this project, however. Absent the remarkable insight and support that this organization provided to Bob, and to the rest of the Population Health program during its life, Section D of this book would not exist. And Bob's involvement in that program, and the insights gathered therefrom, had a profound influence on everything he (and for that matter we) wrote (whether or not specifically about the health of populations) from that point forward.

SECTION A

On Economics and Economists

Foreword

ANTHONY J. CULYER

Two themes inhabit this section. One is about what economists *may* say (legitimately, as economists); the other what they *so often actually do say* (with no legitimacy whatsoever). The latter sins give rise to ample opportunities for rebukes and debunks, and Evans never fails to rise to the occasion. Economists are not especially renowned as aphorism inventors. But he is an exception. I shall distill what I take to be the guts of his teachings on the two themes and illustrate the rebukes and debunks with some choice examples (without spoiling all the reading fun for those who care to venture into the papers in this section).

WHAT ECONOMISTS CAN SAY THAT IS TRUE

What can economics contribute to an understanding of health and health care? Six principles, according to Evans, are the main part of it, and they are woven into the fabric of each of the contributions in this section. "The TSX Gives a Short Course in Health Economics" is a neat summary. They hardly themselves depend on a sophisticated grasp of economic theory, but it takes a different kind of sophistication to avoid falling into the honeyed trap of loving obscure mathematical elegance above all else (on which more anon).

First comes the I ≡ E accounting identity – Income equals Expenditure. A useful warning that the advocates for more E may have their piggy little eyes actually fixed more on the I than the E, irrespective of whether they work in the public or private sector, or whether they are professionals or blue-collared folks. Second comes the distribution of consequences: always unequal, sometimes planned that way, and generally best anticipated (left-wingers note well) by a thorough understanding of the workings of markets. Third, "it's the prices, stupid." Another identity E ≡ PQ. Health care expenditure is necessarily equal to the quantities of things on which it is spent times their prices. Implication: expenditure control does not have to be exercised through service adjustments alone. Equally, increases in public expenditure on health care can easily be swallowed up in prices (including those paid to service providers; see I ≡ E above).

Fourth, the non-inevitability of rising health care expenditures. It should not need saying (but it does) that health care expenditures are always the outcome of choices: choices about the services available in a public (or private) insurance package, about who has access and on what terms, about the types of technology utilized by professionals, about whom to treat, about the prices to be paid, and about the structure of the industry and its regulation. All of these choices are determined by human decisions. As Evans says, "health economists should each be required to write out one thousand times 'The technology does *not* dictate its own range of application.'" The pattern and direction of change in expenditure is not necessarily chosen in an obvious or crudely maximizing way (for some subtleties see "Toward a Healthier Economics"). Amongst determinants other than the prospect of financial gain, "schooling, force of habit and herd instincts are powerful conditioners." But financial gain remains, and there are less subtle sources of influence too – industry can (and does) influence economists (along with everyone else), using myriad enticements and tools; the list of ruses used by pharmaceutical companies is long and well evidenced (see, for instance, Morgan, Barer, and Evans, 2000, which, given space, would have fit comfortably here).

From these considerations arises the fifth principle – expenditure control is as much a political as an economic outcome. Both the regulated and the regulators have their own agendas and often seek to impose constraints on lower-level decision-makers. These will usually be to the benefit of those who constrain (and occasionally may be to the benefit of the clients of the system). However, the political choices must not be *assumed* to be in the public interest, whatever the self-serving protests of the politicians.

The sixth principle is that markets for health care and markets for health insurance don't work well. Textbooks today are full of the reasons why, but Evans played an important early role in exposing them. The major reasons are reviewed in Evans (1984), particularly in the chapter on "Licensure, Consumer Ignorance, and Agency." Despite that, pro-market ideology often rules the day and the public interest requires every new generation to relearn the reasons why public regulation and public finance, though imperfect, are better than the even-more-imperfect unregulated markets (hence the importance of this collection). Some bad ideas about the organization and finance of health care, like zombies, simply refuse to lie down and die, especially when it is in someone's interest to keep them undead. Evans' own views on the potential role of market forces have evolved and "hardened" over the span of his career. Having watched the evidence against markets, however adapted, accumulate for several decades, largely in the United States, Evans now takes a much more skeptical view of their potential benefits. Perhaps his strongest statement of this evolved view can be found in Chapter 3 in this section of the book.

WHAT ECONOMISTS SAY THAT AIN'T TRUE

Oh what a tangled web we weave
When first we practise to deceive.
Walter Scott

"Quantophrenia" is a term coined by Pitrim Sorokin in his critique of *Fads and Foibles in Sociology*. It refers to an obsessive preoccupation with quantifying things without regard for their importance. Robert Heilbroner has said that "mathematics has given economics rigour, but alas, also mortis." The influence of quantophrenia in economics has been much magnified by its coupling with the idea of "positivism" as initiated by Milton Friedman (1953) in *Essays in Positive Economics*. On the face of it, distinguishing between discourse that is value-free and discourse that is value-full is useful. It identifies disagreements that might be resolved by empirical inquiry and those that might be resolvable only by fighting to the death. What distresses Evans, however, is the careless way in which some economists "slouch toward Chicago." "A body of thought that includes normative assumptions is a religion, not an academic discipline, much less a science." He delights in pointing out inconsistencies. The positivists emphasize not only the absence of value judgments but also the pre-eminence of evidence – and then fail miserably to follow their own precepts.

Evidence comes in three forms in positive theory. In propositions of the form "If A and if B then C," A is an empirical prior and C is a predicted consequence (which must be capable of empirical falsification). B is about the domain of the theory – the codling moth maggot in the economic apple. It specifies the empirical circumstances under which C is predicted (such as "given that individuals are fully informed about options available" or "assuming perfect competition" or "assuming a closed economy"). Evans complains, with ample justification, that B is too often based on sloppily assuming that the real world bears a close relationship to the required circumstances or simply asserting that they are a handy simplification that does not affect C.

Under specific circumstances, price systems both convey information and generate incentives governing behaviour in detailed and mutually sensitive ways. The appeal of such decentralized "market" systems is both functional and aesthetic. They also provide suggestive support for those with pre-existing political or philosophical value judgments about the nature of people and the kinds of relationships that *should* exist amongst them. Economists have, of course, thought about this. There are two famous "fundamental theorems" of welfare economics which state, given some very demanding B-type conditions, that all competitive equilibria are Pareto-optimal and, given some further demanding B-type conditions, that all Pareto-optima are also competitive equilibria. However, even if the B conditions applied (which never happens in health care), the subtle shift from positive (if A and given B then C) to normative (C is good so A must be good) is unwarranted. A Pareto-optimum is not the sum total of human well-being; its use lies in the intuition that any change that meets with everyone's approval (or at least one person's and no dissent), is uncontroversial. But that does not exclude many other changes that may also be "good" but are ones upon which the Pareto criterion simply cannot be used. The pseudo-scientific attempt to remove interpersonal and other value judgments from the realm of economics ends up by rendering the procedure for the most part useless.

The alternative, of course, is to be open and upfront about the value judgments one makes. Evans' charge is a general one against all economists, but his heaviest rebukes are for health economists who not only invent their B but *also infiltrate personal value judgments*. This is not being open and upfront about values. It is fundamentally deceptive. Here Evans leans heavily on that great Scot of the Enlightenment, David Hume (*A Treatise on Human Nature*), and his classic posing of what is now generally known as the "is-ought problem." R.M. Hare described what he called "Hume's Law" in this way: an ought-statement cannot be validly inferred from any number of is-statements alone – the is-ought fallacy is the fallacy of drawing an "ought" conclusion from a set of "is" premises. Or, as Evans, quoting his colleague Chris Archibald, briskly puts it, "no ethics in – no ethics out"!

All of this underlines the fact (can it be disputed?) that, though prestige in economics usually goes to those whose modelling is pure mathematics, economics is not a science. Evans is not alone in bewailing economists' scientific pretensions. Deirdre McCloskey (1998) wrote, in *The Rhetoric of Economics*, "The most important example of economic rhetoric ... is metaphor. Economists call them 'models.' To say that markets can be represented by supply and demand 'curves' is no less a metaphor than to say that the west wind is 'the breath of autumn's being.'" Most economists concentrate on a high standard of *mathematical proof* rather than the accumulation of relevant, documented facts. Evans points out one unfortunate consequence: "nifty ideas" get Nobel Prizes (even when they are wrong), and the awarders of the prize don't trouble to make the recipients wait (unlike Einstein, Higgs, et al.) (for more on this, see "What, Me Worry?" in Section D). Evans asks (in "Toward a Healthier Economics") why the International Health Economics Association has an Arrow but not a Kessel Prize, in recognition of the latter's landmark 1958 "Price Discrimination in Medicine" paper. Evans posits, with considerable justification, that Kessel's paper is much more important than Arrow's 1963 paper for anyone trying to understand the economics of health care.

A good example of falling into the "is-ought" morass is the literature on the "excess burden" of health insurance (private or public). That literature provides us with glorious conclusions such as the "fact" that individuals who cannot afford to pay for the health care they need represent an "allocative distortion." That really is what's happening out there in the land of professional economics (at least in some parts of the United States).

The fact that the Pareto criterion is silent on matters of interpersonal distribution or redistribution of income, wealth – or, come to that, health – is frequently interpreted either as a statement that economists ought not to discuss it (eh?) or as a statement that such distributions and redistributions have nothing to do with welfare – a manifest (and empirical) nonsense.

Then there is plain incompetence. Evans cites several examples, from which we can all learn. Two good ones are in cost-benefit analysis, which, with its sister cost-effectiveness analysis, is a rich breeding ground for incompetent work (and not only through explicit bias or from inadequately trained health economists). Exhibit 1 (from "Toward a Healthier Economics"): "Harberger ... states quite explicitly that economists have no special competence in making value judgments or interpersonal comparisons, and then in the same breath proceeds to do precisely that. 'Costs and benefits *should* [Evans' emphasis] normally be added up without regard to the individual(s) to whom they accrue.'" Evidently equal weighting is one particular form of interpersonal comparison. Exhibit 2 (from "Slouching Toward Chicago"): "The number of cost-benefit analyses that have used estimated values of *livelihood* streams as a value for *lives* is too large and too depressing to justify individual citation. If this were the appropriate measure, the social convention in catastrophe would be 'women and children last,' and euthanasia of the elderly would be by an overwhelming margin our most cost-effective public program."

Maybe you can't fool all of the people all of the time, but some, alas, keep trying, which makes it all the more important to heed Bob's timeless reminder: "Hume may be dead, but his principle lives on" (Culyer and Evans, 1996).

REFERENCES

Arrow, K. (1963). "Uncertainty and the Welfare Economics of Medical Care," *American Economic Review* 53(5): 941–73.

Culyer, A.J., and Evans, R.G. (1996). "Mark Pauly on Welfare Economics: Normative Rabbits from Positive Hats," *Journal of Health Economics* 15: 243–51.

Evans, R.G. (1984). *Strained Mercy: The Economics of Canadian Health Care*. Toronto: Butterworths.

Friedman, M. (1953). *Essays in Positive Economics*. Chicago: University of Chicago Press.

Hume, D. (1738). *A Treatise on Human Nature*.

Kessel, R. (1968). "Price Discrimination in Medicine," *Journal of Law and Economics* 1: 20–53.

McCloskey, D. (1998). *The Rhetoric of Economics*. 2nd ed. Madison: University of Wisconsin Press.

Morgan, S.G., Barer, M.L., and Evans, R.G. (2000). "Health Economists Meet the Fourth Tempter: Drug Dependency and Scientific Discourse." *Health Economics* 9: 659–67

Sorokin, P. (1956). *Fads and Foibles in Modern Sociology and Related Sciences*, Chicago: H. Regnery Co.

1

Slouching Toward Chicago: Regulatory Reform as Revealed Religion (1982)

ROBERT G. EVANS

Turning and turning in the widening gyre
The falcon cannot hear the falconer;
Things fall apart; the centre cannot hold;
Mere anarchy is loosed upon the world,
The blood-dimmed tide is loosed, and everywhere
The ceremony of innocence is drowned;
The best lack all conviction, while the worst
Are full of passionate intensity.

* * *

And what rough beast, its hour come round at last,
Slouches towards Bethlehem to be born?

W.B. Yeats, "The Second Coming"

Economists have rather a guilty conscience about values. Many of them aspire to a "scientific" form of analysis, a discipline built solely on positive propositions about how economies function. Such a collection of descriptive, causal statements, "if *A*, then *B*," would serve as the foundation of all

This chapter originally appeared as an article in the *Osgoode Hall Law Journal* in 1982. See R.G. Evans, "Slouching Toward Chicago: Regulatory Reform as Revealed Religion." *Osgoode Hall Law Journal* 20(31): 454. Reprinted with the permission of *Osgoode Hall Law Journal*.

policy analysis. Normative propositions – one (society, the government) ought to do *A* – would then follow from the choice of *B* as a valued objective. Economists might recommend *A* as policy, but strictly speaking their functions as scientific economists end once they have demonstrated the causal linkage from *A* to *B*. Their values with respect to *B* stand on the same footing as those of any other citizen. The role played by the "scientific" economist in policy formation is simply that of establishing the menu of possible choices, the framework of positive constraints, from which a society makes its selections.[1]

The commitment to positive methodology is itself a value strongly held and advocated or preached by a number of economists, although it is interesting that those who profess positivism most loudly are often those who recommend particular policies most energetically.[2] But in fact the possibility of such a radical separation between "is" and "ought" in economics is illusory.

In the first place, as Schumpeter noted, ideology "enters on the very ground floor, into the pre-analytical cognitive act."[3] What we choose to study, how we define the essential properties of the objects of analysis, and what we think are their significant, as opposed to incidental, interrelationships, all depend on our value systems. We begin the positive analysis with a "model" in the broad sense, which establishes intellectual categories, defines boundaries between different phenomena, and in a world where everything depends on everything else in several ways, suggests which sets of dependencies are likely to be worth investigating and which are likely to be accidental correlations. Thus, unfortunately for "scientific" economics, the values are built in before the positive analysis begins. And these values are culturally conditioned, as is strikingly demonstrated by the major differences in underlying models and in research programs followed in different countries in "the same" subdisciplines of economics.[4]

But the impact of values on analysis extends well beyond the pre-analytic phase. The generation and testing of self-sustaining positive propositions, whose validity can be demonstrated either absolutely or probabilistically so as to command universal assent even among economists, turns out to be beyond our capacity. Despite advances in computational, statistical, or mathematical technique, there is no evidence that the situation is improving. We learn more about particular situations, but the "laws of motion" of society elude us. The central methodological problem appears to be that pointed out some years ago by Heracleitus, developed in more detail by Georgescu-Roegen.[5] Positive analysis in practice always embodies a number of simplifying assumptions, empirical judgments, and often just plain guesses, to move it across the gaps in which empirical evidence is missing, or more commonly ambiguous. In this process, of course, value judgments play an inevitable role.[6]

One response to this difficulty, discussed by Archibald in the context of the "realism of assumptions" debate, is to moderate the positivist program by explicit recognition that unambiguous testing of theory in economics is impossible. Instead one can strive for "realism" of both assumptions and conclusions by a process of observation of as wide a range of evidence as possible, and by highlighting the judgmental components and making the value judgments as explicit and open as possible.[7]

An alternative, however, is to follow the sermon notes of the legendary Scottish preacher coping with the problem of the origin of evil – "This point very doubtful – Shout Loudly!!" In economic analysis this takes the form of assigning normative significance to positive propositions themselves. One *ought* to believe that *A* implies *B*. And indeed the development of schools of thought in economic analysis seems to take place around particular sets of positive propositions that are held as items of belief. Free markets, or governments, are alleged to function in certain ways, and if the evidence for such propositions is ambiguous, then assent to the proposition becomes an article of faith.[8]

The assignment of normative significance to positive propositions has great functional value. The individual or group that can set the menu or define the constraints for social choice in economic policy may wield enormous political power. If this set of constraints were as unambiguously established as an astronomical prediction about sunrise, then the analyst's power would be illusory; he would merely be a conduit transmitting the laws of nature. But there are few if any such "laws" in economics. (Astronomers do not argue bitterly over the expected time of tomorrow's sunrise.)

The "scientific" analyst, in claiming such neutral status, is usually supporting a set of normative judgments as well, which either underlie or interpenetrate the positive analysis. And these normative judgments are often of fundamental importance. Cost-benefit analysts, for example, frequently make "scientific" judgments about the value of a human life that are hidden in the footnotes or the technical appendix. (What is ironic is that even on their own terms they get the measure wrong![9]) But the status of the analyst, and his claim to a special role in policy-making, depends on the perception by the rest of the community that the process of analysis is scientific, and "value-free." The positivist claim is thus central to the advancement of the normative interests embedded in the analysis and to the maintenance of a social role for the analyst as something other than a "hired gun" or public relations agent for openly identified interests.[10] Hence the normative significance attached by analysts to the acceptance of particular positive propositions, independent of the quality of the evidence for them.

Indeed the social importance of apparently positive propositions is such that they may be ultimately rendered immune to attack by being embedded in completely circular theories, whose intellectual content is thus nil but whose political appeal is very powerful. At this point, economic analysis meets religion. The faith of Pangloss in Divine Providence is held up to ridicule because it cannot be assailed in any other way. Once one assumes that the world is in fact ruled by Divine Providence, it follows that whatever happens is for the best and cannot be improved. No empirical evidence will serve as refutation; one can only laugh. The similarity to theories of fully informed rational consumers freely transacting in perfectly competitive markets is not accidental. Both are rooted in the same "natural law" tradition, whose foundations are theological, not empirical.[11] More generally, however, one finds in (some) religions great normative importance attached to particular apparently positive propositions. Pagels analyses the conflict in the early Christian church between orthodox Catholics and various forms of Gnostics over such issues as whether Christ was crucified and died in the flesh, or whether the whole transaction was a spiritual shadow play.[12] What was required of the orthodox was neither a positive view (I think, on the basis of the evidence, that a physical death occurred) nor a normative one (it is a good thing for us, that Christ died ... etc.), but rather belief – certain propositions must be accepted as fact if one is to go to heaven. The Apostles' Creed contains a mixture of testable and non-testable propositions, but the whole must be accepted on faith as literally true, and this, rather than the acceptance of normative principles of good and bad conduct, separates sheep from goats. Moral uprightness by itself does not lead to heaven; religion (or at least Christianity) was not and is not now simply a code of conduct.

But the attachment of normative significance to positive propositions is consistent with social and organizational objectives. The Creed was of central importance to the interests of the church as an organizational entity as well as serving to advance the values that Christianity embodied. In the same way, assent to various positive propositions about how economies function serves to maintain the organizational coherence and social status of economists – for a time at least – as well as advancing the values and interests that are smuggled into the positivist analysis. From this perspective it ceases to be surprising that the most ardent advocates of a positivist program of methodology in economic research are also among the most strident and self-confident proponents of radical policy change. When the issue is doubtful, speak loudly.

The mix of value and fact, of ought and is, is inevitable in all economic analysis. Purely formal, mathematical exercises may appear immune, but these only become economic analysis when they are superimposed upon some actual economy, and that superposition cannot be value-free. The mathematical entities must be assigned real-life "objective correlatives" – a discretionary and judgmental process. It would thus be rather naive to imagine that the application of economic analysis to issues in the public regulation of economic activity, or any other field of policy, would permit objective "scientific" discussion and the generation of value-free conclusions as to appropriate action. Economics does not transcend Hume; or in Archibald's paraphrase, "No Ethics In, No Ethics Out."[13]

In fact, the very identification of "regulation" as a separate area of public economic policy itself rests on certain implicit value judgments about the proper or "normal" role of the state in economic life. It presupposes a system of private market institutions which under normal circumstances governs the economic processes of production, distribution, and exchange. The state intervenes in particular situations with authoritative, and ultimately coercive, "regulations" which compel people or organizations to behave in ways they would otherwise not choose to do. Such regulatory intervention may be justified in particular circumstances; what those circumstances might be forms a large part of the economics of regulation. But given an underlying system of values which include individualism and freedom from compulsion, there is an implicit bias, a prior presumption, that places the burden of justification on the proponents of the regulatory intervention, not the free market alternative.

Yet the distinction between the regulatory activities of the state and economic policy in general is far from clear. Most people would recognize as regulation the passage of a law or regulation by a duly constituted governing body, or its delegates, mandating or prohibiting specific actions. But specific taxes, tariffs, or subsidies can achieve similar results. The delegation of "self-regulatory" powers to occupations or supply-managing groups of producers (agricultural marketing boards, taxi cabs) is clearly public regulation at one remove, as is the formation of public corporations – Air Canada, Petrocan, provincial liquor boards. General macroeconomic policy, monetary and fiscal, is not usually referred to as economic regulation, yet all sorts of industry- or group-specific benefits and burdens are implicit in such policy, and many are explicit.

If we focus on the fact that regulations, by changing the opportunities faced by individuals, serve to redistribute wealth or property rights, then it is undeniable that regulation is a form of taxation; it is equally a form of expenditure or transfer payment.[14] But then so is every other form of public economic policy, the tax-transfer effects of an anti-inflationary policy of high interest rates being an obvious example.

It does *not* follow, of course, that since all forms of public economic policy redistribute property rights, therefore "each ... is ... a close substitute for each of the others."[15] Coal, oil, natural gas, wood, and lard are all forms of energy, yet one cannot put lumps of coal in the gas tank of a car, or gasoline in a home furnace. Economic instruments have different comparative advantages, as well as side effects. But the separation of government "regulation" from economic policy in general seems to presuppose some definition of public economic activity that is not regulatory, not interventionist, a "natural" level to which "deregulation" would return us. How that level might be determined is obscure.

Regulation is clearly not everything beyond "anarchy plus a constable" – quite apart from who employs and directs the constable. The idea that the adjudication of property rights and enforcement of contract is somehow non-regulatory, or that one pattern of tax policy or money supply determination represents "regulation" and another does not, requires some concept of a pattern of economic intercourse prior to, or separate from, any form of public regulatory policy. This is certainly fallacious history, and bad, though common, economics – I believe it is also bad law. It would seem that the examination of values in the regulatory process cannot proceed independently of their more general role in economic policy.

And indeed we do find a substantial correlation of attitudes toward macroeconomic policies – fiscal, monetary, trade – with views on "regulatory" policy more narrowly defined. Particularly among the more outspoken universal "deregulationists," it is apparent that the analysis of any particular market or industry is dominated by a more general set of value judgments about the "natural," usually minimal, role of the public sector in economic, or any other, activity. Whatever the state does in the economic sphere (or out of it) will reassign property rights and influence patterns of economic behaviour, and any debate over what the state should or should not do in this regard, whether or not conducted in the rhetoric peculiar to any particular discipline, will involve such conflicting value propositions.

In such debates economic rhetoric has been particularly prominent, because economists have worked out a very detailed set of formal theoretical propositions about how transactors interact with each other in the economic sphere in the absence of formal direction. Their insights as to how systems of prices can in theory, and often do in practice, serve as decentralized coordinating mechanisms, providing "solutions" to otherwise hideously complex social problems of resource allocation and distribution, suggest that broad areas of activity can be carried on not only adequately, but, indeed on fairly general criteria, more satisfactorily, independent of detailed state planning and intervention. Under specific circumstances, the price system both conveys information and generates incentives to govern the behaviour of transactors in a detailed and sensitive way. The appeal of such decentralized systems is both functional and, to their students, aesthetic. They also provide powerful support for pre-existing political or philosophical value judgments about the nature of man and the proper forms of social interaction.

In fact, however, theoretical economics does not in itself provide support for either regulation or deregulation. The famous two "fundamental theorems" of welfare economics demonstrate only that, under fairly restrictive conditions, all competitive equilibria are Pareto-optimal and, under even more restrictive conditions, all Pareto-optima are competitive equilibria.

In other words, in a society in which *all* resource allocation is determined by the behaviour of atomistic, self-interested, perfectly competitive, and fully informed transactors who take prices as parametric, and in which prices adjust freely, and where prices and markets exist for *all* present and future commodities, specific to any uncertain state of nature, then a competitive equilibrium *if it exists* will be such that no one can be made better off without making someone else worse off (the first theorem). Whether such an equilibrium will in fact be reached is another matter. If it is, however, it is optimal in the limited sense that no improvement is possible without sacrificing someone's interests to someone else's. If an economic outcome is not Pareto-optimal, there exists some other outcome that everyone would prefer.

Secondly, if in addition household preferences and firm technologies satisfy convexity conditions, then any such Pareto-optimal position can be reached by competitive processes in free markets from *some* specific initial allocation of resource endowments or property rights (the second theorem). If costless, lump-sum transfers of property rights can be carried out under full information, then any desired Pareto point can, if technically feasible, be reached from any initial rights allocation by a combination of lump-sum transfers and competitive market processes.

While interesting, these results by themselves generate no policy implications whatever ("No ethics in, no ethics out" again). There are many "Pareto-optimal" equilibria, including income/wealth/welfare distributions across the members of a society ranging from completely egalitarian to as unequal as one's index will allow. It is stressed in general equilibrium theory that the pattern of resource allocation and distribution represented by an arbitrarily chosen Pareto-optimal point is not in general "better" than an arbitrary non-Pareto point on whatever criterion is employed for ranking different outcomes. What *is* true is that, under stringent assumptions as to how individual and group preferences are formed, there will for any non-Pareto pattern of prices and distribution be *some* Pareto point(s) which is superior in the sense that some agent(s) has been made better off while no one has been made worse off; but it is simply an error to assume that if one is at a non-Pareto point, perfectly competitive prices and markets will lead to a *better* Pareto point. They will get to some Pareto point, but not necessarily a better one. The second theorem does say that any desired outcome can be achieved through competitive markets, but only if the initial property-rights distribution is such as to yield that outcome. This in turn suggests that if one could flexibly reallocate property rights *ab initio*, and if the other conditions held, then there would be a strong case for unregulated, freely competitive markets as a set of institutions for allocating resources. But if not, such a case would not exist.[16]

But economic analysis itself does not, and cannot, say anything about the appropriate distribution of either property rights or final outcomes. These are value questions pure and simple. Nor does economic theory say anything about the relative political feasibility of *ex ante* redistribution of property rights versus *ex post* reallocation of output through interference in private markets. It is important to stress this fact, because occasionally claims are made that "scientific" economic analysis can provide a basis, other than social value judgments, for particular patterns of income or wealth distribution.

These attempts form part of a historical sequence. The Norman baron replied to Edward's commissioners of *Quo Warranto* that he held his land from his grandfather, who had carried his sword with William the Bastard. As the dynamic instability of this source of rights was fairly clear, the justification for a particular distribution began to shift from might of king to Will of God. Stations in life became divinely ordained. As God's Will became less clear, "natural" rights emerged instead. The appeal to economics as a source of such natural right was based a century or so ago on marginal productivity theory, until it was recognized that marginal products in value terms are dependent on relative prices, which in turn depend on the initial rights distribution. Prices, and therefore marginal productivities, are endogenous.[17]

There is limited ethical appeal to a system in which the distribution of welfare depends critically on unpredictable factors beyond the control of individuals; not merely endowments – heredity and inheritance – but more importantly the effects of shifts in demand, supply, and technology. Services and resources that had a high marginal productivity yesterday may have none tomorrow. And while the investor in physical capital can diversify the portfolio to achieve a desired risk level, the investor in human capital is required to bet most of his net worth on the assumption that the marginal productivity of that human capital will be maintained. It is obviously to the economic advantage of society generally that resource allocation adapt quickly and smoothly to changes in resource availability, tastes, and technology, but transitional costs are inevitable. Resource suppliers may have to take decisions with very long-term consequences, at a point when a reasonable man could not have been expected to make a better judgment. The decision to enter an occupation with a long training period and specialized skills is an important example. Subsequent technological or market shifts may dramatically reduce the value of that investment. But to argue that all the costs of such adjustments should be borne by those who guessed wrong, and that such a redistribution, involving a large part of an individual's livelihood, is *ethically* attractive, seems to confuse a sin with a mistake.

More recently, a rather peculiar allegation has been made that a property rights distribution can be derived from considerations of transactions costs. An attempt to substantiate the claim turns out to apply, however, only to property rights in one's own person and powers, leaving all other forms of rights to property unassigned, and in fact fails even there to do more than assert a "natural" distribution – a predictable result, because economics possesses no settled theory of transactions costs.[18] Even if it did, those costs would still be defined in terms of relative prices that are endogenously dependent on the rights distribution itself. Economic theory will not exorcise Hume; the white coats of "science" may cover value judgments but cannot substitute for them.

A formal framework may, however, serve to display clearly the range of different value judgments that must be made prior to or during the discussion of economic policy. The concept of the social welfare function (SWF), hypothesized as some form of aggregator across the individual interests in a society, is useful in this regard. "Ought" statements about economic policy can then be interpreted as judgments about actions that will increase the social welfare function; "optimal" policy is defined as that which maximizes such a function.

But formalism introduces no new information. Indeed, the SWF as aggregator of individual interests is a restrictive sub-class of more general SWFs, under the assumption that society's welfare, insofar as it can be thought of at all, is some function of that of its component individuals, rather than being specified by the ruling Deity or Party. There is no a priori reason why a society should hold such individual-respecting views – but ours appears to do so. Thus we write: $W = F(U_1 (X^1{}_1 \dots X^1{}_j \dots X^1{}_m) \dots U_i (X^i{}_1 \dots X^i{}_j \dots X^i{}_m) \dots U_n (X^n{}_1 \dots X^n{}_j \dots X^n{}_m))$, which means simply that the overall society is composed of "n" individuals, each of whom has preferences defined over the amounts received, used, owned, perceived by him of "m" different entities. Thus $X^i{}_j$ is the amount of entity X_j that is somehow assigned to person i, and U_i is the welfare level of person i conditional on the pattern $X^i{}_j$. When X_j is a "good," then more $X^i{}_j$ increases U_i – more goods are good – but $X^i{}_j$ can equally be a "bad" to *i* – acid rain on his cottage. Then the function F somehow aggregates all the Ui into a global social welfare level W, and "good" economic policy is that which maximizes F. The maximization takes place, however, under a global production constraint linking the various X_j; the resources available to society limit output and impose tradeoffs. More X_j implies less X_k, once a technical efficiency frontier has been reached.[19]

This structure highlights two different levels of value judgments that are implicit or explicit in any discussion of economic policy, regulation included. The first is the structure of *F*, which includes the range of *i*. Who is included in *n*, and with what weights are they aggregated in *F*? (Non-inclusion implies zero weight.)

Economic analysis generally ignores the issue of the range of *i*, taking for granted that it is defined by and across some social or political unit. Market processes implicitly count people according to their wealth, that is, their initial resource endowments valued at equilibrium prices. Recently there has been a suggestion that weights based on wealth have ethical content as well, which yields the result that persons with insufficient wealth to sustain life should be dropped out of the SWF except insofar as their well-being enters some other, wealthier, person's utility function[20] – which Archibald and Donaldson call the "Dog and Master" approach to income distribution.[21] The notion can be stretched further; inheritance may be "justified" as respecting the wishes of the dead. This then implies that the set i includes dead persons, so long as they "possess" wealth, as well as excluding those of the living who do not.[22] It is hard to imagine a wide appeal for such a set of value judgments, once made explicit. In any case the basis for them cannot be found in economic analysis, which takes the boundaries of i and the structure of F as predetermined. Markets were made to serve man, not man to serve markets. Perhaps support for such ethical judgments could be found in some Plutonian theology, but it would certainly not be congruent with any of the major religions. "Natural" morality of course stretches to fit the values of the proposer.[23]

Second, and at least as important, is the judgment as to what should be included in the sets X^i_j. This in turn includes two types of decisions: (1) what shall j span? and (2) which elements of j enter particular U_i ( )? The second issue, in the form of externalities in consumption or interactive utility functions, has received considerable study – one individual's welfare may depend on that of others, $[U_i(U_k)]$ (non-paternalistic altruism), or on others' specific consumption patterns, $[U_i(X^k_j)]$. This last could be because k's stereo keeps i awake, or because i regrets k's use of cigarettes and the consequent damage to k's health (paternalistic altruism).

Such interactions, whatever their form, are positive questions; people's preferences either do or do not display these characteristics. But it blends into the first issue, the range of j, when we think about *what* counts. So long as X_j are identifiable economic commodities – shoes and ships and sealing wax – that are consumed in identifiable amounts by identifiable people or groups, the situation is clear. But the things that matter to people go far beyond this. One might have – people do have – strong tastes for living in certain types of society. Some value egalitarianism, others prefer inequality. Values are placed on collective perceptions – military strength, athletic fitness, godliness. At the micro level, your church-going behaviour may affect my well-being. The Moral Majority in the US is a dramatic example of a group with very complex utility function interactions, who allege that their welfare is affected by all sorts of activities by others which have no discernible direct impact on them, and who argue that the state, that is, the SWF, should respond to their preferences with regulations to control such behaviour. This seems typical of most religions, and highlights the importance of political processes in determining what shall count in the SWF and what preferences are illegitimate or irrelevant to policy.

What is ironic is the political alliance between those who explicitly adopt such an extended and complex view of the SWF and economic libertarians who at least claim to believe in (or hold as a value) a very simple SWF of a type that makes direct regulation both unnecessary and harmful. If there are no cross-utility function interactions, $X^k{}_j$ does not affect U_i either directly or through U_k, no public goods exist, and all commodities are well-defined and can be traded in markets with well-defined prices (these are the only X_j that do, or should, matter to people), and if the various behavioural and technical conditions outlined above are satisfied, then the two theorems of welfare economics hold, and the SWF can be maximized by private market transactions – but only *if* the initial property rights distribution is the one that will yield that maximum. If not, of course, the best that markets can do is to yield a set of U such that no U_i can be increased without decreasing some U_j; a Pareto point that will not, however, maximize W. There will be feasible non-Pareto sets U that lead to a greater SWF.

In practice, insistence on the Pareto criterion, or of non-comparability of utilities across persons (the "moral monstrousness" of sacrificing one person's interests for others'), amounts to denial of the legitimacy of any economic policy at all.[24] And the advocacy of free markets independent of any form of regulation *without* simultaneous advocacy of wealth redistribution logically implies acceptance, as a value premise, of whatever the current (deregulated) distribution happens to be. (Hegel's children live on; only now the market is the march of God through the world?)[25]

Even then, however, the question of what constitutes economic commodities remains open. By assumption one may rule out such "fuzzy" X_j as egalitarianism, or safe streets, or the nature of interpersonal relationships (the reply to Titmuss' question, "Who is my stranger?" is "Everybody").[26] This can be either a positive assumption (people do not really care about such things), or a normative one (society should not respond to such preferences any more than it should respond to those of sadists). But in analysis it frequently takes on the positive-normative or creedal character mentioned initially – despite counter-evidence one *should* accept the positive proposition that people do not *really* care about non-marketable things, and, in any event, market-like interactions can be dreamed up to explain away any form of evidence (such as families) that appears inconsistent with it.[27] So one should use only analytic tools that apply to commodity X_j and yield conclusions consistent with an all-commodity world. But what is a commodity?

Some reply, "Anything that can be bought and sold," and claim support from economics. But the claim is false. Economics does not say that a market in babies would contribute to social welfare. Babies could be treated as one of the X_j (means) or the U_i (ends), as transactor or transacted object, depending on the value judgments of the society in question.[28] A society that treats babies as ends not means, however, will have to display paternalistic (maternalistic) structures in part, at least, of its SWF. An erroneous judgment that "Economics" supports baby-trading may thus stem from the assignment of normative significance to the positive question of SWF structure – SWFs ought not to be paternalistic, economists ought not to use paternalistic SWFs in analysis, and so babies ought to be objects, not subjects.

Nor does object status necessarily imply commodity status. Societies have prohibited market trading, directly or indirectly, in human blood or organs, sexual favours, or land. And such judgments are neither right nor wrong on economic grounds. The economist may point out that ethical values involve tradeoffs too, and that refusal to treat an entity as a commodity may require the giving up of other valued things, but he cannot judge the tradeoff itself.

But a tradeoff is not inevitable; Titmuss has demonstrated that, in the case of human blood, societies that treat it as a commodity to be allocated in private markets show inferior performance on narrow economic criteria of cost and quality to those in which it is not a commodity.[29] Indeed, it appears that in health care generally (though not universally), full commodity status and private market allocation leads to inferior results on cost, effectiveness, and access dimensions relative to societies in which commodity status is more problematic.[30]

Even more generally, quite apart from the peculiarities of particular commodities, it is simply a theoretical error to suggest that assignment of commodity status to an object necessarily improves overall well-being. Suppose that the production structure of an economy and the preference structure of its participants meet all the requirements for private market transactions to yield a Pareto-optimal point, except that trading is only permitted in $M - 1$ commodities. Markets in commodity M are, for some reason, forbidden, even though M embodies no special ethical considerations. If markets in M are then opened, it follows that those previously constrained by the absence of markets will only transact in such new markets if the transactions make them better off. *Ceteris paribus*, the opportunity to trade would thus improve their welfare, without hurting others. But *ceteris paribus* here does not hold. The critical assumption that trades between "i" and "j" do not affect "k" is false;

the new market in *M* will affect prices and quantities transacted in all other M – 1 markets, and thereby the value of wealth (for any given initial endowment) of all "n" transactors. Hence the Pareto-point reached after market *M* is opened need not be superior to that reached in M – 1 markets, even if commodity *M* has none of the special characteristics of blood or health care. Indeed, the transactors in *M* themselves may be worse off. Free markets (and full information, and absence of externalities, and perfect competition and …) ensure that transactors in *M* are better off after transacting than before, given that an *M* market exists, but not that they are better off than before the market was opened. The overall impact of the new market on other prices and quantities may make them worse off. Thus it is not a priori against the interests of individuals that they are prevented from selling organs, or working in unsafe environments for higher pay, even apart from informational or externality issues. Partial equilibrium analysis may yield invalid answers in a general equilibrum world.[31]

Regulation, then, may be seen as part of the set of social processes which respond to values embedded in the social welfare function but unattainable by, or unrecognized in, or even directly inimical to, the process of arm's-length commodity trading in unregulated markets. This is simply a restatement of the traditional view; public regulation of economic activity serves to remedy failures in markets as resource allocation mechanisms, with the rider that the prior assumption that markets are the "normal" mechanism and regulation is merely remedial is itself a pre-analytic value judgment.

More recent critiques of the regulatory process have pointed out that this "traditional" view rests on two contestable assumptions, that markets do indeed "fail" relative to the optimization of some plausible SWF, and that the political process is capable of remedying such failures.

In contrast, the "deregulationist" school argues that, although the stringent conditions – technical, behavioural, or informational – for optimal market performance would seem to be widely violated in the real world, yet for a variety of reasons markets do not in fact "fail," or at least not often and not by much. Simultaneously, there have developed economic theories of the political process that characterize it in such a way that it is incapable of responding positively to market failure. In the limit some appear to argue, on essentially a priori grounds, that markets cannot in fact be improved upon, there are really no market failures except those *induced* by public intervention, and even if there were, regulation is by its nature unable to do anything but make the situation worse.[32] Pangloss and anti-Pangloss.

The "regulate everything" and "regulate nothing" schools represent polar cases; there is of course an intellectual and policy middle ground that recognizes that social mechanisms for resource allocation do not in fact split neatly into "private" and "public," but rather lie along a continuum from totally unregulated private firms (if there are such) to public institutions totally immune from market forces (if there are such), and a great deal, probably most, of any society's work gets done between these poles. Furthermore, all human institutions have characteristic virtues and vices, and policy-making is a continual struggle for improvement in institutional design under ever-changing circumstances. Thus one can simultaneously advocate more regulation in one area, less in a second, and different in a third. But in any case such advocacy will be built on a blend of positive propositions (believed, more or less well-established, positive judgments based on an often unconscious blend of fact, experience, guess, and wish, and normative assumptions about the good society or the SWF). And intellectual honesty, if not adversarial efficacy, would seem to require continual and diligent effort to separate and identify these different components of any position.

But the attitudinal poles are of considerable interest with respect to their mix of positive and normative bases. The "deregulation" school seems to enjoy the liveliest intellectual life at present, and alleges most energetically its positive foundations and its freedom from arbitrary value judgments. Since these claims cannot be true, the extent to which its policy recommendations serve as stalking horses for particular values is of interest. At the other pole, the extensive regulatory structures that are in place in all developed economies are all proposed and defended as remedies for market failures and responses to a general or widespread social interest; that is, as tending to increase the value of the SWF. Since this too is highly doubtful on the evidence, it is again of interest to inquire what values or interests are served in particular cases.[33]

And finally, a point that appears to have been almost totally neglected, the two poles may, in a perverse way, meet. If, as seems likely, complete deregulation is not politically feasible, and if certain types of regulation – "self-regulation," for example, or those that serve particularly powerful constituencies – are much more resistant to removal, the net effect of a blind drive to deregulate everything may be a much less conspicuous, and perhaps reduced, level of regulation with substantially more harmful net effects.[34] That this concern is serious may be indicated by the enthusiasm with which particular self-regulating occupations in the US greeted the new Reagan administration in 1981, despite its rhetoric of deregulation and "free" competition which would appear to be a very serious threat to their economic status.

This is a particular application of the general problem of the "Second Best." Even if an economy meets all the conditions necessary for private competitive markets to optimize the SWF, it does not follow that a partial move toward more competition is an improvement. Half a loaf may be worse than none, and the whole loaf is rarely attainable in this life at least.

The value foundations of theories and policy recommendations about regulation are most clearly displayed when one considers it as a mechanism of income/wealth redistribution. Economists in particular have long stressed the importance of regulation as a way of suppressing competition and thereby holding up the incomes of suppliers; they have given rather less attention to its role in holding down particular incomes.[35] Advocates of regulation in general attempt either to ignore or to minimize redistributive effects, or else to argue that such redistribution as occurs is justified – the beneficiaries are "deserving," and society benefits as a result. On the other hand, vulgar Marxists such as Stigler and his followers argue that redistribution is the *primary* purpose of regulation, and is demanded by the regulated for that purpose.[36] The most extreme deregulationists go further and argue, in accordance with the two points above, not only that the wealth transfer is unjustified, but that in fact it does not occur. The apparent benefits are all eaten up in dead-weight costs of acquiring regulation, which is thus a policy making no one better off and some worse off.[37]

The vulgar Marxist position has the virtue of being testable; one can look to see if in fact regulation was initiated by the regulated and if they appear to benefit. The answer appears to be yes to both, in many cases, but some very obvious "no's" appear as well. The most strident opponent of food and drug legislation in the US is the drug industry – and it draws energetic academic support from the Stiglerian school.[38] But the argument that regulatory redistribution in fact meets social objectives is rather more difficult to deal with. Middle-ground, wishy-washy regulatory reformers (of whom I think I am one) can reply in several ways. First, the costs of redistribution via market distortion are greater than via direct subsidy, and take the form of both allocative distortions (consumer surplus triangles) and, in a number of cases, sheer technical inefficiency or waste (operation off the production function). If redistribution really is an objective, we could all be better off if subsidies were paid instead. Second, the benefits of regulation become capitalized (taxicab medallions, milk quotas) and go not to the apparent beneficiaries (current suppliers) but to those who received the initial distribution of regulatory assets, who were issued medallions or milk quota rights, without charge, when the regulation was introduced. Third, it is not in fact true that society is aware of the re-distributional effects; regulation is a way of hiding transfers in a world of imperfect information.

To these, pro-regulationists may validly reply that the first response is mistaken; it assumes that the SWF is defined only over commodities, not processes. In fact, recipients of transfers strongly prefer them to be tied to productive activity. Their welfare is lowered by direct transfers. Given this structure, regulation may well be the optimal redistributive device. One can counter this rebuttal in the positive domain, claiming that recipients do not care, but casual empiricism suggests that this is wrong. Or one can move to the domain of values – recipients' preferences *should* not count – and outside that of positive analysis.

On the second point, it is true that some regulatory gains appear to be fully capitalized, but not all are, and in any case, what of it? Society's objective might not be to help farmers in general, for example, but to cushion one generation during a period of rapid technical change that would otherwise lower their incomes sharply. If the desired adjustment is not continuous, but in response to one particular set of events, then a capitalized regulatory asset (production quota) is the appropriate form of wealth redistribution. In any case, deregulation would certainly redistribute away from rights holders, who may have bought these rights at market prices. What is the justification for that?

The would-be deregulator seems to have two possible responses. He could accept the capitalized redistributive effects of regulation as given, and advocate a combination of deregulation plus buyouts of quota or regulatory rights. This removes the allocative distortions resulting from regulation, legitimizes the capital transfer, and avoids penalizing those who bought quotas at market rates.[39] The buyout approach ought to be acceptable in principle, but as Hartle and Trebilcock point out it has in practice serious disadvantages as explicit policy.[40]

The second alternative, then, is to fall back on the information argument. Imperfectly informed citizen voters have accepted a form of redistribution (wealth plus utility from mode) plus associated costs of allocative distortions that they did not in fact want. As Hartle and Trebilcock point out, this does not imply imperfectly informed *policy-makers*; they are likely to be very well-informed indeed. But their calculations must be based on election probabilities, as well as, or instead of, their perception of the public interest. Thus the imperfect-information argument forces on the policy analyst/advocate the task, not of advising the politician, but of educating the voter.[41]

For the absolute deregulator, however, there are at least two dilemmas. First, if he accepts the imperfect-information argument, it is difficult to argue simultaneously that transactors have all the information necessary to make markets work. Fully informed (or very informed) economic man and ill-informed (or stupid) political man have somehow to be crammed into the same physical body. Once widespread ignorance about the effects of particular regulated markets is accepted, perfection of unregulated markets looks a bit schizoid. It looks more like a postulate based on faith – normative-positive – than an empirical conclusion of judgment. Of course it is always possible to argue that redistribution in general or of various types *should* not occur.

Secondly, however, the capitalization of redistributive gains exposes a serious weakness in the argument that all redistribution is eaten up in efforts to acquire the regulatory "assets." In the case of production quotas, it is necessary to assume that lobbying efforts use up resources just equal to the capitalized value of the quotas, or that bribes (of the same value) are competed for by politicians who in total invest real resources in seeking election just equal to the value of bribes expected. All rents get dissipated.

Similarly in the case of non-marketable assets, such as access to a profession, the capitalized value of above-market earnings due to restricted access is assumed to be dissipated in efforts to secure access. If access is free and prices are regulated, entry dissipates the rents.

The problem is that such behaviour again depends on a peculiar assumption about the structure of information. Aspiring professional entrants are assumed to have excellent information on future product/service supply and demand conditions, so as to predict discounted rental streams, but not about present conditions in the "regulation" market – perfect far-sightedness and near-term blindness. For if all applicants were *fully* informed, about the market for "regulation" as well, they would know each other's probabilities (conditional upon effort) of securing entrance. They could then calculate who the winners would be, and once everyone knew this, no one would go to any extra effort. The same holds for lobbyists and bribable politicians, except that to be *seen* by others to be bribable, or to be lobbying energetically, can lower one's effectiveness. "Economic" theories of the political process are not compatible with perfectly informed voters!

Of course information is very far from perfect, which is why people do study hard to get into medical school. But quite apart from whether this activity is a dead-weight loss (surely another value judgment, education is not built on consumer sovereignty!), once one admits imperfect information as a critical component of the "rent-seeking" process, then the dead-weight loss is no longer determined by the value of the discounted rental stream. It can be higher or lower depending on particular conditions.[42]

If regulatory benefits, such as entry to restricted markets, were distributed by lottery, and tickets were auctioned off on the basis of otherwise unproductive effort, then one might expect ticket prices and dead-weight costs to reflect buyers' estimates of the expected value of the discounted rental stream. But no real-life examples of such a mechanism come to mind. This is not to say that regulation will not generate dead-weight losses, obviously it can and does. But the argument that these dissipate all positive redistributional effects rests on implicit informational and structural assumptions about the regulatory process that have no obvious face validity and seem rather to be imposed in order to yield a conclusion desired on other grounds.

The ostensible justification of almost all regulation, however, is not wealth redistribution per se but general improvements in well-being, serving the public interest, however loosely defined. The regulatory activity is proposed as increasing the value of the SWF, quite apart from any incidental redistributive effects it may have. Such increases may result either from the remedy of explicit market failures that constrain private unregulated transactions to sub-optimal results, or from the pursuit of more general social goals, forms of X_j that are valued but cannot be treated as commodities and traded in markets.

In the process, of course, there will usually be some redistribution of income or wealth as regulation creates and destroys property rights. But such redistribution is considered as a side effect, if at all, with some implicit or explicit assumption that, since the overall SWF is to be increased, gainers could afford to compensate losers (though they probably won't). And though common, redistributive side effects do not necessarily follow. Schelling analyzes a number of social processes involving interactive decision-making (such as "prisoners' dilemmas") in which regulatory constraints can make everyone involved better off.[43] Universal compulsory insurance programs in the presence of adverse selection are a prominent example.[44]

There are several forms of market failure that give rise to arguments for regulatory intervention. External effects, natural monopoly (or, more generally, structurally imperfect competition), asymmetry of information between transactors, and the more shadowy "destructive competition" are usually included in such a list.[45] In each of these situations, we find the dual problem that "vulnerable interests," as the Professional Organizations Committee described them, may be unable to protect themselves in private, arm's-length market transactions,[46] and that the outcome of such transactions can be shown to be inefficient in the Paretian sense as well. Those interests benefiting from the outcomes of the allegedly imperfect, unregulated market, who would suffer from regulation, could be compensated (although they probably won't be), and the vulnerable interests would still be better off.

The analysis of such situations could, and does, fill many books. As in the redistribution case, however, assumptions about information and pre-analytic value judgments about process and about wealth distributions seem to play a critical role in determining the outcome of such analysis.

The "deregulationist" school denies either the existence of market failure, or its remediability by public regulation. And their arguments seem to turn on judgments about information. Debates over consumer protection, or occupational health and safety, for instance, usually find the deregulationists assuming, openly or hidden in the equations, fully informed consumers/workers who knowingly accept hazards and are compensated, through competitive market processes, for doing so. No effort is made to determine if transactors really are fully informed. Instead they represent an apparently positive but really, I think, normative assumption about how people ought to behave.

In some cases learning processes of one form or another are tacked onto the model to argue that market interactions will lead to transactor learning and thus full information in the "long run," but this occurs only in a world of stable parameters and arbitrarily long-lived transactors. Both Heracleitus and Keynes are relevant in rebuttal; there are several levels of meaning to: "In the long run we are all dead." In fact, what such arguments boil down to is a judgment that transactors are likely to be adequately, if not perfectly, informed, and in any case better informed than a regulator could be. This may be true in particular cases, but is obviously false in others – unless consumers' interests are assumed to be revealed only by their actions, a version of the Pangloss gambit. People undergo (and in the US pay for) "unnecessary" removal of healthy organs because of the peace of mind this brings?[47] The assumption of full transactor information as a general postulate by deregulationists marks it as a normative-positive postulate, an article of a creed.

The analysis of imperfect competition and natural monopoly similarly depends on informational assumptions. It has been pointed out that the case for regulating natural monopolies disappears if perfect information is taken to its logical limit, because spot contracts can be negotiated between consumers and producers specifying all the pre-set and future behaviour of the monopolist. Moreover, since all relevant information is universally shared, there will be no difficulty in assembling large numbers of transactors on both sides of the market. One can auction off rights to control a natural monopoly, for example, or the constraining features of a structurally imperfectly competitive market, and there will be large numbers of bidders in such an auction because no person or group has inside information.[48]

This argument is useful in turning attention from production structures to information structures, and demonstrating how powerful (and implausible) is perfect information. Counter-arguments are then framed in terms of incomplete rationality/calculability, incomplete foresight, first-mover advantages which lead to small-numbers problems of negotiation and long-term administered contracts, and the public oversight of private "regulation."[49] Arguments against regulation of monopoly, as against anti-combines activity, rest *inter alia* on the assumption that all markets are effectively spot markets with large numbers of potential buyers and sellers, even though at any point they are supplied by a handful, or even one. All supply curves are elastic at or above the present price – if not immediately, then soon, and the hypothetical entrant, implied by perfect information, is always there to make apparently imperfect markets competitive. But the hypothetical entrant is seen clearly only with the eye of faith; lacking such faith one becomes concerned with grubby details of entry barriers, negotiating costs, pre-commitment, and the dynamics of market structure. Some imperfect markets, left alone, may generate self-correcting tendencies, others may not. And the costs of unregulated imperfection vary dramatically, from the cosmetologist to the neurosurgeon, or from monopolies in paper clips to monopolies in oil.

It may seem paradoxical, and is certainly ironic, that among the most energetic advocates of deregulation and reliance on private markets, we also find considerable *apparent* concern for problems of imperfect information. This would appear inconsistent with the statement that the absolute deregulationist position rests on very strong and implausible information assumptions.

But the conflict is more apparent than real. Perfect information, of the sort possessed by Leplace's Demon, is inaccessible to human actors at least. Recast in relative terms, the relevant questions are what sorts of information are generated by different institutional frameworks, and how will transactors behave in the presence of imperfect information? The deregulationist assumptions appear to be twofold: that private markets will in fact generate information which, if not perfect, is the best available given its cost, and that transactors will act on the best available information as if it were perfect. The recognition that information is not perfect in an absolute sense then becomes a way of dealing with empirical evidence suggesting market failure. Observations of price dispersion, or failures of markets to clear (unemployment), are no longer prima facie evidence of failure; they may be consistent with the smooth functioning of markets in all goods, including information. It is also a weapon against public regulation, in that public agencies may be alleged not to have adequate information to regulate effectively.

Of course neither of the above two assumptions holds in general. In conditions of extreme information imperfection, transactors do not act as if they were fully informed, they enter into various forms of non-arm's-length and non-market arrangements.[50] Moreover, information is not a commodity, or if we choose to call it one, it is not a commodity with the characteristics that give private markets an advantage in its efficient allocation. Markets are quite good at producing efficient amounts of some kinds of information; they are very bad at producing others. One can point to numerous examples, many discussed elsewhere in this volume, of the failure of private markets in the production of information.

If one ignores these difficulties, however, and assumes, in the absence of theoretical support and in the face of counter-evidence, that private markets always do yield optimal, if not perfect, information levels, this is equivalent to the assumption of perfect information. Imperfect information is costly, but private unregulated markets minimize these costs – by assumption. A more plausible approach is surely to recognize that imperfect information is a problem under any system of institutions for resource allocation. Better information is costly, but no one set of institutions can be assumed a priori to have informational advantages in all settings.

Of course the pro-regulationist, in particular industries, is not concerned with general cases. He usually has a lively appreciation for the private, as well as the public, benefits that flow from regulation. The Stiglerian Marxist is frequently right. The contrast is particularly striking between directly regulated and "self"-regulating occupations, in terms of the balance of public and private interests served. Self-regulators take care to suppress competitive behaviour within the occupation, and strive to prevent the development of other competitive occupations. Directly regulated occupations show a much richer role structure. Self-regulators see "continuing competence" as a combination of service quality, public relations, and tax-free holidays; the directly regulated have to pass periodic re-examination. Detailed examination of the regulations imposed by self-regulating occupations provides numerous examples of measures promoting the interests of the occupation or its members, independently of or frequently in conflict with the interests of consumers or the wider society.[51] The surrounding rhetoric frequently alleges or takes for granted that whatever is good for the self-regulating group is by definition good for everyone else – the doctrine of Engine Charlie Wilson, or General Bullmoose.

But though regulation frequently serves the interests of the regulated, it does not follow either that it always does so or that it only does so. The irony of the more articulate deregulators in the United States assisting the pharmaceutical industry in its attack on Food and Drug Administration regulations was noted above, to say nothing of the Canadian oil industry's attitude to the National Energy Program! And arguments for deregulation of physicians fall on deaf ears, because the public at large feels that it benefits from such regulation. It is probably right; deregulationists in this field tend to ignore quality issues or to offer pie-in-the-sky alternatives.[52] Similarly the argument that airline safety can be assured by the travelling public's learning to avoid unsafe lines appeals only to those who take the train. In this case, as in medicine, information is costly to have as well as to get, and non-compensable irreversibilities enter in a non-trivial way.

The scope for discussion of particular regulatory cases, and consideration of the balance of positive and normative judgments involved, seems almost endless. But behind myriad specific judgments of fact and value that inform (or cloud) debates over regulation there do seem to be certain abiding values. Articles of a creed can be discerned, even if the whole creed is still unclear. The hypothetical entrants, the generality of transactor information, if not now then soon, the peculiar mix of "perfect information" with specific forms of blindness, the limited cost and reversibility of error, the commodity-like status of all relevant utility function arguments, the absence of utility function interaction among transactors, all represent positive propositions that are accepted on normative grounds, which have limited, or no, empirical support, but which *ought* to be believed.

Behind these, presumably, are more fundamental values, of which a central one may be a peculiarly asymmetric attitude toward coercion. The deregulationist school, or the Plutonian heresy, seem to have a horror of coercion by force. Regulation, the authority of the state resting ultimately on the public sword, is thus at root immoral, with one monumental exception. As pointed out by Steiner, the libertarian quandry is precisely that all property rights themselves rely on this same sword, not on the consent of those constrained to respect such rights.[53]

But to those who do not possess sufficient property rights to sustain life independently, the negotiations surrounding transactions may become indistinguishable from force. This point seems to be passed over in silence, or dealt with implicitly by the assumption that all markets are competitive – or will become so before starvation sets in. The final solution, of simply dropping such unfortunates from the SWF, is one that only a few have been willing to recognize. Posner faces up to this.[54] But he, like the pro-market school generally, seems not to realize that exchange relationships are non-coercive only if one can choose not to participate. In technical terms, the initial pre-trade resource endowment must sustain the transactor. All participants must, like independent peasant proprietors, be able to live off their own. When this is not true, and some must trade to live while others need not, "free" exchange may, depending on market structure, be powerfully coercive. Marx stressed this point, as did Adam Smith.[55] But it has apparently been missed by those who call on his name without reading him.

At this point, the morality of the process whereby a particular structure of property rights has emerged becomes crucial. It appears that, insofar as particular current public regulations can be identified as a source of such rights, then they are not legitimate – deregulate regardless of the distributional consequences. But there seems no corresponding moral obligation to investigate the historical roots of current property rights, particularly ownership of physical capital. Marx's interest in "primary accumulation" would seem to be critical also to deregulationists, but in fact the sources of present rights are either passed over in silence or dealt with by assertions lacking any historical support.[56] This is a serious omission, since the position, "Regulate only with compensation, deregulate without,"[57] must imply a distinction between legitimate and illegitimate property rights. By definition, those acquired as a result of regulation are illegitimate – all the rest are legitimate. Such wholesale ethical ratification of a historical process with some distinctly unsavoury components cannot be the result of mere ignorance.

Moreover, the morality or immorality of the process of rights allocation, its basis in consent or coercion, does not depend only on whether it occurred today or yesterday. Coercion by (public) force is immoral, coercion by fraud or private force is apparently not. Of course extortion or fraud as defined by the law is presumably immoral, since it is at least illegal – *if* it can be proven and redressed, not in some ideal judicial world but in the reality of imperfect information and constrained litigious and judicial resources. But the redistribution that occurs when there is systematic informational asymmetry in a transaction is apparently moral – *caveat emptor* (or in some cases *vendor)*. The stress placed in the creed on assumptions about learning processes or institutional evolution to redress such situations suggests a certain unease at this point, or at least a concern that this value may not be widely shared. But it seems apparent that, as an underlying value premise, redistribution via deceit is at worst a venial sin compared with the mortal sin of regulation.

These asymmetric attitudes toward public and private coercion, force and deceit, find expression in what Archibald and Donaldson call the "Junior Chamber of Commerce Social Welfare Function." Any activity carried out in the private sector (for which no one is convicted) increases the SWF; any carried out in the public sector (possibly excepting those that increase the security of private property rights) reduces the SWF.[58] The task of the analyst in any particular case is merely to explain how.

It is less clear whether the distribution of income and wealth is itself a value, or whether the value judgments cover only the process of rights allocation. Clearly egalitarianism is *not* a value, but is inequality valued for itself, or only as the result of a valued *process*? Most of the deregulation rhetoric is over process, but the fundamental blind spots as to the role of coercion in primary accumulation, in defense of current patterns, or when carried on via informational differentials, strongly suggests that inequality per se is an objective. This in turn could be a Rawlsian value, a preference for inequality even when one is behind the veil of ignorance, but it seems more plausible, given the above, that a particular pattern, the status quo *ante* regulation, is favoured. Such a doctrine has marketable features, as did the Apostles' Creed. There are always enthusiastic and generous benefactors of a doctrine that supports the status quo – the Christian case was a bit more complex.

Whether positivism, objectivity, "science," is also a value in itself is also obscure. Again the rhetoric of positivism suggests that it is, but the normative significance of the creed suggests otherwise. The white coat may be an independent object of veneration, but its application indicates that it is rather more of a cloak.

The usefulness of this cloak, however, depends on the specific values to be defended. Myrdal, for example, argues:

> Quasi-scientific rationalization of a political endeavour may be an effective propaganda weapon; yet its effect at the crucial time, when the ideal has acquired enough political backing to be transformed into practical action, is in a democratic setting almost always inhibiting and disintegrating. I make an exception for completely conservative strivings which seek no more than the preservation of the status quo; from such a political standpoint doctrinaire thinking may be less dangerous.[59]

It is ironic that, while the content of science may be revolutionary, the methodology is highly conservative. Nor is this effect confined to theorizing; Tuohy observes that insistence on the most rigorous scientific standards in cost-benefit evaluations of proposed public policy may so tie up the process that nothing can be done.[60]

In any case non-paternalism is clearly a value – one ought not to interfere with others' behaviour even if one does feel affected by it. This links both to force – one should not impose one's preferences on others, and such preferences are illegitimate (Richard Posner, meet the Moral Majority) – and to wealth – one may distribute charity but there exists no obligation, no *noblesse oblige* to look after others. Paternalism implies both right to interfere and obligation to help – both are denied.

Insofar as a particular wealth distribution *is* a value, and the strong interest of deregulationists in terminating transfer programs suggests that it is, the Plutonian deregulationist closes the circle with the special interest regulationist. Both pursue redistributional goals under a public interest cover story. Both may serve other personal values as well. Neither are wholly detached from the "public interest." There appear to be identifiable situations in which regulation serves interests beyond or other than those of the regulated, general enough to be called public, and other situations in which only the regulated are served. In some of these, again, dead-weight losses may eat up all the gains, so everyone loses.

Between these two poles, the special interest regulationist as he exists in the mind of Stigler and the absolute deregulationist or Chicago Plutonian, the advocate of wishy-washy regulatory reform has few fixed points for guidance. And yet the inhabitants of this large middle ground do routinely terminate their analyses with proposals for improvement and reform. Very few students of regulation, or of economics generally, are motivated solely by intellectual curiosity. Since the impossibility of deriving policy recommendations from analytic economics, of "ought" from "is," applies to such reformers no less than to the Plutonians, one might well ask about the source and content of their (our) values and objectives that are expressed through economic analysis.

The question is not easy to answer. The values expressed through policy recommendations must inevitably be diverse, overlapping, and to some extent contradictory or confused. Following Gordon's criticism of "moral monism,"[61] each analyst/advocate will generally have a number of values in mind, consciously or subconsciously; and the relative weights on each, as well as the range of values admitted, will vary across analysts. In attempting to describe the value bases of non-Plutonian regulatory reform, one runs a significant risk of isolating at best a confused and partial description of the values of one analyst.

Since virtually all regulation redistributes property rights, any policy recommendation implies the existence of values defined over this distribution. The Paretian forbids any redistribution, effectively forbidding policy and freezing the status quo. The cost-benefit analyst usually adds up benefits "to whomsoever accruing," implying indifference to distribution. Explicit distributive weights can be inserted into the analysis, but usually are not. The Plutonian values the status quo *ante* regulation, or the status quo *post* deregulation, distributions (which need not be the same). The reformer generally has a mild egalitarian bent, agreeing with Simons' description of extreme inequality as "evil or unlovely." This is reinforced by concern for the political and social consequences of inequality; like Peacock and Rowley, the reformer is concerned about the "threat to individual freedom ... from concentrations of political and economic power, whether in the hands of *private citizens*, of bureaucrats, or of the state ... [L]iberals are for the most part committed to a more equal distribution of wealth than that which exists, even in countries ... which operate a progressive tax system."[62] The Plutonian, or Chicago liberal, rules out a priori the possibility of private oppression. In their hearts, however, I suspect most regulatory reformers also believe in the diminishing marginal utility of income, despite its analytic problems.

Egalitarianism is, however, tempered by considerations of "transactions costs" in a broad sense. Stability and predictability of individual wealth positions is itself a value, though a value with interesting implications. If unpredictable redistribution is a source of disutility when practised by the state, is it not equally so when it occurs through the market? The suggestion that I have somehow "consented" when my private pension plan is wiped out in the stock market, but not when my taxes are raised, strains the meaning of consent out of recognition.[63] And stability is a frequent and presumably legitimate objective of regulation.

Re-distributional objectives must be balanced against the costs of change as well as incentive considerations.

Moreover there is usually some implicit judgment of "deservingness" – inherited wealth is less deserved than earned wealth. Senior's initial justification of property income against the Ricardian attack made this distinction clearly;[64] and few have been prepared to follow the Plutonians in treating the use of inherited wealth as being consumption or investment on behalf of a dead testator whose interests have as good a claim to protection as those of any living member of society. Some societies engage in ancestor-worship, and allocate resources to the satisfaction of the dead; ours does not.

This indicates the perceived social convention that underlies the analyst's egalitarianism. The reformer bases recommendations not just on his own values but on a perception of social values. All developed countries have progressive income tax systems, on paper at least, indicating a general consensus in favour of moderating inequality. And attacks on the progressive tax system have generally focused, not on this objective itself, but on its alleged side effects with respect to efficiency and growth. Few have been willing to undertake a direct argument in favour of inequality as a value. Apparently progressive tax systems may be more or less so in fact; a system may have relatively few loopholes (Canada) or be so shot through as to have little progressiveness left (the United States) – but its form reflects what the society wants and believes it has. Ultimately the reformer must rest his values on a perceived social consensus, though he may be distinctly uneasy about what a democracy may do.[65] The Plutonian may in effect reject democracy altogether, in favour of divine will, natural law, or socio-biological evolution, but the wishy-washy reformer is squarely caught on the potential conflict between process and outcome values and can only educate – or preach.

The regulatory reformer is thus likely to be more sympathetic to regulation which rather protects the poor than further fattens the rich, though bitter experience teaches that the latter frequently masquerades as the former. It is a common critique of agricultural price stabilization or supply management that it favours the wealthy agribusiness, not the marginal farmer, or of occupational regulation that it protects from competition the highest-earning occupations in the economy, at the expense of their less wealthy customers or potential competitors.

Apart from regulation as redistribution, however, the reformer, like the Plutonian, is concerned with efficiency considerations. Traditionally, this concern has focused on allocative distortions of the "welfare triangle" type, arising from the effects of regulation in constraining supply and elevating price. Increasingly, however, reformer and Plutonian are focusing on real resource costs, technical inefficiency, associated with regulation. The triangles do not appear to be very large; indeed in imperfectly informed and regulated markets they may well not exist.[66] But detailed study of regulated industries indicates extensive resource misallocation in a technical sense. Transport regulation leads to deadheading empty trucks and half-empty aircraft competing by advertising. Professional regulation leads to pharmacists "counting and pouring" and dentists filling teeth. The "high-priced help" uses the regulatory power to hold less costly competitors out of the market. Farmers destroy large quantities of food. The most severe costs of economic regulation turn out, on examination, to be sheer inefficiency and waste. The perverse incentives that are frequently created by regulation lead either to production off the production function, or to production on that function that is non-optimal at current (or any plausible alternative) prices.

The problem is not so much, as the Plutonian analysis has it, that dead-weight losses are incurred in gaining access to rental streams created by regulation, but that regulation distorts the production process itself. This possibility is discounted on a priori grounds by the Plutonians; the simple refutation is to go and look.

This brings out an important methodological distinction between the reformer and the Plutonian deregulationist. The reformer places great weight on specific information, on detailed investigation of what is actually happening in a particular industry. He is prepared to go down on the "shop floor," into the grubby details of whether best practice technique is being used, and if not why not, what are the actual incentives and constraints faced by the key transactors, what sorts of information are in practice available or unavailable, and how do people behave as a result. The deregulationist rises above all this, preferring a priori analysis and indirect evidence, and minimizing the use of specific information.[67] Reliance on indirect information is presumably based on the assumption that all (relevant) direct information, or at least all that is worth acquiring at current costs, is already optimally embodied in the behaviour of the transactors being studied. But this assumption, when formulated as other than a tautology, has neither theoretical nor empirical support.

Detailed investigation of particular industries or markets will often lead to the conclusion that much current regulation is harmful either absolutely, or on balance, or relative to some conceivable alternative. But it requires one to take seriously the issues and problems to which regulation responds.

Whether such a case-by-case, detailed investigation approach is likely to be more effective in achieving change than a doctrinaire anti-public-sector stance based on a priori hypotheses is questionable; it may be true that ignorance is strength. But the logical limit of the deregulationist approach is pure quietism – if there is a "market" in public regulation then presumably that "market" works as perfectly as any other, so whatever is is right in the public sector as well. Reformers hold as a value, or certainly a creedal assumption, that people of good will can in fact respond to public values that to some extent transcend pure self-interest, and can work collectively in public as well as in private to secure general social ends.[68] Conscious amelioration, not just the spontaneous working out of social evolution, is possible. And while there is no lack of examples of regulatory activity that is short-sighted, harmful, or merely a cloak for private interests, there are also examples of regulation that is widely considered successful, or at least necessary, and with good reason.

Finally, most wishy-washy reformers appear to hold as a value a certain conception of intellectual honesty that demands that, insofar as possible, values be brought out in the open, not be hidden in the analysis. Purely value-free analysis may be impossible, but one can comment on the degree of mixture rather than pretend to a spurious objectivity. And one can strive towards objectivity; the impossibility of truly value-free analysis does not obliterate all distinction nor qualify strongly felt emotions as the equivalent of careful intellectual effort. Nor should one apologize if the values thus expressed are a bit vague and frequently in conflict; if they were not so, one could not claim them as representative of the wider society.

Moreover, if the ethical scene is cloudy, there is a silver lining. If regulatory reform must proceed as a series of special cases, with detailed review of the facts and values involved in each, there appears to be a good market for the services of analysts. Given the importance of the field, and the acknowledged wide variation in the quality of work of practitioners, some consideration of licensure seems an obvious priority.

NOTES

1 Robbins, *An Essay on the Nature and Significance of Economic Science* (London: Macmillan, 1932), though the idea goes back at least to Mill.

2 For example, Friedman, "The Methodology of Positive Economics" in Friedman, ed., *Essays in Positive Economics* (Chicago: University of Chicago Press, 1953), 3–43.

3 Schumpeter, *History of Economic Analysis* (New York: Oxford University Press, 1954), 42.

4 Dobb, *Theories of Value and Distribution Since Adam Smith: Ideology and Economic Theory* (Cambridge: Cambridge University Press, 1972), Chapter 1.

5 Heracleitus pointed out that any model which is sufficiently complex to replicate the behaviour of an economic system or of its sub-components will contain a large number of parameters, which in turn will require a large number of observations for their estimation. But this requires either a long time-period of stable structure or a large number of comparable regimes with similar structures. And since history or diversity are constantly changing all such parameters, the process of econometric estimation of a large and complex economic model embodies an "act of faith" that its parameters have been "stable enough" – or have varied only in measured ways – so as to support estimation. But the parameters represent (measure) behaviour, which is inside history in a way the model itself can never be. Thus structure is constantly changing, and the more complex the model, the more implausible the stability assumptions. Or he may have. His views are summarized in the phrase, "*panta rhei, ouden menei*," attributed to him by Aristotle. See also Georgescu-Roegen, *The Entropy Law and the Economic Process* (Cambridge: Harvard University Press, 1971).

6 Myrdal, *The Political Element in the Development of Economic Theory* (New York: Simon and Schuster, 1969). The problem is not unique to economics; Tuohy in "Regulation and Scientific Complexity: Decision Rules and Processes in the Occupational Health Hazard Arena," *Osgoode Hall Law Journal* 20 (1982): 562, refers to "trans-scientific issues," namely, questions which can be *posed* as positive, "scientific" problems, but which cannot be resolved, at present or ever, scientifically. Wicksell, in commenting on the inability of economics to arrive at settled conclusions, drew the religious parallel: "like theology and for approximately the same reasons" economics has failed to arrive at generally accepted results (Inaugural Lecture, University of Lund, quoted by Myrdal, at xiv). But he attributed the difficulty to disagreement over ends and goals of policy. Myrdal's criticism seems well-taken. If the problem were only value conflicts, positive propositions would still command wide assent. Hawks and peaceniks do not disagree about nuclear physics. But in economics, like theology, certain critical pieces of evidence are always lacking, or inadequate, and bridges across such gaps are constructed in both fields from wishes, hopes, and fears.

7 Archibald, "Refutation or Comparison?" *British Journal for the Philosophy of Science* 17 (1966). See also Friedman, note 2 above; Nagel, "Assumptions in Economic Theory," *American Economic Review* 53 (1963): 211; Samuelson, "Discussion." *American Economic Review* 53 (1963): 231.

8 The development of this faith is, I think, the process which Salter, in "The Value Debate in Regulation," *Osgoode Hall Law Journal* 20 (1982): 485, describes as a progression from theoretical, to ideological, and finally to symbolic logic. Symbolic logic is characterized by "highlighting, that is lifting from theory or ideological discussion for that matter, some elements of the analysis and treating these elements as significant in and of themselves" and by "analogical reasoning ... [without] a full empirical and theoretical referent," ibid., 490. Myrdal, note 6 above, at 19, quotes Westergaard speaking of economics as "a science where expressions and metaphors readily engender supposed proofs." Economic analyses of regulation seem particularly prone to this weakness.

9 The number of cost-benefit analyses that have used estimated values of *livelihood* streams as a value for *lives* is too large and too depressing to justify individual citation. If this were the appropriate measure, the social convention in catastrophe would be "women and children last," and euthanasia of the elderly would be by an overwhelming margin our most cost-effective public health program. But you cannot fool all of the people all of the time; see the discussion by Tuohy, above note 6, of the declining credibility of cost-benefit analysis.

10 Economists have, until recently, been predominantly academics with aspirations to scholarship – no insignificant number may indeed be called scholars. The "hired gun," or public relations, role is professionally offensive, being generally considered inconsistent with the pursuit of "truth," or at least of knowledge with some degree of objectivity. For those who come to economics from a legal background, however, adversarial proceedings are perceived more favourably as an investigative approach, and the "hired gun" role seems more comfortable. The analyst-as-advocate is not constrained by the same intellectual rules as the academic; he deliberately makes the best case that selected evidence and plausible analysis will support. The adversarial process itself is supposed to ensure that inconsistent argument and invalid or distorted evidence will be exposed. The tensions between the roles of lawyer-as-scholar and lawyer-as-advocate for whomever pays the fee may become more familiar to economists as the sources of support for analysis shift from universities to clients (public or increasingly private) whose interests are unambiguously adversarial, not intellectual.

11 Becker, *The Heavenly City of the Eighteenth-Century Philosophers* (New Haven: Yale University Press, 1979); see also Dobb, note 4 above, 41. Nor is the linkage from theology to natural law to economic policy of historical interest only; Gordon, "The Political Economy of F.A. Hayek," *Canadian Journal of Economics* 14 (1981): 470, 476–9.

12 *The Gnostic Gospels* (New York: Random House, 1979).

13 University of British Columbia, oral tradition. See also Dobb, note 4 above.

14 "For regulation, in its broadest sense, is the essential function of government. Indeed taxation and expenditures, the other two principal instrumentalities, can be thought of as special cases of regulation." Hartle, *Public Policy Decision Making and Regulation* (Montreal: Institute for Research on Public Policy, 1979), 1. Posner, "Taxation by Regulation," *Bell Journal of Economics and Management Science* 2 (1971): 22, focuses on its relation to taxation in redistributing property rights; Hartle's perspective is broader.

15 Epstein, "Taxation, Regulation, and Confiscation," *Osgoode Hall Law Journal* 20 (1982): 433. The allegation of "close" substitutability permits a verbal transition from regulation as being like taxation, that is, taking "property," to "confiscation," described as a "prima facie wrong" (436) – and finally to "illegitimate tax regulation" (449). But of course regulation *redistributes* property rights, rather than "confiscating" them, and the "illegality" refers to processes which are in accordance with law. The "prima facie wrong" is apparently relative to some natural law standard, while illegal means not counter to law as it is, but counter to law as the author feels it should be. Such personal preferences presumably refer to natural law again, that "diseased and meretricious old drab" (Gordon, note 11 above, 479), which serves so readily as a device to "smuggle authoritarianism in under the cloak of 'nature.'" Epstein recognizes as valid authority neither duly elected legislatures nor courts; he appears willing, like Hayek, to sacrifice democratic process to an ideal of freedom – as defined by ... ? *Quis custodiet?* remains unanswered. (As, for that matter, does *Cui bono?)*

16 Of course, in order to reallocate rights in the first place, one would need to know the entire relationship between initial endowments and final distribution, which raises the question as to what purpose is served by the intermediate market game?

17 This recognition is general, but not universal; there are still some who appear to believe that marginal productivity creates some ethical claim to output; see discussion in Friedman, *Price Theory: A Provisional Text* (Chicago: Aldine, 1968), 196–8.

18 Posner, "Utilitarianism, Economics, and Legal Theory," *Legal Studies* 8 (1979): 103; the attempt to foist responsibility for the initial rights distribution onto "the economist" (125) is certainly novel.

19 I am here abstracting from externalities in production, either positive or negative, which would simply complicate the discussion without affecting the argument.

20 Posner, note 18 above, 128. Posner, however, rejects the Paretian framework in favour of a SWF that maximizes "wealth," a formulation which is somewhat obscure since it cannot be done. His approach involves a confusion between general and partial equilibrum. It is possible to maximize an expression $W = P \bullet X$ where P is an *exogenous* price vector, X a vector of resource/output allocations, and W a global wealth measure; it is then also possible to make individual X_i and X_j allocations so as to increase or decrease W. And one can postulate shadow Pi' where market Pi' are lacking. But one cannot maximize $P \bullet X$ in general, since the essence of general equilibrium theory is that the P and X vectors are simultaneously determined and interdependent, and that *absolute* P• have no meaning. All one can define is an N – l vector of price *ratios* for an arbitrary *numeraire*. The error may arise from a faulty legal analogy – the common law grows by the accretion of precedent, the whole is the sum of the partial decisions of individual courts. But general equilibrium is *not* the sum of its parts; it is an interdependent and simultaneous system. The postulate that wealth maximization can, let alone should, be an objective is a fallacy of composition.

21 Archibald and Donaldson, "Non-Paternalism and the Basic Theorems of Welfare Economics," *Canadian Journal of Economics* 13 (1976): 501–2.

22 Posner, note 18 above, 135.

23 See note 16 above. But divine inspiration helps. Dobb, note 4 above, 23, quotes Longfield, in 1833, "the laws according to which wealth is created, distributed, and consumed, have been framed by the Great Author of our being, with the same regard to our happiness which is manifested by the laws that govern the material world." Longfield, an Irish judge who had turned to political economy, was reacting to the threat to property implicit in Ricardian theory. The phenomenon of lawyer/economists clothing in economic language a transcendental argument for the status quo is not new.

24 "[T]he Pareto principle offers an approach to public policy likely to find favour with those concerned to maintain the status quo," Peacock and Rowley, "Pareto-Optimality and the Political Economy of Liberalism," *Journal of Political Economy* 80 (1972): 476, 479. Posner (note 18 above,

116) is appalled by the "moral monstrousness associated with utilitarianism" insofar as it will "sacrifice the innocent individual on the altar of social need" as well as refusing "to make moral distinctions among types of pleasures." (Of course market-based systems make no such distinctions either, you may pull the wings off as many flies as you can afford.) Put less rhetorically, utilitarianism permits interpersonal utility comparisons, and the trading off of one person's utility against another's. As, in practice, does any form of economic policy, or any ethical system which attempts to justify such policy. Posner's position appears to be that public activity of any feasible sort is morally monstrous – except presumably that of adjudicating and defending pre-existing private property rights.

25 Gordon, note 11 above, 483, makes the same point about Hayek: "If it is meaningless to apply the concept of justice to the market order, then the market order is neither just nor unjust. But the practical import, as far as policy is concerned, is that the distribution generated by the market must be accepted, which is equivalent to regarding it as just." Whatever is, is right. Here Gordon is referring to distribution as a market outcome, not an initial property rights distribution, implicitly assuming away hypothetical costless wealth transfers. Hayek's ultimate value of freedom, spontaneous social order, is the march through the world not of God, but of some social evolutionary process, but it comes to the same thing (as discussed in Gordon, note 11 above, 479).

26 Titmuss, *The Gift Relationship: From Human Blood to Social Policy* (London: George Allen and Unwin, 1970).

27 A critical discussion of the universal self-interest approach is provided in Collard, *Altruism and Economy: A Study in Non-Selfish Economics* (Oxford: Martin Robertson, 1978). The market-like interactions, supergames, and incomplete insurance contracts necessary to rationalize altruistic behaviours and institutions are sufficiently complex as well as implausible that one can no longer defend the self-interest postulate by wielding Occam's Razor. Its appeal must lie elsewhere.

28 Posner asserts (note 18 above, 139) that "the economist" would regard a free market in babies as "much to be preferred to the present system." And so he may – one can find *some* economist who will support anything. But not on the basis of economic theory, because that will not sustain the weight unless buttressed with philosophic or political value judgments, with which other economists would violently disagree. "The economist" appears to be a stalking horse for Posner's personal values, which indeed he has to be, as his "morality is derived from the economic principle itself" (i.e., wealth maximization). But that principle is simply a fallacy of

composition (note 18 above, 135), and even if it were not empty, it would still lack any *moral* content. Posner's "economist" is not a moral monster, but a moral midget – or less.

29 Titmuss, note 26 above.

30 Evans, "The Welfare Economics of Public Health Insurance: The Canadian Example," paper presented to the Arne Ryde Symposium on the Economics of Social Insurance, Lund, Sweden, September 1981, and "Is Health Care Better in Canada than in the US?," paper presented to the University Consortium for Research on North America, Cambridge, MA, December 1980.

31 I am indebted to D. Donaldson for this point, among others.

32 An exception to this general position appears in the analysis of common property resources. The most enthusiastic deregulators seem to recognize this form of market failure, and though some would argue for a reallocation of property rights to "enclose the commons," with or without compensation, others admit that such rights may not be enforceably exclusive, at least with present technology or institutions.

33 See Hartle, note 14 above. See also, Trebilcock, Waverman, and Pritchard, "Markets for Regulation: Implications for Performance Standards and Institutional Design," in *Government Regulation: Issues and Alternatives* (Toronto: Ontario Economic Council, 1978), 28: "[A]n analysis of a limited number of actual forms of intervention indicate that eliminating market failures does not appear to be the sole or even primary motivation."

34 This important point is made by Hartle and Trebilcock, "Regulatory Reform and the Political Process," *Osgoode Hall Law Journal* 20 (1982).

35 Public intervention in the health insurance market in Canada has quite clearly held down physicians' fees and incomes in a way in which private insurance in the US cannot; Evans, note 30 above.

36 Stigler, "The Theory of Economic Regulation," *Bell Journal of Economics and Management Science* 2 (1971): 3. Marx described the (capitalist) state as the executive committee of the bourgeoisie, a collective relationship, while Stigler and his followers treat it as a sort of Mafia contracting with private organizations to sell favourable "regulations" to the highest bidder. Posner, "Theories of Economic Regulation," *Bell Journal of Economics and Management Science* 5 (1974): 335, notes the "odd mixture of welfare state liberals, muckrakers, Marxists and free market economists" supporting capture theories of regulation. He suggests that a carefully articulated neoclassical market analysis of regulation as a commodity which is competitively demanded and (despite appearances) supplied is superior to "interest groups" theory of political scientists which is, he argues, "devoid

of theory" (at 341), or presumably to the class-based Marxist analysis. Since he confesses that "the economic theory is still so spongy that virtually any observations can be reconciled with it" (at 348), the superiority is not of performance. The advantage appears rather to be its commitment "to the strong assumptions of economic theory generally" (at 343) – that is, conformity to a creed. Values attach to the choice of assumptions themselves, regardless of the theory's predictive power.

37 For example Posner, "The Social Costs of Monopoly and Regulation," *Journal of Political Economy* 83 (1975): 807.

38 Peltzman, *Regulation of Pharmaceutical Innovation: The 1962 Amendments* (Washington, DC: American Enterprise Institute, 1974).

39 The argument for deregulation without any compensation seems difficult to justify. When made by those who simultaneously advocate compensation for all who lose from any positive act of government, it seems wholly without ethical or intellectual merit. One can imagine alternating governments of different political stripe first regulating some process with compensation, then deregulating without, indefinitely, until all wealth lay with the "victims" of regulation! But what is regulation and what is deregulation? Again a prior assignment of rights (natural, presumably) is being assumed external to the political process.

40 Hartle and Trebilcock, note 34 above.

41 "[B]y influencing voter knowledge and understanding, and hence voter decisions, the insights of economic research (and social science research generally) can be brought to bear on the ultimate decision making process. Indeed these direct effects of new information may be much more effective than direct information provision to bureaucrats and politicians." Ibid., at 48. Unfortunately, as Keynes pointed out, "the ideas of economists and political philosophers, both when they are right *and when they are wrong* [my emphasis], are more powerful than is commonly understood." Keynes, *General Theory of Employment, Interest and Money* (London: Macmillan, 1971), 383. One would indeed be an optimist to claim that the pamphleteering efforts of economists, taken in total, have made a positive contribution to economic policy in the 1970s, at least in the English-speaking world. But there may be no alternative.

42 The problem is not merely that the relation becomes imprecise or subject to error. Rents may be systematically above the dead-weight cost of their acquisition, depending on the characteristics of the activity or regulation in question, and may remain so more or less indefinitely. They may also be systematically below, if there are continuing biases in entrants' forecasts, as Adam Smith suggested was the case for would-be barristers. In the

professions, each would-be entrant is a new individual (there's one born every minute), so the experience of others cannot be assumed to correct expectations.

43 Schelling, *Micromotives and Macrobehavior* (New York: Norton, 1978).

44 Evans, note 30 above; see also Rothschild and Stiglitz, "Equilibrium in Competitive Insurance Markets: An Essay on the Economics of Imperfect Information," *Quarterly Journal of Economics* 90 (1976): 629; and Wilson, *A Model of Insurance Markets with Asymmetric Information,* Cowles Foundation Discussion Paper #432, Yale University, 29 June 1976.

45 Trebilcock, Waverman, and Pritchard, note 33 above.

46 Ontario, Ministry of the Attorney-General, *Report of the Professional Organizations Committee* (Toronto: n.pub., 1980), 7–11.

47 Pauly, "What Is Unnecessary Surgery?" *Milbank Memorial Fund Quarterly* 57 (1979): 95.

48 Demsetz, "Why Regulate Utilities?" *Journal of Law and Economics* 11 (1968): 55.

49 Williamson, *Markets and Hierarchies: Analysis and Antitrust Implications* (New York: The Free Press, 1975); Goldberg, "Regulation and Administered Contracts," *Bell Journal of Economics and Management Science* 7 (1976): 426; Williamson, "Transaction-Cost Economics: the Governance of Contractual Relations." *Journal of Law and Economics* 22 (1979): 233.

50 Arrow, "Uncertainty and the Welfare Economics of Medical Care." *American Economic Review* 53 (1963): 941, explains the formation of the professional agency role in these terms.

51 Evans and Stanbury, *Occupational Regulation in Canada*, University of Toronto Law and Economics Workshop Series WS-3-17 (April 1981).

52 Few non-economists have been comfortable with Friedman's argument, propounded in *Capitalism and Freedom* (Chicago: University of Chicago Press, 1962), that unregulated health professions would have evolved, under market pressures, alternative and at least as effective forms of quality control and consumer protection. His argument rests on a priori propositions about how perfect markets might function, linked by assertion to actual markets, without supporting evidence of any sort. The discussion of the "quality" problem in professional services in Muzondo and Pazderka, *Professional Licensing and Competition Policy: Effects of Licensing on Earnings and Rates-of-Return Differentials* (Ottawa: Consumer and Corporate Affairs Canada, 1979), similarly rests on assertion and wishful thinking. The contrast with the careful approach to this central problem in

Trebilcock, Tuohy, and Wolfson, *Professional Regulation* (a Staff Study prepared for the Professional Organizations Committee). (Toronto: Ministry of the Attorney-General, 1979), is striking.

53 "A Libertarian Quandary," *Ethics* 90 (1980): 257.

54 Posner, note 18 above, 135. Actually Posner drops those whose post-trade resources do not sustain life. For those whose endowment (such as labour but no capital or land) requires them to trade, the outcome of that trade becomes a life-or-death matter. Whether they are in or out of the SWF depends on market outcomes.

55 *The Wealth of Nations* (London: J.M. Dent, 1910), 59.

56 Several references in Posner, note 18 above, suggest that he is aware of the problem, but his responses are trivial: "lawfully obtained wealth is created only by doing things for other people ... in a well-regulated market economy" (132.) There is a fine confusion between what would happen in an ideal world and what did happen, historically. Similarly "lawfully" may mean in accordance with a moral law, or simply that no one was convicted. Elsewhere (123) the market's response to a buyer's offer for a necklace is given ethical significance because "the buyer's $10,000 was *in all likelihood* accumulated through productive activity" (my emphasis). Likely to whom? It is rather a shaky foundation for an ethical system! One does not have to assume that all primary accumulation is the result of force and fraud, or that property is theft, in order to recognize that such activities played a prominent part in the historical process of rights accumulation [for example, Myers, *A History of Canadian Wealth* (reissued Toronto: James Lorimer, 1972; originally Chicago, 1914)]. And to assert that present accumulation proceeds solely by "understanding and appealing to the needs and wants of others" (136), one must be either naive, or worse.

57 Epstein, note 15 above.

58 University of British Columbia oral tradition. This seems in fact to be the core of Epstein's argument (note 15 above) and of Posner's (note 18 above).

59 Myrdal, note 6 above, xii (preface to 1929 edition).

60 Tuohy, note 9 above.

61 Gordon, note 11 above, 474.

62 Note 24, 480, 482 (emphasis added).

63 To choose *A* over *B* when no other options are permitted does not give *A* any special ethical significance. If I demand "your money or your life," you do not "consent" in giving up your purse.

64 Dobb, note 4 above, 104.

65 Peacock and Rowley, note 24 above, 481, and Gordon, note 11 above, 476–8.

66 Evans, "Professionals and the Production Function: Can Competition Policy Improve Efficiency in the Licensed Professions?" In Rottenberg, ed., *Occupational Regulation* (Washington, DC: American Enterprise Institute, 1980), 225–6; Evans and Stanbury, note 51 above; Trebilcock et al., note 33 above; Evans and Williamson, *Extending Canadian National Health Insurance: Policy Options for Pharmacare and Denticare* (Toronto; University of Toronto Press, 1978).

67 Stigler, in his remarks to the American Enterprise Institute Conference on Occupational Regulation, 1979 (see Rottenberg, note 66 above, 348–54) specifically criticized economists who as amateur technologists tried to understand the technical details of the industries or occupations they studied. Such a criticism might carry more weight if one could demonstrate, as Stigler did not, that economists were incapable of working with, or learning from, people who do have specific technological information about the objects of analysis. But of course they can and do. Stigler's position appears to be a plea for ignorance, and for the disregard of all direct evidence. ("Don't confuse me with facts ... ") In a similar vein, the Reagan administration has slashed public funding for socio-economic research, including that on regulation and its effects, except for "assessments ... in an abbreviated conceptual form only" ["Science and the Citizen: Lesser Immediate Priority," *Scientific American* (September 1981): 104]. The less information, the more reliance on a priorism, the less regulation. Ignorance is strength.

68 The distinction between levels of interest, which re-establishes the possibility of a public interest, is discussed by Sen, "Rational Fools: A Critique of the Behavioural Foundations of Economic Theory," *Philosophy and Public Affairs* 6 (1977): 317.

2

Toward a Healthier Economics: Reflections on Ken Bassett's Problem (1998)

ROBERT G. EVANS

From 1978 to 1990 Dr Ken Bassett practised as a family physician in Invermere, a small town in southeastern British Columbia. As part of that practice, he and his colleagues cared for a number of obstetrical patients. And in managing the delivery process, they would commonly use an electronic foetal monitor (EFM) to check on the condition of the foetus. In this their behaviour was no different from that of most other physicians, in North America at least. But they may have been somewhat unusual in reflecting upon and being troubled by their own behaviour. As they were well aware, there is an extensive research literature on the effectiveness of electronic foetal monitoring that stretches back about twenty years. Over time, the early enthusiasm for this diagnostic tool has given way to the now predominant view that, on balance, EFM provides no benefits for normal deliveries. Yet it continues to be used routinely. And it continued to be used routinely in Invermere, by family practitioners who *knew* that their practice had no scientific basis. Unlike most practitioners (and most other people) they found this discrepancy troubling and tried to understand it.

Evans, Robert G. "Toward a Healthier Economics: Reflections on Ken Bassett's Problem." In *Health, Health Care, and Health Economics: Perspectives on Distribution*, edited by Morris L. Barer, Thomas E. Getzen, and Greg L. Stoddart (West Sussex, England: John Wiley & Sons, Ltd, 1998).

Dr Bassett went further, however, and in 1985 began to study for a doctorate in medical anthropology during winter sessions at McGill University. Not surprisingly, intensive further analysis of EFM from an alternative disciplinary perspective has shown that the application of a particular medical intervention is the result of a wide and quite complex array of interrelated factors (Bassett, 1996). The balance of findings from randomized trials and other forms of "scientific" evaluation of effectiveness is only one of these factors, and is rarely decisive in itself.

Of particular interest was the role of EFM in supporting first an increase and then a decrease in rates of use of "augmentation" (acceleration) of labour through the administration of oxytocin to the mother. This is a highly controversial procedure with some risk to both mother and child. The "objective" data provided by the EFM, available for interpretation by anyone, supported a corresponding sense of a "normal" birth process that could be defined objectively and represented by mathematical models.

Departures from the model, usually taking the form of "prolonged" labour, were then "abnormal," and the intervention was indicated. The EFM could then be applied to ensure that the foetus was not getting into trouble, becoming hypoxic, during the procedure. The technology thus enabled clinicians to act with greater confidence in augmenting more patients.

But when, for a variety of reasons, including the sheer unpleasantness of the procedure and its dubious value, augmentation fell from favour, *the same* "objective" EFM data (which were, in any case, usually rather ambiguous) could be read to show that the foetus was not in trouble during an extended birth, and that no augmentation was necessary. Rates fell. "Only years later did ... local doctors come to see augmentations as almost irresistible opportunities to behave badly, to be impatient, to project their fears onto patients, or to take out their general job frustrations on a particular individual" (Bassett, 1996, 291).

Dr Bassett now works with the BC Office of Health Technology Assessment at the University of British Columbia, where a range of disciplinary perspectives are brought to bear to try to understand *why* particular technologies are adopted, and how to influence the process. Improving these decisions requires far more than simply presenting the findings of research, however relevant or competent.

The processes by which particular technologies come to be employed (or not) in medical practice are of obvious interest to economists, simply because of the impact these decisions have on patterns and levels of resource utilization – costs and outcomes. But that is not the focus of this paper. Much more fundamental, as the Invermere physicians well understood, is the issue raised by the observation of informed practitioners knowingly (and in this case unhappily) applying an intervention that they knew to be inappropriate. I believe that this phenomenon generalizes, and not just among physicians; and I suggest the following label.

KEN BASSETT'S PROBLEM:

> "Why would intelligent and competent professionals routinely behave in ways that they know to be illogical and scientifically unsound?"[1]

My focus will of course be on economics and economists, particularly on economists studying the health care sector. This paper thus complements that by Uwe Reinhardt (this volume), in which he documents quite specifically such behaviour within our own "profession." Like him, I feel best equipped to talk about the inadequacies of the field I know best.

Ken Bassett's Problem, however, refers to a more general process, even if we ourselves have a narrower focus. And while in economics (as in medicine) this behaviour is revealed in the work of particular individuals, we are not or should not be engaged simply in finger-pointing. A systematic pattern of behaviour is unlikely to be explained solely by the lapses and inadequacies of particular individuals; at least this is not the first hypothesis upon which we ought to seize.[2]

Also at the outset we should set to one side, or at least hold in check, a hypothesis that may come most easily to the minds of economists. Ken Bassett and his colleagues were not paid more when EFM was used. The equipment was owned by the hospital, not the physicians, and the hospital was reimbursed on a global budget. They did not do it for the money. We economists are trained and habituated to reach first for economic incentives in explaining human behaviour, and of course such motivations *are* both powerful and widespread. As Morone (1986) has pointed out, however, while incentives are powerful, economists are not very good at predicting their effects.[3] There is usually much more going on than simple financial gain (Giacomini et al., 1996). And indeed (and quite inconsistently) we are much less ready to adopt economic explanations for *our own* behaviour.

In addressing Ken Bassett's Problem in the context of health economics, I am not proposing to argue for the *existence* of this form of professional behaviour in our field. Such behaviour is described elsewhere in this volume, not only by Reinhardt, but also by Hurley and Rice, among others. Nor are they the first to point it out; much of what they say is old news – and yet the patterns they describe persist. Observing this persistence, in economics as in medicine, I am arguing that this behaviour is a systematic phenomenon to be described and understood, not merely an aberration to be deplored. I will also indicate what seems to me to be a relatively effective corrective strategy.

It may, however, be helpful to start by illustrating what I regard as persistent illogical and unsound analysis by competent professionals. Consider the classic summary of welfare economics by Bator (1957). As Reinhardt reminds us, in this volume and elsewhere (Reinhardt, 1992), that paper makes crystal clear a point that every professional economist knows: to rank social outcomes, you need a ranking rule, a social welfare function, embodying a set of values, that cannot be derived from economics itself. If you want to generate recommendations, normative conclusions that state A is better than state B, using economic analysis, then you must introduce those values first, explicitly or more often implicitly.

The Pareto criterion is one such externally imposed ranking rule; it imports a particular set of values into the analysis from outside. The justification may be that these are widely held, "sort of universal" values – surely no one could object to changes that make some better off without making anyone else worse off? Indeed, they could object – the Pareto criterion actually does impose restrictions on individual utility functions (non-malevolence, for one). But maybe in practice they don't? (And anyway maybe malevolent people's values "shouldn't" count?).

As it happens, however, there may be a much more fundamental flaw in the Pareto criterion as a representation of our values. And it is a flaw that health economists, in particular, need to be aware of if they are serious about their subject matter. Consider a pattern of economic growth in which all the gains go to a very small group of people at the top percentile of the income distribution, and everyone else's income is held constant (in real terms). This is not merely a hypothetical case; Krugman (1992), for example, argues that this pattern characterizes growth in the United States over the last two decades.[4] By the Pareto criterion, such growth unambiguously improves overall well-being. But do we approve this trend? Do we think our neighbours would (Rice, this volume)?[5]

More than mere envy is at stake. As van Doorslaer and Wagstaff (this volume) show, inequalities in health status are correlated, across countries, with inequalities in income. If this relationship is causal, then the "Pareto-improvement" above may actually increase the dispersion of health outcomes – life expectancy, disability, morbidity. Do we still approve *this*?

Well we might, if health is related to absolute income. Income gainers become healthier, on average, but non-gainers do not become less so – though it is not so clear that most of us would in fact view with approval a widening gap in, for example, life expectancies. But evidence is now accumulating of a relationship between health and *relative* income status (Wilkinson, 1994; Kaplan et al., 1996; Kennedy et al., 1996). "[T]hese associations ... seem to show that inequality *per se* is bad for national health, whatever the absolute material standards of living." (Davey Smith, 1996). The evidence for this "big idea" (Editor's choice, 1996) is still controversial (Judge, 1995) for a variety of reasons, but it is growing steadily stronger.[6]

If the overall health status of a community *is* in fact lower, *ceteris paribus*, when inequality is greater, that would mean that the "Pareto-improvement" of more for the wealthiest was actually making people, on average, sicker. Do we approve this? If so, would you like to explain to your neighbours, just *why*?[7]

The criterion of Pareto-optimality may thus turn out to be a good deal more ethically troubling than we economists have previously assumed. In any case it does not actually rank very much. Not only does it not permit points on the utility-possibility frontier to be ranked relative to each other, it does not *in general* permit them to be ranked relative to points inside that frontier. Only points northeast (southwest) of a given point in n-dimensional utility space can be declared superior (inferior) to that point.

In the Paretian context, words like "optimal" or "efficient" have very specific technical meanings that are different from, and much more limited than, their meanings in general English usage. Accordingly, as Reinhardt (1992) has pointed out, if economists use such words in their technical sense when communicating with non-technical audiences, they are likely to mislead (whether or not deliberately).

In particular we talk of, and encourage others to believe in, the possibility of an "equity-efficiency trade-off" when in fact no such trade-off exists *when efficiency is used in its Paretian sense*. Nothing is given up – "traded off" – by a move from a Pareto-efficient point in utility possibility space to a non-efficient point, if the latter ranks more highly on the relevant social welfare function. There is an unambiguous welfare gain; that's all.

A trade-off may exist when "efficiency" is used in its more everyday, non-technical sense, as an engineer or a clinician might – trading off total QALYS against their distribution, for example, as Williams describes in this volume. Perfectly legitimate, but quite different from the meaning of "efficiency" when the word is applied to a general discussion of the institutions governing resource allocation – markets and all that. Encouraging others in confusing the two meanings is not honest.[8]

Being well aware of the limits of Pareto, economists have historically tried to extend the range of their analysis by proposing the "compensation tests" associated with the names of Kaldor, Scitovsky, and Hicks. If the gainers from a given policy could compensate the losers, and/or the losers could not bribe the gainers to abandon it, then the policy is "good" *even if no compensation is actually paid.*

This illustrates the point of this paper. How could competent economists, among the most eminent in the profession, imagine that such a test made sense *as economic analysis*? Reinhardt (1992) has skewered the idea memorably as the "unrequited-punch-in-the-nose test"; other economists have, over the years, been equally if less entertainingly scathing. Why should the *losers* find such tests convincing?

The compensation tests embody interpersonal comparisons, value judgments as to whose interests should be sacrificed to whose gain. These are made constantly in the real world of politics and policy; the compensation test is simply one way of making a political choice, suggested by certain citizens with an interest in the political process.

But suppose a majority of economists – or even all of us except Reinhardt – found such compensation tests plausible as a basis for making normative policy recommendations. *So what?* Economists are not priests. Our normative judgments, our political preferences, have no claim to special weight relative to those of our fellow citizens. The relevant question in a democracy (as different from a theocracy) is whether such value judgments are acceptable to the man on the Clapham omnibus, or T.C. Pits, or the median voter. Economists are entitled to one vote each.[9]

Yet the urge to derive normative conclusions from positive propositions, to offer purely objective, scientific recommendations on issues of public policy, remains fully alive and very strong. Just because it is impossible – "No ethics in, no ethics out" in Archibald's paraphrase of Hume – does not stop us from trying, *even though we know it is impossible*![10]

Harberger (1971), for example, states quite explicitly that economists have no special competence in making value judgments or interpersonal comparisons, and then in the same breath proceeds to do precisely that, "costs and benefits ... *should* [my emphasis] normally be added up without regard to the individual(s) to whom they accrue" (785). That is, each individual should be given equal weight. How could an intelligent person and eminent economist miss the obvious fact that equal weighting is one particular form of interpersonal comparison?

Coming down to the present, Mark Pauly (1994a, b; 1996) writes that welfare economics *given its assumptions* permits normative policy conclusions to be drawn. But to support normative conclusions, these assumptions must themselves be normative. So *whose* assumptions are they? *People* have values, and make normative assumptions, but a body of analysis, such as welfare economics, cannot. A body of thought that includes normative assumptions is a religion, not an academic discipline, much less a science (Culyer and Evans, 1996).

When Pauly (1994b) says "Improved health status that results from demand distorted by incorrect information ... *cannot generally be endorsed by welfare economics* [my emphasis]," he is formally correct, because analytic frameworks are not in the business of handing out endorsements of anything. Only people can do that. Pauly is simply attaching the label of "welfare economics" to his personal ideology, no more. He may share that ideology with some other economists, and even some non-economists, but that does not make his values part of "welfare economics."

A critical normative assumption for Pauly (1996) is that the distribution of income is "accepted as ethically correct." This permits one to avoid distributional issues and interpersonal comparisons. But accepted *by whom*? The most that one could ever say, on the basis of economic analysis alone, would be that if *you* believe that the distribution of income (and any health implications associated with it – recall the discussion above) is ethically acceptable, then for you policy A is better than policy B. But if not, not.

In fact matters are a bit more complex than that. Pauly (1996) refers to *the* distribution of income, but particular policies raise distributional questions precisely because they are expected to *change* that distribution in a material way. Otherwise we *could* legitimately abstract from distributional questions (but we might not find many such policies to analyze).

Thus one would have to say that the distribution of income was ethically acceptable *both before and after* the implementation of a policy, suggesting that one was pretty neutral about distribution anyhow, at least over the relevant range. It does not matter if some gain and some lose, or how the gainers and losers are situated. One doubts that many people would share this ethical position with Pauly; and if most people do not accept a particular ethical assumption, what does it mean to say that "welfare economics" does? We're back to religion again.

But is any of this news? A quarter century ago, Arrow (1973) introduced a mathematical analysis of the welfare effects of coinsurance charges for health care by "ignor[ing] distributional considerations and *assum[ing] a single person in the economy* [my emphasis]." Without that assumption, no welfare conclusions could be drawn a priori. One would have to introduce explicit value judgments about interpersonal deservingness – and of course identify interpersonal effects.

And indeed Pauly (1996), in replying to Culyer and Evans (1996), asks what all their fuss is about? Surely all economists know this? Pauly (1997) and Gaynor and Vogt (1997) take the same approach in critiquing Rice (1997a). Why reiterate the obvious as if it were new learning?[11]

Because we know it, and ignore it. At the time Arrow wrote, and ever since, eminent (and less eminent) health economists have been drawing a priori conclusions about the welfare effects of coinsurance charges (e.g., M. Feldstein, 1973; Manning et al., 1987). Never do they mention that these depend upon specific distributional value judgments, let alone identify and justify the ones that they make implicitly.

More generally, the academic literature contains numerous papers by health economists that draw normative conclusions about "efficiency" and "optimality," and approve or reject public policies, without a second thought about the normative content of their work. They assume a spurious objectivity without even bothering to claim it, purporting to be doing economic "science." Yet they are neither stupid, nor ignorant, nor malicious.[12]

This discrepancy between knowledge and practice was one of the most consistent themes of plenary and other sessions at the inaugural International Health Economics Association (iHEA) conference. A common response to this criticism of so much of contemporary economic practice was to mutter about "market-bashing," or simply to ignore the issue and continue with business as usual. Interestingly, these are also the common responses of physicians confronted with questions – however solidly based in scientific research – about the appropriateness of *their* practices. What else is there to do? – the charges are true. So they cannot be answered – but neither are they heeded.

So why do economists knowingly misrepresent the scope of economic analysis, by pretending to draw normative conclusions from positive propositions, and in the process mislead the public, other economists, and themselves?

The news is not all bad, however, in economics any more than in medicine, and I am not trying to be the Ivan Illich of health economics. There are, in fact, some very positive features, of health economics in particular, that can be strengthened and built upon. In important ways we are in better shape than some other branches of economics. We are healthier, and we should strive to stay that way.

From that perspective, one could have chosen two alternative titles for this paper:

"What Do They Know of Economics, Who Only Economics Know?"
and
"Two Cheers for Health Economics."

The first title emerges from the observation that economics per se has remarkably little specific content. One is tempted to say, none at all. Harberger's argument for "equal weighting" was that, without some sort of value judgments as to interpersonal weightings, we as economists can make few, if any, recommendations on policy. Arrow had the same reason for abstracting from distributional considerations, as did the proposers of compensation tests. But the problem runs deeper; on the basis of economic analysis *alone* we cannot say very much of anything.

That, I think, is why we find a definition of economics so elusive. The common ones are vague and over-general – "the study of people in the ordinary business of life," "optimization under constraint," "the study of the allocation of scarce resources among competing wants ... etc." – or trivial – "what economists do."[13] We tend to fall back on references to a way of thinking, or a particular perspective on social phenomena, that leads one to ask certain characteristic sorts of questions and to try to organize the description and prediction of human behaviour in particular ways. But there is in fact no distinct body of *knowledge*, settled or unsettled, that we can point to and say, even provisionally, "That is economics."[14]

The standard jokes about looking for a one-armed economist, or "no matter how many economists one lines up end-to-end, they never reach a conclusion," have a point. Judicial comments on the testimony of economic experts – not "hired guns" but leaders of the profession – have been more brutal, and equally justified. Reputable and defensible economic opinion can be found on every side of almost every public issue, or at least every one that comes to prominence. Nor are disagreements and disputes confined to the leading edges or the fringes of the discipline, where matters might be expected to be unsettled. They persist across the whole range of questions with which economists have concerned themselves. Even when consensus appears to be established for a time, old ideas and controversies break out again in new language. Nothing ever seems permanently settled.[15]

This indeterminacy does not, I think, arise because economists are more confused or more attracted to controversy than practitioners of other disciplines.[16] Insofar as they aspire to "scientific" status, economists seek to generate their own body of positive, "if ... then" statements, that have been consistently confirmed by various forms of empirical analysis. These would therefore command general assent among not only economists but anyone else familiar with "scientific" modes of demonstration.

Armed with such convincingly demonstrable propositions, as well as with a professional consensus as to their validity, economists could then make unambiguous positive statements to their fellow citizens. We could, in Wildavsky's phrase, "speak truth to power," not in the normative form of, "You should do A and not B," but "if you do A, C will follow."

A generation ago this was the great hope. "Give us the data, and we will finish the job!" as the members of the graduate Economic History Seminar proclaimed at Harvard in the 1960s. With new and more powerful mathematical and statistical techniques, new and massive sources of data, and, of course, explosive progress in computing capacity, a rapid increase in the supply of confirmed positive propositions seemed guaranteed – just over the next hill. And these in turn would permit economists to make unambiguous and more or less consensual statements about the impact of different public policies – predictions, not recommendations.[17] Has it come to pass?

Clearly not. Despite the accumulation of empirical studies – particularly multivariate statistical analyses – over the last three decades, it has turned out to be remarkably difficult to confirm or refute hypotheses in a way that is generally recognized as decisive.

What we neglected is that all positive statements have a "third component." Fully specified, they take the form: "If ... [and ...] then ..." The contents of the [and ...] term are absolutely critical; like the gate in a triode or a transistor they amplify or suppress (or reverse) the connection between intervention and response. Under what circumstances does a relationship hold?[18]

But the range of potentially relevant circumstances is exceedingly diverse, and open to all sorts of interpretation and disagreement as to what should be included. Without some sort of restriction, anything can happen. And conclusions of the form "If A ... then anything" are a weak intellectual basis for a science. (They may not elicit much respect or financial support from the rest of society, either). There are two ways of dealing with the contents of the [and ...] term:

1 Go and find out; and
2 Make them up.

The predominant response among economists has been the latter.

We impose radical simplifications on the contents of the [and ...] term, by making substantive assumptions about the circumstances we are studying. (Sometimes we are conscious of this process, and of its significance, but repetition forms habits that economize on scarce cognitive resources.) The resulting "If ... then" propositions refer to abstract transacting entities – "consumers," "firms" – with highly stylized properties, interacting in very specific circumstances. Their relationship to entities in the world of observation and experience is always problematic.

Through this process we are enabled to make certain definite predictions, although the range of unambiguous predictions that can be supported in this way is much more limited than its practitioners – present company not excepted – typically admit. "Demand (supply) curves always slope downward to the right (left), except when they don't." And even such limited results are bought at a very steep price. The substantive assumptions "made up" in traditional economic theory are at best based on radically impoverished and obsolete theories of human behaviour, long abandoned by students of the relevant disciplines. At worst they are in flat contradiction with "reality" as understood by those professionally concerned with such matters.

For example, we can set up an analytic framework postulating that consumer behaviour can be represented as the outcome of maximizing some objective function, but this framework tells us nothing at all about the arguments of that objective function. When we specify them a priori, we are acting as amateur psychologists – and often rather poor ones. Likewise, when we not only hypothesize the existence of the relationships we call "production functions," but try to specify their arguments and functional forms, we are acting as (typically very bad) engineers, or in health economics, epidemiologists or clinicians.

But these specifications matter – minor changes in either the arguments or the functional forms that we use can lead to radically different predictions. (See, for example, Frank, 1985; Frank and Cook, 1995.)

The point is definitely *not* that one should not "build models," in the sense of consciously or unconsciously introducing simplifying assumptions about the processes that we are trying to describe and understand. That would be silly; we cannot *not* do so if we are to think at all, or even to perceive. The full range of possibly relevant impressions is far beyond the capacity of our senses to record, let alone of our brains to manipulate.

The art of simplifying is that of excluding the differences that do not make a difference, of capturing the essence of a process and ignoring the unimportant. Some do and some do not; there are good and bad models. If essential features of the underlying reality are left out of the [and ...] term, the resulting model becomes at best useless, and quite often actively deceptive and mischievous.

But *as economists*, we have no advantage, comparative or otherwise, in choosing the appropriate simplifications. To do that, you actually have to know something about the processes, activities, institutions, people, that you are trying to analyze. Left to his/her own devices, the economist without content knowledge tends to select the simplifications that yield analytic tractability (and follow convention). And if one does not know any better, why not?

More reliable results, however, emerge from the more interesting and productive alternative – to go and find out. This can be done by immersing oneself in the relevant literature from other disciplines, and building their observations and conclusions into economic analyses in a fundamental way. One may also engage in direct observation "on the shop floor."

But the most efficient approach, entailing less effort and greater reliability, is to seek out and work with specialists in other disciplines.[19] Find out what are the relevant "other circumstances" in a particular situation, from those who know. Working closely with people from other disciplines protects economists from a good deal of sin and error, by forcing them to justify their intellectual behaviour to other informed and intelligent analysts. Such people are unlikely to accept, as support for an otherwise implausible assumption, the explanation that many economists have made it before. (That may be why economists, in general, tend to hold themselves and their work apart from other disciplines – arrogance rooted in a deep and justifiable sense of vulnerability.)

Health economists *do* have, I think, an unusual proclivity for following the second route. Many of us work closely with clinicians, epidemiologists, and "social scientists" of various persuasions, on a long-term basis. We are thus more willing – we have no choice! – to modify or abandon, when they do not fit, the traditional assumptions that have been "made up" in formulating the corpus of general economic theory. We also have unusual opportunities to become informed about the technological relationships underlying the production of both health care and health.

But we deserve only two cheers. Not all of us have had that good fortune, or been able to profit from it through a genuine melding of perspectives. More fundamentally, we have come at best only part way in the reconstruction of our theoretical frameworks to accommodate what we have learned from our colleagues in other disciplines. Cross-disciplinary work is not just intellectual "parallel play"; the (relevant) understandings of one field must actually change the content of another. To the extent that this does not happen, we find ourselves working with theoretical frameworks based on the traditional "made up" contents for the [and ...] terms, while trying to grasp the realities of the health care field as we now understand them. Ken Bassett's Problem emerges.

It emerges in a number of specific contexts across the whole field of health economics. I will focus only on a few leading examples that particularly interest me. In each case, we find important discrepancies between what health economists know, and what they assume in much of their theoretical structures – discrepancies that have material consequences for the outcome of their analyses.

But in each area we also find important examples of health economists having learned from other disciplines in ways that significantly improve the quality of our analysis. And as it happens, under each head we can find a nugget or two of illustrative information from Fuchs' (1996) informal survey of economists and physicians, reported in his presidential address to the American Economic Association.

INDIVIDUAL TASTES

"Standard" economic theory postulates that individual consumer behaviour can be analyzed and predicted on the assumption that only commodities (or commodities and leisure) contribute to well-being. If other state variables matter – individual health status, for example – they do not interact with commodities and so can be held in the pound of *ceteris paribus*. They are not in the [and ...] term.

On the other hand it is pretty obvious that the value of the commodity "health care" to a user depends critically on whether s/he is ill or injured, or more generally whether s/he has reason to believe that the care will improve his/her health status. Perceived effectiveness of care is central to the user's decision (when s/he is in a position to decide) to use care.

No one challenges this overtly, at least not in ordinary language.[20] Yet one finds a radical split among health economists as to how or whether this obvious fact should be built into their analyses. On one side of the Atlantic, for example, the centrality of health status is so generally accepted that the consideration of direct utility effects constitutes an extension to the research program. Certain forms of health care, in particular circumstances, may have a value to the user independent of their effects on health status. Health is not *all* that matters.

On the other side, we occasionally find explicit arguments that health effects are, or should be (the normative economist again), irrelevant to the evaluation of resource allocation. The decisions of the (fully informed) consumer, facing prices that reflect opportunity costs, within an ethically acceptable income distribution, are the only relevant criteria (Pauly, 1994a, b).[21] If a particular form of care contributes to such a consumer's well-being, its effect on health is irrelevant; if it does not, *ditto*. Any health effects are subsumed into the (informed) consumer's evaluation.[22] More typically we find this assumption being built into analysis without supporting comment. Health care is treated as just another commodity, a "widget"; health as such is implicitly irrelevant.[23]

Whether or not health status per se is inserted in the utility function for analytic purposes is not, however, simply an academic point. It matters a great deal for the normative evaluation of particular health services, and of the institutions and systems that produce and deliver them. Are they to be judged by their ability to contribute to health, or by their response to the preferences – as expressed, for example, in willingness to pay – of "consumers"?[24]

Research on what people actually want indicates (not surprisingly) that more is not better, that people do *not*, in general, want ineffective or minimally effective care, especially when it is inconvenient, unpleasant, or dangerous. Moreover their judgments as to the effects that matter, and the risks that are and are not worth taking, will often differ from the views of practitioners. The only way to discover these preferences is to go and look for them. Inference from observed utilization is notoriously deceptive.

In any case, people are often not in a position to make their wishes effective, because of either lack of knowledge or lack of effective control. Lack of knowledge is pervasive; loss of physical control typically occurs in extreme situations and not in the general run of patient contacts with the health care system. But a large proportion of health care resources are used up, and costs generated, in just such extreme situations.

When people have been given either greater information or greater control (e.g., Wennberg, 1992; Molloy and Guyatt, 1991), it has been found in certain important cases that they want *less* care, not more. But it is apparently much more difficult than one might think to achieve this; the resistance and simple inertia are substantial (e.g., SUPPORT, 1995). For our purposes, however, there is direct evidence (apart from introspection!) that health care per se – most of it, anyway – is not a direct (positive) argument in the utility function of the normal consumer.[25]

But the role of (perceived) health status is also central to the endless debate among health economists about the role of physicians and other professionals in generating the demand for their own services. (Other students of, and policy makers in, the health care systems of the world have settled this debate long ago. *Of course*, capacity generates use, that is why capacity control – hospital beds, physician supply – is always among the first steps taken in strategies for cost control.) The relationship between health care and health status is a technical "production" relationship about which professional providers are (perceived to be) more knowledgeable than patients. So their advice – recommendations, or still more revealingly "doctor's orders" – powerfully affects use, independent of price.

If these recommendations are themselves endogenous, varying according to the economic circumstances of the provider (workload, income, prices/fees received), then the "demand curve" disappears, or at least becomes endogenous to supplier behaviour. (And it is hard to imagine any sensible economic model of provider behaviour in which their recommendations would *not* be endogenous.) Thus the inclusion of health status in the individual utility function provides the channel through which "supplier-induced demand" operates.

But as we know, this relationship cuts to the positive foundations of standard economic theory, as well as the normative significance typically adjoined to it. It is therefore not surprising that many economists have resisted it, particularly but not exclusively in the United States. What is remarkable is Fuchs' (1996) finding that an overwhelming majority of the economists, as well as the physicians, that he surveyed agreed that *doctors can and do shift the demand curve for their own services*, and are more likely to do so when demand is low. Yet an overwhelming majority of the formal analyses carried out by American economists in particular, and of the normative interpretations given to them, suppress this reality (without comment).

When pressed, analysts in the exogenous demand tradition tend not to deny the existence of such shifting, but to emphasize the empirical difficulties in establishing its existence beyond all doubt, and especially in measuring its extent. Both concerns are valid; they also apply to virtually every (perhaps every) other behavioural relationship that economists study and build into their theories. In this case, however, incomplete information is translated for analytic purposes into a specific assumption – zero effect. This is the Harberger manoeuvre.

Intriguingly, while two-thirds of both health economists and physicians believed that such shifting occurs, among general economic theorists, the proportion was over three-quarters. One is tempted to infer that this reflects the views of the general public, as economic theorists not elsewhere classified have no specific interest in this area. Health economists will be more aware of the extent of the analytic modifications required by such an effect; and physicians may realize – as the leaders of professional associations certainly do – its potentially awkward political implications.

But that is all speculative, and the sample is small. The key point is that – unless Fuchs found a very unrepresentative sample of American health economists – knowledge (or at least belief) and practice appear to diverge at a point fundamental to virtually all of health economics.

But whatever the role of health status in the individual utility function, we cannot legitimately define that function only over arguments pertaining to a single individual. As is well-known, there are "external effects," interactive relationships among people, both in the form of contagion and at more general levels of benevolence. What one assumes about these – including ignoring them – will significantly influence the results of any formal analysis.[26]

Nothing here is new; the theoretical terrain has been mapped for years. Moreover it is now understood that simply inserting interpersonal terms in the individual utility functions leaves us with a "welfarist" social welfare function (Culyer, 1991) that is still quite restrictive.[27] What is new and interesting is the sort of work that Williams (this volume) is doing, in exploring the more detailed structure of these interpersonal concerns in a way that can link them to policy decisions. Rather than simply assuming them away, or assuming that they exist and then weighting each individual, or individual life-year, or QALY, equally on a priori grounds, he has gone to find out.

But the more general question of whether such concerns exist, is easy. People, even Americans, *tell* you when questioned, that other peoples' health matters to them, that people should get the care they need, whether or not they can pay for it, financed through government. And (outside the United States) they vote that way.

Fuchs' (1996) respondents are about two-thirds in favour of a universal health insurance plan for the United States, and well over half of them think it should be tax-based. They are about 85 per cent (physicians and health economists) against charging higher private insurance premiums to people born with costly genetic defects, though much more dubious about requiring general community rating by private insurers. (Physicians are over two-thirds for it, theorists over two-thirds against, health economists split down the middle.) But that could simply reflect the economists' greater understanding of the dynamics of private insurance markets.

Yet those same economists, in their professional lives, will work quite happily with theoretical structures in which "consumers" are completely selfish, and in which tax-based universal (thus, in effect, compulsory) insurance coverage can easily be demonstrated (provided all consumers are identical in all relevant respects) to create a large "welfare burden" for society as a whole.[28] The potential losers from such a policy could easily compensate the potential gainers for abandoning the idea – though they won't, and should not have to.

And what about uncertainty? Do people react to incomplete information by trying to maximize their expected utilities, or do they employ other strategies and heuristics? The answer is known; the psychologists can demonstrate the latter quite conclusively. The departures from E(U) maximization are large, and the circumstances under which they occur are to some extent predictable. (The insurance salesman's maxim is that insurance is sold, not bought.) Yet many economists continue to assume the former.[29] The "efficiency" of markets for risk, where they exist, does rather depend upon how people behave under uncertainty!

The overall point of the above discussion is not that *I* know how individuals' utility functions should be structured in setting up formal models, but that this knowledge:

a matters a lot for the outcome of the analysis; and
b is not and cannot be derived from economics per se; but
c is commonly assumed in economic analysis, often in defiance of evidence generated by non-economist experts,
d despite the fact that most, if not all, health economists know better.

It might be a better idea to go and find out.

TECHNOLOGY

The same four points can be illustrated by the ways in which we understand and model "technology." And here Fuchs' results suggest that health economists well deserve their two cheers. Eighty-three per cent of economic theorists believe that widespread screening and early diagnosis could cut health care costs significantly. And that's a pretty reasonable view – for the 1950s. Ninety per cent of health economists (and even most physicians), however, knew that the evidence is in and that this is a false hope. And indeed economists, working with epidemiologists and clinical specialists, have helped to produce that evidence. A priori reasoning provides no substitute.

Another cheer: *no* health economists identified differential access to health care as the *primary* reason for health status differences across socioeconomic groups. Most of the other economists also understood that (at least on the present evidence) the principal determinants of health lie elsewhere. One does get a little twitchy, however, in recognizing that this is an *American* sample. Class differences in access to (effective) care are especially marked in that country, and *do* appear to contribute to differences in health outcomes. It would be ironic if the health economists' responses were correct for all developed countries *except* their own. But the word "primary" is key.

But then we, or at least Fuchs' sample, go and blow it. Eighty-one per cent of the health economists believed that "technological change" is the primary reason for the increasing share of GDP devoted to health care over the last thirty years! Only 37 per cent of the economic theorists fell for that. The health economists should each be required to write out, one thousand times: "The technology does *not* dictate its own range of application." And that, of course, is why American health care costs have travelled such a different path from those in other countries.

Causality is always problematic; but it is pretty obvious that all the health care systems of the developed world have had access to the same technologies. Indeed, several of the most prominent technological innovations were first developed outside the United States. How extensively those technologies have been used, however, and whether or not they have been translated into escalating costs, has depended upon the ways in which health care has been organized, delivered, and funded in different countries.

Twenty, or even fifteen, years ago one could perhaps claim that, on average, health expenditures were rising as fast (relative to GDP) outside the United States as in it. (There were significant exceptions, like Canada and the United Kingdom.) But that ceased to be true in the mid to late 1970s, and since then the United States has been on a trajectory all its own. As an international common factor, technological change cannot "explain" patterns that show so much cross-national variation.

Again, we all know that. So why would we find not only Fuchs' sample, but also eminent members of the profession, resorting to this "technology" story and presenting something that cannot be true as if it were established fact? Well, it could be that "technology" is shorthand for a more value-laden story. Improved technology has led to more and better care, and people want this new care and are willing to pay for it, individually and/or collectively. Thus use and costs go up, as they should when new and better products meet consumer needs/tastes.

But why, then, is this escalation so much more rapid in the United States? When costs were escalating at similar rates in most countries, one might have argued that some aggregate analogy to an income effect was at work. It could then be claimed that costs were higher in the United States because Americans were wealthier, but that rising incomes were pushing up costs everywhere. Other countries, when they were as rich as the United States, would have similar spending patterns. (They're just a bit backward, that's all.)

But that argument ceased to hold water long ago. As noted above, the gap in health spending between the United States and the rest of the developed world has actually been widening since the late 1970s. And there is no corresponding income gap opening up in Americans' favour; on the contrary, incomes in other countries have, on average, pulled closer to the US level.[30] Now, presumably, one would have to claim that costs do not go up, or not as fast, in other countries because care is being "rationed"; other people are being denied things that they value and would be willing to pay for. So, they are made worse off as a result. The United States does not spend too much; everyone else spends too little.[31]

If this *is* the underlying story, it neatly inverts the evaluation implicit in Abel-Smith's (1985) description of the United States as the "Odd Man Out" or White's (1995) identification of an "international standard" in health care organization and finance from which only the United States departs. It also requires that one bypass the evidence that *prices* for health care are much higher, in relative terms, in the United States (Gerdtham and Jonsson, 1991; see also Fuchs and Hahn, 1990; Nair el al., 1992; Redelmeier and Fuchs, 1993), implying that Americans do not in fact get much more care, but just pay more for it.[32]

In effect, everyone is out of step but Uncle Sam. But Americans are not healthier than people in other developed countries, so the "rationing" that is presumably being practised wherever costs are lower (everywhere else) does not appear to have the health-damaging effects routinely alleged by medical alarmists. It must then be "tastes" for care that are being suppressed by rationing – which brings us back to the questions of the arguments of the individual utility function and, since almost all care is collectively financed anyway, the nature of the interpersonal relationships across utility functions.[33]

But this is all a bit speculative. The positive point is that, on substantive issues of the relationship between health care and health outcomes, health economists have learned from their other professional colleagues, and get the answer right. Only when we get into "technology" in the abstract, are we vulnerable to confusions that may have a political dimension.

The political significance of technological assumptions, however, has deeper roots in economic theory. In microeconomic theory we impose certain substantive assumptions on the shape of the production function, at least in the short run. The average and marginal cost curves had better turn up, beyond some level of output, or else not only is the firm "size" (equilibrium output level) indeterminate in a competitive environment, but marginal cost pricing is impossible. And the normative significance that we attach to markets, and the prices they generate, depends critically upon those prices reflecting opportunity costs.[34]

We all know why we need to specify the technology, the shape of the production function, in a particular way for analytic purposes. But what about the industries we study? If one is producing a drug (or a computer program), the fixed costs of development are extraordinarily high. The marginal costs of producing another batch of pills or another shrink-wrapped box of disks are pretty trivial, and do not rise with output level, at least over a very large range. Average cost per unit will then fall with output, while exceeding marginal cost, over any conceivable output range – except for marketing costs. So how do you price at marginal cost?

You don't. A large proportion, probably most, of the product price is quasi-rent, covering development and marketing cost. Hence the extraordinary efforts pharmaceutical firms put into marketing their products, and suppressing competition through political investments in anti-competitive regulation.[35] They have a very high "demand for regulation" (Stigler, 1971), with exceptional willingness, and ability, to pay. A world of perfect competition, with free entry and prices driven down to marginal costs, would be catastrophic.

Competition among firms is Schumpeterian, taking the form of new product development, which in his famous description bears about as much relation to price competition as an artillery bombardment does to forcing a door. Ranitidine did not simply "compete" with cimetidine – Glaxo convinced physicians that it was a better drug and cimetidine's market collapsed. (SmithKline has reacted by getting regulatory permission, in the United States, to sell it over the counter.)

So what is the "supply curve" for such an industry?

Even if the technology were cooperative, the supply curve and its underlying cost curves and production function all depend for their relevance on the assumption that "firms," or whatever the producing units are, operate *on* their cost functions. Why should they? Well, cost-minimization is a necessary condition for profit-maximization, which is enforced by competition in either or both of product and capital markets. But most "firms" in the health care sectors of most countries are not-for-profit, operating in highly regulated markets, and nothing like price competition occurs. Even where services are provided by independent, fee-for-service practitioners, these typically work under some collectively negotiated fee schedule. When practitioners do have some discretionary power over their own fees, there is typically a good deal of collusion – as one would expect of rational self-interested transactors with highly developed communication skills.

The United States has for a number of years been offered as a counter-example, a system that is, or rather is about to become or has just become, highly price-competitive. But even if that were true, presumably health economics has to be something more than a theory of the American health care system.

Furthermore, if it is the case, as it seems to be, that prices for health care (relative to other commodities) are much higher in the United States than elsewhere, does this mean that the opportunity costs are correspondingly higher? How is it that other countries appear to be able to elicit the necessary resources at lower – sometimes much lower – (regulated) prices? So what *do* the American prices indicate? A priori assumptions about markets are not too helpful; again one has to go and find out where the money is going, to whom and for what.

Are higher prices primarily a distributional phenomenon – yielding higher levels of economic rent? To what extent do they ration access to health services, and with what implications for the use patterns, and the health outcomes, of people in different income classes? Do higher prices reflect higher levels of resource input to perform functions that are carried out in a less costly way in other countries – technical inefficiency? Or are there differences in "quality," as perceived and valued by patients, behind the higher prices? All these effects may be at work; the interesting question is the mix.

All of this discussion, however, has to do with the technology of health *care* production. If we consider instead the production of health, or at least some contribution to health, then any notion of a monotonic positive relationship between inputs and outputs flies out the window. A diagnostic or therapeutic manoeuvre may as easily damage health as improve it – or simply have no effect at all. Health care *can* make you sick – powerful interventions have powerful side-effects. That's why even we economists, in our private lives, rely on clinicians.

And that's why the whole area of clinical epidemiology, technology assessment in health care, and various forms of program evaluation, and behind them the study of why practitioners choose or reject particular techniques, have become critical aspects of health policy. If health status were simply a monotonic positive function of health care input, as some of its marketers would have us believe,[36] no one would be celebrating the work of Archie Cochrane or participating in the extraordinary new international initiative of the Cochrane Collaboration. But it isn't, and they are.

This is also an area to which health economists have made important contributions, both methodologically and in applied studies. But the work is multidisciplinary to its core; the economist alone, relying only on the tools of economics, would be fortunate simply to have no impact.

The way around Ken Bassett's Problem, short of going off to do a PhD in something else, thus appears trivially simple. All one needs to do, is to fill in the [and ...] terms in our "If ... then" propositions with sound information derived from other clinical and social disciplines – or from direct observation. In other words, build this information into the heart of our own models. And the best way of doing this, in that it provides both access to the necessary information and incentive to force one to use it, is truly joint research (not partitioned projects) with people from other disciplines.

So if that is so obvious, why do we keep on repeating old errors?

Well, making things up permits us to control the structure of our models, preserving analytic tractability and simplicity, and facilitating translation into the language of mathematics. Many economists seem to view mathematics much the way medieval scholars viewed Latin, as a language that confers special authority on statements that have been written in it. (Users of these languages were/are able to get away with a good deal of nonsense by avoiding the vernacular.)

Schooling, force of habit, and herd instincts are also powerful conditioners. We make the assumptions that we were taught, that we have always made, and that everyone else makes. Moreover, there is considerable economy in communication when everyone can use the same code. You do not have to explain in detail, let alone justify, what you are doing. An outsider, especially one with substantive knowledge in related fields, might make very trenchant criticisms. But "peer" review and disciplinary self-reference permit one to avoid exposure to such criticism, or to ignore it without penalty. So long as we all make the same assumptions, we cannot be criticized by reviewers.

Quite the contrary, skilful manipulation of an intellectual framework shared by peer reviewers and editors leads to prestigious publication, reputation, research grants, academic promotion, etc., etc. The whole apparatus of a learned discipline comes into play, to preserve the intellectual status quo. In the sciences, experiment and empirical observation periodically force more or less radical revision of the dominant frameworks. But economics is not a science. Or rather, we approximate a science most closely when we "go and find out," and are most vulnerable when we make things up.

There is also another dimension, one that we rarely discuss openly. Whether we wish it or not, the choices we make to fill in the [and ...] terms in our analyses have powerful ideological and political content. Other people with important interests at stake inevitably give considerable attention to how we "make up" the content of these terms, and the analytic results. We have already noted above the way that "technology," in the abstract, has been and is being used as an argument both to explain and to justify ever-growing health care spending.

Such claims emanate from sectors of the health care industry and from their spokesmen.[37] Health expenditures, from whatever source, are their sales revenues and incomes, so they have every reason to resist and subvert public and private efforts at cost control. So long as discussion can be focused on "technology" in the abstract – rather expensive but overall a GOOD THING, and certainly something on which a progressive society should be spending more – such claims cannot be tested in detail. They reduce to "Day by day, in every way, we're getting better and better. Send more money."

But the same interests are involved in the detailed structure of our formal models, again whether we like it or not. Different assumptions about the arguments of individual utility functions, for example, map directly into alternative political programs with powerful (and very different) redistributional effects. If we formulate economic models that embody the observations that users of care really want health, not health care per se, and that they are concerned about each other's health, and that they cannot deal comfortably or very successfully with decision-making under uncertainty, we will be led to a certain "world-view."

Evaluating and improving the effectiveness of health care will be an important public concern, and questions about the distribution of burdens and benefits among the different members of a society will be central to the organization and financing of health care systems. Individual "consumer" choices in private markets will appear not only as unsuitable guides for resource allocation, but in a fundamental sense as undefined.

On the other hand, once one has adopted a standard individualistic, commodity-based utility function, with uncertainty captured in the expectations operator, one is led naturally into a concern with the "efficiency" of "markets" for this commodity. "Optimality" of resource allocation will be achieved by some appropriate structuring of private markets, including private insurance markets. One may add some surrounding textual comment about imperfect information or redistributional concerns, but that is mere window dressing. The central analytic construct holds the centre of the stage.[38]

In the realm of actual public policy, it is clear that the first view is dominant in the industrialized world outside the United States (Abel-Smith and Mossialos, 1994; White, 1995). Within the United States, both policy and the public appear to be quite schizophrenic. But the second view is nowhere completely absent, because the policies that follow from different world views *do* have such important differences in their implications for the distribution of income and wealth.

As we all know, even if we do not always talk about it – and rarely admit it in formal models – the wealthy and healthy are relatively much better off under private forms of finance, while the unhealthy and unwealthy are better off with public tax-based financing (Evans et al., 1994, 1995). (There is more, but this much is obvious, fundamental, and beyond contention.) Well-defined and self-aware interest groups in every society thus have a strong economic interest, in addition to their ideological orientation, in the content of the "world views" that govern health policy (Evans, 1996a, 1997a).

It follows that these same groups have an interest in the structure and content of the economic frameworks that contribute towards – though they are far from dominating – the formulation of those world views. And, as economists, we have a particular professional interest in the way in which economic interests are expressed in action.

Or to put it more bluntly, if economists can choose their assumptions in ways that are crucial to the results of their analysis, and if other people have a strong economic interest in those results, cold-blooded economic analysis itself would seem to predict that economic inducements will be offered to steer those choices. And if so, cold-blooded economic analysis also predicts that some of us, at least, will accept.

Is this happening? That's an empirical question, and is left for the reader.

But to the extent that it *could* happen – and I would welcome any demonstration that it is *not* an obvious economic prediction – this possibility underscores the importance of placing the contents of the [and ...] terms of our analyses on a firmer empirical foundation, and of exposing our work to a wider range of professional criticism. We are going to *need* the input of others, to protect us from external subversion, and from ourselves. And health economists, though I believe we are at the forefront in cross-disciplinary, truly *applied* economics, are also going to come, are already coming, under the heaviest external pressure.

Indeed this may be a backhanded form of compliment – our work has actually been quite useful, so we are worth subverting. We're going to need more allies.

What role might be played by an organization like iHEA? By linking health economists from many countries and institutional environments more closely together, it could encourage and promote intellectual and methodological variety – providing a larger garden in which a hundred flowers might bloom. This will be the more likely if we encourage membership and participation from non-economists who have interests parallel to ours. On the other hand, iHEA could become a vehicle for the enforcement of ideological and methodological hegemony, defining what is and is not "real" health economics on the basis of who does it and/or what methodologies and conventional assumptions (including normative ones) are employed. Such an organization would then become more closely aligned with and supportive of a particular set of ideological and economic interests, interests that are increasingly operating internationally.[39]

It may be worth reflecting upon the fact that iHEA gives an annual prize in the name of Kenneth Arrow, one of the most distinguished theorists of his generation, and indeed his classic 1963 paper is widely and justly cited. But there is another classic paper in this field, "Price Discrimination in Medicine" by Reuben Kessel (1958), that for many years was more widely cited, and that was and is much more important for anyone trying to understand the economics of health care.

Unlike Arrow the theoretician, Kessel went out and studied the actual behaviour of US physicians in considerable detail, and then described and interpreted that behaviour from an economic perspective. Many of his insights are still valid, and not surprisingly they did not and do not all fit comfortably within conventional price theory. His contribution to *our* field, in substance and particularly in method, was far greater than Arrow's single paper, however theoretically elegant. But we do not give a Kessel Prize. Maybe we should.

NOTES

1 One has to be a bit careful with language like "illogical." As Dr Bassett's subsequent anthropological research made clear, there *were* reasons for the pattern of behaviour that he and his colleagues observed and participated in. In Marmor's paraphrase of Hegel, "Nothing that is regular, is stupid." The reasons were not to be found, however, in the overt objectives of the physicians themselves; these did not in general include providing their patients with ineffective care.

2 That would be akin to attributing unhealthy lifestyles such as smoking to the moral inadequacies (or the "tastes"!) of smokers. In fact, we know that smoking is a physiological addiction, taken up in childhood, in response to marketing carefully targeted at children. The presence of a sharp social gradient in this and other "unhealthy lifestyles" reflects more fundamental social processes influencing individual behaviour. Ken Bassett's Problem is similarly indicative of broader social forces at work.

3 "[Law] 4. Beware of incentives. Economists and other rationalists restlessly tinker with peoples' incentives. This is a dangerous game. Although incentives are important for understanding problems and fashioning solutions, they are also tricky devils, always veering off in unanticipated ways ... People are complicated, social systems, almost infinitely so. A great many uninvited incentives lurk in each policy change" (Morone, 1986, 818).

4 In the 1980s, people in the lowest quintile actually became poorer, on average (Krugman, 1992); such a change could not be a Pareto-improvement.

5 And if we think our neighbours *would* approve, why would the editors of the *Wall Street Journal*, among others, argue so strenuously, "display[ing a] ... combination of mendacity and sheer incompetence" (Krugman, 1992, 19), that this "Pareto-improvement" is not in fact occurring?

6 Data on both health status and income distribution, in every country, are not nearly as good as one would like, though they are rapidly improving

(Smeeding and Gottschalk, 1995). The pathways through which a relationship between inequality and ill health might operate, involving "social and cognitive processes, rather than ... [material] effects" (Wilkinson, 1994), have been somewhat obscure, although recent work in neurobiology is rapidly generating candidate possibilities (Evans et al., 1994; Evans, 1996b). The principal reason for the controversy, however, and especially for its intensity, is probably the obvious ideological and political challenge implied by such findings. The interpretation of research, positively or negatively, becomes entangled with advocacy and with well-defined political agendas.

7 A quick answer might be that the Pareto criterion refers to making one or more people better off while making no one else worse off, and if inequality breeds illness, clearly the criterion has not been met. Others *are* worse off. That's true, but it is not what we do. In fact we apply the criterion to models in which individual utility depends only upon commodity (or commodity/leisure) bundles, or indirect functions of incomes and prices. So we *do* use (real) income to stand for well-being.

8 The "equity-efficiency trade-off" is often presented as a claim that egalitarian redistributive social policies may have a cost in total social *output* – the GDP will be lower, for example. That may or may not be so; but it is a statement about *product* space, not *utility* space. The Pareto criterion does not apply to commodities per se, only to the utilities presumed to be derived from them. And again, all professional economists know this.

The persistence of the fallacy is probably rooted in conflicts over the social welfare function itself. Those who would lose from redistribution can be expected to resist with any argument that comes to hand. "We'll all be worse off, if I have to give up anything!" And of course there may be circumstances in which this is true. But a move towards greater equality in utility space, *even if* it involved falling inside the utility-possibility frontier (say, because GDP is lower), might still increase the value of the SWF. It depends on the shape of that function. To assert a *necessary* trade-off is simple political deception, and economists know it.

9 But do any of us believe otherwise? No, or at least I have never heard any economist openly claim special normative insight. So why do we make policy recommendations, qua economists, that implicitly embody just such a claim?

10 We appear to follow Tertullian, the early father of the Church (and later heresiarch) who formulated the "Credo quia impossible!" But are we all so knowledgeable? Styles change in the teaching of economic theory; Reinhardt, in his opening address to the 1996 inaugural iHEA conference, suggested

that a professional economist trained in the major graduate schools of today can no longer be assumed to be familiar with the fundamental theorems of welfare economics. The currently dominant American political ideology, with its emphasis on "markets *über alles*," has sunk so deeply into what is taught as "economic theory" that some in the younger generation *may* in fact simply be ignorant. If he is right, then Ken Bassett's Problem is a question for their instructors.

11 Similar comments were made from the floor about Uwe Reinhardt's presentation at the 1996 iHEA conference.

12 But see Note 10 above. There may be more ignorance around than we think. In this context it is worth reflecting upon a comment by Gaynor and Vogt (1997), highlighted by Rice (1997b), "It is not clear to us in what way an economist saying 'trade barriers make everyone worse off than ...' is any more or less normative than an engineer saying 'bridges made out of cardboard will fall down more frequently than ...'"

Nor are they alone. Fuchs' (1996) questionnaire identifies the statement "Third-party payment results in patients using services whose costs exceed their benefits," as a *positive* statement! Costs and benefits can be defined, indeed evaluated, without introducing any value judgements (we're just doing economic science). And almost all of his respondents dutifully agreed.

13 Jacob Viner's definition is, however, far from trivial in its potential consequences. If economics is "what economists do" then an obvious inference (though not a logical implication) is that "what non-economists do" is, whatever its content and findings, "not economics." The field becomes defined not by its substantive content, but by the identity of its practitioners. If these form a self-identifying club, then economists can achieve something of the monopolistic privileges that other professions have gained through regulation.

14 There is however a body of "tools and techniques" that tends to be the characteristic possession of economists. To the extent that these are exclusive to economists, then defining the field in terms of those tools and techniques leads back to Jacob Viner's definition – see the previous note.

15 Particular *theoretical* propositions that can be given formal mathematical representation are settled, once they are proved or refuted. Thus there is a steady accumulation of information about the properties of such mathematical relationships. But there is no necessary connection between this form of "progress," and our understanding of the behaviour of actual human beings, either individually or in (small or large) groups.

16 They may in fact be either, or both, but I do not think that that is the whole explanation.

17 Friedman (1953) not only laid out this objective, but advocated a particular methodology for reaching it which appeared to liberate economists from the need for any substantive information about the processes they were studying. That "bootstrap" methodology was flawed at its core, and has had no shortage of critics. But it retains a superficial attractiveness, perhaps because it is easy to understand, and offers the illusion of general insights without the effort of acquiring specific knowledge. ("Ignorance is Strength.") Indeed Friedman's proposed methodology may have contributed to Ken Bassett's Problem, in suggesting that it doesn't matter if analysis is based on false assumptions. Go ahead and do things you know are wrong; empirical testing of consequences will sort things out. Well, *that* prediction was thumpingly falsified!

18 This is not quite the same as the traditional *ceteris paribus* assumption. "If A, then B" requires that C, D, etc. not be changing at the same time; *ceteris paribus* isolates the change in a single variable A to focus on its effects alone. But the point here is that the effects of A will depend on the specific pattern of other circumstances, even when these are held constant. And in the real world, these patterns are typically very complex.

19 Few of us are likely to have the opportunity to take Ken Bassett's route, and to *become* a specialist in another discipline. And in any case, even two disciplines is only a beginning.

20 Mathematical formulations, on the other hand, permit one to say things that would be pretty dubious, if not simply silly, in other languages.

21 Does such a consumer exist, has s/he ever existed, *could* s/he exist? Or rather, does this "transacting entity," endowed by assumption with certain properties, and operating in a hypothetical informational and institutional environment, bear a sufficiently close relationship to any human person or family to be of any relevance to the analysis of health care systems in the world around us?

If the answer were "yes," the judgments of such a hypothetical "consumer" might be an ethically plausible guide to resource allocation. Of course there is no way of knowing whether our fellow citizens would agree; and remember, we economists are neither legislators nor priests. But the answer is in fact "no," and the hypothetical situation serves primarily as a distraction from attempts to understand health care systems in the real world.

22 The legendary Muslim (substitute preferred faith) read only the Koran, because other books would either confirm its truth, and be superfluous, or deny it, and be blasphemous.

23 There is a dodge that can be added to this, but it *is* only a dodge. To avoid the obvious absurdity of the insertion of health *care* in the individual

utility function – i.e., that people will want care regardless of their health state ("Take two appendectomies, they're free!"), one can postulate that individuals are indeed concerned not about health care but about their health state. But the latter is then modelled as a "capital stock" in which people "invest" by, *inter alia*, purchasing and consuming health care. This formulation has problems of its own, but it is then augmented by the assumptions that (a) individuals are fully informed about the relation between health care and their "health capital," and (b) more health care always produces more health. Both of these are clearly counter-factual; they serve in effect to reinsert health care into the utility function while camouflaging the absurdity. Health status is introduced into the analysis, but then finessed out again.

24 Implicit in this distinction is the assumption that users of care, though they may know the value of health to themselves, will not, in general, be knowledgeable about how health status is produced from health care. The whole apparatus of professional regulation is built around just this assumption; and if/when an economist assumes perfectly informed "consumers," s/he is very much in the minority. One might speculate about the personal care-seeking behaviour of such economists.

25 A form of mental illness, Munchausen's Syndrome is characterized by seeking out care services, and counterfeiting illnesses in order to undergo various diagnostic and therapeutic interventions. Such people apparently *do* derive direct utility from using health services.

26 Economists can be appallingly stupid about personal interactions. We routinely illustrate the importance of prices by telling the little homily of the group of diners who go out to lunch together and agree to split the cheque equally. Each of them, acting as an independent utility maximizer, eats more than s/he would if s/he had to pay the full cost of his/her meal. All end up eating, and spending, too much relative to what they really wanted. See how bad socialism is, and how much better are private markets? But why did this group decide to eat together (and split the cheque) in the first place? People who act like individual utility maximizers in such settings very soon find themselves dining alone.

27 Archibald characterized this class of models as "dog-and-master" models. The well-being of the dog takes on broader social significance only insofar as the master cares about it. There is no general community concern for equity that might serve as a basis for entitlements for dogs (including stray dogs).

28 Or alternatively provided that a strict interpersonal comparative rule is in effect that "a buck is a buck is a buck" (*pace* Kenneth LeM. Carter) regardless of who gets it – the Harberger SWF.

29 Moreover the economic theorists have shown that expected utility maximization by each individual (argument) in a given "welfarist" SWF will not, except in very special cases, yield the maximum expected value of the SWF itself (Hammond, 1982, 1983). But health economists interested in private insurance markets seem to have ignored this result.

30 The OECD Health Data 96 database (OECD, 1996) assembles a wide range of health-relevant data for these countries from 1960 to 1994. Over the first half of this period, prior to 1977, the US share of GDP spent on health care was rising in parallel with the (unweighted) average of OECD countries, though at the top of the pack. After 1977, however, the average for OECD countries has grown much less rapidly and the United States has pulled away. The share of health spending in GDP in the United States is now about *50 per cent* larger than that in any other OECD country. Over this same period, 1977–94, the (unweighted) average of GDP per capita, measured in purchasing power parities, rose from 71 to 76 per cent of the US level (in the nineteen OECD countries for which data are available since 1960).

31 Indeed, this is precisely the conclusion reached by National Economic Research Associates (NERA) in an international study of health care spending (Hoffmeyer and McCarthy, 1994), with an interesting qualification. "Needs/demands" for health spending were allegedly met (in 1990) in *two* countries – the United States and Switzerland. These two countries spent vastly different shares of their national incomes: 12.4 per cent of GDP in the United States: only 7.8 per cent in Switzerland. Yet both are alleged to have been spending the "right" amount, while all the countries *between* these rates were spending far too little. The United States and Switzerland were the only countries in the OECD (except for Turkey) with a high proportion of private funding, suggesting that NERA's criteria for "meeting needs" depended much less on how much was spent than on how it was spent – and raised.

But even the United States, they claim, should spend a much larger share of its national income on health care by the year 2000, and this will not be politically acceptable. The study then proposes a new international "prototype" model of health care organization and finance, replacing White's (1995) "international standard." In effect, this would ensure that health care costs were once again out of control, so as to escalate as "needed/demanded" by the various national populations. (The percent of GDP spend on health has escalated significantly since 1990 in both the United States and Switzerland.)

The study is critiqued in Towse, ed. (1995): NERA were commissioned by Pharmaceutical Partners for Better Health Care, a lobby group for the international pharmaceutical industry.

32 One might then argue that, if care is higher priced, it must be higher "quality" – a "quality" reflected not in better health outcomes, but, in the minds of the recipients, in greater satisfaction. It must be so, or else higher prices would not be paid. But higher American prices are to a large extent caused by the extraordinarily high costs of administering the *payment system*, not of providing better care (Woolhandler and Himmelstein, 1991). Well, that provides greater "choice," not of care but of mode of reimbursement. Do Americans want that? They must, or they would not pay for it ... And so it goes. There is in fact counter-evidence that might bear on each of these points: but the a priori argument forever slides away into circularity.

33 It also raises a question as to why, if Americans are getting what they want while people in all other countries are having their desires suppressed by "rationing," it is the *Americans* who are so unhappy about their situation (Blendon et al., 1990)?

34 There may be other arguments, good or bad, for markets and for private enterprise (Nelson, 1981). But the stories that we tell on the basis of *economic theory* require that prices correspond to the opportunity cost of resources.

Things get a little fuzzier in the hypothetical "long run." Sometimes we use the traditional argument that coordination costs (or something) lead to a U-shaped average cost curve; other times we fall back on constant returns to scale and let the equilibrium firm size dangle. It does not matter, of course, because so long as firms can enter freely *at any scale, no matter how small,* the threat of entry will hold prices at marginal cost in the long run, even if the industry is monopolized. Public policy to promote competition – anti-trust, anti-combines, whatever – is thus superfluous if not actually harmful ... So the "technological assumption" of constant returns to scale becomes politically significant. Maybe one should try to find out?

35 Members of the industry prefer to speak of "protection of intellectual property." But the label does not matter; the process is the same.

36 Or, more shameless yet, a monotonic function of health *spending*!

37 Recall that NERA's proposals to re-ignite the international escalation in health care costs, that has been largely damped since the late 1970s, were commissioned by the international pharmaceutical industry (note 31 above).

38 It is only from the second perspective that it becomes possible to raise questions like "We do not make groceries free; why should the government provide 'free' health care?" or "Not everyone can afford a Cadillac; why should everyone get Cadillac-style care?" or even "We don't need a special economic theory for car repair, and what really makes medicine different?" and be taken even half-seriously. From the perspective of the first world

view such questions are so crashingly stupid that their being asked at all suggests a deliberate act of intellectual sabotage.

39 The list of contributors to the founding of iHEA makes interesting reading, though Willie Sutton would have understood.

REFERENCES

Abel-Smith, B. (1985). "Who is the odd man out?: The experience of Western Europe in containing the costs of health care." *Milbank Memorial Fund Quarterly* 63: 1–17.

– and E. Mossialos (1994). "Cost containment and health care reform: A study of the European Union." *Health Policy* 28: 89–132.

Arrow, K.J. (1963). "Uncertainty and the welfare economics of medical care." *American Economic Review* 53(5): 941–73.

– (1973). *Welfare analysis of changes in health coinsurance rates*, R-1281-OEO. Santa Monica, CA: The Rand Corp.; republished in *The role of health insurance in the health services sector,* ed. Rosett, R., 3–23. New York: National Bureau of Economic Research, 1976.

Bassett, K. (1996). "Anthropology, clinical pathology and the electronic fetal monitor: Lessons from the heart." *Social Science and Medicine* 42(2): 281–92.

Bator, F.M. (1957). "The simple analytics of welfare maximization." *American Economic Review* 47(1): 22–59.

Blendon, R.J., R. Leitman, I. Morrison, and K. Donelan. (1990). "Satisfaction with health systems in ten nations." *Health Affairs* 9(2): 185–92.

Culyer. A.J. (1991). "The normative economics of health care finance and provision." In *Providing health care: The economics of alternative systems of finance and provision*, ed. A. McGuire, P. Fenn, and K. Mayhew, 65–98. Oxford: Oxford University Press.

– and R.G. Evans (1996). "Normative rabbits from positive hats: Mark Pauly on welfare economics." *Journal of Health Economics* 15(2): 243–51.

Davey Smith, G. (1996). "Income inequality and mortality: Why are they related?" *British Medical Journal* 312(7037): 987–8.

Editor's choice (1996). "The big idea." *British Medical Journal* 312(7037): 985–6.

Evans, R.G., M.L. Barer, and G.L. Stoddart. (1994). *Charging Peter to pay Paul: Accounting for the financial effects of user charges.* Toronto: The Premier's Council on Health, Well-Being, and Social Justice, June.

– M. Hodge, and I.B. Pless. (1994). "If not genetics, then what? Biological pathways and population health." In *Why are some people healthy and others not?* ed. R.G. Evans, M.L. Barer, and T.R. Marmor, 161–88. New York: Aldine de Gruyter.

– M.L. Barer, and G.L. Stoddart. (1995) "User fees for health care: Why a bad idea keeps coming back (or, what's health got to do with it?)" *Canadian Journal on Aging* 14(2): 360–90.

– (1996a). "Marketing the market, regulating regulators: Who gains? Who loses? What hopes? What scope?" In *Health care reform: The will to change*, OECD Health Policy Studies No. 8, 95–114. Paris: OECD.

– (1996b). "Health, hierarchy, and hominids." In *Reforming health care systems: experiments with the NHS*, ed. A.J. Culyer and A. Wagstaff, 35–64. Aldershot: Edward Elgar.

– (1997a). "Going for the gold: The redistributive agenda behind market-based health care reform." *Journal of Health Politics, Policy and Law* 22(2): 423–66.

– (1997b) "Coarse correction – and way off target." *Journal of Health Politics, Policy and Law* 22(2): 503–8.

Feldstein, M.S. (1973). "The welfare loss of excess health insurance." *Journal of Political Economy* 81(2, Part 1): 251–80.

Frank, R.H. (1985). *Choosing the right pond: human behaviour and the quest for status*. New York: Oxford.

– and P.J. Cook (1995). *The winner-take-all society.* New York: Free Press.

Friedman, M. (1953). "The methodology of positive economics." In *Essays in positive economics*, ed. M. Friedman, 3–43. Chicago: University of Chicago Press.

Fuchs, V.R. (1996). "Economics, values, and health care reform." *American Economic Review* 86(1): 1–24.

– and J.S. Hahn (1990). "How does Canada do it? A comparison of expenditures for physicians' services in the United States and Canada." *New England Journal of Medicine* 323(13): 884–90.

Gaynor, M., and W.B. Vogt (1997). "What does economics have to say about health policy anyway? – A comment and correction on Evans and Rice." *Journal of Health Politics, Policy, and Law* 22(2): 475–96.

Gerdtham, U.-G., and B. Jonsson (1991). "Price and quantity in international comparisons of health care expenditure." *Applied Economics* 23: 1519–28.

Giacomini, M., et al. (1996). *Financial incentives in the Canadian health care system – Executive summary*. Hamilton, Ont.: McMaster University Centre for Health Economics and Policy Analysis.

Hammond, P.J. (1982). "Utilitarianism, uncertainty, and information." In *Utilitarianism and beyond*, ed. A. Sen and B. Williams, 85–102. Cambridge: Cambridge University Press.

– (1983). Ex-post optimality as a dynamically consistent objective for collective choice under uncertainty. In *Social choice and welfare*, ed. P.K. Pattanaik and M. Salles, 175–205. Amsterdam: North-Holland.

Harbergcr, A.C. (1971). "Three basic postulates for applied welfare economics: An interpretive essay." *Journal of Economic Literature* 9: 785–97.

Hoffmeyer, U.K., and T.R. McCarthy (1994). *Financing health care*. 2 vols. Dordrecht: Kluwer Academic Publishing.

Judge, K. (1995). "Income distribution and life expectancy: A critical appraisal." *British Medical Journal* 311: 1282–5.

Kaplan, G.A., E.R. Pamuk, J.W. Lynch, et al. (1996). "Inequality in income and mortality in the United States: Analysis of mortality and potential pathways." *British Medical Journal* 312(7037): 999–1003.

Kennedy, B.P., I. Kawachi, and D. Prothrow-Stith (1996). "Income distribution and mortality: Cross section ecological study of the Robin Hood index in the United States." *British Medical Journal* 312(7037): 1004–7.

Kessel, R.A. (1958). "Price discrimination in medicine." *Journal of Law and Economics* 1(2): 20–53.

Krugman, P.R. (1992). "The right, the rich, and the facts: Deconstructing the income distribution debate." *The American Prospect* 11 (Fall): 10–31.

Manning, W.G., J.P. Newhouse, and N. Duan, et al. (1987). "Health insurance and the demand for medical care: Evidence from a randomized trial." *American Economic Review* 77(3): 251–77.

Molloy, W., and G. Guyatt (1991). "A comprehensive health care directive in a home for the aged." *Canadian Medical Association Journal* 145(64): 307–11.

Morone, J. (1986). "Seven laws of policy analysis." *Journal of Policy Analysis and Management* 5(4): 817–19.

Nair, C., R. Karim, and C. Nyers (1992). "Health care and health status: A Canada–United States statistical comparison." *Health Reports* 4(2): 175–83. Ottawa: Statistics Canada (Cat. no. 82-003).

Nelson, R.R. (1981). "Assessing private enterprise: An exegesis of tangled doctrine." *Bell Journal of Economics* 12(1): 93–111.

OECD (1996). *OECD Health Data 96*. Paris: Organization for Economic Cooperation and Development.

Pauly, M.V. (1994a). "Editorial: A re-examination of the meaning and importance of supplier-induced demand." *Journal of Health Economics* 13(3): 369–72.

– (1994b). "Reply to Roberta Labelle, Greg Stoddart, and Thomas Rice." *Journal of Health Economics* 13(4): 495–6.

– (1996) "Reply to Anthony J. Culyer and Robert G. Evans." *Journal of Health Economics* 15(2): 253–4.

– (1997). "Who was that straw man anyway? A comment on Evans and Rice." *Journal of Health Politics, Policy, and Law* 22(2): 467–74.

Redelmeier, D.A., and V.R. Fuchs (1993). "Hospital expenditures in the United States and Canada." *New England Journal of Medicine* 328(11): 772–8.

Reinhardt, U.E. (1992). "Reflections on the meaning of *efficiency:* Can efficiency be separated from equity?" *Yale Law & Policy Review* 10(2): 302–15.

– (1998). "Abstracting from distributional effects, this policy is efficient." In *Health, health care, and health economics: Perspectives on distribution*, ed. M.L. Barer, T.E. Getzen, and G.L. Stoddart, 1–52. London: John Wiley & Sons, Ltd.

Rice, T.H. (1997a). "Can markets give us the health system we want?" *Journal of Health Politics, Policy, and Law* 22(2): 383–422.

– (1997b). "A reply to Gaynor and Vogt, and Pauly." *Journal of Health Politics, Policy, and Law* 22(2): 497–502.

– (1998). "The desirability of market-based health reforms: A reconsideration of economic theory." In *Health, health care, and health economics: Perspectives on distribution*, ed. M.L. Barer, T.E. Getzen, and G.L. Stoddart, 415–63. London: John Wiley & Sons, Ltd.

Smeeding, T.M., and P. Gottschalk (1995). *The international evidence on income distribution in modern economies: Where do we stand?* Working Paper #13, Maxwell School of Citizenship and Public Affairs, Syracuse University, Syracuse, New York.

Stigler G.J. (1971). "The theory of economic regulation." *Bell Journal of Economics and Management Science* 2(1): 3–21.

Support Principal Investigators (1995). "A controlled trial to improve care for seriously ill hospitalized patients: The study to understand prognoses and preferences for outcomes and risks of treatment (SUPPORT)." *Journal of the American Medical Association* 274(20): 1591–8.

Towse A., ed. (1995). *Financing health care in the UK: A discussion of NERA's Prototype model to replace the NHS*. London: Office of Health Economics, 47.

van Doorslaer, E., and A. Wagstaff (1998). "Equity in the finance and delivery of health care: An introduction to the ECuity project." In *Health, Health Care, and Health Economics: Perspectives on Distribution*, ed. M.L. Barer, T.E. Getzen, and G.L. Stoddart, 179–207. London: John Wiley & Sons, Ltd.

Wennberg, J.E. (1992). "Innovation and the policies of limits in a changing health care economy." In *Technology and health care in an era of limits*. Vol. III of *Medical innovation at the crossroads*, ed. A.C. Gelijns, 9–33. "Institute of Medicine Committee on Technological Innovation in Medicine." Washington, DC: National Academy Press.

White. J. (1995). *Competing solutions: American health care proposals and international experience*. Washington, DC: Brookings.

Wilkinson, R.G. (1994). *Unfair shares*. Ilford: Barnardo's.

Williams, A. (1998). "If we are going to get a fair innings, someone will need to keep the score!" In *Health, health care, and health èconomics: Perspectives on distribution*, ed. M.L. Barer, T.E. Getzen, and G.L. Stoddart, 319–30. London: John Wiley & Sons, Ltd.

Woolhandler, S., and D.U. Himmelstein (1991). "The deteriorating administrative efficiency of the US health care system." *New England Journal of Medicine* 324(18): 1253–8.

3

The TSX Gives a Short Course in Health Economics: It's the Prices, Stupid! (2010)

ROBERT G. EVANS

Wednesday, 7 April 2010. The shares of Shoppers Drug Mart (SC-T) closed on the Toronto Stock Exchange at just under $44. The next morning they were trading below $37. Nearly a fifth of the company's market value, about $1.6 billion, had vanished literally overnight. It got worse. On 29 June, Shoppers bottomed at $32.57 a share. The company had lost a quarter of its market value since the evening of 7 April. (Shoppers has since recovered somewhat; on 1 October, it closed at $38.82.)

Lesson One: *Every dollar of expenditure on health services (or anything else) is a dollar of someone's income.*

There is no mystery about where the money went. The minister of health of Ontario announced, on that Wednesday evening, that as of 1 July the Ontario Drug Benefit (ODB) Plan would change the rate at which pharmacies were reimbursed for the ingredient costs of generic drugs dispensed to beneficiaries. By 29 June, it was clear that they were going ahead as planned. Pharmacies had previously been receiving 50 per cent of the price of the corresponding branded and originally patented drug; henceforth they would receive only 25 per cent. At the same time, the

Evans, Robert G. "The TSX Gives a Short Course in Health Economics: It's the Prices, Stupid!" *Healthcare Policy* 6(2)(2010): 13–23. Reprinted with the permission of *Healthcare Policy* and Longwoods.

"professional allowances" (less politely, kickbacks) paid by generic manufacturers to pharmacies would be banned. Shoppers, the largest chain pharmacy in Canada, would see this change come straight off its bottom line – as indeed would every other pharmacy in Ontario – and the stock market reacted accordingly.

The Ontario government estimated that this change would reduce ODB outlays by about $500 million per year, or 12 per cent of the estimated $4.1 billion that the Ontario government spent on drugs in 2009 (CIHI 2009). But private payers in Ontario, both insurers and individual patients, spent another $7.6 billion, and as of 1 April 2012, they too will be paying no more than 25 per cent of the price of the originally patented drug.

Nationally, about a quarter of private spending is for non-prescription drugs and related items. So if one assumes an equivalent 12 per cent saving on generics for private payers, that would amount to $7.6 \times 0.75 \times 0.12 = \$684$ million. The numbers are rough, but the total savings look "not unadjacent to" $1.2 billion per year.[1]

That's an average of nearly $100 for every resident of Ontario. It is also an estimate of the annual revenue lost by Ontario pharmacies. The savings and the loss are opposite sides of the same coin. And the savings/lost revenue will increase over the next few years as several high-volume "blockbuster" drugs come off patent and more generic alternatives become available (Picard 2010; Cutler 2007). The fall in Shoppers' capitalization represents Bay Street's (rather unstable) guesstimate of the present value of its share of that lost stream of future revenue. No wonder Jürgen Schreiber (CEO of Shoppers) was upset.

Lesson Two: *Winners and losers are always unevenly distributed.*

The gainers from this policy change are Ontario taxpayers, patients, and (eventually) privately insured workers and their employers. Patients benefit immediately, taxpayers will gain as the debt burden is lessened, and workers/employers will gain as, if, and when, private insurance premiums fall (or rise less rapidly), leaving more cash on the table to be divided between them.

Investors, in and out of Canada, will lose; the market has already made a preliminary calculation of their loss. Shoppers Drug Mart is a blue-chip stock, popular with mutual funds and exchange-traded funds offering steady growth with good dividends. (It has a beta of 0.40.) These folks have had a nasty surprise. Overall, the net effect has probably been to shift wealth down the income distribution, because stock ownership is highly correlated with income and pharmaceutical use is not.

Pharmacists, qua pharmacists, will probably be little affected. The steady up-trend in prescriptions to be filled will not change, and failing significant technical changes in the dispensing process, pharmacists will be needed to fill them. Assuming that the market for pharmacists' services is reasonably competitive, and chains like Shoppers pay no higher wages and hire no more pharmacists than they have to (they are, after all, for-profit corporations, not charities), then pharmacists' wages and employment are unlikely to change.[2]

Those pharmacists who own their own stores, however, definitely will lose – their profits will fall along with those of corporate pharmacies. They are, in a sense, their own shareholders. But it is the return to store ownership, not the wages of pharmacists, that will fall.[3] Expressions of distress by pharmacists' organizations will reflect this impact on pharmacy owners.

Lesson Three: *It's the prices, stupid!*

Health expenditures are driven by prices as well as quantities: $E = P \times Q$. Q is unchanged; Ontarians are still getting their prescriptions filled. The reforms have cut the prices paid for generic prescriptions, not the quantity provided. Pharmacies have had their profits cut, but have not gone out of business, and it appears that Bay Street has significantly reduced its 29 June estimates of the impact of the reforms. As the price cuts are extended to private payers, there could be some reduction in the numbers of pharmacy outlets, but Ontario is heavily over-endowed with pharmacies, especially in urban areas.[4] Indeed, this density is likely a consequence of the overpricing of generic drugs.

The ODB reforms do contain provisions to protect access to pharmacy services in regions with low dispensing volumes, where lower reimbursement might really threaten patients' access to drugs, but this is a small fraction of the Ontario population. Because the vast majority of prescriptions are filled in markets densely populated with pharmacies, there seems no good reason to let the rural tail wag the urban dog.

Shoppers initially threatened to terminate free delivery services and other benefits to patients, but this move seems questionable. Providing such services is a marketing decision, not an act of charity. If they add to profits, they continue. If not, well, the pharmacy can always offer these services for a price to those willing to pay.[5]

Lesson Four: *Rising health costs are not a law of nature, like the tides. They are responsive to well-crafted policy.*

This episode gives the lie to those who allege that containing health costs must necessarily impose unacceptable cuts to the quantity and/or quality of health services, threatening Canadians' health. Such claims are the basis for the argument that universal public health insurance is "fiscally unsustainable." They are also false.

The interests driving these claims are not difficult to discern; see Lesson One, above. But the implicit assumptions are twofold, and both are wrong. First, they assume that the prices currently paid for health services are determined through some market or other process such that they reflect the real costs of production. Imposed reductions must therefore result in reduced quantity or quality of services. The Ontario reform demonstrates that this is incorrect. The second assumption is that the services currently being provided are all necessary and effective in promoting patients' health. This assumption flies in the face of a vast literature on prescribing appropriateness and clinical variations; for the merest scratch on the surface of the latter, see Evans (2009).

Lesson Five: *Cost containment is primarily a political, not an economic, problem.*

The shares of Jean Coutu, the large Quebec pharmacy chain, also fell on 8 April, from $10 to $9, and bottomed on 29 June at $7.88. Investors expected Quebec to follow Ontario's lead. More generally, Ontario is only about 40 per cent of Canada. If its reforms rolled across the country, could we be seeing national savings – pharmacy revenue losses – in the $2 to $3 billion range? The answer appears to be no, not so much, and the reasons are quite instructive.

The government of British Columbia did react, very quickly. Health Minister Kevin Falcon announced that PharmaCare would negotiate a mutually acceptable agreement with pharmacies to reduce the reimbursement rate for generic drugs. Reductions will apply to private payers as well. But the reimbursement rate was reduced only to 35 per cent of the corresponding previously patented drug, phased in over three years. There would also be additional payments to pharmacists for various other services, of possible value to patients but of clear benefit to pharmacies.

Alberta had, in fact, acted earlier to reduce payments for generic drugs, first for new generics and then, effective 1 April 2010, all generic drugs.

But the cuts were from 75 to 56 per cent of the corresponding branded product (45 per cent for new generics), so that Albertans after their reform are still paying higher prices than the ODB was paying before 1 July 2010.

As the Alberta government's press release notes, disingenuously: "The pharmacy industry indicated it had some concerns with reductions to generic drug prices ... Government recognizes that reducing the price of generic drugs will impact revenues of pharmacy businesses" (Alberta 2010). Well, duh! (Yet again, see Lesson One, above.)

Unlike Ontario, neither Alberta nor British Columbia eliminated kickbacks from generic manufacturers to pharmacies. And both left in place maximum dispensing fees well above Ontario's rate of $8.50 (Alberta, $11.93; BC, $10.50). In short, while recognizing that generic drug prices were too high, both Alberta and British Columbia struck a political compromise between the financial interests of taxpayers and private payers on the one hand, and pharmacies on the other.

There is no economic reason why governments in both Alberta and British Columbia could not have followed Ontario and gone for 25 per cent or even less. The government of British Columbia, in particular, seems proud that they achieved a "negotiated" rather than an imposed settlement. But pharmacies negotiated with a gun at their heads. By leaving so much money on the table, these governments in effect bought ideological comfort and, presumably, political advantage with other people's money. (In BC, some of mine.)

Well, it isn't the first time *that* has happened. The point that comes through loud and clear, however, is that had they wanted to cut drug costs still further, they could easily have done so. Both the previous and the new lower costs of generic drugs are the result of political choices, not economic forces.

Quebec is more involved. Current legislation requires the provincial government to pay no more for a drug than the lowest price available in any other province. That would force them to match Ontario's 25 per cent, and the government says they will. But:

> This same law prohibits private plans from adopting the same control approach as the RAMQ [Quebec's health insurance plan]. Indeed, private plans are obligated to reimburse an original drug at a minimum of 68% of the amount claimed, even if the generic drug is sold to the pharmacist at a maximum of 25% of the price of the original. (Tagsa 2010).

In effect, the government of Quebec is trimming its own costs while leaving private payers exposed to higher charges. And in Quebec, employer-based insurance is de facto compulsory. Employers and employees are thus being milked to subsidize pharmacies – a distinctly perverse approach to cost control!

Nonetheless, pharmacy owners are said to be outraged that they were not consulted. (What, exactly, might they have said? It's a zero-sum game.) They have demanded various forms of compensation, and have taken a page from the Big Pharma playbook. Current or planned generic production in the province will be suspended if their prices fall.

That argument makes no economic sense. Generics are an internationally traded commodity. What possible benefit would there be to Quebeckers at large from paying a premium, directly or indirectly, for local production – and supporting the price of Jean Coutu shares?

But that is an economist talking. The political calculation is likely to be different – as it was in Alberta and British Columbia. At time of writing, the Quebec poker game was still in session. The important point is that it is a political poker game. Whatever emerges, any suggestion that Quebeckers will pay prices for generic drugs that approximate their real economic costs, or are determined by competitive market forces, would be incredibly naive or simply dishonest.

Lesson Six: *In the health services sector, regulation works. Markets don't.*

In October 2007, the Canadian Competition Bureau released a report on generic drug prices (Canada 2008). Bay Street analysts are paid to assess the profit potential of publicly traded corporations. They ignored the Competition Bureau report, if they noticed it at all. A small prize will be given to the reader who can find a response in Shoppers Drug Mart share prices during October 2007.

Yet, the Bureau clearly stated that retail prices for generic drugs were too high. Competition among generic suppliers was effective in holding down prices paid by pharmacies, but not prices charged by pharmacies; the benefits of competition were being appropriated before reaching the retail payer (and hence were capitalized in, for example, Shoppers share prices). The Competition Bureau's report contains thoughtful discussion of the ways in which the competitive market forces of the economic textbooks have been subverted in this market, and hopeful suggestions as to how they might be strengthened and made more effective. The TSX apparently did not fancy their chances.[6]

The report ends on a rather wistful note:

> Individual plan members and persons paying out of pocket can also play a key role in helping to obtain the benefits from competition by being effective shoppers. The more that consumers compare prices and services when shopping for drugs, the more incentive the pharmacies will have to make lower prices and better services available to patients. (Canada 2008)

Indeed. And if wishes were horses, beggars might ride. In the real world:

> it is the cash-paying customer without a drug plan who typically pays the highest price for prescription drugs. Sullivan says many pharmacy computers are set up so that if a regular pharmacy client loses their employer-paid benefits, and that information is entered on the screen, "a completely different" higher price for the prescription automatically pops up. (Silversides 2009)

The central point is that over half of prescription drug costs (55 per cent in 2009), generic and patented, are paid privately and always have been. Yet this private market has not restrained prices. Conceivably, an activist provincial government might try to restructure the drug dispensing process to create genuine market competition, but such restructuring would have to be extensive, complex, politically costly, and highly uncertain of outcome.

Why would any rational government take on such a dubious task when regulatory alternatives are ready to hand? Such a quixotic enterprise might please ideological marketophiles and congenital economists, but the more realistic folk who decry regulation and champion "the market" in health services typically do so precisely because they understand how little threat markets pose to existing price and income patterns.[7] The Ontario government has instead chosen to cut the Gordian Knot. Its example has forced other provinces, perhaps half-heartedly and despite ideological reservations, to follow along.

Lesson Seven (extra credit): *All six of these lessons apply across the whole health system.*

Prescription drugs account for only 13.9 per cent of Canadian health spending, and generics for less than half of that. Even if provinces could pick up, for their residents, all of the $2 to $3 billion in annual savings that might be on the table, that is small change compared to last year's estimated total of $183.1 billion, increasing about $10 billion a year.

But wait! There's more!

When Canada's Medicare was extended to cover physicians' services in the late 1960s, the rate of escalation of physician and hospital costs was dramatically reduced. The universal public system both avoids the very large administrative overheads generated by private insurance (Woolhandler, et al., 2003) and possesses a significant degree of bargaining power in negotiating with providers. The sectoral price inflation endemic to private or mixed financing systems – over and above general inflation rates – is substantially reduced. A universal pharmacare program could do the same.

But in Canada, we still finance prescription drugs on the American Plan – multiple public and private payers, very expensive and highly inequitable. Commentators have noted for years that we incur substantially higher costs as a result. Most recently, Gagnon (2010) calculates that a true pharmacare system similar to Medicare – universal, first-dollar, tax financed, with a single public payer – could reduce total drug costs by as much as $10.7 billion per year, even assuming a 10 per cent increase in utilization. That begins to sound like serious money.

About $1.5 billion could be saved by eliminating most of the administrative overhead, the extra paper pushing (and the tax-expenditure subsidies) associated with private insurance. But the big money comes from aggressive price negotiating with the pharmaceutical industry. When governments are themselves on the hook for drug costs – directly accountable – it concentrates the political mind wonderfully. Promoting industrial policy by giving away their citizens' money to Big Pharma is likely to look less attractive.

These savings are not imaginary; examining New Zealand's Pharmac program for drug purchasing, Morgan (in Evans, et al., 2007) has calculated potential savings for Canada of a similar magnitude. So fierce opposition to a Medicare-type pharmacare program from Big Pharma and the private insurance industry is a given. The potential savings are their revenues – once more, see Lesson One, above.[8]

But there is another source of resistance. In cutting about $10 billion from Canadians' total drug bill, genuine pharmacare would also double the public share. Opposition thus comes not only from anti-tax ideologues and assorted libertarian loonies, but also from quite clear-eyed occupants of the upper income brackets. Tax-financed pharmacare, like Medicare, would transfer some of the overall payment burden from the unhealthy and unwealthy to the healthy and wealthy. The latter are thus natural allies of Big Pharma and the private insurers in protecting our high-cost drug financing system. And they make their dollars count, politically.

Pharmaceuticals are not the only sector where prices are out of line. Payments to physicians account for the same share of health spending ($25.6 billion in 2009) as pharmaceuticals ($25.4 billion), and they have been on a bit of a tear lately. According to the Canadian Institute for Health Information (2009), per capita expenditures have risen 45 per cent in the last ten years, after adjusting for general inflation. This increase is second only to pharmaceuticals (a whopping 74 per cent). But in the last five years, the escalation of payments to physicians has accelerated – 24 per cent above inflation and population growth since 2004, compared with 16 per cent in the previous five years – while in all other major expenditure categories the growth, while still very significant, has slowed. (Pharmaceuticals fell from 46 per cent, 1999–2004, to 19 per cent, 2004–2009; hospitals are down to a mere 11 per cent.)

These are very big numbers. If payments to physicians had merely kept pace with inflation and population growth over the last decade, our annual doctor bill would now be $7.9 billion lower. Similar restraint in prescription drugs would have saved us $11.0 billion.[9]

Research currently nearing completion at the Centre for Health Services and Policy Research at UBC suggests that the growth in physician expenditures is, like that of pharmaceuticals, largely a consequence of increasing relative prices – sector-specific inflation. There is thus considerable scope for cost containment in physicians' services, as in prescription drugs, by focusing on the prices being paid. The real problem is, as always, the political difficulty of containing the income aspirations of powerful actors on the supply side.

The economics is, by comparison, easy.

ACKNOWLEDGMENTS

With thanks to Michael Law for helpful comments.

NOTES

1 The cut to 25 per cent is not the whole story; there are to be a variety of other compensatory payments to pharmacies to cushion the shock. On the

other hand, the proportionate savings to private payers may be even greater than those to the ODB.

2 This prediction assumes that, because the overall volume of dispensing work will not be reduced, requirements for pharmacists will not change, i.e., the average number of prescriptions filled per pharmacist will remain constant. Conceivably, however, efforts to restore the profitability of pharmacies could lead to fewer pharmacies and higher dispensing rates per pharmacist – reducing the demand for pharmacists. Introduction of "robo-pharmacy" could have even more dramatic effects.

3 If the option of opening one's own pharmacy enables pharmacists to bargain for higher wages than the market would otherwise provide for work of similar effort and knowledge, then any such premium would be reduced as store ownership becomes less attractive.

4 A recent analysis of the supply and geographic distribution of pharmacies in Ontario (Law et al., 2011) shows that the majority of the population (63.6 per cent) live within an 800-metre walk of one or more pharmacies, and nearly all (90.7 per cent) live within a five-kilometre driving distance. A randomly distributed cut of 20 per cent in the number of outlets (conservative, since closures would be more likely in pharmacy-dense areas) would have virtually no impact on these access measures.

5 The announcement by Loblaws that they were considering opening dispensaries in their stores took some of the wind out of Shoppers' PR sails, though that may have been just a shot across the bow in response to Shoppers' intrusion into the grocery market.

6 Still, the clear message, from a disinterested public agency, that Canadians were paying too much for generic drugs can only have strengthened the political position of the Ontario government.

7 There are examples of successful cost containment through competition – New Zealand's Pharmac and Medicaid in the United States, or, for that matter, hospital or pharmacy purchasing in Canada. But these are competitive tendering processes at wholesale, by a single buyer or a coordinated group, not a fragmented retail market. Even very large private insurers have been remarkably ineffective, worldwide, in mobilizing their potential market power to restrain price inflation in the health sector.

8 When the United States introduced the Medicare Part D coverage of prescription drugs for the elderly, the pharmaceutical industry lobbied successfully to have the legislation specifically prohibit the Social Security Administration from negotiating drug prices with suppliers. They were well aware of the potential impact on prices of a large public buyer.

9 Of course, the population is also aging. Demography would account for an increase of about 5 per cent.

REFERENCES

Alberta (2010). "Albertans to benefit from reduced prices for existing generic drugs." News release (28 January). Retrieved 12 October 2010. http://alberta.ca/homeNewsFrame.cfm?ReleaseId=/acn/201001/277267697CCF8-C8B8-B2D6-64419AfAE7D72E85.html.

Canada. Competition Bureau (2008). *Benefiting from generic drug competition in Canada: The way forward.* (25 November). Retrieved 10 October 2010. http://www.competitionbureau.gc.ca/eic/site/cb-bc.nsf/eng/02753.html.

Canadian Institute for Health Information (CIHI) (2009). *National health expenditure trends, 1975–2009*. Ottawa: The Institute.

Cutler, D.M. (2007). "The demise of the blockbuster?" *New England Journal of Medicine* 356(29 March): 1292–3.

Evans, R.G. (2009). "There's no reason for it, it's just our policy." Commentary. *Healthcare Policy* 5(2): 14–24.

– C. Hertzman, and S. Morgan (2007). "Improving health outcomes in Canada." In *A Canadian priorities agenda: Policy choices to improve economic and social well-being*, ed. J. Leonard, C. Ragan, and F. St-Hilaire, 291–325. Montreal: Institute for Research on Public Policy.

Gagnon, M.-A. (2010). *The economic case for universal Pharmacare.* Ottawa: Canadian Centre for Policy Alternatives.

Law, M.R., A. Dijkstra, J.A. Douillard, and S.G. Morgan (2011). "Geographic accessibility of community pharmacies in Ontario." *Healthcare Policy* 6(3): 36–46.

Picard, A. (2010). "Patent expiry for some blockbuster drugs presents huge saving opportunity." *Globe and Mail*, 23 June. Retrieved 10 October 2010. http://www.theglobeandmail. com/life/health/patent-expiry-for-some-blockbuster-drugs-presents-huge-saving-opportunity/article1615338/.

Silversides, A. (2009). "Ontario's law curbing the cost of generic drugs sparks changes for pharmacies and other Canadian buyers." *Canadian Medical Association Journal* 181(3–4): 43–5.

Tagsa, A. (2010). "Generic drugs at 25%: False hope for savings affecting private plans in Quebec?" Canada Newswire, 9 August. Retrieved 10 October 2010. http://money.ca/money/surveys/generic-drugs-at-25-false-hope-for-savings-affecting-private-plans-in-quebec.

Woolhandler, S., T. Campbell, and D. Himmelstein (2003). "Costs of health care administration in the United States and Canada." *New England Journal of Medicine* 349(8): 768–75.

4

A New Paradigm for Health Economics? We Already Have Three! (2012)

ROBERT G. EVANS

(Revised, February 2012)

Draft presented at the 8th World Congress on
Health Economics of the International Health Economics
Association (iHEA)
Toronto, July 2011

The inter-sectorial financial flows that characterize all modern health care systems can be represented compactly in the accompanying Figure 4.1. Adapted from the standard National Income Accounting framework, the figure shows the principal "pipes" through which financing flows from the households comprising a nation's population to the intermediate agencies (governments, social and private insurers) that assemble and redistribute collective funds to the various types of provider organizations (public and private clinics and hospitals and for-profit commercial firms) that in turn produce the multiplicity of different health care goods and services. These firms then distribute their funds, directly or indirectly, back to various persons as payment for their "factor inputs" – labour and

Evans, Robert G. "A New Paradigm for Health Economics? We Already Have Three!" *Nordic Journal of Health Economics* 1(1) (2012): 1–16. Reprinted with the permission of *Nordic Journal of Health Economics*.

management skills and the services of various forms of capital. A fundamental feature of this framework is that *all* the financial flows originate with households and return to households – though not of course the same ones. All revenues raised become expenditures, which in turn all become someone's income.[1]

In the heart of the framework are the "real" flows, the quantity and mix of different health care goods and services that are produced by firms, using the factor inputs supplied to them by households, and which flow back to households – though again not in general the same ones.

But Figure 4.1 is a set of accounting relationships, a gross anatomical description that provides no "physiology" to explain how the various components interact, or how those interactions might change in response to anatomical changes. What difference does it make, in terms of patterns of service delivery and cost, of distribution of burdens and benefits among the population, or of population health status, if the mixes of financing and funding flows are rearranged? These questions, sometimes overt, often covert, are everywhere at the heart of debates over health policy.

Attempts to develop such a "physiological" understanding, however, are impeded by the embedded conflicts of interest associated with any policy choice. Research and analysis, no matter how objectively motivated and scrupulously conducted, will if acted upon always have distributional implications, often readily apparent. Representatives of threatened interests will challenge the analysis and propose alternative interpretations of "how things *really* work." These cross-cutting motivations radically compound the ambiguities inherent in trying to understand the behaviour of any complex system. Accordingly there is no single settled body of physiological understanding of health care systems to correspond to the more readily observed anatomy.

One can, however, identify three quite distinct perspectives or "frameworks of understanding" through which people – clinicians, patients, researchers, government officials, politicians, and the general public – interpret the behaviour of health care systems. These we may label:

- The "Naive Clinical";
- The "Mainstream Economic"; and
- The "Eclectic Structuralist."

Casual empiricism suggests that the Naive Clinical is by far the dominant perspective among both clinicians and the general public, and typically exerts its influence over health policy through the sensitivity of

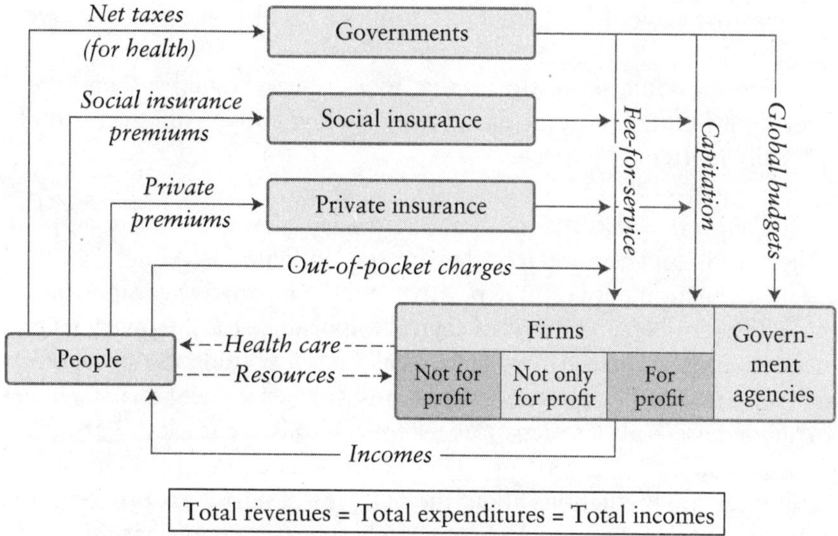

Figure 4.1 Alternative ways of paying for health care

Adapted from: Robert G. Evans. "A New Paradigm for Health Economics? We Already Have Three!" *Nordic Journal of Health Economics* 1(1)(2012): 1–16.

politicians to that professional and public opinion. The Mainstream Economic perspective, by contrast, is held almost exclusively by professional economists or those with conventional economic training. It is predominant in this group (though not among those who specialize in health economics) and derives its influence from the strategic positions they occupy in government economic ministries, in the corporate world, and in the business press. Finally, the Eclectic Structuralist perspective tends to be held by health services researchers (including most health economists), officials in government ministries responsible for health or health care, and administrators/managers of health care institutions (including former clinicians).

These three perspectives – paradigms – each postulate a different pattern of causal connections or perhaps better patterns of influence among the accounting relationships in Figure 4.1, and their relationship to the health of individuals and populations. They are each composed of three distinct elements:

1 A *normative* view of how levels and patterns of health care utilization *should* be determined;

2 A *positive* view of how, under appropriate conditions, they *are* determined; and
3 A corresponding set of stories that focus research, analysis, and policy on a particular sector of the circular flow above – the sector that "really matters."

Each perspective also has its characteristic silences, gaps where no plausible story is told about particular linkages in Figure 4.1.

The distinction between the positive and the normative components of these different perspectives is of central importance for the policy recommendations that emerge from each. As all first-year students of economics are (supposed to be) carefully taught, a positive statement is a statement – true or false – about facts. "Water (pure) boils (at sea level) at a temperature of 100° Celsius," or "The moon is made of green cheese." In effect these are predictions about the outcome of particular observations, to be made under more or less completely specified conditions.

Normative statements, by contrast, contain the words "ought" or "should," either explicitly or in some rhetorical equivalent. They assert that one state of the world is to be preferred to another – is in some sense "better" – and typically include an implication that someone – not necessarily clearly identified – should act to ensure that the better state prevails. The almost universal claim by health care providers that "health care (in our sector or system) is underfunded," for example, is equivalent to "More money should be spent on health care" – a claim that the world would be a better place if expenditures on health care were larger than at present. The total amount of money flowing around the circuit in Figure 4.1 should be larger. (Note that those making this claim are often unclear as to whether they advocate increases in some components of health services, or in the amount paid for them – more care, or higher pay rates.)

One may or may not share the preferences expressed in this statement. But the key point is that it *is* a statement of preferences, a statement about the relative values that the speaker attaches to two different states of the world (one with present spending levels, and one with some higher level). It is not a statement about the world, but a statement about the speaker's attitude toward the world, about her values.[2] The speaker will typically be trying to create and/or mobilize a broader constituency of people who share those values, in order to increase the chances of bringing about the desired change – more money spent on health care.

A common way of building support for change, and neutralizing opposition, is to present the normative statement as if it were a positive one – e.g., "There is a shortage of doctors, and that's just a fact." The number of doctors available to serve a particular population is, subject to questions of definition and measurement, a potentially confirmable or falsifiable fact. So is a claim about the "needs" of a population, in terms of the expected impact of different treatment levels and patterns on health. (The word "need" itself, however, is ambivalent insofar as it asserts an obligation on some other(s) to respond to that need.) But the language of "shortage" is clearly normative, implying that "something should be done" – perhaps open more medical school places – because, if there were more doctors the world would be a better place.

The fundamental logical distinction between normative and positive propositions was spelled out by David Hume in the eighteenth century: "Hume's Law" is that one cannot (logically) derive "ought" from "is." No assembly of valid facts, or of confirmed positive propositions, can serve as a basis for normative claims – or policy recommendations. There has to be brought to that assembly of facts a corresponding set of values and preferences with which to rank alternative states of the world. It is always a logical fallacy – sometimes inadvertent, sometimes deliberate – to claim to base recommendations on "science" – or for that matter "common sense" – alone. But the point deserves emphasis, because that fallacy is so frequently committed, even by professional economists.

The normative component of the clinical perspective is simply that people should get the care they need, as judged by a qualified clinical practitioner, regardless of the cost. The criterion for whether resources should be allocated to produce a particular form of health care, and whether that care should be offered to/accepted by a particular patient is: "On balance, and allowing for uncertainties, is this intervention likely to do more good than harm to the patient's health?" If the answer is believed to be "yes," then the patient needs the care, and that need should be met.[3] This ethical norm is so deeply embedded in professional practice that it is probably no longer recognized as a particular ethical position, among other possibilities. It is simply what you do.

Yet the Mainstream Economic perspective rests on an alternative normative basis, "consumer sovereignty," that could hardly be more different.[4] People *should* get whatever care they are willing and able to pay for, at prices reflecting the resource cost, the real opportunity cost, of producing that care. The impact of that care on their health status is irrelevant, a position symmetric with the disregard of cost in the clinical norm. "Consumers" (not patients!) presumably take account of health effects, among other things, in choosing how to spend their incomes, but if they want and are willing to pay for useless or even harmful care, then they should get it. Conversely, if they are "unwilling" – which includes unable – to pay for desperately needed, even life-saving, health care services, then they should not get those services.

It is "allocatively inefficient," from this perspective, for a society to allocate resources to producing services that people do not value sufficiently to be willing to pay the full cost of producing them. The world will be a better place if those resources are used instead to produce services that someone *is* willing to pay for (Pauly, 1969; Feldstein, 1973). This sounds plausible, until one recalls that "value" in this context refers not just to intensity of preferences but also to ability to pay. "Them as has, gets, and them as hasn't doesn't" is not just a blunt observation about reality but a moral principle – the way things *should* be in the best of all possible worlds. If there is a change in the income distribution, however, then the definition of the "right" pattern of resource allocation and commodity distribution shifts to respond to the new distribution of ability to pay.[5]

Thus both clinical and economic perspectives include well-defined (in principle) concepts of appropriate and inappropriate health care provision. But their concepts are very different. To the clinician, care provided to a particular patient is inappropriate if it is unlikely to do more good than harm for that patient's health. From the mainstream economic perspective, care is inappropriate if the patient would/could not pay for it out of his/her own resources (or voluntary donations by others).

Reinhardt's (1998) hypothetical example of the wealthy Changs and the impoverished Smiths is particularly instructive. His point is not simply that in the American context the Changs will (if they choose) receive for themselves and their children all the health care they want, including care that is of minimal (if any) benefit, while the Smiths may have to forego care of considerably greater potential benefit, putting their health at much greater risk. This is true, but his key point is that much if not most of the formal analysis of health care in the economic literature implicitly adopts as a normative presumption, a moral principle, that this is the way health care *ought* to be allocated (see also Reinhardt, 1992).

Conflicts of moral principle cannot be resolved by rational argument; ultimately they are matters about which people can only fight (or vote).[6] But the normative underpinnings of the mainstream economic perspective set up some extremely interesting cognitive dissonance among economists.

First of all, it is not clear that many economists, if any, actually accept, explicitly and wholeheartedly, this normative position in their non-professional lives. A surprising number, even of American economists, replying to the informal survey described by Fuchs (1996), expressed the view that people should not be denied needed health care because of inability to pay, and that view may be much more general. Only in their academic work do they seem committed to a framework of analysis that rests on the alternative ethical principle. Arrow (1976), perhaps recognizing the rather squalid moral basis for his analysis, states: "In order to avoid distributional considerations, I shall assume that the economy consists of a single individual." He neglected to remind readers that any resulting findings were relevant only on Mars.

But if this is so, the internal ethical conflict seems to have been resolved in a very peculiar way, through the belief that the normative position embodied in the economic perspective is somehow part of the discipline of economics itself, either derived from economic analysis or in some other way inextricably connected with "doing economics right." As a professional economist, one has to adopt this moral position, otherwise one is not doing "real economics." Yet as noted above, Hume's Law points out the logical fallacy of imagining that one can derive "ought" from "is." It is logically impossible for economic analysis to generate the normative presumption that people should get only what they are able and willing to pay for. That principle has to be annexed from outside, as a moral choice by particular individuals.

A group of such individuals – perhaps mainstream economists – may adopt as a convention that "real economics" must include a set of moral principles that they personally find congenial, or perhaps simply convenient for analytic purposes. They may then claim that "economics itself," as they define it, imposes on its practitioners the acceptance of those moral principles. This appears to be the view of Pauly (1996), replying to Culyer and Evans (1996), in which he actually apostrophizes "Economics" as some transcendental entity, demanding that its practitioners accept particular assumptions. But at this point one has crossed the border from an academic discipline to a religion. It is priests, not academic analysts, much less scientists, who are in the business of dictating the normative principles that one is required to hold to belong to a particular community.[7]

There is not much interesting to say about the normative component of the "Eclectic Structural" perspective. In general its practitioners seem to share the clinical position that people should get the care they need. Certainly health services researchers spend a good deal of time and effort studying the impact of different forms of health care on health. But they might argue that this normative view is grounded in the (casual) empirical judgment that this is what the general public (including most economists in their private lives) want the health care system to do (e.g., van Doorslaer et al., 1993). Normative principles should be derived from peoples, not priests (though that itself is a normative judgment). The normative position underlying the clinical perspective, by contrast, appears to be more of a "categorical imperative" for clinicians, not ultimately derived from broad popular or even legal support. Such a moral position may be more priestly than scientific, but most clinicians probably find that dual role quite acceptable.[8]

The positive component of the economic perspective is imported directly from the standard textbook economic theory of "widgets." People will in fact get the care they want and are willing and able to pay for, at prices reflecting its real resource cost – "consumer sovereignty" in its positive sense – if they can/must purchase it freely, at their own expense, in perfectly competitive markets, supplied by for-profit firms. Competition among such firms will ensure that production is technically efficient – no wasted resources – and carried out with the optimal – lowest cost – mix of resource inputs, while the requirement that "consumers" must pay for their own care out of pocket ensures that it goes to those who value it most – as indicated by willingness to pay.

The questions of who pays and who gets paid for care are in this context easily settled: the market will decide. Users of care will (subject to the one qualification below) pay the costs of their own care, while the mix and rates of earnings of factor inputs – the rates of pay of doctors, nurses, and other professionals, and the profits of provider firms, and all the political controversies that vex public systems of health care – will be determined in the decentralized bargaining of competitive private markets. And the answers that emerge will, by definition, be the "right" ones.[9]

The only difference from the standard textbook account of the production and consumption of "widgets" is recognition that individuals' "demand" for health care is subject to random and sometimes quite large fluctuations. One could treat this as fluctuations in "tastes" for a particular commodity, health care, but large and rapid changes in consumer "tastes" might undermine their normative plausibility – why should giving consumers what they want be an ethical principle if their wants are so unstable? Besides, to describe an individual's response to a heart attack or the onset of cancer as a sudden "change in tastes" sounds (and is) artificial and stupid.

Implicitly, then, the Mainstream Economic perspective has to adopt a framework in which health status is subject to random shifts that both lower individual well-being and raise the perceived health payoff from "consuming" health care. For a previously healthy individual in a serious car crash, for example, or diagnosed with cancer, "tastes" for care would jump discontinuously and very suddenly from near zero to some very large value. The rational consumer reorders her consumption patterns accordingly – (much) more health care and less of other things. But the very best that can be achieved from this increase in health care use – rarely achieved in the case of serious illness or injury – is to restore the health status quo *ante*, while the reduction in income available to purchase other commodities and the discomfort and distress associated with the care itself cause a drop, possibly very substantial, in the individual's overall well-being.

By incorporating the experience of illness and the purchase of health care into standard consumer theory in this way, however, the economic perspective introduces another and very important pair of implicit assumptions. In order for the rational consumer to carry out the reordering of consumption patterns required to maximize utility under the new circumstances, she must be in operational as well as strategic control of the "consumption" process – a highly dubious assumption, particularly in the real circumstances of the serious illnesses that account for most of health care use and costs. More fundamentally, however, she must know the relevant marginal utilities. She must not only know how much she values health – the standard assumption in consumer theory – but must also know, if not perfectly then at least better than anyone else, the impact in present circumstances of health care on health status.

For this assumption there is no warrant or precedent in the economic theory of the consumer. In the community at large, including both patients and providers, the standard and seemingly self-evident assumption is that professional experts usually have better, typically much better, information about this relationship. Information is asymmetric between provider and user of care; professionals know patients' needs better than patients do. The Mainstream Economic perspective simply assumes away this asymmetry, typically implicitly, and provides no justification for doing so.[10]

The individual uncertainty created by the possibility of these random fluctuations in health and well-being is, however, assumed to be a "bad" in itself, and people are willing to pay to be relieved of this bad by purchasing "health" insurance that provides monetary compensation for loss of health. Where there is a demand, there will be a supply. Private firms will offer such compensation, in competitive insurance markets, at the "right" price. But there is no market in which one can buy or sell health, and accordingly no way of insuring it. Health insurance subsidizes health *care*, by enabling "consumers" to acquire and use it below cost – perhaps even free. For this, each individual will be charged a premium proportional to his or her risk status, hence individuals continue to pay for their own care in a probabilistic sense.[11]

At this point the economic perspective immediately detects an allocative distortion – an inefficiency. If any commodity is available to consumers at a price below its opportunity cost, they will use "too much" of it, withdrawing resources from more highly valued uses. There is thus, from this perspective, a trade-off between the increased well-being from being able to reduce the "bad" of uncertainty by in effect selling it to the insurer (where it is pooled and disappears), and the loss of well-being from the "overuse" of care in the sense defined above – a definition of overuse in terms not of the effectiveness of care, but of individual willingness/ability to pay.

The existence of such a trade-off is one of the fundamental features – perhaps the fundamental feature – of health care financing as viewed from the Mainstream Economic perspective. Yet unless one accepts the normative principle, the value premises, underlying the mainstream analysis – which few if any do outside academic economics – the "trade-off" vanishes into thin air.

Nevertheless, this imaginary trade-off looms large in the academic literature, particularly in the United States. It has been particularly effective in focusing mainstream economic research on issues of interest to the private insurance industry. A great deal of research effort has been devoted to exploring its terms and suggesting ways of structuring insurance systems so as to minimize, on some metric, the combined costs of uncertainty and allocative distortion. Most of this academic research, however, seems to point (as did Arrow, op. cit.) to the inescapable conclusion that optimizing this trade-off requires some combination of individual and third-party payment – precisely what most public systems of health insurance do not include.[12]

The Mainstream Economic perspective thus focuses attention on the upper left branch of Figure 4.1, the mix of financing channels, and particularly on the level and form of self-payment in the total revenue mix. Since decisions to consume health care are assumed to be made, like any other consumption decision, by individuals responding to the prices they face, the financing mix determines through these consumer choices the level and mix of health care demand. Competitive, for-profit provider firms then respond to these demands in the usual textbook fashion, so that the actual level and pattern of health care utilization – which is measurable – is assumed (subject to the possibility of disequilibrium markets) to be equal to and determined by consumer choices.[13] To meet these consumer demands, providers must purchase resources or factors of production, and their (derived) demand for these inputs interacts with the factor supply functions of households to generate the corresponding income flows back to those households. The causal sequences in Figure 4.1 thus all unfold from the upper left, so that is where the key policy levers are and much of the research by mainstream economists has been concentrated.

Apart from its complete "avoid[ance] of distributional considerations" the most immediately obvious silence in this story is with respect to the rest of the financing mix. Health insurance itself is conceived of and analyzed as a form of commodity, a financial "product" as private insurers like to call it, supplied by private for-profit firms and purchased by consumers. Yet, in high-income OECD countries other than the United States, this form of coverage plays an insignificant role in financing health care, and even in the United States the public sector contributes (directly and through tax-expenditure subsidies) nearly three dollars for every one coming from private insurers. Analysis of the dynamics of real-world insurance markets readily explains the reasons for the disjunction between academic literature and actual coverage (Evans, 2005). But the actual pattern is, from the Mainstream Economic perspective, a major anomaly that cannot be explained, casting doubt on the overall causal story. Why is almost all health insurance public, not private, and what difference does that make for the "physiology" of Figure 4.1?

But this anomaly is by no means the only one. The right-hand side of Figure 4.1 attempts to elaborate a set of categories of firms and payment mechanisms (barely) adequate to reflect the complexities of real-world systems. Most of these firms, and their sources of funding, bear little relation to the competitive for-profit firms, paid per unit of service, that the economic perspective imports, usually implicitly, from the economic theory textbooks. Why is the health care supply-side organized so differently, in every country, and what difference does *that* make?

The assumption that health care simply comes onto the market at prices reflecting its marginal resource cost, to be purchased by consumers who are then reimbursed in whole or in part by private insurers – a surprisingly common implicit assumption in the academic literature – amounts to assuming that the complexities of health care organization and funding are without point and without effect. Not only should they not exist, but for all practical purposes they do not exist. The production of health care, and the determination of product prices and factor earnings, somehow takes place *as if* the industry were made up of for-profit firms operating in perfectly competitive markets, and the resulting patterns of inputs, factor returns, outputs, and prices can therefore be interpreted as they are in standard economic theory, as determined by the tastes of consumers and factor suppliers within the constraints of existing technology and overall resource availability.

Such an assumption suggests serious perceptual difficulties.[14] At the very least, those relying on it should have to carry a very heavy burden of justification. We would recommend rather that one begin from the presumption that these structural complexities are real, not mirages, they have evolved for good if not necessarily sufficient reasons, and that they have important effects, for both good and ill, on the way health care systems operate.

The Naive Clinical perspective provides a ready and powerful answer to the question of why health care provision is organized the way it is. Health care systems are designed to provide people with the care they need, not whatever care they are willing and able to pay for. Different mechanisms serve different objectives. The positive component of the clinical perspective asserts that patients will in fact get the care they need, on three conditions:

1 Care is provided by or under the direction of a qualified professional practitioner;
2 Sufficient resources of all types are available to meet the needs identified by those practitioners; and
3 Patients' access to that care is not impeded by financial or other (language, geography, social distance) barriers.

Give the professionals the tools (and ensure that patients have access to them) and they will finish the job.

This positive claim is rooted in the wholehearted recognition and acceptance of the asymmetry of information assumed away in the Mainstream Economic perspective. When it comes to evaluating the impact of health care on health, not just in general but for a particular patient in particular circumstances, there is a presumption that "doctor knows best." If patients are to get the care they need, they must be able to rely on professionals to act for them, recommending or providing the services most likely to improve their health rather than those most desired by the patient or most profitable for the provider. That in turn requires both that the provision of services be restricted to those having the demonstrated competence to identify and provide what is needed – no free entry – and that they be relieved from the pressures faced by firms trying to maximize profits – or simply survive – in a competitive marketplace.

From this perspective, the flows in Figure 4.1 unfold from the professional identification of needs, of opportunities to improve the health status of particular individuals by the provision of particular services. This defines the "right" level and mix of servicing, and the corresponding requirement for resources. So long as these are sufficient to "meet all needs" such that no person in this society has a health condition that could be improved by the provision of any form of health care, then professional direction of the health care system, at individual and institutional levels, will produce the appropriate care. This requires that provider firms be structured, regulated, and funded so as to ensure that decisions about what to do, for whom, how, and when are firmly in professional hands, and that those hands are guided solely by patient needs rather than by provider motives, financial or otherwise. The consumer sovereignty of the economic perspective is replaced by "producer sovereignty" – it is provider decisions that determine levels and patterns of health care use, but those in turn are determined by patient needs.

The clinical perspective is largely silent on the relationship between the structure of the financing system and the appropriate pattern of care provided, except by implication. If patients are to get whatever care they need, then presumably financing must be structured so as to raise sufficient money to pay for the necessary resources, and no one must be denied needed care because of inability to pay. This would seem to imply wholly or predominantly third-party financing. But since private insurance does not and cannot ever cover more than a relatively small part of the costs of modern health care systems, the clinical perspective would seem logically to imply what in fact we observe – an overwhelming predominance of public funding. The clinical perspective thus does provide straightforward answers, if not spelled out in detail, to the questions: "Why insurance?" and "Why public insurance?" So access to needed care will not be restricted by inability to pay, or insufficient resources.

Yet clinicians themselves have often argued, individually and collectively, *against* public insurance – most notably in the United States. Their resistance is partly rooted in ideological objections that are wholly inconsistent with the clinical perspective as sketched out here. (A surprising number of physicians, particularly in the United States, seem to share the economic perspective – people should *not* get needed care if they cannot afford it.) But there is a more general concern that government financing will never be sufficient to cover all the needs, not because governments cannot pay but because they will not. A political agenda of cost containment will inevitably lead to "underfunding" of health care.[15]

At this point, however, we encounter one of the central silences in the clinical perspective. As emphasized above, and in every first course in economics, dollars are not the same as resources. "Meeting needs" requires health care, and providing health care requires the real resources of human time, skills, etc. But health expenditures are the product of output *and* price levels, $P \times Q$, and price levels are linked to earnings rates or more generally factor supply prices. A claim of "underfunding" may rest on a genuine perception of unmet health needs, and a corresponding need for an increase in services and resources. But it may equally well be a pay claim, an argument for increases in prices to increase the relative incomes of those working in or otherwise supplying resources for health care. The clinical perspective (in contrast to clinicians themselves) has nothing to say about how rates of reimbursement are or should be determined in the health care sector.

The economic perspective, by contrast, has a perfectly coherent story about how wages and other factor returns are determined in competitive markets, where the purchasers are for-profit firms. In such a context, under the usual stringent assumptions about market structure and participant conduct, well-defined factor supply functions rigidly link the quantities of resources supplied to the prices offered for them. Volumes of services demanded, and the factor inputs necessary to produce them, are all determined interdependently with their prices. Once the volume of services demanded is determined by consumer decisions in response to levels of out-of-pocket costs, user charges, then the whole system is determined.

Unfortunately this is a coherent story about an imaginary world. The story goes silent when, as in the health care sector, the purchasers are not competitive for-profit firms, and the resource owners are permitted and even encouraged to limit entry and to collude in price and wage bargaining. Even the major for-profit firms, pharmaceutical marketers, have been permitted to hedge their markets with patent protection so as to suppress direct price competition. Thus the levels of resources supplied and their rates of reimbursement can and do move independently of each other, at least within a substantial range, and are subjects of intense political bargaining between resource suppliers and reimbursers in public payment systems. It is often in the interests of unions or professional associations

– or drug companies – to *claim* that the rigid link between earnings and resource supply postulated in the economic framework actually obtains – higher wages/fees/profits are essential to bring forward enough nurses/ physicians/new drugs to "meet needs." But in the health care sector in particular, even when the claim has some validity, there is always a good deal more to the story.

There is also more to the story of price determination than wage and other factor price levels. Economists conceptualize the relationship between resource inputs and commodity outputs as a "production function." This specifies the maximum level of output that can be produced with currently available technology from any given combination of inputs. But the production function specifies a frontier, a boundary to the "feasible set" – it is always possible to produce less than available resources permit, or equivalently waste resources in producing the current level of output.

The boundary is reached, at least in theory, by a profit-maximizing firm. In order to maximize profits, the firm must produce its outputs at minimum possible cost; this in turn implies using no more resource inputs than necessary.[16] Firms in the real world will conform more or less closely to this theoretical ideal depending upon the intensity of competition in product or factor markets. But there is no basis whatever for assuming that the equality holds in firms organized for purposes other than profit maximization, and/or exempt from product market competition or capital market takeover.

The clinical perspective is completely silent as to what other mechanisms might operate to assure technical efficiency in the health care sector. Yet technical efficiency is implicit in all claims of "underfunding"; service output cannot be raised without acquiring (and paying for) more resources. Conversely pressures for "hospital downsizing," or more generally requests to "do more with less," assume implicitly that for much of health care production there *is* at current resource levels a substantial discrepancy between what is and what could be produced.

There is however another possibility. A given bundle of health care resources may fall short of its maximum potential for improving population health either because the production of health care is taking place at less than full technical efficiency or because the care that *is* being produced is not the most appropriate to meet patients' needs. The positive component of the clinical perspective amounts to asserting that, under the conditions above, the care patients get is the care they need – otherwise it would not be provided – but is silent as to the technical efficiency with which that care is produced. In practice, cost containment efforts focus on both "production functions."[17]

The Eclectic Structuralist perspective, as noted above, includes essentially the same normative position as the clinical; people *should* get the care they need, the care that improves their health, more or less independently of their ability to pay. But it takes dead aim at the central *positive* presumption of the Naive Clinical perspective, i.e. that, under appropriate professional direction, they do. Holders of this perspective have assembled increasingly large and sophisticated batteries of fact and argument to show that the care patients actually receive depends upon much more than evidence of potential capacity to benefit.

Structuralists certainly do not claim that there is *no* connection between patient needs and health care use – demonstrably false and patently absurd. But this perspective focuses attention on the powerful effects of other factors influencing patterns of use by individuals and particularly by populations. Recalling Rose's Law (Rose, 2001), that the causes of rates are not the same as the causes of cases, relative needs may be the primary, indeed the overwhelmingly dominant, factor determining who gets what care *within* a population, and yet play little or no role in determining comparative rates of care *between* populations, or in the same population over time.

How needs are defined and recognized, and especially how and how extensively they are responded to, are highly variable both within and between health care systems, and shift over time, for reasons that have no detectable connection with patient conditions or outcomes. The literature on "clinical variations" has been accumulating for over forty years, showing highly variable patterns of practice among different practitioners, institutions, regions, and countries. This literature has traditionally been dismissed with, in effect, the comment "Who knows which rate is right?" and thus ignored.

In the last decade, however, increasingly sophisticated analysis of very large data sets has shown that, at least in the United States, regions and institutions with higher rates of intervention and cost do not show better outcomes for patients, in either health or satisfaction, and indeed, in aggregate, more can be harmful. The most prominent research program has been the work of researchers assembled by John Wennberg and Elliott Fisher at the Dartmouth Medical School. Fisher (2007) provides a comprehensive and very accessible compilation of their findings.

This is a fundamental challenge to the positive component for the Naive Clinical perspective; so far the collective response of health care systems has been simply to hope that these findings will just go away. "*Underfunding* is the issue; never mind what we do with the money!"

The Structuralist perspective focuses attention on the different forms and amounts of capacity in the health care system, and on the incentives, in particular but not exclusively economic, embodied in the way that that system is organized and financed. Within Figure 4.1, therefore, it emphasizes the importance of the right-hand side – on what terms does money flow to the provider organizations, and what are the motivations of those organizations? A for-profit corporation with the objective of maximizing "shareholder value" (profit) will behave differently from a not-for-profit hospital or the private practice of one or more physician partners – and they do.[18]

It may seem obvious that the behaviour of an individual or an organization will be different, depending upon how that individual/organization is paid and what s/he/it is trying to do – and to Structuralists it is. But acceptance of that "obvious" point implies rejection of the a priori claims that, in practice, health care utilization patterns are solely determined either by clinicians' judgments of need, or by patients' willingness/ability to pay. There remain important questions as to the relative strengths of these different factors in influencing levels and patterns of health care utilization, but those are empirical questions.[19]

The classic example of the Structuralist perspective is "Roemer's Law" of hospitals, that "a built bed is a filled bed." Roemer (1961) observed, from a natural experiment, a strong correlation between the number of beds available in a particular region and the rates of hospital utilization. He inferred that this represented a causal connection. Others argued that a more generally observed correlation between capacity and use might reflect a reverse causality, that areas of high need might build more beds, but subsequent studies confirmed Roemer's interpretation. The primary causal mechanism may operate through the influence of "time and trouble costs" for physicians seeking to admit patients, rather than an absolute capacity constraint. Hospitals typically run at occupancy rates well below 100 per cent, and more bed capacity (beds per capita, age-adjusted) tends to be associated with lower occupancy, but also with increased use rates for the relevant population.

Subsequent declines in the use of hospitals have, however, underlined an implicit qualification to this "Law" – a built *and reimbursed* bed is a filled bed. The introduction of case-based reimbursement in the American Medicare program in 1988, such that the amount of reimbursement a hospital received (under Part A for inpatient care) for a patient with a particular diagnosis was based on a predetermined schedule and no longer linked to actual costs incurred, was associated with an immediate and continuing decline in hospital lengths of stay and a transfer of diagnostic and other procedures to free-standing (and separately reimbursed) facilities.

Fifty years later, the studies of the Dartmouth program (Fisher, 2007) have confirmed Roemer's insight – roughly half of the regional variation in use among the American Medicare population is associated with variation in the availability of facilities and personnel. The remainder seems to be linked to clinical habits and cultures. None of the regional variations could be associated with patient needs or preferences.

SUMMARY

The central concern of all three alternative perspectives, or paradigms, is the determinations of health care utilization. For the naive clinicians, utilization *should* be determined by patients' needs, as judged by clinicians. And it *will* be, subject to the availability of appropriate resources, professionally directed, and the removal of access barriers. This paradigm has very powerful intuitive appeal, to clinicians and patients alike. Research focuses on identifying presently unmet and new needs, and finding better ways to meet them.

For the mainstream economist, utilization *should* be determined by patients' preferences and personal resources, as expressed in their willingness to pay at prices reflecting resource opportunity costs. And it will be approximated, subject to the trade-off imposed by insurance that reduces risk but promotes and reimburses "overuse." The paradigm has minimal normative appeal or positive plausibility even to economists outside their professional work. Its strength derives from the fact that its predictions and prescriptions can be rigorously formulated, and that it yields recommendations with strong and highly regressive distributive implications. Research focuses on measuring a hypothetical "elasticity of demand" so as to optimize a hypothetical "trade-off" between risk and an idiosyncratic concept of "overuse." Holders of this perspective seem ambivalent as to whether this would require dismantling the extensive regulatory structure erected in response to the clinical perspective, or whether that structure is simply a mirage that can be ignored.

Eclectic Structuralists essentially accept the normative position of clinicians, but reject their positive claims on empirical grounds. Extensive analysis of actual utilization patterns shows very powerful effects from capacity levels, and the incentives faced by and the motivations embedded in provider organizations. Research focuses on provider behaviour in differing settings, and its relation to evidence of the effectiveness of care.

NOTES

1 Because this Figure is adapted (much simplified) from the general National Income Accounting framework, we can draw on that much broader framework to reconcile "missing bits," such as the absence of a foreign sector, debt flows, or capital accumulation. They can all be fitted in!

2 Even the most distinguished scholars can occasionally be trapped by the language. In the course of a very clear and powerful exposition on this subject (which deserves reading by every health economist and most of the rest of the profession), Fuchs (1996) carries out an "unscientific" but very suggestive survey of colleagues' opinions as to the validity of a set of positive and normative propositions about health and health care. But one of his "positive" propositions is actually normative. (Its identification is left as an exercise for the reader.)

3 There is a certain ambivalence on the question of disagreement between patient and professional – what if the offered care is rejected? In principle (and in law) the wishes of the (competent, informed) patient are supposed to be determinative. In practice, however, the clinical perspective seems to include a belief that the patient who acts against medical advice is either not fully informed or not fully competent. Patient noncompliance with drug therapy in particular is typically viewed as either a failure of communication by the prescriber, or an inability of the patient to remember and follow instructions. Such deficits should be corrected.

4 "Consumer sovereignty," like "need," has both a normative and a positive sense. It can mean, as here, that people *should* get what they want, or that in fact they do.

5 The normative position underlying the Mainstream Economic perspective is independent of how the distribution of ability to pay comes to be whatever it is. Most people consider theft as an immoral form of redistribution; some of the more extreme advocates of "free markets" seem to regard tax and transfer systems established by duly elected governments as equivalent to

theft. On the other hand, any redistribution occurring through a market transaction (for which no one has been convicted), including some of the amazing transfers in capital markets, presumably makes the world a better place. In any case the allocation of resources should certainly respond to that redistribution. But here we enter the realm of "Natural Law" theology.

6 Better information about the consequences of adopting different positions may eventually influence people's normative views, although unfortunately normative positions also have a strong influence on what is recognized as valid information. "I wouldn't have seen it if I hadn't believed it."

7 Participants in this convention may, if they are able to occupy strategic positions in university departments, academic journals, and research funding bodies, make it very difficult in some countries to "do economics" without accepting their preferred moral principles. The validity of the definition of true doctrine offered by St Vincent of Lérins: "*Quod semper, quod ubique, quod ab omnibus creditum est*," rests implicitly on the power to burn those who disagree.

8 Clinical norms, however, focus more on the individual patient. "People should get the care they need" is a guide for general health policy and financing. But *my patient* should get the care she needs, even if that implies denying care to others in much worse condition.

9 If competition among firms or factor suppliers is impeded by regulations or collusive behaviour, then the obvious answer from the economic perspective is aggressive public policy to promote competition, in health care as everywhere else. *Inter alia*, remove all self-regulatory powers from the professions, along with any other barriers to entry. Some of the more extreme market advocates seem to go farther, however, to suggest that even *this* form of public intervention in private markets is misguided. Perhaps "the market" somehow produces an optimal level of monopoly and collusion?

10 In some analytic frameworks, such as "health capital stock" models in which people are assumed to "invest" in accumulating "health capital" by *inter alia* consuming health care, the assumption is made explicitly that individuals have full, or at least privileged, information about the structure of the (sometimes rather peculiar-looking) health production function. Other frameworks conceptualize the consumer as a "physician-patient pair," a centaur-like being combining the information possessed by the physician with the circumstances and preferences of the patient. But apart from its inherent implausibility, this attempt to justify ignoring asymmetry of information brings serious theoretical difficulties of its own.

11 The shift of language from "uncertainty" to "risk" is significant. Risk is quantifiable; uncertainty is not. The chance of a well-defined event occurring, say one in ten, or one in one hundred, is a measure of risk. Uncertainty implies not only not knowing what is going to happen, but also being unsure about the nature of the possibilities themselves, let alone their relative probabilities.

12 Much confusion can be created at this point by introducing the observation that several European systems – the British, for example, or the German – include a small "upper tier" of private payment by the wealthy for perceived superior-quality services. This partitioning of the population is precisely what the trade-off analysis is *not* about. Rather it focuses firmly on the "representative agent," the hypothetical average individual in the population, and addresses the question of the optimal mix of payment channels for her.

13 The term "demand," at least as used by economists, embodies certain behavioural assumptions. It is the quantity of a commodity that consumers are willing to purchase, at given prices and income levels (and states of expectations about future prices and incomes). "Utilization" of health care refers simply to the observation of what was actually used, with no implications as to whose decisions and actions led to the observed pattern. To use the two terms interchangeably is thus to make an implicit assumption of considerable significance. In general, it is safest and least presumptuous to refer to "utilization" unless one has very solid grounds for doing otherwise.

14 One does find more extreme advocates of free markets accepting that the organization and funding of health care provision is indeed peculiar, relative to more "normal" industries, but that it should not be. The differences do matter, but the world would be a better place if providers were all converted to strictly for-profit status in a truly competitive market environment, and relieved of most of the regulatory and self-regulatory apparatus. This position amounts to assuming that current arrangements have no good justification, that they are the result of a great mistake – or a conspiracy – but at least it recognizes that the real world exists.

15 It might be thought a mark of naïveté to imagine that private insurance could ever finance a significant share of health care expenditures. But the clinical position in practice may be more subtle. De facto large covert subsidies to private insurance, as in the United States and Canada, tap public funds without permitting corresponding accountability or control – the best of both worlds if one's concern is always to get more money into health care.

16 These are necessary, not sufficient, conditions for profit maximization. The profit-maximizing firm must not only minimize the cost of its output, but

also select the right level of output. And cost minimization requires both not wasting resources and choosing the least-cost combination of resources, given their relative prices.

17 The reference to hospital downsizing – the dramatic decline in in-patient utilization in a number of countries over the last quarter of the twentieth century – flags an inherent ambiguity in the definition of "output" or the commodities produced by health care providers, particularly hospitals. Do hospitals produce in-patient days, or treated cases, or simply a wide array of particular services and procedures? Is an unnecessarily long length of stay for a clearly necessary surgical procedure the inefficient production of the commodity "a treated case" or overprovision of the commodities "in-patient days"?

18 It is hard to imagine a private practitioner amassing the string of criminal convictions and billion-dollar fines assembled by Pfizer and treated as simply a business expense (Evans, 2010).

19 The answers can be disturbing. For example, nearly a decade ago American spinal surgeon Edward Benzel conjectured that probably fewer than half of the spinal fusion procedures then performed in the United States were appropriate (Abelson and Petersen, 2003). This is very serious surgery (and very expensive). Yet "The reality is, we all cave in to market and economic forces." (Spinal fusion is also very lucrative.) The reimbursement system is "totally perverse."

REFERENCES

Abelson, R., and M. Petersen (2003). "An operation to ease back pain bolsters the bottom line, too." *New York Times*, 31 December.

Arrow, K.J. (1976). "Welfare analysis of changes in health coinsurance rates." In *The role of health insurance in the health services sector*, ed. R. Rosett, 3–23. New York: National Bureau of Economic Research.

Culyer, A.J., and R.G. Evans (1996). "Mark Pauly on welfare economics: Normative rabbits from positive hats." *Journal of Health Economics*, 15(2): 243–51.

Evans, R.G., (2005). "Preserving privilege, promoting profit: The payoffs from private health insurance." In *Access to care, access to justice*, ed. C.M. Flood, K. Roach, and L. Sossin, 347–68. Toronto: University of Toronto Press.

– (2010). "Tough on crime? Pfizer and the CIHR." [Commentary] *Healthcare Policy*, Vol. 5, no. 4 (2010): 16–25.

Feldstein, M.S. (1973). "The welfare loss of excess health insurance," *Journal of Political Economy* 81(2), Part 1 (March-April): 251–80.

Fisher, E.S. (2007). Pay-for-performance: More than rearranging the deck chairs? Robert and Alma Moreton Lecture, Dartmouth Medical School, 21 May.

Fuchs, V.F. (1996). "Economics, values and health care reform," *American Economic Review* 86(1) (March): 1–24.

Pauly, M.V. (1969). "A measure of the welfare cost of health insurance," *Health Services Research* 4(4) (Winter): 281–92.

– (1996). "Reply to Anthony J. Culyer and Robert G. Evans," *Journal of Health Economics*, 15(2): 253–4.

Reinhardt, U.E. (1992). "Reflections on the meaning of efficiency: Can efficiency be separated from equity?" *Yale Law & Policy Review* 10(2): 302–15.

– (1998). "Abstracting from distributional effects, this policy is efficient." In *Health, health care and health economics*," ed. M.L. Barer, T.E. Getzen, and G.L. Stoddart, 1–53. New York: Wiley & Sons.

Roemer, M.I. (1961). "Bed supply and utilization: A natural experiment," *Hospitals: Journal of the American Hospital Association* 35 (November): 35–42.

Rose, G. (2001). "Sick individuals and sick populations." *International Journal of Epidemiology* 30(3): 427–32.

Roos, N.P., E. Forget, R. Wall, and L. MacWilliam. (2004). "Does universal comprehensive insurance encourage unnecessary use? Evidence from Manitoba says 'no,'" *Canadian Medical Association Journal* 170(2) (January 20): 209–14.

van Doorslaer, E., A. Wagstaff, and F. Rutten, eds. (1993). *Equity in the finance and delivery of health care: An international perspective*, New York: Oxford University Press.

Woolhandler, S., and D.U. Himmelstein. (2002). "Paying for national health insurance – and not getting it," *Health Affairs* 21(4) (July-August): 88–98.

Further Reading

Without intending to be exhaustive, amongst other papers that would have found a comfortable home in this section, but for which there was insufficient space, are:

- Culyer, Anthony J., and Robert G. Evans (1996). "Mark Pauly on Welfare Economics: Normative rabbits from Positive Hats," *Journal of Health Economics* 15(2): 243–51.
- Morgan, Steve, Morris Barer, and Robert Evans (2000). "Health Economists Meet the Fourth Tempter: Drug Dependency and Scientific Discourse." *Health Economics* 9(8): 659–67.
- Evans, Robert G. (2009) "Dismal Science." *Healthcare Policy* 4(4): 19–29.

SECTION B

Health Care Financing

Foreword

JEREMIAH HURLEY

It is an honour to write the introduction to this section highlighting some of Robert Evans' many contributions in the area of health care financing. The selections included in this section – like the pieces throughout this volume – exemplify the characteristics of the author's work that I most admire. First and foremost is his intellectual courage, the courage to forsake established frameworks and ideas when they don't match reality, to challenge conventional wisdom, and to follow ideas fearlessly to their logical conclusion. Evans does not take the intellectual easy road. Second is the sophistication of his analysis, which has always struck me as a counterpoint to the common mistake in economics of equating verbal arguments with simplistic analysis and formal mathematical models with sophisticated analysis. Evans' analyses of health care financing are among the most sophisticated one will encounter, rooted in a clear underlying analytic framework, pursued in a rigorous deductive style, grounded in data and institutional detail, and undertaken using a holistic approach that enables him to integrate relevant phenomena with greater subtlety and insight than is possible in the formal economic mode. In particular, his work incorporates detailed analysis of the distributional effects that are so central to health care financing, but that are neglected in much economic analysis, and the complex connections between insurance markets and health services markets, and among financing, funding, and delivery. Lastly, Evans' contributions to health care financing exhibit an unwavering commitment to the common good and the efficacy of collective action.

The pieces included in this section share a number of themes and analytic perspectives that have preoccupied Evans for decades, but broadly speaking I see them as falling into three important types of contributions he has made to our understanding of health care financing: (a) building the necessary analytic framework within which to ask and answer questions about health care financing; (b) articulating the implications of this framework for the performance of alternative systems of finance, especially in relation to health system expenditures; and (c) analyzing the political economy of health system financing, and in particular, the economic self-interest that so often lies behind calls for greater private finance.

Many of Evans' important contributions to the analysis of health care financing derive from his rejection of the traditional economic model of insurance as inadequate for understanding the welfare effects of universal, first-dollar public insurance, and his associated development of an alternative framework. Market failure in insurance markets is of course real, but if the sole rationale for insurance were risk-reduction, and the sole purpose of government intervention were to "fix" markets for risk-bearing, public insurance as we know it in Canada and many other countries would never have emerged. Rather, the economic rationale for such public insurance can be found in both a broader analysis of market failure in the health care sector and in a broader set of social objectives served by public insurance. Evans developed some of these ideas in early work (Evans and Williamson, 1978; Evans, 1983) that integrated the positive and normative implications of the nature of health care as an economic commodity and the associated operation of health care markets, to demonstrate that, contrary to key conclusions of the standard welfare-economic analysis of insurance, single-payer, universal, first-dollar public insurance makes eminent economic sense. By the mid-1980s, these ideas had matured into an analytic framework that provided the foundation for a series of contributions in which he applied the framework to provide insight into a number of specific questions in health care financing.

"Hang Together or Hang Separately" deconstructs arguments for private financing to reveal their logical and empirical inconsistencies. It also dissects sustainability arguments – the frequent claim that publicly financed health care systems are unsustainable, and hence we must increase the role of private financing. These arguments are proffered in nearly the same form today as they were over 25 years ago when this piece was written. The paper presents some key ideas central to Evans' legacy. I highlight two in particular.

The first is the fallacious nature of arguments based on determinism: the idea that there are unavoidable, external forces pressing on the health care system that force our hand – in this case, the effects of population aging and advances in medical technology. As Evans forcefully argues, such arguments are specious: aging per se is not the problem, it is how we respond to aging; medical technology is not inherently cost increasing – the trajectory of technological development is shaped by the institutions and incentives we create, as is the adoption and diffusion of technology within the system. We are not caught in a deterministic vice; we have policy choices, and it is our obligation to make good ones based on sound analysis.

The second big idea, signalled by the title, is the power, efficacy, and need for collective responses to confront such challenges. Compared to fragmented private finance, public universal systems of finance create both the bargaining power and the institutional mechanisms to control costs, improve equity, and enhance efficiency; these insights were developed further a few years later in "Tension, Compression, and Shear" (Evans, 1990).

Evans has contributed notably to our understanding of the political economy of health care reform, particularly the persistent calls for more private financing, emphasizing the distributional implications of private finance and laying bare the economic self-interest of those calling for more private finance. "User Fees for Health Care" does this in the context of the long history of calls for introducing user charges, and "Going for the Gold" does this in the context of calls for private, market-based reforms to financing. Evans' analysis reveals how specious arguments about the need for private finance to save the public system systematically downplay or ignore distributional issues (abetted by economic models that cannot accommodate distributional analysis) and the associated income gains for many advocates of private financing. As Evans observes, while much policy debate and analysis of public and private finance abstracts from distributional issues, distributional conflicts are central to all arguments for and against private financing. One cannot think sensibly about health care financing without confronting its distributional effects, and the ever-present incentive for system actors to advocate for financing schemes that advance their economic interests.

The last piece in this section, the previously unpublished "Modelling the Benefits of Insurance," elucidates in a more formal way the limitations of the standard insurance model and the centrality of distributional issues in health care financing. Extending the standard economic model of insurance, Evans shows why three facts about real world health care systems – heterogeneous individuals, incomplete insurance markets that only partially compensate individuals for illness-related losses, and systematically lower administrative costs in public systems of financing – reverse the standard conclusion regarding the optimality of deductibles and other forms of cost-sharing. The main messages of the paper are vital to any student of insurance, but I also like the paper because it illustrates the author's knack for zeroing in on crucial false, often seemingly innocuous, assumptions and then drawing out the implications of building a model that reflects better the actual operation of health (care and insurance) markets.

Perhaps the greatest tribute to a scholar is that his or her ideas become so absorbed into common knowledge, and now seem so obvious, that it is difficult to appreciate that they were not always understood, that people use them without even knowing or acknowledging their origin. Such is the legacy of so many of Evans' contributions to our understanding of health care financing.

REFERENCES

Evans, R.G. (1983). "The welfare economics of public health insurance: Theory and Canadian practice." In *Social Insurance*, ed. L. Soderstrom, 71–103. Amsterdam: North-Holland.

– (1990). "Tension, compression and shear: Directions, stresses, and outcomes of health care cost control." *Journal of Health Politics, Policy and Law* 15(1): 101–28.

– and M.F. Williamson (1978). "Public intervention: Objectives and criteria," in *Extending Canadian national health insurance: Options for Pharmacare and Denticare*. Toronto: University of Toronto Press, for the Ontario Economic Council, 3–32.

5

Hang Together, or Hang Separately: The Viability of a Universal Health Care System in an Aging Society (1987)

ROBERT G. EVANS

"To every complex question there is a simple answer – neat, plausible, and wrong."

H.L. Mencken

IS UNIVERSALITY BECOMING "UNAFFORDABLE"?

The line of argument which links the increasing average age of the Canadian population with questions as to the long-run viability of universal, comprehensive public health insurance is generally familiar. Its widespread recognition, if not acceptance, is part of the reason why demographic trends receive prominent attention in all recent discussions of health policy, at all levels. Unfortunately the argument is as fallacious as it is familiar. It starts, however, from two well-documented and universally accepted "facts," or at least statistical generalizations, which *are* valid.

Evans, Robert G. "Hang Together, or Hang Separately: The Viability of a Universal Health Care System in an Aging Society." *Canadian Public Policy* 13(2) (1987): 165–80. Reprinted with the permission of *Canadian Public Policy*.

First, the average age of the Canadian population *is* rising. The collapse of the birth rate in the mid-1960s triggered off this increase; and the acceleration of the downtrend in age-specific mortality rates in the 1970s, including males as well as females in the upper age groups, has reinforced it.[1] Projections vary, depending on assumptions about future trends in birth and mortality rates, but the proportion of the population over 65 is generally expected to rise from roughly 10 per cent in 1980 to roughly 20 per cent in 2020 – and to continue on up. This process will only be nicely started by the year 2000, when the proportion over 65 will still be around 13 per cent – the first baby boomers do not reach 65 until 2011.[2]

Second, it is equally well-known that per capita rates of utilization of health care, and costs, rise with age, subject to some qualifications for the costs of the very young, and child-bearing women. The rate of increase of per capita costs with age, however, differs greatly among different components of health care – consider dentistry and long-term care.

There is room for debate as to the extent to which the upward slope in age-use and age-cost curves (graphs of per capita use against age) is due to the inclusion of costs of terminal care – if one measures only use and costs for persons who are not within several months or a year of death, the average per capita costs of "survivors" does not increase as rapidly with age.[3]

More generally, one can identify high users, who are quite ill, at any age. If one excludes these people, who make up a higher proportion of the elderly population, it can be argued that "healthy" elderly people do not differ much from "healthy" members of the non-elderly population in their use patterns.[4] But while these observations may be a healthy corrective to a tendency to stereotype the elderly as a sickly class, they leave intact the observation that, whatever the mechanism, health care utilization and costs rise with age.

From these two generalizations the argument unfolds smoothly. The aging of the population will place increasing upward pressure on health care use and costs as more and more people fall into the high-cost age groups. Together with the progress of medical technology, which is constantly extending the scope, but also the cost, of effective interventions, demographic changes will enforce, if not an explosion, at least a continued and substantial escalation of health care costs.

But Canadian governments, federal and provincial, are in no position to fund this inevitable expansion. They are trapped by a combination of slow economic growth and taxpayer resistance into mounting deficits and the need to cut public expenditures. They will have great difficulty meeting current spending commitments, let alone coping with the increases in costs which will come with the aging population.

Clearly something has to give. One alternative would be to abandon universality/comprehensiveness of coverage, and allow increased "private funding" to flow into the health care system. This would be a direct repudiation of the principles spelled out and supported in the Canada Health Act of 1984, and, as most Canadians appear to agree, fundamental to the philosophy of the Canadian Medicare system since its inception. The other choice is to maintain the ideological purity of the system at the expense of progressive deterioration, a growth of the backlog of "unmet need," as the resources required to respond to the ever-larger elderly population, at the standards of care dictated by evolving technology, simply are not available. One way or another, openly or covertly, universality has to go. We cannot afford it.[5]

Neat, plausible, and wrong. The argument rests on two major and distinct errors of fact, compounded with a carefully nurtured accounting confusion, and a questionable projection of the bias of technological progress. It converts, and in some hands is specifically designed to convert, a problem of policy choices in an uncertain world into a spuriously inevitable "grim trade-off" or "painful prescription," by distorting or diverting attention from policy options and misstating or prejudging the quantitative implications of current trends.

THE QUANTITATIVE IMPACT OF AGING ON HEALTH CARE COSTS

First, the impact of aging per se on health care costs is readily calculated, and has been calculated by a number of different analysts.[6] One need only project forward the number of people in each age and sex class, then multiply these numbers by constant age-sex-specific average per capita utilization rates or expenditures, defined at a point in time (usually the most recent available for the jurisdiction of interest), and then calculate the rate of escalation of per capita use or expenditure averaged over the population as a whole, as the proportions of the population shift to the "high-end" groups.

This calculation isolates the contribution of demographic change alone to use and costs, holding constant the rate of use of persons at each age. It thus imposes as an assumption that 75-year-olds ten years from now will use, on average, the same pattern of services as 75-year-olds do now, and at the same prices. Per capita costs for the population as a whole will rise as the proportion of 75-year-olds increases, relative to, say, 30-year-olds.[7]

Such computations yield projections of the impact of aging on costs which are quite consistent – and quite small. The increases in per capita costs are in the neighbourhood of 1 per cent per year, for health care as a whole, over the next 20 to 40 years. Moreover, as one would expect, the largest effects are on services which are particularly used by older people – long-term care and home care. In these sectors, demographic forces alone imply increases of 1.5 per cent – 2 per cent per capita per year. For physicians' services, on the other hand, the age-use curve is much less steeply sloped, and the impact of aging per se will only increase use by about one-third of a per cent per year (note 6 supra).

While any compound growth rate will yield impressive increases if maintained over a sufficiently long time, these rates are in fact well within the normal rates of growth of the Canadian economy, and most other developed economies as well. It follows that the increases in health care costs which will result from demographic forces alone will be supportable by the allocation of a constant, or even a falling, share of our national income. They are not nearly large enough to place a strain on our economic resources.[8]

These projected rates of increase are also well below historical trends in health expenditures, indicating that past increases have been driven by forces other than demographic change. Yet it is a widespread perception among health care providers that care of the elderly is becoming an increasingly significant share of their activity, and of system costs. Closer examination of trends in utilization resolves the apparent contradiction.

What is happening is that age-specific per capita utilization among the elderly is rising relative to that of the non-elderly, and for most forms of care in absolute terms as well. Thus the age-use curves are not constant, but are rising and rotating counter-clockwise. The increasing health care utilization of the elderly population is real; but it is a result, not primarily of the increase in their numbers, but of the changing patterns of servicing which they are receiving.

These increases cannot therefore be ascribed to demographic forces external to the health care system; rather they reflect, and raise questions about, the behaviour of the health care system itself. Why are elderly people being treated in an increasingly intensive and costly way, and with what results? It may be that the increases in servicing which they are receiving represent either or both of a reduction in previously unmet needs, or an expansion of the range of potentially effective therapies. But it is also possible that there is increasing servicing of questionable effectiveness, encouraged by the expanded capacity and ambitions of the health care system itself. In either case, the increases are *not* simply a response to demographic changes.[9]

UNIVERSAL COVERAGE AND COST CONTAINMENT

The second error of fact in the argument that we "cannot afford" universal health care is the assumption that a universal public insurance system is more expensive than a system of partial or selective coverage. There are two different sources of confusion behind this error.

The first arises from the lumping of public health insurance together with family allowances, old age pensions, and other public direct payment (transfer) programs as "social programs." A direct payment program will obviously be less expensive, or alternatively will provide higher benefits per beneficiary, if it is targeted to a selected set of beneficiaries rather than being made "universal." Consequently it is argued that scarce transfer dollars go farther in responding to specific needs if they are made "selective" – conditional or categorical – rather than universal.[10]

But if outlays per beneficiary are not under direct program control, and are highly variable and dependent on factors which are difficult or impossible to monitor accurately, as is the case with health insurance, it no longer follows that costs must be lower (or benefits higher) under selectivity. Universality may be an essential factor in maintaining control over total program costs. The experience of the Canadian health care system, and its contrast with that of the US, indicates conclusively that such has been the case.

The second source of confusion arises from analogies with the economic theory of consumer behaviour. Here the variability of outlays per beneficiary is recognized, but the argument is made that comprehensive coverage contributes to additional cost per beneficiary by encouraging the overuse or frivolous use of "free" care. If coverage per beneficiary is partial, on the other hand, users of care will be required to pay part of the cost, and will be motivated to make more careful (i.e., less) use, and perhaps to "shop" more carefully among providers, thereby constraining price increases.

The inadequacies of the analogy between health care utilization and the consumption of a textbook "commodity" are rather involved, and would take us farther into economic theory than is necessary or helpful.[11] A more comprehensive view of the utilization process, however, undercuts the argument for cost containment through partial coverage, and points towards comprehensiveness, along with universality, as conditions necessary to establish a bilateral bargaining relationship between providers and payers, such that costs are in fact better contained than in a hypothetical "free market" – which has never actually been observed in health care in any country.

Regardless of the structure of argument, the basic facts are clear. The Canadian system of universal, comprehensive coverage for hospital and medical costs has maintained control over costs; the US system, with multiple funding sources and a high proportion of out-of-pocket payment by patients, has not. Figures 5.1 and 5.2 display the historical record for the two countries, and identify the years during which the Canadian provinces were introducing first public hospital, and then public medical, insurance, in response to the federal cost-sharing and standard-setting legislation.[12]

These Figures show that Canada has been able to hold health care costs – whether measured by personal health care (PHC) expenditures, or the more comprehensive national health expenditures (NHE) measure – to a relatively stable share of national income for the best part of two decades. The US, on the other hand, has been experiencing a genuine "cost explosion" which does not, despite widespread US opinion to that effect, date from the introduction of their partial Medicare (for the elderly) and Medicaid (for the poor) programs in 1965. The uptrend was well established by that time.

Moreover, the divergence between the two countries' experience begins with the completion of the universal plans in Canada; when our funding system was similar to theirs, our costs escalated at the same rate. Further, the discrepancies in national experience are specifically located in the components of health expenditure, hospital and medical care, for which Canada introduced universal public coverage; there is no significant difference in the (total) performance of the remaining components.[13] Finally the US in the 1980s, having adopted a new, competitive strategy of health funding and delivery, has so far shown *more* rapid cost escalation than in the late 1970s. Erroneous claims to the contrary have been based on "money illusion," an elementary confusion between nominal and real rates of increase.[14]

Indeed the one clear example of a change in US cost patterns, the very sudden and sharp drop in hospital utilization between 1983 and 1984, is a response not to the competitive strategy, but to a change in the public reimbursement system, the shift to admission-based reimbursement,

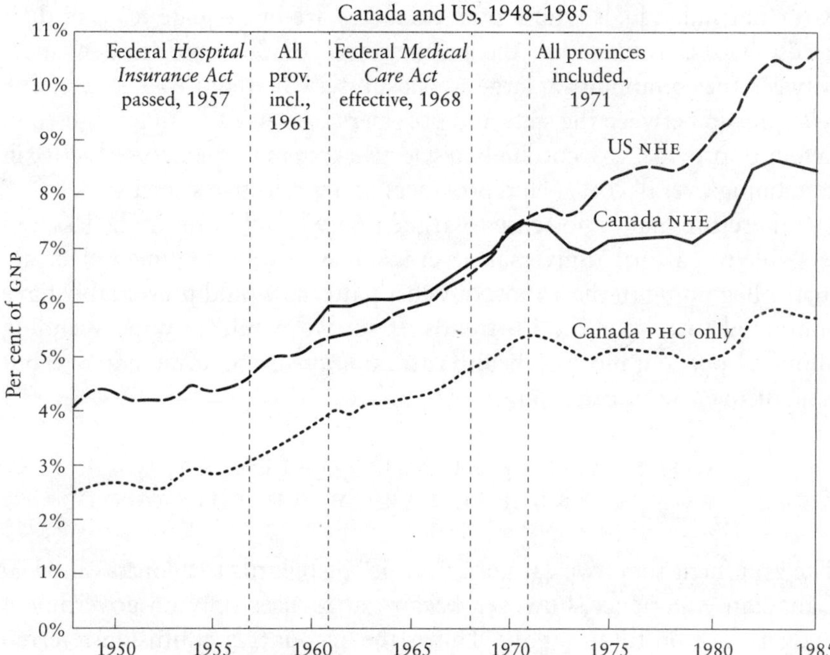

Figure 5.1 Health expenditure as a share of GNP

Adapted from: Robert G. Evans. "Hang Together, or Hang Separately: The Viability of a Universal Health Care System in an Aging Society." *Canadian Public Policy* 13(2)(1987): 165–80.

combined with tougher pre-admission screening. These are "regulatory" mechanisms, imposed by payers, independent of any user choice, and are thus closer to Canadian modes of control. Within their limited sphere of application, they have worked.[15]

It is thus very clear from the Canadian and US comparisons that universality, far from contributing to cost escalation, is in fact associated with effective cost control, and for reasons on which there is now general, if not universal, agreement. In essence, a system of universal coverage uses the public sector as a sort of "consumers' co-operative," a collective organization with which to bargain with providers and their organizations on behalf of all users collectively, not just those with few resources or exceptional needs. This "consumers' co-operative" equalizes the bargaining power, compared with the situation in which individuals confront professionals directly, and thus permits the community to hold down the share of its income which it must make over to providers.

A selective system, on the other hand, treats the public sector as a form of "charity" through which the general community provides assistance to particular individuals whose own resources are inadequate to meet their needs. In this framework, the primary role of the state is to mediate between the community at large, and a sub-set who require assistance. The relationship between the state and providers is secondary, and weighted in favour of providers. Accordingly, a selective system is much less effective in containing overall costs – and providers prefer selective systems.

It therefore makes no sense to argue that we will in future be less and less able to "afford" universal coverage. If we had not "gone universal" by the beginning of the 1970s, our cost patterns would presumably have continued to mirror the US trends. If so, we would now be spending about 25 per cent more on health care, an *increase* of more than $10 billion, or over $400 per capita.

GOVERNMENT BUDGET OUTLAYS – CONFUSING THE PART WITH THE WHOLE

The argument that "we cannot afford it" disregards the contrasting US/Canadian experience, however, because it focuses only on government budgets, not on total outlays. This is the accounting confusion referred to above.

Direct transfer programs, such as family allowances or old age pensions, have a net program cost, *to the community as a whole*, of zero. Money is taken away from one group, in taxes, and given to another, as cheques in the mail. Adding across both groups, gains and losses cancel out.[16] It is common, therefore, and not unreasonable, to look at the program "cost" from the perspective of the government budget, rather than society as a whole, and refer to public outlays as costs, though they could equally well be described as benefits.

In the case of health care, however, expenditures are not simply transfers of wealth, but "exhaustive," in that they go to reimburse the use of real resources – human time, energy and skills, materials, and services of capital – which are used up in the process of providing services. These are net costs to the community as a whole; the resources used up to provide health care are not available for other purposes. Such costs may be financed through the government budget, through "social" or private insurance systems, through out-of-pocket payment, or through private charity, but the cost of health care to the community is the sum total of all such outlays through whichever channel they flow.

It is therefore a simple accounting confusion to imagine that the costs of health care are somehow restricted to the component which goes

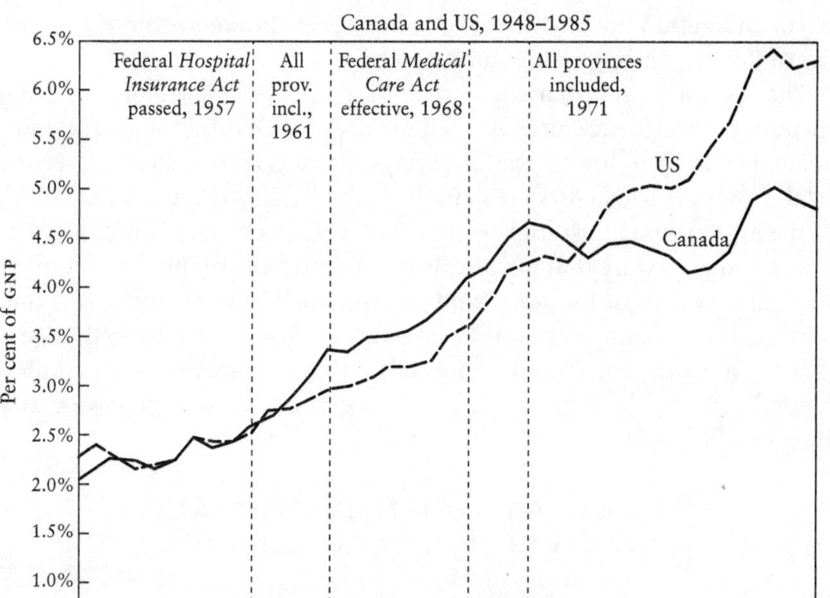

Figure 5.2 Hospital and MD expenditure, as a share of GNP

Adapted from: Robert G. Evans. "Hang Together, or Hang Separately: The Viability of a Universal Health Care System in an Aging Society." *Canadian Public Policy* 13(2)(1987): 165–80.

through public budgets. It is certainly true that, when Medicare in Canada took over the insurance process, premiums which had previously been deducted from payrolls at source and sent to a not-for-profit insurance agency were subsequently sent to a government agency and moved from one set of accounts to another. But that shift per se represented neither a rise nor a fall in the costs of health care.

The argument against universality, however, focuses on government budgets alone, as if there were some special constraint on what the community could afford to pay through this particular channel. It implies, or even states, that we *could* afford to pay more, if we did so as individuals out of pocket, or collectively through private insurance, but we cannot afford to pay more through taxes. Considering that health insurance premiums, like taxes, are for most of the population deducted at source and have identical effects on after-tax income, the distinction is, to say the least, a fine one. At the end of the day, the health care costs of the community must be paid for by the community, regardless of the channel of payment, and do not become less or more, or "different," merely by virtue of flowing through different budgets.

That is not to say that the choice of channel has no effect on total spending; the evidence already cited makes very clear that universal public finance leads to lower overall outlays. But it does not do so merely by relabelling; the total costs are actually lower. And here we get to the nub of the argument against universality. Many of its critics, behind the rhetoric, are quite aware that universality is indeed "affordable," much more so than a system of multiple funding sources. Their argument is rather that health expenditures should be substantially *higher* than they are, that universality leads, not to an overly costly system, but to an "underfunded" one. Spokesmen for medical associations have been particularly clear on this point.[17]

THE REAL CRITICISM: UNIVERSALITY, "UNDERFUNDING," AND TECHNOLOGY

This position shifts and clarifies the argument considerably. The issue is not one of economic constraints on our ability to maintain universality, at least in the overt sense of comprehensive, first-dollar coverage for all. Quite the contrary, to the extent that we believe that economic constraints are likely to be more severe in the future than in the past, maintenance of universality becomes *more* important. But the providers' argument of "underfunding" implies that the community is being harmed by the restraints on health spending which are made possible, and effective, by universality, and would be better off if more were spent.

If in fact the community can "afford" to spend more through private insurance or out-of-pocket channels – and it can, if willing to give up other things – then of course logically it can "afford" to spend more through government budgets as well.[18] The problem of "underfunding," therefore, reduces to providers' perceptions that the community priorities expressed through the political process are "wrong," or at least unacceptable to themselves, and that they would be better able to further their own professional priorities, which they believe are "right," if they could sidestep the political process of allocating resources, and gain access to less closely guarded private funds.

The contrasting US and Canadian cost experiences suggest that this latter judgment is entirely correct.[19] The key issue is the question as to whether the political priorities which control expenditures in a universal system are in fact "wrong" in the sense that not only providers, but the community at large, or at least significant segments of it, would be happier with alternative priorities reflected in a continuing escalation of the share of income devoted to health care costs.

Here we rejoin the component of the "costs of aging" argument which depends on a projection of the bias of future change in health care technology. It is clear from the demographic projections that aging per se will not require us to spend a rising share of national income on health care, just to maintain current (age-specific) levels of provision (unless, of course, future economic growth trends go flat, which is not now projected by most observers).

The claim that technological developments will raise costs is based on the positive assumption that medical technology will generate a steady stream of innovations which are on balance both more effective and more expensive, redefining and expanding the definition of "need," and on the normative proposition that we, as the decent, humane community, ought to be prepared to expand spending on health care to meet these needs.[20] Otherwise universality becomes a hollow boast, "universal access" to an ever more obsolete and inadequate range of services, compared to what the advance of knowledge and technique is making possible.

Indeed the claim that the Canadian system is "underfunded" at present is equivalent to the assertion that the stability of costs (as a share of national income) over the past 15 years has already been associated with declining standards and accumulating "unmet needs." People are being denied access to therapeutically effective interventions, whether or not they are aware of it, as a consequence of expenditure limitations, and the progress of technology can only make this situation worse.

This single issue raises two types of questions. The effects of cost containment up to now are in principle, and to a considerable extent in practice, measurable, although in some sectors they are by no means as securely measured as one might like. The direction of future technology, however, is considerably more speculative. We shall deal with it first, because there is less to be said.

The first point to emphasize, however, is that there is no *necessary* positive linkage between technical progress in health care and cost escalation or increasing unmet need. Innovations may permit expensive salvage – Lewis Thomas' halfway technologies, or effective but expensive "spare parts" replacement. But equally they may permit prevention or early intervention, which in turn may (though it need not) lower overall costs. Innovations in treatment also lower costs, permitting early ambulation and discharge for hospital patients, for example, or drug therapies which substitute for medical or surgical interventions. (Consider the potential impact on long-term care costs of a drug therapy for Alzheimer's

Disease, or on cardiac care of a safe means of dissolving arterial plaque.) It is simply an empirical question what the net effect will be over any time period; one cannot assert a priori that costs must be increased.

Secondly, the direction which technological progress takes, both in development and in field of application, is not independent of the incentives created by the delivery and funding system itself.[21] If, as in the US up to October 1983, the hospital system is essentially cost-reimbursed, there will be a ready market for cost-enhancing technical changes. The impact of the reimbursement system on the proliferation of cardiac care units, for example, is notorious. This not only encourages the R & D industry to focus on innovations which expand reach but add to cost, it also encourages providers to extend the application of new equipment and techniques ahead of their demonstrated effectiveness.

But with the change to case-based reimbursement in US hospitals, it is no longer automatic that a new piece of equipment, if it can be kept busy, is a money-spinner. When reimbursement is detached from specific patterns of care, the costs of extra servicing come straight off the hospital's bottom line – whether or not it is a for-profit institution. This is already having an impact on the market for medical equipment in the US; the key point is that it may also have an impact, over a longer time horizon, on the pattern of innovation. It may be more profitable, in future, to develop and bring to market cost-reducing innovations, and medical practice may extend less rapidly the fields of application and the utilization of new techniques.

The subjunctive is unavoidable; the future is an uncertain place. What one can say with confidence is that the incentive patterns in the "innovation industry" have changed; whether the bias of technological progress in medicine will also shift is less sure. Nor is it clear that the change is entirely beneficial; a redirection of research effort may discourage the development of high-cost technologies which the community would, in fact, have been willing to pay for. (But how would we know?) At this point, however, it is clearly misleading to impose the assumption of a continuing upward bias as if it were a "fact" as secure as, say, the projected aging of the population.

COST CONTAINMENT IN CANADA: PROCESS AND EFFECTS

When we turn to the effects of past cost control in the Canadian system, we have a few more facts to go on. There are two main forms which containment can take, and has taken. Trends in total costs, or expenditures, are the product of trends in utilization, and in unit prices. Again in comparison with the US system, we find that cost containment in Canada has been the result of control over both of these components, but that the emphasis has been different in the two sectors of physicians' services and of hospital care.

In the case of physicians' services, the trends of increase in manpower and utilization are very little different on either side of the border. The major difference, and it has been major, is in the rate of escalation of fees. Since 1970, indices of physicians' fees in Canada (adjusted for differences in general inflation rates) have run about 3 per cent *per year* below corresponding US rates.[22] Thus cost containment in this sector has been entirely a matter of price and income control, and has had no effect on the availability of services to patients. "Underfunding" of physicians' services means, not that patients are suffering from insufficient care, but that physicians would like to earn more money.[23] These income aspirations, legitimate or otherwise, are presented to the rest of the community as a health problem – politically understandable, but no less misleading for that.

In the hospital sector, however, the impact of containment is much less clear. The relative incomes of hospital workers, nurses and others, are an extremely important component of cost trends, but for most of the post-1971 period (as before it) these incomes have been rising. The principal difference between cost trends in Canada and those in the US lies in the growth rates of "servicing intensity," spending per capita or per hospital day, adjusted for changes in input prices. This measures the increases in person-hours, supplies, and use of capital equipment being provided through the hospital system. Such "servicing intensity" has grown much faster in the US than in Canada, and thus represents a real difference in utilization.[24]

But it does not follow that the health of Canadian patients is suffering as a result. There is extensive research documenting the fact that patterns of hospital utilization, and procedural frequency, vary widely across regions and time periods, for reasons which cannot be traced to the underlying health needs of the populations served, and are not reflected in their health outcomes. The less rapid growth of servicing patterns in Canada relative to the US does not necessarily represent accumulating "unmet need"; it is at least as possible that it represents avoidance of (some of) the unnecessary and ineffective utilization which is considered by most observers to characterize the US system. Certainly there is no evidence in aggregate statistics that the health of Canadians is worse than that of Americans, or improving less rapidly. Quite the contrary.

The problem, however, is that utilization patterns in hospitals are not the outcome of careful evaluative research into what works and what does not. A very large part of activity is generally conceded never to have been properly evaluated, either at all, or in particular applications. Rather there is a bias towards: "When in doubt, do something," which has found full expression in the US, at least so long as the many different components of the reimbursement system added up to, in effect, cost reimbursement. Things appear to have changed in 1984. In Canada, the activist urge has been tempered by global budgetary constraints, which seem to express a bureaucratic attitude of: "When in doubt, don't."

But in both systems, much more needs to be known about what is going on. It is conceivable that cost containment is, in fact, resulting in some Canadian patients being denied potentially effective interventions; it is equally possible that there is enough ineffective activity going on, even in the Canadian system, to permit further savings. For that matter, both may be true simultaneously. It would be good to know.

The widely quoted evidence from the US Health Maintenance Organizations (HMOs), indicating that changing from fee for service to capitated medical practice can lead to reductions in hospital utilization of 20 to 40 per cent with no apparent harm to patients, certainly suggests that cost containment is quite compatible with high quality care. It also indicates that, despite its record of successful cost control, the Canadian system is not the last word on the subject.

Up till now, providers have ignored or resisted the external accountability implied by evaluation (based on evidence as opposed to professional opinion), or external comparison. Provincial payers have generally held down the increases in global budgets as best they could, again without relying on detailed evaluative evidence or promoting innovation. They have exemplified Charles Lindblom's characterization of administrative systems – "Strong thumbs, weak fingers."

The result has been a system with a high degree of equity, and relatively successful global control, but little flexibility and organizational innovation. Providers have enough political power to block significant changes, while provincial governments can often block pressures for expansion, or at least retard their effects. The US experience is in contrast on all three points: highly flexible and innovative, but remarkably inequitable, and so far, despite the localized successes of particular organizational innovations, still out of control on global costs. Until such control can be established, further radical changes seem inevitable. The challenge, of course, is to find a way to get the best of both worlds.

The desirability of better evaluation of the interventions being carried on in the Canadian hospital sector, however, or of greater flexibility and innovation in organizational design, does not salvage the fallacious argument that the present universal system is or will become "unaffordable," whether because of population aging or otherwise. If the technologies developed in the future (and those currently available) are carefully evaluated for effectiveness before being put into effect, past experience gives no reason to believe that they cannot be provided in a universal system. A fortiori, if we can apply the information currently available on more efficient and less costly ways to provide care, the future will be even more affordable. (And if we really *cannot* afford it, abandoning universality will not help!)

THE PERSISTENCE OF FALLACY: IDEOLOGY AND SELF-INTEREST

Yet the claim that universality is unaffordable persists, despite its egregious lack of internal validity. The principal source of its appeal may lie in its congruence with two distinct types of ideological bias.

One is a general attitude towards the proper role of the state, which views public activity as per se suspect and private activity as per se meritorious. This sort of "financial press" bias is usually charmingly innocent, i.e., profoundly ignorant, of the institutions, functioning, or performance of the Canadian or any other health care system, but likes the sound of such words as "private," "free enterprise," or "profit." Universality reeks of socialism; its consequences are bound to be bad, whatever they may be.

More interesting to an economist (as opposed perhaps to a political scientist or a social psychologist), however, is the ideological bias which is rooted in a relatively shrewd, if not always clearly articulated, sense of how the health care system actually functions, and which has a strong coloration of plain economic self-interest. As noted above, the argument of "underfunding" in the case of physicians' services reduces not to a problem of insufficient personnel or services, but to a pay claim. Physicians believe they would receive higher fees and incomes under a non-universal system. They are almost certainly right.

But the question of hospital funding is also connected with the economic interests of physicians, as well as of hospital employees. Physicians make their livings by providing specific services for a fee; their ability to do so is (to a greater or lesser degree, depending on specialty) influenced by their access to the "free" capital and personnel provided by the rest of society through the hospital system. The growth of that system in Canada has been limited by public restraints, but the medical schools continue to churn out ever more physicians. The ratio of "doctors per bed," or per the bundle of equipment and personnel which goes with a bed, is rising steadily – each individual physician's access to these "tools of the trade" is being progressively curtailed. It is not therefore surprising that physicians perceive "underfunding," which places pressure on their productivity and earning ability at any given fee schedule.

The attack on universality, which masquerades as a claim that we cannot afford it, and emerges as a claim that we ought to spend more, thus has good solid roots in economic self-interest – not surprisingly, since by accounting definition every dollar of health expenditure is simultaneously a dollar of income to someone providing (directly or indirectly) health services. Cost containment is in aggregate income control, by definition.

But there is a strong ideological component as well. As noted above, universal, comprehensive public reimbursement imposes on the health care system priorities generated through the political process. The overwhelming popularity of Medicare in Canada makes it unlikely that the political system is doing a poor job of reflecting the views of the community at large. But professional ideology does not accept the legitimacy of these priorities. "Health should not be a political football" is an assertion of the superior legitimacy of priorities derived from professional opinion, regardless of what a duly elected government, or its electorate, may want. From this perspective, there is a basic ideological conflict between universality and the traditional professional claim of authority.

This claim, however, is also in conflict with the ideology which underlies the "financial press" hostility to universality. The latter holds that social priorities should be the outcome of decisions by individuals in the marketplace, that people should get what they are willing and able to pay for in a "free" market. (The institutional requirements of a "free" market, and the distributional implications of making access to health care dependent on ability to pay, are commonly either not understood or passed over in embarrassed silence.)

This is in sharp opposition not only to the expression of priorities through the collective, political process, but also to the professional determination of priorities on the basis of need. Few physicians would accept the view that the medical services "market" should be open to anyone who could find a customer, regardless of qualifications, or that people without resources should not receive care, whatever their needs. Both propositions are central to the "free market" ideology. Yet holders of these two conflicting ideologies are often allied in opposition to universality, probably because they have never thought their positions through beyond the rhetorical level, and do not understand their implications.

So far, however, universality in Canada has successfully met the repeated challenges thrown up by professional ideology and self-interest, and the much less serious grumbling by the ideologues of the market. If the analysis thus far is valid, such challenges must be expected to continue, but there is no reason why they should be any more successful in the future than in the past. The objective economic situation, on the other hand, supports rather than undermines universality – it is the best bargain around. Attacks on the costs of universal "social programs" from the business community, if extended to include Medicare, cast serious doubt on the relevance of the principle of enlightened self-interest.

LOOKING FORWARD, NOT BACK: THE REAL ISSUES IN AN AGING SOCIETY

Are there then no problems on the horizon, and can we regard the issue of universality versus selectivity as logically settled in health care? Well, no, not entirely. There are several problems for the health care system generally, which impinge directly on the long-run viability of universality, and which are also bound up with the ongoing aging of the population. These may be grouped under three heads.

First, as mentioned above, Canadian medical schools are currently turning out new physicians at a rate which, combined with residual immigration, is raising the supply by 1.5–2 per cent per capita per year. At the same time, demographic trends are having a comparatively trivial impact on physician use, about 0.3 per cent per capita per year. Population aging requires a redeployment of resources, at least in relative terms, away from physicians' services and over to what the British call the "Cinderella services" – long-term care, home care, mental health – where aging *is* having a significant impact on needs.

Yet the ever-expanding supply of physicians is creating a proportionate expansion in demand for physician incomes, i.e., expenditures on physicians' services. If expenditures are to increase for those services for which population aging does increase needs, and these are real and important, then either new resources must be added to the system as a whole, or physicians' average incomes must fall. Specifically, if per capita expenditures on physicians' services were to rise only at the 0.3 per cent implied by population aging, and numbers of physicians per capita continue to rise at nearly 2 per cent per year, average incomes per physician must fall at between 1 per cent and 1.5 per cent per year, more or less indefinitely. This mathematical inevitability goes far to explain claims of "underfunding."

Indeed what appears to be happening, as noted above, is that utilization patterns are shifting among the elderly in particular, so as to keep occupied the increasing numbers of new physicians. In addition to new procedures and technology, a substantial part of the increase is simply higher rates of office visits to GPs, particularly among older people. Rather than the aging population placing pressure on physician supply and costs, it is the increasing physician supply which is being accommodated by the increase in age-specific utilization rates among the elderly.

It is hard to see how an ever-increasing physician supply can be reconciled with continuing stability of cost patterns in the health insurance system as a whole, much less with expansion of those other services most used by older people. Universality may then be threatened by the "Sorcerer's Apprentice" of manpower policy, which creates (to mix a metaphor) what Reinhardt (1981) has described as ever more place settings at the health care feast. One could, of course, simply restrict the number of physicians permitted to bill the provincial plan – turn some would-be guests away from the table. But is British Columbia's policy still universal coverage? More to the point, if it continues to be upheld by the courts, it is very likely to spread. What happens then, if increasing numbers of physicians cannot gain access to the public plans, anywhere in Canada?

An alternative approach, of course, is to support increased numbers of physicians by withdrawing funds from other parts of the health system – in particular, hospitals. To some extent this may be happening indirectly, as elderly patients with long lengths of stay occupy an increasing share of hospital beds. But while this may mitigate cost problems, by converting acute care beds into de facto long-term care through inserting "bed blockers," it raises the important problem of appropriateness of care. This was discussed above in the evaluation of effectiveness of care. The second major issue to be confronted by a universal, comprehensive system is thus "universal access to what?"

The principle was built into Medicare from the beginning, that it provide universal access to *medically necessary* services. This excludes insurance examinations and other administrative activities, as well as obviously elective cosmetic surgery; it also provides a justification for limitations on the frequency of periodic health examinations. In general, however, medical necessity has been defined implicitly, by the willingness of the physician to provide or recommend a service, and of the patient to accept it. Yet the argument for effectiveness evaluation, or technological assessment, is based on the position that a good deal of current servicing is *not* medically necessary, although it may be provided in good faith.

This in turn implies that the individual clinician's judgment can be improved, with beneficial effects on both outcomes and costs. But how? The search for mechanisms, for transmission belts to carry the results of evaluation of technique into changes in patterns of medical practice, is a major and largely unmet challenge for the Medicare system, which may lead to a redefinition of the concept of universality in practice, though not, as noted above, in principle. Must a universal system reimburse services for which expert opinion judges there to be no evidence of efficacy, if clinician and patient believe them to be necessary? Which experts? ... what evidence? ... and which clinician?

Such questions lead one into the third and perhaps the most difficult area of all, particularly in the care of the elderly, the boundaries of health care itself. For the young and healthy, there is a clear demarcation between health care and "other things," such that there is little room for argument as to where universal entitlements end. But for the frail elderly person, the boundaries become much less clear. Does universal access to a single standard of hospital and medical care imply similar access to long-term care? Personal care? When does home care cease to be a health service and become a convenience or a social lifeline in loneliness and isolation?

The public system is intended to support health, not happiness. But if food, shelter, companionship, and activity are, for part of the population, decisive to health as well as happiness, what is the basis for their exclusion? Lines must be drawn, and are; but services for the elderly which fall into the economically favoured category of "health" may then squeeze out more valued, and even less expensive, services (or direct cash transfers) which do not as clearly meet that test.

These sorts of questions, the demarcation of the boundaries of health care, the determination of necessity of health services, and the reconciliation of manpower policy with spending control and the evolution of needs, are neither new nor surprising, just difficult. But they do represent significant conceptual and operational problems in the application of the principle of universality. They, not hypothetical economic constraints or ancient ideological objections, pose the really interesting problems to be resolved in the future evolution of our health care system.

Such questions are not peculiar to Canada. Virtually every nation in the developed world is facing a similar cluster of issues in health policy. And each, like Canada, is recognizing that the way ahead involves the development not only of programs and policies, but of new intellectual and conceptual frameworks for thinking about health in a broader social context, and about the nature of the interrelationships and obligations among the individual, the family – where one exists – and the wider society.

What distinguishes the Canadian situation, however, is that our solution to the earlier problem, of funding and delivering health care narrowly defined, has been one of the most successful in the world in reconciling and striking compromises among equity, access, quality, and affordability. Some other countries, most notably the US, are still struggling with the problems of the 1960s, although using the rhetoric and institutions of the 1980s. We are now in a position to go forward, and to find explicit ways of dealing with the questions which were left implicit, swept under the rug, in the establishment of the Medicare system.

This is enough of a challenge that we cannot afford to allow ourselves to be distracted by attempts to reopen old issues, and to roll back the progress that has already been made, based on superficial reasoning and faulty or nonexistent data. Nor should we, either explicitly or implicitly, try to "blame" our elderly population (whom we in due course hope to join). The growth in their numbers is focusing and making explicit issues and questions which were inherent in our system from the beginning, but the stresses developing in health care are traceable to the behaviour of that system itself, not external demographic pressures. In a sense, the elderly are the messengers, showing us what the next set of social tasks will be. To succeed, we have to get the message straight.

The research underlying this paper was supported by the National Health Research and Development Program through a Research Scientist Award. The paper was presented at a conference on "Health Care for the Elderly in the Year 2000," November 1986, in Victoria, BC.

NOTES

1 The two factors have quite different effects on the age distribution. A fall in births triggers a rise in the average age of the population, but has no effect on the numbers of elderly people. Falling age-specific mortality among the aged, on the other hand, has immediate effects on the numbers and proportion of

elderly people in the population, even though its influence on the overall average age of the population may be less pronounced.

2 Most projections show the major increase in the proportion of "old-old," 75+ or 85+, taking place by 2000. But these projections are very sensitive to underlying assumptions about future age-specific mortality rates for this group, assumptions which at this point are little more than guesses.

3 The argument is not specific to the Canadian experience; it is in fact a general critique of the possibility or desirability of cost containment in any health care system. In Canada the debate focuses on universality and the role of governments because of the obvious success of the public insurance programs in containing costs. But the "painful prescription" arguments in the US, which allege the inevitability of rationing of access to lifesaving and life-improving interventions, have an identical structure, and offer the same grim trade-off between increasing economic strain and accumulating unmet need.

4 This is not to suggest that anyone believes age-specific use patterns, or costs, *will* in fact remain constant; almost certainly they will not. But the assumption of constancy enables one to isolate the pure effect of aging per se from all the other factors which might impinge on average per capita use or costs.

5 In the zero-growth days of the early 1980s, there was much concern that the future would not be like the past, and that increasing health care costs would have to be funded out of a constant or declining per capita income. But as we emerge from the Great Recession of 1982, historical growth trends are reasserting themselves.

6 There are of course other considerations. Categorical programs may bring in the problems of "means testing" – high administrative overheads, social stigma, and low uptake rates, and arbitrary administrative limitations on access – if eligibility status is difficult to monitor. Moreover, universality maintains political constituencies in support of programs; categorization identifies beneficiaries as "them," not "us," and may lead to progressive erosion of benefits and eventual program emasculation or termination.

7 US data in these charts are drawn from tables provided with a press release, "HHS NEWS," issued 29 July 1986 by the Department of Health and Human Services, containing preliminary 1985 data by expenditure component, and revised total expenditures from 1978. Expenditures by component from 1980 to 1984 are from Table 2 of Levit et al. (1985: 1–35); components from 1965 to 1979 and totals from 1965 to 1977 are from Table 2 of Gibson et al. (1984: 1–29); earlier data back to 1948 are from Cooper et al. (1973). Revised GNP data are from US Department of Commerce (1986: 17–23), with additional minor revisions to the 1983–85 data provided by

K.R. Levit of HCFA, as of August 1986. Canadian data from 1975 to 1985 are pre-publication tabulations of recent revisions and updates made available by Health and Welfare Canada, Health Information Division, as of September 1986. Data from 1970 to 1975 are from Health and Welfare Canada [n.d. (1984)]. Earlier data are from Health and Welfare Canada (1979), and R.D. Fraser, "Vital Statistics and Health" (Series B504-B513), in Leacy, (ed.) (1983). Canadian data on National Health Expenditures (NHE) comparable to those for the US were not compiled prior to 1960; the Personal Health Care (PHC) series shown in Figure 5.1 from 1948 to 1985 includes only costs of hospitals, services of physicians and dentists, and prescription drugs.

8 There is, however, a very large difference in the amount which is spent in each system on the costs of administering the payment process. In 1985, costs of prepayment and administration in the Canadian system (including estimated costs of government programs, as well as remaining private sector insurance) were $20.88 per person (CAD) or 0.11 per cent of GNP. The corresponding US figure was $106.12 (USD) per capita, or 0.66 per cent of GNP. In 1960 the two proportions were almost the same. Thus roughly a quarter of the cost difference between Canada and the US is the much higher overhead costs of running the US system which have developed in the last 25 years.

9 Evans (1987: 585–616); also unpublished data assembled by U.E. Reinhardt, Princeton University. The recession of 1982 reduced incomes in both countries, but hardly touched either health care sector; thus 1982 saw a sharp jump in the health care share of national income on both sides of the border. The recession also significantly reduced the rate of price inflation, world-wide, including the rate of price inflation in US health care. But the key point is that, while all prices are now rising more slowly, US medical prices are still rising more rapidly than the general price level, and by the same or a greater margin.

10 Unfortunately the cost savings were almost entirely offset by increases in prepayment and administration costs, from $14.5 billion in 1983 to $26.2 billion in 1985, suggesting that this mode of control may be effective but a Pyrrhic victory (Evans, 1987). It is, however, early days yet.

11 There are, of course, "dead-weight" costs of administering the program itself, plus potential costs resulting from perverse incentives in the tax or benefit system, but these are of second order or less (Culyer, 1986).

12 Canadian Medical Association, *Evidence Presented to the Special Committee on the Federal-Provincial Fiscal Arrangements*, House of

Commons, Canada, Minutes of Proceedings and Evidence, Issue no. 10, 10–3 to 10–54 and 10A–1 to 10A–44, Tuesday, 12 May 1981, First Session, Thirty-Second Parliament, 1980–81. This is only the most detailed of a number of claims of "underfunding" made by physicians' representatives, with the associated argument that more "private funding" – direct charges to patients with or without private insurance – will remedy the situation. But such claims are commonly unclear as to whether the alleged problem is undersupply of health services, or insufficient incomes for physicians. The most bitterly defended form of "private funding," extra-billing by physicians, addresses only the latter issue.

13 There is one qualification to this point. Conceivably, if public funding were associated with a much larger bureaucratic overhead of administrative and other non-patient care expenses than a private system, the community might not be able, or at least wise, to spend more through the public, tax-financed channel. It is apparently widely believed among providers that this is the case, that the government bureaucracy squanders funds, and is a major contributor to upward pressures on health costs (Taylor, Stevenson, and Williams, 1984). Yet the facts are entirely otherwise – public administration is remarkably cheap (notes 8 and 10 above). By 1985, the multiple funding source US system spent $26.2 billion, or about 6 per cent of all health costs, on prepayment and administration costs explicitly identified. A great deal more was buried in hospital and medical practice budgets. The corresponding Canadian percentage is just over 1 per cent for a substantially larger prepaid share of a smaller total health budget.

14 The process of apparently unbounded cost escalation which seems to be implicit in professionals' priorities may however contain the seeds of its own destruction. This is suggested by the radical transformations occurring in the US health care system, whose consequences will arguably be harmful to professionals and patients alike. But that revolution is still in progress.

15 Interestingly, the assumption is not only that the community *ought* to spend more, but that in fact it would wish to, if not constrained by universality and the misplaced priorities of the political system. This implies a positive, not a normative, critique of the political system, that it fails adequately to aggregate and reflect the priorities of the community, and that professional providers are better able to do so. (Alternatively it could be based on the normative judgment that it really does not matter what the community wants; what they ought to get is what professionals think is good for them, which is different in principle but reduces to much the same thing in practice.) One is reminded of Churchill's observation that

democracy is the worst of all political systems, except for all the others we know about.

16 In this context, it is large markets like the US, Japan, or Germany which matter. Their modes of reimbursement motivate the technology industry, and influence the evolution of "best practice" medicine, which then is carried over into small markets like Canada.

17 Data are in Barer and Evans (1987), and updated in Evans (1987).

18 In principle, this need not be true. Control of fees could lead, for example, to physicians leaving practice, or emigrating, or to reduced enrolments in medical schools, such that capacity and utilization fell. In the event, this has not happened.

19 Hospital utilization is traditionally measured by separations or patient-days per capita; on these measures utilization has always been and still is higher in Canada than in the US. But the service content, the number, complexity, and cost of procedures per patient day, is higher in the US, and the gap has been widening (Barer and Evans, 1987; see also Detsky, Stacey, and Bombardier, 1983).

20 Comparative data on mortality, morbidity, and health services utilization in Canada and the US, and data on the extent of variation in patterns of medical practice in both countries, are extensive but widely scattered through the health services literature. A recent summary of some of the principal comparisons, however, is provided by R.N. Battista, R.A. Spasoff, and W.O. Spitzer, "Choice of technique: Patterns of diffusion in medical practices." in Evans and Stoddart (1987). A survey and interpretation of findings on variations in medical practice patterns, with primary but not exclusive emphasis on the US, is Eisenberg (1986).

21 If, however, multiple-source funding under professional direction results in permanent cost escalation, then the logical outcome of non-universality may be eventual corporate control of medicine, and substantially worse conditions for physicians. But that may lie a (lucrative) generation away. The American physicians who fought off national health insurance in the 1960s and early 1970s will be living on their investments by the time (if) their successors are wage-slaves.

22 Both analysis [A. Williams, "Need: An economic exegesis." In Culyer and Wright (eds.), 1978: 32–45] and US experience suggest, however, that professional priorities of "meeting all needs," in a professionally satisfying manner, provide no upper limit to the size and share of the health care system. If so, then in the long run professional control *must* come under external limitations – the trees do not grow to the sky. The only question is whether these limits will reflect priorities generated through the political

process, as in Canada, or through some restructured private market, such as the US is trying to create. But the results of these two alternatives are very different; moreover a great deal can happen on the way to the long run.

23 If average incomes are rising economy-wide, physician incomes might fall only in relative terms. But the essential mathematical relationship is unaffected; global cost control implies that an increase in numbers of income recipients must lead to a corresponding decrease in average incomes. And universality as applied in Canada is the most effective form of global cost control yet known.

24 The increased numbers of visits to GPs by elderly people, for example (Roch et al., 1985), may be described as "preventive," though no evidence of their effectiveness is provided, and they are reimbursed without question. But social programs which may be equally effective (or ineffective) in preventing physical or mental deterioration are not included in the concept of "universality."

REFERENCES

Barer, M.L., and R.G. Evans (1986). "Riding north on a south-bound horse? Expenditures, prices, utilization and incomes in the Canadian health care system," in Evans and Stoddart (1986).

– R.G. Evans, C. Hertzman, and J. Lomas (1987). "Aging and health care utilization: New evidence on old fallacies," *Social Science and Medicine* 24(10): 851–62

Battista, R.N., R.A. Spasoff, and W.O. Spitzer (1986). "Choice of technique: Patterns of diffusion in medical practices," in Evans and Stoddart (1986).

Cooper, B.S., et al. (1973). *Compendium of national health expenditures data* (Washington: US Department of Health, Education and Welfare), DHEW Pub. No. (SSA), 73–11903.

Culyer, A.J. (1986). "The withering of the welfare state?" and "whither the welfare state?" The E.S. Woodward Lectures in Economics, February 1985. Vancouver: UBC Department of Economics.

– and K.G. Wright, eds. (1978). *Economic aspects of health services* (London: Martin Robertson).

Detsky, A.S., S.R. Stacey, and C. Bombardier (1983). "The effectiveness of a regulatory strategy in containing hospital costs." *New England Journal of Medicine* 309(3): 151–9.

Eisenberg, J.M. (1986). *Doctors' decisions and the cost of medical care.* Ann Arbor, MI: Health Administration Press.

Evans, R.G. (1983a). "We have seen the future and they is us: Health care and the greying of Canada," UBC Department of Economics Discussion Paper 84-02, December.

– (1983b) "The welfare economics of public health insurance: Theory and Canadian practice." In *Social insurance*, ed. L. Soderstrom, 71–103. Amsterdam: North-Holland.

– (1984). *Strained mercy: The economics of Canadian health care*. Toronto: Butterworths.

– (1985). "Illusions of necessity: Avoiding responsibility for choice in health care." *Journal of Health Politics, Policy and Law* 10(3): 439–67.

– (1987). "Finding the levers, finding the courage: Lessons from cost containment in North America." *Journal of Health Politics, Policy and Law* 11(4): 585–616.

– and G.L. Stoddart, eds. (1986). *Medicare at maturity: Achievements, lessons & challenges* Calgary: University of Calgary Press.

Feeny, D., G. Guyatt, and P. Tugwell (1986). *Health care technology: effectiveness, efficiency, and public policy*. Halifax: Institute for Research on Public Policy.

Fraser, R.D. (1983). "Vital statistics and health." In *Historical statistics of Canada* (Series B504-B513) (2nd ed.), ed. F.H. Leacy. Ottawa: Statistics Canada and SSHRC.

Fuchs, V.R. (1986) "'Though much is taken': Reflections on aging, health, and medical care." *Milbank Memorial Fund Quarterly* 62(2): 143–66.

Gibson, R.M., et al. (1984). "National health expenditures, 1983," *Health Care Financing Review* 6(1): 1–29.

Health and Welfare Canada (1979) *National health expenditures in Canada, 1960–1975*. Ottawa: HWC.

– (n.d.) *National health expenditures in Canada 1970 to 1982*. Ottawa: HWC [1984].

Levit, K.R., et al. (1985). "National health expenditures, 1984," *Health Care Financing Review* 7(1): 1–35.

Reinhardt, U.E. (1981). "Table manners at the healthcare feast: 'Regulation' vs 'market,'" *National Journal* 13(19): 855–61.

Roch, D.R., R.G. Evans, and D.J. Pascoe (1985). *Manitoba and Medicare: 1971 to the present*. Winnipeg: Manitoba Health.

Roos, N.P., E. Shapiro, and B. Havens (1986). "Aging with limited resources: What should we really be worried about?" Paper presented at the Economic Council of Canada Colloquium on Aging with Limited Resources, Winnipeg, 5–6 May.

Taylor, M.G., H.M. Stevenson, and A.P. Williams (1984). *Medical perspectives on Canadian Medicare: Attitudes of Canadian physicians to policies and problems of the medical care insurance program*. Toronto: York University.

US Department of Commerce (1986). "Selected national income and product estimates, 1929–85," *Survey of Current Business*. Washington: US Department of Commerce (February).

Williams, A. (1978). "Need: An economic exegesis." In Calyer and Wright (1978).

Woods, Gordon Management Consultants (1984). *Investigation of the impact of demographic change on the health care system in Canada: Final report*. A Study prepared for the Task Force on the Allocation of Health Care Resources, Canadian Medical Association (August).

6

User Fees for Health Care: Why a Bad Idea Keeps Coming Back (Or, What's Health Got to Do With It?) (1995)

ROBERT G. EVANS, MORRIS L. BARER, AND GREG L. STODDART

WHAT'S IT ALL ABOUT?

Calls for user fees in Canadian health care go back as far as the debate leading up to the establishment of Canada's national hospital insurance program in the late 1950s, and they have been with us ever since. The rationales for introducing user fees have shifted around somewhat over the past 40 years; some of the more consistent claims have been that they are necessary as a source of additional revenue for a badly underfunded system, that they are necessary to control runaway health care costs, and that they will deter unnecessary use (read abuse) of the system. In this paper we offer a somewhat different perspective on the longevity of these arguments. There are good and logical reasons for their staying power, but the reasons bear little relation to the claims commonly made for user fees. The introduction of user fees in the financing of hospital or medical care in Canada would be to the benefit of a number of groups,

Evans, Robert G., Morris L. Barer, and Greg L. Stoddart. "User Fees for Health Care: Why a Bad Idea Keeps Coming Back (or, What's Health Got to Do with It?)." *Canadian Journal on Aging/La Revue canadienne du vieillissement* 14(2) (Summer 1995): 360–90.

and not just those one usually thinks of. We show that those who are healthy, and wealthy, would join health care providers (and possibly insurers) as net beneficiaries of a reintroduction of user fees for hospital and medical care in Canada. The flip side of this is that those who are indigent and ill will bear the brunt of the redistribution (for that is really what user fees are all about), and seniors feature prominently in those latter groups.

In subsequent sections of the paper we develop this argument in more detail, we review some evidence from the United States showing the clearly regressive nature of non-tax health care financing, we point out that whether one is for or against user fees reduces to whether one is for or against the resulting income redistribution (that is, it is an issue of values, not analysis), and we offer an explanation for why many well-meaning non-wealthy citizens may, in fact, express support for the idea of having "those who can afford to pay" do so.

In the course of discussing the latter, we analyze a number of non-distributional claims in support of user fees – that they will reduce (increase) total health care costs, that they will improve the appropriateness and effectiveness of health care, and that they will make health care more accessible to those who "really need" it most. These claims can be assessed through analysis and evidence; our judgment is that claims of general benefit do not stand up.

USER FEES AND COST SHIFTING

Many Canadians would benefit from the introduction of user charges for Medicare services. Many others would be hurt. These two propositions are logically linked, and are in no way mysterious. The benefits gained by one group *are* the costs imposed on the other.

The primary effect of substituting user fees for tax finance is *cost-shifting* – the transfer of the burden of paying for health care from tax-payers to users of care. Of course in any given year most of the population both pays taxes and uses care, but different people do so in very different amounts. Taken in total, people pay (all types of) taxes in rough proportion to their incomes, and use health care in rough proportion to their health status or need for care – in general, sicker people use more health care, and richer people pay more taxes.

It follows that when health care is paid for from taxes, people with higher incomes pay a larger share of the total cost; when it is paid for by the users, sick people pay a larger share. If user fees are increased, the amount of taxation required to finance a given level of health care will fall, reducing the burden on those with higher incomes and tax liabilities, and raising the burden on those with greater needs for, or at least greater use of, care services.[1] Some gain, some lose.

The key point to bear in mind is that, as the ecologists and the accountants remind us, it is impossible to do only one thing. If you raise more revenues for health care through user fees, then you will raise less (than you otherwise would have) through some other channel (unless of course total costs go up in response to the user fee – see below). Since the Canadian system, like that of almost every other country in the developed world, is predominantly tax financed, that other channel will be taxation. At any given level of health care spending, the introduction of user fees *must* lead to a need for less tax revenue.

Whether one is a gainer or a loser, then, depends upon where one is located in the distribution of both income – or at least tax liability – and health – or at least use of care services. In general, a shift to more user fee financing redistributes net income (net, that is, of contributions to financing health care, through both taxes and user fees) from lower- to higher-income people, and from sicker to healthier people. The wealthy and healthy gain, the poor and sick lose. Conversely, the introduction of Medicare, a tax-financed system, had the effect of transferring (net) income the other way.

What about the wealthy but unhealthy, or the healthy but unwealthy? Among people at the same level of taxable income, user fees transfer net income from higher users to lower users.[2] Among people at the same level of health – or at least of care use – user fees transfer income from those with lower to those with higher incomes.[3] In general and under quite simple assumptions, you will gain from the introduction of user fees if your share of total tax payments is greater than your share of total health care expenditure, and will lose otherwise (Evans, Barer, and Stoddart, 1994).

If health and income were negatively correlated – people at higher incomes being sicker – the distributional effects of higher fees and lower taxes would tend to cancel out, at least in part. But as it happens, health and income are positively correlated, reinforcing the extent of cost shifting. Note, however, that the cost shifting effect does *not* depend upon this positive correlation. Even if health and income bore no relation to each other, taxes still correlate positively – and quite closely – with income, and care use correlates with illness. So net income will be shifted, on average, from those with high use to those with high incomes.

This pattern of cost shifting is true for *all* user charge schemes which have been proposed. Schemes to exempt those at lowest incomes, or to link charges to taxable income, mitigate but do not reverse the effect. It is not difficult to show (and should be intuitively obvious in any case) that if some are exempt, the same pattern of cost shifting occurs but within the non-exempt group, while if charges are in some way linked to income (as through integrating them with the income tax system) net income is still transferred not only from users to non-users, but also from lower- to higher-income people. Even though user fees linked to income would bear more heavily on them, high-income users also gain more from tax reductions. (Recall that here and subsequently we are referring to reductions in the taxes *required to finance health care*. See note 1.) If your income is high enough, you still come out ahead (Evans, Barer, and Stoddart, 1994).

USER CHARGES, PREMIUMS, AND TAXES: WHO PAYS AND HOW MUCH?

Data from the 1987 National Medical Expenditure Survey in the United States, where user charges are a prominent feature of health care financing, show this effect very clearly. Figure 6.1, reproduced from Rasell, Bernstein, and Tang (1993), provides a breakdown of family expenditures for health care by form of payment (out-of-pocket, insurance premiums, and taxes) and by income level. The authors caution that income data for the lowest 10 per cent of families, #10, may be especially subject to error, so focus attention on the next highest group (#9, families in the bottom 20 per cent of incomes, but not in the bottom 10 per cent) in comparing low- with high-income families. They also divide the top 10 per cent of families into the top 5 per cent and the next 5 per cent, groups 1a and 1b.

When families are ranked by income, there is a pronounced and consistent negative relationship between income level and per cent of income spent on health care. The pattern is strongest for out-of-pocket charges; families in the second lowest decile spend 8.5 per cent of their income on such charges as compared with 1 per cent for the top 5 per cent of families. But insurance premiums are almost as regressive, taking 7.9 per cent of income at the ninth decile, and only 2 per cent at the top end, even though many low-income people (and very few at high incomes) had no insurance coverage.[4] Taxes for health care redress the balance somewhat, but only somewhat. They take a larger share as income increases (except for the rather odd data reported at the bottom end) but are tilted much less steeply than the other forms of health care spending.

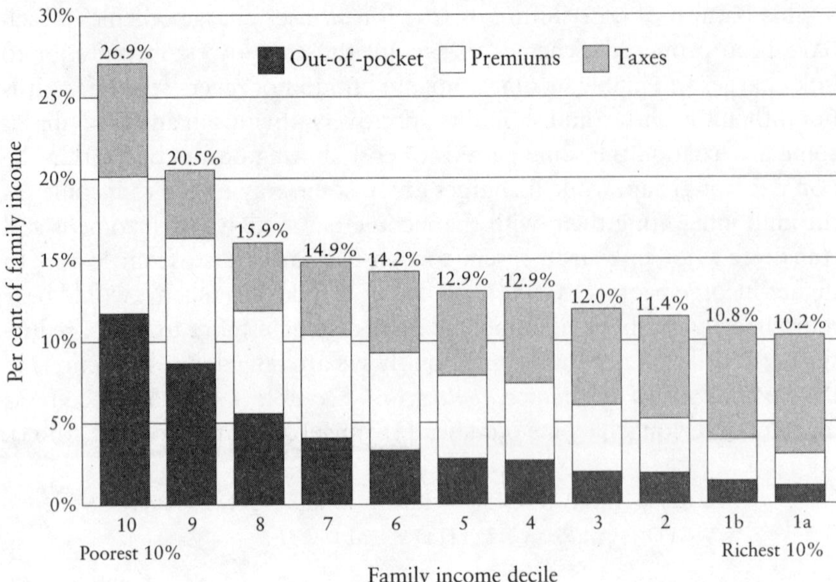

Figure 6.1 US family expenditures for health care, 1987 (by family income decile)

Adapted from: Robert G. Evans, Morris L. Barer, and Greg L. Stoddart. "User Fees for Health Care: Why a Bad Idea Keeps Coming Back (or, What's Health Got to Do With It?)" *Canadian Journal on Aging* 14(2)(1995): 360–90.
Original source: Rasell, et al. (1993). Reprinted with permission of the Economic Policy Institute.

As a result, Americans at the top of the income distribution spend about half as large a *share* of their income on health care as those near the bottom, even though they actually spend much more in dollars. Total spending rises steadily from $1,756 per family in the ninth decile ($960 in the tenth) to $13,234 in the top 5 per cent of families (Rasell et al., 1993), and most of the difference is a result of the higher taxes paid by those with higher incomes. The actual differences in out-of-pocket spending per family, as one moves up the income distribution, are relatively small. The more one relies on out-of-pocket payments to finance health care, the greater the relative burden on those at lower incomes; the more one relies on taxation (at least of income and consumption), the greater the burden borne at upper incomes.

Figure 6.2 disaggregates further, by age of head of household – over and under 65. The regressivity of private funding for health care in the United States is even more marked among the elderly population, despite the fact that the federal Medicare program covers virtually everyone

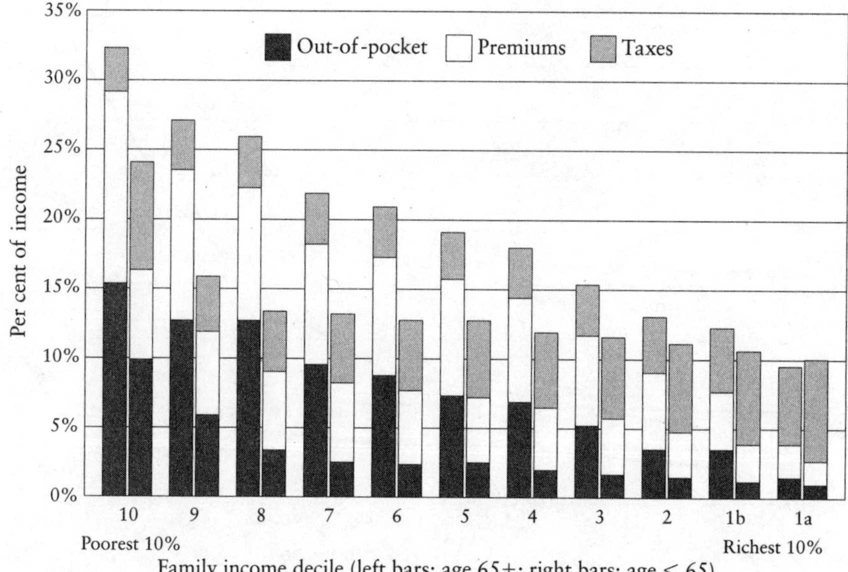

Figure 6.2 US family expenditures for health care by income decile and age of head

Adapted from: Robert G. Evans, Morris L. Barer, and Greg L. Stoddart. "User Fees for Health Care: Why a Bad Idea Keeps Coming Back (or, What's Health Got to Do With It?)." *Canadian Journal on Aging* 14(2)(1995): 360–90.
Original source: Rasell, et al. (1993). Reprinted with permission of the Economic Policy Institute.

over 65. Why? Because that program requires people to pay substantial user fees – deductibles and coinsurance – and in consequence most elderly Americans purchase private "Medigap" insurance to cover some part of those costs.

On average, elderly American families in 1987 paid $1,407 for insurance premiums, almost exactly the same as the $1,471 paid by non-elderly families, to fill in the holes opened in their "universal" public insurance program by user fees! Private insurance expenditures rise with income, and there is surprisingly little difference at each income level between the dollar outlays of elderly and of non-elderly families. Because the average income of elderly families is lower, however, these outlays represented 8.3 per cent of their incomes, compared with 4.9 per cent for the non-elderly.

Despite the combination of the "universal" Medicare program and private insurance to cover its gaps, elderly Americans still spent, on average, $1,239, or 8.3 per cent of their incomes, in out-of-pocket payments for health care, compared with $712, or 3.2 per cent, for the non-elderly. As

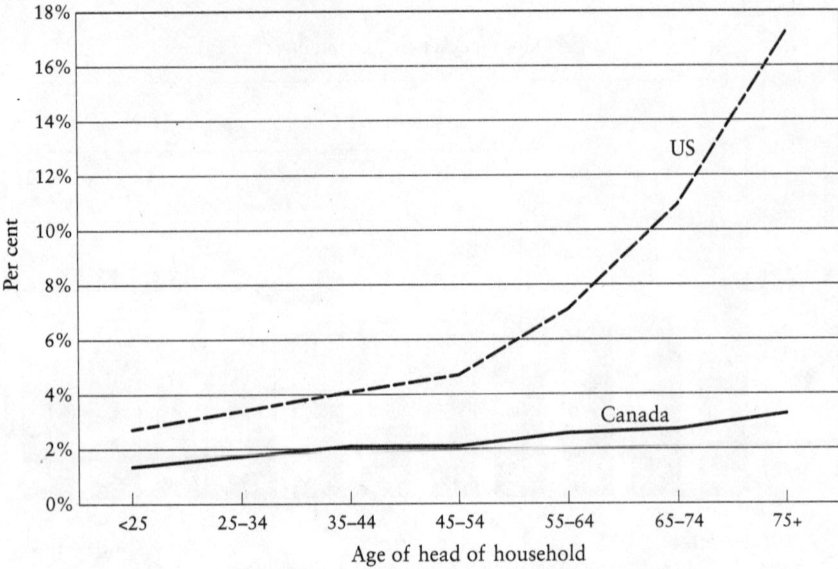

Figure 6.3 Household spending on health care as share of personal consumption, 1986

Adapted from: Robert G. Evans, Morris L. Barer, and Greg L. Stoddart. "User Fees for Health Care: Why a Bad Idea Keeps Coming Back (or, What's Health Got to Do With It?)." *Canadian Journal on Aging* 14(2)(1995): 360–90.
Original source: Torrey and Jacobs (1993), copyrighted and published by Project HOPE/HealthAffairs and archived and available online at www.healthaffairs.org. Reprinted with permission.

a share of their incomes, elderly people in the second-lowest decile spent 12.7 per cent out-of-pocket, compared with 1.5 per cent in the highest-income group. The corresponding values for the non-elderly were 5.9 per cent and 0.9 per cent.

The heavy burden of private health care spending by the elderly has no counterpart in Canada (Barer, Hertzman, Miller, and Pascali, 1992). Torrey and Jacobs (1993) have analyzed data from 1986 family expenditure surveys in Canada and the United States to compare the proportion of personal health care spending to total personal consumption by families with different ages of family head. They report out-of-pocket spending on health care, and health insurance, but not taxes. Their findings are summarized in a graph reproduced here as Figure 6.3.

In both countries, health care and privately purchased health insurance take up an increasing proportion of consumer spending as the household (head) ages. But the percentage in Canada rises from 1.5 per cent for the youngest Canadian families to 3.2 per cent for the oldest; in the United States it starts at 2.8 per cent and rises to 17.1 per cent! The much greater reliance on "user pay" in the American system places a much greater financial burden on those with the greatest needs.

Canadians might draw several lessons from the American experience with private health care financing:

1 The lower (higher) one's income, the larger (smaller) the share taken by private financing, whether user pay or insurance. Only public sector (tax) financing introduces a progressive element;
2 This regressivity is most pronounced among the elderly. In every income class except the very highest, private payments in the United States take about *twice* as large a share from the elderly as from the non-elderly;
3 These shares are *large* in both dollar and percentage terms;
4 Although elderly Americans have (almost) universal public coverage against hospital and medical expenses, the user fees in that system have grown steadily over time and are now large enough to produce the patterns found by Rasell et al. (1993).

COST SHIFTING: PRIMARY OBJECTIVE OR UNFORTUNATE SIDE EFFECT?

Is the pattern of cost shifting which would result from user fees a good thing or a bad thing? Well, where you stand depends to some extent upon where you sit. But most people in the modern world seem to believe, or say when asked, that health care should be available on the basis of need, and paid for on the basis of ability to pay (van Doorslaer, Wagstaff, and Rutten, 1993). That is consistent with the predominance of tax finance.[5]

But if one holds, as a matter of principle or values, that net incomes *should* be transferred from the poor and sick (possibly excluding the *very* poor and the *very* sick) to the healthy and wealthy (with greatest gains to the *very* wealthy and *very* healthy), then there is no analytic basis on which one can disagree. User fees will indeed help to do that job.

The cost shifting effects of user fees are so obvious, once one thinks about them, that there has been very little debate on the subject. Opponents talk about "taxes on the sick"; advocates talk about something else. Even among economists, there has been very little controversy, with advocates analyzing the putative benefits of such fees while "ignor[ing] distributional considerations and assum[ing] a single person in the economy" (Arrow, 1976, 4).[6] Rather, the controversy and the empirical analysis have focused on other effects which user fees are alleged to have on the functioning of health care systems.

Whatever the position that one takes on these more contentious issues, the distributional effects are *always* there, in *any* user fee system. They may be greater or less, depending upon the exact form of the charges and upon the distribution of health care use and of taxable incomes in the population. One may try, empirically, to measure their strength, but one cannot measure or analyze them out of existence, because they cannot *not* be there. Nor can one evaluate them "objectively"; the policy issue boils down to a question of values. Who *should* gain, and who *should* lose? (When people's answers to these questions are stripped of their rhetorical camouflage, they often come down to "Me and my friends," and "You and yours.")

Moreover, the persistence of the topic of user fees on the health care policy agenda, its zombie-like quality (no matter how many times it is killed intellectually, it never goes away), is readily understandable when one considers that a number of people *do* stand to gain, and some to gain handsomely, from the introduction of such fees. Transferring income from one's neighbour's pocket to one's own has always been a popular enterprise. In a time of generally "diminished expectations," a shift in the direction of user fee finance will diminish *someone else's* expectations.

Much of the controversy around the other claimed effects of user fees, positive and negative, arises from the political necessity either of convincing one's neighbour that policies which will have this effect are a "good idea" on more general grounds, or at least of keeping him/her confused and disorganized while one assembles a sufficiently powerful constituency to put through the necessary changes.

But it would be both unduly cynical, and worse, factually wrong, to assume that such a constituency would be made up only of potential gainers, all motivated by a clear understanding of their own interests and a corresponding disregard for those of anyone else. Only economists imagine that the world works that way; others have a more nuanced view. Surveys do reveal a consistent positive correlation between income and support for user fees. But if people's political stances were always and only based on a (correct) appreciation of their own interests, it is doubtful if Medicare could ever have come into being in the first place. (Nor would there be much point in writing this paper.)[7]

A more realistic view might be that while energetic and consistent advocacy of user fees is usually, if not always, powered by hope of gain, there is a further and possibly larger group of more passive supporters of user fees who also see themselves as committed to the *support* of the principles of Medicare. They are willing to make some personal sacrifice to ensure that the health care system has sufficient resources to meet the needs of Canadians. If that personal sacrifice includes a user fee paid by those "able to pay," because public (tax) resources are strained to the limit, well, maintaining an excellent system is worth the price.

In an atmosphere of intense "crisis" rhetoric, focusing on both deficits and health care, such a response appears reasonable, responsible, and even generous. Sadly, it is also profoundly misled. Well-meaning and public-spirited intentions play into the hands of those who *do* have a clear sense of what they hope to gain from user fees – those whom Michael Rachlis has referred to as an "Unholy Alliance" of physician associations, private insurers, and some provincial governments.

Such "well-meaning" or "principled" (non-selfish) support for user fees is based on two distinct types of error. It confuses self-seeking rhetoric with established reality; and it fails to consider certain fundamental accounting relationships. These two forms of error are woven together to create the argument that user fees are needed to "save" Medicare.

The self-seeking rhetoric takes two forms. Providers of care call for ever more resources to meet ever greater needs, while taxpayers grumble and protest that they are "taxed to the limit," that any more taxation will lead to various forms of disaster and ruin. Both claims are ancient, though they have become more urgent and strident as general rates of economic growth have declined. Neither has any empirical foundation. No levels of either health spending or taxation (short of infinity or zero respectively) will ever completely satisfy providers or taxpayers. The real issues are of political choice: "How much do we want to spend, and on what?" and "How and from whom do we want to raise the money?" Claims of "crisis," and of allegedly objective "needs" and "limits," are simply part of the process of political persuasion – "Give us more" on one side, and "Take less from us" on the other.

The accounting relationships which are relevant to this discussion are that, by definition: (1) (health care) expenditures must equal (health care) incomes, and (2) revenues must equal expenditures.[8]

The implications of the second identity have been emphasized above – whatever the level of health expenditure may be, the more money that is raised through user charges, the less need be raised through taxes. So it is not true that user charges are a way whereby those of us who can afford it can help out the health care system, and provide for our less fortunate fellow citizens. We will be helping out some of our fellow citizens, indeed, but as pointed out above, *not* the less fortunate (unless one regards those who pay the highest taxes as the less fortunate). User charges result, not in *shared* sacrifice, but in *shifted* sacrifice.

If the objective is in fact to increase health care spending (that is, to maintain its historic rates of growth) faster than the rest of the economy, then *someone* has to bear the additional burden. But there is no *theoretical* external, binding limit on taxable capacity, and no *empirical* evidence suggesting that we are close to one in practice. The international evidence is conclusive on this latter point – a number of countries impose taxes considerably higher than those in Canada. There may, at any point in time, be (or be a perception of) a political limit on the taxability of the public. But any such political constraint is going to be rather fluid – yesterday's outrageous taxes often look pretty good today.

The political *choice* of more taxation versus user fees is a choice as to who will bear that additional burden. Those who would have the most to lose from increased taxation have an obvious interest in convincing the rest of us that this option is not only undesirable, but impossible – "we're at the limit – it's tax revolt time!"

But who is it who says that health care expenditure *should* be increased? Here the relevant identity is that every dollar of expenditure is simultaneously a dollar of someone's income. More money for health care does not necessarily translate into more health care; it also supports higher prices for health care services, and higher incomes for those who produce them. When "we" all dig a bit deeper to support Medicare, some of us are paying more, others of us are *being paid* more. Again, what is presented as a "shared sacrifice" by those of "us" able to pay, turns out instead to be an income transfer with clearly defined gainers and losers.[9] The argument that health care is "underfunded" has always come from those whose jobs and incomes are in the health care sector.

That is not, of course, the whole story. Although income aspirations are a major component of the "underfunding" claim, and always have been, there is more. What we have called the "principled" (as opposed to the "interested") argument for user fees, still expresses a concern, understandable amid the rhetoric of "health care crises," that some people's health is being put at risk by "shortages," "cutbacks," and inadequate resources. This takes us beyond the re-distributional impact of user fees – their role in transferring money from one set of pockets to another – and into the more murky and contentious area of their effects on health care and on health.

BEYOND COST SHIFTING: WHAT OTHER EFFECTS OF USER FEES?

Advocates and opponents of user fees have alleged any number of positive and negative effects; the assessment of such claims is made difficult not only by their variety but also by the diversity of different forms in which such charges have been proposed. It seems to us, however, that one can group the alleged "other effects" of user fees (other than re-distribution, that is) under three heads. Such charges are alleged to lead to changes in:

- Total health care expenditures or costs;
- Appropriateness or effectiveness of health care; and
- Accessibility of health care to different people.

User Fees and Health Care Costs

A peculiar feature of the discussion of user fees is that they have been advocated as a policy *both* to control or reduce health care costs *and* to remedy alleged "underfunding" by generating more revenues for health care (Barer et al., 1994). It should be obvious that both cannot be true. Yet those who base their advocacy on the first argument never challenge those making the second, nor vice versa; rather, both make common cause.

The standard "cost control" argument proceeds in simple steps:

1 Health care costs are "exploding" out of control, beyond our ability to pay;
2 This is because individuals are making ever-increasing use of the health care system – "demands";
3 If people had to pay some part of the costs of health care out of their own pockets they would "think twice" about using care, and be less likely to "make demands" on the health care system; and,
4 Total utilization and costs of health care would then fall, or at least be less than otherwise. QED.

This "common sense" argument turns out to be much more common than sense. Studies of health care utilization and costs, in Canada and elsewhere, sustain point (3) to some degree (Stoddart, Barer, and Evans, 1994), but refute points (1), (2), and (4). In particular (4) does *not*, as is commonly imagined, follow logically from (3). This assumption is an elementary "fallacy of composition" against which students are supposed to be warned at the beginning of first-year courses in Economics. In fact the national and international evidence shows that user fees are associated with *higher* and less controllable costs; and this relationship appears to be causal.[10]

On the first point, health care costs in Canada are *not* rising faster now than over the past 20 years, and on average have risen considerably less fast since the completion of universal coverage in 1971 than in the previous decades. What *has* happened is that since 1980 the growth of the overall Canadian economy (and that of most other western economies) has slowed markedly. Health care costs are not "exploding," just continuing to rise at the same rate they always have. But our ability, or more accurately our willingness, to pay these ever increasing amounts, in our more straitened circumstances, is now less.

This does not mean that there is not a problem of limiting the growth of our health care system to fit within our more limited capacities – there is, and it is a serious problem. But it has *not* been created by some change in the behaviour of the health care system itself, let alone some change resulting from public financing. On the contrary, public tax-based financing, in Canada and abroad, has been associated with *more* effective cost control than previously (Evans, 1976; Barer and Evans, 1986; Evans, 1992). Widely-held and often-expressed opinions to the contrary may arise from a combination of economic naïveté and statistical ignorance.

As for point (2), individual use decisions have very little to do with overall costs of care. Health care use is driven primarily by capacity. Hospital administrators have been familiar for over 30 years with "Roemer's Law," that "a built bed is a filled bed." But the same processes work for human capital – trained personnel – as for physical capital (Barer and Evans, 1992). Use of physicians' services expands in line with their supply – a licensed doctor is a busy doctor. We have doubled the doctor/population ratio in Canada in the last 25 years, with absolutely *no* tendency for workloads per doctor to fall. And behind both facilities and people, the "know-how" capital embodied in new drugs, equipment, and procedures is constantly expanding, and this form of capacity also adds to utilization pressure.[11]

Thus, the inertial pressure for cost escalation can be traced to the factors that have expanded and continue to expand system capacity – more doctors, more hospitals, more (and more highly trained) staff, more (and more complex) equipment, and more (and more expensive) drugs. The successful policies for cost control, in Canada and abroad, have been those that limit the growth of total capacity and of total budgets. Individuals may make the initial decision to contact the health care system, but the subsequent decisions, over which they have in practice very little control, determine the overall costs of the system.

There *is* evidence to support point (3). Although it is not clear if anyone ever thought otherwise, the RAND Health Insurance Study in the US has shown in a large randomized controlled trial that people will respond to user charges by reducing their contacts with the health care system (Manning et al., 1987). Other studies have found similar results. The commonsense view that people respond to financial incentives is certainly not wrong. But that study did not, and by design could not, show whether this led to an overall *system-wide* reduction in utilization and costs.[12] Where "common sense" goes wrong is in the incomplete and very naive "understanding" of *whose* behaviour and incentives are relevant to the eventual outcome.

Consequently, on point (4), we now have over 20 years of experience in a number of different countries and systems of health care. The *one* (and only one) system whose costs remain out of control – the United States – is also the only one that relies explicitly and quite heavily on user charges to control costs (Evans, 1992; Schieber, Poullier, and Greenwald, 1992). Some other countries have small charges for some forms of hospital and medical care, but they are not taken seriously as a mechanism for cost control. France may be a partial exception, with the rhetoric of the "*ticket moderateur*," the deterrent charge; France has been in recent years the least successful of the European countries at controlling overall health care costs.

The American experience confirms the view that user fees, depending upon how they are structured, can serve to support *more* rapid escalation of health care costs. The key to cost control is, or at least has been to date, the containment of overall budgets, either through a single payer system as in Canada, or a large number of closely coordinated payment agencies as in Germany. But the more independent sources of funding there are, the more difficult is cost control.

Private insurance systems (which in practice depend upon large and uncontrolled public subsidies) are particularly expensive. They have in the United States generated a huge and unproductive bureaucracy whose primary contributions have been to develop more and more sophisticated ways of determining who *not* to insure or reimburse, and of harassing clinicians to distraction. In response, both medical practitioners and particularly hospitals have had to expand dramatically their administrative and financial capabilities to cope with the flood of paper and payment rules imposed by insurers.

The resulting "bureaucratic arms race" between payers and providers now adds about $100 billion "worth" of administrative waste motion to American health care costs (Woolhandler and Himmelstein, 1991; Woolhandler, Himmelstein, and Lewontin, 1993). Things have worked out pretty much the way Justice Hall, in 1964, rather perspicaciously predicted that they would do, when he rejected proposals from the private insurance industry in Canada.[13]

So user fees, or more generally private financing, can increase costs by introducing additional overhead into the payment process. A much smaller Canadian example is given by the physician in North Vancouver who, after opting out of the provincial payment program, announced that he would extra-bill his patients so as to cover the costs of additional office staff to handle his direct billings. Multiple sources of finance add to overhead costs.

But in fact no one knows whether the North Vancouver doctor was really just covering extra overhead costs. He may also have been raising his fees to raise his income. Another significant difference between single- and multiple-source payment is the ability of the former to limit the growth of fees, prices, and costs per unit of service. The argument that user fees will remedy an "underfunded" health care system is, as noted above, at least in part an argument that, once given access to the patient's own financial resources, providers of care will be able to raise their fees and prices more than they can when bargaining with a single reimbursing agency.

Again, the evidence supports this position. Studies comparing Canada and the United States show that physicians' fees have risen much more rapidly (in real terms) in the United States since 1970, and by 1985 were twice as high as in Canada (Barer, Evans, and Labelle, 1988; Fuchs and Hahn, 1990). More recent evidence suggests that the margin has, if anything, grown somewhat (Welch, Katz, and Zuckerman, 1993; Miller, Zuckerman, and Gates, 1993). Charges to patients and "market forces" do not restrict fee escalation; direct negotiation with a single payer does. These fee differences, in turn, translate into higher relative incomes for physicians in the United States.[14]

The point is not that American physicians earn too much, or Canadians too little – how much people "should" earn is partly the outcome of market forces, but in health care is also strongly influenced by value judgments expressed through the political system. Rather, the point is that international comparative evidence indicates that user fees, by diversifying and "privatizing" funding sources, are more likely to lead to higher expenditures (and incomes) through higher prices, rather than to lower costs through lower use. And these effects are again distributional; if fees go up more rapidly, then net incomes of patients (net of fees and taxes for health care) will fall, while those of physicians in particular will rise.

Thus, the people who stand to gain from the introduction of user fees are not only those who will as a result pay lower taxes, but also those who will be able to increase their fees and incomes, as well as those who will find increased markets for their financial services, both private insurance and financial management for providers. How far this will go is difficult to predict, but the direction is clear.

Nor is this the end of the story. Budgetary controls in Canada, as in many European systems, have powerfully limited the growth of markets for equipment, especially "high-tech" equipment. By contrast, the United States is awash in lithotripters, MRI machines, CT scanners, and other expensive innovations, which are on average each used *much* less than their counterparts in Canada (Redelmeier and Fuchs, 1993).[15] This wasted capacity – which the Americans clearly recognize as such – represents a very favourable market for those who develop and manufacture such equipment. If user charges can be a lever to open up the private supply of such services, both the manufacturer and the doctor can benefit (as can parts of the university research community, and those arms of government responsible for job creation and tax revenue, and ...). Total health care costs will rise.

From this perspective the resurgence of interest in user fees in Canada is easily understood. The collapse, in the 1980s, of previous rates of general economic growth has made past rates of growth in health care unsustainable – or at least more costly to sustain than most of us are willing to accept. If Medicare is to remain (almost) entirely tax financed, then either its growth must be slower than in the past or taxes must rise to support the continuation of past growth trends in a flat economy. User charges, by opening up private sources of finance, offer a way out of this dilemma by permitting health care spending to keep rising, while shifting the burden of that rise off the shoulders of taxpayers – precisely the American "solution."

Not surprisingly, then, such policies appeal to higher-income taxpayers, to those who fear restriction of their markets and incomes as health care spending is brought under control, and to those who hope for expanded markets in managing the private component of the funding system. Going back to the initial claim, it seems extremely unlikely that user charges will lead to a reduction in total health care costs, although they may for a time lower the cost to governments/taxpayers by shifting it to users. But even that is not certain.[16] What is *very* sure, from the international evidence, is that a more general reversion to private financing will lead to a substantial *increase* in *total* costs.

The above is something of a "slippery slope" argument. Such arguments are themselves rather slippery, being explicit or implicit predictions that depend upon a number of assumptions. User fees do not necessarily imply private insurance; and few in Canada are openly advocating a wholesale importation of the American system. That system is pretty well-known to be among the worst in the developed world, in coverage, equity, cost, and efficiency.

But we believe that the "slippery slope" argument must be taken seriously. The American predicament is not an accident or an aberration. It is the natural outcome of health care system evolution in response to powerful dynamic forces that are now quite well understood, and that can be checked only by explicit and forceful political action. The American health care system is what happens when such policy fails – and it *may* be irreversible. Their record of "reform" over the past few decades is not encouraging, and the latest round (at the time of writing) is showing increasing signs of being a repeat performance. That system seems unable to produce the very thing it needs the most – explicit and forceful political action.

The "slippery slope" argument in Canada has, we believe, two parts. First, the move from "no" to "some" charges is a discontinuous one, a major change in principle, after which further increases are politically much easier. Indeed, depending upon the form charges take, increases may be virtually automatic – if providers are permitted to bill patients directly, it is difficult to control the amount (and who would have an interest in doing so?)

Second, the fiscal pressures on provincial governments are not going to ease in the near future, nor will "small" user charges do anything much to help. The notion that they will magically deflate expansionary pressures in the health care system – that the people who work there will suddenly become content with lower incomes or happily seek jobs elsewhere (where?) – seems too silly even to contemplate. We predict instead that, under continuing pressure for more revenue from somewhere – anywhere – provincial governments would find continuing increases in user charges impossible to forego. "[A]nyone who thinks politicians would keep user fees at $5 for very long should have their [sic] head examined – free of charge" (*Toronto Star*, 1993).

At some point, the burden of such charges on patients will become sufficiently severe that the ban on private insurance will no longer be sustainable.[17] After that, the spiral of increased user charges, increased private coverage (which again for well-known reasons will be primarily employment-based), and pressure for tax subsidies (such as now enjoyed by dental, pharmaceutical, and extended health insurance), will be very hard to stop. There is a great deal of money to be made from breaking up Medicare.

User Fees and the Appropriateness of Health Care

While there still appear to be a number of people who believe, or at least allege, that they expect user fees to limit the growth of *overall* health care costs, this view now seems to be largely confined to those who have little or no understanding of how health care systems function, or knowledge of their past performance. More informed and sophisticated advocates of such charges now make a more disaggregated case, no longer treating "health care" as some monolithic block of undifferentiated "services."

Instead, the argument is increasingly that a significant proportion of the care currently being provided is "frivolous" or unnecessary, and that people who decide, in response to a user fee, not to seek care, will not incur any additional health risk as a result.[18] The components of this position are that:

1 care is oversupplied, relative to needs;
2 such "unnecessary" use is a result of "frivolous" demands by patients; and that
3 in response to user fees, patients will selectively reduce or eliminate their "frivolous" demands.

Health care will not only be less costly, in total, but on average more effective as the "unnecessary" services are pruned away by the discipline of the market.

Conversely, those who argue that user fees, and private funding more generally, are necessary to remedy public "underfunding," offer a different view on each of these points. They claim that care is *undersupplied*, in total, relative to needs, that this is the result of government decisions, and that, given the opportunity, people will supplement public funds with their own private resources to buy additional care. They hold that care decisions will indeed change, but that *in aggregate* they will and should change in the opposite direction to that predicted by the "frivolous care eliminators."

At the same time, however, this argument has been "hybridized" with points (2) and (3) from the argument of the cost controllers. It is conceded that indeed there *is* a good deal of unnecessary care being provided, in response to "frivolous" patient demands, and that this further strains a health care system that is, in total, inadequate to meet all the *real* needs presented to it. Thus, user fees could have a dual benefit. Not only would they add to the total amount of money available for health care – self-evidently a good thing – but they would, by discouraging "frivolous" demands, free up some of the capacity now being wasted, for those real needs.

In effect, those who claim "underfunding" have taken over the simple-minded argument of the economics texts, that increased user fees will reduce use, and have drawn the teeth that appeared to threaten them with lower expenditures/incomes. But the hybrid argument is curiously silent on just *why* it is that so much of the capacity of the present system is taken up with meeting "frivolous" demands. At most, this argument would appear to apply in primary care, where patients do in fact choose whether or not to contact physicians. From then on, use depends upon referral from the primary practitioner.

In very round numbers, nearly three-quarters of Medicare outlays go to finance hospitals and other institutions, and about one-quarter goes to physician billings. But entry to hospital requires admission by a physician.[19] About 60 per cent of physician billings are for specialists' services, on referral from a primary care practitioner. These latter, directly accessible by the public, thus account for only about 10 per cent of Medicare outlays. Nor is every visit to a primary care practitioner initiated by the patient. Patients are often advised to return, sometimes several times, presumably (in most cases at least) with some reason.

These numbers have two implications. First, they indicate that a very high proportion of Medicare expenditures – over 90 per cent – result from the initiative, or at least the acquiescence, of a physician. But they also suggest that the use of services, and costs, are highly concentrated in the population. Many of us see a primary care practitioner in the course of a year, fewer see a specialist, very few are hospitalized or placed in long-term care, and fewer still are admitted to intensive care, or undergo complex surgery. Most of the costs are thus accounted for by a very small proportion of users – who would then bear most of the burden from significant user charges.[20]

Studies of actual utilization patterns strongly confirm this inference. "It has become common wisdom in both Canada ... and the United States ... that a small minority of the population account for a large majority of health care expenditures. This pattern has been found across all age groups ... (and has) been reported to be consistent through time" (Roos, Shapiro, and Tate, 1989, 347).

In the United States, Berk and Monheit (1992) have recently examined this concentration of use in the 1987 National Medical Expenditure Survey. They found that when people are ranked according to their level of health care expenditure, fully *30 per cent* of expenditures are accounted for by only 1 per cent of the population, and that the highest-using 10 per cent of people account for 72 per cent of all costs. On the other hand, the lowest-using half of the population account for only 3 per cent of expenditures.[21] This concentration of services appears to be increasing over time. Furthermore, among the highest-using 1 per cent of the population 48.2 per cent are elderly and 60.3 per cent report themselves as being in fair or poor health, compared with 11.9 per cent and 16.0 per cent respectively among the general (non-institutionalized) population.

The US Medical Expenditure Survey samples only the non-institutionalized population, in a single year. Roos et al. (1989) examined the usage of hospital and nursing home services, over the period 1970 to 1985, by a representative sample (the Manitoba Longitudinal Study on Aging) of the whole elderly population of Manitoba. They found, not surprisingly, that institutional use is even more highly concentrated than ambulatory: in 1972 the top 5 per cent of users accounted for 65.0 per cent of all hospital and nursing home costs among the sample population, and for 98.8 per cent of nursing home costs alone. On the other hand, three-quarters of the sample had no institutional use at all.

They also found a high concentration over the period as a whole, reflecting the fact that the same people tend to be the high users from year to year. From 1970 to 1985, the top 5 per cent of users in the sample accounted for 27.7 per cent of hospital and nursing home costs, while the top 50 per cent accounted for 92.5 per cent. The other half of the elderly generated virtually no such costs at all – over 16 years!

Moreover, the high users appear to be significantly sicker. Focusing on the 5 per cent of the sample with highest hospital use in 1972, Roos et al. found that 26.5 per cent were dead by the end of that year, and among the survivors, 27.9 per cent were high (top 5 per cent) users in the subsequent year. The corresponding percentages for the remaining 95 per cent of the sample were only 3.6 per cent dying by the end of 1972, and 3.0 per cent among the top 5 per cent of users in 1973. Five years later, at the end of 1977, 68.1 per cent of the 1972 high users were dead, compared with 23.5 per cent of the rest.

Of course the high concentration of use and costs on a small subgroup among the elderly population is partly a reflection of age. Use tends to rise with age, and is particularly high in the year prior to death. But very large variations in use were also found within age subgroups, and after separate identification of use in the year of death.

These findings, along with the observation that hospital and specialist physicians' services account for about 90 per cent of costs in the Canadian Medicare systems, make it clear that most of those costs are generated in caring for a relatively small proportion of the population who are presumably quite ill, and in any case are using a lot of expensive, specialized, mostly hospital-based services. Most of this care requires an explicit physician admission or referral, and some undetermined proportion of the rest are initiated by the practitioner.

This does not leave a lot of scope for savings by reducing *patient-initiated* "frivolous" demands. After all, no one has ever suggested that all, or even a major proportion of, patient-initiated contacts were frivolous. Indeed, the "frivolous use" or "abuse" would only be that share of patient-initiated contacts which the patient could reasonably have been expected to know in advance were unnecessary. The point was well put by a thoughtful clinician: "Necessity is a diagnosis of hindsight."

And while the evidence seems very strong that user charges do discourage people from seeking care, there is no evidence that it leads them differentially to forego the less-needed care. Charges are as likely to discourage contacts which clinicians would regard as "needed," as those judged "unneeded" (Lohr et al., 1986). Once one has contacted the health care system, the subsequent course of treatment commonly depends on the initiative or at least the essential participation of the clinician, for obvious (and generally good) reasons. There are exceptions to this generalization, but they are exceptions. If there is a problem with patterns of care, changing the information and/or the incentives faced by the professional offers a much more effective remedy than imposing a user fee on the patient.

In fact, it appears that when clinicians complain of unreasonable patient demands for "frivolous" care, they often mean that the *form* of care-seeking, not the care itself, was inappropriate. The patient should not have gone to the emergency ward, or called the doctor in the middle of the night, but should have come to the office during regular hours. So if there is scope for reallocating resources to improve the effectiveness of the care currently provided, there is no basis whatever for the claim that this will be assisted by *general* user charges.[22]

The "irresponsible" patient, running to the physician for every little thing, may be largely a myth. But the claim that this person, if he (or she) exists, is placing an unbearable or even a noticeable load on the health care system is *certainly* a myth. Costs may perhaps be too high; some, even much, care may be inappropriate. But to respond by focusing on individual patients seeking primary care is to count the peanuts while ignoring the elephants.

Accordingly, we suspect that those within the health care system who put forward the "hybrid" argument for user charges are in fact primarily interested in their potential as a source of more resources for health care. The story about transferring resources from frivolous to needed care is simply added on to recruit support from a more naive public, understandably worried about both government deficits and the availability of health care, by repeating the rhetoric of cost control and so giving the appearance of concern.

But the argument that additional revenue is needed slides smoothly and swiftly past the conclusions of all of the independent commissions and reviews of health care in Canada over the last five or six years. These have concluded that the Canadian system is adequately, indeed generously, funded in total, but that its priorities are inappropriate and it lacks adequate management and accountability.[23] They have chosen to recommend, not a general expansion in aggregate funding, but rather a reallocation of resources and programs to improve the efficiency and effectiveness of the present systems.[24] Their conclusions can be summarized as "More management, not more money."

In particular, these commissions and review bodies have not recommended general user charges, let alone the introduction of private financing sources and mechanisms, on the understanding that these would have the opposite effect – more money, not more management. This would protect incomes, autonomy, and professional opportunities in health care, whatever the effects (positive or negative) on health care or health.

Accessibility of Health Care to Different People

In any society, Canada included, people are different (from each other). They differ in their incomes, their accumulated wealth, their health status, and their health risk. Accordingly, much of the political controversy over user fees focuses on their impact, not so much on *total* health care use and costs, but on *who* will get *what kind* of care?

Opponents of user fees emphasize their differential deterrent effects, that charges bear more heavily upon those with lower incomes, and consequently will skew utilization away from them and towards those with higher incomes. If one puts together the two propositions – (1) that user fees do not reduce, and depending upon their form are likely to increase, overall use and costs, but (2) that people at lower incomes are more likely to be deterred from seeking care in the first place – the implication is that to the extent that there is any effect on use, people with higher incomes will make *more* use of care, absolutely as well as relatively.

And indeed that is exactly what was found in the original Canadian studies, at the time Medicare was introduced (Barer et al., 1979). The current American experience presents the same story on a much larger canvas – large user fees, uncontrolled *total* use and costs, but large differentials in access by income class and other distinguishing factors, and corresponding differences in health outcomes. Advocates of user fees, on the other hand, argue that by exempting those at lowest incomes and integrating such fees with the income tax system, one could eliminate any differential in deterrent effect.

It is important to distinguish this claim from the point made above about cost shifting. User fees, by substituting for tax finance, will redistribute (net) income from the poor(er) and sick(er) to the healthier and wealthier. This happens, whether or not the charges vary with taxable income. But the influence of such charges on behaviour, on use patterns at different income levels, is a separate question that is more open to opinion.

Indeed it is wide open. We do not know that tax-related charges would have *any* impact on use, by *anyone* – they have never been tried (anywhere, by anyone, though the idea has been floating around in the economics literature for over 20 years). But it is their *differential* impact which is open to debate, not their influence on total costs. If overt, point-of-service user charges do not limit the escalation of overall use and costs, because these are capacity driven, then covert, after-the-fact adjustments to tax liability, months later, are very unlikely to do better.

But as noted above, many advocates of user fees are in fact quite explicit that their objective is to increase the use of certain kinds of services, by some people. They are not always explicit about whether there is to be a reduction in use by others and, if so, whether this would be offsetting. But, occasionally, there is a particularly clear statement of an assumed linkage between appropriateness of use, and willingness to pay. One such statement was provided recently by the premier of Alberta, Ralph Klein, and one of his ministers, Steve West (*Globe and Mail*, 1993). Klein was quoted as suggesting that a "small user fee" would "cut down on abuse," while West did not want to die "on the list for heart surgery," "with half a million dollars in the bank."

Setting aside the fact that all the studies of cardiac bypass surgery indicate that, with the exception of certain conditions which typically have short waiting times, the procedure does not affect life expectancy (Chassin et al., 1986; Naylor, 1991; Rachlis, Olak, and Naylor, 1991; Naylor et al., 1993),[25] these two comments expose the core of the argument over differential access. They express precisely the hybrid argument referred to above: User fees will discourage people from seeking care they do not need, while enabling those who really need care to get it. At present, because care is "free," the system is overloaded with people using services they do not really need, while people with real needs are being denied services, or at least forced to wait, so that their health, and even lives, may be in jeopardy.

But these comments also demonstrate clearly the basis on which need is to be judged. West is troubled, not by the thought that someone might die while on the waiting list for cardiac surgery, but that someone (him) who was *willing and able to pay* for the surgery might die while waiting.[26] Klein is not troubled, unlike the opponents of user fees, by the thought that such fees might deter someone from seeking care they needed: so long as fees are "small," they will only deter "abuse." But since no criteria are offered for distinguishing between "abuse" and "need," it appears that, as a practical matter, he is willing to let the distinction be made after the fact. If people are not willing to pay for care, it cannot have been needed.

Now, in fact, we do know some things about willingness to pay for care. We know, as noted above, that when people must pay out of pocket, they *are* less likely to seek care. But they are as likely to forego "needed" as "unneeded" care, at least as judged by clinicians. There appears to be no evidence to support the proposition that user fees differentially discourage "abusive" care. What they do is differentially discourage care-seeking by people with lower incomes. Furthermore, we know that user fees deter *contact* with the health care system, but do not reduce overall use and cost. And we know that somewhere in the neighbourhood of 90 per cent of Medicare outlays go to pay for care that requires the initiative or at least the approval of a physician. So policies which selectively deter contact by people with lower incomes will tend to increase the share of overall services being received by those who are not deterred – those with higher incomes. In a user fee system, people with higher incomes not only pay a smaller share of the cost of health care, they receive a larger share of the benefits. No wonder the idea never lacks for supporters!

We single out Klein and West only because they have made explicit a position that is, we believe, much more widespread. Superficially, it repeats the argument of the previous section, that user fees will lead to a more appropriate mix of services, better value for money, by deterring "abuse" and permitting the expansion of effective, even "life-saving" services that are now being "rationed." But, in fact, the appropriateness argument is inverted.

Instead of claiming that user fees would lead to a pattern of services which would be more effective or appropriate, as judged by some external standard such as clinical evidence or a version of the Oregon procedure, this argument *defines* appropriateness by willingness to pay. And since willingness to pay is closely linked with *ability* to pay (i.e., with income), it follows necessarily that people with more money must have greater or at least more important needs than people with less.[27] A user fee system leads to "better" patterns of use, not because it discourages ineffective care and supports greater provision of effective care, but because it provides more care to people with more money. The standard for judging the appropriateness of care is not what the care does, but who gets it.

The critical issue is the presence or absence of an external, non-financial standard for judging the appropriateness of care. Advocates of user fees rarely, if ever, offer any way of distinguishing "needed" from "unneeded" services, or even admit that this might be an issue. But a general user fee policy, of "charging something for everything," is in effect based on the assumption either that there *are* no distinctions – that all care is equally "abusive" to some degree – or alternatively that the appropriateness of care can in fact be defined by willingness/ability to pay.[28]

But neither of these assumptions is supported by any evidence, direct or indirect. As noted above, patient responses to both increases and decreases in out-of-pocket charges do not show any tendency for "free" care to result in a higher proportion of "unnecessary" contacts. And the fact that access to so much of health care is by law, as well as custom, restricted by requirements for physician referral or prescription (as well as by the licensure process itself), further emphasizes our collective mistrust of the patient's (our own) unaided judgment. "Doctor's orders" do not (usually) have the force of law; but the phrase is not an empty one, and a sensible person thinks very carefully before acting against medical advice.

Putting these propositions together yields an unfortunate conclusion. If user charges are as likely to discourage "needed" as "unneeded" contacts, and if they serve not to reduce overall use but to reallocate services from those with less ability to pay to those with more, and if at least *some* of the services thus reallocated are not only "needed," as judged by clinicians, but actually effective, then user charges will reallocate health outcomes as well. There is at least a presumption that the present positive relation between income and health status will thus be strengthened. User fees may redistribute not only money and access to care, but health itself, from lower- to higher-income groups.[29]

The argument for user fees looks very different, and for some services (and carefully targeted fees) much stronger, when it is combined with some external standards of appropriateness. As pointed out above, for services which can be identified as having no medical benefit, it seems quite reasonable to charge not only a user fee, but full cost. Medicare has always undertaken to pay for all "medically necessary" care, not for any service provided by a medical practitioner; a sickness absence certificate required by an employer, for example, is by no stretch of the imagination "medically necessary."[30]

If people seek care from inappropriate sources, self-referring to specialists, for example, or taking obviously non-emergency problems to emergency wards when other alternatives are available, user fees may perhaps form part of a strategy to steer them to more appropriate sources. There are some precedents for such "steering" charges; the relevant principle is that the *form or source* of care, the specialist or the emergency ward, rather than the care itself, is not medically necessary.

Other charges, such as those for long-term care, are imposed specifically for their redistributional effect – to take funds away from those on public pensions. Otherwise, they would in effect be receiving maintenance support twice, once in cash and once in kind. An increase in such charges, for those who can afford them, would similarly be explicitly redistributive, removing resources from those in care (or perhaps from their heirs) to the benefit of the general taxpayer. As matters now stand, the general taxpayer is subsidizing the room and board costs of those in long-term care (because costs exceed current charges), whether or not they have resources of their own. If we as a political community believe that reduction or removal of this subsidy would be fair, and are open about it, there seems little basis for objection.

Specialists in long-term care do, however, raise two warning flags. First, such charges generate an obvious incentive for the institutionalized elderly or their representatives to resist transfer from "free" acute care to more appropriate long-term care. This is of course an old problem; possible remedies include the assessment of long-stay patients in acute care and their reclassification as de facto long-stay for purposes of both hospital reimbursement and patient charges (British Columbia, 1991, B102–B110). But the physician plays a key role in acute care; one might anticipate increased pressures on physicians to certify their patients' continuing need for acute care so as to protect them financially.

Secondly, charges for long-term care which are related to a resident's own resources will tend to – and are intended to – draw down those resources. This can foreclose any opportunities for the resident to return to independent living, or threaten the independence of a spouse. The notorious "spend-down" requirements of the Medicaid program in the United States have often been criticized as forcing people to become impoverished, and to impoverish their spouses, in order to qualify for benefits. If the family home has been sold to pay for institutional care, then there is nowhere to return to if one's condition improves, and the spouse may have to be institutionalized as well.

These considerations, we believe, represent warnings rather than decisive counter-arguments. It is not clear how serious such problems may be, in quantitative terms, nor whether effective remedies can be devised. But they emphasize the potential dangers of simplistic solutions based on a priori notions in a complex environment.

CONCLUSION

The diversity and persistence of support for user fees, over many years, despite the inconsistency and inadequacy of the various arguments made for them, has a ready explanation. As Marmor has pointed out, "Nothing that is regular is stupid." User fees would benefit a number of well-defined interests, and those interests are "concentrated," self-aware, and have preferential access to the media and to the formation of the public agenda. Those who would lose are dispersed, "diffuse," and have much less awareness or understanding of what is at stake.

The economic decline has raised the stakes of this debate. Faced with the universal conclusion of public review bodies, that in the present economic climate what is needed is "Not more money, but more management," the traditional advocates of user fees are under increased pressure to open up new channels of finance. They are being forced to cast the call in increasingly clever camouflage, but the intent is still the same: "More money! From wherever!"[31]

We have already referred to Michael Rachlis' "Unholy Alliance." More management means, for provincial governments, difficult and politically dangerous decisions, more conflict with providers, and the necessity of raising taxes if they fail. For providers, both incomes and autonomy are clearly threatened by accountability and restraint. A shift from taxes to user pay enables both to avoid this unpleasant confrontation by externalizing costs to patients. And if the user charges become large enough, private insurers may be able to get back into the game, adding to health care costs (to pay their incomes) while further shifting them from one set of shoulders to another.

Recruiting upper-income taxpayers is not too difficult; for them such a shift is money in the pocket. With user fees, those who can pay will secure a larger share of services for a reduced tax burden. If this results in a pattern of health care which is in total more, rather than less, intensive and costly, well, so be it.

In this recruitment process, the claim of "underfunding" plays a critical role. People can be misled into believing that "shortages," "waiting lists," and other widely publicized problems of access are a consequence of a general shortfall of resources (in the world's second richest system) rather than of inadequate management of the very generous allocation of resources now available, and then frightened into believing that care will not be available when they themselves need it.[32] And, of course, some of the access problems are real, even if the global "underfunding" is not. But for every real access problem in our system there is at least one example of excess capacity or inappropriate care. "Better management, not more money."

User fees seem to offer a response on both the public-spirited and the selfish levels. They would provide more money "from those of us who can afford it" for an excellent but allegedly under-resourced system. But they also offer the expectation that, when not all needs can be met, those of us who "can afford it" will be served. Ability to pay, reinterpreted by fear, becomes greater deservingness – "Me first, I've got the money!"

This work was funded in part by the Ontario Premier's Council on Health, Well-Being, and Social Justice. R.G. Evans was supported by a

National Health Scientist award from Health Canada, and was a fellow of the Canadian Institute for Advanced Research. M.L. Barer and G.L. Stoddart were an associate and a fellow, respectively, of the institute. Helpful comments from Michael Rachlis, Noralou Roos, the members of the Polinomics Research Workshop at McMaster University (and in particular Cathy Charles), and two anonymous reviewers, are gratefully acknowledged.

NOTES

1 This assumes that total spending on health care does not change in response to user fees. More on this below, but note that if total spending should fall, then the total tax liability falls by even more than the revenue from user fees, with even greater gains for higher-income people. We also assume that any reduction in the tax revenue required to finance health care would occur through an equi-proportionate reduction in all tax rates (relative to what they would otherwise have been). In practice, non-proportionate changes could increase or decrease the amount of the transfer to higher-income people. The reduction in tax revenues *required to finance health care* follows logically from the assumption that total health care spending remains constant (or at least does not rise) as revenues from user fees increase. Whether this reduction would be translated into lower tax rates, or deficit reduction, or other spending programs, is a matter of general fiscal policy, not health policy – any number of scenarios is possible.

2 Both save the same amount from lower taxes; the revenue is made up with higher fees from the higher users.

3 Both pay more in fees, but those at higher incomes enjoy a larger reduction in taxes.

4 These data include premiums for the public Medicare program as well as for private insurance. But for the average family in the survey, private insurance accounts for 95.7 per cent of the total, $1,396 compared with $63 for Medicare premiums. Only in the bottom two deciles does Medicare make up more than 10 per cent of total insurance premiums; 15.9 per cent in decile 9, and 23.6 per cent in decile 10.

5 User fees imposed on "those who can afford to pay" are in fact directly in conflict with this principle. Thus they *weaken* the link between ability to pay and share of health care costs borne, even as they *strengthen* the link between ability to pay and use of services.

6 Having said this, Arrow in fact analyses a model with "a very large population" in which "To avoid distributional considerations, I assume that all

individuals have identical endowments and identical utility functions" (5). ("Endowments" include incomes.) Furthermore, the incidence of illness is modelled by assuming that all individuals face identical risks to health, though their actual experience is unpredictable. All "individuals" being assumed identical in all relevant respects, they are in effect multiple copies of a single individual. More recent papers, such as those by Manning, Newhouse, and Duan (1987) and Newhouse (1992), preserve these somewhat unrealistic but analytically essential assumptions. No one since Arrow (or before) seems to have felt it necessary to warn the reader. To those who find these assumptions unduly restrictive, one can only reply that, without them, all conclusions which have heretofore been drawn from formal theoretical analysis would vanish. Conclusions based on such a "single person ... economy" cannot be justified as providing a rough approximation to a more realistic world, because unfortunately they do not. Rather, for reasons which have long been well understood in theoretical welfare economics, they can tell us *nothing at all,* positive *or* negative, about the "welfare effects" of user fees in a world in which people differ in their health status and in their incomes. A formal analysis of *that* world would be substantially more demanding (as Arrow pointed out in 1976), and would require the introduction of explicit interpersonal value judgments. Such an analysis has never been reported.

7 Yet the still small voice of the economist persists. People may *declare* that their motivations are not selfish, and may even sincerely *believe* that they are not. But at the end of the day, the best predictor of behaviour is interest. Do not bother asking people their motivations, just look at what they do. This nasty little voice appears to appeal to observation, but is ultimately a statement of faith; it cannot be refuted. (If people appear to act against their personal economic interests, then we must have misunderstood those interests.)

8 Borrowing can be, for a time, a source of revenue.

9 Provincial medical associations have traditionally and steadfastly supported user fees, in the wholly realistic expectation that increased revenues raised in this way are more likely to support higher payments to their members. Hospital workers' unions, whose members generally serve a less well-off clientele, call for higher expenditure financed from taxation (Barer, Bhatia, Stoddart, and Evans, 1994). Both have the same quite understandable objective, to protect their own incomes in a time of general economic decline. Let someone else take the wage cuts, or the job losses.

10 Causal in both directions, and forming a vicious circle or positive feedback loop. Introduction and expansion of user fees can be a response of fiscal desperation, shifting costs that one cannot control. But the resulting

diversification of funding sources can lead to more rapid cost escalation, and even less control, as has happened to our south.

11 "Know-how" does not come free, nor does it drop from the sky. Very large investments are required to develop new drugs, or major new forms of technology, most of which must be spent *before* the innovation comes into use. These large investments must be recouped in profits from subsequent use; hence the extraordinary efforts devoted to marketing the products embodying "know-how." "Patient expectations" and professional patterns of practice do not drop from the sky either; they are carefully generated and nurtured by skilled marketers.

12 Despite this, it has frequently been misinterpreted (by its authors, among others) as having done so. The fallacy of composition is deep-rooted; and when "an answer" is desperately wanted, and much money has been spent, an answer will be given.

13 "Hence, the decision which Canadians have to make ... is whether they wish to pay $1,020 million ... in 1971 for a program administered by the insurance industry, or $837 million for a program administered by government agencies. In our opinion it would be ... uneconomic ... to spend an extra $183 million ... we must choose the most frugal method ... which we know from our hospital insurance experience is equally efficient" (Canada, 1964, 745). Hall was referring only to expenditures for physicians' services. His estimate of $837 million for 1971 was low; total outlays were actually $1,250 million in 1971 and have since increased to $10.1 billion in 1991. If the cost of insurance industry administration increased at the same rate – a conservative assumption in the light of contemporary US experience – this would yield an extra cost of over two billion dollars for private insurance of medical services alone. (But, one might ask, would costs have escalated less rapidly under private administration? Anything is possible, but since cost escalation was much more rapid in the US than in Canada after 1971, and was less rapid, in real terms, in Canada after the introduction of public insurance, the burden of proof must be borne by anyone making such a claim.)

14 While physicians earn considerably more in the United States, relative to the general population, hospital workers, on average, earn very little more. This appears to be because, although more highly skilled workers earn more in the US, lower skilled workers earn more in Canada (Redelmeier and Fuchs, 1993). Again, the distributional issues are central.

15 There are allegedly about ten times as many MRI machines in Orange County, California (population 2.5 million), as in British Columbia (population 3.5 million).

16 It is worth noting that, despite all the enthusiasm for "private" funding in the US, governments have not been able to prevent *their* health care costs from rising faster than in the private sector, and absorbing an ever growing share of public resources (Letsch, 1993).

17 This is in fact the pattern in both the US and France, in which the rhetorical reliance on user fees in the public system "to control costs," is belied by an extensive system of private insurance – "Medigap," in the US – to cover a substantial part of the user fees. But the private insurance is both more regressive in its costs and substantially more expensive to administer. On top of that, it is supported by tax expenditure subsidies from the public treasury! There is really very little mystery as to why costs in those systems are so difficult to control; the mystery is why such lunatic "systems" persist. And the answer is always the same – every dollar (or franc) of expenditure is also, for someone, a dollar (or franc) of income. And the income earners are more concentrated and self-aware than those who pay them.

18 There is a variant of this line of argument, which dominates the economics textbooks, in which there is no reference to health risks or "necessity" of care. Care is excessive if it is supplied beyond the willingness of the user to pay its full cost, and if not, not. On this criterion it is "inefficient" to provide important and desperately needed care – needed to sustain life or function – if the recipient has not the resources (and is therefore not "willing") to pay for it. On the other hand, an "efficient" economy will provide totally useless and indeed harmful care, so long as the recipient is willing and able to pay the full cost. Presumably economists get away with this sort of nonsense because most people, clinicians included, do not understand what is really being said. Jargon and mathematics, both mainstays of "economic thought," serve to keep the confusion levels high.

19 A portion of hospital budgets goes to finance ambulatory care, some of which is patient-initiated. But the high growth areas, such as surgical and medical day care and various forms of diagnostic testing, are all accessible only on physician referral. The most frequently quoted examples of "patient abuse" are in the emergency ward, and this may well be correct. But such facilities are and always have been a very small proportion of hospital budgets – "Loud cry, and little wool." A number of people are admitted from emergency to inpatient care; but that requires a physician's order, and presumably these are not "frivolous" cases.

20 These data should clarify, if clarification were needed, the difference between services of physicians and hospitals, and "supplementary" services such as those of chiropractors. The latter serve an exclusively ambulatory clientele, and can recommend repeat visits, but do not serve as gatekeepers

to a much larger system. Conclusions drawn from observations of user fees applied to forms of services which are almost entirely patient-initiated have little relevance to the much more complex world of medicine. Confusion arises, we suspect, because the primary care that most of us are familiar with, during most of our lives, accounts for very little of the activity or the cost of a modern medical care system. Drawing on personal experience, we tend to think of visits for primary care as a (quantitatively) significant contributor to the "health care cost crisis." This is an error.

21 We do not have a corresponding Canadian study, but the concentration of costs in our Medicare system may be expected to be even greater, for two reasons. First, the data set used by Berk and Monheit excluded the institutionalized population, a small group of people accounting for a relatively large share of care. And second, they studied *all* health care costs, including dentistry and (prescription and non-prescription) drugs used by patients outside hospitals; neither are covered by Canadian Medicare. These forms of health care are widely used but generate (relatively) small costs per person, so their exclusion would accentuate the degree of concentration reported by Berk and Monheit.

22 The qualification is important. There may be circumstances in which selective user charges can be used to steer people from a less- to a more-appropriate and perhaps less costly setting for care. User charges in an emergency room, selectively imposed only on those for whom equivalent care could have been provided in a nearby clinic (a professional judgment), may be part of a strategy for steering patients to the alternative site. The point here is that "needed" care is freely available; the charge is imposed on those who choose to seek care from the inappropriate, higher-level facility (Barer, Evans, and Stoddart, 1979). Another example arises from the promotion of particular tests (e.g., for blood lipid levels) or drugs (e.g., minoxidil) directly to the public. When these have no medical indication, it seems reasonable to permit, or indeed to require, the physician to bill the patient for these services, in any amount she/he chooses. Rather than imposing a user charge, the public programs should simply not reimburse services associated with these "medically unnecessary" tests or drugs. But there would also seem to be a public responsibility to look rather hard at the corporate marketing practices behind such "patient demands."

23 In the last 30 years, Canadians have almost doubled the share of our national income used to pay for health care, from 5.4 per cent in 1960 to 9.9 per cent in 1991. Per capita expenditure has gone up *four times,* from about $500 to just over $2,000 (in constant, 1986, dollars), and has increased 50 per cent in the last ten years (Evans, 1993). And throughout,

the Canadian health care system has been the most richly supported in the world – always excepting the United States – even though the average age of the Canadian population is significantly lower than that of any European country. Yet despite this massive expansion, the rhetoric of "crisis" and "underfunding" continues – claims of both "unmet needs" and inadequate provider incomes.

24 The "need" for more resources and more funding was a very common theme in submissions to the provincial commissions from provider and patient interest groups. Much less common was any evidence for, or even clear description of, the expected benefits. Awareness of overall resource constraints was rarer still.

25 Rouleau et al. (1993) have recently compared the management of patients with myocardial infarction (heart attack) in Canada and in the United States. They found that, while such patients in the United States are nearly twice as likely to undergo coronary artery bypass grafting (CABG), there is no difference in mortality rates. Over the whole population, CABG rates are about twice as high in the United States, but cardiac mortality is lower in Canada, as it is for most causes of death (Nair, Karim, and Nyers, 1992).

26 As people do, but West falls into the common trap of assuming that they die *because* the surgery was delayed. This is not what the evidence shows. Over time, cardiac surgery is being offered to older and sicker people. The probability of such people dying while waiting is correspondingly increasing. But the procedure itself is not usually life-saving, so there is no reason to believe that they would not have died if they had had the procedure – which itself carries a non-trivial mortality risk. West has apparently been "misinformed"; however much he (or we) might wish it, money won't buy him life. Like the rest of us, he owes God a death.

27 Health status is, however, inversely correlated with income – poorer people tend to be sicker. So one must conclude either that although wealthier people are healthier, the problems they *do* have are more responsive to medical care – hence their needs are greater – or else that caring for wealthier people is simply a higher priority than is reflected in the present system. Of course real needs that are neglected tend to get worse, and may (unless the patient dies) become more expensive to treat.

28 One is reminded of the response of the rather bloodthirsty Christian bishop during the Albigensian Crusade, when asked how the heretics were to be distinguished from the faithful. "Kill them all. God will recognize his own." One hopes so.

29 This possibility is ruled out, for advocates of user fees, by the assertion that "small" charges will discourage only "frivolous" care, and thus have no

impact on anyone's health status. Such charges would thus reallocate money and access to care toward higher-income people, but not health. How small is small? We do know from American experience that, when financial barriers are high enough, those without resources receive substantially less care, and their health does appear to suffer measurably in consequence. If the charges are so small as not to deter use, then they can only be a vehicle for raising revenue – an alternative to taxation. But the administrative costs of collecting small charges are likely to swamp the revenue. And in any case, as noted above, there is no compelling case for more revenue.

30 It turns out, however, that there are few situations as clear-cut as this. The more common situations will involve services which have been shown to be effective for some patients, in some circumstances; or services for which there is not yet evidence of effectiveness (but also no evidence of ineffectiveness); or services which are, in fact, inappropriate (not medically necessary) but for which it would be unreasonable to presume the patient could have been expected to know this in advance. At the end of the day, the situations in which one could justify partial user fees (that is, at levels lower than "full price," which would amount to de-insuring the service altogether) are remarkably scarce (Evans, Barer, Stoddart, and Bhatia, 1994).

31 Advocacy of user fees is a "no lose" strategy. Even when such proposals are defeated, they protect the status quo by diverting scarce public and political attention into revisiting ancient debates and away from the really serious problems of institutional redesign and reform in health care. And since that status quo appears no longer to be sustainable in the long run, diverting any reform process ensures that the same issues will come up again, and the zombies will again come out of their graves.

32 Michael Rachlis, again, has referred to "medical terrorism."

REFERENCES

Arrow, K.J. (1976). "Welfare analysis of changes in health coinsurance rates." In *The role of health insurance in the health services sector*, ed. R.N. Rosett, 3–23. New York: National Bureau of Economic Research.

Barer, M.L., R.G. Evans, and G.L. Stoddart (1979). *Controlling health care costs by direct charges to patients: Snare or delusion?* Toronto: Ontario Economic Council.

– and R.G. Evans (1986). "Riding north on a south-bound horse? Expenditures, prices, utilization, and incomes in the Canadian health care system." In *Medicare at maturity: Achievements, lessons, and challenges*, ed.

R.G. Evans and G.L. Stoddart, 53–163. Calgary: University of Calgary Press for the Banff Centre.

– R.G. Evans, and R.J. Labelle (1988). "Fee controls as cost control: Tales from the frozen north." *The Milbank Quarterly* 66(1): 1–64.

– and R.G. Evans (1992). "The meeting of the twain: Managing health care capital, capacity, and costs in Canada." In *Technology and health care in an era of limits*, Vol. III of Medical innovation at the crossroads, Institute of Medicine Committee on Technological Innovation in Medicine, ed. A.C. Gelijns, 97–119. Washington, DC: National Academy Press.

– C. Hertzman, R. Miller, and M.V. Pascali (1992). "On being old and sick: The burden of health care for the elderly in Canada and the United States." *Journal of Health Politics, Policy, and Law* 17(4): 763–82.

– V. Bhatia, G.L. Stoddart, and R.G. Evans (1994). *The remarkable tenacity of user charges: A concise history of participation, positions, and rationales of Canadian interest groups in the debate over direct patient participation.* Toronto: Ontario Premier's Council on Health, Well-being, and Social Justice.

Berk, M.L., and A.C. Monheit (1992). "The concentration of health expenditures: An update." *Health Affairs* 11(4), 145–9.

British Columbia. Royal Commission on Health Care and Costs (Seaton Commission) (1991). *Closer to Home* (Vol. 2). Victoria, BC: The Province of British Columbia.

Canada. Royal Commission on Health Services (Hall Commission) (1964). *Report* Vol. 1. Ottawa: The Queen's Printer.

Chassin, M.R., R.E. Park, A. Fink, et al. (1986). *Indications for selected medical and surgical procedures: A literature review and ratings of appropriateness.* (R-3204/2-CWF/HF/HCFA/PMT/RWJ) (May). Santa Monica, CA: The Rand Corporation.

Evans, R.G. (1976). "Beyond the medical marketplace: Expenditure, utilization, and pricing of insured health care in Canada." In *The role of health insurance in the health services sector*, ed. R.N. Rosett, 437–92. New York: National Bureau of Economic Research.

– (1992). "What seems to be the problem? The international movement to restructure health care systems." HPRU 92: 8D (November), Centre for Health Services and Policy Research, University of British Columbia, Vancouver.

– (1993). "Health care reform: 'The issue from hell.'" *Policy Options* 14(6): 35–41.

– M.L. Barer, and G.L. Stoddart (1994). *Charging Peter to pay Paul: Accounting for the financial effects of user charges.* Toronto: Ontario Premier's Council on Health, Well-being, and Social Justice.

– M.L. Barer, G.L. Stoddart, and V. Bhatia (1994). *It's not the money, it's the principle: Why user charges for some services, and not others?* Toronto: Ontario Premier's Council on Health, Well-being, and Social Justice.

Friedman, E. (1991). "Insurers under fire." *Health Management Quarterly* 13 (3): 23–7.

Fuchs, V.R., and J.S. Hahn (1990). "How does Canada do it? A comparison of expenditures for physicians' services in the United States and Canada." *New England Journal of Medicine* 323(13): 884–90.

Globe and Mail (1993). "Alberta premier to press for Medicare user fees," 13 January, A3.

Letsch, S.W. (1993). "National health care spending in 1991." *Health Affairs* 12(1): 94–110.

Lohr, K.N., et al. (1986). "Use of medical care in the Rand health insurance experiment: Diagnosis- and service-specific analyses of a randomized controlled trial." *Medical Care* 25(Supplement): 531–8.

Manning, W.G., J.P. Newhouse, N. Duan, et al. (1987). "Health insurance and the demand for medical care: Evidence from a randomized trial." *American Economic Review* 77(3): 251–77.

Miller, M.E., S. Zuckerman, and M. Gates (1993). "How do Medicare physician fees compare with private payers?" *Health Care Financing Review* 14(3): 25–39.

Nair, C., R. Karim, and C. Nyers (1992). "Health care and health status: A Canada-United States statistical comparison." *Health Reports* 4(2): 175–83. Ottawa: Statistics Canada (cat. no. 82-003).

Naylor, C.D. (1991). "A different view of queues in Ontario." *Health Affairs* 10(3): 110–28.

– C.D. Morgan, C.M. Levinton, et al. (1993). "Waiting for coronary revascularization in Toronto: Two years' experience with a regional referral office. *Canadian Medical Association Journal* 149(7): 955–62.

Newhouse, J.P. (1992). "Medical care costs: How much welfare loss?" *Journal of Economic Perspectives* 6(1): 3–21.

Rachlis, M.M., J. Olak, and C.D. Naylor (1991). "The vital risk of delayed coronary artery surgery: Lessons from the randomized trials." *Iatrogenics* 1:103–11.

Rasell, E., J. Bernstein, and K. Tang (1993). *The impact of health care financing on family budgets*. Economic Policy Institute Briefing Paper (April), Washington, DC: EPI.

Redelmeier, D.A., and V.R. Fuchs (1993). "Hospital expenditures in the United States and Canada." *New England Journal of Medicine* 328(11): 772–8.

Roos, N.P., E. Shapiro, and R. Tate (1989). "Does a small minority of elderly account for a majority of health care expenditures?: A sixteen-year perspective." *The Milbank Quarterly* 67(3–4): 347–69.

Rouleau, J.L., L.A. Moyé, M.A. Pfeffer, et al. (1993). "A comparison of management patterns after acute myocardial infarction in Canada and the United States." *New England Journal of Medicine* 328(11): 779–84.

Schieber, G.J., J.-P. Poullier, and L.M. Greenwald (1992). "US health expenditure performance: An international comparison and data update." *Health Care Financing Review* 13(4): 1–87.

Stoddart, G.L., M.L. Barer, and R.G. Evans (1994). *User charges, snares and delusions: Another look at the literature.* Toronto: Ontario Premier's Council on Health, Well-being, and Social Justice.

Toronto Star (1993). "User fee figures (Editorial)," 5 June, D5.

Torrey, B.B., and E. Jacobs (1993). "More than loose change: Household health spending in the United States and Canada." *Health Affairs* 12(1): 126–31.

van Doorslaer, E., A. Wagstaff, and F. Rutten (1993). *Equity in the finance and delivery of health care: An international perspective.* Oxford: Oxford University Press.

Welch, W.P., S.J. Katz, and S. Zuckerman (1993). "Physician fee levels: Medicare versus Canada." *Health Care Financing Review* 14(3): 41–54.

Woolhandler, S., and D.U. Himmelstein (1991). "The deteriorating administrative efficiency of the US Health Care System." *New England Journal of Medicine* 324(18): 1253–8.

– D.U. Himmelstein, and J.P. Lewontin (1993). "Administrative costs in US hospitals." *New England Journal of Medicine* 329(6): 400–4.

7

Going for the Gold: The Redistributive Agenda behind Market-Based Health Care Reform (1997)

ROBERT G. EVANS

SUMMARY PROPOSITIONS

Fundamental economic principles ... put efficient, competitive health care markets in the same class as powdered unicorn horn. – "Health Care without Perverse Incentives," *Scientific American,* July 1993.

1 There is in health care no "private, competitive market" of the form described in the economics textbooks, anywhere in the world. There never has been, and inherent characteristics of health and health care make it impossible that there ever could be. Public and private action have always been interwoven.

2 The persistent interest in an imaginary private competitive market is sustained by distributional objectives. These define three axes of conflict.

   a The progressivity or regressivity of the health care funding system: Who has to pay, and how much?

   b The relative incomes of providers: Who gets paid, and how much?

- c The terms of access to care: Can those with greater resources buy "better" services?

3 The real policy choices fall into two categories.
- a The extent of use of market-like mechanisms within publicly funded health care systems.
- b The extent to which certain services may be funded outside the public sector, through quasi-markets, and under a mix of public and private regulation.

4 Proposals to shift toward more use of quasi-markets, through the extension of private funding mechanisms, are distributionally driven. They reflect the fact that, compared with public funding systems, privately regulated quasi-markets have to date been:
- a Less successful in controlling prices and limiting the supply of services (more jobs and higher incomes for suppliers);
- b Supported through more regressive funding sources (the healthy and wealthy pay less, whereas the ill and wealthy get preferential access);
- c Off-budget for governments (cost shifting in the economy looks like cost saving in the public sector).

5 Market-like mechanisms within publicly funded health care systems constitute a particular set of management tools that might be used along with other more established mechanisms to promote the following generally accepted social objectives:
- a Effective health care, efficiently provided and equitably distributed across the population according to need;
- b Fair but not excessive reimbursement of providers; and
- c Equitable distribution of the burden of contributions according to ability to pay; within
- d An overall expenditure envelope that is consistent with the carrying capacity of the general economy, or rather of its members' collective willingness to pay.

6 These general objectives seem to be widely shared internationally. Their specific content is of course much more controversial – they are fundamentally political statements – and, as usual, God and the devil are in the details. But the key point is that these social objectives have their origins prior to, and at a higher level than, the choice of any particular set of mechanisms for trying to attain them. They are *ends*; the mix and blend of public and private actions are *means* to those ends. (Markets were made for and by men, not vice versa.)

7 Market-like mechanisms, as a class, have no inherent or a priori claim to superiority as mechanisms for achieving these public objectives. Nor is there, to date, any overwhelming empirical support for their widespread use. There are a number of interesting examples, in different countries, of the use of economic incentives to motivate desired changes, and these bear close watching. But this is still very much an experimental technology for system management. Moreover, there are grounds for serious concern about negative side effects from transforming the structure of motivations and rewards in health care.
8 The central role of governments remains that of exercising, directly or more traditionally by delegation, general oversight of and political responsibility for each country's health care system. Governments are increasingly acting as a sort of "consumers' cooperative" or prudent purchaser on behalf of their populations. They should choose whatever managerial tools seem to work best for this purpose, subject to the political constraints created by the fundamental conflicts of distributional interests detailed previously. In particular, they may delegate some parts of this role, but should not be permitted to divest themselves of it. In the one country where a coalition of private interests has prevented government from taking up this responsibility, the results have been spectacularly unsatisfactory.

The proper role of governments in health systems is an ancient debate. Its longevity reflects the permanence of certain fundamental conflicts of economic interest among the different groups involved in the organization and financing of health services. The form and extent of government involvement, and its relation to the activities of nongovernmental agents, significantly affect the balance of advantage in these conflicts.

The current worldwide resurgence of interest in the topic is driven by a number of different motives, covert as well as overt. There is, however, an unfortunate tendency to frame the issue as "government *versus* the market," or "regulation *versus* independent action," as if these were alternative, mutually exclusive, frameworks for economic organization. Such juxtapositions grossly misrepresent the relationships among the various institutions and actors composing modern health care systems.

State and private institutions have always interpenetrated each other, to the extent that in most national systems it is often difficult, and inherently arbitrary, to classify a particular institution as "public" or "private." In reality, there is a continuum along the line from civil service at one end, to the privately owned, strictly for-profit corporation at the other. Most health care, in most countries, is provided by people and organizations that fall into neither category. The public regulatory framework (set by government) typically gives them much more autonomy than civil servants, while conferring both privileges and responsibilities that distinguish them in essential ways from participants in "normal" markets.

The most obvious example of such interpenetration, so obvious that it long ago disappeared from the consciousness of most of those who approach health care systems from a market perspective, is professional self-regulation. Provider associations exercise the coercive authority of the state – the police power – to regulate and sometimes to suppress competitive behaviour among their members. Even more important, they are vigilant in preventing intrusions into their fields of practice by unlicensed persons. This process goes on, one way or another, in all systems, and has very deep historical roots.

The presumption, widely if not universally shared, is that professional self-regulation promotes more general social interests. There is room for considerable disagreement over the balance of public and private interests actually served, in general or in particular circumstances. But in any case, the thing *happens*. Public regulatory authority and (collective) private interest are woven together in a complex way. [1] Where markets for health care exist, they are always managed markets. There may be, at different times and places, bitter political struggles over *who* should manage the market, but no one seriously questions the need for management.[2]

Another example: The state confers monopoly rights, in the form of patents, on the developers of new drugs and devices. This blatant government interference with the free market is traditionally justified as encouraging further innovation: short-run costs for long-run gains. But the traditional story highlights the role of government in responding to "failure" in private markets and regulating in the public interest. Patent-holding firms thus prefer to speak of "intellectual property," implying that there is some sort of "natural right" to exercise monopoly power (and to call upon the state to enforce it) that is prior to, and more fundamental than, whatever interpretation might be given to the public interest by the government of the day. This is legal nonsense, but can be very effective politics.

So are patents regulatory interference with free markets, or simply recognition and protection of private property rights? Certainly, when a government tries to modify patent rights within its own jurisdiction, for example, by introducing compulsory licensure, as Canada did during the 1970s, patent holders worldwide react to this as public intrusion into private markets. They may then be supported by their home governments, essentially claiming a modern form of "extraterritoriality," backed up by a modern form of gunboat diplomacy.[3]

Self-governing professional associations react with equivalent outrage when governments try to modify the (public) legislation from which they derive their power. In general, those who exercise and benefit from delegated public authority come to regard that authority as private property, and try to convince their fellow citizens to share this view. Whether they succeed or fail, the process makes clear the foundation of private property in political consensus. How could it be otherwise?

The long and complex relationship between the state and providers of health care thus goes far beyond the role of public agencies as payers for care. Economic analysts, in particular, tend to focus on the latter as if it were the only point of contact. This restricted view can lead to the representation of the supply-side of health care systems in terms of the traditional categories of the microeconomic theory textbooks. Such an imaginary system may then be hypothesized to be actually or potentially "competitive," in the full textbook sense, with all that that implies for the potential role of private markets. These representations are both analytically convenient and intellectually familiar (to economists) – advantages that seem to compensate for their gross inadequacies as descriptions of actual institutions or behaviour.

But the convenience is not only for the analyst. The pretense that the provision of health services either is, or ever was, or ever could be, organized along the lines of markets for shoes or ships or sealing wax serves to draw a veil over the activities of those who *do* in fact exercise power, and to screen them from public accountability for its use: "Nobody here but us competitors, all obeying the laws of the market." Attempts to modify the institutional rules in order to align private activity more closely with public interests or objectives can then be portrayed, by those with private interests to defend or advance, as simply wrong-headed political meddling in an otherwise smoothly functioning private marketplace.

The primary concern of this article is to identify the economic interests defended or advanced by the extension of private market mechanisms in health care. The companion article by Thomas Rice (1997) in this issue provides a comprehensive survey of an extensive literature demonstrating that the simple-minded application to health care of economic theories about competitive markets is both descriptively invalid and theoretically unsound. Here we consider *why* advocates of the private marketplace might continue to rely on just such analyses.

Standard economic analyses of the market suppress its inevitable distributional implications. If market advocates do, in fact, have a distributional agenda, but one that is not widely shared, then they have an obvious interest in promoting the use of an intellectual framework that makes distributional questions difficult or impossible to ask. If that framework also yields a conclusion (valid or erroneous) that private markets are socially "optimal" in some technical sense (bearing no relation to the common use of the word), so much the better.

Distributional questions may be suppressed in economic analysis, but they remain at the forefront of public policy debates. Private markets have been reduced to a subsidiary role in all developed countries other than the United States, largely on the basis of distributional concerns. This may explain why advocates of private markets tend to make their arguments as if the last forty years had never occurred. The issues that were contentious in the 1950s and 1960s are being dragged out again, with all sorts of old a priori arguments being dusted off, repainted, and presented as new thinking about the role of the private sector.

But we *have* now had several decades of international experience with different mixes of public and private funding systems, and the broad lessons are pretty clear. In the developed world, a general consensus has evolved that White (1995) labelled "the international standard" for health care systems. Behind wide variations in detail, there is a broad similarity of system characteristics (White, 1995: 271):

- Universal coverage of the population, through compulsory participation;
- Comprehensiveness of principal benefits;
- Contributions based on income, rather than individual insurance purchases;
- Cost control through administrative mechanisms, including binding fee schedules, global budgets, and limitations on system capacity.

Although the processes may vary, there seems to have been a progressive convergence in both the mechanisms used for administrative management of system costs and the understanding of system dynamics on which these are based. Cost control is always incomplete; in all countries there are powerful interest groups arrayed on the other side trying to promote continuous system expansion. But in all developed countries, Wildavsky's (1977: 109) law of medical money ("costs will increase to the level of available funds ... that level must be limited to keep costs down") has been understood and acted upon through the development of countervailing public authority (Abel-Smith, 1992; Abel-Smith and Mossialos, 1994).

The turning point seemed to come, for most countries, sometime during the 1970s. Figure 7.1 displays the share of Gross Domestic Product (GDP) spent on health care, averaged (unweighted) across all the countries of the Organization for Economic Cooperation and Development (OECD) for which complete data are available, from 1960 to 1994.[4] This average is bracketed by the experiences of the United States and the United Kingdom, as representing high- and low-cost countries. For the first half of the period, the aggregate international cost experience paralleled that of the United States, with the United Kingdom becoming more and more of an outlier on the low side. But since the mid-1970s, the average experience is of substantially slower growth in health expenditures relative to GDP – roughly paralleling the UK trend – with the United States progressively diverging.[5] Taking 1977 as a mid-point, the OECD average share of health spending in GDP rose 24.8 per cent in the second half of this period, compared with 76.4 per cent in the first.

The United States is of course the exception to White's (1995) generalization, departing in a major way from his "international standard" in both structure and performance. The same point was made ten years earlier by Abel-Smith (1985), observing that the United States was the "odd man out" among modern health care systems. As such, it provides an enormously valuable point of comparison for the rest of us. What happens if a country does *not* move toward a central role for government in the financing of health care? The decade between Abel-Smith's observation and White's review has reinforced the earlier conclusion. The United States has a health care system that is, by most measures, not only unique in the developed world but also uniquely unsatisfactory. Within the United States it may be daring (Blendon et al., 1995) or heretical (Lamm, 1994) to question (publicly) the axiom that "America is number 1," but most external observers (and some internal ones) would put its health care system closer to the *bottom* of the league tables.

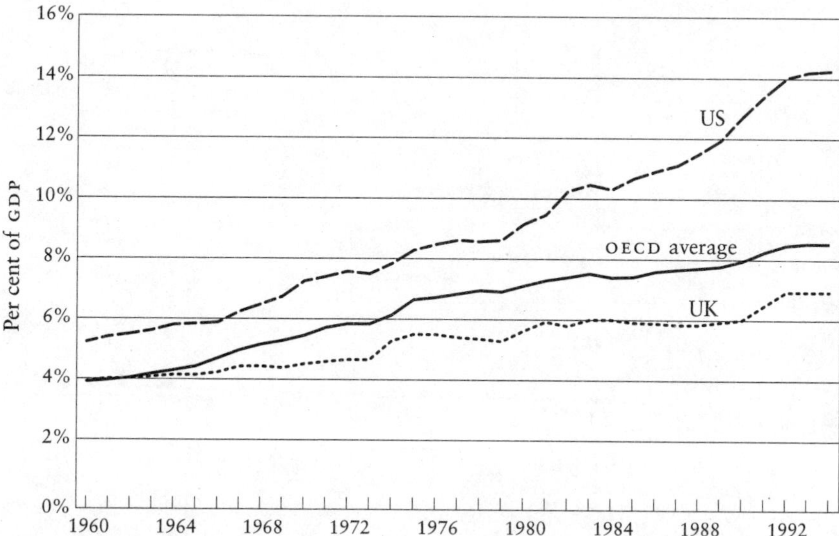

Figure 7.1 Health expenditure over GDP: OECD average, US and UK, 1960–94

Adapted from: Robert Evans. "Going for the Gold: The Redistributive Agenda Behind Market-based Health Care Reform." In *Journal of Health Politics, Policy and Law* 22(2) (1997): 427–65. *Original source:* OECD/CREDES. OECD *Health Data 96: A Software for the Comparative Analysis of 27 Health Systems*. Paris: OECD Health Policy Unit, 1996.

This is not to say that the health *care* provided in the United States is of poor quality. Some is, but much is excellent; some is the best in the world. And American patients typically express a high degree of satisfaction with their own care, as do patients in Canada, or the United Kingdom, or most other countries. But as a *system* for organizing, delivering, and particularly for financing health care, the American approach is, by international standards, grossly inefficient, heartbreakingly unfair, monumentally top-heavy with bureaucracy, and off the charts in both the level and the rate of escalation of costs.[6] And for all that, Americans are not particularly healthy, relative to the rest of the developed world.

Yet, even though the United States maintains the institutional forms and the rhetoric of a private system, it has, over time, shifted more than half its health care funding to the public sector. By 1994, 44.3 per cent of total health expenditure was reported as coming from some level of government (Levit, Lazenby, and Sivarajan, 1996). But the tax expenditure subsidy for private health insurance, the failure to tax employer-paid premiums as income in the hands of the employee, represents an

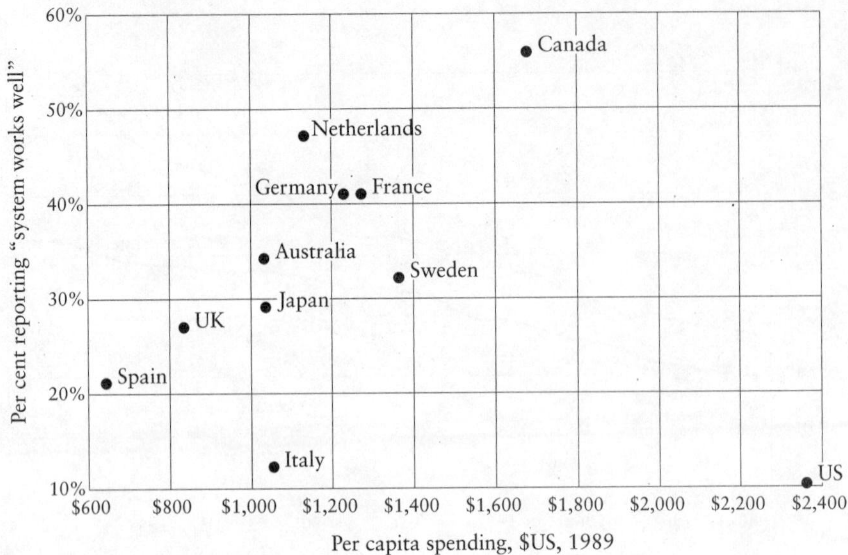

Figure 7.2 Satisfaction with health care: Selected OECD countries

Adapted from: Robert Evans. "Going for the Gold: The Redistributive Agenda Behind Market-based Health Care Reform," in *Journal of Health Politics, Policy and Law* 22(2)(1997): 427–65. *Original source:* Blendon, et al. (1990).

additional public contribution of nearly 10 per cent in the form of foregone tax revenue.

This American reality, in the face of the most powerful expressions of anti-government ideology, suggests that it may simply be impossible to support a modern health care system predominantly from private funds. One can, however, have public funding without comprehensive public oversight and control, at least as long as one is willing to put up with pretty dismal results.

These observations are not always put so bluntly, but their substance is not in dispute. No serious student of health care systems, inside or outside the United States, tries to defend the American status quo. Indeed, American citizens have also figured this out, and give their system very low marks. Figure 7.2 combines responses by citizens of different countries to a standard set of questions constructed by the Harris polling organization (Blendon et al., 1990) with expenditure data from the OECD Health Datafile (OECD/CREDES, 1996).[7] What is most striking is not simply that Americans expressed a relatively low level of satisfaction with their health care system (*not* with their own personal health care), but that they depart so markedly from the pattern found across all other countries surveyed. There is a surprisingly close linear relationship, among the countries that have evolved an institutional framework conforming to White's (1995) international standard, between per capita spending on health care and the average level of public satisfaction with the health care system. More spending leads to more satisfaction.[8] The United States is different, and Americans are not happy about it.[9]

But for them, the international standard appears to be politically inaccessible. Managed care and competition have thus emerged as a sort of lateral move in response to failure and frustration, marketed as an opportunity for the United States to innovate and leap over the experience of other countries to a position of leadership: "If we cannot do what everyone else does, well then we'll do something else. And it will be much better!" Desperation may explain the high level of enthusiasm, despite the lack of any record of success. The triumphs of managed care are still, as they always have been, in the future.

But is the future finally here? American advocates of the market may well see vindication at last in the national health expenditure estimates for 1994. At $949.4 billion, total spending was only 6.4 per cent above its 1993 level: the slowest rate of increase in thirty years (Levit, Lazenby, and Sivarajan, 1996). And the 1993 level was itself only 7.0 per cent above 1992. In both years, increases were lower in the private health insurance sector than in the public Medicare system, with the gap particularly wide in 1994. Quite understandably, this has led some to argue that (whatever else may be going on) the great American cost explosion is finally over – ended by the increasing pressure of market forces.[10] Hair-raising scenarios in which health absorbs nearly 20 per cent of the American GDP by the year 2000 now look decidedly out of date, the products of another era.

And it may be so. But a closer look at the most recent American data suggests continued caution. First, a part of the slowdown is associated with falling rates of general, economy-wide inflation. When one looks at "real" or inflation-adjusted health spending, the increases of the last two years are still low, but there is an interesting historical pattern. Since 1960, there have been three two-year periods of very low rates of increase: 1974–75, 1978–79, and 1993–94. In each of these, major federal initiatives of public insurance and/or cost control were under discussion and close to enactment. In the past, failure of these measures has been followed by a cost rebound. The recent organizational changes in the American health care system have been much more profound than any in the past, but it is too soon to tell whether they have brought about a permanent shift in the growth path.[11]

Furthermore, even if it should be permanent, the United States' "achievement" of 1993–94 looks rather different outside the country. The year 1994 was, after all, one of strong economic growth, and yet health care still increased – albeit very slightly – its share of the American GDP. In Canada, by contrast, the percentage fell from 10.1 per cent in 1993 to 9.7 per cent in 1994. And several European countries (Sweden, Germany, the Netherlands) have been shrinking this ratio for several years. American costs remain extraordinarily high, in international terms, and are continuing to escalate, even if less rapidly than in the past.[12]

Thus, when managed care is offered in other countries as a compromise between public regulation and private action, it looks rather more like a compromise between success and failure. Nobody pretends that other countries do not have substantial problems with their health care systems. But they are typically problems that most Americans would be very relieved to have to face.[13]

So there is a puzzle. The record of the last forty years seems to show that the United States took the wrong road in trying to rely on private action to organize and finance health care. The rest of us groped our way to what now seems to be a reasonably satisfactory road, albeit one needing a good deal of further work. Why, then, would anyone want to rerun the ancient state-versus-market debates of the 1950s? And why, in particular, would other countries be thinking of expanding the role of the private market, and importing American ideas?[14] Have we gotten the military maxim backward: "Expedite failure, and abandon success?"

A good part of the answer, I think, lies in the loose use of *we*. It implies a commonality of interest, suppressing the rather obvious fact that choices with respect to health care finance, as with any other aspect of public policy, have significant distributional consequences. Some gain, and some lose, and the gains and losses can be very large.

The persistence of the same old arguments over health care finance, the resilience of ancient policy proposals in the face of contrary experience, is rooted in the fact that the broad pattern of gainers and losers resulting from particular policy choices in health care has changed little, if at all, over the decades (Barer et al., 1994). The relative size of the particular interest groups is now very different, in different countries, and the stakes are much larger. But the interests are the same.

Figure 7.3 and Equation 7.1 provide an accounting framework – a stripped-down sectoral version of the national income accounts – within which to represent the different interests involved. Abstracting from

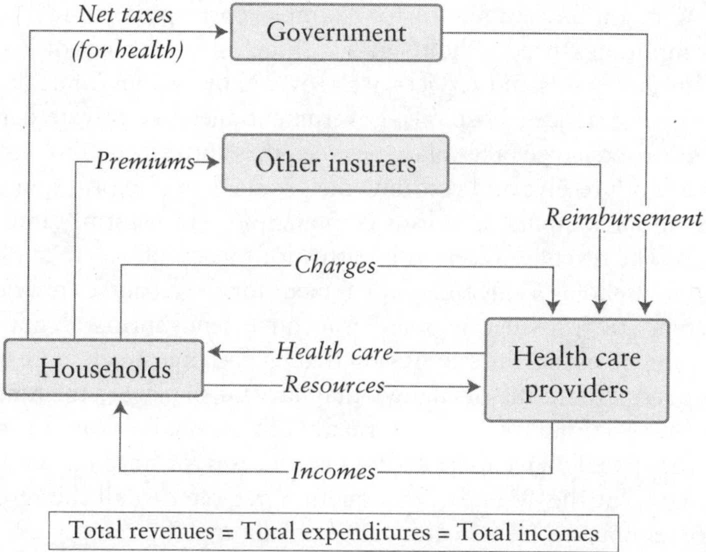

Figure 7.3 Alternative ways of paying for health care

Adapted from: Robert Evans. "Going for the Gold: The Redistributive Agenda Behind Market-based Health Care Reform." In *Journal of Health Politics, Policy and Law* 22(2)(1997): 427–65.

both international trade and changes in asset stocks, there is a fundamental identity linking total *expenditures* on health goods and services, total *revenues* raised to pay for those services, and total *incomes* earned from the provision of services:

$$T + C + R \equiv P \times Q \equiv W \times Z. \qquad \text{(Equation 7.1)}$$

The definition of what does or does not constitute a health service, the basket of commodities included in this sector, is in principle arbitrary, although in practice there is good agreement on the broad categories of medically necessary hospital, medical, and pharmaceutical services. The grey areas are many, but quantitatively pretty small (with the exception of institutional care of the frail elderly or otherwise disabled).

Revenues may be raised through three main channels: taxation (T), direct charges (C), and private insurance premiums (R).[15] Total expenditure can be factored into the unit prices of the various health care commodities, and the quantities of each. P and Q are thus vectors whose elements refer to all the different types of commodities provided in the system. These, in turn, are produced by combining various inputs or resources Z that are paid at a rate per unit W. An element of the vector W might be a wage rate, for example, corresponding to a type of labour input measured in hours and making up an element of Z.

Health care goods and services are provided by various kinds of firms: professional practices, hospitals, government agencies, private corporations. A real exchange takes place between these firms and households, as the latter both receive and consume the products of the former, and supply the resource inputs that firms combine (i.e., "transform") into commodities. The revenues received by firms for their products then all flow back to households as incomes, in payment for the resources provided.[16]

Reference to "provider incomes" is a convenient shorthand, but introduces a source of semantic confusion that has become much more important as a result of the major changes that have taken place in the American health care system. Providers are usually professional persons or institutions who actually give care: doctors and nurses, or hospitals and nursing homes. But the *W* and *Z* in Equation 7.1 refer to all the resources that are reimbursed from health care expenditures. Total incomes earned from the provision of health care include, but are not restricted to, the incomes of providers.[17]

They include, for example, the fees of the lawyer reimbursed by the insurer to whom the physician pays premiums for malpractice insurance. They also include the dividends (and retained earnings) of shareholders in the for-profit managed care firm that contracts with physicians and collects premiums from patients. To the extent that the managed care revolution results in lower fees, salaries, or workloads for particular caregivers, it lowers the incomes of providers as commonly defined. But if total costs continue upward, then the flow of funds through the health care system will have been redirected to benefit a different group of households: suppliers of managerial services and investment capital, marketers, accountants, and the whole administrative overhead of business enterprise. The components of *W* and *Z* will be rearranged – less for some, more for others, but taken in total, incomes earned from the provision of health care continue to increase.

The fundamental point, however, is that the relationship depicted in Figure 7.3 and written out in Equation 7.1 *is* an identity, and must hold, as a matter of logic and mathematical consistency. Any change to one component must be either offset or balanced by corresponding changes elsewhere in the equation.

To this identity, we can annex various side equations, or additional relationships that are postulated to involve components of the basic identity. At a minimum these would include:

1 A health production function that links the outputs of health services Q to the health status of the members of the population. This relationship is both complex and controversial, but the very definition of health services implies that they bear a special relationship to health. Absent that relationship, and most of us would much prefer to forego the services themselves: Consuming health care is not in itself a source of satisfaction.
2 A health *care* production function that links the outputs of services Q to the levels of inputs Z. Dollars do not produce services; but people, know-how, capital, and raw materials do. One cannot make bricks (at least not very good ones) without straw.
3 A demand relationship linking the level of direct charges paid by users, C, to the level of utilization, Q. The typical assumption from the economics textbooks is that as C goes up, Q goes down, and indeed *ceteris paribus* that appears to be true. But the *ceteris* are rarely, if ever, *paribus*, which is why this relationship must be considered in the context of the overall identity.
4 A capacity relation linking levels of service provided Q to some maximum available stock of inputs Z^*. The inputs used and paid for at any point in time do not necessarily represent the full capacity of the health care system. On the other hand, there *is* a strong tendency for patterns of care to adapt so as to use up the resources available: Supply creates its own demand.

The production functions need not hold as equalities; they are boundary conditions that place limits on the possible. But providers of care routinely assert, and often sincerely believe, that both of these boundaries have been reached, and also that there would be a high payoff in improved health from further increasing (the right form of) health care. The system is underfunded! Needs are not being met! Send more resources, and especially more money!

Such claims are part of the political theatre in which struggles over income shares are played out. Occasionally they may be supported with actual examples of unmet needs; rarely are the boundary assumptions made explicit, let alone supported. But whatever its relation to "unmet needs," more expenditure always yields an increase in incomes. ($W \times Z$ goes up, although the split between W and Z will depend on other factors.) This is the driving force behind Wildavsky's law (1977).[18]

There is, likewise, a great deal more assertion about the strength – and normative significance – of the demand relationship than ever appears in actual system experience. In fact, providers in publicly funded systems commonly advocate the expansion of direct charges as a way of *increasing* the total flow of funds into health care, implying that if there is any net negative effect on Q, it will be offset by corresponding increases in P. At the system-wide level, the evidence seems to be consistent with this view.[19] In practice, increases in user charges serve to *shift* costs from one payer to another, while increasing, not decreasing, the total. Providers, and especially their representatives, are not economically naive.

On the other hand, the direct impact of capacity on use is one of the most solidly grounded empirical relationships in health economics. It has been observed for hospital beds, physicians, and new drug products or types of technical equipment. But it is conditional on the availability of payment. Roemer's law, that a built bed is a filled bed, abruptly ceased to hold in the United States when Medicare shifted to case-based reimbursement. And fund-holding general practitioners in the United Kingdom, who have to bear the resulting costs, seem much less willing than previously to hospitalize their patients.

The side equations however remind us that we are dealing with individual people (or households) as well as with commodities and units of currency. Money is fungible, but people are not. If we simply rewrite Equation 7.1 in notation that provides labels for each of the persons, commodities, and inputs involved, it becomes obvious that the identity holds in aggregate, but not for any one individual. Thus,

$$\Sigma_i\{tY_i + \Sigma_j (C_j \times q_{ij}) + R_i\} \equiv \Sigma_{ij} (P_j \times q_{ij}) \equiv \Sigma_{ik}(W_k \times z_{ik}). \quad \text{(Equation 7.1a)}$$

Here persons are indexed by i, health care services by j, and factor inputs by k. In addition, the taxes paid by any individual that are directed toward health care are assumed to be a constant proportion t of that person's income. The user charges paid by an individual are the product of that person's use of a particular commodity, q_{ij}, multiplied by the level of charge, C_j, applicable to that service, and summed over all services. The user charge will typically lie between zero and the actual price/cost P_j of that service, although there is no logical reason why it could not be outside that range.

Stripping off the summations across individuals, the relationships in Equation 7.1a divide the population into two groups according to whether $W \times Z$ for a particular individual exceeds or falls short of both $T + C + R$ and $P \times Q$. The group for whom $W \times Z$ is higher are (net) recipients of health spending; they receive more in income from health care than they contribute to its financing or receive in services. The remainder, with low $W \times Z$, are (net) users of/payers for care: the rest of us.

A change in the funding arrangements for health care that increases expenditure (relative to what it would otherwise be) will typically be advantageous for the first group, and costly for the second.[20] Most obviously, an increase in expenditure that takes the form of rising P and W, however it is financed, unambiguously transfers income from payers/users to providers – no surprises there.

But the user/payer group is not homogeneous; it can, in turn, be subdivided according to whether $T+C+R$ exceeds or falls short of $P \times Q$. The former can be labelled as the healthy and/or wealthy, contributing more to the financing of the system than the value of the services they receive from it. Conversely, those for whom $P \times Q$ exceeds $T+C+R$ are net beneficiaries, at least financially.[21] Again, any change in the sources of funding for a health care system will transfer income between the members of these two groups.

Thus, one finds, for example, that people with higher incomes are more likely to favour greater reliance on user charges as a source of system finance, and less use of general public revenues. A priori it should be pretty obvious that, whereas tax liabilities tend to be more or less proportionate to income, illness is not. For any given level of expenditure on health, more will come out of the pockets of wealthier individuals if the system is tax-financed, and less if it is user-paid. Private insurance premiums, being based on expected use of care, not on income level, also take a bigger share of the incomes of people at lower incomes.

There are, however, two aspects to the regressivity of private insurance financing, as compared with tax financing. Because private insurance premiums are independent of income, lower-income people will have to pay a larger share of their incomes for the same coverage. This will be true even of a community-rated private plan, or a plan covering a large employee group, in which the covered pool is large enough that an individual's premium does not depend upon his or her own illness experience. Tax-financed coverage charges people in some proportion to their incomes.

In small employee groups, however, experience rating by the insurer will imply that the amount of the premium will also be sensitive to extreme individual experiences. Insofar as today's insured outlays are recouped by the insurer in the form of higher premiums tomorrow, insurance becomes, in part, a delayed user charge. This will increase the

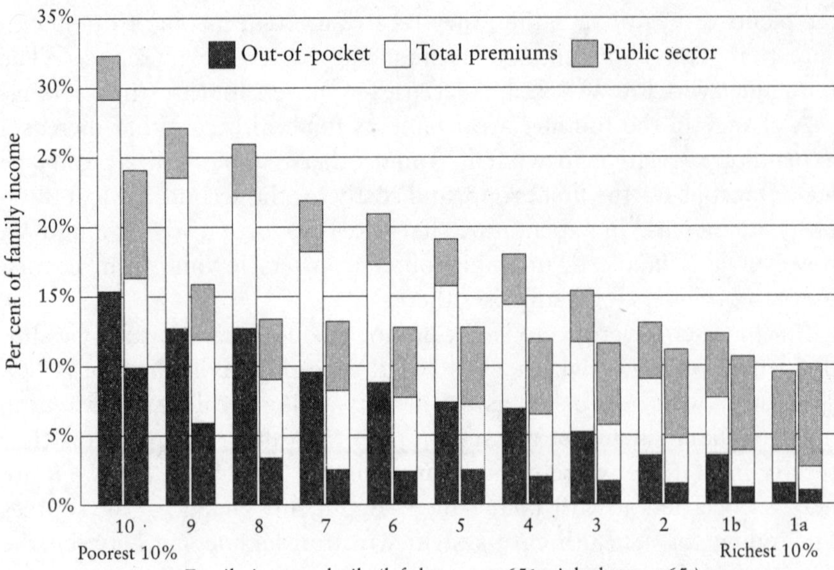

Figure 7.4 Family expenditures for health care by income decile and age of head

Adapted from: Robert Evans. "Going for the Gold: The Redistributive Agenda Behind Market-based Health Care Reform," in *Journal of Health Politics, Policy and Law* 22(2)(1997): 427–65. *Original source*: Rasell, et al. (1993). Reprinted with permission of the Economic Policy Institute.

variance of health care costs as a share of income; to the extent that illness is correlated with low income, it will also increase the regressivity of the financing system. And if and as the labour market evolves away from large employee groups toward smaller firms and individual contractors, this aspect of regressivity will become more pronounced.

Empirical confirmation comes from studies in the United States (Rasell, Bernstein, and Tang, 1993; Rasell and Tang, 1994). As shown in Figure 7.4, the share of health spending that comes through public budgets is progressively distributed, taking a larger share of the incomes of people at higher income levels. But both user fees and private insurance are strikingly regressive, taking a much larger share of the incomes of lower-income people.[22]

Moreover, this pattern is particularly apparent among those over sixty-five, who are virtually all enrolled in the national Medicare program for the elderly. The various deductibles, coinsurance rates, and exclusions in that program, and the corresponding private medigap insurance market, produce a highly regressive financing structure even for this universal public program.

The identity provides the algebra underlying proposals for reform. In Equation 7.1a, if one holds total expenditure constant and makes offsetting changes in t and C, those whose share of total income exceeds their share of total health expenditures (either because their incomes are large or because their expenditures are small) will gain more from tax reductions than they lose from increased user charges (Evans, Barer, and Stoddart, 1994).[23] And these are the people who then advocate, on various grounds and through a multitude of channels, increased reliance on "private" funding (Barer et al., 1994).

Several attempts have been made over the years to confuse this essentially straightforward distributional issue. Proposals for integration of user charges with the income tax, or the creation of medical savings accounts, are financing gimmicks that obscure or appear to change the direction of the income transfer. But when one works through the details, at their core is health insurance with greatly increased deductibles and rates of coinsurance: more user pay and less tax finance. So long as tax liability is related to income, and service use is not, any such changes *must* transfer income from the less to the more healthy and wealthy.[24] Thus, debates over public or private financing, whatever other issues they may draw in, are always and inevitably about who pays what share of the bill.

The standard claim by market advocates has always been that placing more of the cost burden on individual users will lead to lower utilization and more careful purchasing by consumers/patients, more competitive behaviour by providers, and thus to a less costly, more responsive, and more efficient health care system. If this does not occur, it must be because the user charges are not high enough.

As observed previously, the international comparative experience of the last forty years is flatly in contradiction with this claim. But the point emphasized here is that, whether or not the claim is true, it must be the case, from the basic accounting, that shifting the cost burden from taxpayers to users will, on average, redistribute wealth from lower- to higher-income individuals. When people persistently advocate a particular policy by making a claim A, which (I believe) the evidence rejects, while consistently avoiding discussion of effect B, which the policy *must* bring about, one should at least consider that B may be the real objective.

Interestingly, Hsiao (1995) provided a recent evaluation of Singapore's experience with medical savings accounts, as part of a more general reform based on precisely the claims of the market advocates. He concluded that, contrary to those claims, increasing the role of private financing has led to more rapid cost escalation, an overcapitalized system of duplicated and underutilized facilities, and rapid increases in physician incomes. Even when patients are paying prices in nominally "free" markets, hospitals do not compete on price, but on technology, in order to attract the physicians who will bring in the paying patients. Nor can this be blamed on mismanagement; he described the Singapore funding system as carefully planned and well executed. It was the fundamental theory that was in error.

In 1993, Singapore authorities concluded that "the health care system is an example of market failure. The government has to intervene directly to structure and regulate the health system" (quoted in Hsiao, 1995: 263). Their observation is a bit late to be original; indeed, one does wonder, given the accumulation of international experience, how they could ever have imagined otherwise. But it is significant because it follows a decade-long effort, under the most favourable circumstances, to make the market work.[25]

Contributors at different income levels are not, however, the only participants in the conversation over the state versus the market. The split between those who pay and those who are paid has had an even more powerful and long-term impact on the evolution of health care policy. It has always fuelled the conflicting perceptions of system underfunding versus excessive costs that seem to emerge in all systems, whatever the evidentiary base.

The comparative success of governments in developing mechanisms for cost control – although not always in deploying them – has led to increasing efforts by providers to enhance their incomes by drawing in more private funds. These efforts underlie the peculiar "conversation of the deaf" between those who are trying to limit public responsibility for payment by defining "core services," and turning the rest over to the private market, however defined, and those who are trying to improve system management by eliminating ineffective services.

The root of the problem is that people get paid for doing things, whether or not these are effective.[26] If the movement for evidence-based health care leads to a slimmed-down health care system, with fewer ineffective services and lower costs, then, as the identity makes obvious, there will be fewer and/or lower income streams generated. Population health status may be maintained, or even increase, but Q, Z, and T, C, and/or R all fall.

On the other hand, the core services approach finesses the question: Does the service do any good? Health drops out of consideration, and splits Q into two components: *core*, paid for from the public budget, and *non-core*, paid for through direct charges or private insurance. The original bundle of services, or rather types of services, now draws in more money in total. Private funding (*C* and/or *R*) increases; unless there are equal or greater reductions in public funding, the health care system as a whole expands: Prices, incomes, and perhaps jobs are up.

Are the non-core services effective in improving health? Well, once they are out in the private market, who cares? Containing the exuberance of private medicine (or drugs, or dentistry, etc.) is technically difficult and politically expensive, unless there is some egregious public scandal (e.g. thalidomide). Governments – or employers – will only take on the task if they must bear the financial consequences of not doing so. And even then, success is not guaranteed. But if someone else is paying, the prudent response is to hide behind the rhetoric of the "sovereign consumer," who is after all "freely choosing" to spend his or her own money, and perhaps try to promote a voluntary code of ethical conduct by providers.

The key distinction is that the evidence-based approach to classifying services identifies activities that do no good, and thus should not be provided *by anybody, in any setting*. In aiming to reduce total system costs while maintaining or improving population health status, it threatens provider incomes. The core services approach is instead a program for tapping more private funds to supplement those provided by increasingly tough-minded governments: cost shifting rather than cost control. In this way, advocates hope to expand total system costs while limiting or reducing public outlays. Different objectives, different constraints, but again, the debate about private funding turns out to be about incomes.

Not all providers, however, believe that they can successfully draw in private funds. Those who offer well-defined and easily marketable procedures to anxious middle-aged businessmen may do very well, but those whose clienteles have complex problems and few resources would gain little from an opportunity to market their services privately. From them, one hears support for the evidence-based approach, but with the proviso that any savings should be put back into other forms of care to meet other needs. Resources (and incomes) would then be redirected within the health care sector, while blunting the threat to total expenditures/incomes. Unlike the core services approach, however, this does not offer governments a way to limit *their* outlays.

Proposals to expand the role of private insurance link the interests of both providers and upper-income contributors. Governments have proven to be quite tough as budgetary negotiators, and are imposing increasingly stringent controls on health care expenditures as their own fiscal position weakens. Private insurers, on the other hand, have no particular incentive to limit cost escalation – if anything, the contrary – and in any case have not done so. From the point of view of providers, the optimal situation – at least in economic terms – is to have complete freedom to set prices and choose treatment patterns, but to have a high level of insurance coverage in the population so that the resulting bills will be paid.

American experience indicates that a high level of coverage requires very large public subsidies, both directly for the elderly and poor, and through tax expenditures for those with private coverage. But the tax expenditure subsidies for private insurance can be, and in the United States are, structured to yield the greatest benefits for people in higher income brackets. At the same time, the tax-supported public program for the elderly has extensive user charges – deductibles and coinsurance – built into it in the name of cost control. But these charges are in turn covered, in whole or in part, by private medigap insurance policies or through extensions of employer coverage as a retirement benefit. Such private coverage is highly correlated with income.[27]

Thus, increases in Medicare user charges serve primarily to shift costs from a funding source that is related to income (taxes) to one that is not (private insurance premiums). Their deterrent effect, which as argued before has no effect on aggregate system cost anyway, is faced only by those whose employers did not provide (or can no longer sustain) post-retirement coverage, who cannot afford private medigap coverage (or were sold a bad policy), or who are not poor enough for (or do not know about) Medicaid coverage.

Viewed in aggregate, the combination of Medicare user charges to control costs, plus private insurance to cover those charges, plus tax expenditure subsidies for private insurance, all overlaid with the capricious effects of highly imperfect markets, makes no sense at all. Indeed, it borders on lunacy. But, if one looks at the combination instead as a (non-transparent) way of keeping health care expenditures and incomes *up* by fragmenting funding sources while shifting the burden of contributions down the income scale, with a cover story that holds the ill accountable for their "choices" to "consume" health care, then it begins to make sense. The whole system produces much higher costs, and a much more regressive contribution structure, than would be politically acceptable in any single-payer public system funded from general revenue.[28]

But all this administrative apparatus does not come cheap. This point emerged very clearly from an analysis of OECD data by Gerdtham and Jönsson (1991), in which they identified the effects of differences in the

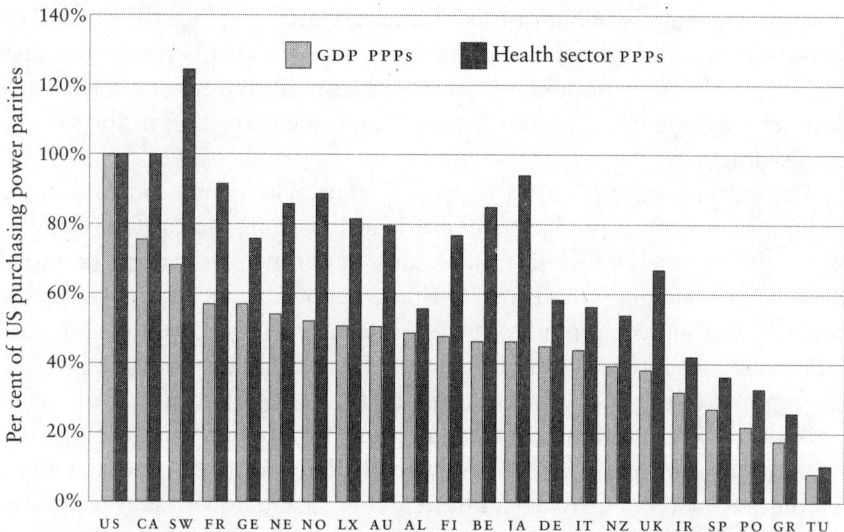

Figure 7.5 Health care spending per capita, 1985, as per cent of US purchasing power parities

Adapted from: Robert Evans. "Going for the Gold: The Redistributive Agenda Behind Market-based Health Care Reform," in *Journal of Health Politics, Policy and Law* 22(2)(1997): 427–65. *Original source:* Gerdtham and Jönsson (1991). Reproduced with permission of Taylor & Francis Ltd, http://www.tandfonline.com

relative prices of health care services, from one country to another, on international comparisons of health care costs. They found, as displayed in Figure 7.5, that a large proportion of the difference in per capita expenditures between the United States and all other countries of the OECD was a result of higher relative prices of health care in the United States.[29]

Americans receive, on average, no more care than Canadians, very little more than Japanese, and much less than Swedes. But they pay much more, relatively, for what they get. In terms of the preceding identity, P (price) is higher in the United States than anywhere else.[30]

Defenders of the American health care system may claim, and even believe, that this price differential corresponds to some unmeasured difference in quality, but the discussion rapidly becomes circular. It is, in fact, a natural extension of the American exceptionalism claim (see note 9): "American health care costs more because Americans face greater threats to their health, and need more care." "But they do not *get* much more care, they just pay much more for it." "Well, then the care they get must be of higher quality." In effect, expenditure is *defined* as quality. The only way out of this (il)logical trap is to place the burden of proof on the apologist. Let him find some evidence of benefit – not just for the wealthy but population-wide, not just inferred from some theory but actually documented – to correspond to the extra cost of the system as a whole.

The extreme case frames the general issue. The expansion of private insurance, within a public system of health care finance, offers benefits to both providers (higher prices) and upper-income payers (a more regressive financing structure). It thus supports a potent political alliance. If, in addition, providers are able (selectively) to recruit people into the private insurance system by offering them the reality, or even just the perception, of superior services, this reinforces the financial advantages.

But the complex administrative mechanisms for achieving these redistributional objectives are themselves costly. They result not only in higher incomes for (some) providers, but in an increasing flow of real resources into the overhead costs of managing the health care system. And this is inevitable. The inherent instability of private health care financing – Wildavsky's law (1977) again – leads to uncontrolled cost escalation. This in turn generates an administrative arms race as each payer struggles to shift the ever-increasing costs onto others. Such efforts are highly rational, indeed necessary for survival, at the level of the individual institution. From the perspective of the society as a whole, they generate an ever-increasing level of pure waste motion.[31]

The dynamics of the relationship between public and private insurance depend upon a number of institutional characteristics that are quite system-specific. God and the devil are both in the details. The point emphasized here is a more general one, that distributional conflicts are central to all arguments for and against private insurance – the relative balance of state and private action. Depending upon how it is structured, expanding private insurance offers opportunities for transfer of incomes both from payers to providers and from the less to the more healthy and wealthy payers. Conversely, the historic shift to public coverage moved incomes the other way, although the amounts were not so large in earlier decades. Associated with these inherently political choices over distribution, however, are significant differences in the real resource costs of system administration, and corresponding income opportunities in the financial services industry.

If governments, and behind them electorates, can be induced to focus their attention on public budgets alone, rather than the balance of costs and benefits from the health care system as a whole, then the stage is set for an unholy alliance in which all three parties can gain by (a) lowering public expenditures, but (b) increasing overall expenditures, and (c) shifting a larger share of costs onto the relatively less healthy and wealthy. A perfectly reasonable public objective of reconstructing a highly dysfunctional health care sector can then be deflected and perverted into a program for regressive income redistribution and protection of health sector revenues, all under the ideological cover of shrinking big government.

All of which is rather banal and obvious (Political Economy 101), and one might reasonably ask whether the whole excursion was necessary. The justification, I think, is that so much of the debate over health care policy, particularly among economists, and particularly over the relative roles of the state and the market, continues to be carried on as if it *were* possible to abstract from distributional issues, when out in the real world, the conflicts are in fact about very little else.

The tone of economic discourse was set about twenty-five years ago, and Arrow (1976) sounded a warning at the time that was generally ignored. In an analysis of the welfare effects of coinsurance rates, originally written in 1973, he declared at the outset that "I ignore distributional considerations and assume a single person in the economy" (4). On the next page, however, he stated: "To avoid distributional considerations I assume that all individuals have identical endowments and identical utility functions. I further assume a very large population" (5).

The confusion is understandable. In a single-person economy, who buys insurance, and from whom? But in an economy of *differentiated* individuals, it is impossible to derive general a priori conclusions about aggregate welfare. Arrow (1976) therefore assumed that the economy consists of many identical individuals. They vary in their actual health experience (or why buy insurance?), but they are identical in their *expectation* of illness, so they have equal access to insurance coverage as well as equal incomes. Moreover, they all work for the same proportion of their time in the "medical" industry. Thus, there is no distinction between providers and users: everyone is both, and to an equivalent degree. Under Arrow's assumptions, Equation 7.1a *does* hold for each of the individuals *i*, not just for the aggregate. One need only substitute an expected value for the actual quantities of services used by each person.

As an approximation to the real world, Arrow's (1976) assumptions were ridiculous – as he very well knew. What he was showing is that *without* such assumptions, one cannot, at the theoretical level, ignore "distributional considerations" and generate any conclusions at all about the desirability or otherwise of any particular policy.[32]

Of course, one can do so if one is prepared to make interpersonal comparisons of well-being, balancing one person's loss against another's gain, and this happens every day in the real world of public policy. But as a number of leading theorists, Arrow included, have pointed out, one cannot do so on the basis of "value-neutral" economic theory. Theory by itself does not, and logically cannot, provide a normative basis for policy prescriptions. Rice's (1997) article in this issue provides a more detailed discussion; see also Culyer (1989), Reinhardt (1992), and Culyer and Evans (1996). Normative judgments, in or out of economics, cannot be derived from positive propositions alone, or in Archibald's paraphrase of Hume: "No ethics in, no ethics out."

Yet respected economic analysts do so routinely, making firm declarations as to the efficiency or optimality of particular arrangements, or their welfare costs or benefits. In doing so they are making value judgments about the relative deservingness of different individuals, and approving or disapproving the transfer of substantial funds from one set of people to another. But these judgments are implicit, unaccountable, and typically unconfessed – sometimes even denied. There is also some reason to believe that the values implicit in proposals for more reliance on private markets in health care are quite unrepresentative of the views of the populations who use and support health care systems. Yet, they are confidently offered as guides for public policy. So, what is going on?[33]

Well, the suppression of distributional considerations through the (implicit) assumption of identical individuals *can* provide an analytic cloak for what would otherwise be a naked redistributional agenda. Deliberately redistributive policies can be promoted as optimal on a priori grounds, allegedly on the basis of value-free economic theory. The essential feature of all such policies is a shift in funding sources in order to link individual contributions more closely to either care use or risk status, while weakening the link to ability to pay. Often they will also give providers greater discretion in price setting, which may include offering patients various forms of preferential treatment in return for additional private payments.[34]

One need not, however, assume that the provision of an analytic cloak for redistributional objectives is the deliberate intent of analysts in the tradition of neoclassical economic theory, even if their work may be useful for this purpose. There is an important distinction to be drawn between two quite different groups of participants in the debate over the role of the state in health services, whom we may label fundamentalists and instrumentalists. The latter advocate particular structures or policies because they expect certain consequences to result; but the former are "advocates without predicates," holding particular forms of economic organization to be good per se. In an earlier day, socialists regarded state control of the means of production, or at least of the "commanding heights" of the economy, as good per se, on a priori grounds. At present, advocates of the market on theoretical grounds enjoy the same absolute conviction.

Debates with fundamentalists about the proper scope of public and private action are ultimately futile. Initial impressions to the contrary, they do not, in fact, base their case for the market on (testable) claims that their preferred institutions or policies will lead to lower costs, or healthier people, or better performance on any other externally defined criterion (Frankford 1992). When pressed, fundamentalists explicitly reject such external standards (e.g., Pauly, 1994a, 1994b). Their position is rather that *whatever* results – prices, quantities, distribution of services, health outcomes – emerge from market processes, such results are optimal *because* they have been generated by those processes. The private marketplace is the source of ultimate objectives rather than merely a means to their achievement. Individual willingness to pay for the products of private, competitive firms is not the best criterion for efficient resource allocation: It is the only criterion.

The fundamentalist argument for private action in health care, although clothed in economic rhetoric, is in fact a form of religion. It converts Side Equation 3, linking the level of use of health care services to the direct charges that users must pay, from a *positive* statement about an (in principle) observable relationship between two variables, into a *normative* statement about how the level, mix, and distribution of health care services, the q_{ij}, *ought* to be determined. But normative statements are the province of priests. (And also of politicians, but those suffer the inconvenience of having to secure public support.) The normative views of economists, qua economists, have no more (or less) significance than those of T.C. Pits.[35]

But these theoretical arguments, mostly in the economic literature, are primarily icing on the cake. Very few people (if any) share the underlying value system on which they are based. When we come to the point, most of us do *not* agree that it is a misallocation of resources when people receive life-saving care that they cannot themselves afford, and that our societies would be in some sense more efficient (better) if this did not occur. We do not want to live in that kind of society, we do not have to, and we will not.

Accordingly, most of those on the political stage who consistently advocate (or oppose) a larger role for private markets in health care do so because they anticipate particular consequences, rather than from religious conviction. These instrumentalists, however, may have very different objectives. Roughly, we may draw a distinction between those whose aims are primarily distributional, and those who are genuinely concerned with system performance.

All, of course, use the rhetoric of system improvement, and of public interest more generally – even the fundamentalists can sometimes be found in this camouflage. And it is a gross oversimplification to suggest that a population can be thus neatly partitioned into two distinct groups. People's motives are usually mixed, and are often far from clear even to themselves. Nevertheless, it is important to recognize explicitly that debates over health policy, and particularly over the role of the state, are motivated by these two quite different classes of objectives.

This article has emphasized the link between extension of the role of private market mechanisms, particularly in the financing of health care, and distributional objectives. The interest groups, which for decades have reiterated the same arguments for private markets, regardless of the evidence accumulated against them, see their own interests clearly enough. Their members hope to earn more (providers), or to contribute less and have preferred access to services (healthy and/or wealthy users).

To the extent that they are right, there is again little to debate. The analyst's role is only to make the proposed redistributional agenda as explicit as possible. Its advocates can then compete directly for broader public support without drawing upon misinterpretations of economic theory or other claims of general public benefit. Because, in practice, people as citizens do not appear to be motivated solely by perceptions of their own economic interests, greater transparency of policy effects may well lead to different, and more satisfactory, collective choices. (If it were not so, interest groups would not be so careful to disguise the full impact of their proposals.)

Moreover, redistributional processes turn out to be more complex than they look, and alternative choices *do* have consequences for the overall functioning of a health care system. Quite clearly, private funding mechanisms can be used to generate a more regressive distribution of contributions, if that is what one wants. But international experience indicates that the overall system will be more expensive, because providers' prices will be higher, because inappropriate use will be harder to control, and especially because the complex mix of public and private financing and management mechanisms will add substantially to the administrative overhead costs of providing care.

The explosion of costs in the United States, for example, has not all gone into the pockets of providers as traditionally defined (discussed previously). An increasing proportion has been appropriated by members of the managerial and financial services industries, who now appear to be cutting into, and pushing down, the incomes of caregivers. The management thus financed has, to date, involved a good deal of extra trouble and work for both caregivers and patients, not all of which is included in statistics on health care costs. But if the most recent data *do* in fact herald a new world of stable or even declining American health care expenditures, the struggle between providers of care and providers of managerial overhead is likely to become increasingly bitter.

In any case, although upper-income Americans may pay a smaller *share* of the costs of their health care system than they would if it conformed to White's (1995) international standard, many of them actually pay more in total, because their system is so much more expensive. Public sector spending on health care in the United States, at $1,599 per capita in 1994, was greater than in any other OECD country except Switzerland, even without accounting for the American tax expenditure subsidy. Canada, for example, with universal public first dollar coverage for hospital and medical care, spent only US $1,444 in public funds; most European countries spent substantially less (OECD/CREDES, 1996). Americans thus pay more *in taxes* for health care, in addition to (or despite) their massive contributions through the private sector.

The more interesting instrumentalist debates arise, however, after it is accepted that the public purpose of health care systems is indeed what most people in every society say it is: the maintenance and improvement of health, and the humane treatment of the ill (Labelle, Stoddart, and Rice, 1994). Indeed, as van Doorslaer, Wagstaff, and Rutten (1993: 11) reported, and as public surveys confirm, most people seem to have a rather Marxist view of health care systems: "From each according to his ability, to each according to his needs." Side Equation 3 then moves from the centre of the stage and we focus instead on Equation 7.1 and Side Equation 2. Are our health care systems efficient producers of effective services? Do they respond to patients' needs in a humane and timely fashion? How can their performance be improved while maintaining fiscal constraints?

If a health care system *were*, in fact, on the frontier of both the preceding health care and health production functions, then there would be a direct link between resource inputs and (someone's) health status. In such circumstances, cutbacks cost lives – or at least put health at risk – as care is long delayed, or denied altogether. And overstrained providers may be brusque, perfunctory, uncommunicative, and inconvenient to access. Faced with such prospects, a majority of our populations might well support more resources for health care, particularly if they perceive themselves personally to be at risk. Nurturing that belief is the cornerstone of the public relations strategy of provider representatives in all countries.

If, on the other hand (as is widely, if not universally, believed by students of health care systems), there is a great deal of inappropriate, unnecessary, and sometimes downright harmful care being paid for in all modern health care systems, and if the process of production is none too efficient either, then the key question becomes one of moving closer to both production frontiers.

The instrumentalist case for systemic reform through private market mechanisms is simply that these could be structured either to embody incentives for greater efficiency in production than is possible in governmentally administered systems, or (which is not at all the same thing) to encourage a more appropriate mix – perhaps less in total – of services, more responsively provided. In the process, of course, these mechanisms must not result in an unacceptable (to whom?) redistribution of incomes, or a re-ignition of cost escalation.

At a very basic level, this proposition does not seem particularly contentious. Opening hospital laundry or dietary services to competitive bids from private firms may raise issues in labour relations, but not for health policy.[36] Implicitly, it is assumed that the quality control problems are similar regardless of the choice of supplier.

Matters become more interesting, however, when the incomes of those making clinical or managerial decisions are linked to the choices they make. Empirically, it is now well established that the therapeutic decisions of providers *are* sensitive to how they are paid, although the terrain is far from fully mapped. When the American Medicare program introduced prospective payment in 1983, for example, and began paying hospitals a predetermined price per inpatient case, treatment patterns promptly changed and inpatient bed use fell. Even more dramatic reductions have since taken place in response to pressures from private payers. In Germany, claims for public reimbursement of prescription drugs fell by 20 per cent in the first six months of 1993, following the government's declaration that drug billings that exceeded a preset target would be paid from the fund for physician reimbursement (Henke, Murray, and

Ade, 1994). When physicians are financially at risk for increased drug bills, they change their prescribing habits.

In general, it seems quite clear that (some) service patterns can be powerfully influenced by linking them directly (negatively) to provider incomes – making *W* depend on *Q*. Aneurin Bevan's comment in 1948 that, if you want to send a message to doctors, you should write it on a cheque, has been confirmed. Furthermore, if you want to make changes in the mix and volume of health care, you *have* to send a message to doctors.

But there are a number of ways of doing this, involving different mixes of economic, regulatory, and educational messages. In the German case, for example, the economic message was combined with closer scrutiny, by professional colleagues, of the prescribing practices of individual physicians (Henke, Murray, and Ade, 1994). Which intervention was critical?

Rates of performance of certain surgical procedures – extracranial/intracranial bypass grafting, carotid endarterectomy, mammary artery ligation – have been powerfully affected by the results of effectiveness trials. (But others, tonsillectomy, for example, or diagnostic procedures such as PSA testing or routine EFM in childbirth, have been remarkably resistant to contrary evidence.) In Canada, the transition from inpatient to same-day surgery proceeded at a slow and stately pace over nearly twenty years after the supporting evidence first became available. The process sped up remarkably in the 1990s, when tighter hospital global budgets forced bed closures.

Economic incentives of various forms, particularly directed at providers of care, are thus only one potentially useful class of tools in the overall mix of mechanisms for health care system management. There is as yet no evidence at the system-wide level to justify a wholesale shift to decentralized decision making based on market-type signals. Moreover, all interventions have side effects. One should never underestimate the power of economic incentives, but neither should one overestimate the ability of economists (or anyone else) to predict how people will respond.[37]

The British experience with general practitioner (GP) fund-holding and hospital trusts is of particular interest in this regard; so far, no close observers of that system seem willing to commit themselves as to whether or not it is working. The introduction of the total package of reforms seems to have been associated with a significant *increase* in system costs, particularly in managerial overhead. There are very clear warnings from the United States that more management may simply mean more money for more managers. Reported declines in waiting lists in the United Kingdom may merely show that with more money, one can buy more services.

The test will be whether the new, more market-like system can deliver better performance, for the same or less money, on meaningful outcome measures. The downside risk, apart from the extra costs of a managerial bureaucracy that fails to pay for its keep, is that it may simply open up new opportunities for income redistribution to providers, and among payers. GP fund holders may find – as American managed-care systems have found before them – that selecting and enrolling relatively healthy patients yields a much higher return than more carefully analyzing the care they give and recommend.

More generally, if subjected to stronger economic incentives, providers will respond. But their responses will probably go beyond what is contemplated or desired by governments, and may be difficult or impossible to control through contracts. As Ham (1994) pointed out, the market will always have to be managed. But the management task may be a good deal more difficult if providers think of themselves less as professionals with public responsibilities and more as private businessmen beating the system any way they can. In the United States, that horse has already left the barn, but not elsewhere, and cooperative relationships, however grudging, should not be lightly put at risk.

In any case, the notion that some sort of automatic, self-regulating market-like structure can be established that will *substitute* for public management and yet achieve public objectives is a fantasy: powdered unicorn horn. In particular, it seems very clear that no incentives at the individual or institutional level, economic or otherwise, will set an upper limit on overall system expenditures. Certainly none ever has. Ultimately, governments have to set these limits and maintain them with whatever mechanisms will do the job.

The use of competition among providers, and market mechanisms generally, as simply one set of tools among others for the pursuit of public objectives seems quite well understood and accepted by many of those responsible for managing the health care systems of western Europe. Morone and Goggin (1995: 568) referred to "guarded optimism about the proposed marriage of medical markets and social welfare universalism. Competition ... may add efficiency and consumer control without subverting traditional collective visions."

It may be that the confusion between market as means and market as end, and the use of currently fashionable private sector rhetoric as a cover for distributional objectives, are more characteristic of North America, at least at the moment. But these ideas *are* being energetically exported, and will find receptive audiences among the same set of potential gainers, in all countries.

The short message of this article is:

- There *are* powerful redistributional motives behind parts of the health care reform agenda, in all countries;
- Much analysis, particularly by economists, misdirects attention by assuming these issues away; and
- Competition, and market mechanisms generally, are particularly suited to both facilitating and concealing the process of redistribution.

Accordingly, to come back to Morone and Goggin (1995: 568), "The great question for the future turns on whether that optimism is justified." Keep your eyes open, and watch your back.

NOTES

1 One of the best treatments of this relationship is Trebilcock, Tuohy, and Wolfson, 1979: Chaps. 2 – 3

2 *Managed markets* is Ham's (1994) term for the interaction between purchasers and providers of health care in the post-reform British National Health Service; in this case "management" is very clearly by the central government, in pursuit of public objectives as interpreted by that government. Kessel (1958) is the classic source in the economic literature for a historical analysis of various forms of collusion and market management among American physicians; there is a large international institutional literature on this subject.

3 The rights of the stronger *do* seem more natural, at least to the stronger.

4 These data are from the 1996 version of the OECD Health Datafile (Éco-Santé OCDE) compiled in Paris by CREDES and the OECD (OECD/CREDES, 1996).

5 It is interesting to note that cost escalation in the United Kingdom seems to have accelerated, relative to the OECD average, in the early 1990s – subsequent to the "internal market" reforms.

6 Although the specific numbers may be controversial, the broad empirical facts do not appear to be in dispute. And these are so glaring as to render the details essentially unimportant.

No one denies, for example, that the uniquely American form of health insurance generates very large administrative costs, much higher than in any other national system. Woolhandler and Himmelstein (1991) have done the most to focus attention on these excess costs; their estimates relative to, say, the costs of administering a Canadian-style universal system would now be well over $100 billion. Others have generated lower estimates, but the point is that, whether unnecessary paper pushing costs Americans $80 billion or $120 billion, the amount is *large*.

Similarly, one can debate whether the number of Americans without health insurance at any point in time is closer to 35 or to 40 million, or whether one should count only those uninsured for a year, or only citizens – and how much care do the uninsured really get anyway? Again, the point is that the number is very large, both in total and as a share of the population, and would not be tolerated in any other developed country.

And while international comparisons of health care (or any other) expenditures are subject to a number of sources of bias and distortion, as well as periodic revision, no amount of statistical adjustment is likely to narrow the gap between the United States, now spending roughly 14 per cent of its national income on health care, and the next most costly countries at about 10 per cent.

7 The Clinton health reform plan was defeated, not because the populace suddenly discovered a new affection for the existing system, but because highly sophisticated and very well-financed disinformation campaigns by those whose incomes would be threatened by reform – $1 trillion fills a lot of large war chests – were successful in generating myths, confusion, and considerable fear of the unknown. These undermined support for any *specific* change, paralyzing the broad consensus that some change was essential (Barer, Marmor, and Morrison, 1995).

8 These observations are not good news for the cost cutters of the 1990s. Moreover, they have the curious feature that reported satisfaction is related to total *spending*. As the relative price of health care varies considerably across countries (see the following), this figure would look quite different if per capita spending were adjusted to reflect the varying per capita quantities of services available in each country. The linear relationship would tend to break down. This implies that Figure 7.2 does *not* simply reflect the crude economic assumption that people are happier when they use more services. What then *is* the connection between spending and satisfaction?

9 The regularity of the international relationship, and the remarkable deviation of the United States, form a context for a claim sometimes made to

explain the American experience: that the threats to health are simply greater in the United States, so the health care system has to work harder and needs more resources. This is the international version of "our patients are sicker" (alternatively, Americans' expectations are higher). Figure 7.2, however, indicates that this American exceptionalism argument requires them to be "very different," not just from some other country, but from the general pattern shown by all developed countries surveyed.

A priori, one might have expected that the differences among "the rest" would have been greater than the differences between the United States and, say, Canada. The only obvious factor differentiating the United States from *all* these other countries is, as Abel-Smith (1985) and White (1995) have pointed out, its health care system.

10 "Whatever else may be going on" covers a vast field, from improved effectiveness, efficiency, and responsiveness to patients at one end, to deliberate underservicing and exploitation of patient vulnerability at the other. A broader discussion is far beyond the scope of this article. A recent and very extensive review by *Consumer Reports*, including a survey of over 30,000 of its members, concluded: "The new age of managed care ... [is] an appealing picture – but today, it's a mirage" (How Good Is Your Health Plan, 1996: 41). Likewise, Zwanziger and Melnick (1996: 190): "The transformation is not yet over. In fact, we are far from the finish, and the process is so complex that we cannot easily predict the outcome."

11 A longer period of experience is available from California, indicating that market forces have exerted sustained downward pressure on cost escalation (Melnick and Zwanziger, 1995). But as Reinhardt (1996) observed, initially very high Californian expenditures have to date simply converged to a national average that has itself steadily risen. And as Glied, Sparer, and Brown (1995) pointed out, the health care market in California has always been strongly promoted and actively managed by the state government. Zwanziger and Melnick (1996), in a discussion of the accumulating American evidence of sustained cost control through managed care, provided a thoughtful assessment of both the issues still unresolved and the critical role for governments in establishing and preserving the conditions necessary for effective competition. Successful private markets will require continued and quite sophisticated public intervention.

12 The most painless way to change the share of health spending in national income is to revise estimates of national income. Recent upward revisions to the American GDP have lowered this share, further reinforcing the sense of easing pressure. The 1993 ratio is now reported as 13.6 per cent; last

year's estimate was 13.9 per cent. Without the GDP revisions, the 1994 ratio would have been 14 per cent. The underlying reality is unchanged, but the "optics" are more optimistic.

13 Most, but not all. Those who work in the private insurance industry, or the rapidly growing managed care industry, know that in any other country their incomes – and the costs they represent – would not exist.

14 Enthoven, one of the most prominent advocates of competitive managed care, declared flatly in 1989 that "it would be, quite frankly, ridiculous ... to suggest that we in the United States have achieved a satisfactory system that our European friends would be wise to emulate" (49). Whatever the changes that have since taken place in the American health care system, the fundamental problems of cost and coverage, efficiency and equity, which motivated his comment, have only become worse.

15 For some purposes, one might wish to subdivide taxes into social insurance premiums and general taxation; alternatively, one can treat that distinction under the general head of the progressivity or regressivity of the overall tax system.

16 Any revenues remaining "in the firm" are attributed back as income to the firm's owners, who are also members of households in this (by assumption, closed) economy. To suppress a swarm of arrows, Figure 7.3 implicitly assumes that no real resources are used up by governments, and no incomes generated therein. One could insert a resource-using process for each financing channel, but the result would be total loss of transparency.

17 Strictly speaking, provider incomes are also not restricted to incomes from health care. They may include earnings on capital investments (outside the health care sector), and other sources of nonprofessional income.

18 Providers, naturally enough, prefer to talk about the "infinite demand" of "consumers." Patient demands may, in fact, escalate pretty rapidly in response to *perceived* threats to life and limb, or health and function. But this demand is endogenous: It depends upon the behaviour of providers themselves.

The cholesterol industry in the United States, for example, has done a remarkable job of creating demand for testing of blood lipids, in complete defiance of the experimental evidence. Those who undergo the tests believe that their life expectancy will be increased by detection and treatment of elevated blood lipids. Understandably enough, they demand the test. Unfortunately, for most of them (the asymptomatic ones), the experimental evidence does not support this belief: ditto mammography in the under-fifty population, ditto PSA testing, ditto routine ultrasound in normal pregnancy, ditto... But there is too much money to be made, not only from testing, but from all the associated services of interpretation, monitoring, and therapy, to let lack of evidence impede medical progress. And then, of course, there is surgery.

19 Emphasis here is on "system." A number of studies have found that the utilization of health care by individuals does seem to respond in the conventional direction when user charges are imposed. But it is a logical error, the fallacy of composition, to infer from this observation that the *overall* costs of a health care system will be lower if patients are required to pay more out-of-pocket. Cross-system observation suggests the reverse, and supports the position taken by providers and their representatives. User charges provide a means of evading the more effective price and quantity controls in public payment systems, and thus of raising overall system costs – and provider incomes.

20 Strictly speaking, this statement depends upon an assumption that the rates of payment for factor inputs in health care exceed their opportunity costs. Because rents and quasi-rents are so pervasive in health care earnings, the assumption is easy to defend. Translated from "economese," the basic idea is that, for a variety of good and less good reasons, people and firms supplying health care tend to be paid prices that are greater, often much greater, than their current costs of production (marginal cost, variable cost), where the latter includes the value of one's own time and skills. They are thus made better off by increases in expenditures that support increases in output at constant prices, as well as those that simply increase prices.

21 Use of words like benefits, however, can obscure the obvious fact that, on the whole, one would prefer not to be among the heavy users of health care! Try it, you won't like it.

22 Both the accounting and the observations are point-in-time snapshots of people moving through a life cycle. Wealth and health change over time; being healthy or wealthy today provides no absolute guarantee for tomorrow. In theory, then, one could imagine that point-in-time status differences might be evened out over the life cycle. But in reality they are not; these states are highly autocorrelated. If you are healthy (or wealthy) today, your chances of being in that state tomorrow are a good deal higher than if you are unhealthy (or unwealthy) today. And the strength of the autocorrelation increases with age. Illnesses become chronic, and wealth becomes predominantly financial assets. Moreover, the two states are cross-correlated. The wealthier (healthier) you are today, the more likely you are to be healthy (wealthy) tomorrow, and this correlation appears to reflect causality in both directions. Life does not even out over time.

23 The assumption that taxes are proportionate to income simplifies the algebra without doing much violence to reality. A sufficiently regressive tax structure would of course reverse this conclusion, but that is all hypothetical. Payroll or other social insurance taxes are less progressive than general income taxes, and revenues from these may be earmarked for health care. But this is simply a labelling exercise if, *at the margin*, public payments for health care come from general revenue sources. In that case, it is the progressivity or regressivity of the tax system as a whole that is relevant, not that of a particular revenue component, whatever its label.

24 There is a qualification here. Poor health is negatively correlated with income, but service use may not be if there are sufficiently large income-related barriers to access. So long as any (positive) correlation between income and use is weaker than that between income and tax liability, however, the transfer is as described.

25 Massaro and Wong (1995) offer a much less critical commentary on the Singapore experience, though drawing upon many of the same observations as Hsiao (1995). Where Hsiao pointed to health care costs outrunning a national income that was itself growing rapidly, they stated that nations "rationally invest" (269) a larger share of their income in health care as they become wealthier, leaving it unclear whether they consider cost control a proper objective in the first place. On the other hand, they suggested that, because costs did not rise as rapidly as they have in some other fast-growing economies, medical savings accounts may have tended to control costs. In any case, "hospitals are profitable and physicians are well paid" (ibid.), and high-technology services are readily available. But that's exactly Hsiao's point: The system is over-capitalized, and (some) providers have made out like bandits.

Massaro and Wong share Hsiao's view that Singapore provided the most favourable environment for competitive markets in health care, and they emphasized the necessary interplay between market mechanisms and detailed public regulation. But they seemed to miss the point that the increasing regulation of physician supply, hospital budgets, and prices/fees in both the public and the private sectors is (according to Hsiao) an explicit response by Singapore authorities to what they regard as failure of the private market system to control costs and promote efficiency. Consequently, they have now adopted the cost control measures that are common in public insurance systems all over the developed world.

As for medical savings accounts, a country with a very small proportion of elderly people, a low birthrate, and a recent very rapid rise in life expectancy would be wise to accumulate savings any way it can. If fear of illness makes people willing to accept a compulsory savings program, then so be it.

26 This generalization is not restricted to fee-for-service payment. Hospital employees may be salaried, and the institution may receive a global budget. But if workloads fall, sooner or later people will be laid off. And eventually, although the adjustment may take some years or even decades, institutions will close.

27 The very poorest are eligible through the Qualified Medicare Beneficiary program for reimbursement of their user charges by Medicaid, if they know about and qualify for the program.

28 Interestingly, France also combines user charges in the public system, the *ticket moderateur*, with private insurance coverage against these charges. The cover story is the same: User charges are needed to hold down costs, but private insurance is needed to ensure access. French health care costs have steadily increased until, by 1995, they were the second highest (relative to GDP) in the OECD. As Marmor says, "Nothing that is regular, is stupid."

29 Gerdtham and Jönsson (1991) began with the usual calculation, converting health care expenditures per capita in each of the OECD countries into US dollars using purchasing power parities (PPPs). When PPPs are based on comparisons of the relative prices of all the commodities in the GDP, one finds very large differences between per capita spending in the United States and in all other countries.

But when other countries' currency was converted into US dollars using PPPs specific to the health care sector, much of this differential disappeared. In this alternative comparison, every country in the OECD moves up relative to the United States, some by a small amount and others by a great deal.

The point is not that prices for health care goods and services are higher in the United States than elsewhere. They are. But what Figure 7.5 shows is that the *ratio* of health care prices to the general price level is higher in the United States than in other countries.

30 Other studies support this inference. Schieber, Poullier, and Greenwald (1994) also showed significantly higher rates of relative inflation of health sector prices in the United States than in other OECD countries. Several comparisons of the Canadian and American health care systems have shown rates of service use that are on average very similar, with Canadians receiving more of some forms of care, and less of others (Fuchs and Hahn, 1990; Nair, Karim, and Nyers, 1992; Redelmeier and Fuchs, 1993).

31 Some have challenged the identification of excessive administrative costs with waste (e.g. Thorpe, 1992). They point to the extraordinarily sophisticated management techniques in the United States, the extent and detail of data generated, and the leading-edge research in health services. In these, the United States clearly does lead the world.

Such responses, however, miss the point. Managerial (and even research) activities are not ends in themselves. They are only valuable insofar as they contribute to the ultimate ends of a more efficient and effective health care system, and a healthier and more satisfied population. As the United States achieves much worse results than systems that spend much less, the extra administrative expenditure is wasted, regardless of how much sophisticated management it may buy. It appears to support a vast negative-sum game of inter-institutional competition over cost transfer and benefit appropriation.

32 Strictly speaking, Arrow (1976) did not ignore distributional considerations. Rather, he imposed very specific distributional assumptions, without which his conclusions have no significance. Nor are there any grounds for arguing that Arrow's results *approximate* what might emerge from a more realistic analysis. They are simply irrelevant to a world of differentiated individuals.

33 Economists who serve as market advocates will sometimes reply that they are simply taking as given whatever distributional outcomes have been generated by the wider society/economy, and are implicit in current arrangements. This argument slides over the fact that changes in health care organization and finance will *change* the pattern of burdens and benefits that the analyst claims to take as given. Preserving the status quo would require offsetting policy changes that are not identified, let alone advocated. In fact, however, their work typically shows little interest in redistributional effects, and even less in the social and political processes that determine underlying patterns.

34 Policies of this form may be described as making more use of the market and of competitive forces to determine the allocation of resources to and within the health care sector. In practice, however, they are always embedded within pseudomarkets, hedged about with extensive regulation and formal or informal collaboration by providers. Much of the regulation may be privately administered, but nowhere outside theoretical analyses does one find anything approximating the free competitive markets of the economics textbooks.

35 The Celebrated Man in the Street, updated. A reference to the common man; see https://www.blogger.com/profile/09213865864534711330

36 Squeezing down costs does not necessarily represent improved efficiency. If private managers achieve their savings by cutting *W* rather than *Z*, then there has been no saving in resource inputs, but only a transfer of incomes from workers in this sector out to whoever enjoyed a decrease in contributions. It is far from clear, at least to me, to what extent contracting out is driven by true efficiency gains as opposed to opportunities to negotiate more favourable input prices. But does it matter: Should we be concerned by the latter?

37 Law 4: "Beware of Incentives. Economists and other rationalists restlessly tinker with people's incentives. This is a dangerous game. Although incentives are important for understanding problems and fashioning solutions, they are also tricky devils, always veering off in unanticipated ways ... People are complicated, social systems almost infinitely so. A great many uninvited incentives lurk in each policy change" (Morone, 1986: 818).

REFERENCES

Abel-Smith, B. (1985). "Who is the odd man out?: The experience of Western Europe in containing the costs of health care." *Milbank Quarterly* 63: 1– 17.

– (1992). "Cost containment and new priorities in the European community." *Milbank Quarterly* 70: 393–416.

– and E. Mossialos (1994). "Cost containment and health care reform: A study of the European Union." *Health Policy* 28: 89–132.

Arrow, K.J. (1976). "Welfare analysis of changes in health coinsurance rates." In *The role of health insurance in the health services sector*, ed. R. Rosett, 3–23. New York: National Bureau of Economic Research.

Barer, M.L., V. Bhatia, G.L. Stoddart, and R.G. Evans (1994). *The remarkable tenacity of user charges*. Toronto: The Ontario Premier's Council on Health, Well-Being, and Social Justice.

– T.R. Marmor, and E. Morrison (1995). "Editorial: Health care reform in the United States: On the road to nowhere (again)." *Social Science and Medicine* 41: 453–60.

Blendon, R.J., J. Benson, K. Donelan, R. Leitman, H. Taylor, C. Koeck, and D. Gitterman (1995). "Who has the best health care system? A second look." *Health Affairs* 14(4): 220–30.

– R. Leitman, I. Morrison, and K. Donelan (1990). "Satisfaction with health systems in ten nations." *Health Affairs* 9(2): 185–92.

Consumer Reports (1996). "How good is your health plan?" *Consumer Reports* 61(8): 28–42.

Culyer, A.J. (1989). "The normative economics of health care finance and provision." *Oxford Review of Economic Policy* 5: 34–58.

– and R.G. Evans (1996). "Mark Pauly on welfare economics: Normative rabbits from positive hats." *Journal of Health Economics* 15(2): 243–51.

Enthoven, A.C. (1989). "What can Europeans learn from Americans about financing and organization of medical care?" *Health Care Financing Review* (Annual Suppl.): 49–63.

Evans, R.G., M.L. Barer, and G.L. Stoddart (1994). *Charging Peter to pay Paul: Accounting for the financial effects of user charges.* Toronto: The Ontario Premier's Council on Health, Well-Being, and Social Justice.

Frankford, D.M. (1992). "Privatizing health care: Economic magic to cure legal medicine." *Southern California Law Review* 66(1): 1–98.

Fuchs, V.R., and J.S. Hahn (1990). "How does Canada do it? A comparison of expenditures for physicians' services in the United States and Canada." *New England Journal of Medicine* 323: 884–90.

Gerdtham, U.-G., and B. Jönsson (1991). "Price and quantity in international comparisons of health care expenditure." *Applied Economics* 23: 1519–28.

Glied, S., M. Sparer, and L. Brown (1995). "Comment: Containing state health care expenditures – the competition vs. regulation debate." *American Journal of Public Health* 85: 1347–9.

Ham, C. (1994). *Management and competition in the new NHS*. Oxford, England: Radcliffe Medical Press for the National Association of Health Authorities and Trusts.

Henke, K.-D., M.A. Murray, and C. Ade (1994). "Global budgeting in Germany: Lessons for the United States." *Health Affairs* 13(4): 7–21.

Hsiao, W. (1995). "Medical savings accounts: Lessons from Singapore." *Health Affairs* 14(2): 260–6.

Kessel, R.A. (1958). "Price discrimination in medicine." *Journal of Law and Economics* 1(2): 20–53.

Labelle, R.J., G.L. Stoddart, and T.H. Rice (1994). "A re-examination of the meaning and importance of supplier-induced demand." *Journal of Health Economics* 13(3): 347–68.

Lamm, R.D. (1994). "Healthcare heresies." *Healthcare Forum Journal* (September-October): 45–6, 59–61.

Levit, K.R., H.C. Lazenby, and L. Sivarajan (1996). "Health care spending in 1994: Slowest in decades." *Health Affairs* 15(2): 130–44.

Massaro, T.A., and Y.-N. Wong (1995). "Positive experience with medical savings accounts in Singapore." *Health Affairs* 14(2): 267–72.

Melnick, G.A., and J. Zwanziger (1995). "State health care expenditures under competition and regulation, 1980 through 1991." *American Journal of Public Health* 85: 1391–6.

Morone, J.A. (1986). "Seven laws of policy analysis." *Journal of Policy Analysis and Management* 5: 817–19.

– and J.M. Goggin (1995). "Health policies in Europe: Welfare states in a market era." *Journal of Health Politics, Policy, and Law* 20: 557–69.

Nair, C., R. Karim, and C. Nyers (1992). "Health care and health status: A Canada–United States statistical comparison." *Health Reports* 4(2): 175–83. (Ottawa, ON: Statistics Canada. Cat. No. 82 – 003.)

OECD/CREDES (1996). *OECD health data 96. Software for the comparative analysis of 27 health systems.* Paris: OECD Health Policy Unit.

Pauly, M. (1994a). "Editorial: A re-examination of the meaning and importance of supplier-induced demand." *Journal of Health Economics* 13(3): 369–72.

– (1994b). "Reply to Roberta Labelle, Greg Stoddart, and Thomas Rice." *Journal of Health Economics* 13(4): 495–6.

Rasell, E., J. Bernstein, and K. Tang. (1993). *The impact of health care financing on family budgets.* Briefing Paper (April). Washington, DC: Economic Policy Institute.

– and K. Tang. (1994). *Paying for health care: Affordability and equity in proposals for health care reform.* Working Paper No. 111 (December). Washington, DC: Economic Policy Institute.

Redelmeier, D.A., and V.R. Fuchs (1993). "Hospital expenditures in the United States and Canada." *New England Journal of Medicine* 328: 772–8.

Reinhardt, U.E. (1992). "Reflections on the meaning of *efficiency*: Can efficiency be separated from equity?" *Yale Law and Policy Review* 10(2): 302–15.

– (1996). "Spending more through 'cost control': Our obsessive quest to gut the hospital." *Health Affairs* 15(2): 145–54.

Rice, T. (1997). "Can markets give us the health system we want?" *Journal of Health Politics, Policy and Law* 22: 383–426.

Schieber, G.J., J.-P. Poullier, and L.M. Greenwald (1994). "Health system performance in OECD countries, 1980–1992." *Health Affairs* 13(3): 100–12.

Thorpe, K.E. (1992). "Inside the black box of administrative costs." *Health Affairs* 11(2): 41–55.

Trebilcock, M.J., C.J. Tuohy, and A.D. Wolfson (1979). *Professional regulation: A staff study of accountancy, architecture, engineering and law in Ontario.* (Prepared for the Professional Organizations Committee). Toronto: Ministry of the Attorney-General of Ontario.

van Doorslaer, E., A. Wagstaff, and F. Rutten, eds. (1993). *Equity in the finance and delivery of health care: An international perspective*. New York: Oxford University Press.

White, J. (1995). *Competing solutions: American health care proposals and international experience*. Washington, DC: Brookings Institution.

Wildavsky, A. (1977). "Doing better and feeling worse: The political pathology of health policy." *Daedalus* 106(1): 105–24.

Woolhandler, S., and D.U. Himmelstein (1991). "The deteriorating administrative efficiency of the US health care system." *New England Journal of Medicine* 324: 1253–8.

Zwanziger, J., and G.A. Melnick. (1996). "Can managed care plans control health care costs?" *Health Affairs* 15(2): 185–99.

8

Modelling the Benefits of Insurance: Here Comes the Insurance Salesman (2004)

ROBERT G. EVANS

In modern health care systems people pay for the care of other people, not for their own. A relatively small proportion – 10 to 20 per cent – of health care expenditures is financed from the out-of-pocket payments of users. Rather, people make contributions, in varying amounts and on varying terms, to "third parties" – public or private agencies that pool these contributions and disburse funds either directly to the providers of care (the predominant approach) or back to individual users to reimburse them for payments previously made. Governments or other public agencies are the dominant actors in this process; in developed countries they typically account for between 75 and 85 per cent of health expenditures (OECD, 2004). In some countries private commercial insurers also play a role, but outside the United States (and to a lesser extent Canada), it is a very small one. And even in the United States, often perceived as having a "private" health care financing system, out-of-pocket payments make up less than 15 per cent of total expenditures, while governments account directly or indirectly for about 60 per cent.[1]

The standard economic interpretation of this universal pattern of "third party" payment is that it arises from "risk aversion," the distaste of individual consumers for risk, and can be understood within the framework of the theory of insurance. It is postulated that risk per se, inability to

This chapter is an edited version of a previously unpublished paper written by the author in 2004. Reprinted with the permission of Robert G. Evans.

predict future circumstances with certainty, is a source of disutility, reducing well-being.[2] Faced with risky futures, therefore, consumers will wish to purchase insurance contracts such that they (or others) will be compensated financially if specified but unpredictable bad things – a house fire, a motor vehicle accident, an illness, a death – should happen.

Private firms can profitably offer such contracts, and do, because while the outcome of any one contract is as unpredictable for the insurance company as for the consumer (subject to qualifications below), the outcome for a portfolio of similar contracts becomes increasingly predictable as the size of the portfolio increases. Pooling risks makes them disappear.[3] Future events remain unpredictable, but their economic consequences for the consumer are reduced or eliminated. Her economic circumstances, at least, become predictable, and her exposure to risk is reduced. Since risk is assumed to be a source of disutility, her well-being is thus improved (depending upon the cost of the insurance contract itself); that is why people buy insurance. "Risk" can be thought of as analogous to any other commodity – it can be bought and sold, and indeed commercial insurers do refer to the various contracts that they offer as "products." The only difference is that risk is a "dis-good" or a "bad," so that the consumer is better off with less of it.[4]

Standard insurance theory has been developed to explain "markets for risk" as they are found in the commercial insurance sector. It will take us a certain distance in understanding the peculiar financing structure of the health care sector, but its reach is actually quite limited. Commercial (private, for-profit) insurance coverage finances a minimal share of health care expenditures outside the United States (and to a lesser extent Canada), and within North America the commercial industry depends on substantial (though hidden) government subsidies and other forms of regulatory support. Furthermore, in North America at least, most commercial health insurance coverage is not bought by "consumers" of economic theory, purchasing from insurers in individual voluntary transactions. Rather it is bought by employers on behalf of their employees, and coverage is a condition of employment over which individuals have little or no choice. (In the United States, however, they may have some choice over the form and extent of coverage.)

Nonetheless it is important to grasp the elementary theory of insurance in order to understand both why "third party" coverage is predominant and why commercial coverage makes up such a small part of this universal (in high-income countries) pattern. Proposals for expanding the role of commercial insurance often appear in debate over the health care financing agenda in a number of countries; these should be considered in the context of the fundamental limits to its scope (in the absence of major public support) and the corresponding limitations of the standard economic analysis.

The theoretical treatment of insurance begins by adding one further assumption to the elementary model of the individual, utility-maximizing consumer. First we write the consumer's utility function in "indirect" form as:

$$U\{Y, P_1, P_2, \ldots P_M\}, dU/dY > 0, dU/dP_i < 0 \qquad \text{[Equation 8.1]}$$

where Y is the consumer's money income and the P are the prices of the M different commodities that the consumer buys. The consumer is assumed always to choose the utility-maximizing bundle of commodities for a given level of income and given commodity prices, so her level of utility will depend on her income, and the prices she must pay. If prices do not change, increasing income enables her to purchase more commodities, and these yield increasing utility or well-being. But if prices rise and income does not, then consumption and utility will fall.

If to this is added the assumption that the benefits of increasing income are always positive but are subject to diminishing returns – $d^2U/dY^2 < 0$, or each successive increment of income adds a smaller amount to well-being than its predecessor – then we can draw the curves shown in Figures 8.1a and b. W or wealth has been substituted for Y, income, to allow for losses that exceed income in any one time period; wealth is equivalent to the discounted present value of future income.

For expositional purposes it is convenient, and common, to begin by assuming that the loss of utility associated with an illness or injury can be expressed in terms of a monetary equivalent, so that a dollar or other currency value can be assigned to the "loss" associated with a deterioration in health. (This nearly universal assumption is, however, neither trivial nor innocuous – see below.) Holding all prices constant, we can express the individual's (maximized) utility as a function of income or wealth and health status, $U = U(W, HS)$. If HS^0 represents an initial baseline level of health, and HS^1 the health status associated with a specific illness or injury, then we define L such that $U(W - L, HS^0) = U(W, HS^1)$. Losing the sum of money L or developing a condition reducing health to HS^1 are equally bad.[5]

This monetary loss will not, of course, be equivalent to expenditure on health care. Only if care of a specific and well-defined amount were instantly and perfectly effective in relieving illness could one represent the consequences of illness for well-being by the dollar cost of care. In general, the money equivalent loss L of an illness will exceed any consequent (change in) health spending by some amount, perhaps very large, which allows for pain and suffering, anxiety, lost wages and/or leisure, and a risk premium for uncertainty of outcome.

Consider a consumer/patient contemplating an uncertain future time period – say a year – in which a specific illness or injury may or may not occur. Let the probability of occurrence be q ($0<q<1$), and of non-occurrence be $1-q$, so that there are believed to be $100q$ chances out of 100 that the illness will occur. If it does, the consequences are judged by the consumer/patient as equivalent to a loss of \$$L$. Holding all other things constant, her well-being during the future period in question will be related (positively) to her wealth, which is expected in the absence of illness to be \$$W$. The occurrence of the illness would thus be equivalent to a reduction in wealth to \$$(W-L)$.

The "expected" level of future wealth, in the sense of the mathematical expectation, labelled $E(W)$, is defined as the sum of the two possible outcomes, each weighted by its probability of occurrence:[6]

$$E(W)=(1-q)W+q(W-L)=W-qL \qquad \text{[Equation 8.2]}$$

If, for example, the probability of the illness occurring over the next year were 5 per cent, then there is a one in twenty chance that the consumer's wealth level will be W – L at the end of the year, and a 19 out of 20 chance that it will be W. The expected value of wealth is accordingly $0.05(W-L)+0.95W$, or $W-0.05L$.

We can similarly describe well-being at the end of the future period as $U(W)$ with a probability of $1-q$, and the lower level $U(W-L)$ with probability q. Representing the expected level of utility as $E(U)$, we can write:

$$E(U)=(1-q)U(W)+qU(W-L) \qquad \text{[Equation 8.3]}$$

Since $U(W)>U(W-L)$, expected well-being is higher, for given W, as L or q are lower. Looking forward, the individual obviously expects to be better off if the possible future illness is either less severe or less likely.

In Figure 8.1a, we represent an individual's well-being on the vertical axis, and wealth level on the horizontal. The curve has positive but declining slope, reflecting the assumed diminishing marginal utility of wealth. More is always better, and there need be no saturation point, but

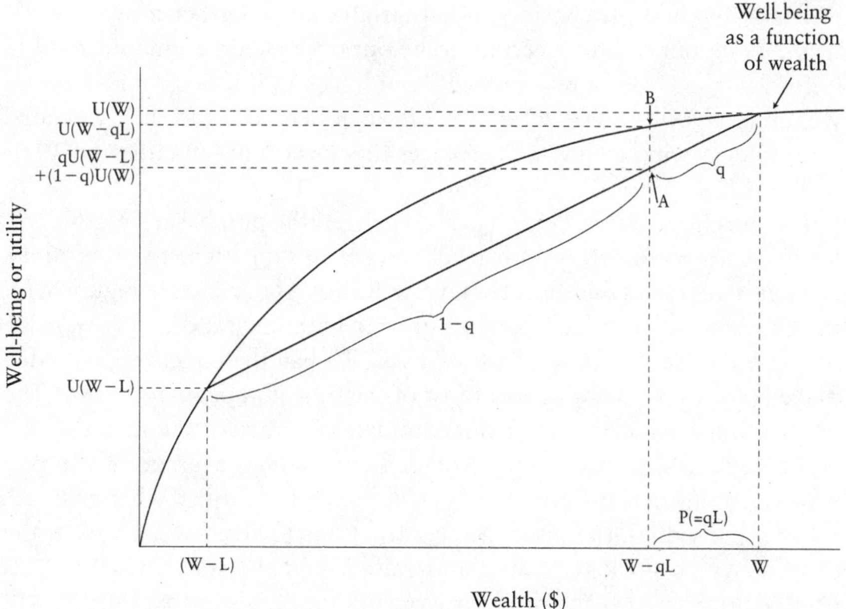

Figure 8.1a

at higher wealth levels a given increment of wealth has a lesser impact on well-being. (People for whom this is not true, do not buy insurance. They gamble a lot.[7])

Insurance contracts can be structured with amazing complexity, but the most elementary form is purchased for a premium $*p* and offers a payment $*R* in the event that a specified event occurs (nothing otherwise). Suppose the individual facing a possible loss L chooses to purchase a contract paying R = L, full compensation in the event of loss. At the end of the year the insurer will pay any one insured individual either $L or nothing, depending on whether that individual suffered a loss. But as the number (call it N) of similar insured individuals increases, the proportion who suffer the loss will converge to q. Thus the insurer's payout will converge to qN individuals times $L, and the average or "expected" payment to each will converge to qL.

As an idealized case we can define an "actuarially fair" contract for which the insurer sets a premium p for each individual contract just equal to the expected payout, $p = qL$. Total payouts over a large number of such contracts will then equal total premium receipts, implying that the insurance agency itself is costless to operate and makes no profit.[8]

The individual purchasing an actuarially fair contract now faces no future uncertainty. She is certain to be out of pocket the amount $p = qL$, but is certain of being reimbursed the full loss L, if it occurs. Her future wealth level will be $W - p$ ($= W - qL$) in either case, and the associated certain well-being $U(W - qL)$ replaces the uncertainty of either $U(W)$ or $U(W - L)$.

The purchase of insurance has not changed the purchaser's mathematically expected future wealth level, except to convert it to a certainty. But it *has* increased the expected level of utility. As depicted in Figure 8.1a, the expected level of well-being is greater with insurance. $U(W - qL) > qU(W - L) + (1 - q)U(W)$, so long as $U(W)$ has the concave shape displayed (which for most people most of the time it appears to have).[9] The gain in utility which results from complete coverage of the whole loss L is the vertical distance from point A, the weighted average of the two possible uninsured utilities, to point B, the certain utility when insured. For the individual, the insurance contract has lowered wealth from the state in which no loss occurs, and raised it in the state in which loss occurs, but because each dollar is worth more – adds more to utility – in the lower income state than in the higher, that transfer adds to total expected utility. The optimal level of coverage is reached when an additional unit of wealth is equally valuable in either state – because wealth is the same regardless of whether loss occurs.

Under the assumptions to this point, individuals are always better off to insure against any risky future event, from a house fire or automobile crash to rain on a proposed picnic. Figure 8.1b, however, introduces an additional consideration. It represents two alternative losses, L_1 and L_2, such that $L_1 > L_2$ but the associated $q_1 < q_2$ such that $q_1L_1 = q_2L_2$. These might represent a low-probability event with large loss, such as a rare but severe illness with hospitalixation and extensive care, and a higher-probability event with smaller loss such as a more common minor illness involving one or two physician visits and a prescription or two. The expected loss in each case, size of loss multiplied by probability of occurrence, is the same, and an actuarially fair insurance contract would charge the same premium, p, to cover either loss.

As Figure 8.1b illustrates, however, the advantage to the buyer of insurance, in terms of the gain in well-being from exchanging a risky situation for a riskless one, is substantially greater in the case of the large, low-probability loss than in that of the small, more probable one. And by extension of Figure 8.1b, we can see that in the limit, if q goes to either zero or one, or if L goes to zero, the gain from insurance becomes

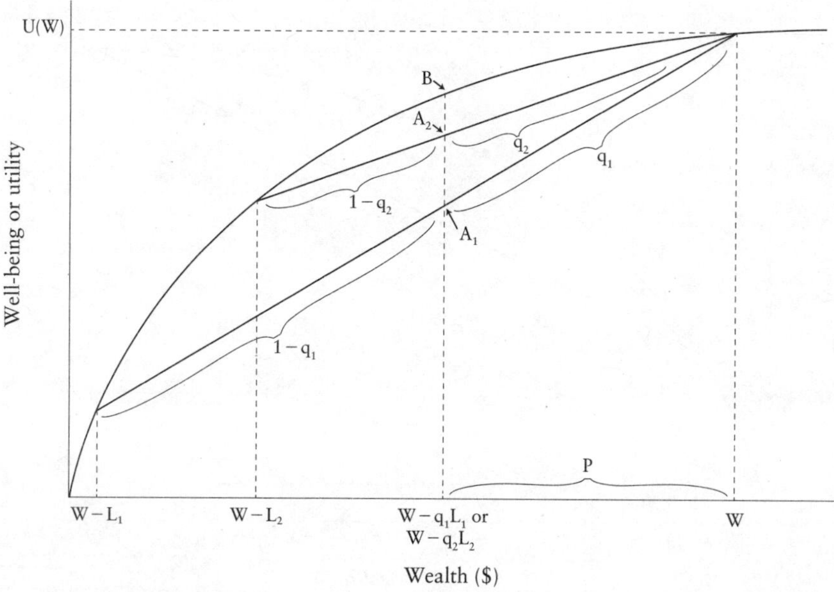

Figure 8.1b

zero, which is as it should be. If an event is certain to occur – or not to occur – then there is no risk and nothing to insure against. A fair premium would equal the loss itself, leaving a purchaser no better off.

In the real world, insuring against certain events would actually leave one worse off, because actuarially fair contracts do not exist. The process of providing insurance coverage is itself costly. Insurance agencies need staff, equipment, and buildings in order to set rates, write contracts, and adjudicate and pay (or dispute) claims. Competitive private companies must also cover marketing expenses and, if for-profit, must on average earn a profit. Premiums collected (or their equivalent in taxes or other payments to public insurers) must exceed claims paid by some additional "load factor," F, large enough to meet the costs of the insurance function itself, thus $p = qL + F$.

The presence of a load factor modifies the implication of Figure 8.1, that all risky events should be insured against. Purchasing insurance now *lowers* the mathematical expectation of the individual's wealth, from $W - qL$ when uninsured to $W - qL - F$ when insured. Insurance coverage is a resource-using service that must be paid for; the question faced by the potential buyer is whether or not the benefit in terms of risk reduction outweighs the cost in terms of lowered (expected) wealth.

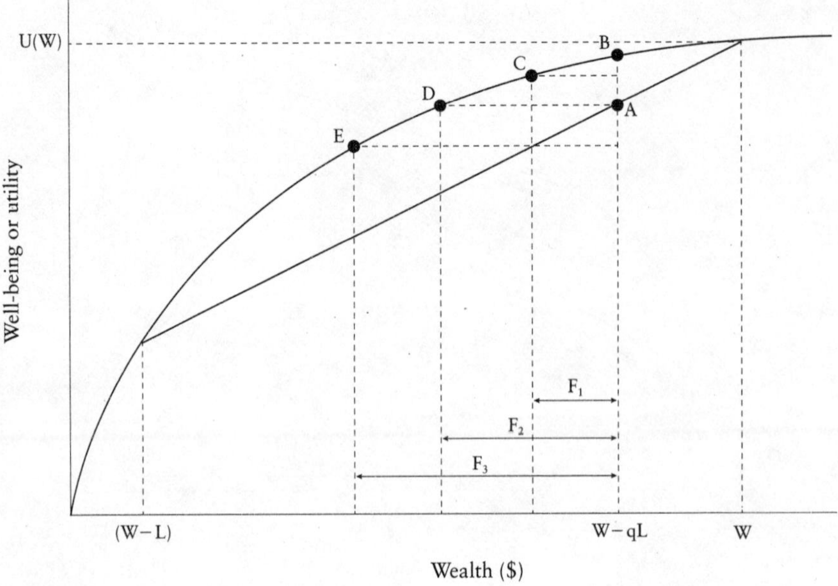

Figure 8.2

Figure 8.2 displays three different possibilities, corresponding to Figure 8.1a but with load factors of different sizes added. All the F values make the insurance purchaser worse off than at point B; the actuarially fair contract is "free" in terms of overhead cost. But with a load factor of F_1, $U(W-qL-F_1)>qU(W-L)+(1-q)U(W)$ and the individual is still better off than with no coverage. Point C is lower on the utility axis than point B, but higher than point A. The larger load factor F_3, however, reduces the individual's utility when insured to point E, where $U(W-qL-F_3)<qU(W-L)+(1-q)U(W)$. This insurance contract is too costly to be worth buying; the individual is better off to take her chances in an uncertain world. At a load factor of F_2 the individual is indifferent between buying and not buying coverage – point D and uninsured point A correspond to the same level of utility.[10]

In order to simplify exposition, three-sector national accounting frameworks outlining the financial flows in health care systems typically disregard the costs of the insurance process itself. But these costs are very real, in both private and public health insurance systems, and can add quite significantly to the total costs of financing health care. Figure 8.3 depicts a generic "third party" financing system that incorporates the resource,

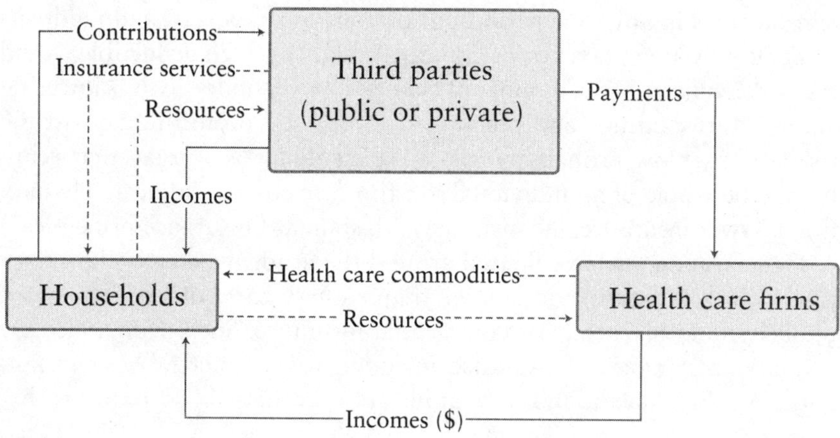

Figure 8.3

service, and income flows associated with the process of insurance itself. Some proportion of the financial flows from households to third-party reimbursing agencies must flow back to households to pay for these "overhead" services rather than going forward to fund the provision of care. The amounts raised to finance health care will all eventually come back to households, but the overhead amounts will become incomes of households whose members provide administrative and financial rather than clinical services.

An individual or small group contemplating buying voluntary health care insurance in a commercial market, and believing (rightly or wrongly) that the decision will not affect either the price of care or their own utilization rates, must compare the proportion of the premium which is load factor, cost of insurance per se, against the gain in well-being from reduced risk. It will obviously be more advantageous to insure large and unlikely losses, because for a given premium, the gains in well-being are greater and (since fewer claims are processed) load factors will presumably be smaller. Coverage for small and frequent claims, on the other hand, provides little benefit in terms of risk reduction and is likely to cost more than it is worth. The individual is better off "self-insuring" – paying for such losses out-of-pocket as they arise.

The analysis to this point supports the arguments of those who recommend that health insurance, public or private, should reimburse individual health care costs only above a "deductible." Insured individuals or households would be better off if they paid the first $X of health expenditures in any time period out of their own pockets, and paid correspondingly lower taxes or premiums. A relatively high deductible would restrict significantly the number of claims to be reimbursed, thus lowering administrative costs – and premiums – while still protecting against the risk of large, low-probability losses. "First dollar" coverage that reimburses the whole of an individual's health care costs is "allocatively inefficient" over-insurance, inconsistent with standard insurance principles.

These arguments have floated around the academic economics literature for a generation, and emerge frequently in the work of right-wing publicists and marketers of commercial insurance. Such deductibles *are* common in commercial insurance, including for commercial health insurance, but they have found little application in the public programs that dominate health care financing in the high-income world. (The United States is, as always, an exception.) On the presumption that "nothing that is regular is stupid" (Theodore Marmor, personal communication), one might infer that there is something wrong with these arguments.

And of course there is, a lot. The analysis represented in Figures 8.1 and 8.2 is highly simplified for expositional purposes. Drawing recommendations for the financing of real-world health care systems from such a tinker-toy model provides another illustration of Pope's oft-quoted verse that "a little learning is a dangerous thing." The model describes the behaviour of "the" insurance purchaser and "the" insurer – representative agents in a world of symmetric and almost perfect information. All that is (temporarily) unknown to both is whether the specified adverse event will occur. These abstractions turn out to be (as usual) crucial; relax them and a very different story emerges.

The first point to note is that, in a world of heterogeneous individuals, the primary effect of introducing (or removing) a deductible is to redistribute wealth. The contributions – premiums or taxes – required to finance the collective payment for care will fall when a significant share of total health expenditures are shifted from third parties to patients themselves. This redistributes costs among households, shifting them from the healthy to the ill, and (since most forms of contribution are income-related) from the more to the less wealthy.[11]

Real resources can thus be reallocated from the insurance process itself to other purposes, at the cost of an increase in the risk (that may perhaps be treated as "relatively small") borne by households. But this raises a further distributional issue. The shape of the utility function sketched in Figure 8.1, derived by annexing the assumption $d^2U/dY^2 < 0$ to Equation [8.1], implies that the greater one's wealth, the smaller the disutility associated with any given degree of risk. Or in plain words, if you are wealthy, you can better afford to take chances. You can bet without losing the rent money, or the farm. The monetary measure of the risk associated with a deductible may be the same at different wealth levels, but the utility cost is not, and it is utility that counts in this analytic framework.

The above considerations, moreover, abstract from the well-known correlation between health and wealth. This implies that the expected monetary cost of a deductible will be greater at the lower end of the wealth distribution. The bottom line is that any system-wide gains in reduced administrative costs will in every real-world system (see note 10) involve losses for some and gains for others, and the pattern of gains and losses will tend to be correlated with wealth. One may still decide that these distributional effects are more than offset by the efficiency gains (or may regard them as desirable per se) but one cannot legitimately claim that the case for deductibles rests on a priori economic principles rather than political choices. Advocates tend to sidestep the distributional issues by assuming a hypothetical representative agent (individual transactors are identical clones), either explicitly (e.g., Arrow, 1976) or implicitly.[12]

Advocates of high deductible coverage also emphasize the putative additional benefits from reduced utilization of services when households must bear a substantial share of the costs of the care that they use. These same alleged benefits are adduced to support arguments for other forms of user charges, such as per visit, per day, or per prescription charges, or "coinsurance" requiring insured users to pay some fixed percentage of the cost of care used. The standard presumption is that raising financial barriers will cause people to forego the least valuable (to them) forms of care, thus freeing up resources to produce other, more highly valued, non-health-care commodities – greater "allocative efficiency." Possible effects on health, like the effects on wealth distribution, do not enter the analysis. In reality the various forms of user charges have little or no effect on overall care use or costs, but serve primarily to redistribute access from the more to the less price sensitive – i.e., from the less to the more wealthy. This is presumably why they are more popular with the latter.

A second problem with the "high deductible" argument arises from a basic confusion among three quite different measures: the monetary equivalent loss associated with illness or injury, the monetary amount that would compensate for that loss, and the monetary expenditures on health care resulting from the loss.

The monetary equivalent of the loss associated with the incidence of illness or injury was defined above as the sum \$L such that $U(W-L, HS^{o}) = U(W, HS^{I})$. The deterioration in health status reduces the

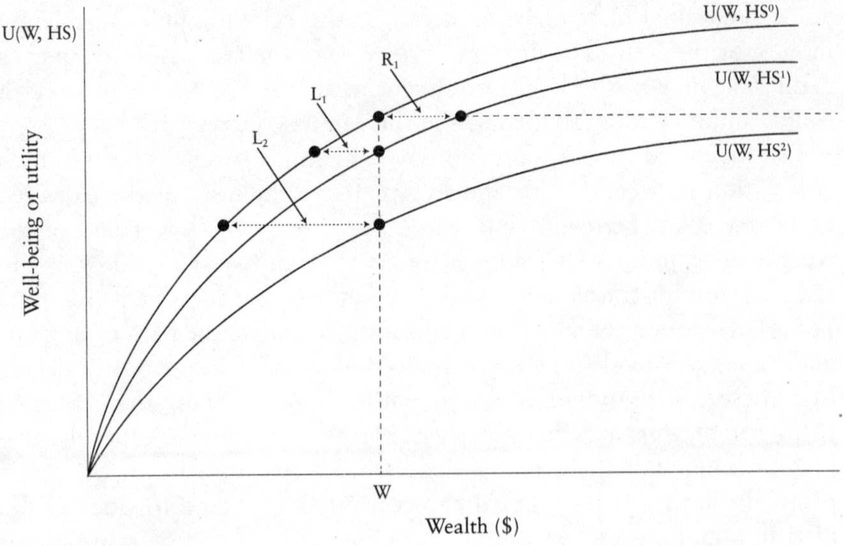

Figure 8.4

individual's utility by as much as a loss of \$L would have done if she had remained healthy. The analysis of Figures 8.1 and 8.2, however, makes a critical simplifying assumption. By treating the monetary equivalent of the health status deterioration as if it were *in fact* a loss of money, the analysis abstracts from explicit recognition of changes in health status and thus assumes that a monetary payment of $R = L$ restores the individual to her initial utility level. This implies that $U(W, HS^{0}) = U(W + L, HS^{1})$. The individual is assumed to be indifferent between being healthy with wealth W and being ill with wealth W + L. In terms of elementary microeconomic theory, we have assumed that the *equivalent variation*, L, is the same as the *compensating variation*, R. This will not be true in general, and if the benefits of increasing income are subject to diminishing returns ($d^2U/dY^2 < 0$) in both the well and the ill states, then the compensating amount must be greater than the monetary equivalent loss – possibly much greater – and may not even have a finite value.

Figure 8.4 depicts the situation of a previously healthy individual contemplating two possible future states of illness or injury, one minor (HS^1) and one severe (HS^2). Both cause a fall in her utility for any given level of wealth. We can define a monetary equivalent loss for each, L_1 and L_2. For the relatively minor ailment there is a sum R_1 that would provide full compensation, restoring the full, pre-illness/injury level of well-being. But it follows from the declining slope of the curve linking wealth to

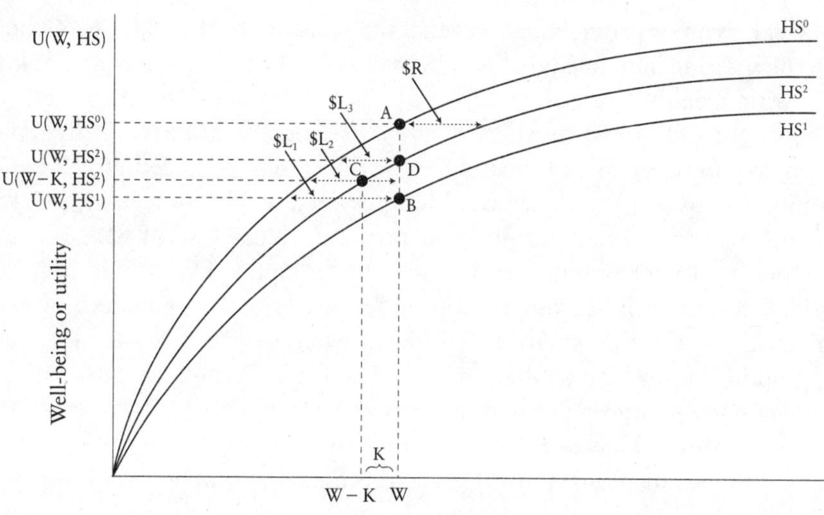

Figure 8.5

utility that this compensating variation R_1 must exceed the equivalent variation L_1.[13] In the case of the second, severe, reduction in health status, however, no finite financial level of reimbursement can restore the original position of well-being.[14]

Whatever the value of the compensating amount, however, it will certainly exceed expenditures on associated health care. People are not indifferent between receiving (free) the best health care imaginable when ill or injured, and not being ill in the first place. Ill-health brings pain and suffering, anxiety, the discomfort and inconvenience of diagnosis and treatment, and temporary or permanent loss of capacities for normal living and enjoyment of life. (It may also threaten income; that loss *is* potentially compensable, but at a cost over and above that of health care.)

Figure 8.5 represents the circumstances of an individual suffering from an illness or injury for whom health care is available, but is not instantly and perfectly effective (the usual case). The curve labelled HS° represents her level of well-being as a function of wealth, for a given, unimpaired level of health. We assign her a particular wealth level $W bringing her to point A on that curve (not the same as A in Figure 8.1). On a bad day she falls ill, leaving her wealth unchanged, but in the absence of health care the whole curve would drop to that labelled HS^1. Her utility would fall to point B, and the monetary equivalent of this loss would be $\$L_1$.

Health care is provided, however, improving her health and raising her to the intermediate line labelled HS^2 at a cost of \$K. Now she is at point C, with wealth reduced to \$W – \$K but a (smaller) total monetary equivalent utility loss of $\$L_2$.[15] Finally, the cost of care \$K is fully covered by public or private insurance, or the care is provided "free" by a public health service, so her wealth is restored to \$W and she moves to point D with a (smaller still) monetary equivalent loss of $\$L_3$. But to restore her to her original level of well-being on line HS° would require additional financial compensation of \$R, additional to payment of her medical and related expenses. This may or may not be possible, depending upon the severity of the illness and the effectiveness of care, but in any case it is not going to happen.

The curves in Figures 8.1 and 8.2, by contrast, assume that it is and it will. Movement along those curves represents a change in well-being resulting not merely from a change in wealth with a constant health status, but from the combined effects of changed wealth (health care costs, lost income), *and* changed health status per se. So the assumption of full insurance against loss in Figures 8.1 and 8.2 implies that the insurance contract does indeed provide a compensating increase in wealth, over and above reimbursing health care expenditures, sufficient to restore the original level of well-being prior to illness or injury.

The point, easily lost in the simplification of Figures 8.1 and 8.2, is that reimbursement of all health care costs still falls short, often far short, of compensating for the losses associated with illness. But no real-world health insurance system, public or private, provides reimbursement for these losses. How would one determine their extent? The size of loss can only be known by the sufferer; it is not directly observable by an external observer. (Recall that we are referring here to the money required to compensate for loss of utility, about which individuals have privileged internal information.) Indeed, the illness itself is rarely monitored by the insurer; while possible in principle, that is usually costly and impractical. Expenditures on health care are taken as a signal that the illness has occurred.[16] But insurance which compensated for total loss of well-being would create powerful incentives for false signalling. Patients would be encouraged to use unnecessary care, i.e., care having no or even harmful effects on health, in order to collect the compensation for putative suffering which did not in fact occur.[17]

Accordingly, health insurance typically covers only actual health care expenditures, rather than losses due to illness.[18] All real-world health insurance provides only partial, and sometimes very partial, coverage against the costs of illness as defined within the theoretical framework above. But the first and second theorems of welfare economics only hold when (among other things) there is a *complete* set of markets for all commodities, including, under conditions of uncertainty, a complete set of markets for contingent claims. Since no such markets exist for some of the most serious welfare losses associated with ill-health, the theoretical demonstration that voluntary exchange transactions in decentralized private markets will lead to an "efficient" allocation of resources (albeit perhaps a morally repugnant one) collapses. Analyses within that framework of the relative merits of full or partial coverage are thus beside the point. Even full first-dollar coverage of care expenses still leaves the insured person at very substantial risk of loss, because loss is defined in terms not only of care expenditures but also of the monetary equivalent of the whole loss of well-being.[19]

It remains true that, in the extension or contraction of the partial coverage represented by health care insurance, there is a potential trade-off between the benefits of risk reduction and the costs of insurance administration. Some insurance is not worth its price. The terms of this trade-off are, however, considerably altered by recognition of the fact that real-world coverage is always incomplete, and is likely to be sub-optimal because of the insurer's limited ability to monitor the circumstances of the insured. If information were perfect, people might wish to buy, and insurers might be willing to provide, coverage that went well beyond the costs of health care per se.

These two points, the inherent incompleteness of the compensation offered by all real-world "health" insurance and the regressive redistributional effects of moving from full to partial coverage, are important in bringing out the limitations of the analytic framework of Figures 8.1 and 8.2 (and policy recommendations based on it). But they leave intact the basic idea that, since the process of insurance is itself costly, resources can be saved by reducing coverage levels – albeit at some cost in terms of increased risk and greater inequity. (Whether or not the latter is a cost or a benefit depends upon one's ideological preferences.) A much more fundamental critique, based on the comparative observation of actual administrative costs, demolishes that hypothesis. It bears the same relationship to the above points, in Schumpeter's famous simile, "as an artillery bombardment does to forcing a door."

The framework represented in Figures 8.1 and 8.2 makes no explicit reference to the motivations of different insurers. Most of the more advanced economic literature, however, assumes that insurance contracts are offered in a competitive marketplace by for-profit commercial insurers, either to individual "consumers" or as a form of "local public good" to groups of employees for whom employers act as purchasing agents. It is then further assumed (implicitly or explicitly) that price competition among (large numbers of) these firms will lead to consumers being offered their most preferred combinations of coverage and required out-of-pocket payment, and that these packages will be offered at the lowest possible load factors. This would achieve an "allocatively efficient" outcome, an optimal trade-off between the risk reduction benefits of health insurance, and its putative costs, the hypothetical "welfare burden" of excessive use of care.

Arguments for the allocative efficiency of private competitive insurance markets for health insurance are at best moot because, bluntly, there aren't any such markets, there never have been, and for good sound economic reasons there never will be, anywhere in the real world. Analysis has been clouded by the presence of large and competitive private insurers in North America, principally in the United States, but the structure of these insurance markets differs in crucial respects from the hypothetical structure imagined in the mainstream economic literature.[20] And in these real-world markets, the presumption that competition among private firms yields minimum load factors has been spectacularly falsified.

Outside North America, the contribution of private commercial insurers to the financing of health care ranges from minimal to none. Each country has its own specific institutional pattern, but in general where private coverage exists it covers a small minority of the population and/or a small share of total expenditures (OECD, op. cit.). In Germany, for example, higher-income people – about 10 per cent – are outside the general *Krankenkassen* system and purchase private coverage, with which they can pay for health services presumed to be more timely or of higher quality. In the United Kingdom everyone has the option of "going private," paying physicians and hospitals for care outside the National Health Service (NHS) – again for more timely or "preferred" services – and some private insurance is available to reimburse these costs. But those who do so remain covered by the NHS, which provides and funds care for serious and costly illnesses. In France a system of *mutuelles* – co-operatives – provides insurance against many of the deductibles and co-payments – the *ticket moderateur* – in the universal public system.[21] Switzerland requires residents to purchase a basic package of private insurance coverage – with prices and content determined not by the market but by government. And so on.

Each OECD country has its own unique features, and these generate varying levels of administrative complexity and costs. Where the overall system must coordinate multiple paying agencies, or administer various premiums or user charges (and mitigate any consequent distributional or deterrent effects), overheads tend to be higher. But only in North America is private commercial insurance a significant source of overall finance.

In Canada, almost all hospital and medical care expenditures are funded through universal public programs, provincially administered, tax-financed, and more or less comprehensive. But pharmaceuticals remain financed through a mix of public and private coverage and out-of-pocket payment. Dental care is largely private, with over half financed through private insurance. Overall, private insurance accounted for 12.2 per cent of Canadian health care spending in 2003. The United States displays a range of different insurance systems for different segments of the population, from direct delivery of free services – truly "socialized medicine" – for veterans, through universal public insurance – quite similar to Canada – for the elderly (American "Medicare"), to nothing at all for about 15 per cent of the population. But a majority of Americans have their primary coverage through private for-profit corporations, as envisaged in the mainstream economics literature. These accounted for 34.6 per cent of total health expenditures in the United States in 2003.

At first glance, then, it might appear that private commercial health insurance is alive and well in North America, and its performance can therefore be analyzed through the standard economic framework. But this is an illusion. The commercial sector, in both Canada and the United States, is heavily subsidized by various governments. Without this tax-payer support, the commercial industry would be very much smaller and might not survive at all.

The public subsidies take the form of tax expenditures for employer-paid health insurance premiums. Premiums paid by employers on behalf of employees are a deductible expense for employers, but unlike wages or other non-health benefits, are not taxable in the hands of employees. This subsidy is equivalent to a tax-financed rebate to households of a portion (in practice about one-third) of private premiums. As noted earlier in this chapter, taking account of this subsidy raises the public share of American health care expenditures to nearly 60 per cent; only about one-quarter of the total is financed through net private insurance premiums. In Canada, the commercial share falls to between 8 and 9 per cent.

Figure 8.6 represents the effect of the tax expenditure subsidy. A portion of tax revenues is diverted before reaching the Treasury, to flow

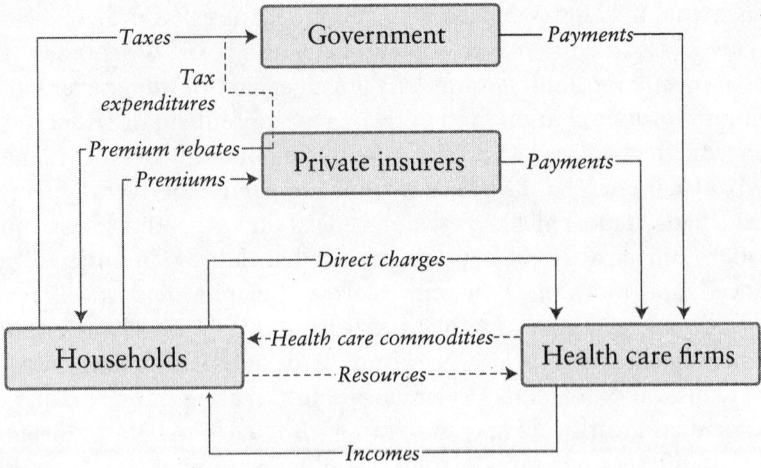

Figure 8.6

through the private insurance system, and returns to households as a discount, effectively a rebate on private premiums.

But this tax-expenditure subsidy is available only for insurance premiums paid by the employer on the employee's behalf. Insurance purchased by individuals is not similarly subsidized; it must be paid for with after-tax dollars. Not surprisingly, therefore, individual insurance purchases account for very little of private commercial health coverage, in either country.

But group insurance contracts do not typically permit individuals to pick and choose as to whether they will be enrolled in the group. To avoid "adverse selection" – the least healthy join, the most healthy stay out – insurers require that all members of an employee group be enrolled. So the imaginary world of individual consumer choice is doubly undermined. Insured individuals do not have a choice as to their coverage; on the other hand, part of the cost of their coverage is indirectly subsidized through the income tax system. As to the extent to which the resulting coverage reflects the personal choices of individuals – and which individuals – that will depend upon the objectives and relative bargaining strengths of particular employers and employee groups. But to suggest that the result would be in some way "allocatively efficient," as the term is understood in economic theory, would be an act of pure faith without grounding in either fact or argument.

One thing is very clear, however. In neither Canada nor the United States does competitive private health insurance tend to minimize load factors. It would be easier to argue that it maximizes them.

A series of publications over more than a decade by Himmelstein, Woolhandler, and their colleagues have compared the administrative overhead costs of the financing systems in Canada and the United States. These studies estimate not only the overhead costs of both public and private insurers – the load factors in the analysis above – but also the administrative costs incurred by provider organizations – hospitals, nursing homes, clinics, and private medical practices – in securing reimbursement from insurers. These latter costs are reported as expenditures on "health care," although the activities they support contribute nothing whatever to anyone's health. As costs of the insurance process itself they are load factors similar to the administrative overheads recognized in insurers' accounts.[22] In the Woolhandler and Himmelstein studies they are found to be as large as the overhead expenditures of private insurers themselves.

The difference in overhead costs between the two systems is huge. The most recent estimates are for 1999 (Woolhandler et al., 2003); taking account of both insurance load factors and provider administrative costs, they show 31 per cent of American health care expenditures being absorbed in this way, compared with 16.7 per cent in Canada. The authors estimate that the excess administrative costs in the United States amounted to $209.0 billion in 1999, or 17.1 per cent of total American health care expenditures. Health expenditures absorbed 13.0 per cent of American GDP in that year, well above that in any other country. Removing these excess administrative costs would reduce the American ratio to 10.8 per cent, comparable to Switzerland and Germany at 10.7 and 10.6 per cent. The American excess accounts for nearly 60 per cent of the difference, with Canada at 9.1 per cent.

These differences in costs arise from differences in the structure of the financing system, and not from the extent or depth of coverage. Canada provides (for hospital and medical care) universal and comprehensive coverage without deductibles or co-payments. In the United States, both public and private insurers impose deductibles and co-payments that add materially to the administrative complexity, particularly for patients. If there are any consequent administrative savings in the form of reduced claims processing costs from these limitations in coverage, they are peanuts lost amid the elephantine impact of differences in the organization of the insurance process itself.

Moreover, overhead cost differences between public and private insurers emerge within, as well as between, these two countries – countries that are otherwise probably as similar as any pair on the planet. In both, the national health expenditure accounts report that private health insurers' administrative overheads average in a range of 16 per cent to 19 per cent of their total revenues. (These include only the overhead costs of insurers, not of providers.) Public programs, by contrast, have overhead rates under 5 per cent.

Private health insurance in Canada, for dental care and pharmaceuticals, thus shows overhead costs similar to those in the United States. Conversely, the low administrative costs of Canada's public insurance for hospital and medical care are also found in the American Medicare program for the elderly. The overall higher costs in the United States result from the much higher proportion of private coverage in that country, not from some uniquely American predisposition to inefficiency.

It is significant that in public health insurance systems the proportion of total revenue actually paid to care providers is known as the "benefit ratio"; in private insurance it is called the "loss ratio." Administrators of public programs (and those to whom they report) regard a high benefits ratio as indicative of an efficiently-run plan, moving funds to providers with a minimum of overhead cost on the way.[23] But for commercial firms, the loss ratio measures the proportion of premium revenue paid out in claims – "lost" to the firm and unavailable for operations, expansion ... or shareholder dividends or profit.

The "load factor" of the simple insurance model presented in Figure 8.2 – the proportion of premium revenue not paid out in claims – is thus the complement of the loss ratio. Profit-maximizing commercial insurers will try to maximize the load factor, and they do. A loss ratio over 80 per cent signals trouble; a commercial insurer that paid out 95 per cent of its revenues in benefits would quickly be in bankruptcy.[24]

But there is still a significant question as to why the overhead costs in the private sector are so much higher. Where does the money go? Commercial firms may *wish* to minimize their loss ratios, in the process of trying to maximize their profits, but economic theory might lead us to expect that competition from other firms will limit their ability to do so. The American insurance market is certainly highly competitive; why are their overheads not forced down to the levels achieved by public agencies, or (since private firms are supposedly more highly motivated) below? And why would the overhead costs of *providers* of care be so much higher in the United States? The answer can be extracted from "standard insurance theory," when we abandon the assumptions of the representative agent and of symmetric information freely available.

First, consider what commercial insurers do. In the hypothetical world of the representative agent, not very much. Every transactor faces the same potential loss or losses, with the same probabilities, and these are known to both buyer and seller of contracts (this is the world analyzed by Arrow, op. cit.). Everyone will want the same coverage, which can be offered for the same premium. Risk assessment need be done for only one representative individual. And claims adjustment is equally boring, since the occurrence of loss and the identity of losers are known to all. There will still be some risks too small to be worth insuring, but not many, because the overhead costs will be trivial. Whether the insurance process is public or private really does not matter much, though perhaps a competitive private market might serve to hold overhead costs down to their minimal level.

The process of insurance underwriting only begins to get interesting when we consider a world of heterogeneous individuals, all of whom face different levels of risk – different sizes and/or probabilities of loss. But it is not very interesting if we retain the assumption of perfect information (other than, *ex ante*, whether the insured event will occur or not, and to whom). In this case, commercial insurers in a competitive environment will set a different premium for each individual (more realistically, each class of similar individuals) equal to her own expected loss "loaded" by a share of the overall administration cost. (That cost is still pretty trivial, on the usual theoretical assumption of costless information.) This pricing pattern will create serious problems for a number of individuals, particularly those with few resources and facing high health risks – the elderly, poor, and chronically ill, for example. They may not be able to afford to cover their expected losses without serious hardship – or at all. The close correlation between health and wealth implies that those with the greatest (expected) needs will be least likely to be able to afford insurance. And without insurance, they are much less likely to get the services they need. On the other hand, this pricing pattern is highly advantageous for the incorrigibly healthy.

From the mainstream economic perspective in which standard insurance theory is rooted, this outcome is perfectly fair and "right."[25] The normative principle embedded in that perspective is that people should get that, and only that, for which they are willing and able to pay. It is allocatively inefficient – wasting resources – for people to have access to care that they cannot afford, regardless of their health needs, and the private insurance market will adjust individual premium levels to ensure that they do not get it. If they did, that would generate a "welfare burden" on the society as a whole.

It must be clearly understood, however, that this perspective is a moral choice, arising not from economic analysis per se but from the ideology (or intellectual conditioning) of the analyst. From other normative perspectives, these inequalities in access to care and in the distribution of costs are unfair, unacceptable, and "wrong."[26] Broad public concerns over such extreme inequalities might lead to the introduction of full or partial public coverage – as historically they have.

But concern over inequalities is not, *under the specified condition of costless information*, a sufficient explanation for the emergence of public coverage. If it was really true that each individual i's expected loss, q_iL_i, was (costlessly) known to both transactors, then one could design a tax and transfer system that transferred wealth from those with lower than average risk to those with higher. Each individual i would contribute or receive an amount T_i sufficient to make $q_iL_i+T_i$ equal to the average value of qL for the whole population. Given the pattern of illness in modern populations, most people would probably have to contribute a relatively moderate amount, while a minority would receive payments ranging from quite to very large indeed. But after paying the premium determined in the private insurance market, each individual would be out of pocket, net, by the same amount qL. In effect, this tax and transfer approach would create the same distribution of net premium costs as "community rating," in which an insurer charges every person in a community the same premium, based on the average risk level in that community.

In an (imaginary) environment of full information and de facto community rating supported by taxation and subsidy, it would not matter whether the insurance function were carried out privately or publicly. Yet, in the real world, advocates, publicists, and lobbyists contend fiercely over the relative merits of private and public coverage. And we observe, in both the United States and Canada, much higher load factors for "benefit" packages offered through private insurance. Obviously the "public/private" choice does matter a great deal, but the reasons cannot be found in theories based on a world of perfect information.

In a nutshell, the story is this. Over the last century, advances in medical knowledge have vastly extended the scope and effectiveness of health care – and its costs. The expected "losses" – health care expenditures – in Figures 8.1a and 8.1b have become much larger, but also much more variable from one individual to another. Analyses based on an assumed "representative agent" have become increasingly wild distortions of reality. An increasing proportion of the population have become "uninsurable," either because their expected losses are too large and unpredictable for an insurer to accept, or because even an actuarially fair premium, if one existed, would exceed their resources. At the same time, insurers have devoted increasing efforts to identifying and excluding "bad risks" from their portfolio of insurees. They have no choice; the survival of for-profit firms in a competitive marketplace dictates this behaviour.

Private health insurance thus becomes increasingly unavailable to those with the greatest risks and least resources – typically also the least healthy. Yet, without insurance, most of the population will be excluded from full (or any) access to a health care system that is, ironically, becoming increasingly effective in protecting life and limb. Access to effective health care matters, and modern populations demand it from their political masters.

Accordingly, most countries in the high-income world have, like Canada, a universal and more or less comprehensive system of public insurance, with or without a small private system supporting preferred services to those willing and able to pay extra.

The United States is unique among high-income countries in having responded to the economic realities of health insurance markets not with a universal public system but with a patchwork of different public programs, plus large subsidies to private insurers. The patches, however, are incomplete, still leaving nearly fifty million Americans with no coverage at all, and many more with inadequate partial coverage.

In the real world, countries face a choice not between public or private health insurance, but between different public systems with a greater or lesser degree of private involvement. The extent of the latter, in turn, depends upon the level of public subsidy or other forms of public support. Truly "free-standing" private health care insurance, sold by for-profit firms in a competitive marketplace, is (as noted above) effectively non-existent.

The chosen structure of different public insurance systems matters, in terms of the way in which the financial burden is distributed across the population. In general, the rich pay more when the system is tax-financed, less when there are compulsory social insurance premiums or other regressive taxes. Overhead costs – the load factors above – also vary depending upon system choice. Where there is a higher proportion of private insurance, the higher load factors associated with that source of financing lead to higher overall system overheads. The extraordinarily high administrative costs in the United State arise from the much higher proportion of private insurance in that country. It is private coverage, not "being American," that is expensive.

That said, the scale of private coverage in the United States does create a very large and lucrative market, in which for-profit insurers are engaged in a constant competitive struggle to identify and avoid insuring high-risk individuals, and when possible to avoid paying claims if the former efforts fail. This has generated a sort of administrative "arms race," in which providers of care – doctors and hospitals – have to go to considerable expense to ensure that their services are reimbursed. The result, as in any arms race, is an extraordinary level of additional overhead costs, resulting not just from private insurance per se, but from the intense competition among insurers and insured that appears to be without parallel outside the United States.

But why would any country abide the continued existence of a health insurance patchwork that is at once so grotesquely inefficient, expensive, and unfair?

The answer is simple. It has been well said that every system is perfectly designed to achieve the results that it does, in fact, achieve. Every dollar that is spent directly or indirectly on health care, in the United States or anywhere else, is a dollar of someone's income. Private health insurance may be an inefficient and inequitable way of spreading health risks across the population, but it functions as a superb generator of incomes, both individual and corporate. The American health insurance system has called into being a very large constituency of bright, articulate, well-connected, and well-financed groups – lawyers, accountants, insurance company executives, actuaries, marketers and information services firms, not a few health economists and, last but not least, investors – whose incomes and/or careers are derived from these extraordinarily high load factors and who are, accordingly and not surprisingly, very committed to defending them. Part of that defence consists of convincing the American population that they enjoy the finest health care in the world – well worth the cost. This goes far to explain the persistence of a financing system that to the rest of the world looks barking mad. You cannot fool all of the people all of the time – but you do not have to.

The standard economic models of insurance cannot begin to encompass these sorts of considerations, and do not try.

NOTES

1 In 2003, out-of-pocket payments covered 13.4 per cent of total national health expenditures in the United States. The share in Canada was slightly higher at 14.4 per cent. (United States, Centers for Medicare and Medicaid

Services, annual; Canadian Institute for Health Information, 2005). The United States *is* home to most of the world's private health insurance, covering 34.6 per cent of national outlays. Canada is a distant second, at 12.2 per cent, primarily covering the dental care and prescription drugs that are outside the national system. In both countries, however, private insurance receives large public subsidies through the "tax-expenditure" mechanism (on which more below). These public subsidies amount to roughly one-third of the health expenditure that flows through private insurers; they bring the true public share in the United States up to well above the officially reported figure of just under 50 per cent.

2 "The basic function of health insurance is the reduction of uncertainty; other things being equal, individuals prefer and are willing to pay for a reduction in their financial risks" (Arrow, 1976, 3).

3 This assumes independence of risks. Insurers may exclude coverage for "acts of God or the King's enemies" – war or natural disasters such as earthquakes – because these events generate a large number of simultaneous losses that would put the financial stability of the insurer at risk.

4 The assumption of non-satiation is, however, violated for "bads"; less is always better, but one cannot have less than zero.

5 A finite sum L need not exist. When a life insurance company pays a claim or a court awards damages in the event of death, it is the beneficiaries or plaintiffs who are compensated, not the decedent. (As far as is known there is no post-mortem individual utility function; the dead have no preferences.) But the assumption serves as a useful starting point; we shall return to this issue below.

6 This is another example of an ordinary-language word used in a very specific technical sense. In the circumstances specified, an actual outcome halfway between the two possibilities would be totally unexpected! Over a number of similar future periods, however, the average outcome would converge towards the mathematically expected level.

7 The obvious co-existence of both insurance purchase and gambling is difficult to reconcile in this framework. Some people may simply be unaware of the size or implications of the odds against them. But many people gamble who are quite aware that it makes no sense as a strictly financial transaction. There are presumably other important psychological effects associated with the process. Buying a lottery ticket permits one to fantasize, and betting seems to produce an adrenalin rush. In some it seems to induce altered, non-rational mental states. But this takes us well beyond the world of insurance.

8 The actuarially fair contract is an abstraction, like a frictionless surface or a perfect vacuum. The term – another example of a discrepancy between technical and ordinary language – should not be taken as implying that premiums

greater than the expected payout are necessarily unfair. At times when nominal interest rates are extremely high, insurers may be able to earn sufficient investment returns on their required reserves (or in this abstract model during the time lag between premium collection and claims payment) to cover operating costs and profits. They can then operate profitably, even if the difference between premium receipts and contract payouts – known as "underwriting gain" – is zero or negative. But these are temporary circumstances.

9 People vary in their tolerance for risk, or degree of risk aversion; this could be expressed as differences in the degree of curvature of the relation $U(W)$. Gains from insurance are obviously greater for those with a higher distaste for risk, or as usually described, lower risk tolerance.

10 With an additive load factor, the individual will either buy or not buy full coverage against the whole loss L. If on the other hand the load is proportionate to the premium, then the rational individual will under these assumptions buy partial coverage. With no load factor, the individual's expected utility is $qU(W - L + R - p) + (1 - q)U(W - p)$, and she chooses the value of reimbursement R to maximize this expression subject to the constraint that $p = qR$. This will be where $R = L$, full coverage. A linear term F added to p drops out of the maximization process, but R now jumps discontinuously from L to zero as F increases. But if the load factor is multiplicative, a factor $f > 1$ proportionate to the expected loss, then expected utility is $qU(W - L + R - pf) + (1 - q)U(W - pf)$, and the optimum R is less than L. The cost of coverage in terms of expected wealth given up is proportionate to coverage, the benefit in terms of reduced risk falls with rising coverage, and so the optimum level is less than 100 per cent and falls as f rises – until it too jumps discontinuously to zero.

11 High-deductible policies raise no *ex ante* distributional issues in an idealized purely commercial, competitive, and unsubsidized insurance system, because (assuming perfect information) each individual's premium would be reduced by exactly the (expected) amount of her additional out-of-pocket payments, plus associated saved administrative costs. She would, of course, carry an additional risk of unreimbursed losses, but individuals could choose among a variety of different levels of coverage with corresponding differences in premium. These conditions may hold, more or less, in markets for property and casualty coverage, but are not even a remote approximation to real-world health care financing systems. Nor could they be – see below.

12 Some schemes for high-deductible coverage do recognize these distributional concerns, and respond by linking the size of the deductible to

individual income levels. This can mitigate the regressive effect to some degree (though not the transfer of costs from well to ill), but in any tax-financed system, those with higher incomes still come out ahead – and the higher one's income, the greater the gain – because tax liability is more "income-elastic" than average health expenditure.

13 Volunteers for clinical trials of new drugs are willing to accept financial compensation for the (presumed minor) health risks involved, and even for undergoing infection with short-term illnesses such as upper respiratory (cold) viruses for research purposes. There may, however, also be altruistic motives in these situations.

14 We might call this the "Superman" tragedy. Try to imagine a finite sum of money that would have compensated Christopher Reeves for his post-accident health state. And his name is Legion.

15 It might be argued that most people recover fully from most illnesses (often without medical intervention). This is true, but treating those who suffer from chronic illness generates a greatly disproportionate share of health care costs. Moreover this analysis is static. Full recovery after pain, distress, and disability (including the inconvenience and distress associated with treatment) still represents a loss of health status, even if only temporary. (One is not indifferent between being ill and being well, even if full recovery is assured.)

16 Major dental care is an exception; the insurer might ask to see the X-rays before authorizing reimbursement for extensive crown and bridge work. And American managed care plans notoriously (to physicians) may require pre-authorization for hospitalization or major procedures, second-guessing the physician's diagnosis and/or treatment plan perhaps on the basis of a (proprietary) computer algorithm. But the United States is again the exception, and it is not at all clear that this approach is cost-effective relative to the more global forms of utilization control used in other national systems.

17 These false signalling problems arise in legal claims for compensation, precisely because the courts do recognize that losses from injury go well beyond the costs of care.

18 Disability insurance goes farther, to provide partial coverage of lost income. In this case the monitoring of the actual state is less difficult, and the scale of loss is sufficient to justify that cost.

19 Arrow's (1976) early attempt to provide a formal argument for the optimality of some level of user charges under health care insurance, in the form of a "coinsurance" rate of some percentage of total outlays charged back to the user, embodies this confusion. Even within his community of identical individuals, the loss associated with illness will exceed outlays for

health care, so that full coverage of those outlays will be substantially short of full coverage of loss. It would be impossible to count how many times that error has been repeated since.

20 The over-representation of American economists in that literature may also play a role.

21 Thereby underlining the role of such user charges as mechanisms for redistributing the burden of health costs rather than for deterring "unnecessary" (or necessary) care use.

22 The official national health expenditures data in both countries thus overstate expenditures on health care services per se, and underestimate administrative overheads. In the United States this misclassification might be of the order of magnitude of 10 per cent of total health care spending.

23 Public plan administrators may in fact overdo this form of "efficiency," insofar as minimal administrative oversight could result in inflated and inappropriate claims and excessive total program costs. But there is in practice no empirical support for arguments that the much higher load factors in private insurance plans are associated with tighter cost control. In fact, the American Medicare program has, over the long term, been more successful than private insurers in controlling total expenditures per capita.

24 In times of high inflation, a private insurer can in fact operate with negative "underwriting gain," but that is another story.

25 Indeed private insurance companies in the United States have been known to argue precisely this in their advocacy advertising, that it is not fair for some people to have to pay for the costs of insuring others.

26 If under these circumstances competitive markets yield outcomes widely judged to be undesirable, the fault lies not with the market but with those who expect market mechanisms to serve purposes they were not designed for and cannot achieve.

REFERENCES

Arrow, K. (1976). "Welfare analysis of changes in health coinsurance rates," in *The role of health insurance in the health services sector*, ed. R.N. Rosett, 3–23. New York: National Bureau of Economic Research.

Canadian Institute for Health Information (2005). *National health expenditure trends, 1970–2005*. Ottawa: CIHI.

OECD (2004). *OECD Health data 2004*. Paris: OECD.

United States, Centers for Medicare and Medicaid Services. *National health expenditure data* (updated annually). Washington, DC: CME.

Woolhandler, S., T. Campbell, and D.U. Himmelstein (2003). "Costs of health care administration in the United States and Canada." *New England Journal of Medicine* 349(8): 768–75.

Further Reading

Without intending to be exhaustive, amongst other papers that would have found a comfortable home in this section, but for which there was insufficient space, are:

- Evans, Robert G. "Tension, Compression, and Shear: Directions, Stresses, and Outcomes of Health Care Cost Control." *Journal of Health Politics, Policy and Law* 15(1)(1990): 101–28.
- – "Baneful Legacy: Medicare and Mr. Trudeau: The Constitution Created by the Trudeau Government Is Now Threatening Canada's Medicare System. What Can Be Done To Defend It?" *Healthcare Policy* 1(1)(2005): 20–5.
- – "Preserving Privilege, Promoting Profit: The Payoffs from Private Health Insurance." In *Access to Care, Access to Justice*, ed. C.M. Flood, K. Roach, and L. Sossin, 347–68. Toronto: University of Toronto Press, 2005.

SECTION C

Health Care Policy

Foreword

THEODORE R. MARMOR

Bob Evans' scholarship has ranged widely, as the editors' (and other) forewords in this volume make clear. My emphasis will be on his contributions to our understanding of the applied world of health care practices – whether examining the industry's structure, how it is financed, its costs, the quality of its services, or how the industry is governed. I have known the author for over forty years, and have had regular and extended contact with him in a wide variety of settings and contexts. Our collegial links began at the 1975 Sun Valley Health Forum on Canadian National Health Insurance (Andreopoulos, 1975). That conference spawned a book that provides a good way to begin to explore Evans' professional contributions to what I will call health care, rather than health policy. (He has had plenty to say about both, but Section D of this collection is devoted to the latter topic).

Evans' role at the Sun Valley conference illustrates nicely the kind of writer, speaker, and advocate he was to become over the next decades. It also provides a helpful perspective on his important place in North American health care policy disputes over many decades. The Sun Valley contribution, for Evans, proceeded from a natural experiment perspective. The starting point was that Canadian and American health care arrangements had been very similar for much of the twentieth century. By 1971, however, Canada's Medicare had insured all citizens for medical and hospital expenses, while in the United States, Medicare and Medicaid were separate patches in a complicated patchwork of private and public insurance which had left substantial numbers uninsured. His chapter in the conference volume asked what explains the similar cost experience of the two countries in the period from 1950 to 1970, but divergence after that. The answer: a public health insurance program with universal coverage and both an operating and capital budget outperforms patchwork systems that discover their expenditure levels rather than choose them.

The approach of natural experiments was only one way in which Evans structured his scholarship. As the articles in this section and this volume illustrate, he has participated in all manner of policy debates. But, it is important to acknowledge that he has had relatively greater influence in Canadian debates than similar debates in the United States, despite the obvious relevance of his scholarship to the latter. Why that is the case is a theme worthy of some reflection, because it cannot be explained by the quality of Evans' work. I return to this matter later.

The premise of this book's publication is that Evans' published record is extraordinary. Part of the explanation is that he has been amazingly active – a scholarly workhorse – in Canadian policy struggles over medical and health care policy. The speeches he has made, the radio and television interviews he has given, the panels on which he has engaged critics, the conference presentations he has offered, which run into the many hundreds, and the public inquiries such as a Royal Commission in which he has been an active participant, have almost all been based in Canada. And a large proportion of his published articles were set in a Canadian context. Yet much of his writing, as I will note shortly, transcends borders.

What then is so special about Evans' contributions in the health care policy arena, and seen in a North American context? I would emphasize two features of the man and the scholar. First and foremost, he is a gifted and amazingly determined public intellectual. By public intellectual, I mean someone who takes very seriously the responsibility to attack mythical and mistaken claims about public policy. In Evans' case, this is evident in how he has responded since the 1970s to a whole series of what he took to be often deliberately misleading, at other times embarrassingly simplistic, analyses and reform recommendations. And, in the campaigns against misguided premises, factual error, and inappropriate policy inferences, he was fearless, often fierce, and punishingly willing to continue an intellectual brawl. But beyond those qualities of tenacity and intellectual command were his modes of public speaking. They made Evans a welcome (or feared) speaker in setting after setting. He brought wit into commentary on topics that would, in others' hands, have received dry, unimaginative treatment. He had a ready supply of biblical allusions for evidence of self-interest, ready references to historical episodes, or quick asides – all of which made him a lively party to a conference, a meeting, or a debate. Finally, he brought a quality of determination to follow the argument through, and to base it in research evidence and defensible research methods, that never failed to impress audiences, whether they be the public or entranced policy-makers.

Precisely those qualities made Evans both controversial and lauded, as the papers collected together in this section illustrate. The article on "Incomplete Vertical Integration," for example, uses the conventional framework of industrial organization to illuminate the fundamental ways in which medical care can be delivered, financed, and regulated. Rather than starting with observations about this or that feature of modern medical care, Evans offers a map of the whole field. His fundamental contention is that incomplete vertical integration among different agents characterizes all health care arrangements – the major players are never either fully independent nor under full administrative direction. He captured the possible relationships in four simplified, but illuminating, models that are as accurate today as the day they were written: a hypothetical free market, a completely professionalized structure, a universal public-health insurance mode, and what Evans calls an "HMO or Consumer Choice Health Plan." In this work Evans provides a guide to how different national policies display different patterns of incomplete vertical integration. At the same time, the article exposes what Evans claims are the propagandistic elements of what he labels as "pseudomarkets" and "pseudopolicies." None of the American health economists lauding the role that market structures and market incentives can play in medical care have paid attention to this fundamental contribution.

The rest of the articles in this section – and other published pieces too numerous to include – offer additional examples of Evans as both an illuminating applied theorist and a scathing critic of sloppy reasoning in health policy debates. One persistent theme in Evans' writing is the widespread tendency of elites to restrict the range of policy choices by appeals to what necessity requires (see, for example, Evans, 1985).The illusion Evans regularly attacked was the pretence that particular choices are just not possible. That perspective is a useful guide to truncated policy debates in today's world, whether exemplified by Pharmacare in Canada or Obamacare in the US.

"Political Wolves and Economic Sheep" (included in this section) illustrates vividly Evans' inclination to take on busting myths as a professional responsibility. Here he addresses the common assertion that public health insurance must of necessity be "fiscally unsustainable." Evans points out, with his usual clarity, that this notion has no convincing empirical basis, but plenty of interested parties who stand to gain from the weakening or elimination of public national health insurance. A similar line of criticism shows up in Evans' writing about the impact of aging on health care costs. The idea that demography is destiny and that aging explains much of the general escalation of medical expenditures has become a "zombie," a false claim that refuses to die. It is Evans' persistence in the role of mythbuster that is remarkable here. Zombies do not die, and policy-makers tend to have short memories; the paper on aging included in this volume, "Aging and Health Care Utilization," is but one of a number written by Evans and colleagues on this topic over his career.

Evans' health care policy papers share forceful language, but not one overarching theme. That is to be expected, given his professional range. Yet the import of his writing is worth emphasizing. I note here just a few of these important contributions. The discussion of "supplier-induced demand" (paper included in this section) is one of Evans' most widely noted articles, a powerful challenge to those who insist on thinking that ordinary market relationships among patient/consumers and physician/suppliers obtain in practice. The reasoning is intricate, but the implications for policy design are crucial. If physicians shape the demand for their services and have both target incomes and the controls necessary to meet those targets, the rules of ordinary market operation will not, indeed cannot, apply.

Evans has also written persuasively on physician supply, the importation of physicians to Canada, and professionalism more generally. The contributions are too many to mention in this foreword, let alone include in this single collection. But it is worth noting Evans' writing in the 1970s about domestic hostility to immigrant physicians (1976). That topic is relevant to contemporary policy debates in most industrialized nations. It took on, as Evans often does, a puzzle from real life: namely, why, amidst concern about a physician surplus, the Canadian government of the time (seemingly paradoxically) chose to restrict the entry of immigrant physicians rather than encourage provinces to reduce domestic training capacity.

Given the wide range and seemingly timeless applicability of Evans' scholarship, one has to wonder why his ideas have not gained more traction in American health care policy debates, despite the obvious relevance of his scholarship to those enduring debates. It would be wrong to picture exclusion; too many of Evans' US colleagues, myself and a number of well-known and respected health-services researchers included, have learned from and cited the body of work. The Baxter Prize noted by the editors of this volume makes that point rather forcefully. But among American health economists in particular his work has largely fallen on stony ground. The reason relates directly to the fact that pro-market economic thinking in health care policy has become more dominant in the US in the last three or four decades. The question is "Why?"

One answer is the general ascendance in American academic writing of economic analyses with a pro-market orientation in the wake of the stagflation the oil crisis of 1973–74 precipitated. The anti-government, anti-regulatory enthusiasms associated with the University of Chicago school moved well beyond that particular "theological" site, providing the intellectual groundwork for wider pro-market and pro-competition thinking. The increased legitimacy of this political ideology – most obviously consequential in traditional areas of governmental regulation like trucking, airlines, and banking – made its application to the medical care industry less problematic than would have been the case early in the 1960s. The Bob Evans who crafted the papers on incomplete vertical integration or supplier-induced demand was a heretic in that context and in those increasingly influential circles.

The setting and timing of Evans' contributions, then, helps us understand the puzzle of his prominence in the Canadian, but not the American, part of North America. Had the US enacted a universal version of Medicare in 1965 (or 1970), Evans' affirmation of public universal health insurance and his critique of free-market thought in health insurance would have been resonant on both sides of the border, and would likely (as has been the case in Canada) have been instrumental in protecting the US system from the buffeting of market zealots. Instead, an intellectual trade barrier emerged by the end of the 1970s, and the United States suffered as a result (and is still paying for the consequences), with a health care system exceptional in its combination of comparatively poor health statistics and comparatively extravagant health care costs.

On the brighter side, however, one could argue that some of Evans' brilliant scholarship has been spurred on by the divergent ideological and policy paths that his country and mine have followed over the past half-century. This grand natural experiment has created remarkably fertile ground for a remarkably fertile intellect. We are all the richer for that.

REFERENCES

Andreopoulos, S., ed. (1975). *National Health Insurance: Can We Learn from Canada?* (New York: John Wiley), 129–79.

Evans, R.G. (1976). "Does Canada Have Too Many Doctors: Why Nobody Loves an Immigrant Physician." *Canadian Public Policy* (Spring): 147–60.
– (1985). "Illusions of Necessity: Evading Responsibility for Choice in Health Care." *Journal of Health Politics, Policy, and Law* 10(3): 439–67.

9

Supplier-Induced Demand: Some Empirical Evidence and Implications (1974)

ROBERT G. EVANS

Everyone knows that physicians exert a strong influence over the quantity and pattern of medical care demanded in a developed economy. The professional status of the physician and the peculiar "doctor-patient relationship" are rooted in the dual roles which the physician must perform. He acts as the agent of the patient, providing expert direction or assistance in the interpretation of the patient's health status, the identification of the capacity of current medical technology to improve that status, and the skilled application of that technology. But at the same time he is a supplier of a particular class of services whose income and work satisfaction are related to the volume of services he supplies and the price he receives for them. In this role the interests of the physician tend to conflict with those of the patient, particularly if medical practice is organized on an entrepreneurial fee-for-service basis. Such a setting creates strong economic incentives for the physician to overemphasize the supply of his own services to the exclusion of substitutes and to bias the patient's "choice" of services towards those which yield the highest net revenue per time unit for the physician. One purpose of the professionalization of

Evans, Robert G. "Supplier Induced Demand: Some Empirical Evidence and Implications." In *The Economics of Health and Medical Care* (proceedings of a conference held by the International Economic Association, Tokyo, 1973), edited by Mark Perlman, 162–73. New York: Halsted Press, 1974.

the physician role is the formation of a set of attitudes which will counteract these incentives.

If physicians were simply entrepreneurs, supplying a particular good, "medical care," then one could analyze the behaviour of the medical market using the conventional theoretical tools of supply and demand analysis. The demand side of the market could be treated as a function of price and consumer characteristics, such as age, sex, income, insurance status, and so on, with efforts made to define and measure demand curves for aggregate or sub-markets. Shifts in demand due to such "policy instruments" as types of insurance coverage could be studied without reference to supply-side behaviour. At the same time the supply side could be handled in a conventional manner, assuming perfect competition or monopoly and investigating the implications of each with or without recognition of the fact that the entrepreneur running the firm is also a principal factor supplier with his own income-leisure trade-off.[1]

What is neglected, however, is the theoretical significance of the other aspect of the physician's role, the patient's agent. The physician can exert direct influence on the demand function of the consumer by altering the patient's perceptions of his needs and of the capacity of medical technology to satisfy them. Thus, the medical service market cannot be simply dichotomized into demand side and supply side, with price serving as the only nexus between the two; rather we must allow for shifts in the demand curve itself in response to supplier behaviour. Market clearing may take place directly through the information which suppliers pass to consumers as well as by adjustments in price.

In such a market, it may no longer be taken for granted that conventional economic propositions hold. If, for example, physicians respond to increases in price by exerting a stronger positive influence on patients' perceptions of their "need" for service, then it is not impossible for the total response of quantity demanded to price to be positive. The *partial* response may be negative as consumer theory predicts, but the *ceteris* do not remain *paribus*. Instead they vary in a systematic way with price.

Similarly, an increase in the physician stock, if physicians have discretionary power over demand, may lead to increases in both output and prices. This is because the power to sell more at the current price (by increasing each consumer's demand) is equivalent to the power to sell the current output at a higher price (by increasing demand and simultaneously raising price). An increase in number of suppliers at a given volume of demand and price will lead to a fall in each supplier's income; he can respond to this change by expanding his effort on demand generation and then either working more or raising prices, or both.[2]

Of course, demand cannot be expanded indefinitely at any given price level. There undoubtedly comes a point where continued increases in supply will lead to the re-emergence of price-competitive behaviour. The usefulness of discretionary models depends on an assumption that such a point is significantly far from where we now are, and that the social costs of reaching it would be relatively large in terms of the negative health impact of "over-doctoring" and quality dilution as well as the economic costs of public investment and subsidy.

A further implication of the same argument has to do with deterrent charges as a device for reducing utilization and moderating cost increases under medical insurance plans. Insofar as such charges are successful in lowering workloads at current prices, they will lower physician incomes. If physicians have discretionary power over demand, they will respond by shifting the demand curve rightward and either raising price or increasing output back to previous levels.[3] The distribution of care may change, but overall expenditures are unlikely to fall.

Thus, the possibility that suppliers can individually or collectively exercise influence over the demand curve can have rather radical implications for the role of prices as market signalling devices on the effects of exogenous shifts in supply and demand on expenditure and price.

By itself, however, the notion that suppliers influence demand does not vitiate any of the conventional propositions of market analysis. If suppliers took no account of economic data in the information which they provided to consumers, e.g., if physicians disregarded prices, their own incomes, and their workloads in making recommendations to patients, then the demand function as a relation between quantity and price could be treated as stable and negatively sloped, because the other parameters of the utility function would still be exogenously determined.[4] Unfortunately, the literature on physician behaviour abounds with references to the responsiveness of physician practice behaviour to economic factors.[5] At the other extreme, if physicians are pure income-maximizers, it is clear that each individual physician will always exert as much influence as he can to increase demand for his own services. In this case, analysis of the medical services market becomes merely a version of the monopolistic competition model with advertising and a rather peculiar advertising cost function.[6] The assumption of income maximization assures that *unexerted* discretionary influence over the demand curve does not exist, hence the demand curve can be treated as exogenous.

In a real world lying between these two extremes, however, discretionary power by physicians may persist. If it is a significant feature of the medical care supply process, then it must be incorporated into models of the medical market; and there appear to be two basic ways of doing this. One can retain the maximizing framework and postulate that physicians have some broader objective function, including the exercise of discretion as well as income and/or workload. Alternatively, one can abandon the maximizing framework for some general "target" model, in which physicians are assumed to have rough targets for both income and leisure (the origin of such targets is unclear, but no more so than the origin of the utility function!) and to adjust prices and/or discretionary behaviour so as to approach these moving targets.

The extended maximizing model can be applied to any market in which *some* price responsiveness by consumers exists due to full or partial self-payment; it cannot explain market behaviour in a full-insurance system such as Canada's Medicare plan. Such a model might specify each physician's utility as a positive function of his income (Y) and a negative function of his workload (W) and the extent to which he exerts discretionary influence (D) to increase demand. D may also be interpreted as a positive preference for nonprice rationing. If we regard each physician as a monopolistic competitor whose market share depends on the population/physician ratio (R), and each of whose patients demands an amount of care negatively related to the price charged and positively related to demand-expanding behaviour, then we may write:

$$U = U(Y, W, D)$$
$$W = R \cdot f(P, D)$$

where W is the physician's workload, $f(P,D)$ is the demand for care by his "representative" patient, and R allows for shifts in workload arising from shifts in the exogenous population/physician ratio. The problem is to maximize U subject to the workload constraint W, by setting price level, workload, and discretionary behaviour. Income is equal to the product of price level and workload, assuming a constant proportion of overhead expense.

The comparative statics of such a model are relatively straightforward, if somewhat tedious, and it turns out that the conditions for a maximum are "reasonable" a priori. But predicted responses to exogenous shifts are not determinate; in particular, an exogenous increase in supply (a fall in R) may well result in a *rise* in price. If the D variable is suppressed, a fall in R for P given lowers both income and workload. The marginal utility of income rises and the marginal disutility of work falls, so the physician cuts price so as to increase workload and income. (Of course, the elasticity of demand for care faced by each physician must be greater than unity to make this model work.) But in the more general model, the physician may increase both P and D to get back to equilibrium. In general, the difficulty is that the D variable introduces an extra off-diagonal term from the Hessian matrix of the constrained maximization problem into each shift-response equation, and nothing is determinate.[7]

A maximizing model extended to include physician discretion is thus able to break the conventional association between rising prices and scarcity of excess demand, but at the cost of giving up all definite predictions about pricing behaviour. A further source of weakness in such models is the structure of the patient demand equation; conditions for a maximum require that the price elasticity of demand faced by each physician must be greater than unity. As noted below, this requires either that most measurements of the elasticity are erroneous, or that physicians are price-competitive with one another. *A fortiori*, such a model will not explain pricing behaviour in a fee-for-service market under comprehensive, universal medical insurance, such as the Canadian Medicare system. The fact that such markets do indeed function, with price behaviour roughly similar to the United States self-paying market, suggests that the maximizing model may be inadequate.

A less formal, non-maximizing model may be constructed if we hypothesize that physicians have rough targets with respect to income and workload, based on their training, expectations, and previous experience. Discrepancies between these targets and actual experience lead to adjustment behaviour; if income and workloads are below targets, demand generation may take place. If physicians feel overworked and underpaid, upward pressure on prices may develop either collectively (revision of fee schedules) or individually (independent adjustments in billing behaviour).

In Canada, revision of fee schedules requires that a large enough number of physicians in any province find target incomes unattainable and seek to put through a uniform schedule revision; the physician whose targets run ahead of his colleagues' can only work harder. In the United States, where individual physicians have more power over their own prices, the factors limiting short-run adjustment are less clear. Nevertheless, there is considerable evidence that price adjustment is only one of several possible strategies a physician may employ in meeting his practice objectives.

The implications of such a model have been developed in more detail elsewhere,[8] but in general they include upward pressure on prices when supply increases, as well as relatively little response of income per physician. Increases in region-wide fee schedules are likely to lower output per physician (although not unambiguously), and thus rising prices are ineffective as a rationing device for clearing markets. The primary function of price is (in conjunction with workloads) to achieve physician income targets. A model of this sort is distressingly fuzzy in its failure to explain the formation of target incomes or the distribution of target shortfalls between price increase and demand generation. It does, however, have the capacity to interpret a number of empirical observations which are anomalous in a conventional supply/demand framework.

If physician influence over demand is a significant feature of the medical service market, we would expect to find relatively little relationship between physician workload and physician density per capita. On the other hand, if demand is exogenous to the physician, workload should vary inversely with density. Within each of the provinces of Canada, physicians are now paid according to a standardized fee schedule; thus, one can use annual incomes of physicians within the same province as indicators of their relative workloads. In British Columbia, annual gross receipts of each physician from the provincial medical insurance plan are published by physician name, and it is thus possible to link up gross receipts with data on physician specialty, length of practice, location, form of practice (solo or group by size), and place of training. Furthermore, since each physician is located by school district and hospital district (the latter being aggregations of contiguous school districts forming a single catchment area for purposes of regional hospital planning), it is possible to measure demographic and other aggregate variables by region and to investigate their significance as predictors of physician gross income and workload.

This database has been investigated for both 1969 and 1971 in order to determine *inter alia* the influence on physician workload of relative physician densities by region.[9] The procedure employed in both surveys has been to reduce the total physician census to a subset assumed to be in full-time medical practice, and then to relate the average incomes of these physicians to a set of independent dummy variables representing professional characteristics. This database consists of 2,279 physicians in 1969 and 2,457 in 1971. Dummy variables are used to control for each of the characteristics listed above, thus enabling one to estimate for any particular set of characteristics the total amount by which the income of the physician which they represent would have exceeded that of the base reference physician (a general practitioner who graduated from the University of British Columbia within the last five years and is in solo practice in Vancouver). Details on the data file are available from the author.

With physician workload (gross receipts) standardized for the characteristics of the physician, it is then possible to introduce measures of the relative availability of medical care in each region. These are unfortunately conceptually fuzzy, for several reasons. Availability is a relation between the exogenous "demand" for medical care (in a fully insured population) and the exogenous "stock" of care in each region. The crudest measures of each are total populations by region and total physician stock. But clearly, people are not homogeneous in their health characteristics; the exogenous demand of a population depends on age, sex, fertility, climate, occupation, socio-economic status, etc. Out of all these factors we carried out a rough standardization for age alone, using relative utilization weights for four different age groups to derive a standardized population for each region. Nor are physicians homogeneous; we therefore calculated physician/(standardized) population ratios for all physicians, general practitioners, and general practitioners and "practising specialists,"[10] and fitted separate equations for each group. The problem of course is to define a subset of physicians who are substitutes for one another (more or less), and there exists no precisely correct procedure. Regional boundaries are a further problem, since one may choose small regions such as school districts, in which case referral across boundaries leads to mis-specification of available supply, or large regions such as hospital districts which may span several medical "markets." We chose the latter to minimize the referral problem: tertiary referrals to the university-affiliated hospitals in Vancouver are missed, but secondary referrals to urban centres are in general within regions.

The coefficients on these physician/population density variables are as follows (*t*-statistics in brackets):

	AMD	GP	GPPS	PS
1969	−0.158	−0.125	−0.179	0.013
	(2.68)	(1.46)	(2.75)	(0.27)
1971	−0.087	−0.274	−0.070	0.061
	(1.27)	(2.28)	(0.88)	(1.06)

AMD is the equation fitted for all physicians of whatever speciality, *GP* are general practitioners only, *PS* are selected specialties (see note 10), and GPPS is fitted on sums from *GP* and *PS*. Equations are double-log, so coefficients represent elasticity. The *PS* equation suggests that interaction among specialists has a positive effect on workload; all other equations indicate weak negative effects from density to workload. This is consistent with the hypothesis that physicians can to a large extent generate enough activity to insulate their workload against supply shifts. Adjustment is not complete, however, so a target income model would also suggest that supply increases generate upward price pressure. Moreover, the incomplete adjustment is consistent with increasing marginal disutility of demand generation.

Shifting "demand" in response to changes in the effective supply of physicians is not of course the only interpretation of these results. One could argue that British Columbia has a physician shortage such that all physicians are working at full capacity regardless of the number available and that some patients are turned away. The plausibility of this argument is weakened by the fact that British Columbia (BC) has far and away the highest ratio of physicians to population in Canada, about 25 to 30 per cent above the national average (depending on definition). Many regions of BC have still higher ratios. Alternatively, one could argue that demand is a function of the shadow price of time and other access costs which are reduced when physician density increases; moreover, demand may vary from region to region due to shifts in non-measured variables, and physicians have simply distributed themselves in response to income differentials in such a way as to even out incomes. Neither of these arguments can be tested directly with aggregate data, since they appeal to unmeasured shadow prices and demand shifts, but they can be indirectly tested by evidence on the particular patterns of medical services supplied as physician density changes.

Data on the mix of services by physician and region in BC were not available for this study. However, a set of data on the operations of the Canadian non-profit private insurance plans which predated the universal federally initiated Medicare program is available from 1957 to 1967. These data indicate that across provinces the relative frequency of physician-initiated services such as consultations tends to be more closely correlated with physician availability than does the frequency of patient-initiated services such as first office or home visits.[11] Moreover, the rapid increases in physician availability in Canada during the period 1957 to the present, due both to increases in manpower and to increases in services per physician,[12] have likewise been associated with increases in the mix of total services accounted for by physician-initiated services. Consultations and diagnostic tests per capita have increased much faster over time than home or office calls; this is not consistent with either the argument that patients are responding to shadow prices or that medical services are merely reducing a backlog of unmet need. In the same context, it is notable that the shift from house to office calls in Canada over the past fifteen years has not been associated with any change in their relative prices. Thus, what evidence we have on inter-regional and intertemporal patterns of service mix is consistent with supplier generation of demand rather than consumer response to implicit prices or exogenous demand-side effects.[13]

If, in fact, discretionary influence over demand is a significant feature of the market behaviour of physicians, then we should expect to find it reflected in price behaviour. And we do discover a general tendency for physician prices to be relatively higher in regions where physicians are plentiful than where they are scarce. While data are sketchy and relative levels are hard to establish, owing to the discontinuous jumps which take place in listed fees, there is a clear tendency for medical care prices to be higher in those provinces of Canada with high physician/population ratios (Ontario, British Columbia) than in those with low (Saskatchewan, the Maritimes). The direction of causality in such an association is by no means obvious: higher prices per unit of output could as easily be the magnet which attracts more physicians. But the problem with this argument is that *income* relationships are much less clear: high prices are associated with both high (Ontario) and low (British Columbia) relative incomes. There is some evidence that higher than average increases in physician density are associated with lower than average increases in income; but the mechanism is clearly not through slower rates of price increase. Rather it appears to be incomplete ability to adjust quantity of workload per physician, perhaps operating with a lag.[14]

If the demand relationship is made subsidiary to supplier behaviour, then one ought to be able to use similar models to interpret United States and Canadian physician behaviour, in spite of the differences in medical care financing. Patterns of organization on the supply side remain relatively similar. The existence of physician discretionary power is indicated by such United States results as Feldstein's inability to derive any sort of "reasonable" demand curve with a negative price term, even in the context of a simultaneous market model under several different price adjustment specifications.[15] His conclusion that physicians may hold prices below market clearing levels to enjoy the utility of non-price rationing is the inverse of the notion that demand generation at given prices is possible but involves disutility. Similarly, Newhouse[16] finds systematic positive correlations between physician density and price in the United

States, rejecting both "competitive" and "monopolistic" models of the market which use price as the only nexus between supply and demand. He notes that rationing by physicians may explain his results. Reinhardt[17] finds that the internal organization of physician practices is inconsistent with income maximization, in that the shadow prices of physician time implicit in fee schedules are much higher than those implicit in physician/aide mixes. He suggests that a state of generalized excess demand creates a "price umbrella," permitting this form of discretionary "inefficiency by preference," but discretionary power over demand is an equally good umbrella. It permits the physician whose preference for income is strong to organize a fast throughput "shop," without squeezing out his less aggressive competitors. Finally, the numerous studies which measure elasticities of demand for medical care at between –1 and zero are rendered plausible: if physicians were income- or income/leisure-maximizers, they should always seek higher prices to raise income and lower workload, and the observed market result would depend on their having insufficient ability to collude so as to raise prices all round. But if in fact each physician generates his own demand, then no stable exogenous demand curve exists to be measured. Price being correlated with demand-generation effort will lead to a reduction in the measured response of demand to price, but the partial response of demand to price, *everything* else held constant, is not being tested.

Thus, there exists a wide range of empirical evidence that the market for physicians' services is not self-equilibrating in the usual sense, that price does not serve primarily to balance supply and demand, because there are important alternative channels of information which perform this function. The primary role of price is instead as an input to supplier incomes, which are not themselves the product of explicit maximizing behaviour, but rather of target-seeking through the manipulation of several different control variables. In this context, as noted above, the explanation of supply, "shortages," utilization, and price and cost behaviour may be very different from the usual market models. To the extent that shortages, prices, or costs are objects of public policy, policy prescriptions must take account of these differences.

NOTES

1 A variety of analyses of demand, some with quite sophisticated analyses of consumer motivation, are surveyed by Cliff Lloyd, "The Demand for Medical

Care: A Selective Review of the Literature," University of Iowa Working Paper Series No. 71–9 (April 1971). The physician's income-leisure trade-off may be handled by estimating demand curves simultaneously with a rising supply curve in which the source of rising marginal cost is the increasing marginal disutility of labour to the physician; this appears to be the rationale for J.P. Newhouse, "A Model of Physician Pricing," *Southern Economic Journal*, 37 (2) (Oct. 1970), as corrected by H. Frech and P. Ginsburg, "Physician Pricing: Monopolistic or Competitive," *Southern Economic Journal*, 37 (3) (Dec. 1970). Similarly, M. Feldstein, "The Rising Price of Physicians' Services," *Review of Economics and Statistics*, 52(2) (May 1970), develops a supply curve embodying a physician work-leisure trade-off which appears to be backwardbending.

2 Such a reaction by physicians should not be interpreted as the deliberate provision of unnecessary care. If physicians as a group believe that the public "needs" more care than it now receives [and there is evidence that they do, e.g., interviews by H. Schonfeld et al., "Number of Physicians Required for Primary Medical Care," *New England Journal of Medicine*, no. 286, (16 March 1972)], then they may well react to lowered workloads resulting from increased density of physicians by attempting to take better care of their patients through more frequent recalls and follow-ups, more extensive testing, consultations, and more services generally.

3 The emphasis on physician responses to overall workload changes indicates that the results of partial and general deterrent charges may be quite different. A small insured group which does not account for a large part of the income of its local medical community may indeed respond to deterrents by reducing utilization. On the other hand, a deterrent fee introduced in a national or provincial insurance plan is much less likely to affect overall utilization and more likely to exert upward pressure on medical prices. R.G. Beck, "An Analysis of the Demand for Physicians' Services in Saskatchewan," unpublished doctoral dissertation (University of Alberta, Edmonton, Spring 1971) emphasizes the reactions of physicians as well as patients to the province-wide deterrent fee introduced in 1968, and points out that this fee happened to coincide with a significant upward revision in the provincial fee schedule, as well as apparently *increasing* utilization by certain classes of patients.

4 If the full information assumption for patients is relaxed, one can still insulate the non-price variables in the demand function from indirect supplier price and income effects by hypothesizing a purely professional physician who considers only technical factors in informing his patients, then wears his entrepreneurial hat when responding to the resulting demand. It is hard

to see how an economist could regard such behaviour as either rational or optimizing.

5 For example, G. Monsma, "Marginal Revenue and the Demand for Physicians' Services," in *Empirical Studies in Health Economics*, ed. H. Klarman (Baltimore: Johns Hopkins University Press, 1970), surveys data on the response of physician practice patterns to rates of payment. U. Reinhardt, "An Analysis of Physicians' Practices," unpublished doctoral dissertation (Yale University, 1970) calculates rates of payment per minute for several types of common activities and notes how these bias activities. *The Task Force Reports on Costs of Health Services in Canada* (Ottawa: The Queen's Printer, 1970) note instances of specific responses to fee schedule revisions – sharp increases in activities whose relative price had risen – as well as general "over-doctoring" in areas with relatively large physician stocks as procedures were multiplied to maintain incomes. The list could go on indefinitely.

6 An advertising model with costless advertising is essentially rather uninteresting, while the usual explicit cost function for demand generation through advertising is implausible in this context.

7 This is a general problem with extended maximizing models, analyzed by: G.C. Archibald, "The Qualitative Content of Maximizing Models," *Journal of Political Economy*, 73(1) (Feb. 1965).

8 R. Evans, *Price Formation in the Market for Physician Services in Canada, 1957–69* (Ottawa: The Queen's Printer, for the Prices and Incomes Commission, 1973), chap. 2.

9 R. Evans, E. Parish, and F. Sully, "Medical Productivity, Scale Effects, and Demand 'Generation'" (mimeo), University of British Columbia, Department of Economics Discussion Paper No. 79 (June 1972), reports investigations with the 1969 data.

10 "Practising specialists" is a concept borrowed from D. Anderson and A. Clough, "The Location of British Columbia Physicians," *British Columbia Medical Journal*, 11 (5) (Sept. 1960). It excludes radiologists, pathologists, anesthesiologists, public health physicians, and rehabilitation specialists, in an attempt to focus only on specialists who are or might be in direct primary contact with patients. The substitution between general practitioner and practising specialist is obvious in the case of a paediatrician: it becomes more strained in the case of a neurosurgeon.

11 Evans, *Price Formation*, chap. 4. It must be confessed that data points are scanty and correlations are not perfect; data cover BC, Alberta, Manitoba, two Ontario plans, and the Maritime provinces, with one observation for each.

12 Ibid., chap. 1. The problem is that price data are thoroughly unreliable, while data on increases in gross income per physician are drawn from taxation statistics and are quite good. The increases in gross receipts must be allocated between output per man and price, allowing for some quality change. Between 1957 and 1970, gross receipts per physician have risen 144.3 per cent, or 7.1 per cent per year. Regardless of how it is split up, this yields very high rates of increases in price or output or both. Over the same period, the Consumer Price Index rose about 2.5 per cent per year, and the stock of physicians per capita (in active fee practice) rose 1.5 per cent per year.

13 Of course, all such evidence can be rationalized in a conventional supply and demand framework. Inter-regional differences in physician availability may lead to differences in implicit costs of physician access, hence different demand patterns. Changes in service mix may be due to changes in patient tastes, operating through the physician as intermediary. Inter-regional variations in "health" or tastes for medical care may lead to bidding up of prices in high-demand regions and drawing in of more physicians, hence a positive correlation between physician density and price. But a model rescued by a succession of ad hoc unobservables is an irrefutable and uninteresting model.

14 Evans, *Price Formation*, chap. 3.

15 Feldstein, "The Rising Price of Physicians' Services."

16 Newhouse, "A Model of Physician Pricing."

17 U. Reinhardt, "A Production Function for Physician Services," *Review of Economics and Statistics*, 54 (1) (Feb. 1972).

10

Incomplete Vertical Integration in the Health Care Industry: Pseudomarkets and Pseudopolicies (1983)

ROBERT G. EVANS

Traditional analyses of market structure presuppose a bilateral relationship between two classes of independent transactors, the producers or suppliers of a particular set of commodities and the buyers or consumers. Indeed the market is defined as the set of exchange relationships between such pairs of independent transactors. Delimitation of specific markets or industries may be made complex by difficulties in identifying clear-cut boundaries between sets of production or exchange activities, or by the presence of intermediate transactors or middlemen. But the essence of the market relationship remains the exchange between two independent, arm's-length transactors.

The health care industry and its marketplaces share the general problems of boundary definition and sequential transactions. Which subset of economic activities constitutes health care production, or its sub-industries, and which exchanges form its markets? It also presents structural features

Evans, Robert G. "Incomplete Vertical Integration in the Health Care Industry: Pseudomarkets and Pseudopolicies." *The Annals of the American Academy of Political and Social Science* 468 (1983): 60–87. doi: 10.1177/000271628346800I005. Reprinted with the permission of SAGE. This article is a revised version of Robert G. Evans, "Incomplete Vertical Integration: The Distinctive Structure of the Health-Care Industry," in *Health, Economics, and Health Economics*, edited by Jacques van der Gaag and Mark Perlman (Amsterdam: North-Holland, 1981).

of an altogether different level of complexity, which cast serious doubt on traditional models of market structure and on policy analyses based upon them. In the first place, the processes of resource allocation, price setting, and revenue raising in health care are a blend of administrative or command and market exchange mechanisms, with the mix varying greatly across different countries. Thus a focus on market structure alone would be incomplete and potentially misleading, even in the United States, where health care markets are still much in evidence. In other countries with a more extensive command system, a focus on markets alone would ignore most, if not all, of the processes whereby health care resources are actually assembled and allocated.

On a more fundamental level, of course, such administrative arrangements are themselves the objects and outcomes of policy decisions, though in practice, history and culture seem to dominate conscious policy. In the United States in particular, the recent resurgence of enthusiasm for competitive and market-incentive policies to address problems of resource allocation and cost control in health care represents an attempt to shift the balance from command to market relationships. The putative benefits of such a shift are derived from various analyses of how a broader market system would be structured and would perform. Thus the analysis of various hypothetical market structures becomes part of the process of evaluating administrative mechanisms.

The administrative institutions that have evolved in every country, to a greater or lesser degree, to modify or supersede the functioning of the private market, are not a purely arbitrary development. They rest on peculiarities of health care markets themselves and of the commodities transacted in them, which limit the applicability of traditional market analysis. Health care markets are pervasively characterized by incomplete vertical integration, in that most exchanges take place between transactors who are not independent or at arm's length from each other, and yet are not under common ownership or management either. Their interests are partially shared and partially conflicting. Moreover, many transactions are multilateral, as managerial and entrepreneurial functions are shared among firms supplying different types of health care. The coordination of transactor behaviour toward common objectives, in the presence of conflicting interests, requires a much richer exchange of information and incentives than is provided through market exchanges.

This pattern of incomplete vertical integration is epitomized by the physician-patient relationship, in which the physician reaches through the market relation – where it exists – to advise or control the patient's utilization of care. The provider thus exercises some or all of the functions of the consumer. On the supply side itself, physicians admit patients to hospitals and direct their treatment there, yet they are, at least in North America, neither employees nor owners of hospitals. They prescribe drugs, to be dispensed by legally independent pharmacists. To characterize and analyze hospital or prescription drug markets as bilateral exchange relationships between hospital- or pharmacy-firms and patient-consumers, neglecting the physician's role, is inaccurate and misleading.

The regulation and insurance of health care use are similarly characterized by incomplete vertical integration. Public regulation of providers takes place not at arm's length, but through delegation of public authority to private self-governing associations to regulate the conduct of their own members and often of other occupational groups as well. Insurance is in some countries sold by private for-profit corporations; but more commonly it is provided by government, or by private non-profit organizations under strong provider influence – for instance, the North American Blue plans or the German sickness funds. The insurance process thus becomes a channel through which other transactors, or regulators, seek their objectives.

The pattern of integration varies greatly across countries. And the particular pattern of linkages observed has very significant effects on the conduct and performance of the health care industry. This article will sketch the more common forms of linkages among the different classes of transactors in the health care market, showing how the observed or alleged patterns of industry performance in different systems can be traced to differences in structure. This in turn leads to questions of performance evaluation and policy response, which are necessarily somewhat more subtle than they are in more conventional industries.

CHARACTERISTIC PATTERNS OF INTEGRATION

Exploration of linkage patterns in health care seems to require at least five different classes of transactors, in contrast to the customary two. These are:

1 consumers, who utilize care;
2 first-line providers, contacted directly by consumers;
3 second-line providers, whose output is either used by consumers under the direction of first-line providers or supplied as intermediate products to first-line or other second-line providers;

4 governments, which exercise or delegate regulatory authority over health care; and
5 suppliers of insurance or purchasers of risk associated with health care use.

These categories do not precisely coincide with the usual partitioning of health care into the sub-industries of physicians' services, hospital care, drugs, and the like. A pharmacy, for example, is a first-line supplier of over-the-counter drugs, but supplies prescription drugs only in response to a patient's compliance with a physician's order. A hospital might operate an emergency ward or an out-patient department as a first-line service. Patients are admitted from these to in-patient wards only on order of a physician, but if the physician is a salaried member of the hospital staff, the line between physician and hospital is tenuous at best. Specialist physicians in referral practice represent an ambiguous middle ground between first- and second-line suppliers; at what point does the consultant take over the patient? Practice varies in different systems. Thus the split between first and second line depends on the directness of the supplier-consumer or provider-patient relation, not necessarily on the identity of the institution or the nature of the service. This logic underlies grouping hospitals with drug and medical equipment manufacturers, for example, because although they are organized very differently, and indeed the last two supply products to the first, the output of all three flows to the ultimate user under the direction of a first-line provider.

A Hypothetical Free Market Model

The linkage among transactors involves the transfer of functions from one transactor to another. These transfers can best be seen relative to a hypothetical model of health care organization (Figure 10.1) in which each class of transactor deals independently and at arm's length with some or all of the others, none exerting any control over the others except through price signals.

Government, of course, would be the exception, in that its function is to define and maintain property rights – in the broadest sense – through orders backed up by a monopoly of coercive power; but it would confine its activity to such orders, and would issue them in pursuit of some general or external interest, not in response to the interests of any one class of transactors. In Figure 10.1 government regulates markets by defining and enforcing contracts and policing fraud, but, assuming property to be defined, it imposes no direct orders on market participants.

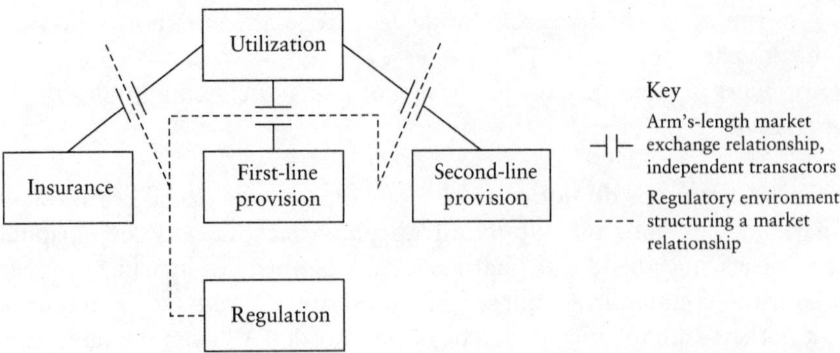

Figure 10.1 Hypothetical free market model: Free exchange among independent transactors

Adapted from: Robert G. Evans. "Incomplete Vertical Integration in the Health Care Industry: Pseudomarkets and Pseudopolicies." *The Annals of the American Academy of Political and Social Science* 468(68)(1983): 60–87.

In this Arcadia, consumers decide upon the level and mix of health care services to be used by responding to price information from suppliers, income constraints, and exogenously determined tastes. Fluctuations in health status – a cold or a perforated appendix – would be represented as changes in tastes for health care, leading to increased demand at current prices and incomes; congenital problems would presumably represent long-run taste differentials. But information from the health care system itself would be restricted to price quotations.

Producers make the key production decisions about the mix of inputs to use and how much to produce, in response to production function information and factor and product prices. Each firm, however, chooses its techniques of production and sets price and output independently, subject only to the information and constraints embodied in market prices. No one firm directly intervenes in another's choices. Government may intervene, but it is strictly exogenous to producers and does not itself produce. Insurance companies exist to formulate and sell a variety of claims contracts that are contingent on health status, or more commonly its imperfect correlate, health care use, but do not intervene in any other market, except through the structure and price of contracts offered. Consumers' use of care will depend on their insurance status, insofar as that status affects the price they pay for care, and thus their choice of contracts and their subsequent use patterns are interdependent. Insurers and providers of care have no direct dealings with each other.

In this hypothetical environment we can speak of health care delivery as governed by consumer sovereignty; the amount and type of care produced is determined by the consumer's willingness to pay. Willingness in turn depends on ability, so wealthier people would receive more. If that were viewed as socially unacceptable, a direct transfer of wealth to people with lower incomes – perhaps negative income tax – is perfectly consistent with the structure of Figure 10.1, so long as the markets for care or insurance are not tampered with: no specific subsidies.

The problem of health care distribution by geographic area or social or income class is simply defined away. What people ought to get is what they are willing to pay for; and the market, if unhindered by regulation, would provide that at the lowest possible price. It is thus further assumed that the unregulated marketplace would be price competitive, such that firms would be forced to be efficient or lose their markets, and providers would be unable to generate above-market incomes from monopoly power. Care would therefore cost whatever it ought to cost, but there would be no cost problem, any more than there is now in the computer industry, where costs – sales – are rising much faster than in health care.

Non-Market Linkages among Transactors

Of course, there is not now and never has been such an Arcadia. In fact, the range and richness of non-price interactions among different classes of transactors yields an embarrassment of analytic opportunity. Perhaps the most fundamental linkages – certainly those with the longest history and the greatest similarity across otherwise different health care systems – are those among patients, first-line providers, and government.

These linkages are expressed in the twin concepts of agency and self-government, both of which involve the transfer of economic functions from their normal holders to the first-line providers. Patient-consumers permit providers to act as their agents in making consumption choices, with respect both to the output of second-line providers and to the agents' own first-line services.[1] Utilization decisions are the outcome of joint decision making, in which the relative influence of provider and consumer varies by type of decision. The provider has integrated forward into the consumer role, acting as both provider and consumer, thus significantly increasing the information, and changing the objectives, reflected in utilization outcomes. Hence it is in general misleading to identify measured utilization of health care with demand in its economic sense of consumer choices responding only to price information and consumer characteristics.

There remains, of course, a demand in the conventional economic sense for treatment of episodes of illness, with first contacts initiated by patients in response to, *inter alia*, price information. With a few exceptions, however, economic analyses have equated measured utilization of services, not episodes, with points on a demand curve. This requires either that utilization patterns, and costs, subsequent to the initial contact in any illness episode are uniquely defined and known to the user before contact is initiated, or that consumers retain full discretion over follow-up treatment and receive only service price information, and offers, from physicians as the case unfolds. Such assumptions appear aggressively counterfactual, yet without them a large part of the health care demand literature in economics rests on misspecified models.[2]

The issue is often obscured by the level of aggregation of analysis – medical, or worse, health care being treated as a homogeneous commodity, so that the episodic structure is suppressed. Empirical studies that use visits or patient days as quantity measures further compound the problem, since such concepts are heterogeneous across providers and are seriously incomplete descriptors of utilization. The amounts and types of services provided in the course of a visit or a patient day are very responsive to how, and how much, providers are paid. The frequently observed sensitivity of physician practice patterns to the structure and level of insurers' fee schedules is an obvious example.

The clinical literature on utilization, in contrast to the economic literature, tends to focus very narrowly on specific procedures or conditions and to assume a dominant role for the physician acting from Hippocratic motives, if not always perfectly informed. Its richer information base frequently permits more reliable causal inferences; but generalizing such inferences requires strong aggregation assumptions. Furthermore, it is clear that the integration between first-line providers and consumers is incomplete and that the professional maintains personal objectives that may conflict with those of the consumer. The essence of professionalism is the internalization and management of this conflict of interest, but the agency relationship is rarely, if ever, perfect.

Paralleling the transfer from patient-consumer to provider, regulatory functions are delegated by the state to first-line providers collectively, in the form of rights to self-government. Individual providers are required to belong to professional organizations, which regulate their conduct, deploying the full coercive power of the state. Although this delegation is in principle subject to review, traditionally the professional organization functions to a significant extent as a private government, enjoying considerable independence in its limited area.

Analyzing this parallelism, Tuohy and Wolfson have shown that self-government is essentially an agency relation in which the providers collectively undertake to act in the interests of the state, for the same reasons of informational asymmetry that lead to agency relations between individual providers and consumers.[3] Further, they argue persuasively that these relationships are mutually supporting and must exist at both levels or neither. Self-government is a political privilege received to support the individual agency relation, and it loses its raison d'être if the latter decays; but without self-government the individual agency is also threatened.

These two forms of functional delegation represent fundamental structural features of the health care market. The conduct of firms is directly influenced, rather than merely induced by traditional structural features, such as the number and size distribution of firms, or by their concentration in particular geographic or other submarkets. Similarly, such structural issues as product characteristics and differentiability or buyer information and demand elasticity are all subsumed in the individual seller's capacity to exercise the ultimate advertising power – to make the consumption decision on the buyer's behalf.

The treatment of self-government in formal economic analysis has focused primarily not on agency, but on the potential for monopoly behaviour created by entry barriers. Implicitly, the argument that the profession functions as a monopoly requires us to treat all self-government as a costly error of public policy. Costs of monopoly are evaluated in the context of consumer demand curves, which requires the assumption that social welfare functions respect consumer sovereignty. But if this standard were relevant, professions as legal entities need not and should not exist. If, however, professionalization is needed to remedy imperfect consumer information, the conventional monopoly critique based on ill-informed demand curves is irrelevant.

In most jurisdictions, moreover, the controls over entry to the professions have been reasserted by governments and are no longer, if they ever were, in the hands of providers. Entry to the professions is now a part of public educational, or even immigration, policy. They are structurally competitive industries, with large numbers of firms and relatively rapid, though not at all free, entry. What is missing is competitive conduct, and it is the self-government over conduct that remains critical. Restrictions vary by jurisdiction and by profession, but in general they extend to how firms may be organized – corporate or noncorporate; who may own the firm – it is considered unethical for a professional to be employed by a non-professional; what production processes may or may not be used – in particular, what may be delegated to other professionals; and, where relevant, what pricing behaviour is permissible. These restrictions are mutually reinforcing and are supported by absolutely restricted access to particular service markets. Indeed access to markets, not to an occupational role, is the crucial entry barrier. The key structural feature is that such access is open only to firms owned by and deploying the services of members of particular occupations; such professionalized natural persons, unlike corporations or entrepreneurs from other backgrounds, are much more sensitive to both formal and informal methods of conduct control. A focus on entry control implicitly assumes that, once entry is achieved, professionals-firms behave like ordinary, unregulated profit-maximizing entities, amenable to the usual forms of analysis; thus such a focus ignores the critical direct impact of collective self-regulation on firm conduct.

Linkage to Second-Line Providers

The largest components of the health care system, in terms of expenditure and employment, are not the first-line providers but the hospitals, drug manufacturers, and equipment makers whose output is directed by the first-line group. The triangular relation of physician, patient, and hospital has been particularly difficult to handle analytically; economic models range from ignoring the physician and assuming that patients buy hospital services directly, to suppressing the hospital as an independent transactor and treating it as an extended physician's office. More recent thinking has moved back toward realism, suggesting that a hospital be thought of as two firms, not one, interacting in a single institution, and transacting as much politically or bureaucratically as economically. No explicit prices or markets govern internal hospital allocation processes, but no single authority relation exists either.

In this relationship, staff physicians exercise a number of the managerial functions – decisions as to levels or patterns of output or mode of production – that are the responsibility of the firm in conventional economic analysis. Yet they do so neither as owners of the hospital nor as managers employed by and responsible to its owners. At least in the North American setting, they are private businessmen who bring in the hospital's patients. Like patient and provider or profession and government, physician and hospital are incompletely vertically integrated, with objectives that partly overlap and partly conflict, and with the power to influence each other's behaviour directly rather than through arm's-length exchange.

Moreover, integration patterns differ significantly across national boundaries, making generalization hazardous. In Canada, the hospital can be thought of as three firms, not two, for provincial governments exercise very significant management powers by determining annual operating budgets and – separately – capital allocations. Here the state has taken over a number of functions of the hospital-firm directly, not merely by regulation, although for a variety of political reasons it chooses not to own and operate the hospitals. But it is questionable whether a hospital per se still exercises enough entrepreneurial functions to be considered a firm after one allows for the decisions delegated to, or taken over by, physicians on one side and government on the other. In the United Kingdom, integration appears to have gone so far that hospitals can no longer be treated as independent firms.

In the United States, most hospitals are managerially independent of insurers, but it is unclear, when one tries to describe the conduct of the hospital industry, just whose conduct is being observed and whose objectives are being sought. The firm as a category in economic analysis does not necessarily correspond either to a legal entity or to a physical/organizational structure, though each may be called hospital. Hence the unsatisfactory state of hospital modelling.

The other second-line providers appear much more distinct in their relations with the rest of the health care system. Manufacturers of drugs and medical equipment are organized as private, strictly for-profit firms with highly differentiated products, and though extensively regulated by government, they have control over their own entrepreneurial functions. Their markets, however, are rather peculiar. Drug manufacturers sell to patients through physicians; equipment manufacturers sell to hospitals and, to a lesser extent, to physicians, who serve patients. Since the ultimate user of services does not generally make the utilization decision, manufacturers market their products to physicians, hospital staffs, and other professional providers. This extensive and sophisticated marketing effort represents yet another form of incomplete vertical integration, as second-line suppliers seek to influence first-line providers' perceptions of optimal technique. They thus reach through the agency role of the first-line provider to influence the ultimate volume and mix of service use.

While the agency role of the first-line provider, with its inherent conflict of interest, is supported by a variety of ethical constraints intended to ensure that patients' interests will be incorporated into providers' objectives, no such agency role binds the for-profit suppliers at the next level. Profit maximizing leaves no room for agency. This places further strain on the agency role of the first-line provider, whose attempts to balance personal and patient interests are subjected to very deliberate and sophisticated pressures designed to shift his or her preferences and perceptions in the direction of more use of specific second-line products or services. Agency at one level must constrain opportunism at both levels.

What is, however, interesting is the relatively limited extent to which first-line providers have integrated backward into pharmacy ownership or drug supply – repackaging companies. Such integration is regarded as unethical, though it is not clear why the conflict of interest for physicians prescribing their own drugs is more severe than that in prescribing their own diagnostic or therapeutic services, or admitting to their own hospital. How and why this boundary has been maintained would be an interesting question that might cast light on the evolution of integration patterns in general.

The widest range of variation across jurisdictions seems to be in the patterns of government and insurance integration with the rest of the health care system. In Canada government has completely taken over hospital and medical insurance, and it plays a significant role in pharmaceutical insurance and a growing role in dental insurance. This control of insurance is a critical lever in controlling current operations and capital formation in the hospital sector; it is thus the vehicle for partial integration of government into second-line supply. Government also engages in first-line supply in such traditional areas as public health and immunization, services in remote areas, and – in Saskatchewan – dental care of children. In the United Kingdom, government seems likewise to have absorbed the insurance function almost completely and to have gone much farther into the management of second-line and first-line supply.

In the United States, in contrast, government has taken over only a part of the insurance function, principally the unprofitable components – insurance for the poor and elderly – which private firms did not want. It appears, from comparing US and Canadian experience, that partial takeover of the insurance function by government does not permit it to reach through to providers in the same way that full takeover does. The ability of government to influence hospital budget/capital investment decisions or physician price formation directly through the payments process is not in proportion to its share of funding when funding sources are multiple and diverse. Hence the apparent failure of hospital and other health cost-control efforts in the United States during the 1970s, in contrast to Canada's successful experience with universal public insurance.[4]

However, integration of transactors through the insurance mechanism can go in several other directions. Many of the early health insurance plans were sponsored and directed by physician or hospital organizations; they served as ways of increasing the flow of payments into the health care industry, enabling it to raise effective prices and/or outputs, as well as redistributing costs. Thus first- and second-line providers integrated backward into insurance. The initiative to integrate can also come from the insuring agency; Goldberg and Greenberg have documented early and recent efforts by US insurers to influence patterns of behaviour among providers.[5] The salient feature of their discussion, however, is that the attempts were complete failures. On the other hand, the successes of health maintenance organizations (HMOs), such as Kaiser or the Seattle Group Health Cooperative in the United States, and the philosophy expressed by Enthoven[6] in his consumer choice health plan, are based on much more extensive forward integration of the insuring organization into delivery by establishing exclusive contracts with closed-panel physician groups and owning its own hospitals.

It is extensively documented[7] that the forward integration of the seller of insurance into care – HMOs – leads to levels and patterns of service utilization and costs very different from those generated when sellers of services integrate backward into insurance – Blue Cross/Blue Shield plans – or when government takes over the insurance function, as in Canada, regardless in each case of the out-of-pocket costs, if any, borne by patients. The US literature on utilization differences between subscribers to closed-panel insurance plans and to arm's-length private or provider-dominated plans emphasizes the importance of provider organization and objectives in influencing utilization levels. As Figure 10.4 indicates, the competitive HMO organizational structure emphasizes the agency role of first-line suppliers and suppresses the market between users and suppliers. It is thus built on assumptions about resource-allocative processes quite different from those underlying the arguments for arm's-length private insurance with large deductibles and coinsurance, which essentially postulate the structure of Figure 10.1. The distinction is blurred by a common rhetoric about private enterprise versus the state.

A Fully Professionalized Model of Health Care

Alternative ways of organizing the production and delivery of health services can be represented as alternative patterns of vertical integration among the five basic classes of transactors, starting from the hypothetical, freely competitive markets of Figure 10.1. In contrast to that abstraction,

Figure 10.2 presents an idealized case of private-enterprise medicine as viewed by first-line providers – mostly self-employed physicians.

In Figure 10.2 the underlying market structure of Figure 10.1 persists, but its resource-allocation functions have been supplemented or supplanted by direct administrative or legal controls emanating from the first-line providers. Markets remain as revenue-raising institutions, but utilization now depends on doctors' orders – the agency role of the professional. The profession collectively exercises regulatory functions over its individual members and would-be members. Insurance plans are either administered by providers – the Blue model, non-profit, and provider-trusteed – or, if private, are restricted to offering contracts acceptable to provider associations. Short-run outputs of hospitals or pharmacies are directed by physicians; longer-run hospital decisions are influenced by medical staffs and physician trustees or owners. Government regulates and subsidizes hospitals, but under professional direction.

This extensive concentration of functions serves the policy objectives of first-line providers in two ways. In the economic sphere it enables providers to promote the flow into health care of resources that are complementary to their own services – for example, expanding the hospital sector – while suppressing potential competitors, such as nurse practitioners or corporate practice. Also the insurance process can be structured to ensure minimal insurer control over either the practice patterns of, or fee setting by, individual physicians, while the self-regulatory power discourages the outbreak of overt price-competitive behaviour. All these serve to enhance provider incomes, as well as professionally approved styles of practice; but the maintenance of professional authority also seems to be an objective for its own sake, an end rather than a means, and this too is promoted in the private-enterprise structure.

What is puzzling is why so much external economic analysis has accepted, largely by default, efforts by industry spokesmen to portray the structure of Figure 10.2 as equivalent in its behaviour to the set of freely competitive private marketplaces in Figure 10.1. Such efforts seem intended, *inter alia*, to discourage direct public intervention.

Universal Public Health Insurance

The public administration of universal health insurance, with negotiated fees and/or budgets, creates quite a different pattern of structural linkages, as can be seen in Figure 10.3. Government now integrates forward to control – that is, to be – the insurer, and all markets and out-of-pocket

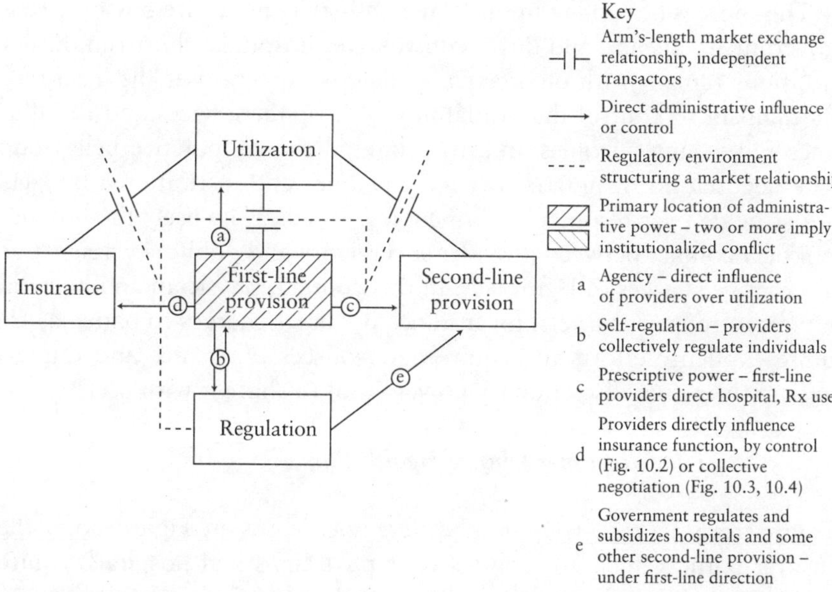

Figure 10.2 Fully professional model: All transactions directly influenced/controlled by first-line providers

Adapted from: Robert G. Evans. "Incomplete Vertical Integration in the Health Care Industry: Pseudomarkets and Pseudopolicies." *The Annals of the American Academy of Political and Social Science* 468(68)(1983): 60–87.

payments disappear. The contrast with Figure 10.2, however, is more apparent than real, for much of the resource-allocation function of markets in Figure 10.1 had already been pre-empted by administrative mechanisms in Figure 10.2. While Figure 10.1 portrays consumer sovereignty, Figure 10.2 represents producer sovereignty, in that providers' objectives and decisions determine what forms of care will be provided, for whom, with what techniques, and at what cost. Figure 10.3 introduces public sovereignty, or at least direct public influence. In addition, in Figure 10.3 the costs of care are raised via taxes, as in Canada, rather than via direct charges or insurance premiums in pseudomarkets, as in the United States.

The integrated regulator-insurer now negotiates fees directly with first-line providers, controls hospitals through budgets as well as regulation, and determines the terms of the insurance contract with users. Utilization is influenced both by doctors' orders and by direct rationing through the hospital system. Patients' preferences have some direct influence on providers, but not through any market.

The sources of conflict in this Canadian-style model are obvious. Self-government, agency, and direct control over hospitals' short-run output decisions remain with physicians, while government uses the insurance mechanism to control the availability of hospital services and to influence physicians' incomes and, to a limited extent, practice behaviour. The negotiation of practitioner fee schedules and institutional budgets – a struggle over resources and incomes – focuses intensely the broader political conflict between provider sovereignty and public sovereignty as alternative sources of legitimacy. In this context, physician and hospital efforts to reopen markets, for instance by direct charges to patients, are quite explicitly efforts to acquire new sources of finance and thus to extend their own discretionary power – not to share it with users.

The Consumer Choice Health Plan

Figure 10.4 represents quite a different case. As in Figure 10.3, the insurer is the vehicle for control over physicians and hospitals. Figure 10.4 represents both as employed or directly administered by the insurer, but one could also envision markets between insurers, physicians, and hospitals. Users transact only with insurers, in markets minimally regulated, as in Figure 10.1, by the state. In practice, however, it turns out that the inherent impossibility of completely specifying the services that the insurer in Figure 10.4 is contracted to provide necessitates a substantial degree of regulation.

Professional self-government and public regulation/subsidy of hospitals remain, as does physician influence on short-run hospital decisions. The key shift from Figure 10.3 to Figure 10.4 is that the user-insurer market substitutes for the state in controlling the resource-allocation process. Insurers competing for sales to individuals and groups will try to assemble and offer combined insurance and service contracts that best match buyers' preferences, at minimum cost, and in the process will try to control provider behaviour.

Whether such a blend of consumer and provider sovereignty can come closer to a social optimum than the political processes of a public insurance system is an interesting and critical question. Of course, powers of self-government must be limited to prevent the first-line providers from taking over or suppressing the activist insurers through that route – a pattern common in US history, and with some Canadian parallels. The fee negotiation between public insurer and collective profession has, in Figure 10.4, been replaced by separate contracts between competitive

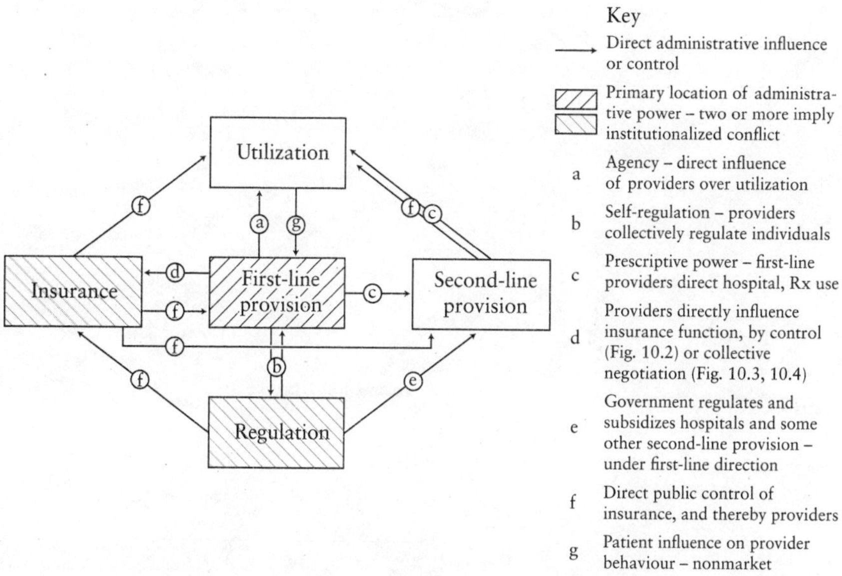

Utilization

Insurance

First-line provision

Second-line provision

Regulation

Key

→ Direct administrative influence or control

Primary location of administrative power – two or more imply institutionalized conflict

a Agency – direct influence of providers over utilization

b Self-regulation – providers collectively regulate individuals

c Prescriptive power – first-line providers direct hospital, Rx use

d Providers directly influence insurance function, by control (Fig. 10.2) or collective negotiation (Fig. 10.3, 10.4)

e Government regulates and subsidizes hospitals and some other second-line provision – under first-line direction

f Direct public control of insurance, and thereby providers

g Patient influence on provider behaviour – nonmarket

Figure 10.3 Universal public health insurance model, Canada: Public – via insurance – and professional influences coexist or conflict

Adapted from: Robert G Evans. "Incomplete Vertical Integration in the Health Care Industry: Pseudomarkets and Pseudopolicies." *The Annals of the American Academy of Political and Social Science* 468(68)(1983): 60–87

insurers and providers as individuals or groups. Thus, depending on the self-regulatory structure, providers' influence might be significantly less in Figure 10.4 than in Figure 10.3.

PERFORMANCE CRITERIA: PROBLEMS OF DEFINITION

Different structural forms lead to different patterns of conduct and performance. The general performance criteria applicable to the health care industry and its components are the same that one would apply to any other industry. The industry can be evaluated by criteria of allocative efficiency – whether its products, at the margin, are valued more than the products of the best alternative use of the same resources; technical efficiency – whether particular patterns of output are produced at minimum resource cost; income distribution effects – whether the industry generates patterns of earnings for its participants that are reasonable in terms of their opportunity costs, or generally viewed as fair; and technical

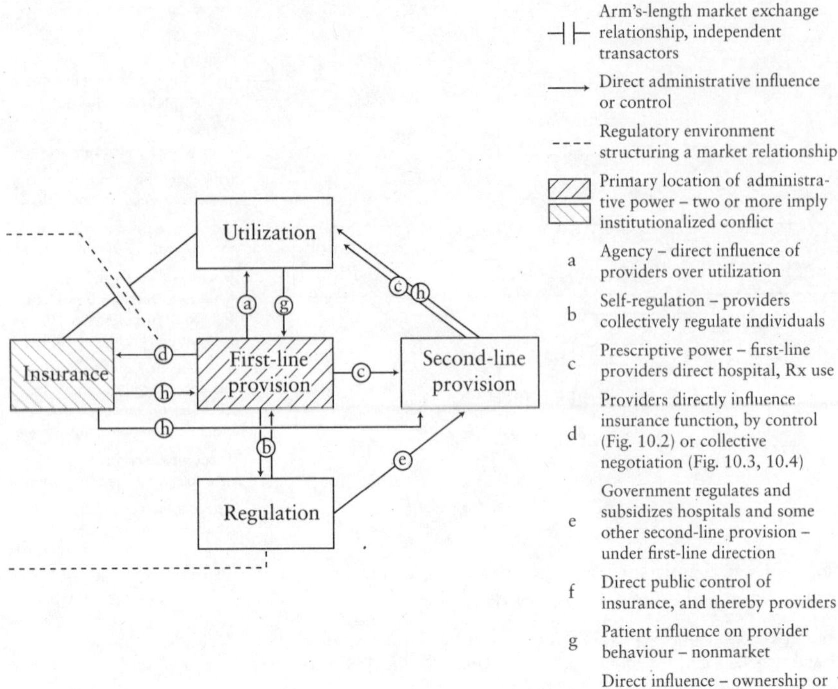

Figure 10.4 HMO or consumer-choice health plan model: Competitive insurers influence or control all other suppliers

Adapted from: Robert G. Evans. "Incomplete Vertical Integration in the Health Care Industry: Pseudomarkets and Pseudopolicies." *The Annals of the American Academy of Political and Social Science* 468(68)(1983): 60–87

progress – whether the industry is advancing in its capacity to offer new products or to produce existing ones at lower resource cost. In the case of health care, however, most societies express additional redistributional objectives, relating to equality of access to care and to the distribution of the burdens of illness and care, which are in principle – but not, it seems, in practice – separable from the evaluation of industry performance itself.

The distinction between allocative and technical efficiency criteria, however, exposes an ambiguity in the definition of the end product – health care. An allocatively efficient system produces the right amount of output; a technically efficient system produces it in the right way. But health care services can be defined at several levels. A diagnostic procedure, for example, may be thought of as an end product or as an input to the production of a spell of hospitalization, which can in turn be thought of as an input to the treatment of an episode of illness. An inappropriate procedure may represent allocative inefficiency in the production of the commodity procedures or technical inefficiency in the production of hospital spells. More generally, most health care is intermediate production – inputs – to the promotion of health status, in intent if not always in outcome. Its direct effect on the user's well-being, if we abstract from anticipated health benefits, is generally negative. Thus inappropriate care is allocatively inefficient health care production, but technically inefficient health production.

This inherent intermediateness is the source of the informational asymmetry between supplier and consumer, which gives rise to the agency relationship and the extensive regulatory structure in health care. While consumers may reasonably be supposed to be the best judges of the value to them of health, they obviously cannot be assumed knowledgeable as to the technical or production relationships by which health care does or does not contribute to health. Health is unfortunately not a traded commodity, hence the abrogation of consumer sovereignty.

The performance of the health care industry is frequently and widely criticized, in many countries, on both allocative and technical efficiency grounds. It is essential to distinguish, however, several quite different performance critiques, which imply different structure/conduct origins. The broad literature, most of it medical or epidemiological, on unnecessary servicing focuses on the provision of health care that has little or no – or even negative – impact on health status. This includes the literature on unnecessary surgery, diagnostic testing, periodic screening or examinations without sickness, drug use, and unnecessarily prolonged hospital stays. The assumption behind such criticism is that health care derives its utility at the individual or social level from its impact on health status – only uninformed consumers use inefficacious care, and they would not do so if they knew – so efficacy is a proxy for value. The allocation of resources to unnecessary care is a reflection of supplier conduct; it results from the structural characteristics of the supply side, in particular the agency influence over the consumer-patient, the provider's direct economic interest in volume of output, and the absence of any systematic mechanism to feed improved information on efficacy back to a fragmented and highly independent group of suppliers. It is not that suppliers deliberately choose to provide inefficacious or harmful services, but rather that the structural pattern induces selective sensitivity to new information. The organization of first- and second-line suppliers is such as to encourage expansion of activity and acceptance of information that supports this expansion. Information that discourages or discredits economically profitable and professionally satisfying activity is much harder to hear.

Alternative patterns of vertical integration, then, are of great importance insofar as they provide different channels for and incentives to the spread of resource-using or resource-curtailing information. When insurance providers integrate forward into supply, they may or may not have – depending on insurance market structure – incentives to reduce unnecessary servicing by attempting to influence providers directly. Governments, in this role, clearly do. Insurance sellers who also supply a full line of services – the HMO model of Figure 10.4 – appear to have had considerable success in restricting inefficient allocation of resources to health care; arm's-length insurers have not.

Governmental experience is similar. Canadian provinces have been relatively successful in controlling real resource inputs in the hospital sector, where they have significant management authority, and much less so in modifying patterns of physician care, except where these depend on hospital access. The potential for system-wide generalization of the US experience with improved allocative efficiency from forward integration of competitive insurers, vis-à-vis the alternative of government integration, is still an open issue.

Two things seem clear, however. First, as long as the insurance structure is controlled by providers – backward-linked – either directly, as in Blue Cross/Blue Shield, or indirectly, through the influence that providers collectively can bring to bear on individual insurers in a fragmented, arm's-length insurance market, whether or not wholly private, then no significant improvement can be made in allocative efficiency. Second, efforts to deal with excessive utilization through manipulating the incentives faced by consumers through various forms of direct charges, coinsurance, co-payment, and so on will be ineffectual. Theirs is not the relevant conduct to be modified by new information.

This is a critical point, and it depends *inter alia* on the identification of allocative inefficiency with overprovision of inefficacious services. There is a more traditional strand of economic literature that defines overprovision, quite independently of efficacy, in terms of consumer willingness to use at particular prices. The marginal social value of care is identified with marginal private values as reflected in assumed consumer choices in response to out-of-pocket costs. In this view, insurance of any sort lowers out-of-pocket costs and induces consumers to overuse care, in the sense that its marginal value to them is below its true marginal resource cost. This view totally ignores the information issue and identifies use with consumer choice; it has the awkward consequence that society loses both when snake oil is regulated off the market and when a child receives a lifesaving operation that his or her family cannot – is not willing to – pay for. More generally, it cannot deal with the very detailed structure of supply-side regulation in health care, and either ignores its existence – assuming prices equal to long-run constant marginal cost – or dismisses it as a policy error to be corrected where possible. Nor does this view cope with the variety of allocative results that emerge from alternative systems of organizing insurance.

The allocative and technical criteria blur into each other, as previously noted, depending on the comprehensiveness of the definition of care, but we reach a central core of technical efficiency questions in the patterns of use of health manpower. An extensive literature in all the main branches of the first-line sub-industry, and to a lesser extent in the second-line, documents the technical inefficiency of the production of services independently of the allocative or efficacy question of whether they should have been supplied at all. This pattern, in turn, can be easily traced to the conduct of the firms supplying such services – in their consistent use of unnecessarily costly combinations of manpower inputs[8] – and to the structures of the relevant markets, which both permit and encourage them to do so.

FROM STRUCTURE TO PERFORMANCE: THE CONDUCT LINKAGES

The integration of providers into regulatory roles enables them collectively to influence structure and conduct in important respects. Historically economists have focused on the use of this power to create entry barriers; indeed, its earlier manifestations were in the form of reduced access to professions and control of numbers. Further, of course, it is definitionally true that supernormal incomes cannot persist and be protected without entry barriers.

As noted before, however, control on entry to professional occupations has in most jurisdictions reverted to the state. Entry, though far from free, has been relatively rapid for many years. Moreover, the analysis of entry processes requires consideration of the role and objectives of training institutions, especially universities, for whom a crude set of objectives would include high rates of entry and overqualified entrants – they sell qualifications – with maximum government subsidy of training, and subsequent regulatory protection of human capital values to ensure future markets. The important uses of self-government are now to restrict access to service markets to firms controlled by members of particular professions, and to control the conduct of those members, so that, even in a structurally competitive environment where there is rapid entry and a large number of firms, price-competitive behaviour can be suppressed and incomes protected, even if more widely shared.

Such protection requires restriction of output-expanding technologies. Individual firms run by a solo practitioner, in dentistry, pharmacy, or many branches of medicine – family practice, obstetrics, anesthesia – can now expand their output per peak professional by up to several hundred per cent, with corresponding increases in net income or reductions in prices, by deploying well-known and tested types of auxiliary workers who are potentially in very elastic supply. When 80 to 90 per cent of the work of a general dentist can be performed at or above professional quality standards by a high school graduate with twenty months' training, the potential exists for dramatic expansions in output per firm. Possible reductions in unit costs have been estimated at about 40 per cent.[9] These could trigger competition destructive of the economic value of professional status and of the investment in its acquisition. By using state authority to ban the use of such technologies, the profession collectively ensures that each individual firm can expand its output only by extending the professional owner-manager's hours of work. The professional is thus discouraged from initiating a price-cutting competitive strategy to expand market share. This, rather than restrictions on price advertising per se, seems to be the critical control mechanism in protecting incomes. Thus the erosion of the power of all professions to control price advertising, which is taking place in the United States, will not likely generate any significant change in competitive behaviour unless regulatory power over technology is dismantled as well.

Even that may not be enough. Conscious parallelism is very powerful among firms all owned and managed by members of the same profession – acutely conscious of their mutual interdependence, their heavy investment in industry-specific skills, and their limited opportunities outside the industry. In such circumstances, the probable responses of other firms to effective price-competitive behaviour, such as matching cuts, are quite easy for each firm to define, and their consequences are equally clear. Add a relatively price-inelastic market demand curve arising from insurance or consumer perceptions of need, and the expected payoff to an individual competitive strategy becomes very low. Since, in addition, agency confers the power to induce utilization and do even more good, when supply expands through rising provider-population ratios, firms are unlikely to be driven to the abyss of price competition unless capacity expands explosively.

Of course firms owned and managed by non-professionals, simply hiring professional services, would take a very different view. The human capital of providers would then become a cost of production, to be minimized – not the principal earning asset of the practice, to be conserved and maximized. Medical or dental practices owned by Sears Roebuck might conduct themselves very differently in the output market, and might even have an interest in changing the locus of regulatory power. Here again conduct of professionals is controlled, in that they may not be employed by non-professionals to supply professional services. All firms in the product market must be owned/managed by an owner of human capital with much to lose if competition breaks out. Thus improvement of technical efficiency in service production by reducing the present substantial and costly overuse of highly trained professionals – feather bedding – appears to require significant change, either in the control of providers over regulation of their own conduct – deintegration in our terms – or in a shift in the patterns of vertical integration to separate management and professional roles.

Direct government supply is one possibility; the Saskatchewan Dental Service uses sixteen dentists, among a staff of several hundred dental nurses and auxiliaries, to provide almost all the services needed by 90 per cent of the province's children. Costs per child are correspondingly low, access is much improved, and quality of care is as good as or better than the private system. But government takeover of supply merely creates the possibility of more efficient input use; it is far from a guarantee. Integrated insurance and care-supply firms – HMOs – have some of the same potential, but they are still severely restricted by professional self-government. Yet, whether one attempts to deal with the technical efficiency problem through increased reliance on markets or through more direct public intervention, it appears clear that the current structure of linkage between professions and government must be significantly modified.

THE LIMITED ROLE OF PRICES

The discussion of allocative and technical efficiency has largely disregarded the role of prices on the ground that, in the health care industry, prices perform primarily an income distributional function. There is still a lively economic literature on the hypothetical resource-allocation role of prices in modifying consumer behaviour, but providers and reimbursers discuss them almost exclusively in income distribution terms. The numerous demand studies and the associated insurance impact and burden studies are all in the context of arm's-length models of the Figure 10.1 type, and they give rather diverse results – not surprising if the model is misspecified.

The emphasis on income distribution is partly due to the almost universal insulation of users of care from all or most of its cost, but this universal phenomenon is in turn rooted in the special characteristics of health care as a commodity. Insofar as prices do play an allocative role, their influence is on provider choices of what to recommend to their patients, and there does seem to be support for the view that relative rates of reimbursement per unit of time affect, though they do not determine, providers' choices of the mix and volume of services to recommend and provide. The literature analyzing this phenomenon is, however, rarely placed in the context of any formal model of supplier behaviour or market functioning; it merely postulates that suppliers will wish to do more of whatever pays better. If, however, prices are endogenous and utilization is supplier-influenced, a consistent formalism becomes rather tricky and requires an extended set of provider objectives.

Patients may, of course, vary the rate at which they contact the health services system in response to out-of-pocket costs; it would be rather surprising if they did not. But this is only one of many factors affecting overall levels of care utilization. In the United States, for example, physician visit rates and hospital days per capita have been relatively stable for a number of years. However, the volume of servicing per visit or per hospital day, in terms of procedures or billings – adjusted for fee, wage, and price increases – has been rising steadily. Changes in what happens to patients after they contact the health care system have been the principal source of utilization and cost increases.

Prices could conceivably have an allocative effect if they influenced either the short-run willingness of providers to supply effort to the industry or the long-run rates of entry and exit. But excess demand for entry at current prices and incomes all over the world is at such a level that industry capacity is likely to depend for the foreseeable future on public decisions about professional school places – provision, as in Canada, or funding, as in the United States – and professional, or perhaps public, decisions about allowable technology, rather than on relative prices. Nor is there much evidence of short-run supply response;

where prices are exogenous, the supply curve appears to be, if anything, backward bending.

In most jurisdictions, a significant share of the health care industry does not even display explicit prices for its products. Hospitals reimbursed on a budget-review basis receive annual grants to cover total operations, and per diems or dollars of expenditure per in-patient day are merely a synthetic ratio of heterogeneous costs over a heterogeneous, and incomplete, output measure. Hospitals reimbursed per unit of service may think of these as prices, but they are hospital-specific prices per unit of intermediate product. The overall price of an episode of care is determined ex post from actual services used and negotiated production costs or charges. Thus, although there is clearly an implicit price for any definition of output, this price is not explicitly identified and does not serve as a critical input to resource-allocation decisions at the micro level. Only for commodities such as drugs or equipment or for the component of professional services reimbursed on fee-for-service are explicit ex ante prices routinely available. The latter, moreover, are less well defined if patients self-pay and collection rates vary.

Emphasizing the income-generating rather than the market-clearing role of – mostly implicit – health care prices leads to the expectation that price levels will respond positively to levels of supply in a market characterized by the typical pattern of agency and self-government. This expectation rests upon complementary perceptions of utilization as strongly supplier-influenced and on a rather general formulation of supplier objectives. Profit maximization is, of course, generally recognized as an untenable objective for self-employed entrepreneurs in imperfect competition, and net income/leisure maximization is both unnecessarily restrictive and, given what we know of health professionals, rather implausible. The primary input to production is the time of the professional, with an opportunity cost rising sharply as hours of work increase. In general, however, the willingness to supply time also depends on income, so prices received for services affect the cost of their production. Effort and output supply may then fall as output price rises. Unless the output market is competitive, of course, this marginal cost curve is not a supply curve anyway; and most conventional models of health providers assume monopolistically competitive structure with limited entry. The casual drawing of firm or industry supply curves, especially positively sloped ones, is thus theoretically unjustifiable. But the demand curve, in an agency world, is no more satisfactory as a central analytic construct, because the quantity of services that consumer-patients demand – are willing to purchase and use – at a given price is not uniquely defined. It depends on the provider's advice. The classical parrot, which once qualified as a political economist by virtue of its ability to say "supply and demand," now has laryngitis.

On the whole, the positive association of supply and price seems to be at least as well supported empirically as the converse, though of course any pattern of observations can be represented by a conventional demand curve with enough unmeasured arguments.[10] Nor is it easy to be sure what is being priced; visits, for instance, are simply not standard measures of output over time, space, or firms.

The combined role of governments and insurers in all major health care markets makes the behaviour and effects of prices in the abstract less interesting and less susceptible to testing. It does appear, however, that received prices and incomes tend to advance more rapidly, the more fragmented and/or provider-dominated the payment process. When suppliers control insurance or when insurance is provided by a number of private firms at arm's length from providers, explicit price levels or unit costs rise more rapidly than if governments integrate forward to control all insurance supply. When sources of funding are multiple, first- and second-line suppliers can maintain greater price-setting or budget-formulating independence, because their inherent monopoly power is not countered by monopsony and because direct charges to consumers are always available as a residual source of payment. So-called usual, customary, and reasonable fees for professionals in the United States seem to be the ultimate in price-setting freedom.

Correspondingly, servicing patterns seem to rise more rapidly in controlled price settings, as a more general model of provider behaviour would suggest. These increases are independent of changes in prices paid by users, if any, and reflect rather a change in the tradeoffs between income, leisure, and other professional objectives when price-setting behaviour is constrained. Whether such increases in servicing imply either proportionately more resource inputs or, more important, increases in health status, are critical but very difficult questions, which can only be addressed at present in the context of particular illnesses and treatment protocols.

The income determination process remains rather obscure, however, in health care as in most other industries. There is still ample evidence, of the unsatisfied-demand-for-entry and rate-of-return-on-investment sort, that providers earn above-market incomes. Excess incomes or profits in the not-for-profit hospital sector are more difficult to identify, showing up as costs, but here too there is evidence of earnings above opportunity cost. These take diverse forms: above-market salaries for employees, perks for physicians, the quiet life for administrators, or even supply contracts let to for-profit firms that are at less than arm's length. These persist not primarily as a result of entry barriers – excess incomes can coexist with underemployment – but as a result of the conduct of firms in the industry, which again comes back to the structural issue: for and by whom are firms managed?

POLICY PARADOXES WITH STRUCTURAL ROOTS

The relative insignificance of prices paid by users as guiders of the level and pattern of health care provided results from the forward integration of providers into direct control over the utilization process. They are able to call the tune, without having to pay the piper – whether the ultimate user pays out of pocket or purchases insurance. Nor, given the extreme asymmetry of information between provider and patient, does any other situation seem possible in practice. Whatever the allocative inefficiencies that result from producer sovereignty, true consumer sovereignty is not a viable alternative.

The failure of health care providers to respond to relative input prices by choosing least-cost processes of service production similarly results from their backward integration into the regulatory process via self-government, enabling them collectively to constrain the economic conduct of individual firms and prevent the substitution of less costly personnel, which would threaten the market for professional services. This form of integration seems in principle more susceptible to modification, though perhaps not in political reality.

Both directions of integration underlie the very peculiar and ambiguous treatment of technical progress in health care. While in general rapid technological advance is viewed as a very positive aspect of industry performance, technology in health care is frequently described as a threat to be limited and controlled.

The key to the paradox is that the combination of direct control over utilization and regulatory power over form of organization and choice of technique can be, and is, used to bias technological advances toward new interventions that add to industry sales or gross revenues, and away from cost-reducing innovations that threaten present economic and professional positions. Yet to society generally, the sales of the health care industry are not a benefit, but the cost of acquiring health. Thus innovation in health care is biased toward cost escalation, with relatively minimal requirements that the innovation demonstrate its efficacy, either at all or, more importantly, in each of its fields of application. Indeed a common pattern of innovation in health care seems to be the development of a diagnostic or therapeutic breakthrough efficacious for a restricted class of problems, whose application is then rapidly and expensively extended to areas of little or no benefit. If individual or social benefit could be inferred, via the assumption of consumer sovereignty, from observed utilization, then the proliferation of technology could only be an advantage. But in a system characterized by producer sovereignty, the inference is groundless.

The problem of technology assessment is now generally recognized as part of the more general question of why particular services are used in health care, and whether they yield increments in health status at all, or at least those sufficient to justify their use. The focus on new technology, however, reflects the fact that in most jurisdictions public agencies have significantly more control over the flow of new capacity – manpower or facilities – into the industry than over the allocation of resources already there. Insofar as new technology is embodied in capital equipment, systems such as Canada or the United Kingdom, in which capital investment is allocated separately from the reimbursement of institutional operating costs, can achieve a certain degree of control over technological proliferation. Regulation independent of reimbursement, as in the United States, seems much less effective.[11]

Over the long run, the most critical form of public management of capacity is manpower policy. The argument for such policy rests on the observation that the quantity and type of services provided by the health care system, and their mode of production, are primarily determined by the types and numbers of professionals available. People do what they are trained to do, and more of them do more. Since health care providers influence utilization levels and patterns directly, controlling their numbers and training may provide the only lever, in the context of the existing US or Canadian structure, for limiting over-servicing and technological inefficiency.

Increasing the supply of particular forms of manpower seems, on the other hand, to lead both to increases in utilization and to upward pressure on prices or fees. Because prices serve an income-generating, not a market-clearing, role, they tend to rise, not fall, when supply increases. At the same time, higher-cost modes of production are promoted to provide employment for the high-priced help; political resistance to less costly substitutes is both more intense and more effective when peak professionals are plentiful.

Incomplete vertical integration of the form of Figure 10.2 thus explains the otherwise paradoxical situation of surgery in the United States: too many surgeons, underutilized to the point that some observers believe quality of care suffers, and overuse of surgery, but maintenance of surgical incomes and prices. The conventional supply-and-demand process, which predicts that low-cost producers replace high-cost ones, that increases in supply lead to bidding down of prices, and that – except through such price changes – suppliers do not influence use, has been superseded. The irony of the health manpower policy debate is that output restriction has shifted from being perceived as a professional tactic that limits competition and maintains incomes to a public policy to improve resource allocation and hold down prices.

Emphasis on the complexity of integration patterns indicates the extent of the structural change that would be necessary to move to a world in which supply increases had their conventional effects. Modification of insurance packages to include more patient payment does nothing whatever to change the locus of managerial decisions. As a pro-competition policy it is bogus and serves only to clothe the structure of Figure 10.2 with the rhetoric of Figure 10.1. At the very least, dismantling of self-government controls over conduct and reallocation of authority within hospitals and other second-line providers, together with significant restructuring of insurance, would be necessary to induce firms at either level to engage in price-cutting strategies in competition over market share.

Whether such a shift would on balance improve welfare, however, is a much more dubious question. Apart from the political feasibility of such revolutionary change, which recent US experience suggests is virtually nil, the central problem of the agency relation persists. It is not exorcised with hand waving about doubtless desirable increases in consumer information, least of all price information. More competitive pressure on providers means that they are less willing/able to protect patient interests. In practice, the feasible alternatives for structural organization of the health care industry can assign agency responsibility entirely to providers – the free enterprise approach; to integrated provider/insurers – the HMO approach; or to both providers and government – intervening through limits on performance or reimbursement of particular procedures, restrictions on forms of capacity, or direct management of supply. Alternative structures give different answers to the central medical question: Whose patient is this? Hypothetical market models do not. Improvements in the allocative and technical efficiency of the health care industry, for which there is substantial evidence of feasibility in principle, seem to wait upon either the creation of new institutions or the more aggressive use of existing ones, to reassign management functions and to change the vertical integration pattern so that incentives and resource-allocation responsibilities can better reflect available information.

Problems of industrial structure in health care thus take us back to the fundamental social policy problem of economics: the design of institutional frameworks so that resource-allocation decisions are assigned to people or groups who possess the necessary information to make optimal decisions – criteria of optimality are necessarily a prior socio-political choice – and who have appropriate incentives to ensure a correspondence of private and social objectives. The alternative structures outlined before represent different assignments of resource-allocation authority, reflecting the inherent informational imperfections of health care markets and the perverse incentives created both by this characteristic and by social responses to it.

To date, the most effective though far from perfect means for achieving this goal have been public, collective responses. The nature of such responses varies markedly across countries. The numerous theoretical attractions of private collective institutions have been associated with some practical success in the United States, but serious concerns about generalizability remain. Still, there remains plenty of room for experiment, since the attempt to reallocate a portion of incomes and of control over utilization from private providers to the public sector through national health insurance seems to be indefinitely stalled; bill paying is probably the least interesting aspect of public insurance. The political feasibility of genuinely pro-competitive change, however, as opposed to a shift in the balance from public to private control over pseudomarkets under the rhetoric of private enterprise, is much more questionable.

In no society, however, are objectives and decision-making powers within the health care industry assigned to the sets of elementary transactors – consumers, firms – on which conventional economic theory is built. The characteristic pattern of incomplete vertical integration – of leaky transactor boundaries – has made the application of economic methodology to health care research particularly difficult and frequently misleading. The task is in the process of becoming even more difficult, because the inherent tendency of structural boundaries in the health care industry to shift across institutions does not stop at research. Since decision-making powers are a form of property rights, their allocation is inherently political. All transactors in the health industry have always operated in the political as well as the economic domain, and from this perspective, research in general – and economics in particular – is just a branch of public relations.

Thus we now observe forward integration of providers, either individual for-profit firms or associations, into the economic research field in order to provide pseudo-scientific justification for structural patterns favourable to their incomes and for decision-making authority. For public relations purposes economic analysis appears both effective and relatively cheap.[12] The objects of analysis enter the analytic process itself, creating methodological problems very different from the hard sciences, where bacteria usually stay on the slide and do not themselves conduct or sponsor bacteriological research.

The structural framework suggested here is not presented with any illusion that it will prove adequate to embody all the complex conduct and performance issues that arise in different sub-industries or systems of organization. But at least it permits one to raise and address a number of the issues that health care analysts find important. In the simplified market model too many important questions appear trivial, or cannot even be posed.

NOTES

1 This concept of agency must not be confused with the agent in the literature on principal-agent problems – for example, sharecropping or defence contracting. In the principal-agent problem, selfish transactors with independent utility functions participate in a non-zero-sum game in which the principal's payoff depends on the agent's action, but the principal can define the payoff framework. In the professional relationship, by contrast, the professional agent's objective function includes the client-patient's health, welfare, or other characteristics. The test question is: If an action that is totally undetectable and that transfers wealth from principal to agent is available to the agent, will it be taken? In the principal-agent literature, yes. In the professional agency concept, no, or at least not always. Otherwise the concept of a professional has no meaning, and its special regulatory status has no justification.

2 Greg L. Stoddart and Morris L. Barer, "Analyses of Demand and Utilization through Episodes of Medical Service," in *Health, Economics, and Health*

Economics, ed. Jacques van der Gaag and Mark Perlman, 149–70 (Amsterdam: North-Holland, 1981).

3 Carolyn J. Tuohy and Alan D. Wolfson, "The Political Economy of Professionalism: A Perspective," in *Four Aspects of Professionalism*, ed. Michael J. Trebilcock, 41–86 (Ottawa: Consumer Research Council, 1977). The importance of the agency concept was clearly brought out by Kenneth J. Arrow, "Uncertainty and the Welfare Economics of Medical Care," *American Economic Review* 53, no.5 (Dec. 1963): 941–73; but it has dropped out of much subsequent work. The application of the label "uncertainty" both to unforeseeable future risks – insurable – and to incomplete present information – requiring agency – was unfortunate. Efforts have been made to support conventional demand analysis by assuming perfect agency – the consumer as physician-patient pair, and thus fully informed – or generalized agency. Perfect agency, apart from the direct evidence against it, undercuts all economic theories of professionals qua principals. Generalized agency is a concept that hovers between perfect agency and nonagency without committing to the critical notion of incomplete agency. Operationally, it seems indistinguishable from perfect agency.

4 Robert G. Evans, "Health Care in Canada: Patterns of Funding and Regulation," in *The Public-Private Mix for Health: The Relevance and Effect of Change*, ed. G. McLachlan and A. Maynard, 371–424 (London: Nuffield Trust, 1982).

5 Lawrence G. Goldberg and Warren Greenberg, "The Effect of Physician-Controlled Health Insurance: US *v.* Oregon State Medical Society," *Journal of Health Politics, Policy and Law* 2 (1977): 48–78. Whether changes in the professional powers and protections conferred by self-government or privately monopolized insurance could enable insurers to monitor service provision effectively is still an open issue. There do not yet appear to be any examples of successful intervention by private insurers in a pluralistic environment, except possibly for some components of dental care.

6 Alain C. Enthoven, "Consumer-Choice Health Plan, Parts I and II," *New England Journal of Medicine* 298 (1978): 650–8, 709–20.

7 Harold S. Luft, *Health Maintenance Organizations: Dimensions of Performance* (New York: John Wiley, 1981).

8 Jane C. Record, *Staffing Primary Care in 1990: Physician Replacement and Cost Savings* (New York: Springer, 1981).

9 Robert G. Evans and Malcolm F. Williamson, *Extending Canadian National Health Insurance: Policy Options for Pharmacare and Denticare*, Ontario Economic Council Research Monograph Series #13 (Toronto: University of Toronto Press, 1978).

10 Alain C. Enthoven, "The Behavior of Health Care Agents: Provider Behavior," in *Health, Economics, and Health Economics: Proceedings of the World Congress on Health Economics,* ed. Jacques van der Gaag and Mark Perlman, 173–88 (Amsterdam: North-Holland, 1981).

11 Theodore R. Marmor, Donald A. Wittman, and Thomas C. Heagy, "Politics, Public Policy, and Medical Inflation," in *Health: A Victim or a Cause of Inflation?* ed. Michael Zubkoff, 299–316 (New York: Prodist, 1976).

12 Stigler has pointed out, with apparent approval, the conservative bias of economic theory; see George J. Stigler, "The Politics of Political Economists," *Quarterly Journal of Ecnomics* 73(1959): 522–33. If one starts from normative assumptions of consumer sovereignty and positive assumptions of complete information, zero transaction costs, and dynamic stability, one moves quickly to the position that whatever is, is right, and the market, like Pangloss' Providence, yields the best of all possible worlds. Some technological questions must be finessed to get to competitive market structure, but if information really is perfect, and transaction costs are zero, then these problems disappear. The only villain in the piece is government. Such analysis is, of course, marketable.

11

Aging and Health Care Utilization: New Evidence on Old Fallacies (1987)

MORRIS L. BARER, ROBERT G. EVANS, CLYDE HERTZMAN, AND JONATHAN LOMAS

Whatever everyone knows, is usually wrong, and common sense is either not common, or not sense. By now, everybody knows that the rapid growth in elderly populations threatens to bankrupt the health care systems of every industrialized country. Unfortunately the rhetoric supporting this belief is much stronger than the evidence.

Populations continue to grow, albeit slowly, and health care utilization and costs tend to rise along with populations. But as populations grow, so does the economic base to sustain increased costs. The relevant issue is the growth of utilization and costs per capita. This distinction is not always clear in much of the rhetoric about aging and health care costs.

These per capita costs *are* rising, and will continue to rise, because the proportion of elderly in the population is also increasing, and the elderly each use more health care, on average, than the rest of the population. The question is, how large will this effect be? The rhetoric would suggest that the magnitude is great enough to justify serious policy concern. Calls for more hospital beds, more physicians, more special care units, more long-term care ... are now commonly justified by reference to these emerging needs. The federal minister of health has identified aging as

Reprinted from M.L. Barer, R.G. Evans, C. Hertzman, and J. Lomas, "Aging and Health Care Utilization: New Evidence on Old Fallacies," *Social Science & Medicine* 24(10): 851–62.

one of the principal policy challenges facing the Canadian health care system (MacDonald, 1986).

But the impact of aging per se on health care use is relatively easily measured. A series of recent Canadian studies has consistently shown that it is, in fact, quite small (Boulet and Grenier, 1978; Stone and Fletcher, 1980; Denton and Spencer, 1975; Woods Gordon Management Consultants, 1984). If one assumes unchanging age and sex specific utilization rates per capita, and projects forward the changing age structure of the Canadian population, it turns out that the increase in the proportion of the population in elderly high-use groups will raise per capita use for the whole population by about 1 per cent per year over the next forty years. For physicians' services, the annual increase is about 0.3 per cent per year. In contrast, historical per capita real cost increases in the 1970s for physicians' services have been about 1.5 per cent per year, and for hospitals 2.6 per cent (Barer and Evans, 1987). In particular sectors, home care, for example, and long-term care, the projections show that per capita use may rise by closer to 2 per cent per year, but these are relatively small components of the total.[1]

These calculations isolate the effect of changing population structure alone on health care costs, abstracting from any changes in patterns of care for particular age groups. They rest on relatively conservative assumptions as to future population growth rates; if a new baby boom should develop, growth in per capita costs would be even slower. No studies suggest cost growth at rates faster than the growth of the general economy is likely to be able to support.

If there is any basis for the rhetoric and the policy concern, therefore, it *cannot* be found in the increasing numbers and proportions of people over 65. Concerns about future cost escalation only make sense on the presumption that costs among the elderly are rising more rapidly than for the population overall.

There could be at least three possible explanations for such a trend. One is that morbidity in each age group among the elderly is increasing. Alternatively, people may not be getting any sicker, but the progress of medical technology may be extending the range of potentially effective interventions. Finally, the health care system may simply be treating patients differently, more intensively, independent of any evidence of improved outcomes.

With respect to the first two possibilities, there are two leading, and competing, scenarios describing the future evolution of morbidity and mortality patterns. In the next section we outline these scenarios and explore the linkages between alternative biological hypotheses, implied patterns of morbidity by age, and the capacity of these projected morbidity patterns to explain future use of health care services by the elderly.

Following this, we compare the implications of the biological explanations with available data on trends in utilization by age. Our objectives here are to determine the extent to which current evidence permits attribution of trends in utilization to changes in morbidity, and to identify the types of data necessary to clarify these relationships.

In our final section, we discuss the possible explanations for the largely unchallenged staying power of the "bankruptcy hypothesis of aging."

WALLS, CEILINGS, AND BIOLOGICAL FOUNDATIONS

The debate in the biological literature on aging pits those who claim that the organism has a preprogrammed lifespan (after which "natural death" occurs) against those who argue that life expectancies can be increased more or less indefinitely.

The former scenario, attributed to Fries and Crapo (henceforth FC) (Fries and Crapo, 1981), has three components – rectangularization of survival curves, compression of morbidity, and "natural death." The rectangularization argument begins with the distinction between "life expectancy" and "lifespan." According to Fries and Crapo, the maximum lifespan is fixed at approximately 115 years.[2] However, life expectancy is increasing but will reach a maximum at approximately 85 years of age within the next few decades. The projection of a maximum life expectancy of 85 years is derived from the observation that the terminal points of age-survival curves over the last hundred years seem to converge at 85, although with progressively steeper slopes. As an increasing proportion of the population survives to the 85 age range, the survival curve will appear to "rectangularize" at this "biological wall." This implies that increasing proportions of the population will die at or near age 85. More specifically, FC predict that, once the "biological wall" of 85 years has been reached, 95 per cent of the population will die between the ages of 77 and 93. However, there will be no increase in the proportion living beyond this age range.

The second component of the scenario is the "compression of morbidity" (Fries, 1983). It envisions a combination of health care intervention and natural changes associated with rising life expectancy leading to a postponement of the onset of clinically detectable and/or debilitating morbidity. When the average life expectancy has risen to its maximum, however, morbidity will continue to be postponed. The effect is one of "compressing" morbidity against the biological wall, as portrayed in Figure 11.1 for chronic diseases.

The final component is referred to as "natural death." Natural death resurrects the concept of "dying of old age" in the context of a high-tech society. Post-mortem studies of the organs of the elderly have revealed that often death cannot be attributed to a specific disease process. Rather, death is often attributable to a general decline in the capacity of the organism to withstand external stressors, such as infection or nutritional imbalance. It is hypothesized that, if health care providers recognize the early signs of impending natural death, they will be less aggressive in their use of life-saving interventions, thus avoiding the prolonged states of ill-health and health care utilization that are often a consequence of such heroic measures.

Thus, the FC theory is a theory about relative endpoints, but posits nothing about the pathway linking them (Hertzman and Hayes, 1985). If the FC scenario proves to be accurate, then we would expect to observe lowered age-specific utilization rates for all age groups (Fuchs, 1984), and a much less pronounced "terminal care effect," wherein large amounts of utilization occur in the last year or two of life (Lubitz and Prihoda, 1984; Scitovsky, 1984; Roos, Shapiro, and Havens, 1986).

The major challenge to this scenario consists of evidence on the pathway between the present and the FC endpoint, rather than on the endpoint itself. While such evidence cannot refute the FC scenario, it nevertheless provides information of particular importance on current trends in morbidity. Schneider and Brody (1983), Grundy (1984), and Brody (1985) (henceforth SBG) examine the extent to which current patterns of morbidity and mortality are moving towards each of the three components of the endpoint scenario laid out by FC. They point out that, rather than rectangularization of the mortality curve, age-specific mortality rates for the very old have been decreasing faster than for younger age groups over the past few decades. In other words, at what FC would call the biological wall, there is a flattening, rather than a rectangularization, of the survival curve (Manton, 1986).

Similarly they can find no evidence to indicate that morbidity is being "compressed" to the tail end of life. In fact, they point out that we are keeping people with chronic conditions alive longer (Gruenberg, 1977). Canadian data compiled by Wilkins and Adams (1983) support this view. They calculate that approximately two-thirds of each year of life

(A)

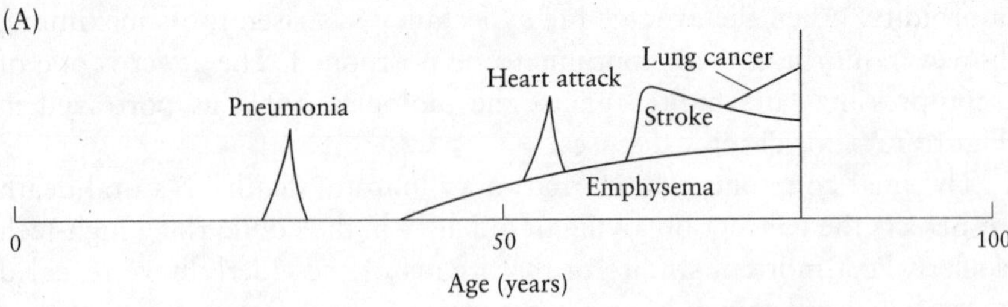

(B)

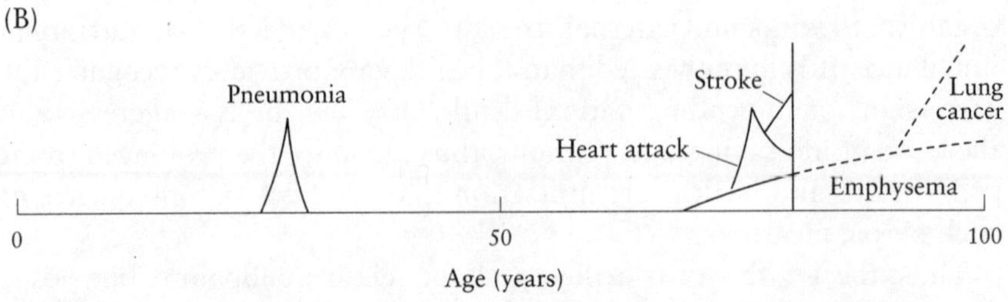

Figure 11.1 The compression of chronic disease. (A) Prototypic lingering chronic illness. (B) Effects of the postponement of chronic disease

Adapted from: Morris L. Barer, Robert G. Evans, Clyde Hertzman, and Jonathan Lomas. "Aging and Health Care Utilization: New Evidence on Old Fallacies." *Social Science & Medicine* 24(10) (1987): 851–62.
Original source: Fries and Crapo. *Vitality and Aging: Implications of the Rectangular Curve*. San Francisco, Calif.: W.H. Freeman, 1981. Reprinted with permission of the authors.

gained between 1951 and 1978 was spent in some degree of disability. Similarly, Verbrugge (1984) reports that National Health Interview Survey (HIS) data for the United States "show rising morbidity for middle-aged and older people since 1957" (Verbrugge, 1984, 505).

Palmore (1986), however, working with the same data set, concludes that between 1961 and 1981 "factors increasing life expectancy also tend to improve health and reduce morbidity." This contradiction in interpretation arises because Palmore focuses on the *relative* health status of the elderly compared to the whole of the population. He finds equivocal results for *absolute* trends in morbidity among the elderly, but assumes that "period effects" – e.g. changes in HIS methodology and increased public awareness of morbidity – bias these trends. He thus concludes that the elderly are in fact becoming healthier. One could equally well infer, however, that morbidity is increasing among the whole population, though less rapidly among the elderly.

Nevertheless, Palmore's results are unequivocal in showing a decline in relative morbidity, by between 10 and 20 per cent on the various indicators examined, over a 20 year span. Moreover, as he notes, failure to adjust for the changing age distribution over 65 implies that his results *understate* the extent of the relative decline. Similar implications emerge from data reported by the American Council of Life Insurance (American Council of Life Insurance, 1986, Table 7).

The problem with the challenges to the first two components of the FC endpoint scenario is that they cannot refute these aspects of it. FC do *not* claim to describe or predict the current trends, yet that is what SBG offer. Hence these challenges are in some sense ships passing in the night. They may end up in the same port eventually, or they may not. All that can be established is that one ship is not presently steaming directly toward the port of call of the second.

In the case of natural death, in contrast, both camps are dealing with the same evidence. However, the evidence is interpreted in diametrically opposing ways, interpretations which have contrasting implications for the extent of health care intervention in the terminal years of life. For instance, Kohn (1982) used an autopsy series of those dying after age 85 to demonstrate that approximately 30 per cent did not have sufficient pathological findings to cause death in a middle-aged person. This implied to Kohn (and to FC) an overall system inability to fend off small threats to internal equilibrium – the concept of "natural death."

However, SBG, while agreeing that the pathologic insults which lead to death among the very old may indeed be insufficient to kill middle-aged persons, argue that, in the absence of these pathologic insults, the very elderly would not have died. The semantic issue is whether these pathologic insults are, in the aged, "natural" events (FC) or "extraordinary" events (SBG). The substantive issue is how the health care system should respond. The critical view of "natural death" espoused by SBG may herald an era in which increasingly heroic measures are applied to increasingly frail elderly in the last years of life (Ginzberg, 1984).

FROM BIOLOGICAL SCENARIOS TO UTILIZATION PATTERNS

These alternative implications for utilization depend implicitly on the assumption that utilization patterns are determined by underlying patterns of morbidity. As emphasized by the semantic disagreement over the concept of natural death, however, a critical additional factor is the way in which the health care system, and the wider society, define and respond to the conditions of the elderly. "Compression of morbidity" into the final stages of life is quite consistent with *either* the "Nunc Dimittis" approach of FC – when the end has clearly come, the wise and humane clinician does not get in the way – *or* the alternative of refusing to permit any patient to die until all conceivable manoeuvres have been attempted.

Furthermore, rectangularization of mortality is consistent with very different trajectories of both morbidity and utilization. FC presume that pre-terminal morbidity will fall as populations become healthier, and that utilization will fall in line. But one could equally well hypothesize that increases in life expectancy are a result, not of people becoming inherently healthier, but of increasingly effective "salvage" activities by the health care system which increase both morbidity and utilization rates. Age-specific utilization rates would rise, as would morbidity at each age, even as mortality was "rectangularizing."

Yet another variant would have "curative" health care becoming increasingly effective, such that morbidity was reduced at each age, but health care utilization and costs were increased. Or again, an extensive array of evidence on the determinants of utilization of health care suggests that the capacity and priorities of the system itself may be more important than the characteristics of the population served.

Thus we must recognize three distinct external forces or classes of factors which interact to generate patterns of morbidity and utilization. These are the underlying health state of the population prior to the impact of the health care system, the effectiveness or technological capabilities of the health care system itself, and the perceptions and attitudes of providers of and users of health care which influence utilization and costs separately from underlying "needs" and therapeutic capabilities.

The range of possibilities is displayed in Figure 11.2. This representation permits us to describe the alternatives which can arise from the two-way linkage between morbidity and utilization. The upper triangles in each of the four quadrants represent the scenarios under which causality runs from morbidity to utilization. The lower triangles show the reverse: causality running from utilization to morbidity. For example, increasingly effective health care technology will be reflected in an increase in utilization followed by either an increase in morbidity – the *salvage* of people who would otherwise have died – or a decrease – the *cure* of people who would otherwise have remained ill.

On the other hand, a fall in morbidity at each age, as suggested by FC's "compression of morbidity," could be reflected either in a fall in utilization

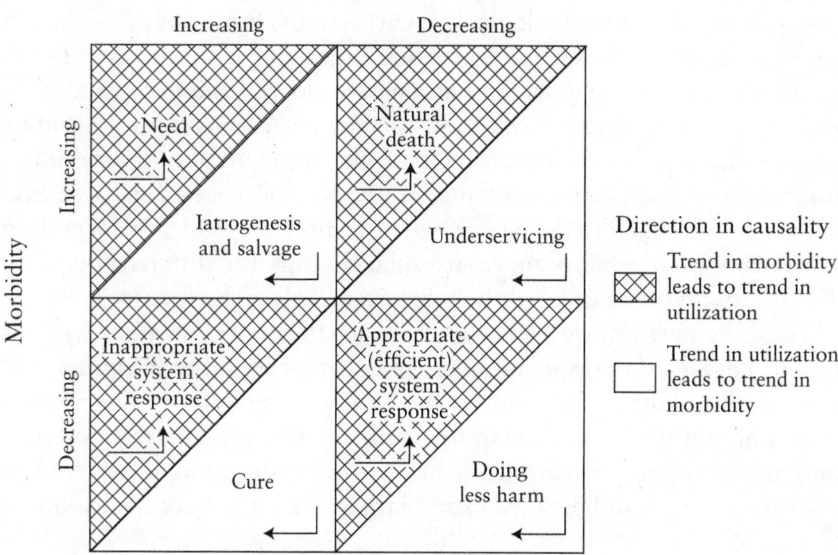

Figure 11.2 Morbidity-utilization relationships

Adapted from: Morris L. Barer, Robert G. Evans, Clyde Hertzman, and Jonathan Lomas. "Aging and Health Care Utilization: New Evidence on Old Fallacies." *Social Science & Medicine* 24(10) (1987): 851–62.

– the upper triangle in the lower right-hand box, *efficient system response*, or a rise – the upper triangle on the lower left, *inappropriate system response*. The actual response will be dependent primarily on the perceptions and attitudes of the providers who respond to the fall in morbidity.

As a third pair of possibilities, a rise in morbidity within the population could lead to a utilization response of *meeting needs* – upper triangle on upper left side, or a recognition of *natural death* – the determination that intervention would no longer help the patient's condition (i.e., a determination that there are no needs). Here the overriding influence is the extant health status of the population.

Finally, a fall in utilization, following for example from a cut in resources, could cause either a rise in morbidity – *underservicing* – or, if targeted to ineffective interventions, could result in a fall in morbidity – *doing less harm*. Here again the predominant determining factor is the attitudes and perceptions of those making the internal system care allocation decisions.

The range and complexity of the different relationships between utilization and morbidity, and the role of the various factors influencing these relationships, makes clear that one cannot argue in any simple or linear fashion from the biological scenarios to the future course of health care utilization and costs. Increasing life expectancies are consistent with either rising or falling morbidity among the elderly; and per capita utilization rates in turn may rise or fall for any given pattern of morbidity. Moreover, there is no reason to believe that the evolution of morbidity-utilization relationships over time will be homogeneous across disease entities. Verbrugge (1984) has provided compelling evidence suggesting a rich mix of morbidity-mortality relationships for different diseases. The morbidity-utilization relationships are likely to be equally diverse.

Thus, the observation of any particular pattern of utilization will not permit backward extrapolation (*noitalopartxe*) to either a unique pattern of morbidity or of underlying biology. Quantifying the relative effects of morbidity, the availability of effective health care technologies, and attitudes and perceptions of health care system providers requires the simultaneous and detailed examination of a number of data sources.

BIKINI DATA: REVEALING AND CONCEALING (AGE-USE) CURVES

An age-use curve plots utilization against age. An historical series of such curves shows the way in which utilization has changed over time independent of changes in the population age structure. Remarkably, such elementary (but crucial) curves, which are readily constructible from existing Canadian data sources, are available only in fragments – for some provinces, some years, and some services. Furthermore, we are unaware of any source which constructs the time series necessary to the identification of the temporal changes. The fact of this informational void, despite the attention being given to the relationship between aging and health care utilization, underscores the point made earlier that the rhetoric and policy recommendations have been innocent of the evidence.

It is not that no data are available on utilization by age. In fact, a number of provincial annual reports provide some form of such data. These data are not reported by individual year of age, but by age classes which are often too broad to permit exploration of age-specific utilization changes over time, or worse, which change with successive annual reports.[3] Furthermore, while data on institutional and medical care are widely available, those for other forms of care (e.g., dental and pharmaceutical) are less readily available. But even within the institutional care data, the mix of utilization reported may change from year to year. For example, in

British Columbia prior to 1983/84, "hospitalization data on long-term care patients occupying acute care beds [had] been separated from acute care data. Commencing with the fiscal year 1983/84, long-term care volume in acute beds [is] included with the acute care data" (British Columbia Ministry of Health, 1986, 4); the information necessary for the user of the reports to bridge this inconsistency was not provided. Finally, the level of detail necessary even to beginning the exploration of underlying causes of change in age-specific use patterns is not even available on source magnetic tapes in many provinces.

As an example of age-use curves that can be constructed from published sources, we compile in Table 11.1 and Figure 11.3 acute and rehabilitation hospital separations and days of care per capita, by 5-year age group, for BC over the period 1971 to 1982/83. It is clear that acute and rehabilitation hospital use in BC fell overall during this period, a result of the concerted efforts to reduce hospital bed capacity (Barer and Evans, 1987). But this overall decline was slowest among the elderly, and slower the older they were. Thus, while patient days per capita for males fell 30 per cent overall in 11 years, the decline for males aged 65 to 69 was a slower 25 per cent; and for males over 80 a *much* slower 10 per cent. Separation rates per capita actually rose over this period for all male age groups over 65. For those 85 and over, the increase was an astonishing 16 per cent, in the face of an overall *decline per capita* of 14 per cent.

The story is much the same for the female population – significant overall per capita reductions in separations (19 per cent) and patient days (28 per cent), but much smaller reductions, or even increases, among those 65 and over. Once again we find an approximate monotonic relationship between age group and relative rate of decline or growth.

This phenomenon is portrayed most succinctly in the final column of Table 11.1. The figures there represent the growth from 1971 to 1982/83 in per capita use by each age group, relative to overall growth. Thus the increase in separations per capita for males 80 years of age and over was 35 per cent faster (or the decline that much slower) than for all males – an increase of 16 per cent versus an overall decline of 14 per cent. The striking relationship between age group and relative use is most vividly portrayed by this ratio. We see monotonic increases with age in the relative growth in use, beginning with the 55 to 59 age group for females. With the exception of slightly lower relative growth among those 70 to 74 than among those 65 to 69, the relationship is equally uni-directional for males. But the relative growth in use among female elderly has exceeded that of their male counterparts. Inter-age variations in use

Table 11.1 BC hospital utilization, selected age groups, 1971–1982/83

						Ratios relative to all					Ratio 1982/83
	1971	*1974*	*1977*	*1980/81*	*1982/83*	*1971*	*1974*	*1977*	*1980/81*	*1982/83*	*over ratio 1971*
MALES: SEPARATIONS PER THOUSAND POPULATION											
15–19	81	85	79	78	70	0.54	0.57	0.56	0.57	0.54	1
55–59	208	225	204	203	194	1.39	1.52	1.46	1.47	1.5	1.08
60–64	247	264	244	247	239	1.65	1.78	1.74	1.79	1.85	1.13
65–69	277	303	291	299	287	1.85	2.05	2.08	2.17	2.22	1.2
70–74	356	349	340	365	363	2.37	2.36	2.43	2.64	2.81	1.19
75–79	398	421	415	433	435	2.65	2.84	2.96	3.14	3.37	1.27
80–84	460	498	502	503	533	3.07	3.36	3.59	3.64	4.13	1.35
85+	500	581	559	555	582	3.33	3.93	3.99	4.02	4.51	1.35
All	150	148	140	138	129						
MALES: DAYS PER THOUSAND POPULATION											
15–19	597	602	481	485	425	0.4	0.43	0.38	0.42	0.4	1.01
55–59	2,334	2,338	2,062	1,815	1,638	1.56	1.69	1.62	1.56	1.56	1
60–64	3,164	3,051	2,764	2,395	2,105	2.11	2.2	2.17	2.06	2	0.95
65–69	3,836	3,948	3,487	3,180	2,870	2.56	2.85	2.74	2.73	2.73	1.07
70–74	5,581	4,805	4,525	4,285	4,027	3.73	3.47	3.55	3.68	3.84	1.03
75–79	6,598	6,602	6,080	5,718	5,343	4.41	4.77	4.78	4.92	5.09	1.15
80–84	8,046	8,435	8,026	7,459	7,238	5.38	6.09	6.3	6.41	6.89	1.28
85+	9,632	10,740	9,861	9,136	8,811	6.44	7.75	7.75	7.86	8.39	1.3
All	1,496	1,385	1,273	1,163	1,050						

FEMALES: SEPARATIONS PER THOUSAND POPULATION											
15–19	185	166	146	136	125	0.91	0.86	0.79	0.77	0.75	0.83
55–59	180	190	177	163	152	0.88	0.98	0.96	0.93	0.92	1.04
60–64	194	208	194	189	180	0.95	1.07	1.05	1.07	1.08	1.14
65–69	222	230	227	223	218	1.09	1.19	1.23	1.27	1.31	1.21
70–74	257	264	261	275	268	1.26	1.36	1.41	1.56	1.61	1.28
75–79	286	304	315	322	329	1.4	1.57	1.7	1.83	1.98	1.41
80–84	327	366	368	390	391	1.6	1.89	1.99	2.22	2.36	1.47
85+	357	361	401	417	438	1.75	1.86	2.17	2.37	2.64	1.51
All	204	194	185	176	166						
FEMALES: DAYS PER THOUSAND POPULATION											
15–19	1,052	866	741	668	597	0.6	0.54	0.48	0.48	0.47	0.79
55–59	2,144	2,078	1,799	1,547	1,311	1.22	1.29	1.18	1.1	1.04	0.85
60–64	2,485	2,475	2,230	2,032	1,737	1.42	1.54	1.46	1.45	1.37	0.97
65–69	3,069	3,024	2,918	2,620	2,390	1.75	1.88	1.91	1.86	1.89	1.08
70–74	3,919	3,847	3,679	3,602	3,163	2.24	2.4	2.4	2.56	2.5	1.12
75–79	4,914	4,861	5,003	4,908	4,494	2.81	3.03	3.27	3.49	3.56	1.27
80–84	5,938	6,554	6,893	6,686	5,867	3.39	4.08	4.51	4.76	4.64	1.37
85+	7,277	7,229	8,255	8,223	7,704	4.16	4.5	5.4	5.85	6.09	1.47
All	1,751	1,606	1,530	1,405	1,264						

Adapted from: Morris L. Barer, Robert G. Evans, Clyde Hertzman, and Jonathan Lomas. "Aging and Health Care Utilization: New Evidence on Old Fallacies." *Social Science & Medicine* 24(10)(1987): 851–62.

Based on data drawn from: British Columbia Ministry of Health (n.d., various years).

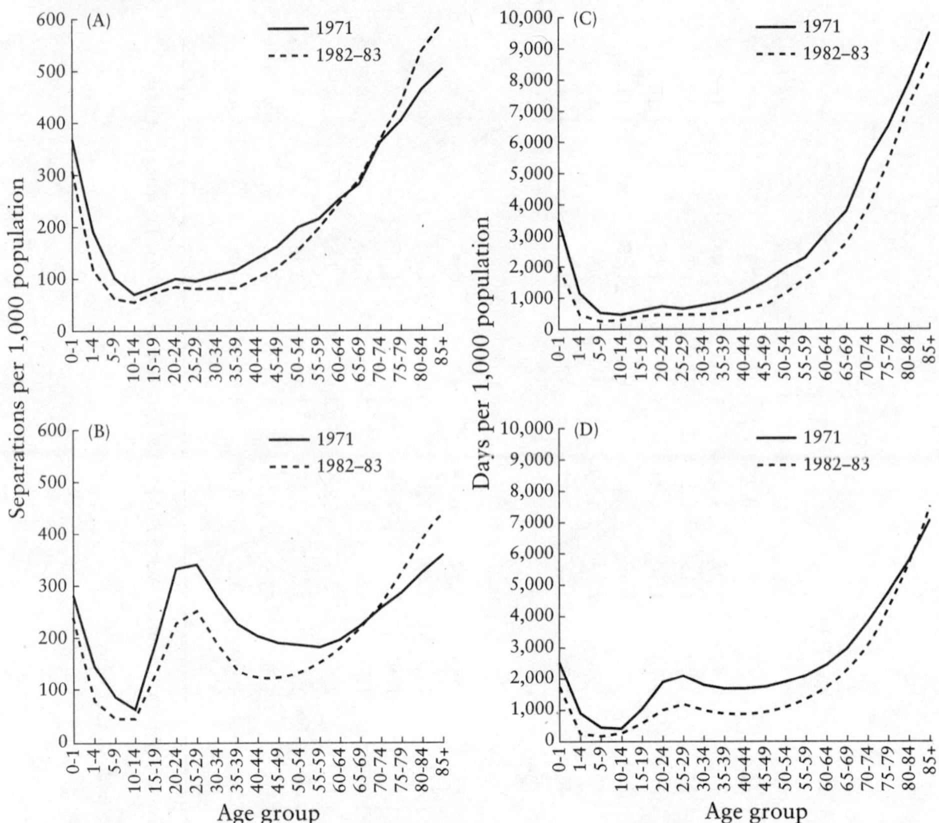

Figure 11.3 Hospital age-use curves, British Columbia, 1971 and 1982/83 (A) Male separations per thousand population. (B) Female separations per thousand population. (C) Male days per thousand population. (D) Female days per thousand population.

Adapted from: Morris L. Barer, Robert G. Evans, Clyde Hertzman, and Jonathan Lomas. "Aging and Health Care Utilization: New Evidence on Old Fallacies." *Social Science & Medicine* 24(10) (1987): 851–862.

among females were less pronounced (although still very evident) than among males in 1971; since then the age-specific differences have widened for females relative to males, although the absolute differences still remain far more distinct among males of different age groups.

The distinction between this right-most column, and any one of the other columns, cannot be overemphasized. Each of the other columns shows that at any point in time hospital use is a clear and unequivocal function of age. Males 85 and over, for example, used three times the number of days per capita of males 60 to 64, in 1971. The right-most

Table 11.2 Fee-for-service payments per capita, BC, 1981/82–1983/84

	(1)	(2)	(3)	(4)	(5)	(6)
				Relative to "all"		
	1981/82	*1983/84*	*(2)/(1)*	*1981/82*	*1983/84*	*(5)/(4)*
MALES						
0–4	165.9	224.7	1.354	0.859	0.854	0.994
5–9	107.1	141.4	1.32	0.555	0.537	0.969
10–14	92.2	119.3	1.294	0.477	0.453	0.949
15–19	96.7	128.8	1.332	0.501	0.489	0.977
20–29	108	136.7	1.266	0.599	0.519	0.929
30–39	126.9	165.2	1.302	0.657	0.628	0.955
40–49	150.2	198.6	1.322	0.778	0.755	0.97
50–59	210	280.1	1.334	1.088	1.064	0.979
60–64	281.3	390.6	1.389	1.457	1.484	1.019
65–69	326.5	441.4	1.352	1.691	1.677	0.992
70–74	396.1	546.8	1.38	2.051	2.078	1.013
75–79	461.9	640.3	1.386	2.392	2.433	1.017
80–84	520.5	715.2	1.374	2.695	2.717	1.008
85+	570.5	815.5	1.429	2.954	3.098	1.049
FEMALES						
0–4	151.3	195.7	1.293	0.784	0.744	0.949
5–9	93.2	123.7	1.327	0.483	0.47	0.974
10–14	88.3	114.3	1.294	0.457	0.434	0.95
15–19	162.1	209.2	1.291	0.839	0.795	0.947
20–29	262.2	356.8	1.361	1.358	1.356	0.998
30–39	251.7	340.4	1.352	1.303	1.293	0.992
40–49	229.3	305.4	1.332	1.187	1.16	0.977
50–59	240.2	324.7	1.352	1.244	1.234	0.992
60–64	266	363.6	1.367	1.378	1.381	1.003
65–69	294.1	403.7	1.373	1.523	1.534	1.007
70–74	324.3	462.4	1.426	1.679	1.757	1.046
75–79	338.7	509.9	1.505	1.754	1.937	1.105
80–84	349.4	533.8	1.528	1.809	2.028	1.121
85+	362.9	537.9	1.482	1.879	2.044	1.087
All	193.1	263.2	1.363			

Adapted from: Morris L. Barer, Robert G. Evans, Clyde Hertzman, and Jonathan Lomas. "Aging and Health Care Utilization: New Evidence on Old Fallacies." *Social Science & Medicine* 24(10) (1987): 851–62.

Based on data drawn from: Barer and Wong Fung (1983), Table 46, for column 1, and Barer and Wong Fung (1985), Table 44, for column 2.

column reflects the fact that in 1982/83 males 85 and over were again intensive users relative to those 60 to 64. In fact, they now received almost 4.2 *times* the number of days of care *per capita*. Thus, the inter-age relationships have retained their ordinality, but the cardinality has undergone remarkable shifts, and more so among females than among males.

This gradual intensification of age-related use rate differences is reflected as well in Figure 11.3. The age-use curves have all shifted down, reflecting the overall decline in per capita use rates. But the slopes of those curves have been steepening over time past about the age of 55, and in three of the four curves there is a utilization "cross-over point" among the elderly.

Lest one be tempted to dismiss this as an isolated phenomenon, among specific types of care or institutions, we show in Table 11.2 the fee-adjusted medical service expenditures per capita for BC over the period 1981/82 to 1983/84 (Barer and Wong Fung, 1983; Barer and Wong Fung, 1985). The period is short because we could find no published Canadian data on medical care use by detailed age class covering a longer period of time.[4] But the brevity of the period makes more remarkable the emergence of any trend.

The columns are structured in a similar manner to those of Table 11.1. The first two columns simply show actual fee-for-service medical expenditure per capita in each year and age-sex group.[5] The stories there are familiar – high servicing for the very young, falling to a minimum among the 10- to 14-year-olds, and then increasing monotonically (with the exception of the maternity years for females) with age group thereafter. Again the ordinality is unchanged. But as the right-most column illustrates, growth in per capita medical expenditure for the elderly has been faster than for the rest of the population, even over a period as short as two years. The trend is particularly marked for females, where for those 75 and over expenditures per capita have grown over 10 per cent faster than for the entire population. For males over 85, expenditures per capita have grown 5 per cent faster than overall, while growth among all those 60 and over has been faster than growth among those under 60. The ratios are not nearly as dramatic as the institutional-based ratios of Table 11.1, but they represent emerging trends over a much shorter period of time. In fact, if one returns to Table 11.1 and computes, say, comparable ratios for 1982/83 over 1980/81, the magnitudes of relative growth are not dissimilar.

Some corroborative evidence over a longer period of time, but without the fine age-sex-related detail, comes from a recent study of Manitoba's experience with medical insurance over the 10 years 1971 to 1981 (Roch, Evans, Pascoe, 1985). Table 11.3 is adapted from data published in that report, and shows average medical care cost per discrete patient for Manitoba, by broad age group.

These data are slightly different than those in the previous table, in that they are patient rather than population based. The denominators include anyone who saw a physician at least once during the relevant year. The data are also fee-deflated, and thus reflect implied utilization per patient. The latter makes no difference. The fee index used to deflate expenditures in Table 11.3 was not an age-group and region-specific fee index, so the figures in column (5) would be the same if columns (1) and (2) contained expenditure data rather than "utilization" data. The use of discrete patients as a denominator means that the data are not strictly comparable to those in Table 11.2, but they provide revealing information nevertheless.

An examination of columns (1) to (4) reveals the now familiar story of use increasing with age, except that in this case it is use among the ever-users. The elderly who receive medical care receive more of it than the young. Our focus is, again, on the right-most column (5), which represents relative rates of growth in use among users. Over this 10-year period, utilization of those over 85 increased 19 per cent faster than overall; for those 65 to 84 the relative growth was 7 per cent over average. Even more remarkable was the relative utilization boom for those over 85 in Brandon and Winnipeg, but the tale of two cities is told elsewhere (Evans, Roch, and Pascoe, 1986).

It is, of course, possible that the ratio of users to population in the older age groups fell relative to the ratio for the Manitoba population as a whole. This would mean that on a denominator of population rather than patients the effect shown in column (5) might disappear, or at least be less pronounced. Over this 10-year period, the number of discrete patients increased almost 8 per cent faster than overall population (Roch, Evans, and Pascoe, 1985; Table V-7). But the report does not disaggregate this relative growth by age group. Only an absolute decline in discrete patients per capita among the over-65 group would offset this effect. Furthermore, the fact of dramatic *relative* growth in *per patient* utilization among the elderly is in itself of direct relevance to the issues set out in the Figure 11.2 framework. Among those making contact with the medical care system, growth in utilization per "contact-patient" was most rapid among those over 65, and particularly among those over 85. Was each patient who made contact sicker? If nothing else, the data are suggestive, but also beg more detailed examination.

The general trend, showing a direct and positive relationship between age and *growth* in utilization per capita, is not even restricted to medical and acute/rehabilitation hospital care. Stark (1985, Table 4) shows the proportions of those in each of three elderly age groups (65 to 74, 75 to 84, 85+) in BC who were "in care" within that province's long-term care program over the period 1980 to 1984. Again, not only do the proportions "in care" at each point in time increase with age, but the *growth* in those proportions over the five years was increasing with age group (from 5.2 to 5.6 per cent for those 65 to 74; from 19 to 21 per cent for those 75 to 84; and from 46 to 55 per cent for those 85+). Furthermore, the trend of relative growth in utilization or health care expenditures among the elderly is not an isolated Canadian phenomenon (Waldo and Lazenby, 1984).

At this point, we may be relatively comfortable "retiring" two heretofore debatable points. First, growth in the numbers of elderly will not swamp our health care system, if relative use rates remain stable and we are able to sustain rates of general economic growth at or near our historical experience. But, second, recent history shows those relative use rates to be anything but stable, at least for hospital, medical, and long-term care in selected provinces. This suggests that the debate could productively shift away from demography and toward relationships between morbidity and utilization. The search for evidence would involve a closer examination of the underlying components and determinants of the relatively rapid increases in hospital and medical care among the elderly (Roos, Shapiro, and Havens, 1986).

To return to Figure 11.2, what is required is a determination of whether these utilization data correlate (either positively or negatively) with morbidity trends. Once this is established, the direction of causality may be addressed. The data explored here support a focus on the left-hand side of Figure 11.2; they do not begin to differentiate between the four morbidity utilization combinations associated with increasing relative utilization rates among the elderly.

We are unaware of any Canadian data which would support such differentiation. The American data reported by Palmore (1986), however, do bear on this issue. If these data should characterize Canada as well, and if Palmore's interpretation of falling morbidity among the elderly is correct, then we would be located in the lower-left quadrant of Figure 11.2. But we would still be faced with the question of direction of causality. Is the increased relative utilization among the elderly "curing" morbidity that would otherwise emerge, or is the health care system

Table 11.3 Average fee-adjusted cost (implicit utilization) per discrete patient, by age and region, Manitoba, 1971/72 to 1981/82

	(1)	(2)	(3)	(4)	(5)
			Relative to total		
	1971/72	*1981/82*	*1971/72*	*1981/82*	*(4)/(3)*
WINNIPEG RESIDENTS					
Age group:					
0–14	76.84	91.74	0.616	0.604	0.981
15–64	146.94	167.93	1.179	1.106	0.939
65–84	227.27	304.55	1.823	2.006	1.101
85+	232.59	360.94	1.866	2.378	1.274
BRANDON RESIDENTS					
Age group:					
0–14	64.85	86.8	0.52	0.572	1.099
15–64	128.35	141.65	1.03	0.933	0.906
65–84	205.04	249.65	1.645	1.645	1
85+	195.8	295.11	1.571	1.944	1.238
RURAL RESIDENTS					
Age group:					
0–14	69.28	82.48	0.556	0.543	0.978
15–64	117.99	129.24	0.946	0.851	0.9
65–84	179.78	218	1.442	1.436	0.996
85+	204.84	259.81	1.643	1.712	1.042
MANITOBA RESIDENTS					
Age group:					
0–14	73.06	87.47	0.586	0.576	0.983
15–64	134.66	152.37	1.080	1.004	0.929
65–84	205.78	267.27	1.651	1.761	1.067
85+	219.38	316.98	1.76	2.088	1.187
Total	124.67	151.8	1.000	1.000	1.000

Adapted from: Morris L. Barer, Robert G. Evans, Clyde Hertzman, and Jonathan Lomas. "Aging and Health Care Utilization: New Evidence on Old Fallacies." *Social Science & Medicine* 24 (10) (1987): 851–62.
Original source: Columns (1) and (2), Roch, Evans, and Pascoe (1985), Table V-2, 59.

"responding inappropriately" by servicing more intensively a population that is getting healthier for other reasons?

As noted above, however, Palmore's interpretation rests on the assumption that "period effects" bias the trends in absolute morbidity. His assumption overestimates the health status of the elderly if there has been an overall decline in population health status over the period 1961 to 1981. In any case, health care utilization among the elderly has been rising faster than among the general population, even as their relative health status has been improving.

This leaves the question of how one might identify the quadrant with more certainty, and disentangle the direction of causality. As a start, one might begin to disaggregate the changes in hospital use over time by diagnosis and procedure, in an attempt to develop a picture of the shifts in underlying morbidity. It is clear that lengths of stay have fallen for all age groups. But separation rates are up among those over 65 in British Columbia. What diagnoses and procedures may we identify with this growth, and is there then evidence of other sorts from other sources that could be used to validate or cross-check this diagnosis-specific information (Verbrugge, 1984)? Is the mix of procedures and treatments associated with any given illness shifting over time (Scitovsky, 1985)? Here, we suspect, the HMRI (Hospital Medical Records Institute) databases could prove remarkably rich.

On the medical care side, relatively faster growth in servicing of the elderly may be disaggregated by specialty of provider, by region, by fee item, and (in some provinces) by diagnosis. Again the process is one of homing in on the underlying phenomena – is it shifting patterns of morbidity, or shifting patterns of system- or patient-response to unchanged age-specific morbidity, or ... ? The data reported by Wilensky and Rossiter (1981) may be relevant in this regard. They found that the proportion of office visits *initiated by the physician* increased dramatically with age of the patient, from 23 per cent for those under 13 years of age, to almost 50 per cent for those over 65. While such descriptive data may be interpreted in a number of ways, they are at least consistent with a system response explanation for part of the relative changes in use rates. This still leaves an extensive future research agenda, but such research is essential if we are to replace rhetoric with reason and evidence in planning for our care of the elderly.

THE POLITICAL ECONOMY OF AGING

In preceding sections we separated the impending "crisis" of our aging population into three distinct components – the increasing numbers of elderly, their actual level of health or morbidity, and the intensity of the services delivered to them by the health care system. The increasing numbers do not, by themselves, imply an impending crisis. Furthermore, the health of the elderly, while difficult to estimate precisely because of the paucity of data, certainly does not appear to be getting worse at a rate that suggests a future crisis; in fact, it may actually be improving. However, the relative intensity with which the health care system is treating the elderly *is* rising dramatically. Hence, if there is an impending crisis, it would appear to be this increasing intensity of servicing of the elderly, overlaid on the increasing numbers of elderly.

Of course the crucial question, which cannot be answered without additional data and analysis, is whether this increased intensity of servicing is an appropriate response to levels of morbidity among the elderly. It would be appropriate either if specific types of morbidity for which the health care system has effective interventions were increasing or if existing morbidity from previously untreatable disorders could now be treated effectively. It would be an inappropriate response if it were based either on misguided perceptions of the effectiveness of the extra services (Wershow, 1977), on income aspirations of providers, or on demands from patients unrelated to underlying health care needs. Even without an answer to this question, it is important to note that the focus of the policy debate is shifted significantly when the "crisis" of the elderly is framed in this fashion.

If it were a crisis of numbers – the oncoming elderly hordes – we would have no control over the source of the problem. The system could only respond by increasing efficiency or increasing resources. The degree of flexibility in policy selection would depend on where the health care system sits relative to the technical efficiency frontier. If there is significant room for efficiency gains, then the increasing numbers of elderly could be "absorbed" without additional resources, although a changing mix of resources would be essential. If the system is operating on or near the frontier, then additional resources would be needed. But even then throwing money at the system rather than targeting those resources may move one away from the frontier again.

The effect of a crisis, instead of increasing morbidity among the elderly of every age, is much the same. Sufficient "efficiency slack" could mean that there was room to handle the increasing needs through redeployment of existing resources. In the face of an already "taut" system, more resources would be necessary. But again, it is likely that the efficient resource mix would require fine tuning – tax breaks for home conversions for the disabled, more homemaker services, perhaps more chronic care beds, income supports for the chronically ill or their informal caregivers, and so on [although there appears to be some disagreement in the literature as to the effectiveness of the last of these (Walker, 1986; Doty, 1986)].

Finally, if the crisis is being generated by the intensity with which the health care system and its providers are servicing the existing patterns of morbidity among the elderly, then policies that scrutinize service patterns and allocate resources on the basis of service effectiveness may be the most appropriate response. Recall from Figure 11.2 that increased age-specific utilization rates in the face of unchanged or decreasing morbidity levels represents an inappropriate system response that should only be addressed by policy initiatives that move the system toward a more efficient use of existing resources.

The policy implications of each scenario now become clear. If the only "crisis" is the impending growth in the numbers of elderly (that is, if one assumes the system already deals efficiently with what is there), then additional resources of some variety will be necessary. But normal rates of economic growth should provide the necessary resource base. If, in addition, there is a crisis of increasing morbidity (*ceteris paribus*), selective supplementary resources will be needed. The third "crisis" system response is in fact a crisis of internal resource misallocation, and is amenable to non-resource-increasing solutions.

This helps explain why the policy debate on aging continues to focus on the numbers of aged. The first of the three scenarios is the only one for which there seems to be irrefutable evidence. Evidence on morbidity patterns is, as we suggested above, a key component to the sorting out of the morbidity-utilization linkages. But the necessary evidence does not currently exist. Similarly, debate, evidence, and counter-evidence on the behavioural dynamics of the health care system continue to abound. But the policy uptake of information on system inefficiencies is painstakingly slow.

Why has the policy debate continued to focus on the numbers of elderly, when evidence showing that numbers per se are no crisis has been available for nearly a decade? There is clearly a vested interest on the part of system providers to couch the debate in terms that will imply the need for increased funds for existing services, or to portray the solutions as health care rather than social support, tax, or other system initiatives. The data presented in this paper suggest that care of the elderly has become the new growth sector in the health care system. There is, as yet, little justification for health care responses to what may well be non-health problems or, worse still, health problems generated not by the elderly but by the health care system itself.

What is not as clear is why governments have been (and largely continue to be) complicit with this miscasting of the debate. It may simply be that they have not yet come to recognize the relatively unimportant role that the increasing numbers will play. It is not uncommon for the left hand of government to know nothing of the right hand's activities. Hence, the message from the Economic Council of Canada (Boulet and Grenier, 1978) has apparently not penetrated to the appropriate decision-makers, or perhaps just cannot be heard above the clamour of providers.

At the same time, they have not yet come to recognize the relatively important role that morbidity trends may play. In the United States, morbidity trends can be followed through the National Health Interview Survey (Verburgge, 1984). In Canada, the equivalent (Canada Health Survey) was "killed" for apparently capricious reasons after one outing. It has not been replaced by an ongoing morbidity survey. Rather, a series of uncoordinated initiatives by different government agencies have sprung up in the last few years in response to various consumer and policy needs. While each initiative involves a disability survey component, the sampling strategies and methods of data collection have not been arranged to yield comparable information. Without an ongoing survey to provide periodic age-specific morbidity data, it will be difficult to assess the role of morbidity in observed Canadian utilization trends.

Alternatively, and slightly more optimistically, governments may see the inevitability of the growing numbers of aged as a useful "lever" in prying increased efficiency from the health care system. It may be convenient to perpetuate the idea that the "problem" is not amenable to change, and that the consequence is such a huge increase in resource requirements that the health care system as it is currently structured cannot be sustained. The only "solution," the argument might go, is to make major structural changes in the system to improve its efficiency – a goal long-coveted but little-pursued by governments in the past.

An example of this line of reasoning comes from an unlikely source, the Canadian Medical Association's Task Force on the Allocation of Health Care Resources (1984). This task force surprised many (including the CMA!) with a number of its recommendations. Having stated that "The Task Force does not support the contention that there is underfunding generally in Canada" (Task Force on the Allocation of Health Care Resources, 1984, 116) , it highlights (and agrees with) government's response to the spectre of increasing numbers of elderly: "In responding to the projections many provincial governments emphasized that not only *can* the types of changes in the health care system suggested by the scenarios [of improved efficiency] have a major impact on future utilization and costs, they *must* be introduced to enable the provinces to continue to provide the high quality of health care that currently exists" (Task Force on the Allocation of Health Care Resources, 1984, 29).

If this is the "hidden agenda" of governments, then perhaps we should all put a finger to our lips and quietly say "sshhh" to those (such as the present authors) who would point out that we may not have a crisis of numbers. We can all then stand quietly by and watch as governments gradually lever the system toward more cost-effective modes of health care delivery. However, we may, if we adopt this approach, be putting too much faith in either the ability of the system to respond appropriately or the political will of governments to apply the requisite force to the lever. The danger is that small efficiency-improving battles may be won while the war is lost and more aggregate resources get funnelled into the health care system. Of particular concern is the evidence presented here that with increased attention to the oncoming hordes has come dramatically increased servicing of their forerunners. If this reflects increasing morbidity, then the government policy responses may be misdirected. If it does not, then the magnitude of the system's exploitation of fertile new "grey areas" thus far, is a vivid portrayal of the extent of the policy challenge.

If there is a crisis, it is the disproportionate growth in the use of health care services by the elderly, not the growth in the numbers of potential elderly users. Policy-makers are already being forced to confront head-on the reality of limited resources for the care of the elderly. If these limits are set in the context of controlling expenditures for perceived needs of increasing numbers of elderly, cost-restraint will be greeted by the population at large with howls of protest and accusations of unreasonable rationing. The alternative is limits imposed in the context of increasing per capita utilization of health care services by the elderly, at least some of which is of questionable effectiveness. This has the dual virtues of being politically palatable and, more important, consistent with current evidence.

ACKNOWLEDGMENTS

The financial support of Health and Welfare Canada, through career awards 6610-1231-48 and 6610-1440-48, and of the Ontario Ministry of Health, through career award 01356, are gratefully acknowledged. An earlier version of this paper was presented at the Third Canadian Conference on Health Economics, Winnipeg, 29 May 1986. We are grateful to Tony Culyer and the participants at that conference for helpful comments.

NOTES

1 These studies each adopt age-sex specific utilization rates at a particular point in time. The choice of base year can affect the results of the study, if utilization rates of different age-sex groups are changing at different rates. In Canada, the per capita utilization of the elderly has been rising relative to that of the rest of the population, so that the more recent the study, the larger the measured effects of changes in population structure over time. (If current trends persist, our great-grandchildren may be able to project quite different implications of a changing population structure.) In addition, each study adopts a particular set of assumptions about the evolution of age-sex specific mortality rates. As these have been falling over time, more recent studies tend to project more rapid increases in the proportions of the elderly. Thus the study using the most recent patterns of use and mortality rates, Woods Gordon (1984), projects a greater impact of aging per se than do Boulet and Grenier (1978). But the differences are small – Woods Gordon projects an increase of about 1.4 per cent per year, while Boulet and Grenier's figure is about 0.65 per cent – certainly not of a magnitude that would reverse this conclusion over the foreseeable future.

2 This rectangularization argument is analogous to the earlier in vitro observations of Hayflick and Moorhead (1961) that human fibroblast cells have a limited lifespan in tissue culture. This suggests that some human biological functions have built-in time limits, which would be consistent with the concept of a limited human lifespan.

3 For example, the published annual reports of the Saskatchewan Medical Care Insurance Commission began to provide some age and sex disaggregation of medical care services and payments as early as 1964. But the disaggregation is limited (< 1, 1–4, 5–14, 15–24, 25–44, 45–64, 65–69, 70+); furthermore, for a period of time the < 1 was combined with the 1–4 age group (Saskatchewan Medical Care Insurance Commission, n.d.)

4 Saskatchewan has reported payments per capita since about 1965, but those 70 years of age and over are not disaggregated, and only seven or eight age classes in all are provided (Saskatchewan Medical Care Insurance Commission , n.d.).

5 These data are based on *payments* to physicians in each fiscal year, not payments for services rendered during the fiscal year. While this is an important distinction if one is interested in absolute levels or growth rates, here the focus is on relative rates of growth. Only if one believed that the degree of date of payment versus date of service discrepancy varied with age and/or sex would this be of concern here. We could think of no compelling reason for this to be the case.

REFERENCES

American Council of Life Insurance (1986). "The life and health of older Americans." *Datatrack* 15.

Barer, Morris L., and Robert G. Evans (1987). "Riding north on a south-bound horse? Expenditures, prices, utilization, and incomes in the Canadian health care system." In *Medicare at maturity: Lessons from the past, challenges for the future*, ed. Robert G. Evans and Greg L. Stoddart. Calgary: University of Calgary Press.

– and Patrick Wong Fung (1983). *Fee practice medical service expenditures per capita, and full-time-equivalent physicians in BC, 1981–1982. HMRU Report* 83:1. Vancouver: University of BC, Division of Health Services, Research and Development.

– (1985). *Fee practice medical service expenditures per capita, 1983–1984 and full-time-equivalent physicians in British Columbia, 1979–80 to 1983–84. HMRU Report* 85:1. Vancouver: University of BC, Division of Health Services, Research and Development.

Boulet, J.A., and G. Grenier (1978). *Health expenditures in Canada and the impact of demographic changes on future government health insurance program expenditures.* Discussion Paper no. 123. Ottawa: Economic Council of Canada.

British Columbia Ministry of Health. *Statistics of hospital cases discharged during 19xx.* Victoria: Hospital Programs, Ministry of Health, n.d., various years.

Brody, Jacob A. (1985). "Prospects for an ageing population." *Nature* 315: 463–6.

Denton, Frank T., and Byron G. Spencer (1975). "Health-care costs when the population changes." *Canadian Journal of Economics* 8: 34–48.

Doty, Pamela (1986). "Family care of the elderly: The role of public policy." *Milbank Quarterly* 64: 34–75.

Evans, Robert G., D. Roch, and D. Pascoe (1986). "Defensive reticulation." Paper presented at the Third Canadian Conference on Health Economics, Winnipeg, MB, 29–30 May 1986.

Fries, James F. (1983). "The compression of morbidity." *Milbank Quarterly* 61: 397–419.

– and Lawrence M. Crapo (1981). *Vitality and aging: Implications of the rectangular curve.* San Francisco: W.H. Freeman.

Fuchs, Victor R. (1984). "Though much is taken: Reflections on aging, health, and medical care." *Milbank Quarterly* 62: 143–66.

Ginzberg, Eli (1984). "The elderly are at risk." *Inquiry* 21: 301–2.

Gruenberg, Ernest M. (1977). "The failures of success." *Milbank Quarterly* 55: 3–24.

Grundy, Emily (1984). "Mortality and morbidity among the old." *British Medical Journal* 288: 663–4.

Hayflick, Leonard, and Paul S. Moorhead (1961). "The serial cultivation of human diploid cell strains." *Experimental Cell Research* 25: 585

Hertzman, Clyde, and Michael Hayes (1985). "Will the elderly really bankrupt us with increased health care costs?" *Canadian Journal of Public Health* 76: 373–7.

Kohn, Robert R. (1982). "Causes of death in very old people." *Journal of the American Medical Association* 247: 2793–7.

Lubitz, James, and Ronald Prihoda (1984). "The use and costs of medicare services in the last two years of life." *Health Care Financing Review* 5: 117–31.

MacDonald, N. (1986). "Health care linked to economy: Epp." *Ottawa Citizen*, 20 February 1986.

Manton, Kenneth G. "The linkage of morbidity and mortality: Implications of increasing life expectancy at later ages for health service demand." Paper presented at Economic Council of Canada's Colloquium on Aging with Limited Health Resources, Winnipeg, MB, 5–6 May 1986.

Palmore, Erdman B. (1986). "Trends in the health of the aged," *The Gerontologist* 26: 298–302.

Roch D., R.G. Evans, and D. Pascoe (1985). *Manitoba and Medicare, 1971 to the present.* Winnipeg: Manitoba Health.

Roos, N.P., E. Shapiro, and B. Havens (1986). "Aging with limited resources: What should we really be worried about?" Paper presented at Economic Council of Canada's Meeting on Aging with Limited Resources, Winnipeg, MB, 5–6 May 1986.

Saskatchewan Medical Care Insurance Commission. *Annual Report 19xx.* Regina: MCIC, various years, n.d., 1966 to 1981.

Scitovsky, Anne A. (1984). "The high cost of dying: What do the data show?" *Milbank Quarterly* 62: 591–608.

– (1985). "Changes in the costs of treatment of selected illnesses, 1971–1981." *Medical Care* 23:1345–57.

Schneider, Edward L., and Jacob A. Brody (1983). "Aging, natural death, and the compression of morbidity: Another view." *New England Journal of Medicine* 309: 854–6.

Stark, A.J. (1988). "Seven years of co-ordinated long-term care in one Canadian province: What will be its future?" in *The Future of Health and Health Systems in the Industrialized Societies*. ed. Bui Dang Ha Doan, 140–58. Praeger: New York.

Stone, L.O., and S.A. Fletcher (1980). *A profile of Canada's older population.* Montreal: Institute for Research on Public Policy.

Task Force on the Allocation of Health Care Resources (1984). *Health – A need for redirection.* Ottawa: Canadian Medical Association.

Verbrugge, Lois M. (1984). "Longer life but worsening health? Trends in health and mortality of middle-aged and older persons." *Milbank Quarterly* 62: 475–519.

Waldo, Daniel R., and Helen C. Lazenby (1984). "Demographic characteristics and health care use and expenditures by the aged in the United States: 1977–1984." *Health Care Financing Review* 6: 1–28.

Walker, Allan (1986). "Meeting the needs of Canada's elderly with limited health resources: Some observations based on British experience." Paper Presented at the Economic Council of Canada's Colloquium on Aging with Limited Health Resources, Winnipeg, MB, 5–6 May 1986.

Wershow, Harold J. (1977). "Comment: Reality orientation for gerontologists: Some Thoughts About Senility." *The Gerontologist* 17: 297–302.

Wilensky, Gail R., and Louis F. Rossiter (1981). "The magnitude and determinants of physician-initiated visits in the United States." In *Health, Economics, and Health Economics: Proceedings of the World Congress on Health Economics,* ed. Jacques van der Gaag and Mark Perlman, 173–88. Amsterdam: North-Holland.

Wilkins, Russell, and Owen Adams (1983). *Healthfulness of Life.* Montreal: The Institute for Research on Public Policy.

Woods Gordon Management Consultants (1984). *Investigation of the impact of demographic change on the health care system in Canada – Final Report.* Prepared for the Task Force on the Allocation of Health Care Resources. Toronto: Woods Gordon.

12

Political Wolves and Economic Sheep: The Sustainability of Public Health Insurance in Canada (2005)

ROBERT G. EVANS WITH MARKO VUJICIC

INGENUITY: SUSTAINING OURSELVES IN AN UNFRIENDLY WORLD

In its simplest terms, "sustainability" refers to nothing more than a comparison of rates of change. If a resource stock – a fishery, a forest, an aquifer, a bank account – is being drawn down faster than it is being replenished, then that stock, or better, that pattern of rates, is not indefinitely sustainable. Continuous accumulation is equally unsustainable – the trees do not grow to the sky. Human nature being what it is, however, the latter form of unsustainability typically presents as some form of pollution or accumulating "bad," while the former involves running out of "goods."

While the simple arithmetic of trend projection is beyond dispute, its relevance in any particular situation is not. The time horizon is critical. Economists, in particular, tend to be congenitally suspicious of mechanical projections, for reasons well illustrated in the controversies over the "limits to growth" in the 1970s (Meadows et al., 1972). Computer models of resource use and pollutant generation used in the study commissioned by

Evans, Bob, and Marko Vujicic. "Political Wolves and Economic Sheep: The Sustainability of Public Health Insurance in Canada." In *The Public-Private Mix for Health*, edited by A. Maynard, 117–40. Oxon, UK: Radcliffe Publishing Ltd, 2005. Reprinted with the permission of Nuffeld Trust.

the Club of Rome showed rigorously that the world was approaching, in the relatively near future, absolute limits to economic growth. Worse, even then-current levels of output and income in rich countries were unsustainable in the long run. But critics emphasized that the very definition of a "resource" depends on the tastes and technology of the day, and that the latter, at least, was endogenous.

Natural resources do not "run out," they simply become increasingly expensive to locate and extract. But rising prices create powerful incentives to innovate around the tightening constraint, using an increasingly costly resource more efficiently and finding substitutes. Accordingly, depletion of any one resource need not constrain the whole complex economic system. Successful innovation will be reflected in stable (or falling) prices for the commodity that was previously "running out." Long-run resource price data seem to support this view; the economist Julian Simon, for example, challenged exponents of "limits" models to find any natural resource whose price, over the long run, has risen in real terms.

More recently, however, students of sustainability have developed a broader, "neo-Malthusian" perspective. The environments to which human societies adapt tend to become more hostile over time, sometimes from natural changes but especially from the activities of humans themselves – Malthus' point. On the other hand, human societies have always been ingenious in finding ways to advance their purposes even in the face of this deterioration. Successful societies generate a "supply of ingenuity" sufficient to meet the challenges thrown up by both the external environment, and the consequences of their own (or others') activities.[1] But an "ingenuity gap" can open up, with potentially serious consequences, if the supply fails to keep pace with the demand (Homer-Dixon, 2000).

This concept of ingenuity includes but goes far beyond advances in technical capacity, to include most importantly the institutional frameworks within which economic and social activity take place – and which also serve to mobilize ingenuity itself. Fiduciary currency, double-entry bookkeeping, and limited liability corporations were fundamental advances in ingenuity. Price systems and markets are powerful institutional mechanisms, operating automatically to create incentives for technical innovations – or behavioural changes – to relax the constraints of any particular depleting resource. Pollutants become a problem when no institutional framework motivates a corresponding supply of ingenuity to limit their accumulation. "Pollution markets," in which rights to pollute could be traded at varying prices, have been suggested as such a possible framework.

Markets are only one form of social mechanism for mobilizing ingenuity – or indeed for promoting any other social objective. Public regulation, for example, is more typically used for pollution control. The most appropriate institutional choice will depend on the context, and is ultimately an empirical question. There is no one "right" institutional response to every social challenge.[2] Nor, most importantly, is there any God-given guarantee that the supply of ingenuity itself will be sufficient to deal with emerging social problems. In the idealized world of economic theory, automatic, self-equilibrating mechanisms always take a society to the "best of all possible worlds" (so long as they are not perturbed by misguided government interventions). But in the real world, societies may not find a satisfactory institutional answer to their problems, becoming more or less "failed" societies, with increasing suffering and misery and, in extreme cases, dissolution.[3]

Societies split by deep tribal, ethnic, religious, or economic divisions, and having weak or non-existent unifying institutions, are at particular risk. A deteriorating environment may increase internal conflict, both diverting and dissipating the supply of ingenuity. The incentive to innovate is weakened when there is little security of reward; worse, plundering one's neighbours may become the most profitable application of ingenuity. In the most extreme cases, external challenges to deeply divided societies generate a vicious circle of violent internal conflict, deepening divisions, and further deterioration. Unable to hang together, the population hang each other separately.

These extreme observations heavily underline the critical importance of political ingenuity as an essential basis for other forms of advance, in designing and maintaining institutions for mitigating internal conflict and bridging fissures in the body politic. Absent these, and a whole society can become "unsustainable." Figure 12.1 (Homer-Dixon, Boutwell, Rathjens, 1993) provides a compact representation of the dynamics of violent conflict over renewable resources within rather than between states.

States do not generally collapse in high-income countries with highly developed, more or less democratic, political systems and massive resources of ingenuity.[4] Conflicts are typically political and legal rather than military; dramatic transfers of power and shifts in priorities take place not through coups d'état but by the election of a Margaret Thatcher or a George Bush. Nevertheless, the general framework seems to have very broad applicability. Social advance in the most general sense requires a sufficient supply of appropriate ingenuity to meet the challenges of a deteriorating environment. And that supply is threatened by internal

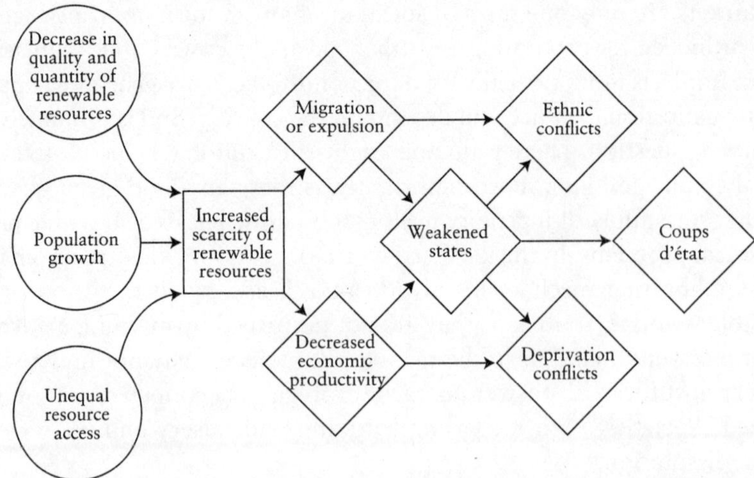

Figure 12.1 Some sources and consequences of renewable resource scarcity
Adapted from: Bob Evans and Marks Vujicic. "Political Wolves and Economic Sheep: The Sustainability of Public Health Insurance in Canada." In *The Public-Private Mix for Health,* edited by A. Maynard, 117–40. Oxon, UK: Radcliffe Publishing Ltd, 2005.
Original source: Homer-Dixon, Boutwell, and Rathjens (1993). Reprinted with permission of the illustrator (Jared Schneidman).

divisions that divert ingenuity from promoting collective advantage into escalating political conflicts among competing interests. In particular, this framework seems to provide an interpretation for the seemingly endless conflicts over health care policy in high-income countries (Evans, 1998). In this chapter we address the recently reignited debate over the "sustainability" of the current system of universal public health insurance in Canada, showing that certain anomalous features of that debate can be readily understood within the neo-Malthusian framework.

FINANCING CANADIAN HEALTH CARE THROUGH FAT AND LEAN

The long-run economic environment in Canada has deteriorated significantly since the early 1980s. Figure 12.2a plots Canadian GDP per capita (adjusted for inflation) since World War II, fitting a log-linear trend to 1947–81 and projecting it to 2002.[5] Figure 12.2b shows the ratio of actual to fitted or projected values over this fifty-five-year period.

The closeness of actual experience to this trend prior to 1982 is remarkable, with a discrepancy greater than 5 per cent in only four years

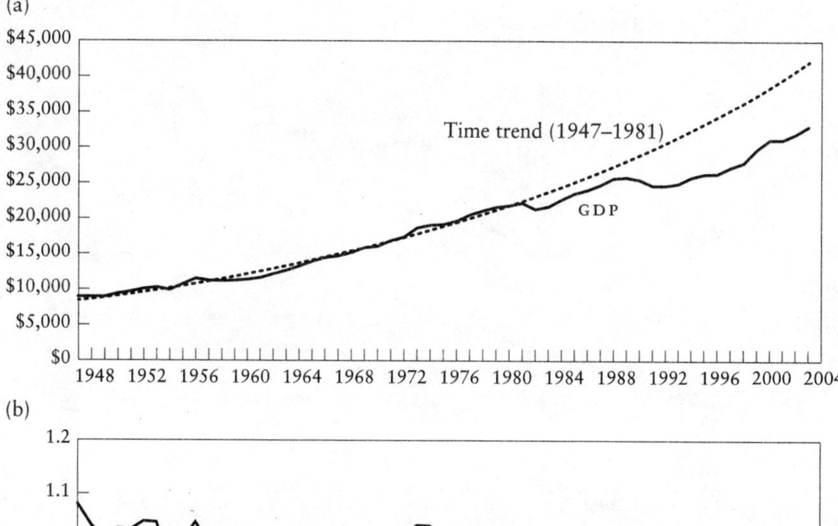

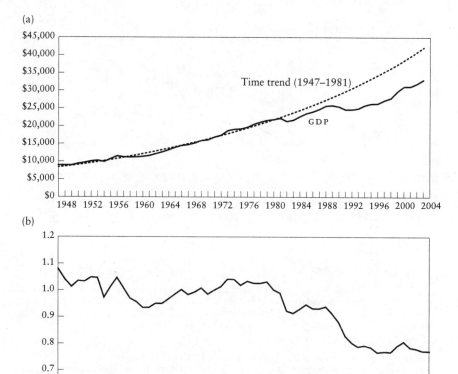

Figure 12.2 (a) Real GDP per capita $1992, 1947–2004; (b) Real GDP per capita over trend $1992, 1947–2004

Adapted from: Bob Evans and Marko Vujicic. "Political Wolves and Economic Sheep: The Sustainability of Public Health Insurance in Canada," In *The Public-Private Mix for Health*, edited by A. Maynard, 117–40, Oxon. UK: Radcliffe Publishing Ltd., 2005.

out of thirty-five, and never reaching 10 per cent. Recessions in 1954 and 1957–61 were followed not only by resumption of growth but also by recovery to the previous path – making up the lost ground.

The recession of 1982 was different. Real income per capita not only dropped sharply, but also failed to recover. Growth resumed in 1983 on a trend line parallel to that of 1947–81, but nearly 10 per cent lower, and after the even more severe recession of 1989–92, was along a still lower path. Canadians are not poorer now than in the past; average GDP per capita in 2002 was higher than ever before, and growing (between recessions) at roughly the same rate as in earlier decades. But that average is

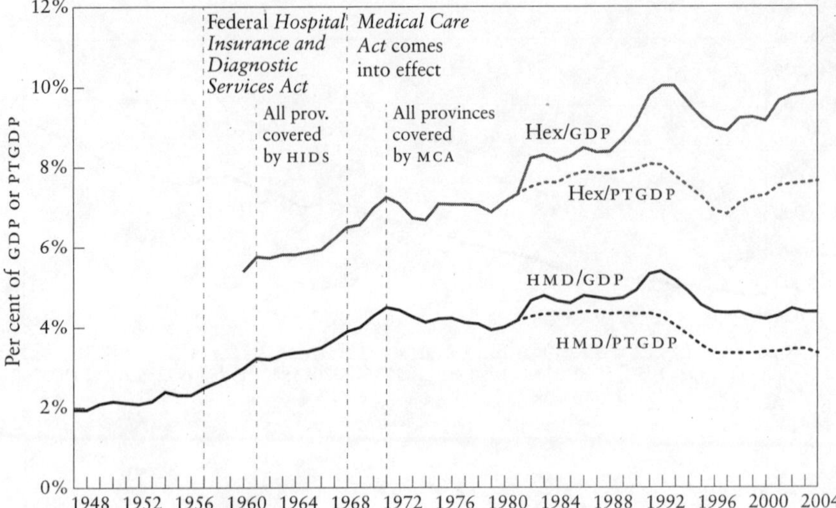

Note: Hex = Total healthcare expenditure; HMD = Hospital and physician services expenditure; PTGDP = Pre-1982 trend GDP

Figure 12.3 Total health, and hospital and physician expenditure, over GDP and trend GDP projected, 1947–2004

Adapted from: Bob Evans and Marko Vujicic, "Political Wolves and Economic Sheep: The Sustainability of Public Health Insurance in Canada," In *The Public-Private Mix for Health,* edited by A. Maynard, 117–40, Oxon. UK: Radcliffe Publishing Ltd., 2005.

now more than 20 per cent below where it would have been if the last two recessions had each been followed by real recoveries. For whatever reasons, the ground lost in recent recessions appears permanently lost.

This implies, among other things, a permanent reduction in the income base from which to meet the demands of an expanding health care system. Figure 12.3 displays the ratio to GDP of Canadian expenditure (public and private) on hospitals and physicians' services from 1947 to 2002, and of total health care expenditure after 1960. It includes hypothetical lines, showing what these ratios would have been, after 1981, if GDP had continued to grow along its pre-1982 trend while health spending had evolved as it did.

The hospital and physician data are of particular relevance because only these sectors are covered by the federal-provincial public insurance programs – Medicare – whose "sustainability" has been challenged. Administered by provincial governments, according to federal standards and with federal financial contributions, these provide universal comprehensive coverage without deductibles or coinsurance. Other components of health care, such as drugs, dentistry, and long-term care, are covered through various mixes of out-of-pocket payment, public and private insurance, and direct public delivery.

Perhaps the most striking feature of Figure 12.3 is the remarkable stability of the share of national income devoted to the public insurance programs. Provinces introduced these in different years, but coverage for hospital care was nationwide by 1961 and for physicians' services by 1971. The latter date was marked by a sharp break in the previous pattern of continuing cost escalation. Universal, comprehensive coverage was not more expensive than the previous fragmented mix of public and private insurance coverage and out-of-pocket payment. Consolidation of expenditures in the hands of a single payer made possible the control of rates of escalation, through a variety of different mechanisms (Evans, 1982). From 1970 until 1981, the share absorbed by the Medicare services fluctuated in a narrow band between about 4 and 4.25 per cent of GDP.

Nor was the Canadian experience unique. By the 1970s public universal and comprehensive health service or health insurance systems were in place in all the high-income countries of the OECD. All developed, at some time during the 1970s or early 1980s, more or less effective mechanisms of cost control (Evans, 2002). The pattern is sufficiently consistent that White (1995) refers to it as "the international standard." The one exception, on both counts, is the US, and even there the federal Medicare program for those 65 and older has been more successful than private insurers in controlling hospital and medical costs over the long term (Boccuti and Moon, 2003). Single-payer public financing creates an institutional environment, encouraging the supply of ingenuity to contain costs. These are higher in multi-source funding systems where ingenuity is diverted into shifting costs onto someone else (Evans, 1990).

The early 1980s increase in the Canadian ratio was largely a denominator effect. Health spending stayed on its trend path through the recession, but national income fell. Since the previous income trend was never regained, the share of income spent on hospitals and physicians remained permanently higher. Had there been no recession, or a full recovery, the hospital and medical spending share would have remained in the neighbourhood of 4.25 to 4.33 per cent for another decade.

The ratio began to follow the same pattern in the next recession, rising sharply to 1992 but again maintaining a constant share of the pre-1982 GDP trend. This time, however, the fiscal exigencies faced by both provincial and federal governments forced a quite dramatic response. Public expenditures were frozen or cut across the board after 1992, including, for the first time, actual cuts in hospital spending. By 1997, hospitals and physicians' services were absorbing the same share of GDP as they had in 1971; if it were not for the persistent effects of the two recessions, that share would have been back to early 1960s levels.

The pattern for total health care spending is roughly similar, but with a long-term upward trend. Shares of national income devoted to total health care expenditure in 1971, 1982, 1992, and 2002 were 7.2, 8.1, 10.0, and 9.9 per cent respectively, while hospitals and physicians' services accounted for 4.5, 4.6, 5.3, and 4.3 per cent. The year-to-year movements are strongly influenced by the general business cycle, but the 30-year trend indicates that cost containment has been much more successful in the Medicare programs than in the other health care sectors.

Expenditures on prescription drugs, in particular, which are outside Medicare and reimbursed through a combination of public and private insurance and out-of-pocket payment, have been growing very rapidly over the past two decades, more than tripling their share of national income since 1980 (Figure 12.4). This pattern of rapid growth parallels the experience of the whole Canadian health care system prior to 1971 (and the American experience prior to 1992 and the "managed-care revolution"), again illustrating the link between fragmented funding sources and rapid cost escalation.[6]

ADAPTING TO ADVERSITY: PUBLIC SUCCESS, PRIVATE FAILURE

The deterioration of the Canadian economic environment after 1982 posed a challenge for the financing of health care. That challenge was met initially by allocating a larger share of national income to the health care system. The still larger shock of the early 1990s, however, triggered unprecedented reductions in public funding. Controversy has focused, then and subsequently, on the extent to which this mobilized ingenuity to provide care more efficiently and effectively, or whether it simply reduced the level and standard of care provided and left real needs unmet.

We will bypass this question here, except to note that, however one interprets their impact on the health of Canadians, reductions in expenditure must necessarily correspond, as a matter of elementary accounting, to a reduction in total payments to those working in or otherwise supplying resources to the health care system. There is an inevitable element of conflict of interest between those who are paid for providing

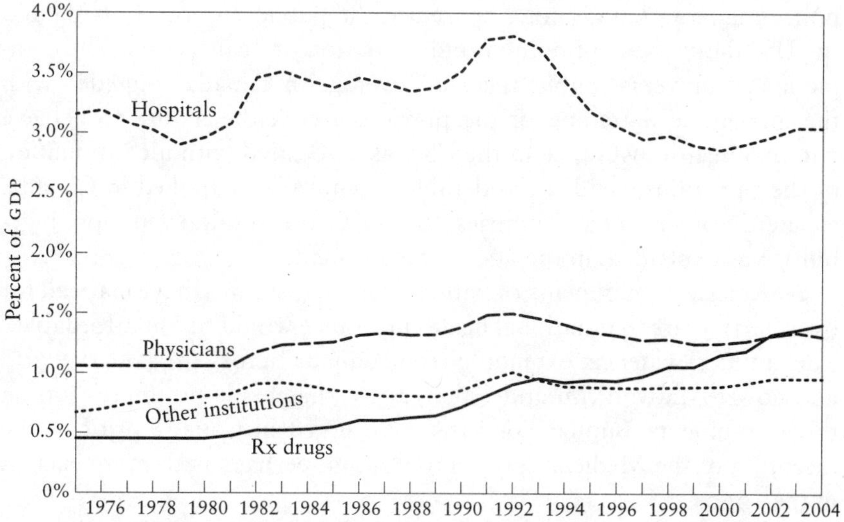

Figure 12.4 Health expenditures: selected components as a percentage of GDP, 1975–2004

Adapted from: Bob Evans and Marko Vujicic. "Political Wolves and Economic Sheep: The Sustainability of Public Health Insurance in Canada," In *The Public-Private Mix for Health,* edited by A. Maynard, 117–40, Oxon. UK: Radcliffe Publishing Ltd., 2005.

care and those who pay for it. Mobilizing ingenuity to improve efficiency, if it lowers total expenditure, threatens the interests of the former even as it benefits the latter. The deterioration of the overall economic environment has tended to widen this division, intensifying the political and rhetorical conflict and clouding efforts to establish – and communicate – what actually happened.

For better or worse, however, the Canadian public insurance programs did (have to) adapt to the general fiscal circumstances after 1992. Coincidentally, and through different mechanisms, so did US health care. The projection by the US Congressional Budget Office (1992) that by 2000 the US would be spending 18 per cent of its GDP on health care was spectacularly falsified; that percentage flattened in 1992 and remained between 13 and 14 per cent until 2001 (Levit et al., 2003). As with the "limits to growth" modelling of the 1970s, linear projections that fail to take account of the adaptability of complex systems are likely to be misleading. The trick is to create the institutional environments that most effectively mobilize the ingenuity necessary to support that adaptation.

Indeed, Canada's experience at the beginning of the 1970s makes the same point. At the end of the 1960s there was growing concern among policy-makers (though not, apparently, the public) in both Canada and the US, about the continuing rapid escalation of health costs. The completion of universal public medical coverage in Canada coincided with the immediate flattening of the previous trend; the failure to achieve national health insurance in the US was associated with a continuation of their previous trend. Considerable ingenuity was applied in Canada, as later in other OECD countries, to achieve this result; even more ingenuity was expended, in the US, in frustrating it.

Yet American opponents of national health insurance have claimed for over thirty years that national health insurance would be "unaffordable." The counter-evidence, extending from Canada across the OECD world and now to Taiwan (Lu and Hsiao, 2003), has made no impression on these arguments. Similar concerns were urged in Canada prior to the inception of the Medicare programs, though perhaps with more excuse, in the 1960s.

Their resurgence in recent years, however, presents us with an obvious anomaly. Why would those alleging the financial unsustainability of Canadian health care focus on the public insurance programs, on Medicare? Why would any rational person, concerned about cost escalation, advocate transferring costs from government budgets back onto patients, either directly or through increased private insurance contributions? On all the available evidence, accumulated across nations and decades, such a shift would almost certainly lead to more rapid escalation.

As the Yale political scientist Ted Marmor reminds us, "Nothing that is regular is stupid." If apparently intelligent and well-informed people (in Canada and the US) continue, in the face of the evidence, to revive the argument that universal public health insurance is "unsustainable" and to advocate diversifying funding sources to increase private payments, then presumably they are either looking at different evidence, or have objectives other than cost control.

THE PUBLIC FISC: STILL AFLOAT AFTER HEAVY WEATHER

One explanation might be that for governments, and especially their treasurers, the GDP or its provincial equivalent is something of an abstraction. What is "real" (subject to the creativity of the public accountants) is the government's own fiscal situation.

GDP patterns certainly affect that situation, insofar as they translate into public sector revenues and expenditures. The 1982 recession ushered

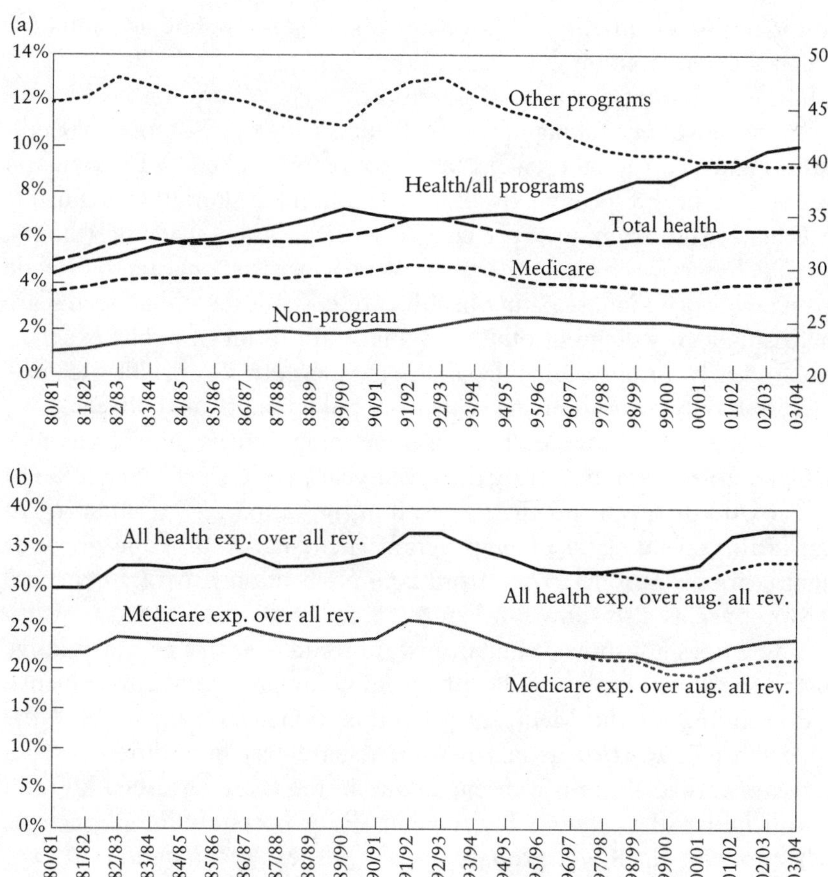

Figure 12.5 (a) Provincial government expenditure as a percentage of GDP, 1980/81 to 2003/04; (b) All provincial government expenditure on Medicare and on all health programs as a share of total revenue with and without tax cuts, 1980/81 to 2003/04

Adapted from: Bob Evans and Marko Vujicic. "Political Wolves and Economic Sheep: The Sustainability of Public Health Insurance in Canada," In *The Public-Private Mix for Health,* edited by A. Maynard, 117–40, Oxon. UK: Radcliffe Publishing Ltd., 2005.

in a decade of continuing public sector deficits and growing debt and debt charges; the 1989–91 recession accelerated this fiscal deterioration and raised the spectre of actual bankruptcy for some provincial governments. The harsh public expenditure cuts of the 1992–97 period, combined with subsequent more rapid economic growth, reversed this situation, generating substantial surpluses at the federal level and a falling aggregate public debt. But important as national income trends may be for the fiscal situation of governments, it is the public accounts for which they are accountable.

In those accounts, provincial government expenditures on health care programs have been taking up a rapidly increasing share of total expenditures (Figure 12.5a, right scale).[7] In the six years between FY1995/96 and FY2001/02, health spending by all provincial (and territorial) governments in Canada rose from 34.8 per cent of total program spending (that is, net of debt service charges) to 41.1 per cent. This trend appears to provide strong evidence that escalating health care costs in the public sector are increasingly crowding out other and important forms of public expenditure – clearly an unsustainable situation. Allegedly, this problem can be addressed only by transferring costs from public to private budgets.

Equally clearly, however, there is something unusual about this particular six-year period. During the seven-year period from FY1988/89 to FY1995/96 there was no change at all in the ratio of aggregate provincial health spending to other program spending. And in the previous eight years the ratio had risen from 29.6 per cent only to 34.7 per cent.

Moreover, as also shown in Figure 12.5a, aggregate provincial health spending does not show a similar upward trend over this period, relative to national GDP. Both total health spending by provincial governments, and spending on the Medicare programs alone, took up roughly the same share in 2001/02 as in 1995/96, a share very little different from 20 years earlier. There is a recent uptick in the share absorbed by total provincial health spending, but none at all for hospitals and physicians. (This uptick, which will probably persist in next year's data, raises the question of whether the future will be different from the past, whether the public system has just now become unsustainable. We will try to address this more speculative question below, noting here only that such claims have a long history.)

It follows that provinces must have been cutting back on their non-health spending, and indeed they were. Provincial government spending on other programs took up a roughly constant share of national income from 1980/81 to 1995/96, between 11 and 12 per cent. It has since fallen steadily, to just over 9 per cent in 2001/02. Yet this quite dramatic reduction was not in fact driven by an "unsustainable" surge in health spending.

There could still be "crowding out," if cuts to aggregate spending were being forced by a declining revenue base while political considerations made it difficult or impossible to impose these cuts on health. Other programs might have had to bear more severe cuts because of the inflexibility of the health care as presently structured. But this would imply that health spending was rising as a share of provincial revenues as well as of program expenditures. This is not so (Figure 12.5b).

Between 1995/96 and 2001/02, when provincial government health spending was rapidly increasing its share of program expenditures, its share of revenues was virtually flat. Only in the last year do we see the same uptick as in Figure 12.5a. Taking the longer view, health spending now takes up roughly the same share of provincial revenue as it did 20 years earlier.

Moreover, several provincial governments have been taking deliberate steps to reduce that revenue. Starting in 1996/97, they began to introduce a variety of fiscal measures, including, in particular, reductions in their rates of personal and corporate income taxation. By 2003/04, the resulting foregone revenue is estimated at about $23.1 billion annually – $24.9 billion in income tax cuts, less $1.8 billion from increases in other tax rates and fees. This reduction represents nearly 15 per cent of aggregate provincial government own-source revenues (excluding federal transfers). Had provincial governments not chosen to use the reviving economy as an opportunity to cut tax rates, the share of provincial revenues devoted to the Medicare programs would now be lower than it was in 1995/96 (Figure 12.5b, augmented all revenues) – the year in which provincial health spending began to take a rapidly increasing share of total program spending. In fact, that ratio would have been lower, in the last three years, than in any other year since 1980/81.

Even apart from the impact of these tax cuts, there is no evidence that health spending is placing an increasing strain, over the long term, on the provincial revenue base. The recessions at the beginning and end of the 1980s certainly reduced that base, and each resulted in, among other things, a jump in the proportion of total revenues going to health care. Since the economic ground lost in those recessions was never really recovered, that ratio stayed up through the 1980s. In the 1990s, (politically difficult) cuts and rationalizations in the Medicare sector brought the ratio back to its long-term level, consistent with the now lower path of economic growth.

But if health spending has been taking a relatively stable share of revenue while increasing its share of program spending, then the ratio of revenue to expenditure must have been rising. And it has been, for nearly a decade (Figure 12.6a). Provinces reacted to the recession of the early 1980s by running persistent deficits; the 1989–91 recession exacerbated their weak fiscal positions.[8] By 1992/93 aggregate revenues were nearly 20 per cent below expenditures (including debt service). This was unsustainable, and serious expenditure cutting began in both the health and non-health sectors. Figure 12.5a shows the corresponding downturn in both spending components, relative to GDP.

But the persistent deficits that were a hangover from the 1980s have now been eliminated (Figure 12.6a). The provincial total is inflated in 2000/01 by a spike in resource revenues, particularly in Alberta; the aggregate ratio drops back to balance in the next year. But Figure 12.6a also shows what provincial revenues would have been, in the absence of the income tax cuts and other fiscal changes that began in 1996/97. Provincial governments would, in aggregate, have reached fiscal balance five years ago, and several would now be rolling up large surpluses.

(And others would not. The unequal distribution of economic development and particularly of resource revenues results in very large disparities between so-called "have" and "have-not" provinces. While wealthier provinces have been cutting their taxes and driving the aggregate data, fiscally weaker provinces are still struggling to keep their heads above water. They are also under political pressure to compete in the "tax cut" game. These disparities generate severe political strains within the federation.)

FEDERAL-PROVINCIAL FISCAL RELATIONS – OF COURSE

There is another dimension to the story. The federal government transfers money to the provinces, both as "tax room" – tax rate reductions to permit provinces to raise their rates – and as block grants of cash, to help provinces support health, education, and social welfare programs. These transfers are a source of continuing friction. Without delving into the fascinating arcana of federal-provincial fiscal relations, the critical point is that after a number of years of chipping away at the cash grants, the federal government introduced a major restructuring, effective 1996/97, that consolidated several of them into one item – the Canadian Health and Social Transfer (CHST) – but significantly reduced the overall amount (Figure 12.7b).

Between 1995/96 and 1997/98, federal cash transfers fell by about $5 billion, or nearly 20 per cent, leaving a substantial hole in provincial budgets. Critics argued, with some justification, that the federal government was fighting its own deficit "on the backs of the provinces." That federal battle was outstandingly successful: the Government of Canada has been recording surpluses ever since 1997/98 and, barring major recession, seems likely to do so for the indefinite future.

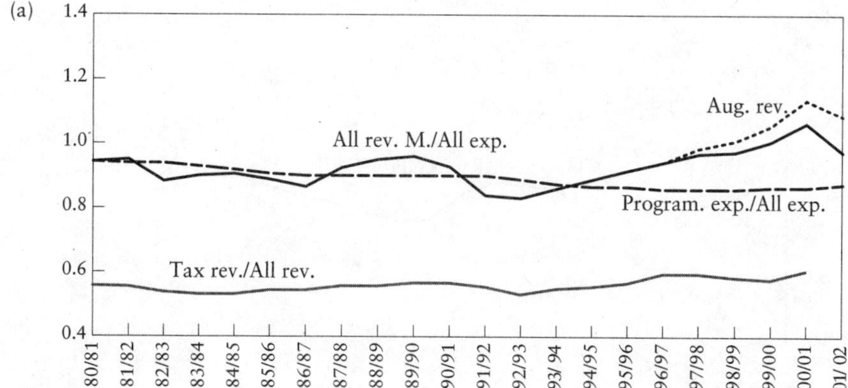

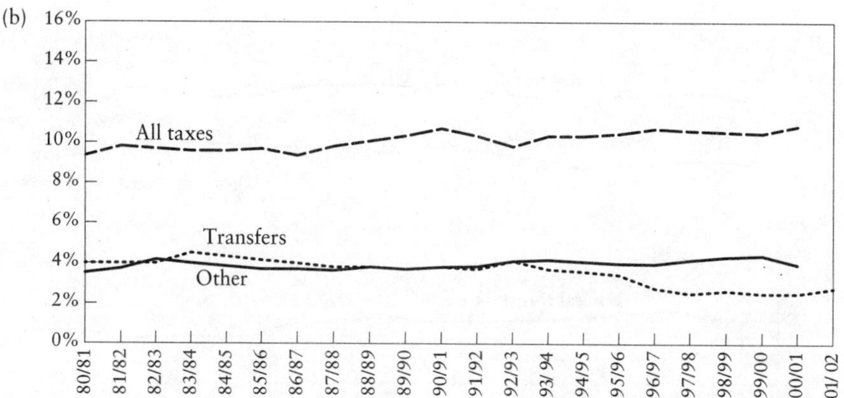

Figure 12.6 (a) Ratios; (b) Provincial government revenue as a percentage of GDP
Adapted from: Bob Evans and Marko Vujicic. "Political Wolves and Economic Sheep: The Sustainability of Public Health Insurance in Canada," In *The Public-Private Mix for Health*, edited by A. Maynard, 117–40, Oxon. UK: Radcliffe Publishing Ltd., 2005.

Rather than restoring the cash grants to their pre-CHST rate, the federal government began in 1998/99 to cut its own income tax rates. By 2003/04 the annual federal revenue foregone is estimated to be about equal to the total of the provincial government cuts in that year – $24 billion – and is budgeted to rise to $29.6 billion in 2004/05. The total cumulative revenue foregone through these federal tax cuts is estimated by the Department of Finance to reach $101.5 billion by that year; in comparison, total spending on health care in Canada in 2002 is estimated at $112.2 billion, with public sector spending accounting for $79.5 billion.

(a)

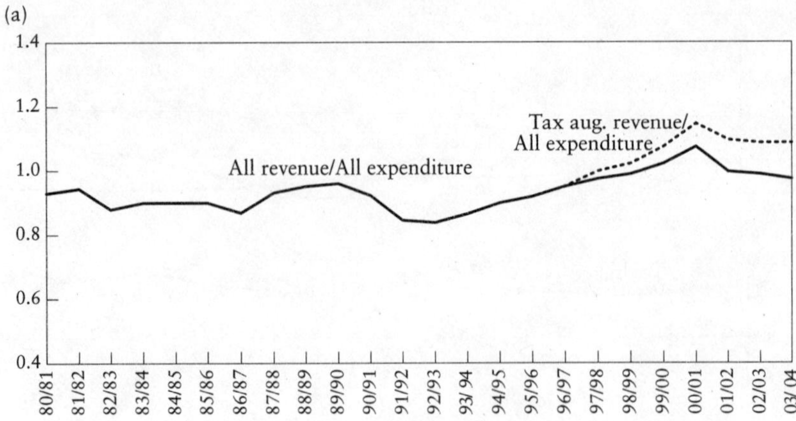

(b)

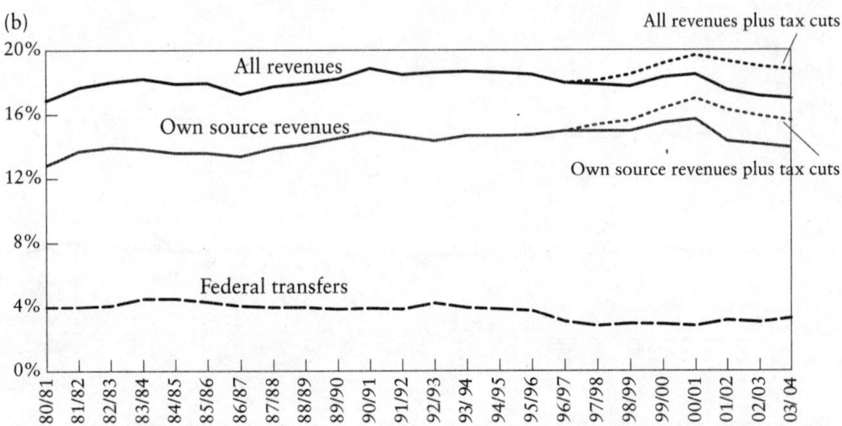

Figure 12.7 (a) Provincial governments, total revenues over total expenditures, 1980/81 to 2003/04; (b) Provincial government revenue, total and components as a percentage of GDP, 1980/81 to 2003/04

Adapted from: Bob Evans and Marko Vujicic. "Political Wolves and Economic Sheep: The Sustainability of Public Health Insurance in Canada," in *The Public-Private Mix for Health,* edited by A. Maynard, 117–40. Oxon, UK: Radcliffe Publishing Ltd., 2005.

It is hardly surprising that provincial governments have demanded restoration of the cash transfers unilaterally reduced by the federal CHST.[9] A substantial amount of new federal money has since begun to flow, but as Figure 12.7b shows, this has not restored the previous relationship of federal transfers to GDP. On the other hand, the federal government seems to have taken the (also understandable) view that there was no benefit to either the health care system or its own political fortunes from transferring more revenues to provincial governments whose principal priority was cutting their own income tax rates. The government of Ontario, in particular (ideologically at odds with the federal government during this period), will by 2003/04 have cut a cumulative total of $61.9 billion out of its own revenue base.

Amid the continuing intergovernmental wrangling, one fact is prominent. Between 1996/97 and 2003/04 the federal and provincial governments have between them cut personal and corporate income tax rates so as to remove $170.8 billion from public sector revenues. In 2003/04 the annual public revenue foregone will amount to an estimated $48.9 billion – over 60 per cent of current public sector expenditure on health care.

In summary, the Canadian federal and provincial governments have, over the past decade, succeeded in restoring fiscal positions undermined by unfavourable developments in the general economy. But this process has had two distinct phases. Prior to 1996/97, provincial health and non-health expenditures were both being reduced, relative to GDP. In the more recent period, there was a resumption of the flow of public funds into health care, more or less in proportion to the rise in GDP, while the shrinkage of non-health programs has continued. Hence the rise, after 1996/97, in the share of health in provincial program spending.

But the cuts to non-health programs in the more recent period were no longer being driven by the need to balance provincial budgets. That job, difficult and important, had been done. The tax cuts after 1996/97 were a fiscal choice by right-wing governments in several of the larger provinces, a choice that then necessitated continuing expenditure cuts to maintain the fiscal balance previously achieved. Presumably, finding it politically more difficult to make further cuts in the health care sector, these governments made deeper cuts to non-health programs. One could argue that in this way health care was in fact now "crowding out" other programs. But the source of the pressure was no longer fiscal exigency generated by poor overall economic performance, rather it was the political decision to take advantage of an improved fiscal situation to cut tax rates rather than to maintain spending on public programs (or to pay down debt).

Governments are elected to make choices, fiscal and otherwise, and the provincial governments making these choices have been duly and democratically elected. But it would be erroneous, and misleading, to claim that an unsustainably expensive public health care system has been the source of the pressure on other public programs. The argument that the public health programs are economically "unsustainable" has no more basis in the public accounts than it has in the national accounts.

WHAT'S THE REAL ISSUE? THE INEGALITARIAN AGENDA

So the anomaly remains. These data are perfectly well-known in provincial and federal finance ministries; indeed these ministries are their source. They are not known to most of the public; that raises a whole other set of issues as to the role of the media during this period. (The awareness of politicians is always an open question.) So what are the real motives behind the claims of unsustainability?

An important clue lies in the pattern of some of the recent provincial tax changes. Figure 12.8 is calculated from the federal and provincial income tax returns for single residents of Ontario and British Columbia. Between 1997 and 2002, individuals in both provinces with annual taxable incomes of $15,000 and $25,000 (and no other complications) had their tax liabilities reduced by about 4 per cent, with roughly equal reductions in federal and provincial taxes. But the percentage reductions increase steadily with annual income, reaching nearly 9 per cent (Ontario) and 10 per cent (BC) at $100,000. Beyond this point the federal reductions decline as a share of income, but the provincial reductions continue to increase. In Ontario, these increases are quite small, and do not offset the federal decline. But in British Columbia they do, reaching nearly 8 per cent for a taxable income of $1,000,000. At that level, after-tax income would be larger in 2002 by $104,097 ($78,754 from the province, and $25,342 from the federal government). After-tax income at the $15,000 level in British Columbia would rise by $645 ($327 provincial, $317 federal). The comparable provincial amounts for Ontario are $49,293 and $255.

Rate changes immediately introduced by the British Columbia government newly elected in mid-2001 account for most of the increased inequality of after-tax incomes. Later changes in other taxes reinforced this effect.[10] British Columbia, like the neighbouring province of Alberta, levies compulsory health insurance "premiums" (unrelated to risk status). Public coverage is not, however, conditional upon payment; the "premiums" are actually a form of poll tax. In May 2002 they were raised by 50 per cent, or $216 for a single individual.[11] Figure 12.8 shows this premium increase as a proportion of taxable income; it

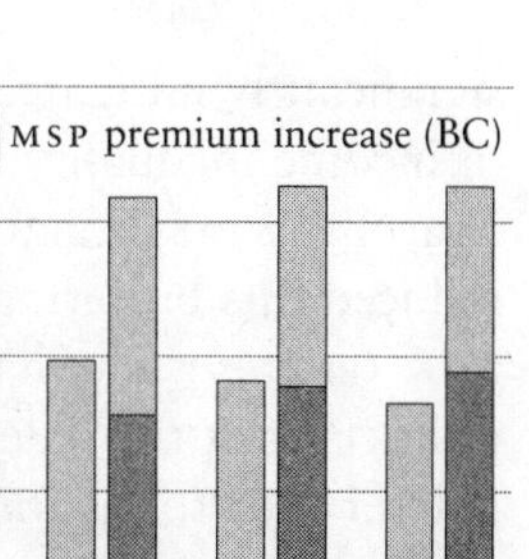
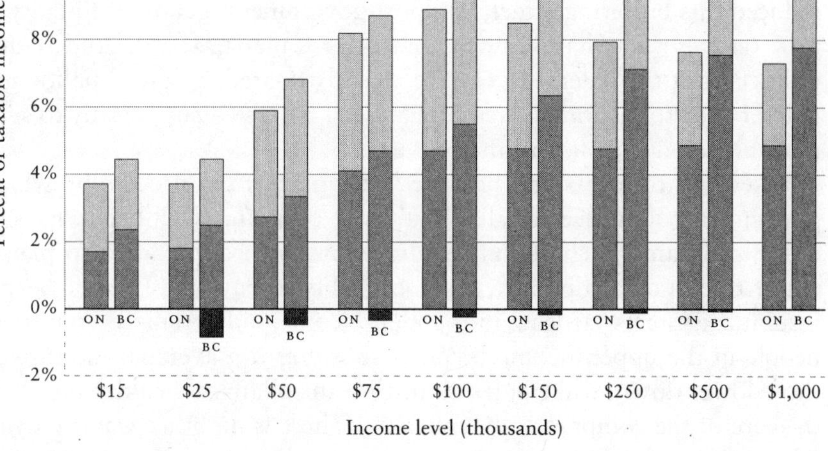

Figure 12.8 Income tax reductions in Ontario and British Columbia, 1997–2002, as a percentage of taxable income, by income level.

Adapted from: Bob Evans and Marko Vujicic. "Political Wolves and Economic Sheep: The Sustainability of Public Health Insurance in Canada," in *The Public-Private Mix for Health*, edited by A. Maynard, 117–40. Oxon, UK: Radcliffe Publishing Ltd., 2005.

offsets over one-third of the income tax cut at $25,000 per year, 4 per cent at $100,000, and a quarter of a per cent at one million.

The Government of Alberta also increased its health care premiums in 2001, by about one-third, but its approach to income taxation was even simpler. On 1 January 2001, Alberta introduced a provincial "flat tax" of 11 per cent of taxable income above a basic exemption level, substituting for the previous percentage of the (relatively progressive) federal liability. This approach twists the whole tax schedule above the basic exemption level to decrease the relative burden on the wealthy and increase it on middle incomes.

In all three provinces, the higher the income, the greater the percentage gain from income tax reductions. In addition, the cuts to public expenditures imposed in these provinces, along with a variety of additional fees for public services, were significantly regressive in their impact.

One has to conclude that these provincial governments were pursuing, for whatever motive, an agenda of regressive income redistribution.[12] Nor are they alone. Historically, Canadian governments have significantly mitigated, through taxes and financial transfers, the degree of income inequality that is generated in the marketplace (Wolfson and Murphy, 1998). Changes since the mid-1990s, however, appear to have reduced this buffering effect, and post-government income inequality is now on the rise (Sharpe, 2003; Statistics Canada, 2003). And senior politicians at the federal level have recently floated, as a trial balloon, a federal "health insurance premium" – read poll tax – supposedly to support increased transfers to the provinces.

Taxes and transfers are, however, only part of the process by which governments influence the distribution of economic well-being. Expenditure programs, such as public education and health care, also play a major role in detaching benefits from ability to pay. In all public health insurance systems (at least in the high-income, industrialized countries) people in the upper-income brackets subsidize (on average) the care of those lower down, while at the same time the relatively healthy subsidize the care of the comparatively unhealthy. There is no other way to maintain a modern health care system – at least none is known.

But considerable variation occurs among national systems in the nature and extent of this subsidization. The Canadian Medicare programs, covering hospital and physicians' services, are almost entirely financed from general taxation and provide care "on equal terms and conditions" to the whole resident population. In the US, in sharp contrast, people of different incomes receive care on very different "terms and conditions," depending on their employment status, age, and ability to pay. Most European systems make care available on more or less equal terms and conditions to the whole population, but several (unlike Canada) permit providers within the public system to sell, to those willing and able to pay, more timely access to a perceived higher standard of care. Purchasing these advantages for themselves, the better-off are not required to contribute to a similar standard for the rest of the population – that is the whole point of "two-tier" care.

Moreover, the distribution of the cost of health care across the population varies considerably among national systems (Wagstaff et al., 1999; van Doorslaer et al., 1999). Financing raised through direct taxation tends to distribute the burden more or less in proportion to income, indirect taxation is more regressive, and social insurance programs can be either more or less proportional (France) or quite steeply regressive (Germany, the Netherlands), depending on their structure. But private payment, whether through private insurance or directly out of pocket, is by far the most regressive. Low-, middle-, high-, and very high-income people pay the same amounts for the same services, but these payments represent very different shares of their respective incomes.

Since health is correlated with wealth, on average lower-income people would pay an even larger share of their incomes for health care through private payment – if they were to get equal service for equal need. But of course they do not. Higher-income people spend more on health care through private payments, and get more services, but spend a much smaller proportion of their incomes in this way. This pattern is similar for both private insurance and self-payment, because private insurers in a competitive market must set their premiums according to the estimated risk of the insured. For equivalent coverage, healthier people will pay less, regardless of their incomes, and sicker people will pay more.

Thus the "public-private" debate about financing sources is, in all modern health care systems, fundamentally a debate about *Who Pays?* and *Who Gets?* The Canadian universal tax-financed system requires higher-income people to contribute more to supporting the health care system, without offering them preferred access or a higher standard of care (Mustard, Shanahan, and Derksen, 1998; Mustard et al., 1998). Any shift towards proportionately more private financing, through user charges with or without private insurance, would reduce the relative burden on people with higher incomes. Insofar as private payments also limit access by people with lower incomes, they also open better access for those willing/able to pay. Relative to universal, fully tax-financed public insurance, an expansion of private payment would thus enable the wealthy to pay less (in charges, private premiums, and taxes) and get more (in volume, quality, and/or timeliness). The converse would be true for those with lower incomes. This conflict of economic interest is real, unavoidable, and permanent in all systems, which is why the "public-private" debate is never resolved (and why it is typically so occluded with "econofog").

Cutting across the income spectrum, there is a third and equally deeply entrenched conflict feeding the endless "public-private" financing debate – *Who Gets Paid?* and how much.

Private insurance systems, for example, incur heavy administrative costs to conduct underwriting and set premiums, to market policies, and to adjudicate and pay individual claims, as well as to reward investors and (sometimes spectacularly) senior executives. These overhead costs absorb between 15 and 20 per cent of the revenues of Canadian private insurers. In addition, there are substantial costs imposed on providers of care and beneficiaries or their representatives, in negotiating with insurers and trying to ensure that claims are in fact paid.

In the US, the only country with significant private coverage, these overheads were recently estimated (Woolhandler, Campbell, and Himmelstein, 2003) at 31 per cent of total health care expenditure in 1999. In a universal public system, most of these costs vanish; the comparable estimate for Canada was 16.7 per cent, which includes extensive private insurance for dentistry and drugs. The excess administrative costs in the US were estimated at $209 billion, or 17.1 per cent of total US health expenditures. But all these billions represent income for insurers, benefits managers, and administrative and financial staff in hospitals and clinics. In a universal public insurance system, most of these jobs would not exist.

Payments to care providers raise exactly the same issue. Insofar as public single-payer systems have been relatively more effective in controlling overall costs of health care, they have, to the same extent, controlled the incomes of providers. Hence, the intense opposition to such coverage in North America from economically motivated providers, most notably the for-profit pharmaceutical industry. Again, the conflict of interest is real and fundamental; for a firm whose products have high fixed costs of development but are sold at prices far above variable cost, any reduction in prices comes straight off the bottom line.

Not all providers thrive in a private funding system. Health and wealth are correlated; a high proportion of costs are generated by a relatively small proportion of people with above-average morbidity and below-average incomes. The income base of the provider community as a whole depends on a high proportion of public funding. Even in the "private" US, about 60 per cent of health care expenditure comes directly or indirectly from public funds (Woolhandler and Himmelstein, 2002). But a multi-source financing system, with supplementary private financing and public sources that are indirect and difficult to control, provides the best income opportunities for providers – i.e. higher health care expenditures.

POLITICAL WOLVES MASQUERADING AS ECONOMIC SHEEP

These embedded conflicts of economic interest over *Who Pays?*, *Who Gets?*, and *Who Gets Paid?* play roles analogous to the tribal, ethnic, or religious divisions in the framework of Figure 12.1. They are always present, but tend to flare up into more intense and self-reinforcing political conflict under economic stress. Such conflicts may pose a real threat to the sustainability of Canada's Medicare. But it is a threat from private interests pursuing a redistributive agenda, rather than from expenditures outrunning public resources.

The relative deterioration of the economic environment in Canada since 1981 with its particularly powerful impact on the public fiscal situation, has resulted (among many other things) in a number of relatively successful efforts to "do more with less."[13] On the other hand, a number of policy proposals for structural "reform" represent, in reality, the application of ingenuity to redistribute burdens and benefits – to eat the other fellow's lunch. Efforts to promote – and to expose and combat – such "reforms" distract from the very real needs for improved system management and adaptation to a less favourable environment.[14]

The wealthy in the modern world may be increasingly reluctant to accept a single standard of care for the whole population, with no preference for themselves, while contributing a relatively larger share of the cost. Private financing quite genuinely offers them "more, for less," while offering the rest of population "less, for more." It may lead to a less efficient and more expensive system overall, through increased overhead costs, weaker control over prices, and reduced potential for managing care patterns, while a diversion of care from those with greatest need to those with greatest resources will result in a less effective distribution of services. But the wealthy still come out ahead.

It also appears that, in several countries, including Canada (and for reasons well beyond the scope of this chapter), political systems have become increasingly sensitive to the priorities of the wealthy. Claims that Canada's Medicare is economically or fiscally unsustainable represent part of a broader propaganda campaign to advance those priorities, "softening up" a generally skeptical and unsympathetic public to accept that the current form of public health insurance (which most Canadians still strongly prefer) is simply impossible to maintain. The agenda is being advanced by right-wing governments in the larger provinces, with sympathetic coverage from the country's dominant newspaper chain. In these circumstances, the political sustainability of the public system is very much an open question. But the claims of economic unsustainability appear from the data to be themselves wholly unsustainable.

THAT WAS THEN, THIS IS NOW?

Or are they? Unsustainability is a claim about the future, not the past, and that claim is buttressed by current fiscal projections showing public health care spending growing much faster than provincial revenues. As noted above, the most recent data available at the time of writing do show a resumption of more rapid rates of cost escalation. Is there now a real economic wolf at the door?

The future is an uncertain place, and all forecasts will be falsified. But why should the future be different from the quite sustainable past? A standard triad of reasons is typically offered – and has been for decades. They are classic examples of "Zombies" – ideas and arguments that are intellectually dead but will not stay buried (Evans, et al., 1994; Barer et al., 1998), and are repeatedly disinterred to advance interests that are very much alive.

The triad consists of interlinked claims about trends in demography, technology, and public attitudes, each asserted to be generating increasing needs or demands (the distinction is typically fuzzy) for increasingly expensive health care. Aging populations have greater needs; advancing technology creates ever more expensive possibilities for intervention; and "public expectations" of the health care system are ever increasing. People just want more, and want it now. But (it is further asserted) no government can afford to meet these ever-expanding needs/demands. So we should, indeed must, limit the public liability, and let those who can, buy more for themselves if they wish. There is really no alternative. QED.

When one unpackages these broad generalities, however, and looks at the actual data, a very different picture emerges.

The "Zombie" of the aging population, a.k.a. "apocalyptic demography," has been studied in particular detail. The average age of modern populations is rising, and elderly people generally do have greater health needs requiring more costly care. But it is not true that these patterns will place an unsustainable burden on public health care systems (Barer et al., 1998; Barer, Evans, and Hertzman, 1995; Evans et al., 2001). Holding age-specific per capita use and cost rates constant, Canadian population forecasts indicate a rise in per capita costs of about 1 per cent per year – well within the range of prevailing rates of economic growth. Use and cost are primarily driven not by changing age structure, but by changing patterns of care use – what is done to and for patients. These patterns obviously respond to the evolution of scientific knowledge and technical capacity, but the link is neither simple nor direct (Bassett, 1996). New technologies may be inherently either cost-enhancing or cost-reducing – there are many examples of each – but it is the way in which they are taken up and applied that determines their impact on costs. That process of uptake and application is primarily controlled by clinicians, and the cost-enhancing bias of technology arises, *inter alia*, from the economic incentives that they face.

There is extensive evidence of the provision of questionable or simply inappropriate services, old and new, at unnecessarily high cost. But efforts to evaluate outcomes, eliminate ineffective or questionable practices, and restrain the exuberant proliferation of interventions have typically met indifference from clinicians, if not active resistance. Apart from issues of professional autonomy and pride (and the urge to "do something"), this reaction has roots in the ineluctable reality that cost containment must always threaten someone's income.[15]

The potential for transferring a large proportion of in-patient care to ambulatory or day care facilities, for example, has been well documented in Canada since the early 1970s. But large-scale uptake was slow until the rigorous budgetary restraints of the 1990s. The transfer eliminated jobs; widespread claims of "underfunding" and threats to patient health have not been substantiated.[16] If substantial additional funds flow into the health care system, the incentives for improved efficiency are likely to be relaxed.

The clearest examples of inappropriate and excessively costly choice of intervention can be found in the pharmaceutical sector. In Canada, the principal driver of rapid cost escalation is the replacement of older, off-patent drugs with new patented ones at prices that may be ten times higher. These are marketed as superior, but the regulatory process does not require new drugs to be tested against those they will replace, only against placebo. In some recent trials, high-profile (and high-cost) new drugs have shown no additional benefits (Furberg and ALLHAT Investigators, 2002; Rossouw and Women's Health Initiative Trial Investigators, 2002). Large additional expenditures, stimulated by intense marketing, are in effect buying nothing.

But what about public demand for the newest and the best, at any cost? Again, the pharmaceutical experience is instructive. Manufacturers have always engaged in intense and highly sophisticated marketing, primarily targeting physicians. More recently the industry lobbied successfully to eliminate American regulatory restrictions on advertising directly to the public, and in 2000 spent $2.5 billion to manipulate public expectations. Such advertising does change physician prescribing behaviour (Mintzes et al., 2003) – why else would a for-profit industry spend the money? American pharmaceutical manufacturers – for whom data are available – now spend twice as much on marketing as on research

(Families USA, 2001). In this environment, to speak of "public expectations" as if they represented independent consumer choices is at best dangerously naive, and at worst deliberately deceptive.

Managing patient expectations has always been a significant part of the professional role. The difference between a physician and a for-profit firm is that the former is responsible for the health of patients, the latter for the earnings of shareholders. In both cases, expectations management has very significant effects on trends in health expenditures, but those effects depend on the incentives created by the institutional environment in which the process takes place. That environment is determined by public and private policies and is always politically contested – as the pharmaceutical example makes clear.

Such matters as technology assessment, medical practice guidelines, and efforts to promote the practice of "evidence-based medicine" are highly political, interacting with the economic incentives embodied in the different structures for reimbursing physicians and hospitals. Medical and other professional associations and unions take a very active interest in these matters; advancing the economic interests of their members is one of their principal responsibilities. The recent uptick in Canadian health care costs includes some very successful physician fee bargaining. To pretend that trends in health care use and costs are determined by impersonal forces external to the industry itself is just that, a pretence.[17]

Whether or not the recent rise in Canadian Medicare expenditures presages a period of more rapid longer-term escalation is a critical question, but the answer does not depend on external factors. Rather it will, as in the past, depend on the outcome of political and administrative contests between those who pay and those who are paid for delivering or financing care. Projecting cost trends is akin to predicting the outcome of the Stanley Cup, the ice hockey cup final; there is certainly relevant information, but it is not a scientific exercise.

PRIVATE MORALITY AND PUBLIC CHOICES – AND CONSEQUENCES

In the end, though expenditure trends loom large in the public debate, the question of "sustainability" may not be about expenditure trends at all. Reinhardt (2001) argues that sustainability is actually a moral issue, a debate about what the members of a society owe to each other.

To illustrate, suppose the preceding argument is incorrect, and we are in fact entering a new era in which advancing medical technology really does offer dramatic improvements in health – at dramatically increased expense. Citizens might quite rationally accept this bargain, with health care spending rising as a share of GDP – why not? That is exactly what happened in Canada when universal public insurance was introduced; there was consensus (rightly or wrongly) that more spending would produce better health for everyone. At root, the arguments for cost containment have always been about seeking value for money, containing price inflation, and paring away waste, not about foregoing effective care.

But who should pay, and who should get the care? Under public insurance, the burden would fall on taxpayers and the benefits would go to patients. Government expenditure on health care would rise, as would taxation. The claim that such increases would be "unsustainable" is tantamount to saying that this pattern of burdens and benefits is morally wrong. People should not get care that they cannot afford. And people who can afford a higher standard of care for themselves should not have to contribute, through taxation, to support a similar standard for others.

This moral position does not appear to be widely shared by the Canadian public. Nor can its advocates credibly claim that governments "cannot afford" such increased expenditures, while simultaneously advocating and carrying through substantial cuts to income taxes. Considerable ingenuity must therefore be devoted to finding general harms from an expanded public sector.[18] This ingenuity might more constructively be directed towards improving the efficiency and effectiveness of the health care system. But those who allege unsustainability largely ignore the evidence on waste and inappropriate care, and implicitly or explicitly also allege "underfunding" – thus coming into alliance with provider interests.

Reinhardt's comment (2001) on the US Congress is worth quoting:

> That no one in the US Congress shows much interest in the glaring inefficiencies that could easily be addressed within the current Medicare program [in the US, covering only those sixty-five and over] speaks volumes about the true, but hidden, agenda that actually drives the quest for privatizing … Crisply put, the objective is to shift responsibility for health spending on older persons from the general taxpayer onto the older people themselves. (201)

Canada's universal system has done a much better job of mobilizing ingenuity to deal with these "glaring inefficiencies," but a much better job than the US still leaves a lot to be desired. More significant reforms continue to be stalled by the political struggles over *Who Pays?*, *Who Gets?*, and *Who Gets Paid?* Claims that the Canadian public system is both economically unsustainable and underfunded seem driven by the same agenda that Reinhardt identifies in the US – containing public outlays while letting private expenditures go where they will. Such a mixed system would be more expensive and less efficient overall, as the US example has shown, escaping the price restraints imposed by the public single payer and bearing significantly increased administrative overheads. But it would be better for the wealthy.

Hence Reinhardt's assertion that "sustainability" is actually a moral issue, of defining the mutual obligations of the members of a community. Public choices are private morality writ large. There *is* a wolf at the door of the Canadian Medicare system. But it is a political wolf dressed in phony economic clothing to deceive the sheep.

NOTES

1 The idea is not entirely new. H.G. Wells referred to civilization as a race between education and disaster, and Arnold Toynbee built a theory of history around the success or failure of different civilizations' responses to successive challenges.

2 Advocates of market mechanisms tend to presume on a priori grounds that private markets always generate the right or "optimal" answer – a position typically buttressed against empirical challenge by the implicit assumption that whatever outcome is generated by such markets is by definition optimal.

3 "And presently word would come, that a tribe had been wiped off its ice field, or the lights had gone out in Rome."

4 The ingenuity requirement to manage an increasingly complex global environment – "tightly coupled" physically, financially, and even psychologically – does appear to be increasing rapidly, and it is far from clear that our political institutions in particular have the capacity or can even recognize the need to meet that growing demand. But that, O Best Beloved...

5 Here and subsequently, calendar year data on GDP and health expenditure back to 1975 are from CIHI (2001). Data back to 1960 can be found in OECD (2003), sources for pre-1960 data are given in Barer and Evans (1986).

6 The pharmaceutical industry and its advocates claim that this increase has made possible the reduction in hospital costs; the claim is spurious. It rests on little more than a correlation in trends, and cannot withstand any serious empirical scrutiny. But that is again another story.

7 Here and subsequently, FY data on provincial and federal public accounts are from the federal Department of Finance, Economic and Fiscal Reference Tables (October 2002), updated and augmented with additional data from Finance Canada staff. FY health expenditures are from CIHI (2001).

8 They may quite reasonably have anticipated a recovery to the long-run growth path, as in previous recessions. That did not happen.

9 It is difficult to know how much of the rhetoric of "unsustainability" is simply part of the never-ending provincial campaign for larger federal transfers.

10 The provincial budget went from a $1.4-billion surplus in 2000/01 to a $1.2-billion deficit in 2001/02. A number of other fiscal changes were made, generally regressive in effect but not so directly linkable to income level.

11 The premium is discounted for those with incomes under $25,000, falling to zero at $15,000.

12 This agenda was spelled out explicitly by Conrad Black (2001) in an editorial bitterly critical of Canadian governments for "taking money from people who have earned it and redistributing it to those who haven't." As owner of most of the major newspapers in Canada, he had taken the opportunity energetically to promote his personal political views.

13 The spread of "managed care" in the US during the 1990s can be similarly interpreted as the application of ingenuity to deal with an increasingly unsatisfactory environment – somewhat less successfully.

14 Medical Savings Accounts provide a leading example. They would serve no useful purpose in the Canadian context, merely providing a cover for increases in both user charges and health expenditures. But debunking the claims of their advocates has taken up a significant amount of research effort (e.g., Hurley, 2000; Forget, Deber, and Roos, 2002), and diverted public attention from more constructive topics.

15 Accordingly, when technologies emerge that are both therapeutically superior and less costly per patient treated, they are often associated with rapid proliferation – and increased total cost.

16 A similar pattern was observed in the US when the Prospective Payment System was introduced in 1983. Patterns of care respond to economic incentives.

17 "[T]he Pharmaceutical Research and Manufacturers of America, known as PHRMA, will spend at least $150 million in the coming year" on political lobbying activities including "spend[ing] $1 million for an "*intellectual echo chamber of economists – a standing network of economists and thought leaders to speak against federal price control regulations through*

articles and testimony, and to serve as a rapid response team" and "allocates $1 million "*to change the Canadian health care system*" (Pear, 2003; italics are quotes from industry documents).

18 Economists have been particularly helpful in this quest, being ingenious in providing rigorous demonstrations – from faulty assumptions – of the general benefit from smaller government and greater inequality. This pays.

REFERENCES

Barer, Morris L., and Robert G. Evans (1986). "Riding north on a southbound horse? Expenditures, prices, utilization and incomes in the Canadian health care system." In *Medicare at maturity: Achievements, lessons, and challenges*, ed. Robert G. Evans and Greg L. Stoddart, 53–163. Calgary: University of Calgary Press.

– Robert G. Evans, and Clyde Hertzman (1995). "Avalanche or glacier? Health care and the demographic rhetoric." *Canadian Journal on Aging* 14(2): 193–225.

– Robert G. Evans, Clyde Hertzman, and Mira Johri (1998). *Lies, damned lies and healthcare zombies: Discredited ideas that will not die*. Health Policy Institute Discussion Paper 10. Houston, TX: University of Texas (Houston) Health Science Center.

Bassett, Ken (1996). "Anthropology, clinical pathology, and the electronic fetal monitor: Lessons from the heart." *Social Science and Medicine* 42(2): 281–92.

Black, Conrad (2001). "The most boring election in history (editorial)." *National Post*, 1 December.

Boccuti, Cristina, and Marilyn Moon (2003). "Comparing medicare and private insurers: Growth rates in spending over three decades." *Health Affairs* 22(2): 230–7.

Canadian Institute for Health Information (2001). *National health expenditure trends: 1975–2002*. Ottawa: Canadian Institute for Health Information.

Evans, Robert G. (1982). "Health care in Canada: Patterns of funding and regulation." In *The public-private mix for health: The relevance and effects of change*, ed. Gordon McLachlan and Alan Maynard, 371–424. London: Nuffield Provincial Hospitals Trust.

– (1990). "Tension, compression, and shear: Directions, stresses, and outcomes of health care cost control." *Journal of Health Politics, Policy, and Law* 15(1): 101–28.

– (1998). "Healthy, wealthy, and cunning? Profit and loss from health care reform." In *The Vancouver Institute: An Experiment* in *Public Education*, ed. Peter N. Nemetz, 447–86. Vancouver: JBA Press.

– (2002). "Financing Health Care: Taxation and the Alternatives." In *Financing Health Care: Options for Europe*, ed. Elias Mossialos, Joseph Figueras, and Joe Kutzi, 39–58. Buckingham: Open University Press.

– Morris, L. Barer, Gregory L. Stoddart, and Vandna Bhatia (1994). *Who are the zombie masters and what do they want?* Toronto: The Ontario Premier's Council on Health, Well-being, and Social Justice.

– Kimberlyn McGrail, Steve Morgan, Morris L. Barer, and Clyde Hertzman (2001). "Apocalypse no: Population aging and the future of the health care system." *Canadian Journal on Aging* 20, Supp. 1: 160–91.

Families USA (2001). *Off the charts: Pay, profits and spending by drug companies.* Washington, DC: Families USA Foundation Publication, 1–104.

Forget, Evelyn L., Raisa Deber, and Leslie L. Roos (2002). "Medical savings accounts: Will they reduce costs?" *Canadian Medical Association Journal* 167(2): 143–7.

Furberg, Curt D., and the ALLHAT Investigators (2002). "Major outcomes in high-risk hypertensive patients randomized to angiotensin-converting enzyme inhibitor or calcium channel blocker vs diuretic." *Journal of the American Medical Association* 288(23): 2981–97.

Homer-Dixon, Thomas F. (2000). *The ingenuity gap.* Toronto: Alfred A. Knopf.

– Jeffrey H. Boutwell, and George W. Rathjens (1993). "Environmental change and violent conflict." *Scientific American* 268(2): 38–45.

Hurley, Jeremiah (2000). "Medical savings accounts: Approach with caution." *Journal of Health Services Research and Policy* 5(2): 30–2.

Levit, Katharine, Cynthia Smith, Cathy Cowan, Helen Lazenby, Art Sensenig, and Aaron Catlin (2003). "Trends in US health care spending, 2001." *Health Affairs* 22(1): 154–64.

Lu, Jui-Fen Rachel, and William C. Hsiao (2003). "Does universal health insurance make healthcare unaffordable? Lessons from Taiwan." *Health Affairs* 22(3): 77–88.

Meadows, Donella H., Dennis L. Meadows, Jorgen Randers, and William W. Behrens III (1972). *The limits to growth.* London: Earth Island.

Mintzes, Barbara, Morris L. Barer, Richard L. Kravitz, Ken Bassett, Joel Lexchin, Arminée Kazanjian, Robert G. Evans, Richard Pan, and Stephen A. Marion (2003). "How does direct-to-consumer advertising (DTCA) affect prescribing? A survey in primary care environments with and without legal DTCA." *Canadian Medical Association Journal* 169 (5): 405–12.

Mustard, Cameron, Marian Shanahan, and Shelley Derksen (1998). "Use of insured health care services in relation to income in a Canadian province." In *Health, health care, and health economics: Perspectives on distribution*, ed. Morris L. Barer, Thomas E. Getzen, and Gregory L. Stoddart, 39–58. Chichester: John Wiley.

– Morris Barer, Robert Evans, John Horne, Teresa Mayer, and Shelley Derksen (1998). "Paying taxes and using health care services: The distributional consequences of tax financed universal health insurance in a Canadian province." Presented at the Centre for the Study of Living Standards Conference on the State of Living Standards and the Quality of Life in Canada, Ottawa, October 1998. Available from URL www.csls.ca/oct/must.pdf

OECD (2003). *Health data file, 2003*. Paris: Organisation for Economic Cooperation and Development.

Pear, Robert (2003). "Drug companies increase spending to lobby congress and governments." *New York Times*, 31 May.

Reinhardt, Uwe E. (2001). "Commentary: On the apocalypse of the retiring baby boom." *Canadian Journal on Aging* 20 (Suppl. 1): 192–204.

Rossouw, Jacques E., and the Women's Health Initiative Trial Investigators (2002). "Risks and benefits of estrogen plus progestin in healthy postmenopausal women." *Journal of the American Medical Association* 288(3): 321–33.

Sharpe, Andrew (2003). "Linkages between economic growth and inequality: Introduction and overview." *Canadian Public Policy.* 29 (Jan. Supp.): S1–S14.

Statistics Canada (2003). "Family income, 2001." *Daily Mail*, 25 June.

United States Congressional Budget Office (1992). *Projections of national health expenditures*. Washington, DC: Congressional Budget Office.

van Doorslaer, Eddy, Adam Wagstaff, Hattem van der Burg et al. (1999). "The redistributive effect of healthcare: Some further international comparisons." *Journal of Health Economics* 18(3): 263–90.

Wagstaff, Adam, Eddy van Doorslaer, Hattem van der Burg et al. (1999). "The redistributive effect of health care finance in twelve OECD countries." *Journal of Health Economics* 18(3): 291–314.

White, Joseph (1995). *Competing solutions: American health care proposals and international experience*. Washington, DC: Brookings.

Wolfson, Michael C., and Brian B. Murphy (1998). "New views on inequality trends in Canada and the United States." United States Bureau of Labor Statistics. *Monthly Labor Review* (April): 3–21.

Woolhandler, Steffie, Terry Campbell, and David U. Himmelstein (2003). "Costs of health care administration in the United States and Canada." *New England Journal of Medicine* 349 (8): 768–75.

– and David U. Himmelstein (2002). "Paying for National Health Insurance – and not getting it." *Health Affairs* 21(4): 88–98.

Further Reading

Without intending to be exhaustive, amongst other papers that would have found a comfortable home in this section, but for which there was insufficient space, are:

- Evans, Robert G. "Does Canada Have Too Many Doctors?: Why Nobody Loves an Immigrant Physician." *Canadian Public Policy/ Analyse de Politiques* 2(2)(1976): 147–60.
- – and M.F. Williamson. "Public Invervention: Objectives and Criteria." In *Extending Canadian Health Insurance: Options for Pharmacare and Denticare*, 3–32. Toronto: University of Toronto Press, 1978.
- – "Professionals and the Production Function: Can Competition Policy Improve Efficiency in the Licensed Professions?" In *Occupational Licensure and Regulation*, ed. S. Rottenberg, 225–64. Washington, DC: American Enterprise Institute, 1980.
- – and G.C. Robinson. "Surgical Day Care: Measurements of the Economic Payoff." *Canadian Medical Association Journal* 123(9) (1980): 873.
- – "Licensure, Consumer Ignorance, and Agency." In *Strained Mercy: The Economics of Canadian Health Care*, 69–91 (chap. 4). Butterworths and Company, 1984.
- – "Illusions of Necessity: Evading Responsibility for Choice in Health Care." *Journal of Health Politics, Policy, and Law* 10(3) (1985): 439–67.
- – "Squaring the Circle: Reconciling Fee-for-Service with Global Expenditure Control" (unpublished), 1988. Retrieved from: http://circle.ubc.ca/bitstream/handle/2429/50352/Evans_RG_Squaring_the_circle.pdf?sequence=1

SECTION D

Population Health

Foreword

JOHN FRANK AND ALAN BERNSTEIN

It is a great pleasure and privilege to have the opportunity to co-author a foreword for this remarkable collection. Each of our lives has been influenced by the author, because of his later-in-career interest in the determinants of health of populations (the subject of the papers in this section). John Frank was introduced to Evans through participation in the Program in Population Health (PHP) of the Canadian Institute for Advanced Research (then CIAR, now CIFAR), a program for which Evans served as inaugural director but, more importantly, intellectual leader. In his role at CIAR in the 1980s and early 1990s, Evans brought together a diverse and brilliant group of scholars to examine in detail the emerging evidence that socioeconomic status was a critical but overlooked determinant of health. The result of that unique multidisciplinary collaboration was profound: two books, hundreds of articles, and the creation of an entire new field of investigation. To a considerable extent, these stand as a testament to many of Bob's qualities and hallmarks: a focus on data and evidence ("theories divide, data unite"), insistence that experts be able to communicate their knowledge in terms that other experts from different disciplines can understand, an amazing ability to synthesize across disciplines in his reading, understanding, and writing, and the leadership he showed and the respect he garnered from his colleagues. Taken together, these attributes kept a group of "stars in their own right" pulling together for a common purpose. In a brilliant move early in the life of that program, its Fellows and Associates decided as a group that the most effective way of coalescing their work in a way that would have enduring impact would be to focus their discussions, common purpose, and direction around the idea of writing a book together. That book, *Why Are Some People Healthy and Others Not?* (Evans,

Barer, and Marmor, 1994), became a classic, arguably spawning the new field of "Population Health." In Evans' own words, "[t]he book made the program and the program made the book." Julio Frenk, the former minister of health for Mexico and at the time dean of the School of Public Health at Harvard, told Alan Bernstein not long ago that this book had been *the* standard textbook for Harvard students in population health!

As a fellow in that program, John Frank was privileged to co-author, with Evans and the late Clyde Hertzman, one of the chapters. The collaboration on that chapter was interesting, not only because of the way in which three quite unique sets of expertise were woven together in ways that none of us could have imagined at the outset, but more importantly because it also turned out (in retrospect) to have been an opportunity for Evans to teach Frank and Hertzman how to write – clearly, succinctly, and entertainingly. To physicians trained in quantitative research methods, but inexperienced with the pen, Evans' tutelage was a revelation. As but one example, Evans questioned our use of the stock-in-(epidemiological)-trade phrase, "the prevention of mortality," noting that it was illogical because "only postponement is on offer."

The book also continued a Canadian tradition of sentinel contributions to the world's understanding of the determinants of health in human populations, following in the footsteps of the landmark Lalonde Report (Lalonde, 1974).

Alan Bernstein's first meeting with the author came much later, in the mid-2000s. By that time Evans had been appointed as one of only two CIFAR Institute Fellows, in recognition of his seminal contributions to scholarship and to CIFAR. Evans was outspoken, iconoclastic, sarcastic (mostly about the economics profession), brilliant, and warm; it was no mystery as to why he had been made a Fellow.

Bernstein (though without knowing it at the time) would, within a few years, become the organization's president and CEO. But Evans' influence on his career had been cast in stone much earlier, through the PHP and its considerable influence. Among other things, that program served as an incubator for two direct-descendant CIFAR programs, Successful Societies, and Child and Brain Development. Both programs have continued the legacy of excellence established by Evans and his colleagues in the PHP. But the more important influence in terms of its impact on Bernstein had come from outside CIFAR. Parliament's decision to create the Canadian Institutes of Health Research (CIHR) in 2000 to replace the Medical Research Council (MRC) was based to a considerable extent on the federal government of the day having come to embrace this broader view of the determinants of health and disease. The MRC philosophy had focused largely on understanding disease and its biological origins. CIHR's mandate and programs, in contrast, reflected a broader perspective, best articulated in the PHP book, that a person's health and disease status reflect the complex interplay of a wider array of influences, including not just inherited biology, but also early life experiences, lifestyle, environment, community influences, and socioeconomic status. The CIHR was built around thirteen institutes, one of which was the Institute of Population and Public Health (and John Frank had the honour and privilege of serving as its inaugural director). It is not just a bit ironic that Alan Bernstein became the inaugural president of CIHR, and then more recently the president of CIFAR.

Rereading these four seminal book chapters and articles by Evans was a distinct pleasure and a cause for celebration. As with the works in earlier sections, they are entertainingly written, superbly thought-out, and unrelentingly critical of bad scholarship. In short, they demonstrate how a great and nimble academic mind grasps and conveys to others the key issues in a complex field. The result is a set of timeless analyses, still viewed as key contributions to the field of population health one to two decades after most of them were written.

In the writings in this section of the book the eclectically curious Evans voraciously consumes and integrates all manner of scientific publications in the biological, epidemiological, and sociological aspects of health and its determination, with major excursions en route in primatology, the psychoneuro-immunology and -endocrinology of stress, as well as the field of child development. The result is a remarkable achievement for a scholar originally trained in economics, with a strong personal interest in and broad knowledge of history. These papers present cogent and strikingly original syntheses of what were, at the time of writing, refreshingly new insights from these "hard sciences," illuminating the "upstream" origins of disease, disability, and premature death over the life course. They remain core to the field of "Pop Health."

What is it about Evans' thinking and writing that makes his work refreshing, relevant, and stimulating to read, decades later? Four key characteristics of his way of tackling complex issues stand out:

- a distinct disrespect for conventional wisdom – especially wherever he found it to be unduly influenced by special-interest groups ("rent-seekers," in the parlance of his discipline);

- an encyclopedic knowledge of pretty much everything, with a steel-trap memory that seemed never to lose or misplace any new information in his vast cerebral files – complemented by an insatiable appetite to know even more;
- an uncanny ability to find connections between seemingly disconnected dots, to synthesize across quite diverse areas of scholarship; and finally,
- a special gift for witty word-smithing, at a level reached by few academics, punctuated by the clever and unexpected juxtaposition of words for humorous effect.

The result is a unique writing style that can usually be spotted merely from the title. The selected writings in this book provide many examples.

The first three papers in this section arose from Evans' decade as director of the PHP. They focus on heterogeneity in health status within populations. The fourth was written twenty years later and was originally presented as a memorial lecture for a former colleague, Gideon Rosenbluth. The first paper, "Producing Health, Consuming Health Care," develops a conceptual framework for bringing together the broad categories of determinants of health of populations and identifying potential causal pathways. While not denying the importance of medical care in determining why people get well once ill, it shifted attention to why people get ill in the first place. It was a remarkably cogent attempt to provide in one place, and in one systematically developed framework, a template for assembling and integrating evidence on patterns and correlates of variations in the health of groups from a wide range of disciplines that might otherwise have not been seen as related.

The second offering in this section is the first chapter of *Why Are Some People Healthy and Others Not?* In it, Evans highlights and links important pieces of evidence regarding socioeconomic status and health, that is, the socioeconomic gradient. A particularly important contribution of this paper was to point out that social hierarchies are important not just in human populations, but in the populations of many non-human primates. It draws out lessons from animal studies of the effects of hierarchies on health, for human organization and interaction.

"Health, Hierarchy, and Hominids," the third paper chosen for this section, showcases Evans' remarkable intellectual reach. It also opens the way to understanding a central question in the study of the social determinants of health – how does the social context get "under the skin" to become biologically embedded as resilience or vulnerability to disease. Evans was perhaps the first to recognize the significance of the deep parallels between two very important but apparently totally disparate long-term research programs – Sir Michael Marmot's "Whitehall" studies of the UK civil service, and Robert Sapolsky's studies of olive baboons in the Serengeti region of Kenya. Both were "free-ranging" populations of male hominids with complex social structures and well-defined status hierarchies. The Whitehall studies showed a clear relation between rank and health status; the Serengeti studies complement them by showing the biological link between status and stress response.

In the final paper in this section, the focus has shifted to the population as a whole and the "social context" – the intellectual and political context within which societies address – or fail to address – environmental threats to their collective health. The intellectual framework offered by economics and by economists – often not the same thing! – receives particular attention, since both Evans and Rosenbluth were academic economists with a somewhat skeptical view of conventional economic theory. In that sense, this paper brings us full circle, back to the first section of the book.

In summary, the offerings in this section of this book are wonderful examples of the author's ability to communicate with the pen, to achieve both precision and provocation in equal measure. But our debt to the author extends beyond the sorts of contributions found in these pages. We are equally indebted to him for his contributions as an iconoclast who has consistently challenged accepted wisdoms that needed challenge, and for his roles as public conscience and commentator, and as mentor to, and inspiration for, the next generation of young scholars. This book is a very fitting tribute to a great Canadian, a brilliant scholar and a wonderful human being.

REFERENCES

Evans, R.G., M.L. Barer, and T.R. Marmor, eds. (1994). *Why are some people healthy and others not? The determinants of health of populations*. New York: Aldine de Gruyter.

Lalonde, M. (1974). *A New Perspective on the Health of Canadians*, Ottawa: Minister of Supply and Services Canada.

13

Producing Health, Consuming Health Care

ROBERT G. EVANS AND
GREGORY L. STODDART

INTRODUCTION

People care about their health, for good reasons, and they try in a number of ways to maintain or improve it. Individually and in groups at various levels – families, associations, work groups, communities, and nations – they engage in a wide range of activities which they believe will contribute to their health. People also attempt to avoid activities or circumstances that they see as potentially harmful. Implicit in such behaviour are theories, or more accurately loosely associated and often inconsistent collections of causal hypotheses, as to the determinants of health.

In particular, but only as a subset of these health-oriented activities, modern societies devote a very large proportion of their economic resources to the production and distribution of "health care," a particular collection of commodities which are perceived as bearing a special relationship to health. The "health care industry" which assembles these resources and converts them into various health-related goods and services is one of the largest clusters of economic activity in all modern states (Schieber and Poullier, 1989; OECD Secretariat, 1989). Such massive efforts reflect a widespread belief that the availability and use of health care is central to the health of both individuals and populations.

Reprinted from R.G. Evans and G.L. Stoddart, "Producing Health, Consuming Health Care." *Social Science and Medicine* 31 (12), 1347–63. Copyright 1990, with permission from Elsevier.

This concentration of economic effort has meant that public or collective health policy has been predominantly health *care* policy. The provision of care not only absorbs the lion's share of the physical and intellectual resources which are specifically identified as health-related, it also occupies the centre of the stage when the rest of the community considers what to do about its health.

Health care, in turn, is overwhelmingly *reactive* in nature, responding to perceived departures from health, and identifying those departures in terms of clinical concepts and categories – diseases, professionally defined. The definition of health implicit in (most of) the behaviour of the health care system, the collection of people and institutions involved in the provision of care, is a negative concept, the absence of disease or injury. The system is in consequence often labelled, usually by its critics but not unjustly, as a "sickness care system."[1]

Yet this definition of health was specifically rejected by the World Health Organization (WHO) more than forty years ago. Its classic statement, "Health is a state of complete physical, mental, and social well-being, and not merely the absence of disease or injury," expressed a general perception that there is much more to health than simply a collection of negatives – a state of *not* suffering from any designated undesirable condition.

Such a comprehensive concept of health, however, risks becoming the proper objective for, and is certainly affected by, *all* human activity. There is no room for a separately identifiable realm of specifically health-oriented activity. The WHO definition is thus difficult to use as the basis for health policy, because implicitly it includes *all* policy as health policy. It has accordingly been honoured in repetition, but rarely in application.

Moreover, the WHO statement appears to offer only polar alternatives for the definition of health. Common usage, however, suggests a continuum of meanings. At one end of that continuum is well-being in the broadest sense, the all-encompassing definition of the WHO, almost a Platonic ideal of "The Good." At the other end is the simple absence of negative biological circumstances – disease, disability, or death.[2]

But the biological circumstances identified and classified by the health care disciplines as diseases are then experienced by individuals and their families or social groups as illnesses – distressing symptoms. The correspondence between medical disease and personal illness is by no means exact. Thus the patient's concept of health as absence of illness need not match the clinician's absence of disease. Further, the functional capacity of the individual will be influenced but not wholly determined by the perception of illness, and that capacity too will be an aspect, but not the totality, of well-being.

There are no sharply drawn boundaries between the various concepts of health in such a continuum, but that does not prevent us from recognizing their differences. Different concepts are neither right nor wrong, they simply have different purposes and fields of application. Whatever the level of *definition* of health being employed, however, it is important to distinguish this from the question of the *determinants* of (that definition of) health (Marmor, 1989).

Here too there exists a broad range of candidates, from particular targeted health care services, through genetic endowments of individuals, environmental sanitation, adequacy and quality of nutrition and shelter, stress and the supportiveness of the social environment, to self-esteem and sense of personal adequacy or control. It appears, on the basis of both long-established wisdom and considerable more-recent research, that the factors which affect health at all levels of definition include but go well beyond health care per se (Dutton, 1986; Levine and Lilienfeld, 1987; Marmot, 1986; McKeown, 1979; McKinlay, McKinlay, and Beaglehole, 1989; Townsend and Davidson, 1982).

Attempts to advance our understanding of this broad range of determinants through research have, like the health care system itself, tended to focus their attention on the narrower concept of health – absence of disease or injury. This concept has the significant advantage that it can be represented through quantifiable and measurable phenomena – death or survival, the incidence or prevalence of particular morbid conditions. The influence of a wide range of determinants, in and beyond the health care system, has in fact been observed in these most basic – negative – measures.

Precision is gained at a cost. Narrow definitions leave out less specific dimensions of health which many people would judge to be important to their evaluation of their own circumstances, or those of their associates. On the other hand, it seems at least plausible that the broad range of determinants of health whose effects are reflected in the "mere absence of disease or injury," or simple survival, are also relevant to more comprehensive definitions of health.

The current resurgence of interest in the determinants of health, as well as in its broader conceptualization, represents a return to a very old historical tradition, as old as medicine itself. The dialogue between Asclepios, the god of medicine, and Hygieia, the goddess of health – the external intervention and the well-lived life – goes back to the beginning.

Only in the twentieth century did the triumph of "scientific" modes of inquiry in medicine (as in most walks of life) result in the eclipse of Hygieia. Knowledge has increasingly become defined in terms of that (and only that) which emerges from the application of reductionist methods of investigation, applied to the fullest extent possible in a "Newtonian" frame of reference (Reiser, 1978).

The health care system has then become the conventional vehicle for the translation of such knowledge into the improvement of health – more, and more powerful, interventions, guided by better and better science. Nor have its achievements been negligible in enhanced ability to prevent some diseases, cure others, and alleviate the symptoms or slow the progress of many more. Thus by mid-century the providers of health care had gained an extraordinary institutional and even more an intellectual dominance, defining both what counted as health, and how it was to be pursued. The WHO was a voice in the wilderness.

But the intellectual currents have now begun to flow in the other direction. There has been a continuing unease about the exclusive authority of classically "scientific," positivist methods, both to define the knowable and to determine how it may come to be known (McCloskey, 1989; Dreyfus and Dreyfus, 1988), an unease which has drawn new strength from developments in sub-atomic physics and more recently in artificial intelligence and mathematics.[3] In addition, the application of those methods themselves to the exploration of the determinants of health is generating increasing evidence – in the most restricted scientific sense – of the powerful role of contributing factors outside the health care system (House, Landis, and Umberson, 1988; Dantzer and Kelley, 1989; Bunker, Gomby, and Kehrer, 1989; Renaud, 1987; Sapolsky, 1990).

Simultaneously, the more rigorous evaluation of the health care system itself has demonstrated that its practices are much more loosely connected with scientific or any other form of knowledge, than the official rhetoric would suggest (Banta, Behney, and Willems, 1981; Eisenberg, 1986; Feeny, Guyatt, and Tugwell, 1986; Lomas, 1990). And finally, the very success of that system in occupying the centre of the intellectual and policy stage, and in drawing in resources, has been built upon an extraordinarily heightened set of social expectations as to its potential contributions. Some degree of disappointment and disillusion is an inevitable consequence, with corresponding concern about the justification for the scale of effort involved – the rhetoric of "cost explosions."

There is thus a growing gap between our understanding of the determinants of health and the primary focus of health policy on the provision of health care. This increasing disjunction may be partly a consequence of the persistence, in the policy arena, of incomplete and obsolete models, or intellectual frames of reference, for conceptualizing the determinants of health. How a problem is framed will determine which kinds of evidence are given weight, and which are disregarded. Perfectly valid data – hard observations bearing directly on important questions – simply drop out of consideration, as if they did not exist, when the implicit model of entities and interrelationships in people's minds provides no set of categories in which to put them.

There is, for example, considerable evidence linking mortality to the (non)availability of social support mechanisms, evidence of a strength which House, et al. (1988) describes as now equivalent to that in the mid-1950s on the effects of tobacco smoking. Retirement, or the death of a spouse, are documented as important risk factors. Similarly some correlate or combination of social class, level of income or education, and position in a social hierarchy is clearly associated with mortality (Dutton, 1986; Marmot, 1986). None of this is denied, yet no account is taken of such relationships in the formulation of health (care) policy.

Such policy is, by contrast, acutely sensitive to even the possibility that some new drug, piece of equipment, or diagnostic or therapeutic manoeuvre may contribute to health. That someone's health may perhaps be at risk for lack of such intervention is prima facie grounds for close policy attention, and at least a strong argument for provision. Meanwhile, the egregious fact that people are suffering, and in some cases dying, as a consequence of processes not directly connected to health care, elicits neither rebuttal nor response.

The explanation cannot be that there is superior evidence for the effectiveness, still less the cost-effectiveness, of health care interventions. It is notorious that new interventions are introduced, and particularly disseminated, in the absence of such evidence (Banta, Behney, and Willems, 1981; Eisenberg, 1986; Feeny, Guyatt, and Tugwell, 1986). If (some) clinicians find it plausible that a manoeuvre might be beneficial in particular circumstances, it is likely to be used. The growing concern for "technological assessment" or careful evaluation *before* dissemination, is a response to this well-established pattern. But those who might wish to restrain application, fearing lack of effect or even harm, find themselves bearing the burden of rigorous proof. If the evidence is incomplete or ambiguous, the bias is towards intervention.

This heavy concentration of attention and effort on a subset of health-related activities, and de facto dismissal of others, may be a product of the conceptual framework within which we think about the determinants of health. A simple mechanical model captures the causal relationships from sickness, to care, to cure. The machine (us) is damaged or breaks, and the broken part is repaired (or perhaps replaced). Although this mental picture may be a gross oversimplification of reality, it is easy to hold in mind.

By contrast, it is not at all obvious how one should even think about the causal connections between "stress" or "low self-esteem," and illness or death – much less what would be appropriate policy responses. The whole subject has a somewhat mysterious air, with overtones of the occult, in contrast to the (apparently) transparent and scientific process of health care.[4] There being no set of intellectual categories in which to assemble such data, they are ignored.

In this paper, therefore, we propose a somewhat more complex framework, which we believe is sufficiently comprehensive and flexible to represent a wider range of relationships among the determinants of health. The test of such a framework is its ability to provide meaningful categories in which to insert the various sorts of evidence which are now emerging as to the diverse determinants of health, as well as to permit a definition of health broad enough to encompass the dimensions which people – providers of care, policy-makers, and particularly ordinary individuals – feel to be important.

Our purpose is *not* to try to present a comprehensive, or even a sketchy, survey of the current evidence on the determinants of health. Even a taxonomy for that evidence, a suggested classification and enumeration of the main heads, would now be a major research task. Rather, we are trying to construct an analytic framework within which such evidence can be fitted, and which will highlight the ways in which different types of factors and forces can interact to bear on different conceptualizations of health. Our model or precedent is the federal government's White Paper, *A New Perspective on the Health of Canadians* (Canada, 1974), which likewise presented very little of the actual evidence on the determinants of health, but offered a very powerful and compelling framework for assembling it.

We will also follow the White Paper in offering no more than the most cursory indication of what the implications of such evidence might be for health policy, public or private. Policy implications will arise from the actual evidence on the determinants of health, not from the framework per se. If the framework is useful, it should facilitate the presentation of evidence in such a way as to make its implications more apparent.

But there is of course much more to policy than evidence; "the art of the possible" includes most importantly one's perceptions of who the key actors are and what their objectives might be. We will be addressing these issues in subsequent work, but not here.

Finally, we must emphasize that the entities which form the components of our framework are themselves categories, with a rich internal structure. Each box and label could be expanded to show its complex contents. One must therefore be very careful about, and usually avoid, treating such categories as if they could be adequately represented by some single homogeneous variable, much less subjected to mathematical or statistical manipulations like a variable. Single variables may capture some aspect of a particular category, but they are not the same as that category. Moreover, in specific contexts it may be the *interactions* between factors from different categories of determinants that are critical to the health of individuals and populations.

DISEASE AND HEALTH CARE: A (TOO) SIMPLE FOUNDATION

We build up our framework component by component, progressively adding complexity both in response to the demonstrable inadequacies of the preceding stage, and in rough correspondence to (our interpretation of) the historical evolution of the conceptual basis of health policy over the last half century. The first and simplest stage defines health as absence of disease or injury and takes as central the relation between health and health care. The former is represented in terms of the categories and capacities of the latter. The relationship can be represented in a simple feedback model, as presented in Figure 13.1, exactly analogous to a heating system governed by a thermostat.

In this framework, people "get sick" or "get hurt" for a variety of unspecified reasons represented by the unlabelled arrows entering on the left-hand side. They may then respond by presenting themselves to the health care system, where the resulting diseases and injuries are defined and interpreted as giving rise to "needs" for particular forms of health care. This interpretive role is critical, because the definition of "need" depends on the state of medical technology. Conditions for which (it is believed that) nothing can be done may be regrettable, and very distressing, but do not represent "needs" for care. The patient feels the distress, but the health care system defines the need.

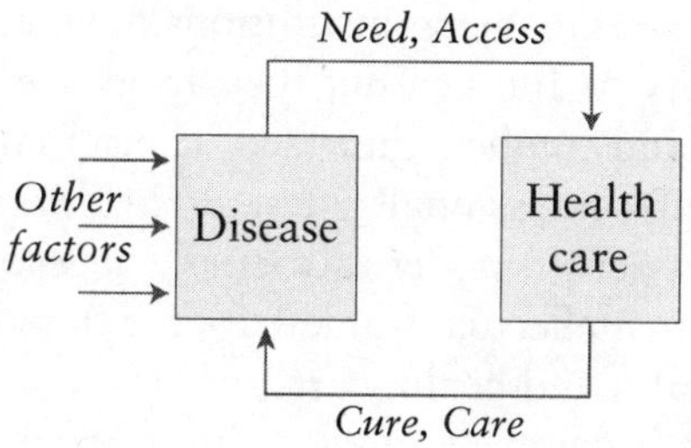

Need, Access

Other factors → Disease → Health care

Cure, Care

Figure 13.1

Adapted from: Robert G. Evans and Gregory L. Stoddart. "Producing Health, Consuming Health Care." *Social Science & Medicine* 31(12)(1990): 1347–63.

Potential "needs" for health care are, however, pre-filtered before they reach the care system, an important process which is reflected explicitly neither in Figure 13.1 nor in most of health policy.[5] Whether or not people respond to adverse circumstances by contacting the health care system, seeking "patient" status, will depend on their perceptions of their own coping capacities and their informal support systems, relative to their expectations of the formal system. These expectations and reactions are thus included among the "other factors" that determine the environment to which the health care system responds.

The health care system then combines the functions of thermostat and furnace, interpreting its environment, defining the appropriate response, and responding. The level of response is determined by the "access" to care which a particular society has provided for its members. This access depends both on the combination of human and physical resources available – doctors, nurses, hospitals, diagnostic equipment, drugs, etc. – and also on the administrative and financial systems in place, which determine whether particular individuals will receive the services of these resources, and under what conditions.[6]

The top arrow in Figure 13.1 thus reflects the positive response of the health care system to disease – the provision of care. But the form and scale of the response is influenced, through a sort of "two-key" system, both by the professional definition of needs – what should be done to or for people in particular circumstances, suffering particular departures from health – and by the whole collection of institutions which in any particular society mobilize the resources to meet the needs, and ensure access to care.

Those organizing and financing institutions have very different structures from one society to another, but their tasks are essentially similar, as are the problems and conflicts they face. The actual technologies, and the institutional and professional roles, in health care also show a remarkable similarity across modern societies, suggesting that those societies share a common intellectual framework for thinking about the relationship between health and health care.

The feedback loop is completed by the lower arrow, reflecting the presumption that the provision of care reduces the level of disease, thereby improving health. The strength of this negative relationship represents the effectiveness of care. These effects include: the restoration and maintenance of health (providing "cures"); preventing further deterioration; relieving symptoms, particularly pain; offering assistance in coping with the inevitable; and providing reassurance through authoritative interpretation.

The important role of health care in providing comfort to the afflicted fits somewhat ambiguously in this framework, since services which can clearly be identified as making people feel good, but having no present or future influence on their health status however defined, can readily be seen to include a very wide range of activities, most of which are not usually included as health care (Evans, 1984).

The provision of services which *are* generally recognized as health care should obviously take place in a context that preserves a decent consideration for the comfort of those served. There is no excuse for the gratuitous infliction of discomfort, and patients should not be made any more miserable than they have to be. But for those services which represent *only* comfort, it is important to ask both: Why should they be professionalized, by assigning "official" providers of health care a privileged right to serve? and Why should the clients of the health care system be awarded privileged access to such services? There are many people, not by any sensible definition ill, who might nevertheless have their lives considerably brightened by comforting services at collective expense.[7]

In this conceptual framework, the level of health of a population is the negative or inverse of the burden of disease. This burden of disease in Figure 13.1 is analogous to the temperature of the air in a house in a model of a heating system. The health care system diagnoses that disease and responds with treatment; the thermostat detects a fall in air temperature and turns on the furnace. The result is a reduction in disease/increase in room temperature. The external factors – pathogens, accidents – which "cause" disease are analogous to the temperature outside the house; a very cold night is equivalent to an epidemic. But the consequences of such external events are moderated by the response of the heating/health care systems.

The thermostat can, of course, be set at different target temperatures, and the control system of the furnace can be more or less sophisticated depending on the extent and duration of permissible departures from the target temperature. Similarly access to care can be provided at different levels, to meet different degrees of "need" and with tighter or looser tolerances for over- or under-servicing.

The systems do differ, insofar as the house temperature can be increased more or less indefinitely by putting more fuel through the furnace (or adding more furnaces). In principle the expansion of the health care system is bounded by the burden of remediable disease. When each individual has received all the health care which might conceivably be of benefit, then all needs have been met, and "health" in the narrow sense of absence of (remediable) disease or injury has been attained. Health is bounded from above; air temperature is not. The occupants of the house do not of course *want* an ever-increasing temperature, whether or not it is possible. Too much is as bad as too little. Yet no obvious meaning attaches to the words "too healthy." More is always better, a closer approximation to the ideal of perfect, or at least best attainable, health.[8]

The differences are more apparent than real, however, since in practice the professionally defined needs for care are themselves adjusted according to the capacity of the health care system, and the pressures on it. The objective of health, René Dubos' mirage (Dubos, 1959), ever recedes as more resources are devoted to health care. As old forms of disease or injury threaten to disappear, new ones are defined. There are always "unmet needs."[9]

Furthermore, obvious meanings *do* attach to the words "too much health care," on at least three levels. First, too much care may result in harm to health in the narrow sense – iatrogenic disease – because potent interventions are always potentially harmful. But even if care contributes to health in the narrow sense – keeping the patient alive, for example – it may still be "too much." Painful interventions which prolong not life but dying are generally recognized as harmful to those who are forced to undergo them. More generally, the side effects of "successful" therapy may in some cases be, for the patient, worse than the disease.

Second, even if the care *is* beneficial in terms of both health and well-being of the recipient, it may still represent "too much" if the benefits are very small relative to the costs, the other opportunities foregone by the patient or others. If health is an important, but not the only, goal in life, it follows that there can be "too much" even of effective health care (Woodward and Stoddart, 1990).

And finally, an important component of health is the individual's *perception* of his or her own state. An exaggerated sense of fragility is not health but hypochondria. Too much emphasis on the number of things that can go wrong, even presented under the banner of "health promotion," can lead to excessive anxiety and a sense of dependence on health care – from annual checkup to continuous monitoring. This is very advantageous economically for the "health care industry,"[10] and *perhaps* may contribute in some degree to a reduction in disease, but does not correspond to any more general concept of health (Illich, 1975; Haynes et al., 1979; Toronto Working Group on Cholesterol Policy, 1989).

Unlike a heating system, however, health care systems do not settle down to a stable equilibrium of temperature maintenance and fuel use. The combination of the "ethical" claim that all needs must be met, and the empirical regularity that, as one need is met, another is discovered, apparently ad infinitum, leads to a progressive pressure for expansion in the health care systems of all developed societies. It is as if no temperature level were ever high enough, more and more fuel must always be added to the furnace(s).[11]

CONCERNS ABOUT COST, EFFECTIVENESS, AND THE MARGINAL CONTRIBUTION OF HEALTH CARE

The result is shown in Figure 13.2, in which the top arrow, access to health care, has been dramatically expanded to reflect a "health care cost crisis."[12] A comparison of international experience demonstrates that the *perception* of such a crisis is virtually universal, at least in Western Europe and North America. It is interesting to note, however, that the countries which perceive such a crisis actually spend widely differing amounts on health care, either absolutely or as a proportion of their national incomes (Schieber and Poullier, 1989; OECD Secretariat, 1989).

Nevertheless, whether they spend a little or a lot, in all such countries there is an expressed tension between ever-increasing needs, and increasingly restrained resources. Even in the United States, one finds providers of care claiming that they face more and more serious restrictions on the resources available to them (Reinhardt, 1987), despite the egregious observation that the resources devoted to health care in that country are greater, and growing faster, than anywhere else in the world.

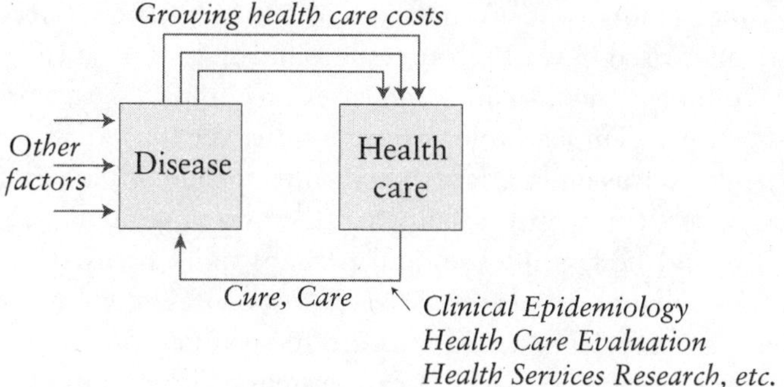

Figure 13.2

Adapted from: Robert G. Evans and Gregory L. Stoddart. "Producing Health, Consuming Health Care." *Social Science & Medicine* 31(12)(1990): 1347–63.

We interpret this observation as implying that perceptions of "crises" in health care finance arise from conflicts over the level of expenditure on health care (and thus by definition also over the levels of incomes earned from its provision). Such conflicts develop whenever paying agencies attempt to limit the rate of increase of resources flowing to the health care system. They are independent of the actual level of provision of health care to a population, or of its expense, let alone of the level of health, however defined, of that population. They also appear to develop independently of the particular form taken by the payment system in a country.

Nor, as the American example shows, does it matter whether the attempts to limit cost escalation are successful. Perceptions of crisis emerge from the attempt, not the result. Accordingly, one should not expect to find any connection between the health of a population, and allegations of "crisis" in the funding of its health care – or at least not among the countries of Western Europe and North America.

On the lower arrow, and intimately connected with the perceptions of "cost crisis," we find increasing concern for the effectiveness with which health care services respond to needs. The development and rapid expansion of clinical epidemiology, for example, reflects a concern that the scientific basis underlying much of health care is weak to non-existent. More generally, the growing field of health services research has accumulated extensive evidence inconsistent with the assumption that the provision of health care is connected in any systematic or scientifically grounded way with patient "needs" or demonstrable outcomes (Banta, Behney, and Willems, 1981; Eisenberg, 1986; Feeny, Guyatt, and Tugwell, 1986;

Lomas, 1990; Ham, 1988; Andersen and Mooney, 1990). Accordingly, the greatly increased flow of resources into health care is perceived as not having a commensurate, or in some cases any, impact on health status. Nor is there any demonstrable connection between international variations in health status and variations in health spending (Culyer, 1988).

If there were a commensurate impact, then presumably efforts to control costs would be less intense (and perhaps more focused on relative incomes). As Culyer (1989) emphasizes, "cost containment in itself is not a sensible objective." The rapid increase in spending on computers has not generated calls for cost caps. A care system which could "cure" upper respiratory infections, colds, and flu, for example, would have an enormous positive impact on both economic productivity and human happiness, and would be well worth considerable extra expense. So would a "cure" for arthritis. Offered such benefits, we suspect that few societies would begrudge the extra resources needed to produce them; indeed these resources would to a considerable extent pay for themselves in higher productivity.[13]

The combination of virtually universal concern over cost escalation, among payers for care, with steadily increasing evidence from the international research community that a significant proportion of health care activity is ineffective, inefficient, inexplicable, or simply unevaluated, constitutes an implicit judgment that the "expanding needs" to which expanding health care systems respond are either not of high enough priority to justify the expense, or simply not being met at all.

It is not that no "needs" remain, that the populations of modern societies have reached a state of optimum health – that is obviously not the case. Nor is it claimed that medicine has had no effect on health – that too is clearly false. The concern is rather that the remaining shortfalls, the continuing burden of illness, disability, distress, and premature death, are less and less sensitive to further extensions in health care – we are reaching the limits of medicine. At the same time, the evidence is growing in both quantity and quality that this burden may be quite sensitive to interventions and structural changes outside the health care system.

These concerns and this evidence are by no means new – they go back at least two decades. Yet most of the public and political debate over health policy continues to be carried on in the rhetoric of "unmet needs" for *health care*. There is a curious disjunction in both the popular and the professional "conventional wisdom," in that widespread concerns about the effectiveness of the health care system, and acceptance of the significance of factors outside that system, coexist quite comfortably with continuing worries about shortages and "underfunding."

The current "shortage" of nurses in Canada, and indeed in much of the industrialized world, provides a good example. Nursing "shortages" have been cause for periodic concern in Canada for more than a quarter-century. Yet throughout that period, there has been virtually uniform agreement among informed observers that utilization of in-patient beds in Canada is substantially higher than "needed," and efforts have been ongoing to reduce such use. Taking both positions together, this suggests that there is a "shortage" of nurses to provide "unnecessary" care!

The significant point is not the validity or otherwise of either perception, but the fact that they do not confront one another. In terms of the thermostatic model, public discussion still consists almost entirely of claims by providers (with considerable public support) that the room temperature is not high enough, or is in danger of falling, or that a severe cold spell is on the way ... but in any case it is imperative that we install more and bigger furnaces immediately, and buy more fuel. Meanwhile payers – in Canada provincial governments – wring their hands over the size of the fuel bill and seek, with very little external support, ways of making the existing heating system more efficient.

A more efficient heating system is indeed a laudable objective, although it is understandable that the providers of health care, as the owners of the fuel supply companies, may give it a lower priority than do those who are responsible for paying the bills. But there is a much more fundamental question. The people who live in the building are primarily concerned about the level and stability of the room temperature, not the heating system per se. They become drawn into an exclusive focus on the heating system, if they perceive that this is the only way to control the room temperature. But as was (re)learned in North America after the oil shock of 1974, this is not so.

Similarly the health care system is not, for the general population, an end in itself. It is a means to an end, maintenance and improvement of health (Evans, 1984). And while few have followed Ivan Illich (1975) in arguing that the health care system has no positive – and indeed net negative – effects on the health of those it serves, nevertheless as noted above, the evidence for the importance of health-enhancing factors outside the health care system is growing rapidly in both quantity and quality.

But the intellectual framework reflected in Figs 13.1 and 13.2 pushes these other, and perhaps more powerful, determinants of health off the stage and into the amorphous cluster of arrows entering from the left-hand side of the diagram. By implication they are unpredictable, or at least uncontrollable, so there is no point in spending a great deal of intellectual energy or policy attention on identifying or trying to influence them. For most of the twentieth century, rapid advances in the scientific, organizational, and financial bases of health care have encouraged, and been encouraged by, this dismissal. We have given almost all our attention to the heating contractor and the fuel salesman, and have had no time or interest to consider how the house is insulated.

By the early 1970s, however, all developed nations had in place extensive and expensive systems of health care, underpinned by collective funding mechanisms, which provided access for all (or in the United States, most) of their citizens. Yet the resulting health gains seemed more modest than some had anticipated, while the "unmet needs," or at least the pressures for system expansion, refused to diminish.

Simple trend projections indicated that, within a relatively short span of decades, the health care systems of modern societies would take over their entire economies. As public concerns shifted from expansion to evaluation and control, the alternative tradition began to reassert itself. In such an environment, a growing interest in alternative, perhaps more effective, hopefully less expensive, ways of promoting health was a natural response.

The resurgence of interest in ways of enhancing the health of populations, other than by further expansion of health care systems, was thus rooted both in the observation of the stubborn persistence of ill-health, and in the concern over growing costs. The latter development has been particularly important in "recruiting new constituencies" for the broader view of the determinants of health. Financial bureaucrats, both public and private, have become (often rather suspect) allies of more traditional advocates (Evans, 1982; McKinlay, 1979).

THE HEALTH FIELD CONCEPT: A NEW PERSPECTIVE

The broader view was given particularly compact and articulate expression in the famous Canadian White Paper referred to above, which came out, presumably by complete coincidence, in the same year as the first "energy crisis." Its "Four Field" framework for categorizing the determinants of health was broad enough to express a number of the concerns of those trying to shift the focus of health policy from an exclusive

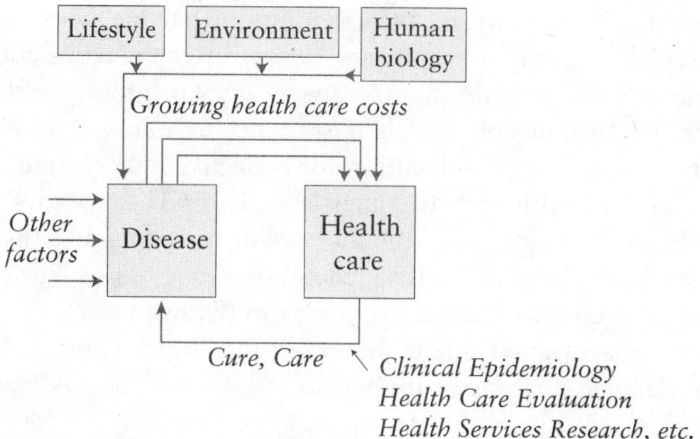

Figure 13.3

Adapted from: Robert G. Evans and Gregory L. Stoddart. "Producing Health, Consuming Health Care." *Social Science & Medicine* 31(12)(1990): 1347–63.

concern with health care. In Figure 13.3 this framework is superimposed upon the earlier "thermostat/furnace" model of health care and health.

The *New Perspective* proposed that the determinants of health status could be categorized under the headings of Lifestyle, Environment, Human Biology, and Health Care Organization. As can be seen in Figure 13.3, the first three of these categories provided specific identification for some of the "other and unspecified" factors entering on the left-hand side of Figures 13.1 and 13.2. By labelling and categorizing these factors, the White Paper drew attention to them and suggested the possibility that their control might contribute more to the improvement of human health than further expansions in the health care system. At the very least, the health field framework emphasized the centrality of the objective of *health*, and the fact that health care was only one among several forms of public policy which might lead towards this objective.

The White Paper was received very positively; no one seriously challenged its basic message that who we are, how we live, and where we live are powerful influences on our health status. But the appropriate policy response was less clear, because the document could be read in several different ways. At one end of the ideological spectrum, it was seen as a call for a much more interventionist set of social policies, going well beyond the public provision of health care per se in the effort to improve the health of the Canadian population and relieve the burden of morbidity and mortality.

At the other end, however, the assumption that lifestyles, and to a lesser extent living environments, are *chosen* by the persons concerned could be combined with the White Paper framework to argue that people are largely responsible for their own health status – have in fact chosen it. If so, then the justification for collective intervention, even in the provision of health care, becomes less clear.[14] This appears to have been far from the intention of the authors of the paper, but the framework in Figure 13.3 lends itself to "victim-blaming" as well as to arguments for more comprehensive social reform (Evans, 1982).

Whatever the original intent, however, the White Paper led into a period of detailed analysis of *individual* risk factors, that is, both individual hazards and individual persons, as contributors to "disease" in the traditional sense.[15] The potential significance of processes operating on health at the level of groups and populations was obscured, if not lost (Buck, 1988). Smoking, for example, was viewed as an individual act predisposing to specific diseases. Specific atmospheric pollution contributes to lung disease. Genetic defects result in well-defined genetic diseases. The central thermostatic relationship is preserved, with health as absence of disease, and health care as response to disease in order to provide "cures" or relieve symptoms, individual by individual.

To illustrate the distinction, one can formulate health policy to address cancer across a spectrum from the individual to the collective. One can increase facilities for the treatment of cancer patients, a wholly individualized, reactive response. One can increase research on cancer treatment, an activity with a "collective" focus only insofar as the specific recipients of new treatments may not be known in advance. One can launch anti-smoking campaigns, trying to induce certain individuals whose *characteristics* are known – they smoke – to change their behaviour voluntarily. These campaigns may in turn be wholly individualized – paying or otherwise encouraging physicians to provide counselling, for example – or advertising campaigns aimed at the general population. Or one can try to limit involuntary exposures by regulating the presence of carcinogens in the environment, establishing mandatory smoke-free zones (hospitals, restaurants, aircraft, workplaces ...) or regulating industrial processes.

The focus on individual risk factors and specific diseases has tended to lead not away from but back to the health care system itself. Interventions, particularly those addressing personal lifestyles, are offered in the form of "provider counselling" for smoking cessation, seatbelt use, or dietary modification (American Council of Life Insurance and Health Insurance Association of America, 1988; Lewis, 1988). These in turn are subsumed under a more general and rapidly growing set of interventions attempting to modify risk factors through transactions between clinicians and individual patients.

The "product line" of the health care system is thus extended to deal with a more broadly defined set of "diseases" – unhealthy behaviours. The boundary becomes blurred between, for example, heart disease as manifest in symptoms, or in elevated serum cholesterol measurements, or in excessive consumption of fats. All are "diseases" and represent a "need" for health care intervention. Through this process of disease redefinition, the conventional health care system has been able to justify extending outreach and screening programs and placing increased numbers of people on continuing regimens of drug therapy and regular monitoring.

The emphasis on individual risk factors and particular diseases has thus served to maintain and protect existing institutions and ways of thinking about health. The "broader determinants of health" were matters for the attention of individuals, perhaps in consultation with their personal physicians, supported by poster campaigns from the local public health unit. The behaviour of large and powerful organizations, or the effects of economic and social policies, public and private, were not brought under scrutiny. This interpretation of the White Paper thus not only fitted in with the increasingly conservative zeitgeist of the late 1970s and early 1980s, but protected and even enhanced the economic position of providers of care, while restricting sharply the range of determinants, and associated policies, considered. Established economic interests were not threatened – with the limited exception of the tobacco industry.

This tendency was reinforced by attempts to estimate the relative contribution of the four different fields or sets of factors to ill-health. As Gunning-Schepers and Hagen (1987) have pointed out, a simple partitioning of sources of mortality, morbidity, or care utilization into four discrete "boxes" is fundamentally misguided. Nevertheless, "expert opinion" suggested that, of the three fields external to the health care system, "Lifestyle" had the largest and most unambiguously measurable effect on health. "Lifestyle" – diet, exercise, substance use – was also the factor most readily portrayed as under the control of the individual. It thus lent itself to the politically innocuous, inexpensive, highly visible, and relatively ineffective intervention of health education campaigns – carried on through the public health arm of the health care system.

Smoking cessation provides a partial counter-example, which illustrates the difficulty of breaking out of the disease–health care intellectual framework. Tobacco is not only toxic, but addictive, and addiction most commonly commences in childhood. Consequently, the presumption that users rationally and voluntarily "choose" smoking as a "lifestyle" is particularly inappropriate. Furthermore, the observation that smoking behaviour is very sharply graded by socioeconomic class undercuts the argument that it represents an individual choice, and indicates instead a powerful form of social conditioning.[16]

Partly for these reasons, Canadian health policy has gone beyond educational campaigns to spread information about the ill effects of smoking and includes limitations on the advertising and marketing of tobacco products. The political resistance to these limitations has been much more intense, suggesting prima facie that the marketers of such products fear that they might be effective. But the broader question, of the social determinants of tobacco use, is still left open.[17]

The intellectual framework of the White Paper, at least as it has been applied and as represented in Figure 13.3, has thus supplemented the thermostatic model of health as absence of disease, and health care as response, but has failed to move beyond the core relationship. Since as noted above, "disease" is defined through the interpretation of individual experience by the providers of health care, it is perhaps not surprising that the Health Care Organization field tended to take over large parts of the other three when they were presented as determinants of disease.

EXTENDING THE FRAMEWORK: HEALTH AND ITS BIOLOGICAL AND BEHAVIOURAL DETERMINANTS

Yet in the years since the publication of the White Paper, a great deal of evidence has accumulated, from many different sources, which is difficult or impossible to represent within this framework. The very broad set of relationships encompassed under the label of "stress," for example, and factors protective against "stress" (Dantzer and Kelley, 1989; Sapolsky, 1990), have directed attention to the importance of social relationships, or their absence, as correlates of disease and mortality. Feelings of self-esteem and self-worth, or hierarchical position and control, or conversely powerlessness, similarly appear to have health implications quite independent of the conventional risk factors (Dutton, 1986; Marmot, 1986; House, Landis, and Umberson, 1988; Sapolsky, 1990).

These sorts of factors suggest explanations for the universal finding, across all nations, that mortality and (when measurable) morbidity follow a gradient across socioeconomic classes. Lower income and/or lower social status are associated with poorer health.[18]

This relationship is not, however, an indication of deprivation at the lower end of the scale, although it is frequently misinterpreted in that way. In the first place, the socioeconomic gradient in health status has been relatively stable over time (Townsend and Davidson, 1982), although average income levels have risen markedly in all developed societies. The proportion of persons who are deprived of the necessities of life in a biological sense has clearly declined. But even more important, the relationship is a *gradient*, not a step function. Top people appear to be healthier than those on the second rung, even though the latter are above the population averages for income, status, or whatever the critical factors are (Marmot, 1986).

It follows that the variously interpreted determinants of health which lie outside the health care system are not just a problem of some poor, deprived minority whose situation can be deplored and ignored by the rest of us. *De te fabula narratur*, we are all (or most of us) affected. And that in turn implies that the effects of such factors may be quantitatively very significant for the overall health status of modern populations. The issues involved are not trivial, second- or third-order effects.

Moreover, the fact that gradients in mortality and morbidity across socioeconomic classes appear to be relatively stable over long periods of time, even though the principal causes of death have changed considerably, implies that the underlying factors influence susceptibility to a whole range of diseases. They are general rather than specific risk factors. Whatever is going round, people in lower social positions tend to get more of it, and to die earlier – even after adjustment for the effects of specific individual or environmental hazards (Marmot, Shipley, and Rose, 1984).

This suggests that an understanding of the relationship between social position, or "stress," and health, will require investigation at a more general level than the aetiology of specific diseases. It also raises the possibility that disease-specific policy responses – through health care or otherwise – may not reach deeply enough to have much effect. Even if one "disease" is "cured," another will take its place.

An attempt to provide a further extension to our intellectual framework, to encompass these new forms of evidence, is laid out in Figure 13.4.

In Figure 13.4, two major structural changes are introduced. First, a distinction is drawn between disease, as recognized and responded to by

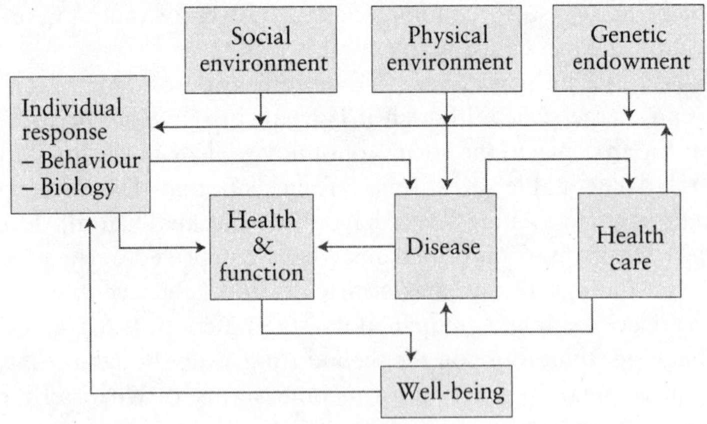

Figure 13.4

Adapted from: Robert G. Evans and Gregory L. Stoddart. "Producing Health, Consuming Health Care." *Social Science & Medicine* 31(12)(1990): 1347–63.

the health care system, and health and function as experienced by the individual person. Such a distinction permits us to consider, within this framework, the common observation that illness experienced by individuals (and their families or other relevant social groups) does not necessarily correspond to disease as understood by the providers of care. Persons with "the same" disease, from the point of view of the health care system – similar biological parameters, prognoses, and implications for treatment – may experience very different levels of symptoms and distress, and very different effects on their ability to function in their various social roles. Arthritis, and musculo-skeletal problems more generally, are leading examples of conditions for which the patient's sense of "illness" bears no very close relationship to the clinician's interpretation of "disease."

This is not to say that one perspective is "right" and the other "wrong"; the two modes of interpretation simply have different purposes. The clinician's concept of disease is intended to guide the appropriate application of available medical knowledge and technology, so is formulated in terms of that knowledge and technology. The patient, on the other hand, is ultimately concerned with the impact of the illness on his/her own life. The clinician's disease may be an important part of that impact, but is by no means the only relevant factor.

Moreover, from the point of view of the individual's well-being and social performance – including economic productivity – it is the individual's sense of health and functional capacity which is determinative – as shown in Figure 13.4. The "diseases" diagnosed and treated by the health care system are important only insofar as they affect that sense of health and capacity – which of course they do. But health, even as interpreted by the individual, is not the only thing in life which matters. Figure 13.4 introduces the category of "well-being," the sense of life satisfaction of the individual, which is or should be (we postulate) the ultimate objective of health policy. The ultimate test of such policy is whether or not it adds to the well-being of the population served.

Going back to the original WHO definition of health, we are relabelling that broad definition as well-being. Our concept of health is defined, in narrow terms but from the patient's perspective, as the absence of *illness* or injury, of distressing symptoms or impaired capacity. Disease, as a medical construct or concept, will usually have a significant bearing on illness, and thus on health, but is not the same thing. Illness, in turn, is a very important (negative) influence on well-being – but not the only one. The WHO broad definition of "health" is, as noted above, so broad as to become the objective, not only of health policy, but of all human activity.

Hypertension screening and treatment gives a clear and concrete example of this distinction, as well as bringing out the limitations of the static framework expressed in all the accompanying figures. It is sometimes said that hypertension does not hurt you, it only kills you. Target organ damage proceeds silently and without symptoms; a sudden and possibly fatal stroke announces both the presence of the long-term condition, and its consequences. Until that point, the individual concerned may have no illness, although a clinician who took his/her blood pressure might identify a disease.

Studies of the impact of hypertension screening and treatment programs, however, have made it clear that the fact of *diagnosis*, "labelling," makes the patient ill, in ways which are unambiguous and objectively measureable (Haynes et al., 1979). Treatment exacerbates the illness, through drug side effects, although those who comply with treatment may suffer less severe labelling effects. Screening and treatment of hypertension thus spread illness among the beneficiaries and reduce their functional capacity, in a real and literal sense, even as their disease is alleviated.

Of course such screening is not carried out from clinical malice! The long-term consequences of hypertension as a disease may be expressed in very definite forms of illness, including death. The immediate consequences of discovery and treatment of disease may be increased illness; the longer-term consequences are reduction in illness, and very severe illness at that, for some of those under care. There is substantial evidence that screening and treatment of moderate to severe hypertension have very significantly reduced both morbidity and mortality from stroke; this is widely regarded as one of the leading "success stories" in clinical prevention (Hypertension Detection and Follow-up Program Cooperative Group, 1979). But regardless of their relative strength, the static framework of Figure 13.4 does not reflect this pattern of offsetting movements in different time periods.

Indeed there is an implicit time structure to all of the figures. "Cures" are rarely instantaneous, so health care has its negative effect on disease only with a time lag of variable length. The lifestyle and environmental factors displayed in Figures 13.3 and 13.4 have long-term and cumulative effects on health/disease. But the extra problem in Figure 13.4 arises because the relationship being displayed may reverse itself over time. Health care can have a negative effect on health in the short term, and a positive one in the longer term.[19]

The possibility of "long-term gain" may, but does not necessarily, justify the "short-term pain," and analysts and evaluators of preventive programs are acutely aware of the necessity of weighing the health benefits and health costs against each other. Overzealous intervention can do significant harm to the health of those treated, even if at some later date it can be shown to have "saved lives" or, more accurately, postponed some deaths.

The debate over cholesterol screening, and the contradictory recommendations arising from "experts" in different jurisdictions, is a current case in point (Toronto Working Group on Cholesterol Policy, 1989; Moore, 1989; Anderson, Brinkworth, and Ng, 1989). At issue are not merely differing interpretations of the epidemiological evidence, or different weightings of "lives and dollars" – program resource costs versus mortality outcomes. The prospect of converting a quarter of the adult population of North America into "patients" with chronic illness requiring continuous drug therapy gives at least some clinicians (and others!) pause.

The framework of Figure 13.4 enables, indeed encourages, one to consider this distinction. Large-scale cholesterol screening and drug therapy, in this framework, would represent an epidemic of new illness, with negative impacts on health and function from both labelling effects and drug side effects. As the hypertension studies remind us, these negative effects are real and concrete, measurable in people's lives. Against this, there would be a reduction in disease, as measured first in serum cholesterol, and subsequently in heart disease. The latter would then contribute positively to health, but the conflicting health effects of disease reduction, i.e., deterioration in health now, improvement later, must be weighed against each other in assessing their net impact on well-being.

In addition to distinguishing explicitly "disease" from "illness," Figure 13.4 extends the categorization of the determinants of health provided in the White Paper framework. This permits us to incorporate within the framework the diverse and rapidly-growing body of research literature on the determinants of health which does not fit at all comfortably within the White Paper categories.

The key addition is the concept of the individual "host response," which includes but goes beyond the usual epidemiological sense of the term. The range of circumstances to which the organism/individual may respond is also wider than is usually encompassed within epidemiology (Cassel, 1976), This "host response" now includes some factors or processes which were previously assembled under the labels of "Lifestyle" and "Human Biology."

The implications of this change can be seen when one considers (yet again) smoking behaviour. In the White Paper framework, tobacco use is labelled as a "Lifestyle," from which one can draw the implication that its use is an "individual choice." That in turn leads not only to victim-blaming, but also to an emphasis on informational and educational strategies for control, which are notoriously ineffective. The powerful ethical overtones of "choice," with its connections to "freedom" and "individual self-expression," introduce not only political but also intellectual confusions into the process of control of an addictive and toxic substance.

Yet it is widely observed that tobacco use is powerfully socially conditioned. Income, status, and prestige rankings in modern societies have become strongly negatively correlated with smoking, such that differential smoking behaviour is now a significant factor in the social gradient in mortality. This was not always so; prior to the widespread dissemination of information about its health effects, smoking was positively correlated with status. It seems clear that, far from being simply an "individual" choice, smoking is an activity engaged in – or not – by groups of people in particular circumstances. Understanding why some people smoke, and others do not, and a fortiori developing successful strategies to discourage this self-destructive behaviour, requires that one explore these group processes, and their conditioning circumstances. To treat smoking as "individual choice" is simply to throw away the information contained in the clustering of behaviour.

This is not to reduce the individual to an automaton, or deny any role for individual choice. Nor is smoking the only activity which is socially conditioned – far from it. But the well-defined clustering of smoking and non-smoking behaviour within the population suggests that such behaviour is also a form of "host" (the smoker) response to a social environment which does or does not promote smoking. Heavy tobacco advertising promotes, for example, while legislated smoke-free environments discourage, quite separately from the "individual choice."

The psychological dynamics of status and class may have even more powerful, if subtler, effects. The sense of personal efficacy associated with higher social position encourages beliefs both in one's ability to break addictions, and in the positive consequences of doing so. Beliefs in the effectiveness (or lack of it) of one's own actions are both learned and reinforced by one's social position.

The distinction between social environment and host response also permits us to incorporate conceptually factors which influence health in much less direct and obvious ways than smoking. It has been observed that the death of a spouse places an individual at increased risk of illness, or even death. This may be due to a reduction in the competence of the immune system, although the causal pathways are by no means wholly clear. Evidence is accumulating rapidly, however, that the nervous and immune systems communicate with each other, each synthesizing hormones that are "read" by the other, so that the social environment can, in principle, influence biological responses through its input to the nervous system. Data from animal experiments have shown the power of these effects (Dantzer and Kelley, 1989).

Biological responses by the organism to its social environment are not restricted to the immune system. Forms of stress which one feels powerless to control – associated with hierarchical position, for example – may be correlated with differences in the plasma levels of reactive proteins such as fibrinogen (Markowe et al., 1985), or with the efficiency of the hormonal responses to stress (Sapolsky, 1990). The adequacy or inadequacy of nutrition in early infancy may "program" the processing of dietary fats in ways which have consequences much later in life (Barker et al., 1989; Birch, 1972). The range of possible biological pathways is only beginning to emerge, and is at present still quite contentious, but it seems clear that the sharp separation between "Human Biology" and "other things" is crumbling.

Accordingly we have in Figure 13.4 unbundled that field, and restricted it to the genetic endowment. This endowment then interacts with the influences of the social and physical environments, to determine both the biological and the behavioural responses of the individual (Baird and Scriver, 1990). Some of these responses will be predominantly unconscious – few of us are aware of how our immune systems are performing (unless they are overwhelmed), much less can deliberately affect them. Other responses will be behavioural - smoking, for example, or buckling seatbelts. Both forms of response, or rather the continuum of such responses, will influence the ability of the individual to deal with external challenges, either to resist illness or to maintain function in spite of it. They will also affect the burden of disease, separately from illness, insofar as the decision to seek care, compliance with therapy, and response to therapy (or to self-care) are also part of the host response.

An example of the significance of changes in such host responses may be given by the decline in tuberculosis in the United Kingdom over the last century. This dramatic change in mortality patterns occurred prior to the development of any effective responses from either public health measures or medical therapy (McKeown, 1979). Sagan (1987) notes that the decline was apparently *not* due to a reduced rate of exposure to the bacillus, as the majority of the population continued to test positive for the TB antibody as late as 1940. The resistance of the population simply increased. McKeown offers improved nutrition as an explanation, but the issue still seems to be open (McKeown, 1979; Sagan, 1987).[20] The point for our purposes is that the *biological* response of the organism is malleable.

Indeed, progress in genetics is also extending the older picture of a fixed genetic endowment, in which well-defined genetic diseases follow from single-gene defects. It now appears that particular combinations of genes may lead to predispositions, or resistances, to a wide variety of diseases, not themselves normally thought of as "genetic." Whether these predispositions actually become expressed as disease, will depend *inter alia* on various environmental factors, physical and social (Baird and Scriver, 1990).

The insertion of the host response between environmental factors and both the expression of disease and the level of health and function provides a set of categories sufficiently flexible to encompass the growing but rather complex evidence on the connections between social environment and illness. Unemployment, for example, may lead to illness (quite apart from its correlation with economic deprivation) if the unemployed individual becomes socially isolated and stigmatized. On the other hand, if support networks are in place to maintain social contacts, and if self-esteem is not undermined, then the health consequences may be minimal.

The correlation of longevity with hierarchical status may be an example of reverse causality – the physically fitter rise to the top. But it is also possible that the self-esteem and sense of coping ability induced by success and the respect of others results in a "host response" of enhanced immune function or other physiological strengthening. The biological vulnerability or resilience of the individual, in response to external shocks, is dependent on the social and physical environment in interaction with the genetic endowment. While, as noted, the biological pathways for this process are only beginning to be traced out, the observed correlations continue to accumulate. Figure 13.4 provides a conceptual framework within which to express such a pattern of relationships.

In this extended framework, the relationship between the health care system and the health of the population becomes even more complex. The sense of self-esteem, coping ability, powerfulness, may conceivably be either reinforced or undermined by health care interventions. Labelling effects may create a greater sense of vulnerability in the labelled, which itself influences physiological function. Such a process was an important part of Ivan Illich's message. Yet the initiation of preventive behaviour, or of therapy, may also result in positive "placebo" effects, perhaps reflecting an increased sense of coping or control, independently of any "objective" assessment of the effectiveness of such changes.

The possibility that medical interventions may have unintended effects is inevitable. Our framework includes both placebo and iatrogenic effects in the causal arrow from care to disease. But there is also a potential effect, of ambiguous sign, from care to host response.

At yet another level, the protective sense of self-esteem or coping ability seems to be a collective as well as an individual possession. Being a "winner," being on a "winning team," or simply being associated with a winning team – a resident of a town whose team has won a championship – all seem to provide considerable satisfaction, and may have more objectively measurable influences on health.

A FURTHER EXTENSION: ECONOMIC TRADE-OFFS AND WELL-BEING

But there is still another feedback loop to be considered. Health care, and health policy generally, have economic costs which also affect well-being. Once we extend the framework, as in Figure 13.4, to reflect the fact that the ultimate objective of health-related activity is not the reduction of disease, as defined by the health care system, or even the promotion of human health and function, but the enhancement of human well-being, then we face a further set of trade-offs, which are introduced in Figure 13.5.

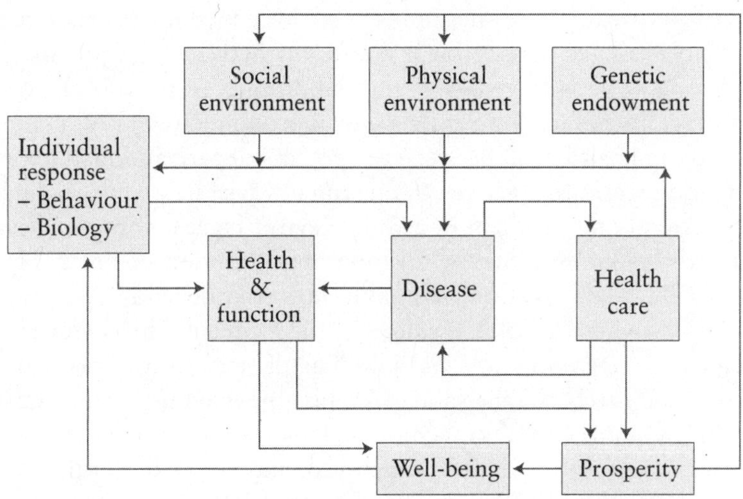

Figure 13.5

Adapted from: Robert G. Evans and Gregory L. Stoddart. "Producing Health, Consuming Health Care." *Social Science & Medicine* 31(12) (1990): 1347–63.

Health care is not "free"; as noted above, the provision of such services is now the largest single industry or cluster of economic activities in all modern societies. This represents a major commitment of resources – human time, energy, and skills, raw materials and capital services – which are therefore unavailable for other forms of production. To the extent that health care makes a positive contribution to health, it thereby contributes to human happiness both directly and through the economic benefits of enhanced human function and productivity.

The latter effect is frequently referred to as an "investment in health"; spending on health care may even pay for itself through increased capacity of the population to work and produce wealth. The increasing concentration of health care on those outside the labour force, the very elderly or chronically ill, has however severely weakened this form of linkage. For most health care now provided, the benefits must be found in the value of the resulting improvements in health, not in some further productivity gains.

Whatever the form of the payoff to health care, the resources used in its provision are inevitably a net drain on the wealth of the community. The well-being and economic progress of the larger society are thus affected *negatively* by the extension of the health care system per se. The fallacious argument frequently put forward by the economically naive, that health care, or any other industry, yields economic benefits through the creation of jobs, rests on a confusion between the job itself – a resource-using activity or cost – and the product of the job, the output. It is in fact an extension into the general economic realm of a common confusion in health care, between the process of care and its outcome.[21]

Yet "job-creation" is very easy; one can always hire people to dig holes in the ground and fill them in again. (Keynes suggested burying bottles filled with banknotes, thereby creating opportunities for profitable self-employment.) The creation of wealth, however, depends upon the creation of jobs whose *product* is valued by the recipient. This understanding is implicit in references to "real jobs," as distinct from make-work, or employment purely for the sake of keeping people busy – and remunerated. In a complex modern economy, large numbers of people can be kept busy, apparently gainfully employed, and yet adding little or nothing to the wealth of the population as a whole.[22]

This distinction between the cost of an activity, its net absorption of productive resources, and the benefits which flow from it in the form of valued goods and services, is not unique to health care. It applies to any economic activity, as reflected in the generality of the techniques of cost-benefit analysis. The situation of health care is different, however, for a variety of complex and interrelated reasons which are implicit in the chain of effects from health care, to disease reduction, to improved health and function, to well-being.

As a commodity, health care has characteristics which make it intrinsically different from "normal" commodities traded through private markets, and this is reflected in the peculiar and complex collection of institutional arrangements which surround its provision. As a consequence both of these intrinsic peculiarities, and of the institutional responses to them, the mechanisms which for most commodities maintain some linkage between the resource costs of a commodity and its value to users are lacking.

These problems are discussed in detail in the literature on the economics of health care (e.g., Evans, 1984, Chaps. 1–5). For our purposes, however, the important point is that overexpansion of the health *care* system can in principle have negative effects not only on the well-being of the population, but even on its *health*. These dual effects are shown in Figure 13.5.

The possible negative impact of overprovision on well-being is straightforward. As emphasized, the provision of health care uses up economic resources which could be used for other valued purposes. Canadians spend nearly 9 per cent of their national income on health care – 1 dollar in 12 – and these resources are thus unavailable for producing consumer goods like clothing or furniture, or building rapid transit systems, or improving the educational system, etc. (expanding the capacity of the Toronto airport!) In the United States, nearly 12 per cent of national income is spent on health care; in Japan, about 6 per cent. The Japanese correspondingly have a larger share of their income available for other purposes, the Americans a smaller proportion.

Less obviously, but implicit in Figure 13.5, the expansion of health care draws resources away from other uses which may also have health effects. In public budgets, for example, rising health care costs for the elderly draw funds which are then unavailable for increased pensions; rising deficits may even lead to pension reductions. Increased taxes or private health insurance premiums lower the disposable income of the working population. Environmental cleanup programs also compete for scarce resources with the provision of health care.

Once we recognize the importance and potential controllability of factors other than health care in both the limitation of disease and the promotion of health, we simultaneously open for explicit consideration the possibility that the direct positive effects of health care on health may be outweighed by its negative effects through its competition for resources with other health-enhancing activities. A society which spends so much on health care that it cannot or will not spend adequately on other health-enhancing activities may actually be *reducing* the health of its population through increased health spending.

Two points of clarification may be helpful here, along with one of qualification.

First, we are *not* referring to iatrogenesis, the direct negative effects of health care on health. Powerful interventions have powerful side effects; the growing reach of medical technology often brings with it increased potential for harm.[23] Clinical judgment includes the balancing of probabilities for benefit and harm; the best care will sometimes work out badly. Moreover, all human systems involve some degree of error – inappropriate and incompetent care, or simply bad luck. Expansion of the health care system thus carries with it a greater potential for harm as well as good, as a direct result of care, but that is not the point here.

Second, the potential effects we are postulating are the economist's *marginal* effects. The global impact of health care, on either health or resource availability, is not addressed. Perhaps Ivan Illich is right, and the health care system as a whole has a net negative impact on the health of the population it serves. But we do not know that, and we do not know how one could come to know it.

The point we are making is a much more limited one, and one which within the framework of Figure 13.5 may be self-evident. The health of individuals and populations is affected by their health care, but also by other factors as well. Expansion of the health care system uses up resources which would otherwise be available to address those other factors. (Whether they would be so used or not, is another matter.) It follows that an expansion of the health care system may have negative effects on health. A *health* policy, as opposed to policies for *health care*, would have to take account of this balance.

The qualification, however, arises from the fact that, when we speak of the health of a population, we are aggregating across all the individuals in it. Different policies benefit different individuals. A decision to reallocate resources from health care to other health-enhancing or productivity-enhancing activities might indeed result in a population which was in aggregate both healthier and wealthier, but particular individuals in it will be worse off. Most clearly, of course, these will include persons who either make or intended to make their living from the provision of health care. But in addition, health care services respond to the circumstances of identified individuals, in the present. A more limited commitment of resources to health care might leave such persons worse off, even though in future there might be fewer people in their position.

Such trade-offs, between the interests of those who are now ill and those who may become so, may be inevitable. In any case it is important to note their possibility, because they are hidden from view in the aggregate framework. But conversely, it should also be noted that there is no obvious ethical, much less prudential, basis for resolving this trade-off in favour of more health care. We need to be clear as to whether we have, as a community, undertaken a collective obligation of concern, and support, for each other's *health*, or only for those aspects of health which can be enhanced through *health care*. If the latter, we may find that we are as a society both poorer, and less healthy, than we could otherwise be, and we may want to rethink the details of our (self-imposed) ethical obligation.

In this context, as in so many others, the Japanese experience is startling, and may provide an illustration of the feedback loop from prosperity to health included in Figure 13.5. The extraordinary economic performance of Japanese society is not a new observation; the phenomenon goes back forty years, and indeed a similar period of extraordinary modernization and growth began after the Meiji restoration in 1868. What is new is that within the last decade Japan has begun to shift from the very successful copying of innovations elsewhere in the world, to being increasingly on the leading edge of both economic growth and technological change.

Over the same period, there has been a remarkable growth in Japanese life expectancy, which in the 1980s has caught up with and then surpassed that of the rest of the developed world (Marmot and Smith, 1989). Like the Japanese economy and per capita wealth, average life expectancy is continuing to rise on a significantly faster trend than in other industrialized countries. This experience is now setting new standards for the possible in human populations.

On the other hand, the Japanese health care system absorbs one of the lowest shares of national income in the industrialized world, and has been described by a recent American observer as "an anachronism" in the context of modern Japanese society (Iglehart, 1988). And the popular external image is that life in Japan is very crowded, highly stressful, and quite polluted. How then does one explain the extraordinary trends in life expectancy?

One causal pattern suggested in Figure 13.5 would lead from outstanding economic performance, to rapid growth in personal incomes and in the scope and variety of life, to the greatly enhanced sense of individual and collective self-esteem and hope for the future. A number of observers, concerned not with comparative health status but with international economic competitiveness, have noted the extraordinary Japanese sense of self-confidence and pride arising from their rapid progress towards world economic leadership. Individually and as a nation the Japanese are seeing themselves as harder-working, brighter, richer, and just plain better than the rest of the world; could this attitude be yielding health benefits as well?

Conversely, the centrally planned economies of Eastern Europe and the Soviet Union have on most measures of economic success performed dismally for many years, to the extent that their rulers as well as their populations have been willing to undertake a massive and indeed revolutionary political restructuring. Corresponding to this extended period of economic decline, measures of life expectancy in those nations have been stagnant or even falling, in marked contrast to the universal improvements in Western Europe (Hertzman, 1990).

Uncontrolled environmental pollution and unhealthy lifestyles are commonly-cited explanations, but the observation is at least consistent with the hypothesis of a relationship between collective self-esteem and health – a relationship which could be expressed in part through unhealthy lifestyles.

The factors underlying the shift in world economic leadership are no doubt complex and diverse. One of several recurring explanatory themes, however, is the Japanese advantage in access to low-cost long-term capital, which is channelled into both research and development, and plant and equipment investment embodying the latest technology. This low-cost capital is generated by the very high savings rates of the Japanese people. The United States, by contrast, reports a savings rate close to zero, and now relies heavily on savings borrowed from the rest of the world – particularly Japan.

To maintain a high savings rate, one must limit the growth of other claims on social resources – such as health care.[24] The difference between Japanese and United States rates of spending on health care amounts to over 5 per cent of national income, and could account for a significant proportion of the large difference between Japanese and American aggregate savings rates. (The difference in military spending accounts for another large share.)

Very speculatively, then, one can suggest that, by limiting the growth of their health care sector, the Japanese have freed up resources which were devoted to capital investment both physical and intellectual. The consequent rapid growth in prosperity, particularly relative to their leading competitors, has greatly enhanced (already well-developed) national and individual self-esteem, which has in turn contributed to a remarkable improvement in health.

It must be emphasized that this is a rough sketch of a possible argument, not a well-developed case, much less a "proof." There are other candidate explanations for Japanese longevity – diet, for example, or the peculiar characteristics of Japanese society which may be protective against the ill effects of stress. (On the other hand, there are different forms of stress, and the stress of success is much less threatening to health than the stress of frustration and failure.)

Equally problematic, there is good evidence that environmental effects on morbidity and mortality may operate with very long lags, so that present Japanese life expectancies may reflect factors at work over the past fifty years. And in any case, what has been observed is that the Japanese live a long time; whether they are relatively healthy in any more comprehensive sense is another matter. On the other hand, the Japanese gains in life expectancy are occurring across the age spectrum, with both the world's lowest infant mortality, and extended lives among the elderly, consistent both with some contemporaneous effects, and with more general increases in health.

Whatever the explanation, it is clear that something very significant is happening (or has happened) in Japan – something reflected in trends in life expectancy which are remarkable relative to any other world experience. These observations are at least consistent with the rough sketch above. A good deal of closer investigation would seem warranted.

It is not our intent in this paper to lay "The Decline of the West" at the feet of the health care system of the United States, or even those of North America and Western Europe combined. Rather our point is to show that the framework laid out in Figure 13.5 is capable of permitting such a relationship to be raised for consideration. Its network of linkages between health, health care, the production of wealth, and the well-being of the population is sufficiently developed to encompass the question, without overwhelming and paralyzing one in the "dependence of everything upon everything."

FRAMEWORKS IN PRINCIPLE AND IN PRACTICE

As noted above, the test of such a framework will be the extent to which others find it useful as a set of categories for assembling data and approximating complex causal patterns. The understanding of the determinants of population health, and the discussion and formulation of health policy, have been seriously impeded by the perpetuation of the incomplete, obsolete, and misleading framework of Figure 13.1. There is a bigger picture, but clearer understanding, and particularly a more sensible and constructive public discussion, of it requires the development of a more adequate intellectual framework. The progression to Figure 13.5 is offered as a possible step along the way.

In this paper we have suggested several important features of such a framework. It should accommodate distinctions among disease, as defined and treated by the health care system, health and function, as perceived and experienced by individuals, and well-being, a still broader concept, to which health is an important, but not the only, contributor. It should build on the Lalonde health-field framework to permit and encourage a more subtle and more complex consideration of both behavioural and biological responses to social and physical environments. Finally, it should recognize and foster explicit identification of the economic trade-offs involved in the allocation of scarce resources to health care instead of other activities of value to individuals and societies, activities which may themselves contribute to health and well-being.

To date, health care policy has in most societies dominated health policy, because of its greater immediacy and apparently more secure scientific base. One may concede in principle the picture in Figure 13.5, then convert all the lines of causality into "disease" and "health and function" into thin dotted ones, except for a fat black one from "health care." That is the picture implicit in the current emphasis in health policy, despite the increasing concern among health researchers as to the reliability and primacy of the connection from health care to health.

One lesson from international experience in the post–Lalonde era is that appropriate conceptualization of the determinants of health is a necessary, but not a sufficient, condition for serious reform of health policy. Intellectual frameworks, including the one offered here, are only a beginning. Simply put, to be useful, they must be used.

ACKNOWLEDGMENTS

We wish to thank colleagues in the CIAR Population Health Program, the Health Polinomics Research Workshop at McMaster University, and the Health Policy Research Unit at the University of British Columbia for stimulating comments on earlier versions of this paper. We take responsibility for remaining errors or omissions.

NOTES

1 The rhetoric of "prevention" has penetrated the health care system to a significant degree; reactive responses to identified departures from health may be labelled secondary or tertiary prevention insofar as they prevent further deterioration of an adverse condition. But even when components of the health care system move from a reactive to a promotive strategy – screening for cholesterol, for example, or hypertension – the interventions still consist of identifying departures from clinically determined norms for particular biological measurements, and initiating therapeutic interventions. Elevated blood pressure or serum cholesterol measurements become themselves identified as "diseases," to be "cured."

2 The representation of mental illness is always troublesome – where is the borderline between clinical depression and the "normal" human portion of

unhappiness? The difficulty of definition persists, however, across the whole continuum; the WHO definition of health does not imply perpetual bliss.

3 This does not represent a rejection of rational modes of inquiry; the universe is still seen as, on some levels, a comprehensible and orderly place. But there appear to be fundamental limits on its comprehensibility – not just on our ability to comprehend it – and the relevant concepts of order may also be less complete than was once hoped. Whether or not Nietzsche turns out to be right about the death of God (Hawking, 1988), Laplace's Demon appears definitely defunct (Dreyfus and Dreyfus, 1988; Gleick, 1987; Holton, 1988). (But has he met his maker?)

4 The actual interventions themselves may be very far from transparent; "medical miracles" are an everyday occurrence, and the processes are presented as beyond the capacity or ken of ordinary mortals. But the application of a high degree of science and skill is still within the conceptually simple framework of a mechanical model – fixing the damaged part.

5 To the extent that overt policy does recognize this process, it tends to respond with marketing activities encouraging people to seek care. A surprising proportion of so-called "health promotion" includes various forms of "see your doctor" messages, and might more accurately be called "disease promotion." Measures to encourage "informal" coping should *inter alia* include recommendations *not* to contact the health care system in particular circumstances; the latter are virtually unheard of.

6 The experience of the United States is a clear demonstration of the distinction between the resource and administrative/financial dimensions of access. The United States devotes a much larger share of its national resources to producing health care than does any other nation, and spends much more per capita (Schieber and Poullier, 1989; OECD Secretariat, 1989). Yet the peculiarities of its financing system result in severely restricted (or no) access for a substantial minority of its citizens. On the other hand, nominally universal "access" to a system with grossly inadequate resources would be equally misleading.

7 Providers of care, particularly nurses, often emphasize their "caring" functions. The point here is not at all that caring is without importance or value, but rather that it is by no means the exclusive preserve of providers of health care. Furthermore, the "social contract" by which members of a particular community undertake collective (financial) responsibility for each other's health narrowly defined, does not necessarily extend to responsibility for their happiness. "Caring" independently of any contemplated "curing," or at least prevention of deterioration, represents an extension of the "product line" – and sales revenue – of the health care system. If collective buyers

of these services, public or private, have never in fact agreed to this extension, its ethical basis is rather shaky.

8 Best attainable health begs the question of by which *means* health may be attained. A hypothetical situation in which the members of a population had each received all the health *care* which might benefit them, might nevertheless be one in which the population fell well short of attainable health because other measures outside the health care system were neglected.

9 A classic example has been provided by the response of paediatrics to the collapse of the baby boom in the mid-1960s. The "New Paediatrics" – social and emotional problems of adolescents – was discovered just in time to prevent underemployment. At the other end of the paediatric age range, progress in neonatology will ensure a growing supply of very low-birthweight babies surviving into childhood, with a complex array of medical problems requiring intervention. We do not suggest that these system responses are the result of conscious and deliberate self-seeking by providers; such is almost certainly not the case. But the outcome is what it is.

10 The quotes are needed because the health care system, and the people in it, are not simply an "industry" in the sense of a set of activities and actors motivated solely by economic considerations. But to the extent that they are – and it is undeniable that economic considerations *do* matter, even if they are not the exclusive motivations – then this observation holds.

11 If building environmental standards were set by fuel-supply companies, would we have similar problems with the regulation of thermostats?

12 The rhetoric of "cost crises" rarely if ever recognizes an extremely important distinction between expenditures or outlays, and the economist's concept of resource or opportunity costs. Expenditures on health care may rise (fall) either because more (fewer) resources of human time, effort, and skills, capital equipment, and raw materials, are being used in its production, or because the owners of such resources are receiving larger (smaller) payments for them – higher (lower) salaries, fees, or prices. The arrow from health care to disease represents a response in the form of actual goods and services provided – real resources. But much of the public debate over "underfunding" and "cost crises" is really about the relative incomes of providers of care, not about the amount and type of care provided. For obvious political reasons, income claims are frequently presented as if they were assertions about levels of care (Evans, 1984; Reinhardt, 1987).

13 There might still, however, be quite justifiable interest in the patterns of prices and incomes generated by such care (see note 11). A competitive marketplace can generate intense pressures which automatically control prices and incomes, as the computer example has demonstrated. Health

care, however, is nowhere provided through such a market (not even in the United States), and has not been for at least a hundred years. There are excellent reasons for this (see Evans, 1984; Culyer, 1982), and the situation is not in fact going to change in the foreseeable future. It follows that other mechanisms, with associated controversy, will remain necessary to address issues of income distribution.

14 *Not* nonexistent. There is no basis in ethical theory or institutional practice for the proposition which creeps into so much of normative economics, that individual choice is the ultimate, and even the only, ground of obligation (Etzioni, 1988).

15 We do not mean to imply that the authors of the White Paper had the relatively limited view which we present below, still less that all of their subsequent interpreters have been so intellectually constrained. But it is our perception that the principal impact of the White Paper framework on debates about, and the development of, health policy *has* been limited in the way we describe.

16 None of which is news to tobacco marketers.

17 One should note, however, that the very limited experience in the early 1970s with *anti-smoking* advertising on television appeared to be sufficiently successful that tobacco companies were willing voluntarily to abandon this medium in order to get the "opposition" off the air.

18 Wilkins (1989) and Wolfson (1990) provide recent Canadian data.

19 One might point out that this is true of much therapy. Surgery, for example, typically has a very powerful negative effect on health and function in the immediate intervention and recovery phase, while (when successful) yielding later improvements. In the hypertension case, however, healthy individuals are introduced to prolonged low-level illness, in order to receive large but uncertain benefits in the farther future. Such a difference of degree becomes one of kind.

For people with short time horizons, painful or disabling interventions with longer-term payoffs may not be justified. Elderly people, in particular, will quite rationally discount future benefits more heavily. The finding that elderly cancer patients are more likely to choose radiation treatment over surgery, even if the latter has a greater five-year survival rate (McNeil, Weichselbaum and Pauker, 1978), illustrates the point. The enthusiasm among dentists to provide "optimum" oral health to residents of nursing homes, raises similar concerns. Would you want to spend a day in a dentist's chair if you expected to die tomorrow? Next week? Next month? ...

20 "Improved" nutrition is ambiguous. For impoverished and deprived populations, better is simply more, and more nutritious. But for a high proportion

of modern populations, better is probably less, and particularly less fats. It is not clear when in the historical record "better" shifted from more to less, for the majority of industrialized populations, such that (from a health perspective) nutrition may have begun to deteriorate.

21 The operation was a success, but the patient died.

22 The common identification between private-sector jobs as by definition "real," and public-sector ones as "unreal," is however simply ideological nonsense – "real" and "unreal" exist in both sectors, wherever activity is being carried on with no output, or none of any value. It includes, but is not restricted to, the caricature of the lazy or obstructionist bureaucrat.

A strong argument can be made, for example, that most of the jobs in the private health-insurance sector in the United States – complex, demanding, and highly paid – are not "real jobs," because they actually yield nothing of value, and in all other health care funding systems are dispensed with. That is, of course, another story, but one which emphasizes the invalidity of an equation between "unreal jobs" and "lazy public servants." One can work quite hard and conscientiously, both individually and as a group, and yet be completely useless or even get in the way. Parallels with public bureaucracies in centrally planned economies are not inapt.

23 Often, but not always. Improvements in the techniques of diagnostic imaging, for example, have reduced the degree of risk and distress associated with earlier forms of diagnostic imaging; and the substitution of lithotripsy for kidney surgery has yielded similar benefits. On the other hand, less risky or uncomfortable procedures tend to be offered to many more patients.

24 It would, of course, be quite possible for a nation to maintain both high savings rates and high spending on health care – or the military – simply by cutting back on consumption. But there is strong resistance at both bargaining table and ballot box to a reduction in current consumption through higher taxes or lower wages. Citizens do not want to accept a reduction in present living standards to pay for more health care.

A neo-classical economist might argue that the living standard is *not* reduced; what is given up in smaller houses, poorer roads, or fewer electronic gadgets is gained in more cardiac bypass grafts, laboratory tests, MRI procedures, and months in nursing homes. But the average individual is, quite rightly, unconvinced. Health care, like military spending, is not valued for its own sake. What, after all, are the direct satisfactions from a tonsillectomy, or a tank? Each is simply a regrettable use of resources, a service for which in a better world one would have no need. Hence the tendency for health spending increases to be drawn from savings, whether through government budget deficits or reduced corporate retained earnings.

REFERENCES

American Council of Life Insurance and Health Insurance Association of America (1988). *INSURE project – Lifecycle study*, Press Kit, 25 April.

Andersen, T.F., and G. Mooney, eds. (1990). *The challenge of medical practice variations*. London: Macmillan.

Anderson, G.M., S. Brinkworth, and T. Ng (1989). "Cholesterol screening: Evaluating alternative strategies." *HPRU* 89 (August): 10D, Health Policy Research Unit, University of British Columbia, Vancouver.

Baird, P.A., and C.R. Scriver (1990). *Genetics and the public health*. Internal Document No. 10A, Program in Population Health, Canadian Institute for Advanced Research, Toronto, Jan. 1990.

Banta, H.D., C. Behney, and J.S. Willems (1981). *Toward rational technology in medicine: Considerations for health policy*. New York: Springer.

Barker, D.J.P., P.D. Winter, C. Osmond, et al. (1989). "Weight in infancy and death from ischaemic heart disease." *Lancet* (9 Sept.): 577–80.

Birch, H.G. (1972). "Malnutrition, learning, and intelligence." *American Journal of Public Health*. 62: 773–84.

Buck, C. (1988). "Beyond Lalonde: Creating health." *Canadian Journal of Public Health* 76 (Suppl. 1): 19–24.

Bunker, J.P., D.S. Gomby, and B.H. Kehrer (1989). *Pathways to health: The role of social factors*. Menlo Park, CA: The Henry J. Kaiser Family Foundation.

Canada (1974). *A new perspective on the health of Canadians* (Lalonde Report). Ottawa: Department of National Health and Welfare.

Cassel, J. (1976). "The contribution of the social environment to host resistance." *American Journal of Epidemiology* 104: 107–23.

Culyer, A.J. (1982). "The NHS and the market: Images and realities." In *The public-private mix for health: The relevance and effects of change*, ed. A. Maynard and G. McLachlan, 23–55. London: Nuffield Provincial Hospitals Trust.

– (1988). *Health expenditures in Canada: Myth and reality, past and future*. Toronto: Canadian Tax Foundation.

– (1989). "Cost containment in Europe." *Health Care Financing Review* (Dec. Suppl.): 21–32.

Dantzer, R., and K.W. Kelley (1989). "Stress and immunity: An integrated view of relationships between the brain and the immune system." *Life Sciences* 44: 1995–2008.

Dreyfus, H.L., and S.E. Dreyfus (1988). "Making a mind versus modeling a brain: Artificial intelligence back at a branchpoint." *Daedalus* 117: 15–43.

Dubos, R. (1959). *Mirage of Health*. New York: Harper & Row.

Dutton, D.B. (1986). "Social class and health." In *Applications of social science to clinical medicine and health policy*, ed. L.H. Aitken and D. Mechanic, 31–62. New Brunswick, NJ: Rutgers University Press,

Eisenberg, J.M. (1986). *Doctors' decisions and the cost of medical care.* Ann Arbor, MI: Health Administration Press.

Etzioni, A. (1988). *The moral dimension: Toward a new economics.* New York: The Free Press.

Evans, R.G. (1982). "A retrospective on the 'new perspective.'" *Journal of Health Politics, Policy, and Law* 7: 325–44.

– (1984). *Strained mercy: The economics of Canadian health care.* Toronto: Butterworths, Chap. 1.

Feeny, D., G. Guyatt, and P. Tugwell (1986). *Health care technology: Effectiveness, efficiency and public policy.* Montreal: Institute for Research on Public Policy.

Gleick J. (1987). *Chaos: Making a new science.* New York: Viking.

Gunning-Schepers, L.J., and J.H. Hagen (1987). "Avoidable burden of illness: How much can prevention contribute to health?" *Social Science and Medicine* 24: 945–51.

Ham, C., ed. (1988). *Health care variations: Assessing the evidence.* London: The King's Fund Institute.

Hawking, S. (1988). *A brief history of time.* Toronto: Bantam Books.

Haynes, R.B., D.L. Sackett, D.W. Taylor, E.S. Gibson, and A.L. Johnson (1979) "Increased absenteeism from work after detection and labeling of hypertensive patients." *New England Journal of Medicine* 229: 741–4.

Hertzman, C. (1990). "Poland: Health and environment in the context of socioeconomic decline." *HPRU* 90 (Jan.): 2D. Vancouver: Health Policy Research Unit, University of British Columbia.

Holton, G. (1988). "The roots of complementarity." *Daedalus* 117: 151–97.

House, J., K.R. Landis, and D. Umberson (1988). "Social relationships and health." *Science* 241: 540–5.

Hypertension Detection and Follow-up Program Cooperative Group (1979). "Five-year findings of the hypertension detection and follow-up program, I: Reduction in mortality of persons with high blood pressure, including mild hypertension." *Journal of the American Medical Association* 242: 2562–71.

Iglehart, J.K. (1988). "Japan's health care system – Part Two: Health policy report." *New England Journal of Medicine* 319: 1166–72.

Illich, I. (1975). *Medical nemesis: The expropriation of health.* Toronto: McClelland & Stewart.

Levine, S., and A. Lilienfeld (1987). *Epidemiology and health policy.* London: Tavistock Press.

Lewis, C.E. (1988). "Disease prevention and health promotion practices of primary care physicians in the United States." In *Implementing preventive services* (Suppl.) *American Journal of Preventive Medicine* 4: S9–16.

Lomas, J. (1990). "Promoting clinical policy change: Using the art to promote the science in medicine." In *The challenge of medical practice variations*, ed. T.F. Andersen and G. Mooney, 174–91. London: Macmillan.

Markowe, H.J.J., M.G. Marmot, M.J. Shipley, et al. (1985) "Fibrinogen: A possible link between social class and coronary heart disease." *British Medical Journal* 291: 1312–14.

Marmor, T.R. (1989). *Healthy public policy: What does that mean, who is responsible for it, and how would one pursue it?* Internal Document No. 6A, Program in Population Health, Canadian Institute for Advanced Research, Toronto, August.

Marmot, M.G. (1986). "Social inequalities in mortality: The social environment." In *Class and health: Research and longitudinal data*, ed. R.G. Wilkinson, 21–33. London: Tavistock Press.

– M.J. Shipley, and G. Rose. (1984). "Inequalities in death: Specific explanations of a general pattern." *Lancet* 1 (May 5): 1003–6.

– and G.D. Smith (1989). "Why are the Japanese living longer?" *British Medical Journal* 299: 1547–51.

McCloskey, D.N. (1989). "Why I am no longer a positivist." *Review of Social Economy* 47: 225–38.

McKeown, T. (1979). *The role of medicine: Dream, mirage, or nemesis?* 2nd ed. Oxford: Blackwell.

McKinlay, J.B. (1979). "Epidemiological and political determinants of social policies regarding the public health." *Social Science and Medicine* 13A: 541–58.

– S.M. McKinlay, and R. Beaglehole (1989). "A review of the evidence concerning the impact of medical measures on recent mortality and morbidity in the United States." *International Journal of Health Services* 19: 181–208.

McNeil, B.J., R. Weichselbaum, and S.G. Pauker (1978). "Fallacy of the five-year survival in lung cancer." *New England Journal of Medicine* 299: 1397–1401.

Moore, T.J. (1989). *Heart failure: A critical inquiry into american medicine and the revolution in heart care, Part II: Prevention.* New York: Random House.

OECD Secretariat (1989). "Health care expenditure and other data: An international compendium from the Organization for Economic Cooperation and Development." *Health Care Financing Review*, Supplement: 111–94.

Reinhardt, U.E. (1987). "Resource allocation in health care: The allocation of lifestyles to providers." *Milbank Quarterly* 65: 153–76.

Reiser, S.J. (1978). *Medicine and the reign of technology.* New York: Cambridge University Press.

Renaud, M. (1987). "De l'epidemiologie sociale à la sociologie de la prevention: 15 ans de recherche sur l'etiologie sociale de la maladie." *Revue d'Epidemiologie et Santé Publique* 35: 3–19.

Sagan, L.A. (1987). *The health of nations.* New York: Basic Books.

Sapolsky, R.M. (1990). "Stress in the wild." *Scientific American* 262: 116–23.

Schieber, G.J., and J.-P. Poullier (1989). "Overview of international comparisons of health care expenditures." *Health Care Financing Review,* Supplement: 1–7.

Toronto Working Group on Cholesterol Policy (1989). *Detection and management of asymptomatic hypercholesterolemia.* Prepared for the Task Force on the Use and Provision of Medical Services, Ontario Ministry of Health and Ontario Medical Association, Toronto.

Townsend, P., and N. Davidson, eds. (1982). *Inequalities in health: The Black Report.* London: Penguin.

Wilkins, R., O.B. Adams, and A. Brancker (1989). *Mortality by income in urban Canada, 1971 and 1986: Diminishing absolute differences, persistence of relative inequality.* Joint Study, Health and Welfare Canada and Statistics Canada, Ottawa.

Wolfson, M.C., G. Rowe, J.F. Gentleman, and M. Tomiak (1990). *Earnings and death: Effects over a quarter century.* Internal Document No. 5B, Program in Population Health, Canadian Institute for Advanced Research, Toronto, February.

Woodward, C.A., and G.L. Stoddart (1990). "Is the Canadian health care system suffering from abuse? A commentary." *Canadian Family Doctor* 36: 283–9.

14

Introduction (Chapter 1) to the Book *Why Are Some People Healthy and Others Not?* (1994)

ROBERT G. EVANS

The prudent text-books give it
In tables at the end –
The stress that shears a rivet
Or makes a tie-bar bend –
What traffic wrecks macadam –
What concrete should endure –
But we, poor Sons of Adam,
Have no such literature,
To warn us or make sure!

Kipling, *Hymn of Breaking Strain*

Top people live longer. Moreover, they are generally healthier while doing so. This is not exactly news. Many studies, in many countries, over many years, have shown a correlation between life expectancy and various measures of social status – income, education, occupation, residence (Wilkinson, 1992). Studies of the living, while fewer because decent

Originally published in Evans, Robert G., Morris L. Barer, and Theodore R. Marmor, eds. *Why Are Some People Healthy and Others Not?* New York: Aldine de Gruyter.

All "Chapters" referred to by Evans herein are from *Why Are Some People Healthy and Others Not?*

health information is so scarce (see Chapter 11 by Wolfson), show that health status is also correlated with social status. And such studies confirm what most people knew anyway – poverty is bad for you. As Sophie Tucker said, "I've been poor, and I've been rich. Rich is better."

Yet this commonplace observation, when examined in detail, raises complex and important questions about the determinants of health, for individuals and populations.[1] Or in short, Why? Moreover, the correlation between social status and health is only one leading example of a much larger class of observations, of large differences in health status not just among individuals, but among well-defined groups: populations and sub-populations, both human and animal. Such aggregate observations, the "heterogeneities" discussed in Chapter 3 by Hertzman, Frank, and Evans, lead naturally to attempts to identify the group characteristics associated with good and bad health, in the hope of finding and then influencing the underlying causal factors.

At quite an early stage in any such analysis, it becomes apparent that many of the conventional explanations of the determinants of health – of why some people are healthy and others not – are at best seriously incomplete if not simply wrong. This is unfortunate, because modern societies devote a very large share of their wealth, effort, and attention to trying to maintain or improve the health of the individuals that make up their populations. These massive efforts are primarily channelled through health care systems, presumably reflecting a belief that the receipt of appropriate health care is the most important determinant of health.

But if this is not so, if the principal determinants of the health of populations lie elsewhere, then we may well have left undone those things that we ought to have done, and have done those things that we ought not to have done. And there will in consequence be less health in us than there could be. We may also, as a result, be less wealthy.

Nor is this situation likely to be improved by efforts to expand "preventive" activities, if these are also based on shaky assumptions about the determinants of health. The hypotheses about causality that underlie arguments for prevention are often no more able to explain differences in health status between different groups of people than are those which attribute all or most differences to the availability of "curative" services.

There is, of course, still a very real and important role for medical and other health care services in preserving life, relieving suffering, and maintaining or restoring function. It is difficult to understand the faintly sneering tone with which health care systems are sometimes dismissed as "illness care systems." Is caring for illness, usually effectively, something to be ashamed of? Health care services, and the people and institutions that provide them, have earned the high regard in which they are generally held, even though, as shown in Chapter 9 by Roos and Roos, the expectations of both providers and users are often greater than can be justified on the available evidence. But while they may be decisive in individual cases, the availability of such services – or their lack – cannot begin to explain observed differences among the health of populations. Nor is this any surprise to thoughtful clinicians, past or present.

In this chapter we introduce and link together a selection of studies that either report or bear upon various aspects of the relationship between status and health. This linkage permits us to extract and focus upon a series of propositions that, taken together, constitute at least the beginnings of a much more complex and comprehensive, yet coherent, understanding of the determinants of health. They are intended to provide a thread through what is now a vast labyrinth of particular findings. The subsequent chapters explore the underpinnings and implications of this synthesis. In the process, we consider how a true health policy based on an understanding of the relative importance of the various determinants of health might differ from the health care policies that predominate today.

We start our story with the work of Marmot (1986; Marmot, Kogevinas, and Elston, 1987, see especially 126–8). His Whitehall Study has followed more than ten thousand British civil servants for nearly two decades, accumulating an extensive array of information on each of the individuals in the study. The data set is thus person-specific and longitudinal, offering important advantages over the many studies of status and health based only on group average data, at a single point in time. Moreover, it is readily and unambiguously divisible into status groupings; the hierarchy of income and rank in the civil service is well-defined.

Marmot found that the (age-standardized) mortality, over a ten-year period, among males aged forty to sixty-four was about *three and a half times* as high for those in the clerical and manual grades, as in the senior administrative grades (Marmot and Theorell, 1988). The correlation between status and health is alive and well in Whitehall. But that is only the beginning of the story.

There was an obvious *gradient* in mortality from top to bottom of the hierarchy. Mortality was significantly higher in the second rank, professional and executive personnel, than in the top, administrative, grades, and increased further as one went down the scale (see Figure 14.1). But in none of these groups are people impoverished or deprived (at least according to the common understanding of those concepts). All are

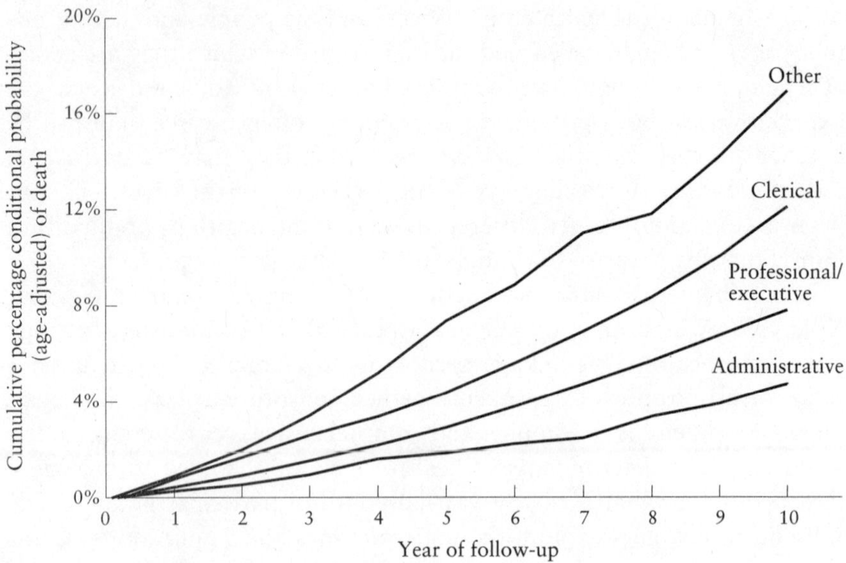

Figure 14.1 Whitehall study: All-cause mortality among total population by year of follow-up

Adapted from: Robert G. Evans. "Introduction" (Chapter 1), in *Why Are Some People Healthy and Others Not?* edited by Robert G. Evans, Morris L. Barer, and Theodore R. Marmor, 3–26. New York: Aldine de Gruyter, 1994.
Original source: Marmot (1986). Reproduced by permission of Taylor & Francis Books, UK.

employed, most in office jobs with low risk from the physical environment (or at least at no greater risk than those in the classes above them), and the professional and executive grades are relatively well paid compared with the general population.

Thus a common interpretation of the correlation between socioeconomic status and health – that "the poor" are deprived of some of the material conditions of good health, and suffer from poor diet, bad housing, exposure to violence, environmental pollutants, crowding, and infection – cannot explain these observations. Indeed a focus on poverty can block progress in understanding, because it can be dismissive of further questions.

For some (on the right), "the poor ye have always with ye." One can never remove social differentiation; some people are just better than others, and some will always be at the bottom. Health differentials are thus inevitable (and probably deserved). "What can't be cured, must be endured." Fortunately, most of us have the intestinal fortitude to bear with good grace the sufferings of someone else. For others (on the left),

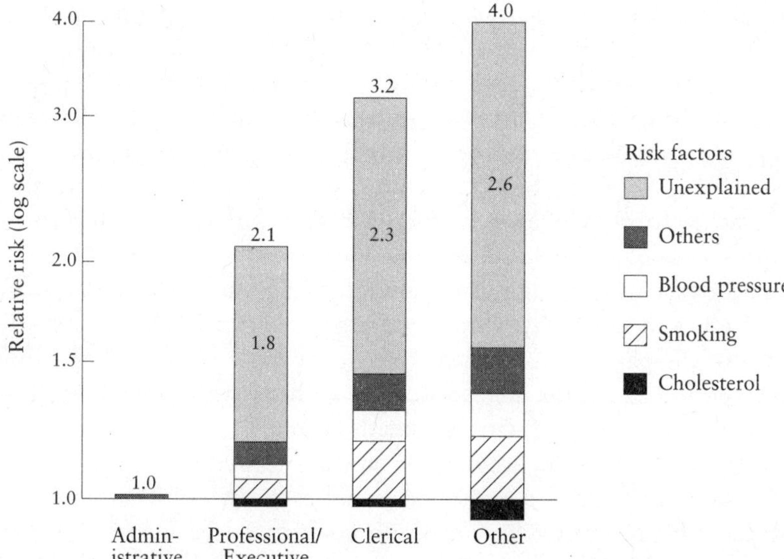

Figure 14.2 Relative risk of CHD death in different grades "explained" by risk factors (age-standardized)

Adapted from: Robert G. Evans. "Introduction" (Chapter 1), in *Why Are Some People Healthy and Others Not?* edited by Robert G. Evans, Morris L. Barer, and Theodore R. Marmor, 3–26. New York: Aldine de Gruyter, 1994.
Original source: Marmot, et al. (1978). Reproduced with permission from BMJ Publishing Group Ltd.

health differentials are markers for social inequality and injustice more generally, and are further evidence of the need to redistribute wealth and power, and restructure or overturn the existing social order.

Both preconceptions miss the main point of Marmot's findings, that there is *something* that powerfully influences health and that is correlated with hierarchy per se. It operates, not on some underprivileged minority of "them" over on the margin of society, to be spurned or cherished depending upon one's ideological affiliation, but on all of us. And its effects are *large*.

There is more. A gradient in mortality was found in each of a number of different diseases or causes of death (but not all).[2] Some were clearly correlated with smoking behaviour: top people rarely smoke; bottom people often do. (That in itself is a very systematic pattern with major health implications. It cries out for explanation, rather than trivialization as "personal choice.") But a gradient was also observed in other causes of death that have no known relation to smoking (see Figure 14.2

and Tables 14.1 and 14.2). Moreover those few top people who did smoke were much less likely to die from smoking-related causes.

Nor is smoking behaviour the only "individual" risk factor that failed to explain the gradient.[3] On average, people in the lower grades were at greater risk for heart disease, because they had higher levels on the established triad of smoking, blood pressures, and cholesterol. But differences in mortality from heart disease persisted after adjustment for all these factors.

These observations suggest some underlying general causal process, correlated with hierarchy, which *expresses* itself through different diseases. But the particular diseases that carry people off may then simply be alternative pathways or mechanisms, rather than "causes" of illness and death; the essential factor is something else.[4]

These two ideas – the gradient in mortality, and the disease as pathway rather than cause – are also suggested by a number of other studies of differential mortality by socioeconomic class (see Chapter 3). The British data (Table 14.3) on mortality rates by social class reviewed in the Black Report [Office of Population Censuses and Surveys (OPCS), 1972; Black, Morris, Smith, Townsend, and Whitehead, 1988; Wilkinson, 1986] are of particular interest, because they are available decade by decade over most of the twentieth century. They too show a gradient, but most interestingly they show it persisting, with not much change, over most of the period since the first data were collected in 1911, and apparently increasing in recent years.

Yet during that period the causes of death have changed radically. At the beginning of the century infectious diseases were the great killers, and (age-standardized) mortality rates were higher in the lower classes. At the end of the century heart disease and cancer are the killers, and they too hit harder the people lower in the social hierarchy. While death is ultimately quite democratic, deferral appears to be a privilege correlated with rank. The diseases change, the gradient persists, again suggesting (from a completely different data set) an underlying factor, correlated with hierarchy and expressing itself through particular diseases.

There has been another major change in the last fifty years. All developed societies have greatly expanded their health care systems, and (with the exception of the United States) have introduced systems of financing designed to make that care accessible to the whole population, regardless of ability to pay. And the use of health care has correspondingly increased dramatically, and become more equal across social classes. Yet the longitudinal data from the United Kingdom show no evidence that

Table 14.1 Age-adjusted relative mortality* in ten years by civil-service grade and cause of death

Cause of death	*Administrators*	*Professional & executive*	*Clerk*	*Other*
Lung cancer	0.5	1	2.2	3.6
Other cancer	0.8	1	1.4	1.4
Coronary heart disease	0.5	1	1.4	1.7
Cerebrovascular disease	0.3	1	1.4	1.2
Chronic bronchitis	0	1	6	7.3
Other respiratory	1.1	1	2.6	3.1
Gastrointestinal diseases	0	1	1.6	2.8
Genitourinary diseases	1.3	1	0.7	3.1
Accidents and homicide	0	1	1.4	1.5
Suicide	0.7	1	1	1.9
Non-smoking-related causes				
Cancer	0.8	1	1.3	1.4
Non-cancer	0.6	1	1.5	2
All causes	0.6	1	1.6	2.1

* Calculated from logistic equation adjusting for age
Adapted from: Robert G. Evans. "Introduction" (Chapter 1). In *Why Are Some People Healthy and Others Not?* edited by Robert G. Evans, Morris L. Barer, and Theodore R. Marmor. New York: Aldine de Gruyter, 1994.
Original source: Marmot (1986). Reproduced by permission of Taylor & Francis Books, UK.

Table 14.2 Age-adjusted mortality in ten years (and number of deaths from coronary heart disease and lung cancer) by grade and smoking status

Cause of death	*Administrators*	*Professional & executive*	*Clerk*	*Other*	*Total*
Non-smokers					
CHD	1.4	2.36	2.08	6.89	2.59
Lung cancer	0	0.24	0	0.25	0.21
Ex-smokers					
CHD	1.29	3.06	3.32	3.98	3.09
Lung cancer	0.21	0.5	0.56	1.05	0.62
Current smokers					
CHD	2.16	3.58	4.92	6.62	4
Lung cancer	0.35	0.73	1.49	2.33	2

CHD: Coronary heart disease

Adapted from: Robert G. Evans. "Introduction" (Chapter 1). In *Why Are Some People Healthy and Others Not?* edited by Robert G. Evans, Morris L. Barer, and Theodore R. Marmor. New York: Aldine de Gruyter, 1994.
Original source: Marmot (1986). Reproduced by permission of Taylor & Francis Books, UK.

Table 14.3 Mortality by social class, 1911–1981 (Men, 15 to 64 Years, England and Wales)

	Social Class				
	Professional	*Managerial*	*Skilled manual and non-manual*	*Semi-skilled*	*Unskilled*
Year	*I*	*II*	*III*	*IV*	*V*
1911	88	94	96	93	142
1921	82	94	95	101	125
1931	90	94	97	102	111
1951	86	92	101	104	118
1961[a]	76 (75)	81	100	103	143 (127)
1971[b]	77 (75)	81	104	114	137 (121)
1981[c]	66	76	103	116	166

a Figures are SMRs, which express age-adjusted mortality rates as a percentage of the national average at each date.
b To facilitate comparisons, figures shown in parentheses have been adjusted to the classification of occupations used in 1951.
c Men, 20 to 64 years, Great Britian.

Adapted from: Robert G. Evans. "Introduction" (Chapter 1). In *Why Are Some People Healthy and Others Not?* edited by Robert G. Evans, Morris L. Barer, and Theodore R. Marmor. New York: Aldine de Gruyter, 1994.
Original sources: Marmot (1986) and the Office of Population Censuses and Surveys (1978). Reproduced by permission of Taylor & Francis Books, UK.

the introduction of the National Health Service has reduced the mortality gradient. There *is* some evidence in some countries of a reduction of the gradient in, as well as the rate of, infant mortality in response to more, and more generally accessible, health care, but it is far from conclusive (Wilkins, Adams, and Brancker, 1990). Whatever underlies the gradient does not seem to be very sensitive to the provision of health care.

This observation links the data on social class gradients with the well-known work of McKeown (1979) in historical epidemiology. He showed that the very large reductions in mortality from the principal infectious diseases, which have occurred over the last two centuries, took place prior to the development of any effective medical therapy. His data on tuberculosis are of particular importance (Figures 14.3A and 14.3B).

A common response is that public health measures, rather than medical therapy, were decisive. But the TB bacillus is not waterborne, so the decline cannot be attributed to clean water supplies – at least not directly. It may be that greater general cleanliness, made possible by clean water and sewage removal, played a role.

In particular, as Szreter (1988) points out, tuberculosis mortality could have fallen because people were less weakened by other infections whose

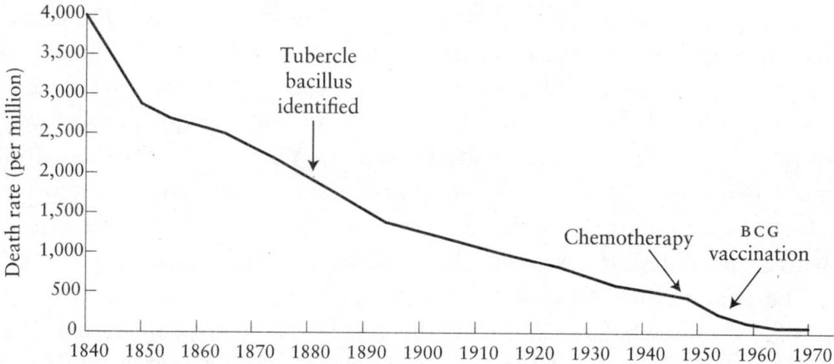

Figure 14.3A Respiratory tuberculosis: Mean annual death rates (standardized to 1901 population), England and Wales, 1840–1970

Adapted from: Robert G. Evans. "Introduction" (Chapter 1). In *Why Are Some People Healthy and Others Not?* edited by Robert G. Evans, Morris L. Barer, and Theodore R. Marmor, 3–26. New York: Aldine de Gruyter, 1994.
Original source: McKeown (1979). Reprinted with permission of Princeton University Press.

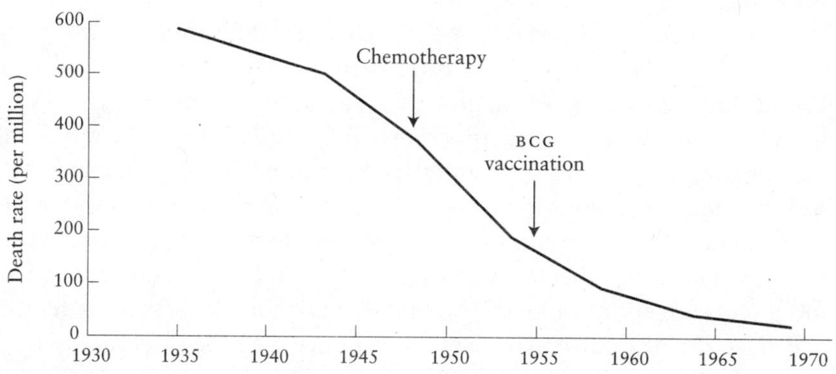

Figure 14.3B Respiratory tuberculosis: Mean annual death rates (standardized to 1901 population), England and Wales, 1935–1970

Adapted from: Robert G. Evans. "Introduction" (Chapter 1). In *Why Are Some People Healthy and Others Not?* edited by Robert G. Evans, Morris L. Barer, and Theodore R. Marmor, 3–26. New York: Aldine de Gruyter, 1994.
Original source: McKeown (1979). Reprinted with permission of Princeton University Press.

incidence *was* reduced by public health measures, if not by medical care per se. He emphasizes that McKeown's own "explanation" for the TB decline – rising incomes and improved diet, with no significant influence from public health or other deliberate human agency – was at best a "diagnosis of exclusion," which appears to be unsustainable in the light of more recent evidence.

In any case, even as late as the 1940s most adults in the United Kingdom still showed evidence of having been exposed to the bacillus at some time. Unlike their ancestors, few of them developed the disease, and fewer died. One is still left with the interesting question of why people who were exposed to the "cause" of TB – the bacillus – in one century developed the disease, and in the next did not. And McKeown's central point – that the major decline in mortality from most infectious diseases predates effective therapy – remains unchallenged.

The tuberculosis data illustrate another important point, however, which is somewhat obscured in the long-term historical picture. The development of effective therapy in the 1940s *was*, in fact, a significant factor in the further reduction in mortality. The decline at that point was about 50 per cent in a decade, a very large proportionate fall, so there is no argument here for therapeutic nihilism. But these gains are swamped, in the historical record, by the much larger impact of something else operating outside the health care system. The role of medicine was very real, but limited. While it accelerated the speed of decline, it was not the initiating force.

Thus McKeown observed very large changes in mortality in a society over time, and Marmot and the authors of the Black Report found very large differences among social groups at particular points or over shorter periods in time, in each case apparently independent of medical knowledge or care use. In each case, improvement in health is associated with improvement in economic position, but at least in Marmot's data it is clear that this is not a result of an escape from poverty. And in each case, while people always die *of* something – this is both a cultural convention and a requirement of modern systems of vital statistics – there is reason to believe that the particular diseases recognized by medical science may not be the fundamental causes.

So what is going on?

Actually, this question has two quite distinct parts. First, what are the causal factors – status? empowerment? stress? coping skills? future orientation? other factors? – that are correlated with hierarchy and thus with health, and can they be changed? Second, what are the biological pathways through which these causal factors operate? We do not believe in spooks and the supernatural; disease and death are biological phenomena. Whatever factors lie upstream in the sequence of causes, at some point in the chain there must be biological processes at work.[5]

Possible answers to these questions are only beginning to emerge, with pieces of the puzzle being supplied, in a relatively uncoordinated fashion, from the research of a number of different disciplines. The incomplete, tentative, and sometimes controversial nature of the answers to "What is going on?" must not, however, be permitted to obscure the fact that *something* is going on. While death rates are admittedly incomplete measures of health, they are unambiguous and "hard-edged" measures of difference. And a three-to-one difference, emerging from large numbers of individual observations, deserves attention. The lack of an adequate explanation for the phenomenon in no way negates the reality or the importance of the phenomenon itself.

Taking the second (biological) question first, some remarkable results are now coming from animal studies, both experimental and observational. Social hierarchies are not peculiar to humans. Other primates have them as well, both in their natural state and in experimental colonies.

Sapolsky (1990) has been observing the social relationships among free-ranging olive baboons in Kenya, taking physiological measurements in a way that would probably be unacceptably intrusive for most human subjects. He finds that a dominance hierarchy is readily identifiable among male baboons, and that there are, on average, significant differences between dominant and subordinate males in the functioning of their endocrine systems. In dominant males, the physiological responses to stress – the "fight or flight syndrome" – are turned off more rapidly after the stressful event has passed. In subordinate animals, there seems to be a break in the feedback loop, and the stress response continues. Top baboons thus cope with stress better than their subordinates, who seem to be in a continuous state of low-level readiness or anxiety. (Interestingly, there is a very similar break in the cortisol feedback loop for humans suffering from some forms of depression; see Chapter 6 by Evans, Hodge, and Pless.)

Prolonged stress, or rather the responses it engenders, are known to have deleterious effects on a number of biological systems and to give rise to a number of illnesses. Could this be happening in other primate populations, such as free-ranging British civil servants? Interestingly, Marmot has found that, on average, all ranks in his study have similarly elevated blood pressure when at work (see Figure 14.4). But the blood pressure of senior administrators drops much more when they go home. They seem to be better able to turn off the stress response. There also appear to be systematic differences in the levels of fibrinogen circulating in the blood, which may be a marker for other differences in stress response.[6]

Another study of primate social hierarchies, among female macaques in an experimental setting, was primarily focused on the animals' responses

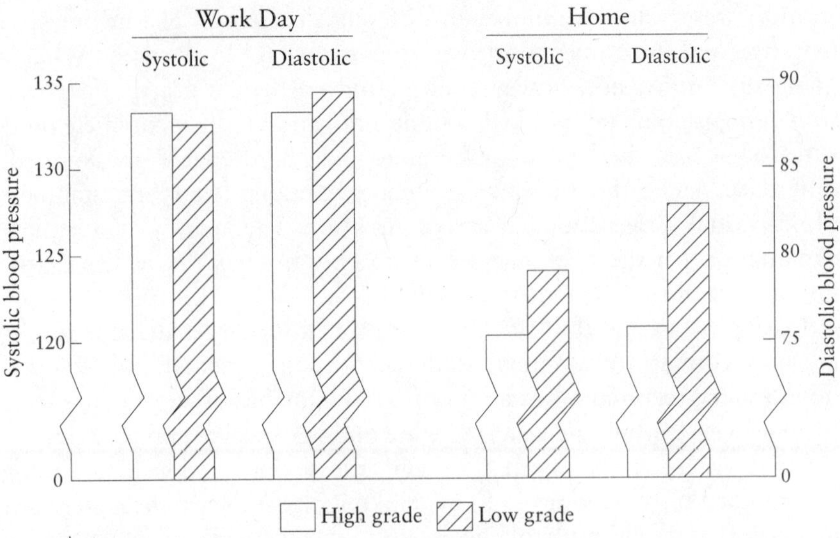

Figure 14.4 Blood pressure in British civil servants

Adapted from: Robert G. Evans. "Introduction" (Chapter 1). In *Why Are Some People Healthy and Others Not?* edited by Robert G. Evans, Morris L. Barer, and Theodore R. Marmor, 3–26. New York: Aldine de Gruyter, 1994.
Original source: Marmot and Theorell. "Social Class and Cardiovascular Disease: The Contribution of Work." *International Journal of Health Services* 18, no. 4 (1988): 659–74. Reprinted with the permission of SAGE Publications.

to high-cholesterol diets. The intent was to induce heart disease, and this indeed occurred. But a striking finding was that the degree of stenosis of the coronary arteries was nearly *four times* as severe among the low-status as among the high-status monkeys. The possible physiological pathways to this outcome are discussed in Chapter 7 by Marmot and Mustard; in general terms, prolonged stress can lead to injury to the arterial walls, and this in turn to clotting, atherosclerosis, and stenosis-coronary heart disease (CHD). CHD, of course, is the leading killer of human primates.

The external social environment, as interpreted by the various receptors of the nervous system, the senses, induces a generalized response by the endocrine system. This stress response, which we commonly experience as a burst of adrenalin, can if inappropriately prolonged result in a variety of forms of physiological damage, including heart disease. Still other animal experiments, with a variety of different subjects, have demonstrated that experimentally generated, prolonged, and unavoidable stress can lead to a variety of illnesses, and eventually death (Dantzer and Kelley, 1989).

But the stress response need not be inappropriate. The low-status baboons and macaques may have good reasons for continued anxiety – as may the low-ranking civil servants. You never know when some higher-ranking animal is going to turn up and drive you away from a meal or a female, or make some other threat to your sense of well-being. The "learned helplessness" that is experimentally induced in animals may also be a response by low-status humans or other free-ranging primates to a rather unsatisfactory social environment, and may be the behavioural counterpart to biological processes.

The endocrine system has the characteristic that it is strongly responsive to the nervous system, and induces a wide range of physiological changes in various parts of the organism. It is thus a natural place to look for an underlying process that is expressed in a number of different diseases and responds to the external physical or social environment.

Recent findings in immunology have shown that the immune system is another possible channel of influence, again with the potential for very general effects.[7] It is now well-known that the brain communicates directly with cells in the immune system, both through neuropeptides in the blood, and through the nerves themselves. There is a two-way "conversation" going on, discussed in Chapter 6, through which the immune system can be influenced by information about the outside world, although what is being said, and with what effect, is another matter. But it is now solidly established that the immune system does much more than simply respond mechanically to encounters with "foreign" cells or molecules.

The observations of reduced immune function in students during exam time, accountants at income tax time, and people who have lost a spouse now begin to fit into the story. Studies of other primate populations once again provide support; they too have complex social structures, and respond to loss of a "social object" (a technical term for one's mate?) with a depression of immune function. (The response may include other generalized unhealthy "behaviours" – see Chapter 2 by Evans and Stoddart.) If immune status is compromised by stressful events, then this may be an alternative pathway through which social status can have generalized health effects.[8]

So the biological pathways appear to be there, although there are still many careers to be made, and Nobel prizes to be won, in elucidating them in detail. But this brings us back to the prior question: What is it about hierarchies, or social structures more generally, that triggers the biological responses, and can anything be done about it? Our discussion has suggested that rank correlates inversely with stress, or with ability to cope with stress.

A common reaction, particularly among those who are themselves near the top of the social hierarchy, is that such a relationship is inevitable, inherent in either genetic endowment or human social structure. Fitter people rise to the top, and are also healthier – genetic selection. Alternatively human societies must have hierarchies – that's just how primates are – and the health effects follow. (The inevitability of both hierarchy and its rewards is usually more clearly visible from the top.) But is this reaction justified? As for most really interesting questions, the correct answer seems to be, yes and no.

On the "no" side, there is ample, indeed striking, evidence for the malleability of population health status, over time spans far too short for any change in genetic endowment. Studies of migrant populations demonstrate that, as they take on the social patterns and customs of the host country, they take on its disease patterns as well. These changes can be very large indeed, over one or two generations (Doll and Peto, 1981). The classic study (Chapter 7) of Japanese in the home islands, in Hawaii, and in California shows very clearly the effects of successive migrations to social environments that pose greater risks of heart disease (Marmot, et al., 1975; Marmot and Syme, 1976).

Indeed the Japanese in Japan itself have in the last thirty years demonstrated that the health status of an entire population can change very rapidly, and that the current experience of Western countries does not represent an upper bound on the possible. Since 1960, Japanese mortality statistics (male and female life expectancy, infant mortality) have improved from markedly below most European countries to markedly above, and the trend may be continuing (see Figures 14.5A and 14.5B). The dramatic improvements of the nineteenth century, which were analyzed in detail by McKeown, are not matters of historical interest only.

Also paralleling the tuberculosis story, the extraordinary increase in Japanese life expectancy does not appear to follow from better medical care (Marmot, 1992). All countries were greatly expanding their health care systems over this period, and Japan was not in the forefront. Nor does the physical setting in which most Japanese live and work match our usual conception of "healthy environments." (Even stranger, Japanese smokers seem less likely to develop lung cancer than their western counterparts [Hirayama, 1990].) Yet *something* lies behind the undeniable increase in their longevity. Unique features of the Japanese diet, or of social structure, have received considerable attention, but these of course

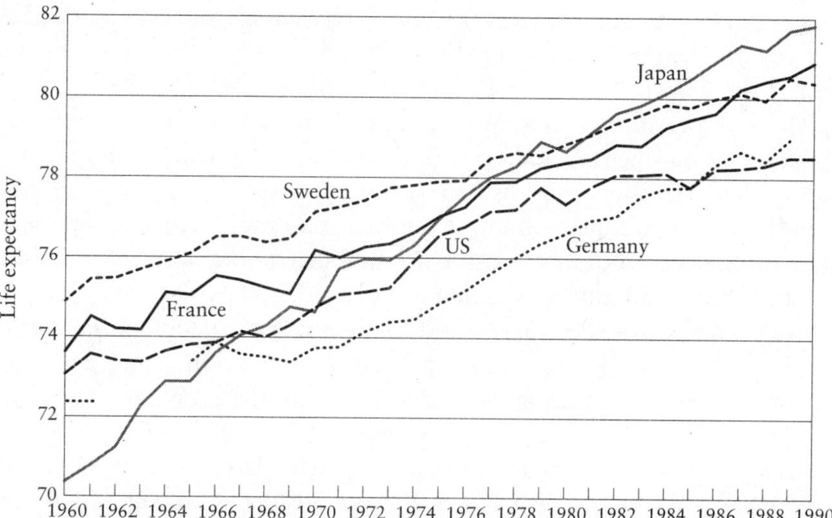

Figure 14.5A Trends in female life expectancy. Selected OECD countries, 1960–1990

Adapted from: Robert G. Evans. "Introduction" (Chapter 1). In *Why Are Some People Healthy and Others Not?* edited by Robert G. Evans, Morris L. Barer, and Theodore R. Marmor, 3–26. New York: Aldine de Gruyter, 1994.
Original source: Schieber, Poullier, and Greenwald (1992).

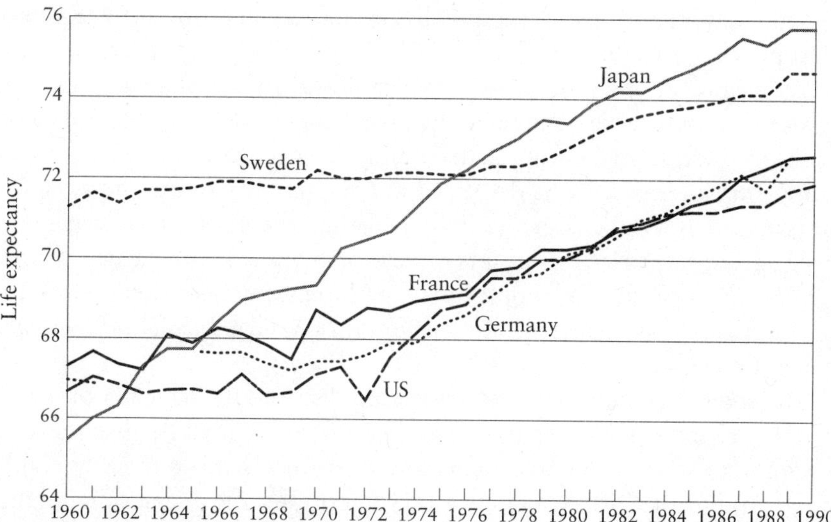

Figure 14.5B Trends in male life expectancy. Selected OECD countries, 1960–1990

Adapted from: Robert G. Evans. "Introduction" (Chapter 1). In *Why Are Some People Healthy and Others Not?* edited by Robert G. Evans, Morris L. Barer, and Theodore R. Marmor, 3–26. New York: Aldine de Gruyter, 1994.
Original source: Schieber, Poullier, and Greenwald (1992).

have *not* changed rapidly over the last thirty years. What *has* changed is the hierarchical position of Japanese society as a whole relative to the rest of the world.

These observations demonstrate the extremely large influence of "macro-environmental" factors, both social and physical, on illness patterns. They also show that disease patterns and health status can change rapidly, and by a large amount, when these external factors change. But they leave open a question as to the mutability of hierarchical patterns, of both status and illness, within a population.

Addressing this issue, Vagero and Lundberg (1989) applied the methodology of the Black Report to the Swedish population, using the same set of occupational categories as developed by the registrar-general in the United Kingdom. They found Swedish males (aged twenty to sixty-four) show an inverse gradient of age-adjusted mortality with socioeconomic class, just as the British do. But the Swedish gradient was much less pronounced. Moreover, mortality among the lowest social class of Swedes was lower than among the highest class of Britons.

These findings suggest that aspects of the social environment can powerfully moderate or accentuate the relationship between status and mortality. Hierarchy per se may be a marker for the underlying causal factor(s). We have examples of societies that are (nominally) hierarchical but healthy (Japan) and others that are (nominally) egalitarian but unhealthy (Eastern Europe).

Yet despite all the evidence for malleability, the role of genetic factors in health differentials cannot be dismissed. And indeed, one should not fall into the trap of viewing genetic and environmental explanations as competing alternatives. As discussed in Chapter 5 by Baird, the advance of genetic knowledge is increasingly revealing the importance of genetic predispositions, based on clusters or networks of interacting genes, whose expression depends in a complex way on the environment experienced by the individual. The genetic endowment may be fixed at birth, but its effects generally are not.

Moreover, the expression of genetic predispositions depends on environmental influences over the *history* of the individual. As discussed in Chapter 3, previous environments and particularly those in early childhood (and before birth) can play a very important role in determining the subsequent status of the individual, both health and socioeconomic. But their influences will depend in part on their interaction with the genetic endowment.

Looking again at the animal studies, Sapolsky found that the superior physiological functioning of the dominant males in his study population

– their ability to turn off the fight-or-flight syndrome more quickly and completely – was impaired when the dominance hierarchy was disrupted. When status was uncertain, all the animals began to show the continuing anxiety and low-level stress response characteristic of subordinates. This indicates the importance of contemporaneous circumstances, rather than that some are "born to rule." It is supported by other animal studies showing that deliberate manipulations of a hierarchy – removing and inserting dominant animals – have measurable and reversible physiological effects. Physiological function follows status, not the other way around.

On the other hand, Sapolsky also found that only a subset of the observably dominant animals showed the more effective endocrine response. Others were physiologically more similar to subordinates. The "true" dominants shared a cluster of personality traits that did appear to be inherited.

The relationship between personality and reaction to stress has been explored in considerable depth by Suomi (1991), working with rhesus monkeys in both experimental and free-ranging environments. He has identified about 20 per cent of his primate population as having "highly reactive" personalities, and has shown that this behaviour pattern is inherited. These animals show extreme reactions, both behavioural and physiological, to stress. Interestingly, while their behavioural reactions differ at different stages in the life cycle, the underlying physiological reactions are the same.[9]

Suomi's findings clearly establish a genetic basis for differential responses to stress, with extreme reactions being associated with symptoms similar to clinical depression in humans. On the other hand, he also found that the adverse health and social consequences of the reactive personality could be mitigated or avoided if the animals were reared by a particularly nurturing mother (not necessarily biological). An exceptionally supportive early environment could offset the effects of a genetic predisposition.

These findings recall those of the cohort study, still under way, of all of the children born on the island of Kauai in 1955. The Kauai Longitudinal Study (Werner and Smith, 1982; Werner, 1989) has focused on the long-term consequences of prenatal and perinatal stress, and the effects of adverse early rearing conditions, on various aspects of child development. One of the findings has been that children who suffer moderate or severe perinatal stress, but are subsequently reared in "good" environments (as measured by family stability or high socioeconomic status), suffer little or no disadvantage in development at twenty months.[10]

Children with no perinatal stress likewise showed little disadvantage, despite poor, unstable households. But two negative factors together had quite severe consequences for child development.

Other recent studies have shown that very early intervention programs can compensate for a deprived rearing environment. Educational day-care (starting between six and twelve weeks of age) has been found to be protective for children at high risk for intellectual impairment, especially those with mentally retarded mothers (Martin, Ramey, and Ramey, 1990; see also Chapter 3). And both nutritional supplementation and psychological stimulation were found by Grantham-McGregor, Powell, Walker, and Himes (1991) to have significant and independent beneficial effects on the mental development of growth-retarded children.

Thus an initial disadvantage, whether reactive personality (Suomi) or perinatal stress (Werner), can be buffered by a sufficiently supportive early environment. At the same time, an inadequate early environment can be remedied by specific interventions. Genetic and congenital factors are not unimportant, but the expression or non-expression of their effects depends on the social environment. This offers a possible reconciliation of the old "nature/nurture" debate. Even if genetic or congenital problems were equally distributed across the population, their expression would still depend to some extent upon buffering factors whose availability and strength in turn is correlated with socioeconomic position.

In reality, of course, such "initial" problems or predispositions are not equally distributed across social groups. Birth outcomes depend on the condition and behaviour of the mother, and possibly the father as well, and these are affected by social factors. Most obvious is the social-class gradient in maternal smoking; still more extreme and tragic are the children of crack addicts. What is "nature" for the individual is influenced by the social environment of the parent – again no one is an island.

How such buffering factors might work, and have their long-term effects, is unclear. One thinks naturally in terms of "learned" responses, of people consciously or unconsciously adopting styles of behaviour and ways of responding to their environments. But one must be careful not to allow the use of words like "learning" to lead us to confuse this process with learning the multiplication table. Who (or what) learns and what does he, she, or it learn?

For example, it has been shown that *immune systems* can "learn," and not just in the obvious sense of learning to recognize and attack foreign material. The immune systems of mice can be classically conditioned, by feeding them saccharin and cyclophosphamide (an immunosuppressive drug), such that when they are later fed saccharin-flavoured water alone, their immune systems do not respond to challenge. Some part of the nervous system of the mouse receives the taste sensation ... and something happens. Is this true of men as well as mice? Can various forms of experience condition the human immune system (or the endocrine system) – perhaps quite independently of consciousness? If so, then this might provide a pathway for very long term effects of experience on health, through a wide array of different diseases.

An analogy from engineering may be helpful in pulling these threads together. Suppose we think of people becoming ill, or injured, or dying, as similar to the failure, in whole or in part, of a material or structure. That failure is in response to some external force – some stress – acting either all at once, or over a long period of time, or both. The individual, like the material or the structure, responds to an external force by becoming strained, deformed to some degree. But how much it is strained, and with what consequences, will depend both upon the amount of stress and the characteristics of the material itself.

Neither stress, the external force, nor strain, the response of the person or material, is necessarily harmful. For both persons and materials there is a range of "working strain" that is normal and healthy. Over this range, deformations are reversible and the material is resilient. Some have introduced the terms *eustress* and *distress* to distinguish "good" and "bad" stress. These terms reflect the important point that stress is not per se bad. But what is eustress for one person may be distress for another, so we prefer to focus on the extent of the strain response, which depends on what one is made of.

Trouble arises when the strain is too great, and one is (irreversibly) "bent out of shape," or broken. This unfortunate outcome can be prevented either by avoiding overloading – do not let the stress level get too high – or by using stronger materials or construction. The strength of the materials themselves depends on their inherent characteristics, and on how they have been worked and processed. These may be analogous to genetic endowment and early rearing environment, which interact to influence the resilience of the individual, just as they do for steel, wood, or plastic. (Heat treatment and tempering can toughen steel; it is not recommended for wood.)

But one can also make a structure more resistant to stress – reduce the degree of strain – by the way in which it is supported. A horizontal beam can carry much larger loads if it is part of a structure, supported at several points along its length, than if it is simply fastened at one end and otherwise projecting into empty space. The same is true of people – a supportive environment helps one to bear heavier loads without breaking.

From this perspective, Marmot's data indicate a social gradient in the degree of breakage. Is it because people in the lower ranks are under greater stress, or because they are in themselves less able to bear the strain that follows from stress, or because their environments, at work or at home, do not provide the supports that would permit them to transfer some of the strain? These possibilities are, of course, interactive, not mutually exclusive.

There is now a very large literature on the third point, the supportiveness of the social environment in assisting the individual in coping with stress. House, Landis, and Umberson (1988), for example, report widespread and strong correlations between mortality and social support networks – friends and family keep you alive. They interpret the evidence as suggesting that the sheer number of contact persons is protective, regardless of the nature of the interaction. Others, however, emphasize the "quality" of the social interaction, its cultural context and interpretation (see Chapter 4 by Corin). More is not always better; social contacts can generate as well as mitigate stresses.[11]

Syme, Karasek, Theorell, and others focus in particular on the nature of the work environment and the characteristics of the job (Karasek and Theorell, 1990; Johnson and Johansson, 1991). They find a connection between job demand and job latitude, and morbidity and mortality. Looking at heart disease among male workers, they show that people in jobs that impose unpredictable and uncontrollable demands, yet that leave very little room for individual discretion in responding, and that in addition underutilize the individual's skills and abilities – no opportunity for personal growth – tend to have higher rates of heart disease, and death.

In Marmot's Whitehall study, lower-ranked workers are more likely to report that their work is dull and underutilizes their abilities – perhaps not surprising. And experimental animal studies confirm that exposure to stress (e.g., electric shock) that is unpredictable and uncontrollable imposes much greater strain – and health damage – than stress that the animal can learn to predict and control.

Such findings suggest, plausibly, that it may be the quality of the "microenvironment," both social and physical, that is critical to health, rather than some mechanical connection between "health and wealth." Prosperity and health are certainly highly correlated, whether one looks at different income groups within a society or trends over time, or compares different societies. Increasing prosperity is both an indicator of past success in coping with one's environment and a basis for future possibilities – a source of both self-esteem and empowerment. And it may be difficult to maintain high-quality microenvironments in a society where overall income levels are static or declining. But as discussed in Chapter 3, one can find examples of both "health without wealth" and "wealth without health," not only among individuals, but across societies.

Caldwell (1986) shows that, within the strong cross-national correlation between health and wealth, certain societies achieve aggregate health status measures that are much higher than their income levels would "predict," while others are much lower. He also notes that there are particular social characteristics (in particular, high levels of maternal education) that seem consistently to be associated with good population health even at low levels of average income. Wilkinson (1992) presents evidence that the health of a population depends upon the *equality* of income distribution, rather than the *average* income, so that rising average incomes can be associated with declining health, if the resulting wealth becomes concentrated in fewer pockets. Or, as Sir Francis Bacon observed: "Money is like muck – not good unless it be well spread."

And so on. Our purpose here is not to try, in an introductory chapter, to summarize this vast literature, or collection of potentially related literatures. Rather we have tried, through a selection of leading studies and findings, to sketch out the basis for an argument that factors in the social environment, external to the health care system, exert a major and potentially modifiable influence on the health of populations, through biological channels that are just now beginning to be understood.

The interpretation of these observations and their translation into health policy represent a massive challenge, to which the subsequent chapters of this book attempt to offer a first response. But the observations themselves are facts, which cannot be dismissed simply because they are incompletely understood. They do not fit comfortably, or at all, into the simplistic "repair shop" model of health and health care on which most current health policy is based.

Relative to that simplistic view, the observations outlined above are "anomalous findings" on the determinants of health. They emerge from a number of different disciplines whose members rarely, if ever, read each other's work. They do not follow the same journals, or use the same jargons or metaphors. Yet we believe that enough such anomalous results have now been observed that, if they could be assembled and interpreted in a common framework and related to one another in a coherent way, they would be seen, in Kuhn's terms, to justify a paradigm shift.

Such shifts of perspective, however, do not occur in response to exhortation. They only occur when enough people find the old perspective unsatisfactory – because of a growing awareness of its lack of explanatory power – *and* find a new one more interesting as well as more enlightening.

Many of the "anomalous findings" described above have long histories, though new observations are accumulating rapidly. But, to the best of our knowledge, this diverse set of observations has never been brought together and examined within a single coherent framework. Yet they appear all to be pieces from the same large and complex jigsaw puzzle. This book is a start at assembling that puzzle, and at drawing out some of the implications for social policy of the resulting (still sketchy) picture.

It must be admitted that at present these implications are far from clear. We cannot offer a detailed prescription of "What is to be done," and much remains to be learned about the development of effective health interventions. But the evidence does suggest that the potential for improvement, in directions not addressed by conventional health care systems, is great. And relevant new knowledge is emerging rapidly, from both the biological and the social disciplines.

ACKNOWLEDGMENTS

This introductory chapter, written by R.G. Evans, is to be understood as a collaborative effort, growing out of the continuing research and seminars of the Population Health program of the Canadian Institute for Advanced Research.

NOTES

1 Our work proceeds from a particular notion of "health" about which it is important to be clear at the outset. For the most part, we simply assume that health is the absence of disability or disease. That is, when free of illness as experienced by patients (e.g., aching muscles or sinus congestion associated with cold or flu), of disease as understood by clinicians (e.g., arthritis, diabetes, or cancer), or of injury (e.g., broken leg or hip fracture), one is "healthier." For any given state of disease or illness, capacity to function may vary dramatically among individuals, and it is this functional capability, in combination with the absence of clinically defined disease, that is implicit throughout.

There are, of course, other conceptions of health. It is by now pretty well accepted that the WHO's broader definition – a state of complete well-being

– is rather unhelpful operationally. Health, on that conception, is everything, and hence nothing in particular. But there is in some contemporary intellectual circles productive ferment about different understandings of health.

2 Sooner or later, the reader should question the rather morbid focus on death rates, as (inverse) measures of health. There is, after all, much more to good health than simply being alive. But for research purposes, deaths have the advantage of being quite unambiguously countable, and partly for that reason have been widely collected for a long time. Measurements of illness rates are much less complete, and more subject to differences in concept and definition over time and across regions. Measurements of health status are still more debatable conceptually, and are only sporadically collected.

But patterns of illness are also hierarchical. Marmot's later studies have found a gradient in morbidity, as measured by rates of sickness absence, which is at least as steep as the mortality gradient (North et al., 1993). It would have been rather surprising if the people who died earlier died in better health.

3 Are *any* risk factors truly "individual"? Donne is a better guide than Defoe. "No man is an island," and Robinson Crusoe is fiction.

4 The relation of this "something else" to one's position in a hierarchy may recall Maslow's concept of a "hierarchy of needs." All those in Marmot's study may have enough to eat, clothing and shelter, and personal safety. But the levels of "self-actualization" and self-esteem are probably quite different, on average, from top to bottom. So high status may correlate with satisfaction of high-level needs. But what exactly is low self-esteem (if that is the something else), and how does it kill you? It is somewhat easier to measure starvation or exposure and to understand their mechanisms of action.

5 In the subsequent discussion, we focus primarily on the possible relationships between hierarchy, stress, and health. But the reader should keep in mind that hierarchy is simply one example of the more general concept of heterogeneities. As discussed in Chapter 3, one also observes systematic differences in health status among cultures, geographic areas, and the sexes. And even in the explanation of differences within hierarchies, we have no basis for assuming a priori that stress is the only biological pathway.

6 Fibrinogen, in conjunction with thrombin, produces fibrin, which promotes normal clotting of blood. This may be very helpful, if one has sustained or is about to sustain a physical injury. It is much less so if the "clots" are on the interior walls of the arteries. In Marmot's studies, lower-ranking civil servants had on average higher levels of circulating fibrinogen, although the differences are not, in themselves, large enough to explain the differences in heart disease rates.

7 These are not alternatives; hormones released by the endocrine system may enhance or depress the functioning of the immune system.

8 Norman Cousins has done much to disseminate to clinicians and the general population the significance of brain-body links. But his emphasis seems to be on "self-improvement" and small-group support in a clinical context, rather than on the influence of broader social structures and networks, on predispositions as well as outcomes. Like many of the "health promoters" of the 1980s (see Chapter 8 by Marmor, Barer, and Evans), he focuses on the attitudes and behaviour of the individual rather than the physical and social environment from which that behaviour arises. Similarly, Friedman (1991) describes "jobs that are disturbing and uncontrollable" as giving rise to "psychological impotence," but then, without pausing for breath, attributes this latter to the "disease-prone personality" (p. 43)! Both thus fit their work comfortably into the "medical model," in which the individual patient has (is) a problem, and one-on-one or small-group therapy is the solution. No challenges are raised to the existing social and economic order.

9 Perhaps coincidentally, Offord, Boyle, Fleming, Blum, and Grant (1989) found in the Ontario Child Health Study that 18.1 per cent of the child population met the study criteria for presence of some degree of psychological problem.

10 One of the most well-known findings of the Kauai Study has been the identification of a small group of "vulnerable but invincible" or "indomitable" children who, despite "high-risk" perinatal experiences and home environments, grew into successful adults. The common characteristics seemed to be close bonding with and high level of attention from *some* adult – not necessarily a parent or even a family member – very early in life. But these children also had personalities that "elicit positive responses" – presumably enabling them to "recruit" emotional support.

11 Again there is a mechanical analogy. In the case of the simple beam above, more supports lead to greater strength. But in complex structures, with each part transferring stresses to others in an overall pattern that is difficult to deduce a priori, reinforcing one part may in fact weaken the whole structure. Hence Seppings' maxim: "Partial strength produces general weakness" (quoted in Gordon, 1978: 69).

REFERENCES

Baird, P.A. (1994). "The role of genetics in population health." In *Why are some people healthy and others not?* ed. Robert G. Evans, Morris L. Barer, and Theodore R. Marmor, 133–59. New York: Aldine de Gruyter.

Black, D., J.N. Morris, C. Smith, P. Townsend, and M. Whitehead (1988). *Inequalities in health: The Black Report: The health divide.* London: Penguin.

Caldwell, J.C. (1986). "Routes to low mortality in poor countries." *Population and Development Review* 12:171–220.

Corin, E. (1994). "The social and cultural matrix of health and disease." In *Why are some people healthy and others not?* ed. Robert G. Evans, Morris L. Barer, and Theodore R. Marmor, 93–132. New York: Aldine de Gruyter.

Dantzer, R., and K.W. Kelley (1989). "Stress and immunity: An integrated view of relationships between the brain and the immune system." *Life Sciences* 44: 1995–2008.

Doll, R., and R. Peto (1981). *The causes of cancer: Quantitative estimates of avoidable risks of cancer in the United States today.* New York: Oxford University Press.

Evans, R.G., M. Hodge, and I.B. Pless (1994). "If not genetics, then what? Biological pathways and population health." In *Why are some people healthy and others not?* ed. Robert G. Evans, Morris L. Barer, and Theodore R. Marmor, 161–88. New York: Aldine de Gruyter.

– and G.L. Stoddart (1994). "Producing health, consuming health care." In *Why are some people healthy and others not?* ed. Robert G. Evans, Morris L. Barer, and Theodore R. Marmor, 27–64. New York: Aldine de Gruyter.

Friedman, H.S. (1991). *The self-healing personality.* New York: Holt.

Gordon, J.E. (1978). *Structures, or why things don't fall down.* London: Plenum.

Grantham-McGregor, S.M., C.A. Powell, S.P. Walker, and J.H. Himes (1991). "Nutritional supplementation, psychosocial stimulation, and mental development of stunted children: The Jamaican study." *Lancet* 338 (July 6): 1–5.

Hertzman, C., J. Frank, and R.G. Evans (1994). "Heterogeneities in health status and the determinants of population health." In *Why are some people healthy and others not?* ed. Robert G. Evans, Morris L. Barer, and Theodore R. Marmor, 67–92. New York: Aldine de Gruyter.

Hirayama, T. (1990). *Lifestyle and mortality: A large scale census-based cohort study in Japan.* Basel: Karger.

House, J.S., K.R. Landis, and D. Umberson (1988). "Social Relationships and Health." *Science* 241 (July 29): 540–5.

Johnson, J.V., and G. Johansson (1991). *The psychosocial work envrionment: Work organization, democratization and health.* Amityville, NY: Baywood.

Karasek, R.A., and T. Theorell (1990). *Healthy work: Stress, productivity, and the reconstruction of working life.* New York: Basic Books.

Marmor, T.R. (1992). "Japan: A sobering lesson." *Health Management Quarterly* 14(3): 10–14.

– M.L. Barer, and R.G. Evans (1994). "The determinants of a population's health: What can be done to improve a democratic nation's health status?" In *Why are some people healthy and others not?* ed. Robert G. Evans, Morris L. Barer, and Theodore R. Marmor, 217–30. New York: Aldine de Gruyter.

Marmot, M.G. (1986). "Social inequalities in mortality: The social envrionment." In *Class and health: Research and longitudinal data*, ed. R.G. Wilkinson, 21–33. London: Tavistock.

– (1992). "Coronary heart disease: Rise and fall of a modern epidemic." In *Coronary heart disease epidemiology: From aetiology to public health*, ed. Michael Marmot and Paul Elliott, 1–19. Oxford: Oxford University Press.

– S.L. Syme, A. Kagan, H. Kato, J.B. Cohen, and J. Belsky (1975). "Epidemiological studies of coronary heart disease and stroke in Japanese men living in Japan, Hawaii and California. Prevalence of coronary and hypertensive heart disease and associated risk factors." *American Journal of Epidemiology* 102: 514–25.

– and S.L. Syme (1976). "Acculturation and coronary heart disease in Japanese-Americans." *American Journal of Epidemiology* 104: 225–47.

– G. Rose, M.J. Shipley, and P.J.S. Hamilton (1978). "Employment grade and coronary heart disease in british civil servants." *Journal of Epidemiology and Community Health* 32: 274–6.

– M. Kogevinas, and M.A. Elston (1987). "Social/economic status and disease." *Annual Review of Public Health* 8: 111–35.

– and T. Theorell (1988). "Social class and cardiovascular disease: The contribution of work." *International Journal of Health Services* 18: 659–74.

– and J.F. Mustard (1994). "Coronary heart disease from a population perspective." In *Why are some people healthy and others not?* ed. Robert G. Evans, Morris L. Barer, and Theodore R. Marmor, 189–214. New York: Aldine de Gruyter.

Martin, S.L., C.T. Ramey, and S. Ramey (1990). "The prevention of intellectual impairment in children of impoverished families: Findings of a randomized trial of educational day care." *American Journal of Public Health* 80(7): 844–7.

McKeown, T. (1979). *The role of medicine: Dream, mirage or nemesis?* 2nd edition. Oxford: Basil Blackwell.

North, F., S.L. Syme, A. Feeney, et al. (1993). "Explaining socioeconomic differences in sickness absence: The Whitehall II Study." *British Medical Journal* 306 (February 6): 363.

Office of Population Censuses and Surveys (1972). *Occupational mortality: The Registrar General's decennial supplement for England and Wales*, Series DS No. 1. London: Her Majesty's Stationery Office.

– (1978). *Occupational mortality: The Registrar General's decennial supplement for England and Wales*, Series DS No. 1. London: Her Majesty's Stationery Office.

Offord, D.R., M.H. Boyle, J.E. Fleming, H.M. Blum, and N.I. Rae Grant (1989). "Ontario child health study: Summary of selected results." *Canadian Journal of Psychiatry* 34(6): 483–91.

Roos, N.P., and L.L. Roos (1994). "Small area variations, practice style, and quality of care." In *Why are some people healthy and others not?* ed. Robert G. Evans, Morris L. Barer, and Theodore R. Marmor, 231–52. New York: Aldine de Gruyter.

Sapolsky, R.M. (1990). "Stress in the wild." *Scientific American* 262(1): 116–23.

Schieber, G.J., J.-P. Poullier, and L.M. Greenwald (1992). "US health expenditure performance: An international comparison and data update." *Health Care Financing Review* 13(4): 1–87.

Suomi, S.J. (1991). "Primate separation models of affective disorders." In *Neurobiology of learning, emotion and affect*, ed. J. Madden, 195–214. New York: Raven.

Szreter, S. (1988). "The importance of social intervention in Britain's mortality decline, c. 1850–1914: A re-interpretation of the role of public health." *Society for the Social History of Medicine* 1(1): 1–37.

Vagero, D., and O. Lundberg (1989). "Health inequalities in Britain and Sweden." *Lancet* 2 (July 1): 35–6.

Werner, E.E. (1989). "Children of the garden isle." *Scientific American* 260 (4 April):106–11.

– and R.S. Smith (1982). *Vulnerable but invincible: A longitudinal study of resilient children and youth*. New York: McGraw-Hill.

Wilkins, R., O.B. Adams, and A.M. Brancker (1990). "Changes in mortality by income in urban Canada from 1971 to 1986." *Health Reports 1989* 1(2): 137–74. Canadian Centre for Health Information, Statistics Canada, Cat. #82-003 quarterly, Ministry of Supply and Services, Ottawa.

Wilkinson, R.G. (1986). "Socio-economic differences in mortality: Interpreting the data and their size and trends." In *Class and Health*, ed. R.G. Wilkinson, 1–20. London: Tavistock.

– (1992). "Income distribution and life expectancy." *British Medical Journal* 304: 165–8.

Wolfson, M.C. (1994). "Social proprioception: Measurement, data, and information from a population health perspective." In *Why are some people healthy and others not?* ed. Robert G. Evans, Morris L. Barer, and Theodore R. Marmor, 287–316. New York: Aldine de Gruyter.

15

Health, Hierarchy, and Hominids: Biological Correlates of the Socioeconomic Gradient in Health (1996)

ROBERT G. EVANS

POLITICAL EPIDEMIOLOGY: SOCIAL INEQUALITIES IN HEALTH

Top People live longer, and they are healthier while doing so. Fifteen years after the pioneering work of the Black Report (Townsend and Davidson 1988), nearly twenty years after the observations of growing health inequalities that led to the appointment of the Research Working Group, the correlation of health with social status is now so extensively documented and so widely recognized that it has even come to the attention of *The Economist* (1994a). The efforts by the UK government in 1980 to suppress the Black Report, presumably in the hope that its findings would go away, have been spectacularly unsuccessful. The study of health inequalities is now a significant research sub-industry; and socioeconomic gradients have turned up in every country where researchers have looked for them.

Although the existence of the correlation is no longer in question, the interpretation remains highly contentious. *Why* are class differences so

Evans, Robert G. "Health, Hierarchy, and Hominids," in *Reforming Health Care Systems: Experiments with the NHS*, edited by Anthony J. Culyer and Adam Wagstaff, 35–63. Cheltenham, UK, and Northampton, MA: Edward Elgar Publishing Ltd., 1996. Reprinted with the permission of Edward Elgar Publishing Ltd.

strongly correlated with the prevalence of disease and the risk of death, and what, if anything, can or should be done about it? Interpretation has from the very beginning been tightly entangled with political ideology and economic interest.

The logical sequence from observation, to explanation, to response, is often turned on its head. Conflicting views of what constitutes a well-ordered society (depending in large part on one's position in that society) determine preferences for particular social policies, and these in turn influence the choice of explanations.

For those on the Left, health inequalities are clear evidence of material deprivation, symptoms of an unjust society.[1] Only by a more equitable distribution of both life chances and rewards can one hope to improve the health of the least healthy, and this in turn is the key to improving the overall health of the population. To become healthier, we must remake our societies. Among other things, this will require a significant redistribution of wealth and power from the more to the less fortunate. The improvement of health, for which there is widespread public support, can thus be recruited to advance a broader and more contentious social agenda.

To those on the Right, however, this looks like a fool's errand. The first knee-jerk reaction is that the correlation is spurious, that health status determines social position rather than the other way around. Fitter, healthier people rise in a just society that rewards performance. As to *why* they are fitter – perhaps because of genetic superiority or early life experience – well, that is just the way life is. And anyway, people lower down the social scale actually *choose* their unhealthy circumstances. They smoke, eat bad diets, do not get enough exercise, and in general fail to look after themselves. (This is clearly the explanation favoured by *The Economist.*) If they are sicker, and die sooner, it is their own fault. Medical care is provided at public expense; but there is not much more that can, or in any case should, be done, except perhaps to lecture the badly behaved about "taking more responsibility for their own health."

Each of these lines of interpretation has significant problems of fact and logic, and in both political preferences for particular remedies – income redistribution or laissez-faire – clearly influence the favoured perceptions of mechanism. But the debate has already generated a large literature and a further critique in this paper would add little. Moreover it is difficult to enter the discussion without simultaneously becoming involved in the political controversy that must inevitably surround claims of "inequalities" – particularly inequalities with mortal consequences. Instead, I shall try to reframe the discussion of class and health in a way which may hold the political and ideological issues at arm's length, at least for a time, while also broadening the range of relevant evidence.

HETEROGENEITIES IN HEALTH: MORAL OFFENCE OR RESEARCH OPPORTUNITY

Socioeconomic status (SES) is only one among any number of measures by which to partition a population, and not an unambiguous one at that. The British are commonly regarded as suffering from a morbid fascination with social class, giving it the sort of attention that in other countries would be reserved for sex, or federal-provincial fiscal relations. Elsewhere it is less clear what "class" means, or how it should be identified, perhaps using measures of income, education, occupational status, or public esteem.

In practice, people are grouped on the basis of some measurable indicator variable or variables which are accepted as standing for the more abstract notion of SES. (In the US a key indicator seems to be race.) But one could equally well categorize a population by region, or sex, or ethnic status, or religious affiliation, or height, and so on. If one found systematic differences in health between the sub-populations thus defined, one could then refer to "health inequalities" across these divides as well. Such language, however, automatically combines an observation of differentness with an implicit judgment of unfairness that may or may not be appropriate. It is well known, for example, that women in industrialized societies live, on average, significantly longer than men. But this "health inequality" generates little or no political controversy; to my knowledge no government has ever tried to suppress the evidence.

A more neutral term, *heterogeneities*, captures the generic observation that, when populations are partitioned by some variable of interest, significant health differences are frequently found between the groups (Hertzman et al., 1994). Comparing these sub-populations may then provide clues to determine the causal factors in differences in health, without simultaneously implying (or denying) that these differences represent "inequalities" in the sense of indicators of injustice. Inequalities are goads to action; heterogeneities are merely guides to research. "[T] here is a tremendous potential to exploit heterogeneity in populations as a wedge for greater understanding" (Sapolsky, 1993).

Such greater understanding, once achieved, may indeed have significant moral or political implications. But the more neutral language is less likely to trigger ideological immune systems at the very beginning of the process.

A focus on heterogeneities as "a wedge for greater understanding" then leads us to consider *mechanisms* rather than remedies. What are the pathways through which some groups of people become healthier than others? Material deprivation is certainly one possible explanation, and has the attraction that the links between deprivation and ill-health – hunger, exposure, crowding, environmental toxins – are relatively easy to imagine. But so are the "self-abuse" explanations of the Right – smoking, overeating, and too much television.

Political debates select the simple, easily communicated explanation, which is usually seriously incomplete, if not outright wrong. In reality, the pathways through which heterogeneities in health status emerge seem to be a good deal more complex than is contemplated, or caricatured, by either side. But the quick, easily understood, politically comfortable "explanations," with their associated prepackaged policy remedies, tend to crowd out the messages that are emerging from more wide-ranging and subtle efforts to understand the relation between status and health.

The third step in seeking a more neutral stance is to broaden our interests from heterogeneities in *human* populations to include consideration of other primates closely related to ourselves. The old-world monkeys are particularly well adapted for these comparisons. Apart from genetic and physiological similarities, they have complex and sophisticated social structures with readily identifiable status hierarchies. There are several long-term research programs studying different species, some in the wild and some under experimental conditions, that have generated findings remarkably consistent with those emerging from observations in the human species.

This paper will draw particularly heavily on findings from two remarkable programs of research with free-living primate populations. Both populations have a well-defined hierarchical structure, and in both one finds strong connections between this hierarchy and factors related to health. The research design and procedures are, however, very different and are in important ways complementary. When taken together each study provides important insights that are missing from the other, because interventions and modes of data collection that are impossible in one are possible in the other.

Robert Sapolsky has for fourteen years been studying a population of wild baboons in the Serengeti ecosystem of East Africa, and has assembled a remarkable array of information on the relationship between physiology and social structure. For an even longer period, Michael Marmot has been studying the experiences of a group of over 10,000 British civil servants in the Whitehall ecosystem of London.

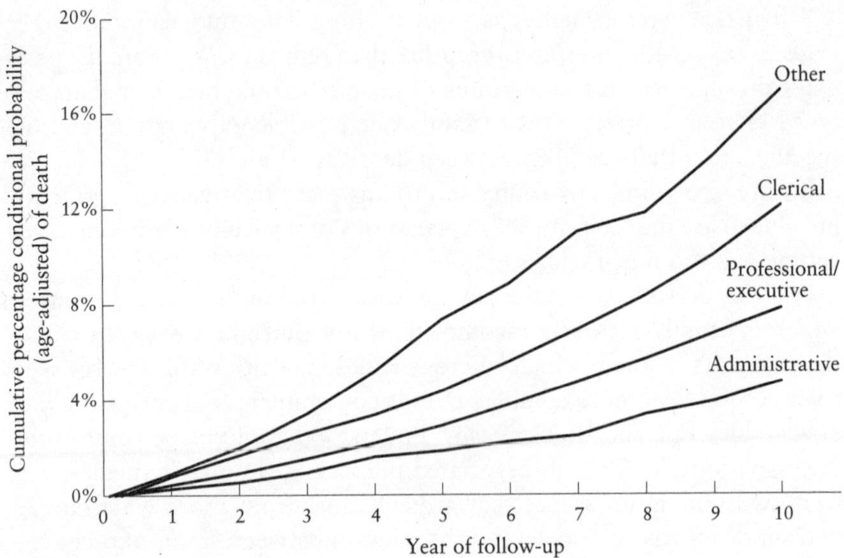

Figure 15.1 Whitehall study: All-cause mortality among total population by year of follow-up

Adapted from: Robert G. Evans. "Health, Hierarchy, and Hominids." In *Reforming Health Care Systems: Experiments with the NHS*, edited by Anthony J. Culyer and Adam Wagstaff, 35–63. Cheltenham, UK, and Northampton, MA: Edward Elgar Publishing Ltd, 1996.
Original source: Marmot (1986), Reproduced by permission of Taylor & Francis Books, UK.

HIERARCHY AND HEALTH AMONG THE HOMINIDS OF WHITEHALL

Perhaps the clearest message to emerge from the first decade of the Whitehall studies was that there is a correlation between status and mortality, and it is *large*. Figure 15.1, which has been widely reproduced, shows that, when (male) individuals were followed over a ten-year period, those in the lowest civil service grades had three times as large a probability (age-adjusted) of dying as those at the top. More recent work has shown that this gradient has persisted through the 1980s, and is observed for measures of illness as well as death, and for females as well as males (Marmot et al., 1991; North et al., 1993).

These observations are of particular importance because they are *person-specific* as well as *population-based*. They are drawn from the experience of a large population of identified individuals, followed through time. Other studies correlating mortality and SES, and particularly the data from the British Office of Population Censuses and Surveys (OPCS) which were drawn upon in the Black Report, have been subjected to a number of methodological criticisms. Some have been based on aggregate data, comparing averages among groups that were not always strictly comparable, rather than following the experience of actual individuals. Their messages are powerfully confirmed by the Whitehall findings.[2]

Marmot's work, however, also highlighted two other features of the relationship between hierarchy and health which deserve special attention. The first is that it is a *gradient* and not a threshold, and the second is that it is observed for most (though not all) causes of death.

As shown in Figure 15.1, the mortality curves improve steadily as one moves up the hierarchy. Death rates are lower in the top administrative grades than in the professional and executive grades just below them. But people in the latter can hardly be described as living in destitution. Indeed, all those in the study are employed, and in jobs which do not expose them to the same occupational hazards as, say, lumbering or fishing. Material deprivation cannot explain the observations in Figure 15.1. This is not to say that deprivation does not exist, or that it is not harmful to health. But there is clearly a process at work by which hierarchy influences health status directly, independently of deprivation.

The understanding of this gradient in health status is not assisted, therefore, by the automatic assumption that it is a problem of "the poor," those folks over there, who are to be cherished or spurned according to one's political predilections but are, in any case, "other." There is more to health inequality than poverty; *de te fabula narratur*, this story is about us.

Furthermore, in the modern world people are required to die *of* something. ("Visitation of God" is no longer fashionable on death certificates.) Aggregate mortality differentials should be reflected in differentials in causes of death from particular diseases, and (as shown in Table 15.1) they are. What is interesting is that there are gradients in mortality rates for almost all diseases. There is no preferred channel of effect. This suggests that hierarchical position may be associated with some sort of underlying vulnerability or vitality that is expressed through a number of different diseases. The diseases themselves are not the critical mechanisms.

Of particular importance, the gradients are found for both the smoking- and non-smoking-related diseases (Tables 15.1 and 15.2). As everyone knows, the lower classes smoke and the middle and upper classes do not. Smoking causes lung cancer, emphysema, and bronchitis, and is a risk factor for many other diseases, especially heart disease – tobacco is an addictive, toxic substance. So they bring it on themselves – what can one do? Well, before throwing one's hands in the air, one might at least

Table 15.1 Age-adjusted relative mortality* in ten years by civil-service grade and cause of death

Cause of death	*Administrators*	*Professional & executive*	*Clerk*	*Other*
Lung cancer	0.5	1	2.2	3.6
Other cancer	0.8	1	1.4	1.4
Coronary heart disease	0.5	1	1.4	1.7
Cerebrovascular disease	0.3	1	1.4	1.2
Chronic bronchitis	0	1	6	7.3
Other respiratory	1.1	1	2.6	3.1
Gastrointestinal diseases	0	1	1.6	2.8
Genitourinary tliseases	1.3	1	0.7	3.1
Accidents and homicide	0	1	1.4	1.5
Suicide	0.7	1	1	1.9
Non-smoking-related causes				
Cancer	0.8	1	1.3	1.4
Non-cancer	0.6	1	1.5	2
All causes	0.6	1	1.6	2.1

* Calculated from logistic equation adjusting for age

Adapted from: Robert G. Evans. "Health, Hierarchy, and Hominids." In *Reforming Health Care Systems: Experiments with the NHS*, edited by Anthony J. Culyer and Adam Wagstaff, 35–63. Cheltenham, UK, and Northampton, MA: Edward Elgar Publishing Ltd, 1996.
Original source: Marmot (1986), 25. Reproduced by permission of Taylor & Francis Books, UK.

Table 15.2 Age-adjusted mortality in ten years (and number of deaths from coronary heart disease and lung cancer) by civil-service grade and smoking status

Cause of death	*Administrators*	*Professional & executive*	*Clerk*	*Other*	*Total*
Non-smokers					
CHD	1.4	2.36	2.08	6.89	2.59
Lung cancer	0	0.24	0	0.25	0.21
Ex-smokers					
CHD	1.29	3.06	3.32	3.98	3.09
Lung cancer	0.21	0.5	0.56	1.05	0.62
Current smokers					
CHD	2.16	3.58	4.92	6.62	4
Lung cancer	0.35	0.73	1.49	2.33	2

CHD: Coronary heart disease

Adapted from: Robert G. Evans. "Health, Hierarchy, and Hominids." In *Reforming Health Care Systems: Experiments with the NHS*, edited by Anthony J. Culyer and Adam Wagstaff, 35–63. Cheltenham, UK, and Northampton, MA: Edward Elgar Publishing Ltd, 1996.
Original source: Marmot (1986), 25. Reproduced by permission of Taylor & Francis Books, UK.

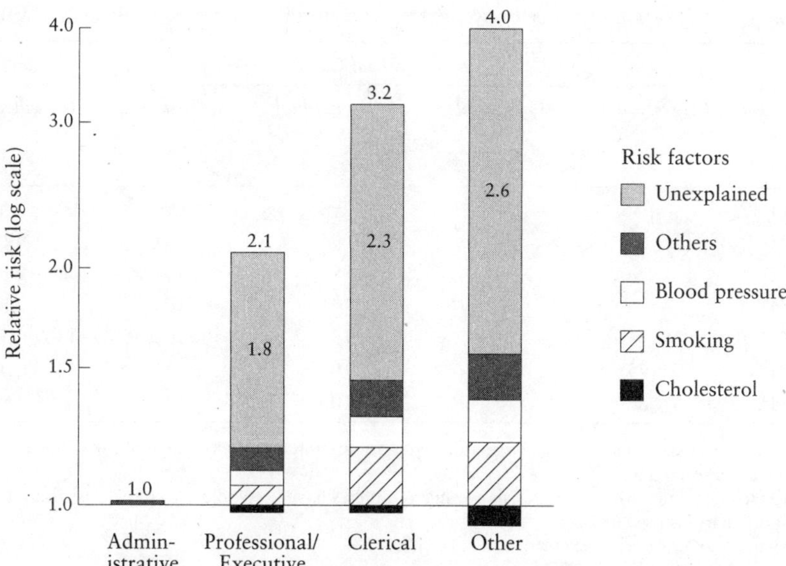

Figure 15.2 Relative risk of CHD death in different grades "explained" by risk factors (age-standardized)

Adapted from: Robert G. Evans. "Health, Hierarchy, and Hominids." In *Reforming Health Care Systems: Experiments with the NHS*, edited by Anthony J. Culyer and Adam Wagstaff, 35–63. Cheltenham, UK, and Northampton, MA: Edward Elgar Publishing Ltd, 1996.
Original source: Marmot, et al. (1978). Reproduced with permission from BMJ Publishing Group Ltd.

wonder *why* smoking is now so clearly socially graded, in all our societies. If it were simply a "taste," or even a genetic predisposition to addiction, one would expect smoking behaviour to be spread more equally across the population, not concentrated at the low end. But that is a separate issue. The main point is that the Whitehall gradient is not explained by differences in smoking behaviour.

The correlates of cardiovascular disease, which is the largest single cause of death, have been extensively explored. Marmot and his colleagues (1978) have partitioned the gradient in cardiac mortality according to the differences in the three individual characteristics – smoking, hypertension, and blood lipid levels – which are most widely accepted as risk factors. The results are shown in Figure 15.2. These factors *do* explain a portion of the difference in death rates between those at the top and those at the bottom of the hierarchy, but what is most apparent is how much they leave unexplained. Something else, something important, is at work.

Table 15.3 Mortality by social class, 1911–81 (men, 15 to 64 years, England and Wales)

	Social Class				
	Professional	*Managerial*	*Skilled manual and non-manual*	*Semi-skilled*	*Unskilled*
Year	*I*	*II*	*III*	*IV*	*V*
1911	88	94	96	93	142
1921	82	94	95	101	125
1931	90	94	97	102	111
1951	86	92	101	104	118
1961[a]	76 (75)	81	100	103	143 (127)
1971[b]	77 (75)	81	104	114	137 (121)
1981[c]	66	76	103	116	166

a Figures are SMRS, which express age-adjusted mortality rates as a percentage of the national average at each date.
b To facilitate comparisons, figures shown in parentheses have been adjusted to the classification of occupations used in 1951.
c Men, 20 to 64 years, Great Britian.

Adapted from: Robert G. Evans. "Health, Hierarchy, and Hominids." In *Reforming Health Care Systems: Experiments with the NHS*, edited by Anthony J. Culyer and Adam Wagstaff, 35–63. Cheltenham, UK, and Northampton, MA: Edward Elgar Publishing Ltd, 1996.
Original sources: Marmot (1986), 2. Reproduced by permission of Taylor & Francis Books, UK, and the Office of Population Censuses and Surveys (1978), 174.

This large hierarchical gradient in mortality, not apparently linked to material deprivation, and expressed through a number of different causes of death, also emerges in the longitudinal data from the OPCS that were used in the Black Report. Differential mortality by social class can be found, as shown in Table 15.3, at least back to 1911. But the principal causes of death have changed radically over that period, implying that the factor or factors underlying the gradient have been independent of the diseases themselves. Whatever diseases are the chief killers, people lower down in the hierarchy are always more at risk.

The historical data also span a period of remarkable expansion in the medical care services – expansions in scale and capacity, technical sophistication and access. Whatever criticisms one may make of health care systems in the UK or anywhere else, it is undeniable that, over the last century and particularly over the last half-century, their reach has been extended as never before. While it would be naive to claim that class differences in access have disappeared as a result, access has at least become a great deal less unequal. And without accepting the more extreme claims of the medical miracle marketeers, there is obvious evidence of improved effectiveness in cure, care, and contribution in quality of life. Yet the social gradient, in the UK at least, persists and even grows wider.

Most modern health care is in fact illness care. This is nothing to apologize for; illness care is obviously worth doing, and is often done very well. But if hierarchy influences health in some way more fundamental than the particular illnesses through which differences in health are expressed, then we should not perhaps be surprised if they are unaffected by responses to illness per se. Thus the apparent insensitivity of the SES gradient to the massive expansion of the health services, over a period of decades, is not evidence that those services are not doing their job. But it is at least suggestive that there is something else going on that may be beyond their reach.

The historical persistence of the SES gradient in the OPCS data also supports the Whitehall studies, in undercutting explanations based on material deprivation. The present economic environment, with slow growth and a growing disparity of incomes between rich and poor, raises the possibility of an absolute decline in living standards for those low down the social scale. It is tempting to correlate this with the growing disparities in health status. Over the century as a whole, however, absolute living standards have obviously risen a great deal, even for those at the bottom. It should then be clear from the historical record that the declining prevalence of deprivation, in absolute terms, leads to declining health inequalities. But as shown in Table 15.3, it does not.

Again it should be emphasized that this is *not* to imply the irrelevance of material conditions. *The World Development Report 1993*, issued by the World Bank (1993), provides a dramatic comparison across countries of the relation between average incomes and mortality (Figure 15.3; see also Preston, 1976, 67). At the lowest income levels the relation between mortality and income is very clear. But over time an increasing number of countries are reaching a plateau where more income does not appear to be correlated with further reductions in mortality.[3]

Within a single country, greater affluence can contribute through a number of channels to better health. But the fact that the *gradient* in mortality in the UK has not been reduced, even during times when living standards were improving across the whole population, weakens any explanation in terms of absolute deprivation. Wilkinson (1992) considers the UK experience in the context of several different sets of data on income and mortality in developed societies. These suggest quite strongly that life expectancy is correlated, not with the level of income per se, but with how equally it is distributed. This in turn implies that it is relative, not absolute, income that matters within each country.

So we are led to think about factors or processes associated with hierarchy, which can exert a powerful influence on health status independent

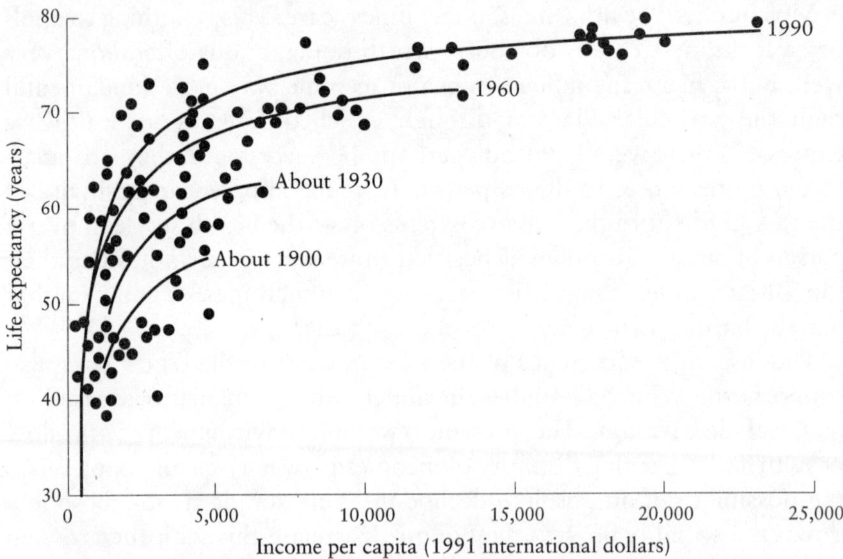

Figure 15.3 Life expectancy and income per capita for selected countries and periods
Adapted from: Robert G. Evans. "Health, Hierarchy, and Hominids." In *Reforming Health Care Systems: Experiments with the NHS*, edited by Anthony J. Culyer and Adam Wagstaff, 35–63. Cheltenham, UK, and Northampton, MA: Edward Elgar Publishing Ltd, 1996. Reproduced under terms of Creative Commons Attribution License (CC BY 3.0 IGO).
Original source: World Bank (1993). © World Bank.

of material conditions, or even of "lifestyles" as traditionally represented, expressed through a number of different diseases. At this point, we shift our attention to the second major study of free-ranging primates, that of the Kenyan olive baboons.

HEALTH AND HIERARCHY AMONG THE CERCOPITHECIDS OF KENYA

Sapolsky's studies begin from an interest in endocrinology and stress physiology, and the growing body of evidence indicating that people's physiological responses to stress are profoundly influenced by their emotional makeup, their personalities, and their positions in society (Sapolsky 1990). Ideally, to understand these relationships would require simultaneous observation of the structure and interactions of an entire social group, and various physiological measures of its members.

But there are severe restrictions, both ethical and practical, on what is possible in the study of human populations. Many of the interesting interactions – mating, grooming, feeding, confrontation, and conflict – take place under cover, not on the open plain. Even if one could follow an individual continuously, one would miss most of the group action. Moreover, Sapolsky's basic technique consists of anaesthetic darting of subjects, as unobtrusively as possible, so as to take physiological measures in particular circumstances. It is difficult to imagine a researcher being permitted to dart a senior, or even a middle-level, civil servant during a particularly stressful meeting, in order to measure hormone levels.[4]

On the other hand, caged animals under experimental conditions are already under stress and in artificial environments, and it is hard to know how severe an effect this has on their baseline physiological status and patterns of response.

Free-ranging animals offer a middle ground for research, being more accessible than humans and less "contaminated" than caged populations. As for the baboons:

> These intelligent animals are good stand-ins for human subjects in part because their primary sources of stress, like those of humans in modern society, are psychological rather than physical. Food is plentiful; the baboons spend only a few hours each day feeding. Predators are few, and infant mortality is low. With the luxury of plentiful resources and free time, the animals can devote themselves to distressing one another. I study the males, who are quite adept at that activity. (Sapolsky, 1990)

The individual interactions within the troop are not, however, a simple "war of all against all," but rather a highly complex social web with a well-defined dominance hierarchy. Status among females tends to be inherited and maintained over the lifetime. But males typically rise in rank as they mature, winning higher positions through overt aggression, holding them through "threats, psychological harassment, and bluff" (Sapolsky, 1993), and then being displaced as their strength declines with age. The competitive interactions may be individual, but may also involve alliances and combinations – it is good to have friends – which are nonetheless rather unstable.

When the population is divided into dominants and subordinates, the top and bottom halves of the rank order, there are systematic physiological differences between these groups. "[W]hen the dominance hierarchy is stable (as it usually is), the workings of nearly every physiologic system I have examined differ between the dominant and subordinate males"

(Sapolsky, 1990). In particular, their endocrine systems function differently in response to stress, as expressed in the "fight or flight" syndrome.

Like ourselves, or any other animal, the baboons respond to an actual attack or injury or a perceived threat by mobilizing physical and intellectual resources to respond – to fight back or to run away. The neural system interprets the external threat and triggers the release of hormones that direct this process. Maintenance, repair, and "investment" (growth, development, and reproduction) are shut down while all available metabolic resources are used to cope with the immediate threat.

But mobilization is expensive. Tissues and organs that are held in a high state of readiness, and denied maintenance and repair, become fatigued and eventually atrophy. The suppression of immune function, which is energy-intensive, puts the individual at greater risk of infection. It is therefore advantageous to be able not only to turn on the "fight or flight" response rapidly, but also to turn it off when the threat is past. In general, dominant animals are better able to turn off their stress responses.[5]

Subordinate animals appear to be living in a chronic state of stress response that, by analogy with engineering usage, we might refer to as chronic strain.[6] The physiological threats come not so much directly from the external environment, but from their own responses to that environment. Recall that most of the stress experienced by these animals is generated by their social interactions rather than by external threats such as predators or lack of food. Moreover most of those stresses are psychological – threats, bluff, and harassment rather than outright attack. What really bothers subordinates is not so much being attacked by a leopard, or even worrying about being attacked by a leopard. It is being yawned at by a higher-ranking male (showing very large canine teeth) from a distance of three feet, whenever one is trying to enjoy one's dinner or mate.

The hormonal patterns associated with chronic strain are also associated with a number of different diseases. The suppression of immune system function has already been noted. Sapolsky also finds that the ratio of HDL to LDL, high- to low-density lipoprotein, is lowered in low-status males. Elevated LDL concentrations are risk factors for heart disease in both humans and baboons, and high concentrations of HDL are protective. Moreover, there is experimental evidence that sustained glucocorticoid overexposure can suppress HDL:LDL ratios; and basal levels of cortisol, the primate (and human) form of glucocorticoid, are higher in the subordinate baboons.

With proper allowance for scientific caution, what *can* be said is that these studies have demonstrated a *potential* pathway leading from hierarchical position, through differential endocrine responses to stress, to differences in basal hormone levels which are consistent with differential risk status for a number of diseases. These results are in a sense the mirror image of Marmot's findings, where the endpoints are firm – hierarchy correlates unambiguously with mortality – but what is going on between them is much less clear. Working with non-human primates, Sapolsky can characterize in much more detail the physiological characteristics of subjects at different levels in the hierarchy. But the unambiguous connection between status and survival is not so clear.[7]

In neither population is material deprivation a significant part of the story. The dominant primates in both populations get the choicest bits of food, but everyone gets enough to eat. However, the subordinate civil servants also show some physiological signs suggesting chronic strain. Marmot and Theorell (1988) report that both high- and low-ranking civil servants have higher blood pressures when at work than when at home. But while their pressures at work are on average similar, the drop in pressure on going home is significantly greater in the higher-ranking workers.

HIERARCHY AND HEALTH IN CAPTIVE (NON-HUMAN) PRIMATE POPULATIONS

Experimental studies with captive populations offer more opportunities for intervention. Hamm, et al. (1983) showed that feeding a "moderate" cholesterol diet to cynomolgus macacques will induce heart disease. But when the animals were kept caged in single-sex groups, and their status hierarchies observed, it was found that the degree of occlusion of the coronary arteries in the lowest-status animals in each group was much greater than in the high-status group – twice as high for males, and nearly four times for females.[8] Part of this difference was associated with lower ratios of HDL:LDL in submissive animals – paralleling Sapolsky's findings – and part seemed to be an independent effect.

The degree of occlusion was significantly greater for males than for females: dominant males had about the same degree of occlusion as submissive females (23.1 per cent vs 24 per cent) while submissive males had 44 per cent occlusion, and dominant females only 6.9 per cent. So both diet and gender matter, as they do for humans. But so, independently and significantly, does hierarchical position.

There is a substantial and growing literature, reviewed by Cox (1993), on the relationship between psychosocial factors and immune function in non-human primates. Experimental findings go back nearly thirty years, demonstrating that "the formation and disruption of social relationships should be viewed as significant psychobiological events with many immunological sequelae, especially for the young monkey." The endocrine system has traditionally been considered to be the "mediating pathway," but more recently attention has shifted to the sympathetic nervous system (Cox, 1993: 299). Virtually all these findings, however, are under experimental conditions. Sapolsky extends them to free-living conditions, and focuses particularly on the psychosocial consequences of hierarchical position in a way that provides a direct link to the correlations between status and health in hominid populations.

WHICH COMES FIRST, SOCIAL STATUS OR HEALTH STATUS?

The obvious question, of course, is that of causality. If dominants and subordinates differ in their endocrine function, as they do, and if this has significant implications for their health, as it might, is this a *consequence* of their differential status, or simply an indicator of differential fitness? Are some "born to rule"? (This interpretation is quite popular with those of high status in human populations – the cream rises to the top, and the universe unfolds as it should.)

Like all good questions, this one turns out not to have a simple answer – or rather, the simple answer is "Yes and No."

The Stress of Social Circumstances Induces Physiological Responses

In the first place, the subordinate baboons' greater difficulty in regulating their basal cortisol levels, in turning off the "fight or flight" response, seems to be induced rather than innate. Experiments in other animals (including humans) have shown that "[p]rolonged or repeated stressors will elevate basal glucocorticoid concentrations and cause feedback resistance" (Sapolsky, 1993, 444). This mechanism may also be at work in the subordinate baboons, such that the stressfulness of their social status leads, through frequent triggering of the fight or flight response, to blunting of feedback sensitivity and permanently elevated basal cortisol levels.

Consistent with this, observations of dominant males during periods in which the status hierarchy is disrupted and status is uncertain show that they have the high basal cortisol levels and physiological response patterns characteristic of subordinates. Even though they remain dominant as a group, the uncertainty of their individual status leads to reduced efficiency of endocrine function, and symptoms of chronic strain. "[T]he optimal hormonal profile seen in dominant males during stable times is an effect and not a cause of one's high rank" (Sapolsky, 1990, 121).

Again these findings can be reinforced from the study of captive populations under experimental conditions. A number of studies of dominant males in unstable captive social groups (cited in Sapolsky, 1993, 459) have found that dominant males do not have the low basal cortisol levels typically observed during more peaceful times.

Cohen et al. (1992) demonstrated a direct link between instability and vulnerability. They randomly assigned male cynomolgus macacques to "stable" and "unstable" living conditions, and followed them over a 26-month period. The animals were housed in groups of four or five and, for half the population, these groups remained the same throughout the study. But for the other half, the housing groups were "shuffled" every month. The animals had repeatedly to adapt to living with a new set of companions. At the end of the period, it was found that their immune responses were significantly depressed, relative to those who had been living in stable social conditions.

The endocrinal differences among the baboons were directly linked to the frequency and outcomes of "personal" confrontations. Dominant animals that were being challenged from below, and whose status was in question, showed chronic strain patterns even though they might still be winning the majority of their confrontations. On the other hand, frequent confrontations with those of *higher* rank, and occasional reversals of status, do not seem to lead to chronic strain – moving up is good for you.

In one particular instance, however, a male changed troops and adopted a strategy of aggressively "going for dominance" in the new troop. This significantly increased the overall hormonal evidence of strain in the members of the new troop. But *individuals* in that troop showed greater or lesser responses, according to the frequency of their interactions with the newcomer. Of particular importance, the highest cortisol concentrations and lowest lymphocyte counts in the troop were shown by the newcomer himself. The highly aggressive strategy was costly in physiological terms. Far from being "born to rule," the newcomer was engaged in a very stressful gamble that, if successful, would put him in a position to relax and enjoy the benefits, endocrinal and otherwise, of rank.

There is thus clear evidence that hierarchical status influences physiology, in ways that could influence vulnerability to a whole range of diseases. But the linkage from status to sickness is not simple, direct, or complete. The physical effects on the individual depend upon how that status is experienced. Dominance that is stable, and maintained by the occasional reminder of showing one's large teeth, is much more restful than dominance that is under constant challenge, with uncertain outcomes.

Subordination, however, implies (among other things) being the recipient of "displaced aggression" – being attacked out of the blue by a higher-ranking male who has lost a confrontation higher up the line. But the frequency of these events varies from group to group and year to year; there are definitely better and worse times and places to be a subordinate.

The Place of Innate "Personality"

The powerful evidence of the importance of social environment, however, does not rule out a role for individual characteristics as well. While hormonal function is related to rank, it is also clearly related to what can only be described as "personality." The "optimal hormonal profile" is found only in some of the dominant animals; others are much more similar to subordinates. And there is a well-defined set of personality traits and behaviours associated with this profile. They include ability to read social situations accurately, to distinguish real threats from behavioural "noise," and to respond actively and successfully to such threats. If unsuccessful, "displace your aggression" – if you lose a confrontation or a fight, get it out of your system by beating up someone else.

But "true dominants" also spend more time playing with infants, and are more likely to have female "friends" as distinct from mates; they spend more time grooming and being groomed by non-estrus females. (Rates of sexual contacts, however, as opposed to affiliative ones, were not associated with cortisol levels.) Baboons with this more "laid-back" personality spent a longer time in the dominant cohort of the troop – recall that dominance in males is not permanent but rather gained and lost over the life cycle. But this style is not a learned behaviour: "the lower basal cortisol trait is present in the very first season of such males' long tenures; it is a predictor, rather than a consequence of such social success" (Sapolsky, 1993, 465).

Again the captive studies offer supporting evidence. Cohen et al., comparing macacques in "stable" and "unstable" social settings, found that various forms of "affiliative behaviour" were more common in the unstable environments, and that the animals engaging in such behaviour showed far less depression of immune function. Those able to increase their affiliative behaviours were *largely* protected against the effects of social instability. Some are better than others at making friends and, in an unstable environment, this can be good for your health.

Sapolsky (1993, 465–6) provides a particularly apt summary:

> although social rank is an important predictor of some physiological parameters, just as important can be the type of society in which that rank occurs, and the way in which one experiences such a rank ... [moreover] ... the filters of personality with which an individual views these events and the varying strategies available for coping with them are probably immensely important variables as well.

Coming back to the hominids, research shows that "in the face of overt and undeniable external stressors, the magnitude of the physiological stress response can be modulated enormously by psychological factors ... by increasing the individual's sense of control, of predictability, by providing outlets for frustration, and by strengthening social support networks."

Is Biology – or Sociology – Destiny?

The importance of "personality" leaves open the question of malleability. To what extent are people, or baboons, born with protective or vulnerable personalities, as part of their genetic makeup? How much of personality is acquired through life experience, and how? Can "coping styles" be modified to decrease vulnerability to "the stress of life"?

There is a related question of malleability at the societal level. All human societies have hierarchies. Are their effects on health therefore inevitable, simply a part of the human condition, or are the individual experiences of dominance or subordination, and the corresponding physiological effects, quite as variable among hominids as they appear to be among baboons?

Some Hierarchies Are Rougher than Others

The second question seems easier to answer, at least in part. Vagero and Lundberg (1989) have categorized the Swedish population by the same social class measures as used in the UK by the OPCS and presented in the Black Report, and have calculated the corresponding class-specific mortality rates. A gradient emerges even in egalitarian Sweden, with higher age-standardized mortality (for middle-aged males) as one goes down the class ladder. But the difference from top to bottom is much smaller in Sweden, and the mortality rates among the lowest class of Swedes is lower than among the highest class in the UK.

Kunst and Mackenbach (1992) have studied mortality gradients among men in several countries in Western Europe, using both education and occupational status as measures of SES. All countries show status gradients, but the slope of the gradient is much greater in some than in others. Moreover, the countries themselves show a consistent ranking in their slopes. The gradients tend to be flattest in Denmark and the Netherlands, growing larger as one moves to Norway and Sweden, then to Finland and England and Wales, larger again in the US, with France and Italy having the steepest gradients of all.

As they point out, gradients in mortality depend on both the degree of inequality in the underlying measure and the extent to which these inequalities are translated into health differences. A steep mortality gradient could be observed either because of large inequalities on the SES measure used or because such inequalities as exist have a relatively large impact on mortality (or both). Kunst and Mackenbach conclude that the former is true of the US, and the latter of France and Italy.

The implication seems to be that gradients in health status are *not* an inevitable part of the human condition – at least not on the scale which we now observe. Societies can be organized in ways which accentuate or buffer the effects which give rise to those gradients – that seems to be beyond debate. But there is still ample room for controversy over what exactly are the critical features of different societies that determine the slope of these gradients, not only because our knowledge is incomplete, but because here we come back to the inherent conflicts of interest between people at different levels in the hierarchy.

It may be worth emphasizing, however, that the baboon studies do not show that you have to remake the society from top to bottom in order to mitigate the health effects of hierarchy. It may be enough to reduce the extent to which those of lower status have their faces rubbed in it. What seems to be physiologically harmful is the chronic strain, the elevated cortisol level, and other elements of a "sub-optimal hormonal profile" that come from being subjected to frequent and unpredictable attack, both physical and particularly psychological.

Genetics Matters – but Is Not Predestination

The malleability of the individual, even in principle, is, however, a more complex question. Could one identify and inculcate "coping styles" and personality traits that leave people less vulnerable to external stress? Or are these genetically predetermined?

Studies of other primates again suggest part of the answer. Working with rhesus monkeys, Suomi (1991) finds that about 20 per cent of the population have "reactive" personalities such that they experience extreme behavioural and physiological responses to external stresses (see also Cox, 1993, 301). There are certain stages in the animal's life that are periods of high stress – separation from the mother when she resumes breeding, or (for males) expulsion from the natal troop. The behavioural responses to these stresses by highly reactive animals differ at different stages of the life cycle: "teenagers" behave differently from infants, but the underlying physiological patterns are the same. Extreme reactions to stress can put at risk the health and even the survival of the animal.

Suomi and his colleagues have shown that this pattern of reactivity is inherited; they have even been able to breed for reactivity. This suggests that "coping styles" for dealing with stress may also be inherited in the baboon, or the human.[9] But they also found that reactive infants that received particularly competent nurturing, from their own or from foster mothers, did not display the extreme physiological and behavioural responses to stress, and indeed might be more capable as adults. Conversely, several studies reviewed by Cox (1993) found that disruption of normal rearing conditions very early in the life of young monkeys led to long-term reductions in their immune competence.

There seems little support for the proposition that human social classes, however defined, represent genetically distinct populations. A more promising line of argument generalizes from Suomi's observation that genetic vulnerability can be socially buffered. Geneticists increasingly emphasize the interplay between genetic predisposition and environment, as opposed to older notions of genetic determinism (e.g., Baird, 1994). Whether or not a genetic predisposition will in fact be expressed depends upon the experiences of the individual organism, particularly in early life. Genetic advantages and disadvantages may be equally distributed across the population, but the environmental resources necessary to compensate for disadvantages (or to exploit advantages) are not.

The Biological "Embeddedness" of Early Experience

This perspective finds support in the Kauai longitudinal study of the 1955 birth cohort from that island (Werner, 1989a). One of the findings has been that children who suffer moderate or severe perinatal stress, but are reared in "good" environments (as measured by family stability or high socioeconomic status) suffer little or no disadvantage in development at

20 months. Children in unstable households, but with no perinatal stress, likewise showed little disadvantage. But perinatal stress *plus* poor rearing environment had quite severe consequences for child development.

Studies of the effects of childhood exposure to lead on intellectual development show a strikingly similar pattern. In general, the more exposure, the more impairment. Severe exposure impairs intelligence severely, regardless of the quality of the rearing environment. But for children with "moderate" exposure, the degree of impairment is much less if the rearing environment is of high quality (Bellinger et al., 1993).

The Kauai and lead studies do not address the issue of genetic endowment versus environment, but they do show that superior rearing environments can compensate for the effects of adverse exposures at or shortly after birth. They parallel, "in the human," the non-human primate studies showing that the early rearing experience can have long-term effects on physiological functioning. The impact of the early psychosocial environment thus seems to be just as "real" as that of the physicochemical environment, with a similar potential for becoming permanently embedded in the biology of the individual.

One of the best-known findings of the Kauai study has been the identification of a small group of "vulnerable but invincible" or "indomitable" children who, despite "high risk" perinatal experiences and home environments, grew into successful adults (Werner and Smith, 1982; Werner, 1989b). The common characteristics seemed to be close bonding with and high level of attention from *some* adult – not necessarily a parent or even a family member – very early in life. But these children also had cheerful, outgoing personalities that "elicit positive responses," presumably enabling them to recruit emotional support, and again emphasizing that the question "nature *or* nurture?" is profoundly misleading.

By their early 30s, however, these "vulnerable but invincible" people were showing a significantly higher proportion of self-reported health problems, of a sort consistent with stress (Werner, 1989b). One is reminded of Sapolsky's observation of the baboon who changed troops and made a very aggressive bid for status; his hormonal profile suggested the highest level of strain in the troop. Compensation may have a biological price.

THE DETERMINANTS OF HEALTH AND THE SOURCES OF THE SES GRADIENT

The emerging evidence on the determinants of health, coming from a wide range of disciplines, is surveyed in detail in Evans et al. (1994). The introduction to that volume offers an engineering example as a metaphorical summary. The strength of a beam under a load – an external stress – will depend upon what the beam is made of, how it has been made, and how it is supported. The load-bearing characteristics of steel differ from those of wood or glass, but each can be shaped and treated during fabrication in ways which dramatically change performance. And a beam with several supports distributed along its length will carry much more weight before distortion or failure than one that is fastened at one end only, and then extended into space. Metaphorically, we could refer to the beam's genetic endowment, the quality of its early-life rearing, and the supportiveness of its current social environment.

Obviously humans do differ in their genetic endowment. The primate studies strongly suggest that these differences make some people much more vulnerable to being "bent out of shape" by stress, but that this vulnerability can be compensated by high-quality early life rearing, or increased by poor-quality nurturing. Whether or not vulnerability becomes translated into illness then depends upon the physical and social environment in which the individual finds himself, or herself. Furthermore, the human life course tends to be a good deal more complex than that of most other animals, even our near relatives. Present vulnerability or resilience will depend upon the accumulation of experiences all along the way, but the very early life period appears to be particularly critical for us as well as our relatives (Hertzman, 1994).

The resulting variation in individual experiences could then aggregate into the observed correlation between socio-economic class and health, but not because there are differences in *genetic* makeup between classes. Rather, those higher up in a hierarchy are less exposed to the sorts of psychosocial stresses that induce the endocrinal and neural responses that constitute chronic strain, and lead to a number of forms of physiological damage. They also have more resources, social and economic, with which to respond. Moreover, in so far as higher status among humans tends to be inherited, those of higher rank may on average receive higher-quality early nurturing, and a higher proportion of positive than of negative experiences thereafter, and thus be less vulnerable to, and better able to cope with, whatever stresses they do face. They can carry more stress, with less strain.[10]

Such a general explanation still leaves room for the tough and resilient individual from a deprived background, or the fragile child of privilege. Status, however measured, is a determinant of health only in a statistical sense; good (and bad) genes and nurturing may be found all across the social spectrum. Nor does it rule out the confounding effects of social mobility: robust and healthy individuals *are* more likely to move up, and the sickly to move down. But the non-human primate studies, in which this is *exactly* how status is gained and lost, support the conclusions from studies of human populations, that this cannot be more than a partial explanation for the SES-health link, and that there is a very obvious causal arrow from status to physiological functioning.

The study of non-human primate populations tells us a good deal about the biological processes that link hierarchy with health, and fills in some of the gaps that are inevitably left by studies in human populations. Observations to the effect that the psychosocial environment becomes embedded in the biology of the individual, and that that environment is principally made up of relations with other individuals, seem to generalize fairly smoothly from one primate population to another.

But the precise environmental characteristics that influence health need not be the same in different species. Human and non-human infants probably have similar needs for maternal contact, but different requirements for vocalization: only the humans learn to speak. And it is doubtful if removing the canine teeth of adult males would greatly influence the hierarchical structure of the UK civil service. Thus one should not expect a collection of detailed policy prescriptions for modifying the human social environment to emerge from comparative primatology.

The simple-minded explanations of the Left and Right, with all their faults, lead fairly directly to proposals for action (or inaction). The more complex interplay of genetic predisposition, early-life experience, current stress exposures, and "learned" or biologically embedded physiological and behavioural response patterns leaves us with equally complex questions as to appropriate interventions. Nevertheless, some generalizations seem at this point to be defensible.

HEALTH AND INCOME: SHARE THE WEALTH, OR GO FOR GROWTH?

For most people in affluent societies, there is no simple mechanical linkage between health and income (Wilkinson, 1992). The health gradient appears to be a consequence, not of material deprivation – "cold, dampness, filth, malnutrition and starvation, overcrowding and endemic infectious diseases" (Charlton, 1994)[11] – but of patterns of interpersonal relations within a hierarchy. All the primates in the studies above, human and non-human, captive or free-living, were adequately fed and housed; the stresses they faced were generated by their fellows. The resulting physiological strains they displayed depended both on the extent of these stresses and on their own personal interpretations and reactions.

But if material deprivation does not explain the health gradient, then there is no reason why making everybody richer should *in itself* eliminate it, or raise the average level of health in the group. There *are* very impoverished populations in which absolute deprivation is an important determinant of health, and there are people even in affluent societies whose absolute standard of living places their health at risk. But for most of us income appears not to be a determinant of health in a functional sense, but rather a marker (one of many) both for exposure to stress and for the availability of coping resources and other mechanisms for buffering its physiological effects.

The absence of a simple functional relationship between health and wealth is not, however, the end of the story. It is not hierarchy per se, but the way in which status is *experienced* by the members of the hierarchy, that affects their physiological and behavioural responses. There would seem to be at least two channels through which the overall wealth of a society might influence the health of its members, and moderate the social gradient, quite independently of any form of absolute deprivation.

First, affluent societies maintain institutions to protect their members against external threats, supplementing the resources of individuals and families. Such collective buffering mechanisms are costly, and inevitably require some degree of redistribution of resources. But they also affect the extent to which participation in the society is dependent upon status, as expressed in income or otherwise.

Of course the rich have bigger cars, but is there also decent public transportation? Of course the rich can enjoy more expensive vacations, but does everyone have the same access to the same quality of medical care? What about the educational system – do the bright and hard-working from every stratum have equal chances? As among the non-human primates, some are always bigger, stronger, and more aggressive than others, but how often and how severely do the subordinates get their faces rubbed in that fact? It seems to make a difference.

A second potential channel of influence has to do with the perception of progress. Economic growth, even if it lifts all the boats together, gives each individual the sense of progress and of hope. Tomorrow will be better than today. This seems to be an important component of psychological well-being, which also translates into physical well-being.

Economic decline both darkens the perceived future of each individual and erodes collective support for the social mechanisms that buffer stress. If the future is not going to be better than the past for *all* of us, then I want to be sure that I'm all right (Jack). And if that requires pushing you down, too bad.[12] It is no accident that the attack on the welfare state has coincided with the decline in economic growth rates throughout the Western world.

HEALTH CARE SERVICES: PART OF THE SOLUTION, AND OF THE PROBLEM

Health care in the modern world is largely illness care. In so far as differences in status lead to differences in illness rates, the health services have to deal with the consequences of the gradient. But it is unlikely that they can do much to change it – in any case they do not appear to have done so up to now.[13] One might use differences in SES as a basis for allocating care services across a population, but only as a proxy for differences in needs for care, which it would be preferable to be able to measure directly, not with any expectation that such services would in themselves change the underlying processes at work.

Yet observed health gradients are large, relative to the effects of specific illnesses that the care services do respond to. Flattening the social gradient in mortality, by raising the life expectancy of those at the bottom towards those at the top, could have a greater impact on overall longevity than the complete elimination of a major disease such as cancer. We do not know how to do so; but then we do not know how to eliminate cancer either. Nevertheless, massive resources are devoted to biomedical research; the Americans alone have spent $25 billion or so on a self-declared "War on Cancer" that is now charitably described as "not won" (Beardsley, 1994). Since the social gradient in health is increasingly being provided with a respectable biological basis to link together what have previously been strong but ill-understood correlations, it might repay investigation on the same scale as the more traditional biomedical sciences.

Indeed, the study of the sources of heterogeneity in health status raises some distinctly worrying questions about current trends in the health services, particularly about the futuristic technological fantasies of the Buck Rogers set (*The Economist*, 1994b). It is well understood, since the work of McKeown (1979), that medical technology can take much less credit for past improvements in health status than its celebrators have claimed.[14] But this common knowledge does not extend to the general public, or their political representatives. The popular will to believe in miracles is as strong as ever, and the technology marketeers take full advantage.

The steady increases in care costs, against which all developed countries have been struggling with varying success over the last 20 years, are largely a consequence of the ever more intensive servicing of increasingly elderly patients with increasingly sophisticated techniques. All our systems are spending a larger share of their resources treating the elderly, not because there are more of them (the usual claim), but because more and more is being done to each.

But age increases vulnerability to the hormonal changes associated with stress. Animal studies show that, among other things, elevated cortisol levels actually kill off neurons. Worse, they seem to target the very neurons involved in coping with stress (Sapolsky, 1992). These studies thus provide biological support for the clinical impression that placing very elderly people in institutions, even for acute care, may render them incapable of independent living thereafter. If "first do no harm" is to guide medical interventions, the potential for permanent harm from the stress of the intervention itself must be taken into account along with all the other, better-known ways in which too much, or the wrong sort, of care can lead to iatrogenic illness (Stoddart and Lavis, 1994).

At the society-wide level, there is still much controversy among economists over the proposition that an overextended health care system may actually weaken a nation's economy and reduce its rate of economic growth. Simple stories about fringe benefit costs and threats to international competitiveness seem easy to refute; the linkages through savings and investment rates and participation in technological change raise deeper questions. At some point, nations that devote ever more of their scarce resources of time, energy, and capital to servicing the oldest members of their population, and extending their lives regardless of condition, must find this activity cutting into the resources available for both current consumption and future investment (Evans, 1994).[15]

In any case, the health care services compete, within the public budget, with other programs and institutions that can serve in different ways to mitigate the consequences of hierarchy and stress. Public budgets are under pressure everywhere, and health care systems, described by one observer as "the hyena gnawing on your foot," tend to have privileged access to such resources as are available. Whatever insights we may gain, from animal studies or elsewhere, about the determinants of health, the prospects of doing much about them are limited if this requires (public) money. Hypertrophy of the health care system thus has, in principle, the potential to be a hazard to health.[16]

On the other hand containment of health care costs tends in practice to be focused on the *public* services; expansion of the private sector has in recent years been treated with benign neglect. Yet the social gradient in health is real. Whether or not its sources lie beyond the reach of the health services, those services respond to real problems. Redirecting our health care systems so as to provide more services to those with lesser needs but greater incomes – which is what private systems inevitably do – seems questionable policy, to say the least.

LIFE IS LONG, AND THE PAST IS PERPETUALLY PRESENT

What then can be concluded from these studies? Well, a powerful advantage of studies of non-human primates is their ability to take a comprehensive view, both of the life cycle of the individual and of the social structure in which that life cycle is played out. Seen in that perspective, three features of health and hierarchy stand out that are relevant to human social policy:

1 the existence of developmental "windows of vulnerability";
2 the length of the time periods over which the psychosocial environment has its effects; and
3 the potential for the environment to buffer or compensate for both genetic vulnerabilities and physicochemical insults.

The observation of biological embeddedness clearly reinforces arguments for the importance of the experiences of very early life, and their potential influence over the whole of the life cycle. What happens in the year after (and the year before) birth can have permanent effects. This observation recalls the work of Barker et al. (1986; 1987; 1989; 1990), showing correlations between the health and circumstances of human infants at birth and during the first year, and mortality differences 50 years later.

But there are other windows. For the male animals, changing troops is a highly stressful time, exposing the psychological and physiological vulnerabilities of each individual. In some species adolescent males are routinely forced out of the natal troop, and some do not survive the re-entry process elsewhere. The parallel is obvious with the human transition to adulthood, and entry into the workforce, as a time of particular stress and risk with significant long-term consequences. Job change, likewise, has parallels with changing troops in mid-life, especially if one is forced out of one troop and must fight one's way into another. (Survival in isolation is, for social primates, a very dubious proposition.) Loss of employment, for adult male humans, is associated with increased risk of mortality (e.g., Morris et al., 1994).

Finally, the deterioration with age of the physiological mechanisms for coping with stress is found in a number of animal species. In later age a vicious circle is thus set up in which stress makes one more vulnerable to further stress. But the accumulated experiences of early life, both behavioural and biological, seem to exert a significant influence on the degree of vulnerability even in late age. The extension of these findings to humans is not yet clear, but it has recently become accepted that the level of education in early life is to some degree protective against Alzheimer's disease, decades later (Hertzman, 1994).

Demonstrating long-term effects "in the human" is difficult for both institutional and biological reasons. It is hard to keep research projects going for decades, and some of the subjects will outlive the investigators. But there are several long-term cohort studies whose study populations are moving into the age ranges at which significant health differentials might begin to appear. These may be of exceptional importance. And there is at least one striking example of a randomized trial of intervention in early life – the Perry High/Scope Preschool Study – that has found very significant benefits 20 years later, effects that were not obvious in the early going (Schweinhart et al., 1993).[17]

Other shorter-term studies have shown that very early intervention programs can compensate for a deprived rearing environment (e.g. Martin et al., 1990; Grantham-McGregor et al., 1991). There may, however, be a warning in some of the non-primate rearing studies reviewed by Cox. Infant monkeys separated from their mothers and reared by humans – a compensatory program – do not show the depressed immune responses of those reared in isolation. But they do show other "behavioural and central nervous system abnormalities" and "increased susceptibility to gastrointestinal pathogens."

It is thus possible that there is no true substitute for the real thing, and that social policy should be aimed at protecting and supporting the "normal" primate-rearing environment, with a compensatory program a second-best option. But this possibility could raise a great many difficult and politically explosive questions across the whole range of modern social and economic organization.

People are not, however, monkeys: over-enthusiastic extension of these findings to humans could be as misleading as failure to take them into account. For the moment, what can be said is that there is increasingly solid evidence, from both human and non-human primates, of biological effects on the individual from the psychosocial environment. These effects are potentially significant for the health of individuals; moreover, they appear to provide a biological foundation for observed differences in health status across the SES gradient in the population as a whole. Since these health gradients are large, in some societies at least, it follows that any measures that could equalize the health of the whole population to that of its most fortunate or successful members would have large health payoffs.

We do not at present know how to do this, and there is a real risk that effective policies, when we find them, will turn out to be too contentious and ideologically threatening to be acceptable. Indeed if they require a significant degree of sacrifice by some members of society, resistance will be quite understandable. But it must be recognized that continuous expansion of the care services also requires significant sacrifices (although the pattern of gainers and losers is different) in order to deal with the diseases and injuries that increasingly appear as the consequences, as much as the causes, of ill-health. The message from the animals is that a broader, more "upstream" view of the determinants of health is biologically respectable as well as potentially more productive. At the very least we might be wise to spread our bets.

This paper draws heavily on work by the members of the Program in Population Health, Canadian Institute for Advanced Research, which is presented in more detail in R.G. Evans, M.L. Barer, and T.R. Marmor (eds.), *Why Are Some People Healthy and Others Not? The Determinants of Health of Populations*. New York: Aldine de Gruyter, 1994.

NOTES

1 Left and Right are used here as labels for particular stylized perspectives, rather than groups of people. There are no doubt many who would identify themselves as Left, or Leftish, who are quite aware that material deprivation is not an adequate explanation of health experience in the developed societies. There are also doubtless Right-leaning people who go beyond the observation that some people are just "better" than others, in all sorts of ways, to ask "Why?" People on these paths risk convergence.

2 A recently published Canadian study, also person-specific and population-based, dwarfs even the Whitehall studies. Wolfson et al. (1993) examined the

mortality experience of nearly half a million beneficiaries of the Canada Pension Plan, over the ten years following their retirement, and related this to their pre-retirement incomes as derived from tax records. Again a clear gradient emerges, with significantly higher probability of survival for those with higher incomes. Disability status is also recorded in the pension records; the result holds for those without reported disability.

3 The upward shift in the curve is interpreted by the authors of the *World Development Report* as reflecting improvements in other determinants of health, such as medical technology, public health, and public education and understanding of how to use available technologies.

4 This is misleading. In reality the principal problem is to obtain valid *basal* measures for each animal, which requires measures to be taken at the same time of day and season, avoiding animals that are sick or injured, or have just mated or been in a fight, or (for some purposes) eaten. Still, it would probably be difficult to dart one's civil servant just before breakfast or lunch, take him aside for a set of studies, and hold him in a cage overnight for recovery and release. Someone would notice, and eventually questions would be asked.

5 The "fight or flight" response begins with, among other things, a rapid buildup of the adrenal hormone cortisol in the blood. A critical part of the control process is a feedback loop whereby the hypothalamus detects the level of circulating cortisol and regulates its rate of release. In subordinate animals, the feedback "signal" is weakened, so that the hypothalamus underestimates the level of circulating cortisol and production is not turned off appropriately. The subordinate animals consequently have higher basal levels of this hormone. In response to stress, however, the dominant animals can rapidly increase cortisol concentrations to levels equivalent to those in subordinates.

6 For the engineers, stresses are the external forces acting on a material or structure, and strain is the extent to which that material or structure is deformed, "bent out of shape," as a result. "Stressor" seems to have been introduced in those disciplines that have also used "stress" to refer to the organism's physiological reactions to stress.

7 It is not possible among the baboons, as it is among the civil servants, to follow animals of different status through time and to compare standardized mortality rates and causes of death, because "among [male baboons] ranks change over time and in idiosyncratic ways." This has not historically been true in the UK civil service; one does not lose status as physical powers fail. One might study the female baboons, whose status tends to be stable over the lifetime. But because mature female baboons spend much of their lives

either pregnant or nursing, it would not be possible to anaesthetize them without risk to mother or baby.

8 Such measurements are not, of course, available to the student of free-living populations. Ethical and legal constraints discourage the removal of subjects' arteries for detailed analysis.

9 Interestingly, Offord et al. (1989) found, in the Ontario child health study, that about 20 per cent of the child population suffered from some form of mental disorder.

10 Responses to stress are both physiological and behavioural. One probably should not draw too sharp a line between stress responses that are biologically embedded – e.g. in the endocrine system – and those that are overtly behavioural – lighting up a cigarette, or getting drunk. How should one classify panic?

11 It is not clear to what extent anyone studying health inequalities actually holds the views that Charlton (1994) describes as "The model implicit in work on health inequalities" – his source is a publication from 1936. He assumes that health status *is* a mechanical function of (absolute) income, and claims that others do likewise. He then points out, correctly, that if the first differential of such a function is positive over its whole domain, rather than going to zero as income increases, then any redistribution of income must lower the health of losers while raising that of gainers. But Charlton seems to confuse the persistence of a positive first differential – no health plateau – with the existence of a non-negative second differential – no diminishing returns to income. The first does not imply the second. If the second differential is negative throughout the domain of the function, then total health will still be increased, on balance, by income redistribution. Charlton cites no evidence that the second differential is non-negative. The real problem, however, is that in affluent societies the functional relationship between health and income is itself highly implausible.

12 This process shows up clearly in the present international movement for health care reform. In a time of declining economic expectations, some are concerned to improve the efficiency and effectiveness of health care systems. But others advocate various forms of "privatization" simply to redistribute both access to care and the burden of paying for it: more and better care for the (relatively) healthy and wealthy, at lower cost (in taxes), and less and poorer care, at greater cost (in charges), for the rest. Sharing is a luxury; "we" cannot afford it now.

13 An exception to this broad generalization may be infant mortality rates, which do appear to have become much less unequal in some countries, but here the range of interventions goes beyond medical care narrowly defined.

14 Public health, however, is another matter (Szreter, 1988).

15 There is increasing evidence to support what should in any case be obvious, that in many cases elderly people themselves do *not* want life-extending interventions in terminal care. But the decision has usually passed beyond their control.

16 We should obviously look first for signs of this in the US, where health care now takes up over 14 per cent of national income and is rising uncontrollably. But private versus public funding is almost certainly a red herring in this discussion. In the first place, all modern health care systems depend, and must depend, primarily on public funding. Even in the US, while most people rely primarily upon private coverage, about half the costs come directly or indirectly from public funds. Second, even where significant amounts of funds flow through "private" insurance channels, they are to the individual payroll deductions, job-related and largely involuntary, and look very much like taxes.

17 The Perry High/Scope Preschool Study actually demonstrates large improvements in the experimental group in social adjustment – school completion, job-holding and income, reduced rates of teenage pregnancy (females) and crime (males) – rather than health per se. But it is powerful evidence for the significance of long-term effects. One probably should not expect to observe health differences among a population still in their mid-twenties.

REFERENCES

Baird, P.A. (1994). "The role of genetics in population health." In Evans et al. (1994).

Barker, D.J.P., A.R. Bull, C. Osmond, and S.J. Simmonds (1990). "Fetal and placental size and risk of hypertension in adult life." *British Medical Journal* 301: 259–62.

– and C. Osmond (1987). "Inequalities in health in Britain: Specific explanations in three Lancashire towns." *British Medical Journal* 294: 749–52.

– and C. Osmond (1986). "Infant mortality, childhood nutrition, and ischaemic heart disease in England and Wales." *The Lancet* 327(8489): 1077–81.

– P.D. Winter, C. Osmond, B. Margetts, and S.J. Simmonds (1989). "Weight in infancy and death from ischaemic heart disease." *The Lancet* 334(8663): 577–80.

Beardsley, T. (1994). "A war not won." *Scientific American*, 270(1) (January): 130–8.

Bellinger, D., A. Leviton, C. Watemaux, H. Needleman, and M. Rabinowitz (1993). "Low-level lead exposure, social class, and infant development." *Neurotoxicology and Teratology* 10: 497–503.

Charlton, B.G. (1994). "Is inequality bad for the national health?" *The Lancet* 343(8891): 221–2.

Cohen, S., J.R. Kaplan, J.E. Cunnick, S.B. Manuck, and B.S. Rabin (1992). "Chronic social stress, affiliation, and cellular immune response in nonhuman primates." *Psychological Science* 3(5): 301–4.

Cox, C.L. (1993). "Psychosocial factors and immunity in nonhuman primates: A review." *Psychosomatic Medicine* 55(3): 298–308.

Economist, The (1994a). "The unhealthy poor." 4 June: 55–6.

– (1994b). "Peering into 2010: The future of medicine survey." 19 March: 3–18.

Evans, R.G. (1994). "Health care as a threat to health: Defence, opulence, and the social environment." *Daedalus: Journal of the American Academy of Arts and Sciences* 123(4) (Fall): 21–42.

– M.L. Barer, and T.R. Marmor, eds. (1994). *Why are some people healthy and others not? The determinants of health of populations*. New York: Aldine-de Gruyter.

Grantham-McGregor, S.M., C.A. Powell, S.P. Walker, and J.H. Himes (1991). "Nutritional supplementation, psychosocial stimulation, and mental development of stunted children: The Jamaican Study." *The Lancet* 338(8758): 1–5.

Hamm, T.E., Jr., J.R. Kaplan, T.B. Clarkson, and B.C. Bullock (1983). "Effects of gender and social behavior on the development of coronary artery atherosclerosis in cynomolgous macacques." *Atherosclerosis* 48: 221–33.

Hertzman, C. (1994). "The lifelong impact of childhood experiences: A population health perspective." *Daedalus: Journal of the American Academy of Arts and Sciences* 123(4) (Fall): 167–80.

Hertzman, C., J. Frank, and R.G. Evans (1994). "Heterogeneities in health status and the determinants of population health." In Evans et al. (1994).

Kunst, A.E., and J.P. Mackenbach (1992). *An international comparison of socio-economic inequalities in mortality*. Rotterdam: Department of Public Health and Social Medicine, Erasmus University, Rotterdam.

Marmot, M.G. (1986). "Social inequalities in mortality: The social environment." In *Class and Health*, ed. R.G. Wilkinson, 21–33. London: Tavistock Publications.

– G. Rose, M. Shipley, and P.J.S. Hamilton (1978). "Employment grade and coronary heart disease in British civil servants." *Journal of Epidemiology and Community Health* 32: 244–9.

– and T. Theorell (1988). "Class and cardiovascular disease: The contribution of work." *International Journal of Health Services* 18: 659–74.
– Stansfeld, C. Patel, F. North, J. Head, L. White, E. Brunner, A. Feeney, and G. Davey Smith (1991). "Health inequalities among British civil servants: The Whitehall II Study." *The Lancet* 337(8754): 1387–93.
Martin S.L., C.T. Ramey, and S. Ramey (1990). "The prevention of intellectual impairment in children of impoverished families: Findings of a randomized trial of educational day care." *American Journal of Public Health* 80(7): 844–7.
McKeown T. (1979). *The role of medicine: Dream, mirage, or nemesis?* Princeton: Princeton University Press.
Morris, J.K., D.G. Cook, and A.G. Shaper (1994). "Loss of employment and mortality." *British Medical Journal* 308(6937) (30 April): 1135–9.
North, E., S.L. Syme, A. Feeney, J. Head, A.J. Shipley, and M.G. Marmot (1993). "Explaining socioeconomic differences in sickness absence: The Whitehall II Study." *British Medical Journal* 306 (6874): 361–6.
Office of Population Censuses and Surveys (1978). *Occupational mortality: The Registrar General's decennial supplement for England and Wales*, 1972, Series DS No. 1. London: HMSO.
Offord, D.R., M.H. Boyle, J.E. Fleming, H.M. Blun, and N.I. Rae Grant (1989). "Ontario child health study: Summary of selected results." *Canadian Journal of Psychiatry* 34(6) (August): 483–91
Preston, S.H. (1976). *Mortality patterns in national populations*. New York: Academic Press.
Sapolsky, R.M. (1990). "Stress in the wild." *Scientific American* 262(1): 116–23.
– (1992). *Stress, the Aging Brain, and the Mechanisms of Neuron Death*. Cambridge, MA: The MIT Press.
– (1993). "Endocrinology alfresco: Psychoendocrine studies of wild baboons," *Recent Progress in Hormone Research* 48: 437–68.
Schweinhart, L.J., H.V. Barnes, and D.P. Weikart (1993). *Significant benefits: The High/Scope Perry Preschool Study through age 21*. Ypsilanti, MI: The High/Scope Press.
Stoddart, G.L., and J. Lavis (1994). "Can we have too much health care?" *Daedalus: Journal of the American Academy of Arts and Sciences* 123(4) (Fall): 43–60.
Suomi, S.J. (1991). "Primate separation models of affective disorders." In J. Madden ed. *Neurobiology of learning, emotion and affect*. New York: Raven Press.
Szreter, S. (1988). "The importance of social intervention in Britain's mortality decline c. 1850–1914: A re-interpretation of the role of public health." *The Society for the Social History of Medicine* 1(1): 1–37.

Townsend, P., and N. Davidson, eds. (1988). "The Black Report." In *Inequalities in Health* ed. Black et al., 29–213. London: Penguin.

Vagero D., and O. Lundberg (1989). "Health inequalities in Britain and Sweden." *The Lancet* 334(8653): 35–6.

Werner, E.E. (1989a). "Children of the garden isle." *Scientific American* 260(4) (April): 106–11.

– (1989b). "High risk children in young adulthood: A longitudinal study from birth to 32 years," *American Journal of Orthopsychiatry* 59(1) (January): 72–81.

– and R.S. Smith (1982). *Vulnerable but invincible: A longitudinal study of resilient children and youth*. New York: McGraw-Hill.

Wilkins, R., and O. Adams (1983). *The healthfulness of life*. Montreal: The Institute for Research on Public Policy.

Wilkinson, R.G. (1986). "Socio-economic differences in mortality: Interpreting the data on their size and trends." In *Class and health*, ed. R.G. Wilkinson, 1–20. London: Tavistock Publications.

– (1992). "Income distribution and life expectancy," *British Medical Journal* 304: 165–8.

Wolfson, M., G. Rose, J.F. Gentleman, and M. Tomiak (1993). "Career earnings and death: A Longitudinal analysis of older Canadian men." *Journal of Gerontology: Social Sciences* 48(4) (July): S167–S179.

World Bank (1993). *World development report 1993: Investing in health*. New York: Oxford University Press for the World Bank. Licence: Creative Commons Attribution licence (CC BY 3.0 IGO).

16

What, Me Worry? The Second Annual Gideon Rosenbluth Memorial Lecture (2013)

ROBERT G. EVANS

Gideon Rosenbluth was my colleague and friend for most of my professional life, ever since I came to UBC over forty years ago, so there is really quite a lot I could say about him. But that is not my remit here; my task is not to praise Gideon, much less to bury him. But I would like to emphasize that he was the type of public intellectual that I aspired to be when I began my career. He combined intellectual reach and rigour with passionate and energetic engagement in public issues. I thought when I came to UBC, and think now, that is the way an academic life should be lived.

Now to the talk at hand. This gave me a chance to explore something that has been sticking in the back of my mind, literally since 1975. It is a line from a paper by Gideon called "Economists and the Growth Controversy." Towards the end of that paper he writes: "we economists really have no business being so god damn cheerful." He was talking about environmental issues.

Now Gideon was not a person who used profanity lightly, and certainly not in a professional paper. This is a serious comment by a serious man, about a significant issue. And it is this issue that will be the focus and theme of this lecture. My concern is not so much with the environment

This article is an edited (2014) version of a public presentation (not previously published) delivered by Robert G. Evans as the 2nd Annual Gideon Rosenbluth Memorial Lecture on 23 October 2013. The event was sponsored and hosted by The Canadian Centre for Policy Alternatives (CCPA) and UBC's Vancouver School of Economics. Published with permission of the CCPA.

per se but rather with the way economists have dealt with it. Of course, it does not apply to everybody, and there are lots of stellar exceptions to any generalization, but Gideon goes on to conclude that if we (economists) seriously take on the issues that arise from the growth controversy, the controversy between the people he called the growth men and the doomsters (this is going back to the 1970s and the limits-of-growth debates, which a lot of people around here probably still remember; in fact the same issues are still with us), we might succeed in re-establishing the reputation that economics is the dismal science.

Well that's something to look forward to.

The doomster competition has become much keener since Gideon's paper. In 2013 Alan Weisman published a book called *Countdown: Our Last, Best Hope for a Future on Earth?* Weisman focuses on the way in which the continuing population explosion will lead, as with every other species, into a collapse. The question then is whether or not our species would survive in truncated form after the collapse. Weisman quotes analyses from biological sources indicating that the optimal carrying capacity of the planet, at present high standards of living, is about one and a half billion people. We are currently at a little over seven billion and projections are for nine to 11 billion by mid-century and as many as 16 billion by the end of the century. So Weisman is really saying that we probably have a mass die-off coming here, folks. I don't think Malthus was quite that grim; more dismal, perhaps, but much less dramatic.

Weisman is only the latest large-scale doomster. In 2006 James Lovelock said, cheerfully, that by the end of this century the population of this planet will probably be down by about 90 per cent. Now Lovelock has no further credibility since he published the Gaia hypothesis. This imaginative extended metaphor was misinterpreted as some sort of mystical tract and got him classified with crystal gazers, mappers of ley lines, and other assorted kooks. So we don't need to pay attention to him, except that he was also a serious scientist who made his career in the study of the evolution of planetary atmospheres. Could be relevant.

Current evidence, however, suggests that Lovelock was wrong. The earth is not heating up nearly as fast as he thought. But it *is* heating up, and will continue to do so as long as we continue to pump more and more carbon dioxide into the atmosphere, so it is just a question of timing. The mass die-off may threaten our great-grandchildren, and particularly someone else's, but for this century there will be only increasingly extreme weather, shortages of food and water, and rising sea levels. Nothing really serious.

But I am in no way a specialist in climate change, knowing no more, and perhaps less, than I read in the papers. Better then to take up the lead that Gideon had provided about economists and the growth controversy, and address economists and economics more generally. On that much more manageable front (for me, at least), the first point is that it is wrong and dangerously misleading to call economics a dismal science, because it is simply not a science at all, dismal or otherwise. Now of course we do have Nobel prizes in economic science, and some universities have departments of economic science, so the trappings are there. But these are simply marketing exercises.

To make my point, let me draw your attention to Peter Higgs. Everybody knows something about Peter Higgs and the Higgs boson and all that stuff, though most of us know very little. There may well be people in this room who know more about it and could actually talk about it sensibly, and I'm not one of them. But we all know that it is extremely important, and we probably all know that Peter Higgs and François Englert got the 2013 Nobel Prize in physics for a proposition that they and others made on theoretical grounds back in 1964. Note that that was nearly 50 years ago. Did it really take the Nobel committee that long to figure out that this postulated particle is pretty significant? Well the answer is no, of course not. But it took other scientists that long to actually demonstrate experimentally that they were right. The particle whose existence that they postulated fifty years ago, as necessary to pull together the subatomic "particle zoo," actually exists. In other words you don't get Nobel prizes in the real sciences for very nifty ideas, you only get the Nobel Prize when your very nifty idea has turned out to be confirmed by experiment or other rigorous observation. One of Einstein's prizes was held up until there was an opportunity to observe the transit of Venus. Fortunately the weather was good, his theory was confirmed, and he received his prize.

I want to underline the stark contrast between that and the prize in economic sciences, in which there is no necessity to demonstrate rigorously that your nifty idea was actually correct. Indeed, I can provide a telling example in which it was rigorously demonstrated to be false. But that came after the prize had been awarded, and it was not given back.

But first, consider Gunnar Myrdal and Friedrich von Hayek, who shared the prize in economic sciences in 1974. Gunnar Myrdal was an advocate for the welfare state, a Swedish economist, and a progressive one. Von Hayek was at the other end of the political spectrum and had written a bitter polemic, *The Road to Serfdom*, against the welfare state. The committee apparently decided to split the difference and let them share the prize. Yet, the notion that either of them structured his arguments and reached his conclusions based on something recognizable as economic analysis, was simply wrong. Myrdal then wrote quite a persuasive essay, arguing that there should not be a prize in economics for anybody. He was right. It is not a science. And the Nobel Prize in Economics is not a real Nobel either, because it is not given by the Nobel Foundation. It is given by the Swedish Central Bank, a bunch of economists, in memory of Alfred Nobel. It is a deliberate attempt to enhance the public perception of economics as a science, and the trick seems to have worked. It is an example of what my colleague Ted Marmor calls "persuasive definition." Give it a label and maybe people will think it is real. There is a lot of that about, and not just in the advertising industry. The most notorious example is creation science, which should be more honestly called anti-science. There are other examples. Christian science has kind of faded into the background. Most of you have probably not heard about nursing science, but it's also out there. Political science, well, we all agree politely not to push the issue, but of course no one really thinks it is a science.

So that's the tipoff. When something is called a science, like the prize in economic sciences, watch it, you are dealing with persuasive definition. And the purpose of that is to advance the status of economics and economists, and the credibility of their analysis and their pronouncements. Well that is a perfectly understandable thing for economists to want to do, but you should not be taken in by it.

I think the Myrdal/von Hayek case is pretty clear evidence that there is something wrong here. Having said that, I don't want to leave you with the impression that there is no good economics being done, or that none of it has been recognized with Nobel prizes. There is some very brilliant stuff. There is also some stuff which is somewhat less brilliant, names perhaps supplied on request. I have enormous respect for some of the economists who come home with Nobel prizes. But that does not make economics a science.

Perhaps the most damning evidence is a proposition that was rewarded with a Nobel Prize in Economic Science and then subsequently refuted by a real-life experiment. There is a thing called the Black-Scholes Equation, for which Myron Scholes and Robert Merton got the Nobel Prize in 1997. Fischer Black died before the prize was given (and prizes are not given posthumously). This equation enables you, using some really nifty math, to predict the proper value of options for a whole raft of different financial assets. And if you can predict those reliably, then you can identify when markets are slightly out of whack – the options are priced too high or too low – and you can go in and bet that the necessary price adjustments are coming. Sell them short, if they are too high, and buy them if they are too low, and you can make a killing! So they organized a hedge fund called Long-Term Capital Management in 1974. For a considerable period of time, things went well. The fund made squazzillions, and it made that fortune by very high-risk bets, on which they said, well it is really not all that risky, because we've got the math that says we know what we're doing. The group was up about five billion dollars with investments, gambles in fact, amounting to hundreds of millions. They were heavily leveraged by the time they got the prize – that was in 1997. A year later, the fund was wound up. They were bust. The markets had turned bad, and their equation didn't work. They were not asked to give back the prize. The point, however, is that the elaborate mathematical framework that they had put together at the time of the prize had not been fully tested. When the markets did finally arrange for a test, it flunked. The financial historian Niall Ferguson at Harvard has quite a good chapter on this, with a variety of reasons why things went wrong. I'm not going to go into those; the point I want to underline is that being called economic sciences and getting Nobel prizes and all that good stuff does not a science make, or, as the clown says in *Twelfth Night*, "*Cucullus non facit monachum*" – "The cowl does not make the monk."

So why not and so what? Does it matter? Well it does, because I think that one of the problems that economics has, is that the efforts by economists to establish themselves as real scientists lead them to rely rather too heavily on really complex and elaborate mathematics, which doesn't necessarily correspond to the reality that they are trying to explain. The Black-Scholes Equation is a case in point, and it's a point emphasized by Gideon at the end of his paper on economists and the growth controversy.

Another economist who "found a flaw" was Alan Greenspan. Remember him? He learned his economics from the rational expectations school in the 1970s and 1980s and was inspired also by Ayn Rand. We know where that led – into the largest international financial crisis since 1929. As Chairman of the United States Federal Reserve System he concluded that there was no real need for public regulation of financial markets.

The identification of economics as a science is an example of a category mistake. Now why is it a category mistake? Because, as Neil Postman noted, there is an important distinction between processes and practices. Processes are phenomena in the natural world, which repeat themselves under constant conditions and are susceptible to scientific investigation and prediction. The practices of human communities on the other hand evolve in a historical context. They have histories and they change through time. You don't necessarily have to be able to do experiments to find processes that operate under constant conditions. Astronomy, for example, became a science long before anyone could do any experiments with it. It was careful, precise observation, from the Mesopotamian astrologers through to Tycho Brahe, of processes that repeated themselves under constant conditions. You didn't necessarily require elaborate mathematics (although it evolved that way with celestial mechanics). Eratosthenes gave us a tolerably accurate estimate of the circumference of the earth not quite 2,000 years before Columbus sailed. He did it looking down a well in Syene and measuring the angle of a shadow in Alexandria – nothing elaborate, just a really clever guy. I'm still left wondering, since every educated person in Columbus' day knew of Eratosthenes' work, what was really going on with Columbus and the Spanish crown? The kids' story that we are told cannot be right – it doesn't make any sense; but I don't know what the real story is. There must be some back story, and maybe some clever historian will someday figure it out.

Practices on the other hand describe the behaviour of human communities, which is what economics purports to do. Practices evolve over time and vary from one place to another. They are not consistent, they are not like the temperature necessary to boil water, so the techniques for studying them are fundamentally historical, not traditionally scientific, and just adding more math to your model doesn't make it any more realistic. You really have to think about how these processes change. You might say economics goes astray when it follows Democritus, who brought us the concept of the atom, rather than Heraclitus, who said (poetically rendered) "it is impossible to step into the same river twice." What he actually said was "all things flow, nothing is static." That's I think the mindset that you have to bring into economics.

When you don't do that, I think you can get into trouble. Now, economists tend to focus closely on incentives. Jim Morone, a political scientist at Brown, describes them as "tinkering restlessly with incentives. This is a dangerous game." A host of unintended consequences lurk in every incentive. His point could be summarized as "you should never underestimate the power of an incentive, or overestimate the ability of an economist to predict which way it will go."

There are in fact several things that you have to keep track of besides incentives; one is information, and that is really central to health economics. There is an awful lot of foolish and dangerous stuff that comes out of mainstream economics about health care systems, because the practitioners of the pseudo-science make no serious attempt to take account of limitations on information flows. That is something I have spent much of my professional career tracking. One of the most distinguished economic theorists of the twentieth century, Kenneth Arrow, has written an important and influential essay on health economics, which is in fact just nonsense, because he was working within an intellectual framework which took no sensible account of the role of information and power imbalances. No one can take away from Arrow's towering reputation, and yet he has probably done more to retard our understanding of health economics than any other single economist. Other prominent American economists have also "darkened counsel" through ignoring the effects of information, institutions, and ideologies. The effects are still resonating in the United States in the current arguments over Obamacare. They are still out there causing trouble. It does look as if on this one the retrograde economists may have won the battles within the mainstream of the profession, but have in fact lost the war, because Obamacare was enacted, and is still in place. But it's hard to be sure, because wars like this really never end.

I want however to dodge back now, because in some cases and in some times the economists get it absolutely right. There are situations where the models work. And one of those can be found in the controversy about the limits to growth. In the 1970s the engineers and the Club of Rome were telling us about the limits to economic growth. There was much concern that the current rate of drawdown of the earth's resources, category by category, would soon exhaust the available supply. We're running out. We are reaching the end of growth and it's over, or will be soon. It's going to be terrible. The economists, most of them, looked at this, and said, "Aw, nuts! You guys just don't understand price systems; you don't understand incentives. What happens is, when there is a scarcity emerging, the prices go up, more efforts go into exploration and more efforts go into innovation to get around the problem. All kinds of things happen in response to changes in relative prices." And the economists were dead right. The engineers were wrong. Does anybody remember peak oil? Now it seems we are drowning in "unconventional oil" or other hydrocarbons. We are told that shortly North America will be self-sufficient in fossil fuels. The phrase "Saudi-America" has emerged.

In British Columbia we are told that we can all get rich by exporting liquefied natural gas, but we had better hurry up, because otherwise the rest of the world will catch up. In Alberta they are desperate to export "dilbit" (dilute bitumen) from the Tar Sands, even if it gets smeared all over the North Pacific coast. We've got to sell it any way we can, and if that means it ruins the environment, well, what the hell! What did the environment ever do for us?

Be that as it may, the fact remains that we have not run out of oil, and it doesn't look as though we will for some time to come. So we should never underestimate the impact of price systems and incentives.

But the broader problems remain, of the externalities, the unintended and undesired consequences of continuing growth. Sure we have lots more fossil fuel than we thought we had, but there are some near-term problems, some of them sitting on rail lines in Alberta at the moment. Some of them turned up in rather dramatic form in Quebec. We can't have that continuing, and yet if you want to know whether it's going to continue or not, go out and track, over the last year or two, the stock prices for CN Rail and CP Rail. The stock market is telling you they think there's just going to be an awful lot more oil going down those rail lines and, while much could be done to try to make it safer by spending more money but reducing the profits, the stock markets don't think that's going to happen. Meanwhile, the Northern Gateway Project grinds slowly ahead, driven by a single-minded prime minister wholly committed to the oil industry.

But these, like the risks of polluting important habitats along the coast of BC, are local problems. There are much bigger issues out there. If we have lots more fossil fuels than we thought we had, that will just contribute more carbon dioxide to the atmosphere. Well, that's a little bit of a problem. Remember Lovelock?

The Intergovernmental Panel on Climate Change (IPCC) tells us, yes the earth is heating up, yes we are doing it, but no it's not happening as fast as we previously thought. That's good news, isn't it? So, is it going to stop? Ahhh … no, not so long as we continue in the present form, not unless we find some way of not adding more carbon dioxide to the atmosphere. Well, what could we do?

Ultimately there are no long-term solutions that don't involve just burning less stuff. Maybe we can expand alternative energy sources such as fusion power. There have recently been some promising results in the technology of fusion power, and maybe in another 30 or 40 years we could be "burning" hydrogen and producing water as a by-product.

But as Gideon pointed out, quoting John von Neumann from 1955, that will still add heat to the planet, albeit more slowly. Widespread diffusion of fusion technology would give us little hydrogen bombs or, more accurately, little suns all over the planet. Wind power is expanding rapidly but may simply not be sufficient or come close to meeting our energy requirements. Ultimately, the only way to generate energy without heating the planet has to be tapping into solar power.

Lo and behold, within the last month, Jillian Buriak, who has a Canada Research Chair at the University of Alberta (there is a certain irony in that), has discovered that using nanoparticles of zinc phosphide, you can produce solar cells much more cheaply than the old silicon stuff. Silicon-based cells are expensive, because silicon is difficult to work with and the cells are not very efficient. The zinc phosphide material is much more malleable. It can be produced in sheets, and we can even imagine someday being able to wear it as clothing. This new technology does have a couple of flaws. It is still quite inefficient, but that just says more research is needed. That's normal in this kind of game. The second flaw is they don't seem to know how to transfer the power to the grid, to get at the energy that is being produced from this source of solar power. In other words, it's working away all right, but there is no place to plug in your kettle; here again, these are problems that deserve careful attention, and I am pleased to say that the Canadian Institute for Advanced Research (CIFAR) has taken an interest in this work, since this seems to be an opportunity that really needs to be pushed.

Solar technology, while it seems to be the only long-run solution, is still a long way from providing any significant proportion of humankind's energy needs; in the meantime we are continuing to heat up the atmosphere. We still need to figure out how to burn less stuff. A logical policy combination would be to try to limit carbon emissions in the near term (ideally immediately) while ramping up research for the longer-run use of solar power.

We have, however, a mechanism to address the near-term problem. Pricing and taxing carbon emissions creates the incentives for all participants in the economy to figure out how to burn less stuff. Alas, the institutional and ideological structure within which the price system is embedded makes this policy extremely difficult to implement. In British Columbia we made a start down that road by imposing a carbon tax to discourage the use of fossil fuels. And, in fact, every serious student of the problem of global warming understands that this is the way to go. The ideological and institutional response in Canada has been hysterical, particularly from the Harper government.

The carbon tax has two major flaws. One, it actually seems to work. The alternative, cap and trade, which doesn't, is thus obviously superior, if your primary objective is to sell fossil fuels. The second flaw is that carbon taxes impose costs on businesses and create revenues for governments. Cap and trade on the other hand creates opportunities for corporate profit. If you are pro-business and anti-government, the choice is not difficult. Then of course one could always just do nothing. The fossil-fuel industry is just too important to risk interfering with its growth.

So that's where the political institutions and the ideologies intervene to make it difficult to apply even those solutions which we can find. The problem is not so much in economics itself, as with some economists and particularly in the way the economics is (and economists are) used. So long as we don't pretend that it is some kind of exact mathematical science, you can actually find economists saying some remarkably sensible things. Indeed, we are celebrating one of those economists tonight. But the overall political and ideological framework and the institutional framework in which these problems and issues are embedded make it extremely difficult to actually come to grips with what we recognize as real threats.

So the carbon tax provides an example of a more positive view of the "dismal science," but it really does depend on the institutional framework responding in such a way as to push the promising policies forward, and not to spend all our efforts trying to run more oil down rail lines, through populated communities. That just seems so blindingly obvious, until you get to the point of asking, well, who profits from the present framework?

As with every other public issue, economists can be found on all sides of environmental questions. You think about somebody like Ken Boulding who wrote "The Economics of the Coming Spaceship Earth" back in the mid-1960s, again referenced in Gideon's paper. It turns out to have been misleading to think of "spaceship earth" as having a limited supply of resources in its hold that we were going to run out of very soon. But if we think about it instead in terms of the environment of the passengers on the spaceship – the atmosphere and the water – then that is quite an enlightening way of looking at it. So you could pick up from Boulding, who was a rather unusual economist, this basic idea that we must carry forward, now that we have left behind an "engineering" view of growth as limited by scarcity of specific resources. On the other side of the coin, however, you've got those economists who have provided a great deal of ammunition, as I see it anyway, to the politics of anti-tax and anti-regulation. Milton Friedman, who was the inspiration for the rational expectations school of the 1970s and 1980s, provided the intellectual underpinnings for Alan Greenspan's view that financial markets are essentially self-regulating, that government regulatory intervention is ineffective when it isn't actually harmful. You don't need to regulate financial markets, because no rational individual would put their corporations at risk by taking reckless bets on garbage assets. He was the chief regulator who oversaw a long period of deregulation in financial markets, which brought us to the near collapse of the world financial system in 2008. The system was saved only by massive government intervention and government money. Much of the necessary public money went to prop up the very firms – and now very wealthy individuals – that had orchestrated the collapse. So much for self-regulation.

More broadly, and this is where we come back and intersect with Ken Arrow and health economics, "mainstream" economic theory purports to show rigorously that public regulation and taxation create something called a welfare burden (or how to make a burden out of welfare). This was a central concept in much of the American economic literature on health care finance.

The welfare burden story works like this: Say you are ill and there exists an effective medical treatment that can help you. But you can't afford it. Some meddlesome government comes along and imposes taxes on "hard-working" Canadians (Conservative code for wealthy Canadians), using the revenue to buy you effective health care. The story line (backed up by mathematics, of course) is that that creates an "allocative distortion," and a welfare burden. That makes the whole society in some rather exiguous sense worse off; it lowers the overall welfare of society when people have access to health care or any other commodity that they would not be willing to pay for, whether or not they could afford it. If you are wealthy enough to pay for that care, however, and would have been willing to do so if you had not received it at public expense, then there is no welfare burden, no loss of overall aggregate social welfare.

The welfare burden only arises if care is provided to a person who needs it but is not able to pay for it. This represents an "allocatively inefficient" oversupply of health care to a person who should not be receiving it.

Now those of you who are not professional economists, which is probably the majority, are thinking: Can you be serious? And the answer is, in the old expression, "I kid you not." That really is what's happening out there. There *is* a logic behind it, but it is the logic which keeps coming back from the Fraser Institute to justify why we need more user charges in health care. As Romney's chief health advisor, Mark Pauly, said, the only way to fix health care in the United States is to "get more skin in the game" – by skinning the patients' wallets. That will prevent them from using services that they can't afford, and thus lower health care costs.

The whole economic concept of the welfare burden of health insurance, public or private, makes no reference at any point to whether the foregone health care is useful, irrelevant, or harmful? The answer in the conventional economic analysis is "No." The real answer is that many economists don't understand economics. There is, in fact, a well worked out theory of welfare economics that demonstrates the fallacy of the welfare burden analysis. It has been available for over 50 years (references available upon request). In fact, several former members of the UBC Economics Department, including Gideon Rosenbluth, have made significant contributions to this literature. But the concept of the welfare burden, theoretically unsound as it is, remains a very powerful instrument for advancing the political agenda of the right wing (and the "1 per cent"). It appears to provide a basis in economic theory for opposing public policies to mitigate increasing economic inequality, let alone, God forbid, to roll it back. We do know how to do this, through taxes and transfers and public programs with universal benefits – such as public health insurance.

This brief excursion into health care economics is partly because it is the field in which I have spent most of my professional life. (Everything reminds me of health economics.) More importantly, though, it provides a leading example of the way in which economic interests and political ideologies enter into economic analysis at a fundamental level, emerging as pseudo-scientific justifications for the policies advocated by the analyst (or his/her sponsors). The welfare burden story that dominates most conventional economic analysis, particularly in North America, suppresses the central institutional realities of health care systems, and evaluates their financing against artificial criteria ("allocative efficiency," rather than consequences for population health) shared by few, if any, in any society.

Returning to "Economists and the Growth Controversy," I think Gideon is pointing to the same fundamental flaws. The conventional treatment of growth fails to take into account the institutional framework of the real world, and the ideologies and interests at play. Economics originally earned its reputation as the dismal science through Malthus' analysis of population growth and food supply. Gideon suggests that, if we take seriously the issues that arise from the study of economic growth, we can restore that dismal reputation. Malthus is back.

Gideon identifies two major challenges to the survival or at least the happiness of the population on this planet. We have to slow the rate of economic growth in the wealthy world, and we have to stop the growth of population in the non-wealthy world. Taken together, these would permit living standards in the non-wealthy world to catch up. Those are the two key tasks. Remarkably, we seem to have achieved the first, except for the notorious "1 per cent" (and especially the .001 per cent), whose incomes continue to grow quite nicely thank you. We've now moved to a low-growth world. Everybody is praying and hoping that we will get back onto the growth track. Gideon has pointed out, essentially, that no you actually don't want to do that. That's not going to work for the long term. (The World Meteorological Office reported, at the beginning of December 2014, that the average world temperature for 2014 will be tied with 2010 for the highest on record, and that fourteen of the fifteen hottest years on record have been in the twenty-first century.)

So it would be more important, I think, for economists to be spending more time figuring out how you organize a well-functioning low-growth world, with a zero rate of greenhouse-gas emissions, rather than creating complex and misleading mathematical models of non-existent worlds. It seems to me that within the spirit of Gideon's approach to this, that's where a serious focus on the problems raised by the economic growth controversies might lead economists to think very hard indeed. How do we go about making a decent, humane, well-functioning society, without constantly relying on growth to get us past any of the roadblocks? Right now the "1 per cent," or better the .001 per cent, seem to be getting away with absorbing pretty much all the growth in the high-income world, and our political systems seem unable or unwilling to rein them in.

The really hard part is containing population growth, and there economists have not been terribly helpful. They have put forward theories that rest heavily on economic determinism. Once people become wealthy enough, they stop having babies of their own accord. They find better things to do with their time, apparently. The problem of population growth thus becomes part of the problem of economic growth; if the latter proceeds fast enough, the former will go away. There is no need for public policy specifically directed at population.

There is certainly some basis for this view. We know that populations in the high-income world have been stable, or even declining, for a generation. In North America it would be declining were it not for the high rates of immigration into Canada from Southeast Asia and China, and into the United States from Latin America.

If these declines were worldwide and sustained for a long time, we might eventually get back down to the one and a half billion identified by Alan Weisman as maintainable for the long run at a high standard of living. But these observed declines in the high-income world were not in fact a consequence of economic growth. The historical record is quite clear that the development of the birth control pill brought the postwar baby boom to a dramatic halt in 1964–1966. The breakthrough in technology combined with the changing status of women were the driving factors.

The Chinese have done a remarkable job of containing their population growth by an explicit policy to limit family size, in marked contrast to India or Pakistan, where it has just exploded. There has been a lot of hand wringing in the West about draconian Chinese policies, as well as the economic problems that will arise as they must support an overhang of elders. But these criticisms seem silly. Should they have kept on adding more and more and more people just to float off their elders? It just doesn't make any sense, but we keep getting that kind of rhetoric.

Overall, the picture is not good. When Norman Borlaug, the father of the Green Revolution, gave his acceptance speech for the Nobel Peace Prize in 1971, he said, "I have bought you 40 years." He meant that the Green Revolution would hold off widespread famine for a generation. The 40 years are up, and so are the population trends.

When you look at Africa, both Niger and Nigeria are at the top of the list of the world's fastest-growing countries, with rates of growth of over 3 per cent per year. If women in these countries had their druthers, the rates would probably not be anything like that. But they do not control their own reproduction and do not in fact have access to the kinds of birth control technologies that are taken for granted in the high-income world. The social structure of these countries matters.

As for economic motivations and incentives, there is an interesting new organization called Walk Free, which is bankrolled by a very successful Australian mining entrepreneur. This organization is dedicated to the documentation and rolling back of slavery in the world. They have just published an index of slavery which reports, by their count, that there are currently about 30 million slaves in the world. This is, amazingly, more than there have ever been. They are highly concentrated in India, Pakistan, and equatorial Africa. Now a slave is an earning asset to the owner, thus the economic incentives are to keep producing more of them.

The extremely high birth rates in these countries do not necessarily reflect the preferences and choices of the population – and particularly not of the female population. These are the brutal realities behind the theories of economic determinism. The interests of the dominant members of the society are then powerfully reinforced by religious and cultural conventions.

These conventions obviously differ among countries and can change over time. The determination of the Roman Catholic church to suppress any form of birth control, other than abstinence, has broken down quite dramatically over the past generation in Quebec and also in Italy. More generally, many practising Catholics in high-income countries are also practising birth control, despite the stern admonition of their church hierarchy. On the other hand, the church retains a tight grip in the Philippines and Mexico, as reflected in their population growth. Islamic ideology still has a strong hold in Pakistan. Islamic extremists respond to the threat of female education by kidnapping and murder. Such problems of ideologies and institutions do not figure large in economic theoretical frameworks, but they are in reality critical.

Gideon says at the end of his paper that he'll come clean, he's a bit of a doomster, because he does not see us overcoming these kinds of institutional problems. He does not see the kinds of assumptions that underlay the Black-Scholes equation – smoothly functioning, continuously adjusting markets, rational people, far-sighted, well-meaning politicians who actually have the power to go beyond the single election – as offering much help in understanding real world circumstances. These are the things that he would argue economists have to come to grips with, and it seems to me that it is worth thinking about that, because it is not so very different now.

Further Reading

Without intending to be exhaustive, amongst other papers that would have found a comfortable home in this section, but for which there was insufficient space, are:

- Evans, Robert G., Matthew Hodge, and I. Barry Pless. "If Not Genetics, Then What? Biological Pathways and Population Health." In *Why Are Some People Healthy and Others Not?* ed. Robert G. Evans, Morris L. Barer, and Theodore R. Marmor, 161–88. New York: Aldine de Gruyter, 1994.
- – 2002. *Interpreting and Addressing Inequalities in Health: From Black to Acheson to Blair to…?* London: Office of Health Economics.
- – and Greg L. Stoddart. "Consuming Research, Producing Policy?" *American Journal of Public Health* 93. (3)(2003): 371–9.
- – "From World War to Class War: The Rebound of the Rich." *Healthcare Policy* 2(1)(2006): 14–24.
- – "Fat Zombies, Pleistocene Tastes, Autophilia and the 'Obesity Epidemic.'" *Healthcare Policy* 2(2)(2006): 18–26.

Editors' Postscript

As we noted in our editors' foreword, the task of choosing papers for this collection was made extremely difficult both by the sheer volume of Evans' publications, and by the overall outstanding quality of the scholarship. Therefore, one book cannot capture the full extent of the author's reach and the impact of his contributions. As partial compensation, we have included a "Further Reading" list at the end of each Section of the book. These lists are populated largely by papers that had to be culled in the final round of decisions that took us from what would have been over thirty chapters (!) to sixteen. Those entries have been supplemented by a few other papers that cover additional important territory within a Section theme.

Those interested in reading even more Evans are invited to visit the following website: www.chspr.ubc.ca/publications/publications-by-author/Robert-Evans

There, links to (almost) his entire published record can be found.
Happy reading.

The Editors

Contributors

MORRIS L. BARER is a professor at the Centre for Health Services and Policy Research in the School of Population and Public Health at the University of British Columbia.

ALAN BERNSTEIN is president and chief executive officer of the Canadian Institute for Advanced Research.

ANTHONY (TONY) J. CULYER is a professor emeritus in the Department of Economics and Related Studies at the University of York (England). He is also an adjunct professor at the Institute of Health Policy Management and Evaluation at the University of Toronto.

ROBERT G. EVANS is a professor emeritus in the Department of Economics and at the Centre for Health Services and Policy Research in the School of Population and Public Health at the University of British Columbia.

JOHN FRANK is director and a professor at the Scottish Collaboration for Public Health Research and Policy at the University of Edinburgh.

CLYDE HERTZMAN (1954–2013) was the director of the Human Early Learning Partnership and a professor in the School of Population and Public Health at the University of British Columbia.

JEREMIAH (JERRY) HURLEY is a professor in the Department of Economics and the Centre for Health Economics and Policy Analysis, and dean of Social Sciences, at McMaster University.

JONATHAN LOMAS is a professor emeritus in the Department of Clinical Epidemiology and Biostatistics and at the Centre for Health Economics and Policy Analysis at McMaster University.

THEODORE (TED) MARMOR is a professor emeritus of Public Policy and Management in the Yale School of Public Health, Yale University.

KIMBERLYN M. MCGRAIL is an associate professor at the Centre for Health Services and Policy Research in the School of Population and Public Health at the University of British Columbia.

CHRIS B. MCLEOD is an assistant professor at the Partnership for Work, Health and Safety in the School of Population and Public Health at the University of British Columbia.

GREG L. STODDART is a professor emeritus in the Department of Clinical Epidemiology and Biostatistics and at the Centre for Health Economics and Policy Analysis at McMaster University.

MARKO VUJICIC is the chief economist and vice-president of the Health Policy Instititute at the American Dental Association.

Index

Page references followed by "t" indicate a table; page references followed by "f" indicate a figure.